THE ORIGINS OF FRANCO'S SPAIN

THE ORIGINS OF FRANCO'S SPAIN

The Right, the Republic and Revolution, 1931–1936

Richard A. H. Robinson

UNIVERSITY OF PITTSBURGH PRESS

First published in England 1970
by David & Charles (Publishers) Limited

Manufactured in Great Britain
by Latimer Trend & Company Limited Plymouth

Contents

Preface   9

Introduction   THE RIGHT, 1814–1930   14

Chapter 1   THE RIGHT IN DISARRAY   30
January 1930–July 1931

Chapter 2   LEGALITY AND CONSPIRACY   59
July 1931–September 1932

Chapter 3   UNITY IN DIVERSITY   105
September 1932–December 1933

Chapter 4   THE REPUBLIC AND THE REVOLUTION   152
December 1933–October 1934

Chapter 5   THE CEDA-RADICAL PARTNERSHIP   193
October 1934–December 1935

Chapter 6   'DESCENSUS IN AVERNO'   238
December 1935–July 1936

Epilogue   291

References   294

Appendix 1   Attempts at Dynastic Reconciliation   411
August 1931–January 1932

Appendix 2   Component Organisations of *Acción Popular*
and the CEDA   415

Appendix 3   Social Composition of the Minorities of the
Right, *Lliga* and PNV   425

Bibliography   428

Acknowledgements   455

List of Abbreviations   456

Note on Titles   457

Note on Place-Names   457

Index   458

FOR MY MOTHER

The Englishman or the American will have every right to pass judgment on what has happened and ought to happen in Spain, but this right will be a *wrong* if he does not accept a corresponding duty: that of being well informed about the Spanish Civil War, the first and most important chapter of which is its origin; the causes which have brought it about.

José Ortega y Gasset,
Epílogo para los ingleses

Preface

THE PURPOSE of this book is to provide a comprehensive study of the Right in Spain from the beginning of the Second Republic in April 1931 up to the outbreak of the Civil War in July 1936. Pride of place has been given to the CEDA (and its antecedents *Acción Nacional* and *Acción Popular*) because this was the biggest and most important of the parties of the Right in this period. The term 'Right' has been taken to signify those parties which did not proclaim themselves Republican, ie principally the Catholic CEDA, the Monarchist groups and the 'Fascist' *Falange*. Consideration has also been given to two important institutions usually believed to be 'on the Right': the Church and the Army.

Concentration on the CEDA in the book is felt by the writer to be fully justified, not only because of that party's size and importance for the history of the Republic, but also because it has been so neglected by historians. This neglect is perhaps attributable to the fact that its leaders were *personae non gratae* both to the Left and to the victors in the Civil War.

The book endeavours to explain why the various parties existed, to trace the development of each of them and to give an account of relations between them. The attitude of each to the Church and to the Army is also discussed. In addition, an attempt is made to examine the policies, ideology and strength of each and, so far as is possible, to indicate socially and geographically whence came their supporters. The absence of adequate biographical information has however hindered a proper study of the economic interests represented by them.

The book also attempts to set the Right's activities firmly within the broader context of the history of the Republic and the events leading up to the Civil War. For this reason the chronological approach has been preferred: the events of the years

9

1931–6 in Spain are comparable in their complexity to those of, for example, the years 1789–99 in France. Furthermore, the activities and development of the Right were to a considerable extent dictated by this kaleidoscopic sequence of events in which, by and large, the Left held the initiative. The chronological approach also brings out the cumulative effect of events, which helps to explain the causation of the Civil War.

The content of the book has naturally been limited by the sources available. Historians of Spain in the 1930s have a mass of raw material to use, but it is not as complete as that available to students of German, Italian or British history in the same period. Ministerial archives are not open to inspection and it is very difficult to gain access to private papers—where these have survived. The papers of D. Antonio Goicoechea, the Monarchist leader who died in 1953, are in the exclusive possession of D. José Gutiérrez-Ravé, whose full-length biography of this politician has been 'forthcoming' for some time. Another Monarchist, D. Pedro Sáinz Rodríguez, has a flat in Lisbon full of papers in a state of some disorder, from which some day he intends to write memoirs. D. Geminiano Carrascal, a leader of the CEDA, said in 1964 that he would have been delighted to make available the archives of his party as well as his own papers, but all had unfortunately been burned or looted and lost during the Civil War.

For these reasons the book is perforce somewhat limited regarding sources of finance for the Right and also on 'manoeuvring behind the scenes'. Nevertheless it must be stated that politicians interviewed were sometimes curious to know how the writer had obtained certain pieces of information and seemed genuinely surprised that these had been gleaned from careful study of the newspapers of the time.

The principal sources have been the press of the period and the record of parliamentary debates. The writer believes that he is the first historian to have read meticulously and *in toto* the main Catholic daily (*El Debate*), the main Monarchist daily (*ABC*) and *El Socialista* for the years 1931–6, as well as the *Diario de sesiones de las Cortes*. These sources have proved most rewarding and revealing and have been grossly neglected. The non-parliamentary speeches of leading politicians were fully reported in at least one of the aforementioned dailies. It has been possible to evaluate reporting of events by comparing the Right's versions with those of *El Socialista*. However, *El Debate* had the only proper nation-wide news service and its wealth allowed it to print many more pages than *El Socialista*; this fact could make for a distorted interpretation by over-reliance on *El Debate* as a source of information. The writer believes that he has retained a sense of objectivity thanks to the parliamentary record, where both sides had equal opportunity to state and argue their cases. Nevertheless the writer has formed the impression from the latter source that the Right got the better of the argument in the majority of cases. Macaulay observed that the true history of a people is to be found in its newspapers, and in this case they have acted as an insurance against the writer getting the importance of what contemporaries thought significant out of proportion.

Published memoirs by politicians prominent during the period studied are relatively few. Some, such as Largo Caballero's *Mis recuerdos*, are disappointing. Miguel Maura's *Así cayó Alfonso XIII* is illuminating on the early months of the Republic, while Lizarza's *Memorias de la conspiración* is revealing on Carlism in Navarre. Two very useful and informative memoirs are Aguirre's *Entre la libertad y la revolución* and Lerroux's *La pequeña historia*. The former, an indispensable source on Basque Nationalism (a movement 'objectively' on the Right until 1933), has been accepted as generally accurate by anti-Basque Nationalist writers. The latter, written in Portugal in 1937 without access to his papers by the leader of the Radical Party, which moved from Centre-Left to Centre-Right during the Republic, has proved more accurate than its polemical tone suggests. The first volume of memoirs by the Catholic leader Gil Robles, *No fue posible la paz*, is an indispensable source on the CEDA; he wrote it in Portugal in 1936–7 from memory, his papers having been destroyed in July 1936, and revised the text with the help of the press and other sources before publication in 1968.

Secondary works written about the period inside and outside Spain often distort as much as they explain. Nevertheless they often include important pieces of evidence which are helpful. Such is the case with Arrarás's four-volume *Historia de la segunda República española* which, despite its bias, is a mine of information since it is largely a succession of quotations from primary material. The lengthy 'official history' of the CEDA—Monge Bernal's *Acción Popular*, written at the end of 1935 by a party member—is also useful in this way.

For military conspiracy secondary works, for the most part biographies written with a clear propagandistic intention, are virtually all that is available. Nevertheless some, such as Pemán's life of Varela (*Un soldado en la Historia*), are based on diaries and papers and contain valuable information. When the 'authorised biographies' and 'official histories' are compared there appears a plethora of discrepancies, yet the writer thinks that it has been possible from such works to put together a reasonably coherent account of what happened.

Renewed interest in the Anglo-Saxon world in the recent history of Spain has led to the appearance of several scholarly works since research for this book began. Professor Carr has met the need for a good general history of modern Spain with his volume in the 'Oxford History of Modern Europe' series. Professor Jackson's *The Spanish Republic and the Civil War* provides a fairly detailed account of the period from a Centre-Left standpoint, but it unfortunately contains inaccuracies. Professor Sánchez's monograph on the Church, *Reform and Reaction*, is useful if at times rather highly coloured, while Mr George Hills has produced a well-documented biography of General Franco. The prolific Professor Payne's *Politics and the Military in Modern Spain* is a major work; his earlier history of Spanish Fascism, *Falange*, is a very useful monograph, but it does not place the *Falange* satisfactorily within the context of the Right as a whole and it is perhaps rather too favourable to Primo de Rivera.

This book is intended as a further contribution to the study of the Second Republic and the background to Franco's Spain. With regard to the interpretation of the history of the Republic and the causes of the Civil War, the writer believes that two crucial points have clearly come to light. Firstly, given that the future of the Republic depended on the Socialist movement and the Catholic party, it is important to recognise that it was the former and not the latter which abandoned democratic methods and appealed to violence. Secondly, it is clear that the Left Republicans themselves dealt the democratic Republic a serious

blow by equating the form of government with their own ideological predilections. In the light of these conclusions, certain
assumptions still quite widely held outside Spain concerning the
responsibility of the Right for the tragedy of July 1936 must be
reconsidered.

R. A. H. R.

POSTSCRIPT

The first volume of Ricardo de la Cierva's *Historia de la guerra
civil española* (Madrid, 1969) unfortunately appeared too late for
consideration in this work.

Introduction THE RIGHT
1814–1930

A SPANISH extremist once observed that 'the historical charac-
teristic of Spaniards is exaggeration in all things'.[1] Probably the
conflict between Right and Left has been longer-lasting, more
bitter and more profound in Spain than in any other European
country. Ideological battle has been repeatedly joined in the nineteenth and twentieth centuries between 'those wishing to correct
the effects of isolation, by adapting the life of the Peninsula to that
of the rest of Europe, and those of the opposite tendency who wish
to maintain intact the ancestral heritage of culture'. Each of these
'two Spains' has tried to wipe out the other. Religion has been the
constant around which the storms have raged and it could be
argued that the distant origins of the Civil War of 1936–9 lie in
the second half of the eighteenth century when the reforming
pays légal sought to impose 'enlightened absolutism' on the
traditionally minded and essentially Catholic *pays réel*.[2]

The history of the Spanish Right as an organised political force
began in 1814 with the presentation of the 'Manifesto of the
Persians' to Fernando VII. The 'Persian' Royalists were a group
of deputies to the Cortes of Cádiz who asked the King to abolish
the Constitution of 1812, which enshrined the revolutionary principle of popular sovereignty. They interpreted the War of Independence against Napoleon as a struggle by the people for the
traditional alliance of throne and altar. They therefore objected to
a paper constitution drawn up by Cortes meeting as a single
assembly in a liberal sea-port. Their positive programme was
rather vague: a return to the 'traditional' constitution, under
which the Monarch was 'absolute' yet 'limited' by respect for
Natural Law, the historic Cortes and established custom—in

particular the *fueros* (liberties, laws and usages) of the regions. They knew more surely what they did not want: the liberal programme, inherited and adapted from the bureaucrats of Carlos III, but now revolutionary, Republican and bourgeois in spirit. The 'Persians' rejected centralisation, uniformity, economic individualism and any encroachment on the moral status or material position of the Church, including the Orders. Hostility to the foreign ideas of the Enlightenment and the principles of 1789, and defence of the old Catholic Monarchy, were then the keynotes of the emergent Right.[3]

Though Fernando set aside the liberal constitution in 1814, he ignored the plea for a return to traditional Monarchy and ruled as an 'absolute despot'. When he was saved by French intervention in 1823 (after the liberal revolt of 1820), he again rejected the demands for a return to the 'ancient constitution' from the 'Pure' or 'Apostolic' Royalists who had fought for him in the north and east. During the last decade of his reign these 'Apostolic' Royalists were as disenchanted with Fernando as the French *Ultras* had been with Louis XVIII. They came to seek their Charles X in Fernando's younger brother Carlos. The liberals' expulsion of the Jesuits in 1820 and their attack on other Orders led many clerics to espouse the 'Apostolic' cause.

Fernando, however, managed to stymie his brother's hopes, and with them 'Apostolic' hopes. In 1830 he set aside the Salic Law (introduced in 1713), thus excluding Carlos from the succession. When his new Queen, María Cristina, gave birth to a daughter, Isabel, the Carlists declared Fernando's arbitrary Pragmatic Sanction invalid. In the faction-fighting at court, the anti-Carlists emerged as the victors and by the time Fernando died the military and administrative organs of the State had been purged of Carlists. Carlos V nevertheless raised his standard and civil war began. Although the Queen-Regent was not anti-clerical, she was driven to ally with the liberals because the most fervent Catholics supported Carlos. This alliance was cemented by Mendizábal's confiscation of monastic property in order to finance the war, and by the subsequent sales of the Church's land. Thus the dynastic schism was superimposed on other, more fundamental issues: the place of religion, respect for *fueros* and the type of Monarchy.[4]

Carlism was the product of the clerical and lay traditionalist

opposition to Fernandine absolutism and of the elements purged
by María Cristina's faction in 1832–3. It also represented a rural
reaction against urban liberalism in the north and east. With the
Army, the bureaucracy, the towns, the 'enlightened' ruling class
and foreign sympathies on the side of the Queen-Regent, the
Carlists were not surprisingly defeated. They could find no support outside the north and east because their programme of legitimacy coupled with Catholic unity did not appeal to others. The
personal cause of Carlos V was only accidentally tied to the defence
of regional *fueros*. Similarly, even though the Virgin of the Sorrows
was the supreme commander of the Carlist forces, the cause of
religion was only accidentally harnessed to Carlos V. The alliance
between Carlist throne and altar depended on the virulence of
liberal anti-clericalism.[5]

After the First Carlist War of 1833–40 the political situation
became more fluid. The alliance of the throne of Isabel II with
the Church was now desired by both the ecclesiastical hierarchy
and the Moderates, the Queen's more conservative supporters who
constituted the liberal Right. Some Carlists hoped that the young
Queen would marry Carlos V's heir, thereby ending the dynastic
schism and facilitating the union of Isabelline and Carlist Catholics against the anti-clerical Progressives. One of the leading proponents of fusion was a Catalan, Fr Balmes. His hopes for a
peaceful solution that would bring Carlism within legality came
to nothing, as did all other attempts at fusion during the century.
This failure was followed by an unsuccessful revolt in Catalonia
on behalf of Carlos VI.[6]

The career and ideas of Balmes were nevertheless of great
significance for the future development of the Spanish Right. He
was a Carlist and believed in hereditary 'pure Monarchy'; government by discussion was doomed to failure, while liberal parliamentarianism opened the door to demagogy. Though he upheld
the twin principles of Catholicism and Monarchy as the ideal, his
real contribution to Rightist thinking lay in the sphere of means.
He was remembered as the theorist of 'possibilism', or 'the policy
of the lesser evil'. 'A just policy does not sanction what is unjust,
but a sensible policy never ignores the force of facts. . . . If they
are indestructible, it endures them by compromising with dignity;
it plucks the best advantage from difficult situations and tries to

match the principles of eternal justice with the designs of political convenience.' The essential traditional principles had to be preserved, but without blind opposition to 'the spirit of the age', which might contain 'wholesome' elements. Balmes thought 'if not everything, at least something' was a wiser political rule than 'all or nothing'.

This idea of accepting the established system as the framework within which to operate for the attainment of one's ideals—the evolutionary tactic—was taken up by Pope Leo XIII, upon whom Balmes was possibly an influence, and in the twentieth century by social-Catholics in Spain. The latter could also look back to Balmes as a precursor on the social question. He denounced the abolition of guilds and condemned economic liberalism because it made the rich more selfish and the poor more numerous. Religious regeneration must be the foundation for political and social regeneration and not vice versa.[7]

If the Carlist Balmes failed to build a bridge between the two Spains, the Isabelline Moderates and Pius IX were more successful. The Concordat of 1851 established Catholicism as the sole religion of the State. All education was to conform to Catholic doctrine. The Church accepted the confiscation of its land, while the State undertook to pay the stipends of the clergy and permit the entry of two specified and one unspecified Order. The ambiguity of the clauses regarding the Orders was to lead to controversy. Anti-clericals argued that only three Orders were allowed in Spain, but Catholics said that the State had undertaken to support three Orders and that, by implication, any other Order could set itself up in the country. By and large, the latter interpretation prevailed. The Concordat brought about the reunion of Church and State. The liberal Monarchy was to protect the Church and support the Hierarchy, while the Episcopate now had a vested interest in the Isabelline State and pinned its hopes on the constituted power as a bulwark against revolution.[8]

An exaggerated manifestation of the conservative tendencies of some Moderate liberals was provided by the speeches and writings of Donoso Cortés. His pronouncements were prompted by horror of the European revolutions of 1848 and by a desire to defend Narváez's dictatorship. However, his words, like those of Balmes, were remembered by Rightists and were therefore of more than

B

transitory significance. Donoso was the exponent of 'catastrophism', the consequences of which represented the antithesis of the 'possibilism' of Balmes.

Donoso started his political life as a conservative liberal, but by 1848 he was converted to fervent Catholicism and political reaction. He now believed that European society was dying because of the diminishing influence of religion. Spain was on the eve of cataclysmic socialist revolution: 'the catastrophe' was inevitable. Yet the catastrophe could be postponed by recourse to dictatorship, which was a legitimate form of government in such circumstances. 'Liberty is finished!': the 'dictatorship of government' must forestall the 'dictatorship of insurrection'. Liberalism was doomed: henceforth the battle would be fought between socialism, the consequence of liberalism, and its antithesis, Catholicism, which would teach the poor to be patient and the rich to be compassionate. In short, society could only be saved by a wholehearted return to religion, protected by dictatorship. In his last writings he moved towards a more traditionalist position, attacking parliamentary Monarchy for being the sick seed of that greatest religious error of modern times, 'the independence and sovereignty of human reason'. Rotten 'parliamentarianism' must give way to a parliament acting simply as a check on the Crown and not seeking to suppress social hierarchies.[9]

The Monarchy of Isabel II survived until 1868. The leadership of the Right was then assumed by the Neo-Catholics Aparisi Guijarro and Cándido Nocedal. The Neo-Catholics represented a reaction against the anti-clericalism of the biennium following the revolution of 1854. These Isabelline Traditionalists stood for Catholic unity and were hostile to the parliamentarianism of the liberal oligarchy with its 'accursed parties'. Religion was the answer to the social revolution which would surely come as a result of *laissez faire* policies. When Isabel was duly overthrown, they went over to Carlos VII since he opposed the liberalism which condemned Spain to the evils of anarchy or dictatorship. The parties of the Centre were said to be doomed to extinction. People must choose between order and revolution, between Jesus and Barabbas. The true answer to Spain's troubles was the traditional constitution adapted to modern needs.[10] Aparisi explained what this meant: 'Catholic unity, a king who both rules and governs;

true Cortes in the Spanish tradition, decentralisation, and a real life of the municipality and of the province; and above all the Catholic spirit, living in the institutions, in the laws, in the customs.'[11]

Nocedal clung to 'possibilism' for as long as he could, in the hope that the Carlists would be legally voted into power on the wave of reaction to revolutionary instability. In 1872, however, the supporters of the newly imported Monarch, Amadeo of Savoy, resorted to electoral malpractice and Nocedal was obliged to yield to the Carlist activists' desire for a rising. The Traditionalist cause was again defeated in the Second Carlist War of 1872–6, and this time the defeat was definitive. The reasons for the failure of Carlism in the 1870s were basically the same as those for the failure in the 1830s. The revolutionary chaos of the First Republic of 1873–4, which associated that form of government in conservative minds with social and political anarchy, irreligion and national disintegration, redounded to the benefit of Isabel's son. Army officers and the conservative classes remained anti-Carlist and so military men successfully 'pronounced' in favour of Alfonso XII at Sagunto in 1874.[12]

The architect of the restored Monarchy was Cánovas del Castillo, a conservative liberal who disapproved of this premature military action. He was the heir to the Moderate Catholic tradition which sought to build a bridge between the two Spains. His aim was to take advantage of the exhaustion of the Left after the sterility of the preceding quinquennium in order to create a political system within which Right and Left could co-operate, or at least coexist peacefully. With the help of Sagasta, his opposite number on the Left, he successfully installed a liberal Monarchy based on the co-sovereignty of Cortes and King. Cánovas and Sagasta rendered military intervention unnecessary by devising the practice of 'pacific rotation' in office for their respective parties, the Liberal-Conservatives and the Liberals. As in contemporary Italy, parliamentary majorities were 'made' from the Ministry of the Interior by patronage and the manipulation of local political bosses (*caciques*)—a system known in Spain as *caciquismo*. Cánovas's system lasted until 1923, though it began to break down around the turn of the century.

If Cánovas's liberal régime were to be comprehensive, it clearly had to embrace the Church and as many Catholics as possible in addition to the throne, the oligarchy and the Army. The Church had refused to accept the short-lived Constitution of 1869 which permitted toleration of non-Catholic sects and Alfonsine propaganda presented the restoration as a return to religion after persecution. The Constitution of 1876 therefore reaffirmed the provisions of the Concordat of 1851 with modifications—Article 11 allowed freedom of worship in private to non-Catholics. This compromise did not please the more fervent Catholics or anticlericals, but the defeat of Carlism and the election of Leo XIII in 1878 ensured that there would be no serious challenge to the settlement from the Right.[13]

After its second failure in the field the Carlist movement began to disintegrate. First to leave the Catholic-Monarchist Communion was a group of 'possibilists' led by Pidal Mon, who founded the *Unión Católica* for the defence of the Church within legality. To the disgust of Carlists who refused to accept Article 11 of the Constitution even as a starting-point, Leo XIII gave his blessing to the movement and the Primate became its president. Pidal and the Vatican still hoped for dynastic reconciliation, but Pidal's followers and the Carlists engaged in bitter polemics. The Church came down firmly on the side of established institutions and in 1883 the Pope approved of the group joining Cánovas's party. Pidal put the theorising of Balmes into practice. The slogan of the *Unión Católica* was: 'Wish for what one ought and do what one can.'[14]

More important for the history of the Right than the group's political activities were the ideas and writings of its chief intellectual, Marcelino Menéndez Pelayo. He provided Catholics and the Right with a thorough historical interpretation of Spain to counteract growing laicist intellectual influence and his contribution to the Right has been likened to that of Fichte to German nationalism. Catholicism was the great and essential unifying factor in Spanish history. The Catholic Kings were the most genuine representation of Spain. In their Golden Century the Spaniards, 'a nation of armed theologians', were the chosen instrument of God's will. 'Spain, evangelist of half the globe; Spain, hammer of heretics, light of Trent, sword of Rome, cradle of St Ignatius; this is our greatness and our unity: we have no other. . . .

Two centuries of unceasing and systematic work artificially to produce the Revolution, here where it could never be organic, have brought about, not the renewal of the national way of life, but the vitiation, confusion and perversion of it.' He believed the *pays réel* to be still basically healthy, but if its 'slow suicide' were to be averted it must return to its Catholic culture and to the old Monarchy with its regional variety. An old people, denying its traditions, ignorant of its history, was condemned to senile imbecility, if not to death.[15]

The second group to leave the Communion were the followers of Ramón Nocedal. He expected to become Carlos VII's Delegate in Spain on his father's death, but he was not appointed because Carlos did not approve of the virulence of his attacks on the 'liberalism' of the Episcopate and Nuncio, and therefore indirectly of the Pope. In 1888 Nocedal founded the Integrist Party to uphold the cause of 'God and Country' instead of 'God, Country and King'. Devoted to Christ the King, its members were more intransigent than Carlos VII and more Papist than Leo XIII or St Pius X.

The Integrists wanted to continue the history of Spain 'from that point at which it was interrupted by the devastating invasion of foreign novelties which destroy and pervert it'. They were fierce advocates of Catholic unity and mortal enemies of liberalism, a sin worse than robbery, murder or adultery. Under no circumstances was it licit to co-operate with liberals who had created an absolute and despotic State which oppressed society as never before. Society was defined as 'an organism of families, municipalities, provinces, classes, institutions, corporations, each having its own life . . ., not subject to the caprices of any man, but ruled by its own particular laws'. For Integrists Cánovas's party was 'the greatest evil', because liberal Catholics were 'liberals *per se* and Catholics *per accidens*'. Though the Integrist Party lost its political importance by 1906 with the desertion of its Jesuit supporters, it bequeathed to others a tradition of extreme intransigence. It also demonstrated that Traditionalist principles could be upheld without a king.[16]

From the 1890s the mainstream of Carlism was revivified by the work of a great orator, Vázquez de Mella, who codified and developed its ideology along Thomist lines. He campaigned for a 'representative and federative Monarchy' that was neither absolute nor parliamentary, as was the Alfonsine system which was founded upon 'an absurd combination of the most contrary principles' and was but a staging-post on the road to Republican democracy. Since religion was the foundation of liberty he advocated the moral union of Church and State, but their economic and administrative separation. The King would reign and rule, limited and aided by corporative Cortes representing material, spiritual and intellectual interests. Society was 'polyarchic', being composed of a series of 'intermediary republics' (guild, municipality, region) between the 'monarchies' of the State and family. Social reform on the lines of *Rerum Novarum* (1891) was necessary because *laissez faire* capitalism was tyrannical, lacking in justice and charity, and would surely lead to a 'new Apocalypse' by comparison with which the French revolution would seem an idyll. Catholic corporativism was the answer to Socialism and Anarchism. He also saw the historic regions as tributaries flowing into the river of the nation. They should retain their juridical personalities and enjoy 'autarchy' (internal self-government) within a 'federative union' including Portugal. Centralisation and separatism he abhorred. The idea of 'federative imperialism', and 'spiritual federation' with former colonies, appeared in the political will of Carlos VII, which also called for Spanish rule in Gibraltar and Morocco.[17]

These ideas on foreign policy led Vázquez de Mella to be Germanophil during the First World War. His attitude brought about a rift with Jaime III, the liberal-minded and pro-Allied successor to Carlos. In 1919 Vázquez de Mella and most of its other leading personalities left the Communion, which now consisted of Navarrese and Catalans loyal to Jaime's person.[18] The Jaimists were an insignificant political force enjoying 'the static tranquillity of a sensuous Nirvana'.[19] Typical was the Marqués de Oñate, who kept relics of the last Carlist war in a glass case and refused to go to the opera when 'the Institutions' (ie Alfonso XIII) were there.[20]

Vázquez de Mella's concept of regionalism did not however satisfy the aspirations of most Catalans in the twentieth century. Restitution of *fueros*, which had been taken up by the Carlists, gave way to ideas of modern nationalism, the product of various factors: dislike of Castilian liberal centralisation coupled with the defeat of Carlism, cultural revival in the region, and the protest of industrialists against the ruling landed oligarchy. In nineteenth-century Catalonia Traditionalist regionalists nostalgically looked for a return to the medieval liberties lost in 1714. By the 1890s, however, this organic 'non-revolutionary' regionalism, propounded by such as Bishop Torras Bages of Vich, was losing its appeal. Educated Catalans in the towns were beginning to expound the very type of regionalism that the Bishop detested: federalism based on 'enlightened' theories of contract, or 'revolutionary nationalism'.

Although Prat de la Riba and Cambó, who founded the *Lliga Regionalista* in 1901, spoke of decentralisation and autonomy within Spain, it soon became clear that their 'Catalanism' was not of the Traditionalist type. After obtaining a measure of self-government (the *Mancomunidad*) in 1913, Cambó went on to raise the question of the 'integral sovereignty' of Catalonia. If doctrinally a separatist, Cambó the pragmatic politician and businessman always sought an autonomist solution based on compromise with Madrid. By 1923, however, more radical nationalists were emerging, prominent among whom was the overt separatist Maciá, who came from a Carlist family.[21]

Whereas Catalan nationalism was the creation of intellectuals and town-dwellers, Basque nationalism was the work of intellectuals and peasants. The Basques had supported Carlism against liberal centralisation so as to keep their *fueros*. In 1839 they had surrendered to the Queen-Regent's forces at Vergara on condition that their *fueros* were respected, but within two years Madrid had abolished the *pase foral* (the right of local authorities to allow or disallow Spanish laws). After 1876 nothing remained to them but the 'economic arrangement', a tax quota. With the second failure of Carlism the Catholic Basques sought other remedies against liberal centralisation.

The first Basque nationalist club was founded in 1894 by Arana Goiri, who, like Maciá, was raised in a Carlist home. Arana was a fervent Catholic who wanted to free the Basques from capitalist exploitation by non-Basques. He interpreted restitution of *fueros* as meaning independence, first for Biscay and later for the invented territory of Euzkadi. In 1906 the Basque Nationalist Party was founded to propagate an ideology in which autonomy, integral Catholicism and race (Aranzadi's contribution) were consubstantial. It became strong in Biscay and Guipúzcoa, and after 1918 a split occurred in the leadership between those demanding outright independence and the 'collaborationists' who preferred a con-federal Iberian pact. In Navarre, however, the party made very little progress; there the population preferred loyalty to Jaime.[22] 'Basque nationalism represented centrifugal traditionalism and the Navarrese centripetal traditionalism. The former wanted not to depend on Spain for anything; the latter wanted the whole of Spain to depend on them.'[23]

Peripheral nationalisms were not, however, the only challenge to Cánovas's system at the turn of the century. Defeat in the disastrous war of 1898 with the United States brought forth cries for 'regeneration' on all sides. The laicist intellectuals of the 'Generation of '98' saw the answer to national problems in speedy 'Europeanisation', but few were as practical as Costa with his ideas for agrarian reform and strong government. There was also a revival, if not of Republicanism, of the 'Republican spirit' and anti-clericalism, which was taken up by Liberals. Industrialisation led to the growth of Socialism in Madrid and Bilbao, and of Anarcho-Syndicalism in Barcelona. Overpopulation and bad con-ditions produced Anarchism in the countryside of the south. Furthermore, with the passing of Cánovas and Sagasta the system of bi-partisan rotation started to break down as their parties dis-integrated into factions. 'Regenerationism' on the Right appeared in two guises: one non-political, social-Catholicism; the other political, *Maurismo*. Both failed to meet the challenge of the 'other' Spain of laicism and revolution.[24]

Catholicism in the late nineteenth century was strongest in the north and east, the areas from which Carlism had drawn its following. The Church had succeeded in winning the allegiance of the ruling oligarchy and the provincial middle class, but, in general, it failed to grasp the full significance of the drift to the towns. To the urban working class it seemed a 'bourgeois' institu-tion. The clergy as a whole lacked ideas on social problems, but there were important exceptions and something of a Catholic revival can be discerned at the turn of the century.[25]

As early as 1864 the Jesuit Fr Vicent had begun to found mixed workers' and employers' *Círculos Católicos* dependent on the Hierarchy. His immediate aim was to prevent the apostasy of the masses by securing for them just wages, education and the means to save. He hoped that out of the *Círculos* would grow 'guild-corporations' to regulate production, competition, distribution, consumption and wages. He was helped in his task by the Marqués de Comillas, a wealthy philanthropist who started a bank to provide cheap credit. Although many *Círculos* were set up, Fr Vicent's corporative dream did not come true. Employers considered the *Círculos* useful recreation centres but strongly opposed the creation of workers' unions. Those priests who tried to organise unions were denounced for not sticking to their last. By 1912 Fr Vicent and Comillas recognised their failure: they had been wasting time on too ambitious a project.[26]

Inspired by Fr Vicent's example others attempted to found industrial workers' unions and agrarian organisations. In 1911 the Catholic unions in the Basque provinces formed the *Solidaridad de Obreros Vascos*, which, however, soon went over to Basque Nationalism. About the same time the Dominican Fr Gafo began organising his free Catholic unions in the north which were eventually wrecked by disputes over confessionalism. Fr Paláu's efforts in Barcelona to develop *Acción Social Popular* were thwarted when its members were refused permission to participate in a just strike. Similarly, Canon Arboleya's activities in Asturias met with hostility from the *beati possedentes*, who short-sightedly denounced such priests to the Bishops as revolutionaries and even on occasion demanded their excommunication. When a national confederation of Catholic workers' unions (CNSCO) was finally established in 1919, it consisted of 60,000 miners and railwaymen, compared with a membership of 200,000 for the Socialist UGT and 700,000 for the Anarcho-Syndicalist CNT. Nor were the non-confessional *Sindicatos Libres*, founded in Barcelona in 1920, any more successful.[27]

In the countryside of Castile and León, however, social-Catholicism did meet with success. The smallholders' syndicates of the area were in 1917 organised into a confederation, the CNCA, among the aims of which was opposition to Socialism, usury, *caciquismo* and 'the pagan principles of liberalism'. By 1920 the confederation claimed to have 600,000 members.[28] This success was to provide a solid base of support for the political Catholicism of the 1930s.

The political response of the Right to the new challenge was *Maurismo*. Antonio Maura, like Polavieja and Silvela before him, was a Conservative 'regenerationist'. He believed that the *pays réel* was 'sound' and therefore sought to put through a 'revolution from above' to forestall revolution from below. Opposed to *caciquismo*, insincere elections and oligarchy, he tried to reform local government to create the conditions necessary for democracy and he also tried to come to terms with the regional 'regenerationists' of the *Lliga*. He assumed that the masses would follow a democratic Conservative *caudillo* who succeeded in getting things done, but he did not bargain for the alliance of the increasingly anti-clerical dynastic Liberals with Leftist parties which did not accept the Monarchy. In the crises of 1909 and 1912 Alfonso XIII (who had come of age in 1902) decided to appease the Leftist bloc rather than risk tying the Monarchy's future to Maura. In 1913, with Maura in effect boycotting the Crown, the King gave power to another Conservative, Dato, whereupon the Conservative Party fell apart; Maura's vision of Conservative democracy faded.[29]

As a result of Dato's 'treason' the Young Conservatives rallied to Maura's personal cause and programme. The *Maurista* movement was founded in the autumn of 1913 by the Aragonese Conservative Ossorio Gallardo and *Juventudes Mauristas* sprang up under the presidency of Goicoechea. Maura himself was a sincere Catholic, a sincere Alfonsine Monarchist and a sincere liberal; he declined to espouse clericalism, ally with Jaimists or countenance dictatorship, which he thought would be suicide for the Monarchy. Yet, although he could do no wrong in the eyes of his romantic young followers, the style and tone of 'street *Maurismo*' was combative and authoritarian in its contempt for the 'old politics'. With their anthem and catechism the 'civic *guerrillas*' tried to shock the 'neutral masses' from their slumbers and 'make politics moral'. When the *caudillo* was entrusted with leadership of a national coalition government in 1918 the movement lost its *raison d'être*, and with his failure to produce results *Maurismo* went into decline. Many of its young followers were to be prominent under the Dictatorship and as authoritarian Monarchists in the 1930s. Calvo Sotelo, a young lawyer keenly interested in social problems and founder of the *Mutualidad Obrera Maurista*, said that *Maurismo* was neither of the Right nor of the Left, but a synthesis of the best elements in both.[30]

In the confusion and disorder of the years between the abortive revolutionary movement of 1917 and the military *coup* of 1923 an attempt was made to revivify and unify the Right within a Christian-Democratic framework. The three most prominent supporters of Christian-Democratic ideas in Spain were Ángel Herrera, the energetic social-Catholic editor of the daily *El Debate*, who since 1909 had helped to create an association of Catholic propagandists, Spanish Catholic Action, the *Editorial Católica*, the CNCA and the Catholic students' confederation; Severino Aznar, President of the *Grupo de la Democracia Cristiana* (a non-political study-group) and organiser of the 'social weeks' of 1906–12; and Mgr Tedeschini, an advocate of Sturzo's *Partito Popolare* in Italy who was appointed Papal Nuncio in 1921. They really prepared the ground for the foundation in 1922 of the *Partido Social Popular*.

The PSP was formed from men with differing political backgrounds who were united on fundamentals. It claimed to represent 'the essence of Traditionalism, *Maurismo* and regionalism' and was open to all desiring 'the regeneration of Spain within Christian channels'. This 'austere and reforming citizens' movement' was intended as a third force between Marxism and oligarchic liberalism. It stood for the purification of politics, for 'sound traditional Christian regionalism' and, above all, for social reforms based on the 'social and popular' teaching of the Gospels as interpreted in the Encyclicals of Leo XIII. Among those who rallied to this united Catholic front were disappointed *Mauristas* such as Ossorio and Vallellano, and the Traditionalist Pradera. One of its speakers was a young Catholic propagandist, José María Gil Robles, the son of a Carlist deputy and ideologue. The PSP was virtually still-born, for in September 1923 the military took over; nevertheless, it was clearly the precursor of the Catholic political organisation of the 1930s.[31]

From 1814 military intervention was a constant feature of Spanish politics. The Army was the mainstay of liberalism against the Carlists and from the middle of the nineteenth century became increasingly associated with the maintenance of order and the power of the centralised State. The dependence of governments

upon military loyalty meant that the Army saw itself as the reposi-
tory of the general will of the nation as well as the defender of its
own professional interests. When a government was felt by officers
no longer to represent 'opinion', or when it could not keep order,
these officers made a 'pronouncement' against the politicians in
power. If the rest of the Army did not positively support the
government—a phenomenon known as the 'negative pronouncement'—the *pronunciamiento* was successful.[32]

Having precipitated the restoration of the Monarchy in 1874,
the Army remained in the background as the nation's last resort
in time of need; Cánovas had ended its function as the instrument
of political change by his system of 'pacific rotation'. After the turn
of the century, however, the Army began to show signs of re-
emerging on the political scene as the guardian of national integrity
and public order. As heirs to the liberal centralising tradition
military men detested Catalanism. Anti-militarist sentiments and
the campaigns in Morocco made officers hostile to the Left and
social radicalism. The enthusiastic patronage of Alfonso XIII also
flattered their sense of importance. These factors led bureaucratic
junior officers in 1916–17 to form *Juntas de Defensa* to press for
better conditions for themselves and a strong government for the
nation. When the Army in Morocco, which had little liking for the
chairborne *Junteros*, was defeated by tribesmen at Annual in 1921
and politicians who could not keep order at home sought scape-
goats in the King and the military leadership, General Primo de
Rivera decided that it was time to 'pronounce' against the unpatriotic professional politicians who were ruining a perfectly good
country.[33]

Primo de Rivera ruled Spain by 'intuitionism' from 1923 to
1930, though in 1925 the Military Directory made way for the
Civil Directory.[34] When he took power he announced that his
dictatorship would only be a parenthesis in the constitutional life
of the country during which order would be restored and politics
purged of self-seeking politicians. The bluff Andalusian was a
simple patriot who saw his task as national regeneration under the
Monarchy, a regeneration based upon the 'iron surgery' recommended by Costa and the 'revolution from above' preached by
Maura. His slogan, 'Country, Religion, Monarchy', was vague,
while the Dictatorship's official organism, the *Unión Patriótica*

with its eclectic programme, claimed to be 'apolitical' and 'not a party'. Like the Somatén (civic militia), it was open to 'all men of goodwill'. It was joined by time-servers as well as idealists.

The Dictator solved the Moroccan problem with French help, gave the country order and gained the co-operation of the Socialist UGT, which seized the opportunity to build up its strength. While favourable economic conditions prevailed his civilian nominees did much useful work. Calvo Sotelo's financial reforms permitted Guadalhorce to embark on an ambitious programme of public works, while Aunós set up a corporative system of industrial arbitration with the UGT. The tragedy of the Dictatorship was that Primo de Rivera could find no political solution. The UP was a flop. The consultative National Assembly convoked in 1927 was a failure, not because it was boycotted by intellectuals or the old politicians, but because the Socialists, now the only real political force in Spain, refused to attend. The Socialist decision to follow a policy of alliance with Republicans, as advocated by Prieto, and not to help draw up a new constitution for the Monarchy, as advocated by Besteiro, was a most important turning-point in twentieth-century Spanish history.[35]

Since the Dictator could not now create a 'new legality', he and those associated with him were politically doomed. He had alienated the old political class by suspending and dispensing with the Constitution of 1876. He had alienated intellectuals and students by his support for clerical education and by his haphazard censorship. He had alienated opinion in Catalonia and the Basque Country by his rigorous suppression of regionalism. He had alienated important sections of the armed forces by his attacks on the artillery corps. He had alienated conservatives and economic interests by his interventionism and his paternalistic social justice. He had even alienated the Church by his mild regalism and his favouritism of the UGT to the detriment of Catholic unions. The King who gently edged him from power was left compromised by his acceptance of the 'illegal' régime. The Right, weak in 1923, was left powerless, discredited and in disarray in 1930.

Notes are on pages 294–6.

Chapter I THE RIGHT IN DISARRAY
January 1930–July 1931

THE LAST months of Alfonso XIII's reign proved to be the prologue to the Second Republic in more than a chronological sense. The Monarchy was invertebrate. The forces upon which it depended—the Army, the Church, the conservative classes, the political establishment—all considered the form of government of secondary importance. The preservation of their own particular interests was what they considered essential. None supported Alfonso wholeheartedly and all were willing to give the Republic a try. From the end of the Dictatorship the King was on the defensive and even went so far as to try and reach agreement with his imprisoned opponents. Thus, when in April 1931 the 'neutral masses' of the towns voted against him and the forces of order staged a 'negative *pronunciamiento*' against him, he had no alternative but to leave.

The components of the new Republican government were disparate. The Socialists provided its real strength although they participated only to further their own interests. The Left Republicans were a collection of bourgeois radicals with the negative aim of getting rid of the 'old Spain' of King, Church and Army. These radical elements were hidden behind the moderate façade of 'respectable' politicians who wanted little more than the replacement of a king by a president. Surprised to find themselves in power so suddenly, the Republicans and Socialists at first moved cautiously, but in so doing they alienated those who wanted a revolutionary break with the past.

The burning of *conventos* in May by small bands of extremists proved to be an indelible stain on the Republican record. The episode raised dramatically the two basic issues that were to plague the history of the régime: religion and public order. Divisions of opinion inside and outside the government hardened, with the result that in the elections in June the liberal-Catholic *via media* propounded by the leaders of the Republican-Socialist coalition, who had failed to keep order in May, suffered a defeat. In the absence of a real Right conservatives voted as a *pis aller* for the 'historic Republicans' of Lerroux, who emerged as a conservative by contrast with the triumphant Socialist and Left Republican reformers.

The Right proper was weak and disorganised. Although there was a general feeling that the Republic meant revolutionary change, two different schools of thought emerged. Some said that only the Monarchy could safeguard the Church, national unity and the social order. Others, more numerous, followed the policy of the Church in rejecting the idea that the causes of Monarchy, Catholicism and Spain were inseparable. They believed that Catholic and patriotic interests could best be defended within the newly established régime. Thus there was controversy on the Right from the start of the Republic over the validity of 'accidentalism' (indifference to forms of government). The Right proper did poorly in the elections because it had insufficient time in which to organise. Furthermore it was harassed by Republicans who wanted to make sure of an overwhelming majority in the Constituent Cortes.

In January 1930 Alfonso had two alternatives before him: he could either become dictator himself, like Alexander of Yugoslavia, or he could endeavour to return to the Constitution of 1876.[1] He chose the latter course and appointed General Dámaso Berenguer to preside over a *Dictablanda* which was to make the transition from the *Dictadura* of Primo de Rivera. To achieve their purpose, King and General needed the collaboration of Primo de Rivera's political opponents. Still smarting from the humiliation of a spell of enforced retirement, the politicians did not rally round immediately. The Duque de Maura and Cambó, leaders of the Conservatives and the *Lliga* respectively, refused to join this government, while the Conde de Romanones and his Liberals, offended at not being asked to join it, kept up an opposition that proved fatal to the General's efforts.

A section of the political class was prepared to forgive Alfonso in order to re-create the network of *caciquismo* destroyed by the Dictator. By February 1931 these politicians had decided that circumstances demanded a temporary closing of ranks and a new government was formed, including Maura, Romanones and Cambó's lieutenant, Ventosa Calvell. The problem now was to 'make' the elections for the Cortes; but since the Liberals and their Catalan and Conservative rivals who formed themselves into the Constitutional Centre Party, could not agree upon the ideal result, it was decided to hold municipal elections first.[2] To ensure fair play, the two crucial positions in the new government were filled by non-party men: Admiral Aznar was the Premier with the Marqués de Hoyos at the Ministry of the Interior.

Those willing to co-operate with Alfonso and confident of their ability to reconstruct the constitutional system, represented only a part of the old political class. A second group preferred to remain on the margin of loyal opposition to the Monarchy. These 'Constitutionalists' included former Liberal and Conservative leaders like Santiago Alba and Burgos Mazo, the Reformist chief Melquíades Álvarez, and other rebels against the Dictatorship. Their leader was the ex-Conservative José Sánchez Guerra.

They adopted, in effect, the Reformist policy: belief in a liberal Constitution was essential; forms of government were of secondary importance. They advocated Alfonso's abdication rather than a Republic and called for the election of Constituent Cortes to judge the King for his actions since 1923. Posing as spokesmen for the discontents of the 'neutral masses' they sought to gain their end by withdrawing from Alfonso's governments the prestige which they believed their names still represented. Typical among them was Ossorio, who now described himself as a 'Monarchist without a King'.[3]

The opponents of Alfonso, said a Monarchist speaker, could be divided into three groups: Republicans, Socialists and 'Monarchists who have grown tired of being Monarchists and intellectuals who have grown tired of being no more than intellectuals'.[4] Meeting in San Sebastián in August 1930, lifelong Republicans, newly converted Republicans, Socialists and Catalan Leftists agreed to join together against the Monarchy with a programme of general reform, including autonomy for Catalonia, to be carried out under a Republic.[5]

The 'historic' Republicans, the Radicals, were led by Alejandro Lerroux, a reputedly corrupt professional politician who had begun his career with violent anti-clerical outbursts and attacks on society, but who now advocated a Republic of orderly conservatism. To his Left were new converts like Manuel Azaña and the 'Jacobin' Radical-Socialists, who wanted a more radical bourgeois parliamentarist Republic with pronounced anti-clerical characteristics. Apart from the Radicals, who had some organisation, the Republicans had no political organisation apart from cliques of friends. They had therefore to ally with the Socialist Workers' Party (PSOE), which had a nation-wide organisation thanks to the protection given by the Dictatorship to its union, the UGT. By tradition Republicans, the Socialists believed a Republic would give them greater scope and open the way to Socialism.[6]

To mask any impression of social and anti-Catholic revolution and so reassure the 'neutral masses', the leaders of this Republican-Socialist coalition were two Catholics converted to Republicanism since the end of the Dictatorship: Niceto Alcalá-Zamora, a former Liberal Minister, and Miguel Maura, a son of Antonio Maura. In contrast to the Left Republicans, Alcalá-Zamora promised a conservative Republic led by ex-Monarchists like himself, which would even allow the Primate to sit in its upper chamber.[7] The manifesto of his Liberal Republican Right mentioned authority, the gradual separation of Church and State by negotiation, and recognition of the rights of property, albeit subject to modern needs.[8] The two politicians had joined the Republicans and Socialists because they deemed it unwise 'to leave the Left alone in the Republican camp'. They intended to fight the revolution by leading it.[9]

They succeeded in imposing their views on the others in the electoral manifesto of the coalition, which promised a tolerant Republic with a maximum religious programme of freedom of religion so as to emancipate Spain from 'discreditable clericalism'.[10] A more spectacular manifesto was that of the 'Intellectuals in the Service of the Republic', who declared that the Monarchy of 1876 had failed to take root in the nation and thus become one with its needs, though they admitted that the Monarchy was dying from

C

internal causes and was not being killed off by the opposition.[11]
The Republican Committee did not expect the fall of the Monarchy as a consequence of the municipal elections.

The strongest opposition to the Republican-Socialist coalition
came from groups on the Right which were in virtual opposition to
the governments of Berenguer and Aznar. By implication they
disapproved of the policy chosen by the King, whose throne they
were ardently defending. The most important of these groups—
which, like all parties except the Socialist, lacked masses—was the
Unión Monárquica Nacional. It appeared in April 1930, succeeding
the Dictator's *Unión Patriótica* as the organisation incorporating
those who remained loyal to his memory and aspirations. Its
leaders were the ex-Ministers of the Dictatorship and the General's
eldest son, José Antonio, all under the direction of the Conde de
Guadalhorce. Its manifesto rejected the idea of a new dictatorship
and proposed instead constitutional reforms to strengthen the
prestige of the executive power.[12] However, the group's chief
intellectual, Ramiro de Maeztu, believed a 'military Monarchy'
would be a necessity for at least two generations to make the
transition to a resuscitated Catholic traditional Monarchy. 'The
notion of Parliament', he added, 'is foreign to the Spanish national
genius.'[13]

Such views, together with the denigration of the Dictatorship by
parliamentary Monarchists, made the formation of single Monarchist lists difficult although these were seen to be necessary.[14] On
the other hand, the character of the UMN encouraged Integrists to
join actively in the fight. The Integrist daily *El Siglo Futuro* made
propaganda for the supporters of Alfonso XIII, and in San
Sebastián the Monarchist list was an Integrist-UMN coalition.[15]

Another group, the *Juventud Monárquica Independiente* led by
Eugenio Vegas Latapié, made efforts to rouse Monarchists from
their apathy by organising demonstrations. It also tried to keep
what little enthusiasm there was from being dissipated in a proliferation of even smaller bodies calling themselves grandiosely
*Acción Monárquica, Acción Nobiliaria, Partido Socialista Mon-
árquico 'Alfonso XIII'*.[16] Such was the lack of enthusiasm among
moneyed supporters of the Monarchy that Vegas could not even
collect sufficient funds to start a review in October 1930.[17] Although the Alfonsine daily *ABC* warned that the coalition stood

for social revolution, separatism and anti-Catholicism as well as a Republic,[18] *Reacción Ciudadana*, the electoral body of the Monarchists in Madrid, existed in little more than name. It collected only 22,000 pesetas and was therefore unable to employ sufficient staff to check the electoral roll.[19]

At a more popular and 'Right radical' level, two attempts were made to start a nationalist revival. A Spanish version of the French *Camelots du Roi* was founded in April 1930 by a former Freemason and neurologist, José María Albiñana. The members of his *Partido Nacionalista Español* (*Legionarios de España*) saluted in the Roman manner and came to blows with anybody who shouted 'Long live the Republic'. Such energetic behaviour was frowned upon by the authorities, who considered shouts for King or Monarchy more provocative than shouts for the Republic.[20] The policy of the PNE was violently nationalist and authoritarian but was otherwise negative.

Another attempt was made in February 1931 by the signatories of the manifesto of *La Conquista del Estado*, a small group including Ramiro Ledesma Ramos and Ernesto Giménez Caballero. The manifesto proclaimed their desire for 'revolutionary action for a State of radical novelty' to be founded upon 'Hispanic values' and a syndicalist economic structure in which 'all power belonged to the State'. The group produced the first number of their review in March 1931. *La Conquista del Estado* did not take sides, however, in the elections, which it termed a farce for *señoritos*. Ledesma declared that the group would fight against whichever faction won.[21]

With no organised masses upon which to rely, there remained for Alfonso, at least in theory, the Army and the Church. In the armed forces the Dictatorship had left divisions like those in the political class. Officers who had quarrelled with Primo de Rivera were ripe for conspiracy. The Director-General of Security, General Mola, observed that the Air Force, the artillery corps, which the Dictator had dissolved, and the navy, precisely those branches of the armed services enjoying royal favour and the slackest discipline, were those most affected by conspiratorial activities. Yet when the Republican military revolts at Jaca and Cuatro Vientos took place in December 1930, hardly anybody supported General Queipo de Llano, Captain Galán or the aviator Major Ramón Franco. The small Air Force was disbanded and the

army and navy remained obedient until 14 April.[22] The great
majority of officers wanted to stay in barracks and out of politics in
order not to increase the unpopularity gained by the Army as a
result of its political interventions. Political opinions were sacrificed to keep the officer corps united.[23]

In 1929 the Pope told Spanish Catholics that they could belong
to any political party not of a revolutionary character. The Bishops,
appointed by the King, true to Papal doctrines of obedience to the
constituted power, took the side of the Monarchy. Given the anti-
clerical, when not anti-Catholic, tradition of Spanish Republicanism, they had little choice even if their attitude was 'not based
primarily upon an attachment to monarchical government *per se*'.[24]

While the Bishops could not conduct propaganda campaigns,
the laity could and did. The leader of the *Grupo de la Democracia
Cristiana*, Severino Aznar, spoke up for the Monarchy because a
Republic ruled by anti-clericals and Socialists would suppress the
Catholic unions.[25] Ángel Herrera, however, pointed out to his
Propagandists a notable example of loyalty to Papal advice: the
immediate acceptance of the Weimar Republic by German Catholics, in contrast to the disloyalty of some French Catholics to the
ralliement, an error which led to a victory for anti- clericalism.[26] As
long as the Monarchy continued the Propagandists nevertheless
supported it as a guarantee of order. *El Debate* warned that 'the
Republic in Spain would be the opening of an era of anarchy in
which Religion, property, the family, in short, everything upon
which society is based, would be the object of experiments *à la
russe*'.[27]

The municipal elections took place on 12 April 1931 under the
supervision of Hoyos, who claimed that no political pressure was
exerted;[28] 80,280 councillors were to be elected. The reports of the
provincial Governors forecast a Monarchist victory with slender
Republican majorities in some capitals—a not unprecedented
situation.[29] The results known by the early hours of 14 April,
mostly those from the towns, showed the election of 22,150
Monarchists compared with 5,875 Republicans and Socialists.
The Monarchists won only nine of the fifty provincial capitals, but
to judge by the trend of the first results from the *pueblos*, an
overwhelming majority of the remaining 52,255 councillors would
have been Monarchists.[30]

The complete results, however, did not interest the King's Ministers, who thought solely in terms of the towns where the 'neutral masses' voted. The prevailing political outlook was qualitative, not quantitative: the votes of over 70 per cent of Spaniards who lived in the country were considered insignificant. The psychological effect of the urban results, giving the Republican coalition a bigger vote than expected, left the government thunderstruck. With one or two exceptions, its members deemed that all was lost.[31]

On the morning of 14 April Alfonso ordered a car to be prepared for his departure.[32] The decision was not surprising. On the 13th Romanones advised him to leave, while the Duque de Maura declared that the first results robbed the Monarchy of its legitimacy.[33] On the same day Berenguer at the War Ministry circularised the Captains-General, telling them, in effect, to maintain the internal unity of the Army by avoiding political compromises and awaiting developments. Already, on the 12th, the Director-General of the Civil Guard, General Sanjurjo, had warned Ministers not to count on the Civil Guard.[34] On the Republican side, no immediate changes were expected. Not until the morning of the 14th did the Republican Committee realise that events had moved in its favour; its members were surprised that the Monarchists had 'presented them with power'.[35]

In the early hours of the 15th, Alfonso boarded a cruiser at Cartagena and set sail for Marseilles and an exile he expected to be brief. He left behind three parting messages, two of which thanked the Army and Navy for their past loyalty and bade them now serve Spain. In the third message, to the country, the King recognised that he had lost the love of his people. His conscience informed him, however, that the aversion would not be definitive, and forgiveness would follow. While he justified his departure on the grounds that bloodshed had thereby been avoided, Alfonso XIII remained 'the King of all Spaniards . . . I renounce none of my rights'.[36] In fact he had made rather an important psychological error.

At about the same time as the King left Madrid various ex-Ministers of the Dictatorship met at Guadalhorce's house and held their inquest on a régime which seemed to have fulfilled Metternich's dictum: 'If Monarchies disappear, it is because they themselves surrender.' Some fixed the blame on the person of the King, others on the government of Berenguer; Maeztu blamed constitutionalism. Before their own departures for France or Portugal to avoid Republican retribution, they agreed that 'a school of up-to-date counter-revolutionary thought' must quickly be created to give political leaders faith in Monarchy and arguments with which to justify it.[37] The principal Alfonsine daily, while still believing that 'the Monarchy . . . is the history of Spain', followed the advice of the Duque de Maura, who said it was not the moment to attack 'the first Republican dictatorship, which is to-day the government of Spain'. *ABC* promised not to encourage acts of military rebellion: 'We are constitutional and parliamentary Monarchists and we seek to attain victory for our ideals by lawful means.'[38]

In contrast to both these views was the policy chosen by Herrera's *El Debate*. On the 14th it asked Alfonso not to abandon his inheritance and to await the full results, but its editorial on the 15th, which cited texts from Encyclicals and which was entitled 'Before a constituted power', was quite different. The Catholic daily acknowledged the Republic to be 'the form of government established *de facto* in our country. Consequently our duty is to obey it. . . . We shall obey it in a loyal and active manner, contributing what we can to aid it in its task. . . . Men of the Monarchy, men of the Republic, must join together in a common ideal . . . which is Spain . . . because the nation is above forms of government. To do otherwise would be treason.'[39]

A new charter for Spanish politics was drawn up on 15 April by the Provisional Government of the Republic: the Juridical Statute, moderate in tone and content, representing the minimum aspirations of the Republican-Socialist coalition. The Statute reflected the rather vague views of Radicals and Liberal Rightists. It proclaimed the inauguration of a State based upon 'a plexus of norms of justice', pending the voting of a constitution by Constituent Cortes. Until such time, the Provisional Government assumed full powers, subject to the examination of its conduct by the Cortes. It announced that judgment would be passed on the last governments of the Monarchy. The third clause proclaimed complete freedom of religion, thus implicitly revoking the Concordat of 1851. Private property rights were guaranteed, though reference was made to agrarian reforms. Individual rights and the right of association were recognised although individual rights were for the time being subject to governmental whim so that the nascent Republic should not be defenceless against any who might choose to oppose its consolidation.[40]

This liberal charter enabled the Right to organise in the defence of its interests. Stimulation was provided by the assurance of early elections for Constituent Cortes which would give definitive shape to the Republic. The threat to the *status quo ante* 14 April was obvious from a government composed mainly of anti-clericals, if not anti-Catholics, and for the first time including three Socialists, all in important Ministries. The installation of the Republic, however, left the old parties and factions of the Monarchy, with the exception of the *Lliga*, mere handfuls of isolated and discredited individuals deprived now of the possibility of reconstructing their former organisations from the Ministry of the Interior. The change of régime also dashed the hopes of the Constitutionalists, who found themselves in a similar predicament. To such politicians there remained only the fame, or notoriety, of their names, and perhaps some friends in the provinces with influence in a few *pueblos*. The old parties of the Monarchy simply disappeared. The only Monarchist group which continued to function was Vegas's JMI, and it was quite insignificant. Clearly new organisations and new men were urgently needed on the Right.

The process of organisation began as early as 15 April, when Herrera addressed an ordinary meeting of Young Propagandists in Madrid. He asked them to make renewed efforts while 'seeking in all systems of government the glory of God and the salvation of souls', so that forces of defence might be organised for the coming struggle.[41] *El Debate* proposed the idea of a single organisation for 'all the anti-revolutionary elements' in the coming elections. Its slogan should be 'Religion, Country, Order, Family, Property', omitting 'Monarchy' so that conservative Republicans as well as Monarchists could participate.[42] *ABC*, however, was shocked by the omission: 'The Monarchy also meant Religion, Order, Property, etc. . . . The Republic is the Revolution. . . . The concept of the accidental nature of forms of government, if in doctrine immoral, is in practice absurd. . . . Monarchy defines better than anything else the opposite of revolutionising, and under it we ought all to gather.'[43]

Herrera was not deterred. On 26 April an assembly of Young Propagandists decided to create *Acción Nacional*, an organisation to breathe new life into Spanish Catholicism. Propagandists dispatched to the provinces to survey the situation there did not bring back glowing reports; Catholic Action alone would not suffice.[44] On 29 April, *El Debate* therefore announced the formation of *Acción Nacional*, 'an electoral organisation to bring together the elements of order. . . . It is not a new political party.' On the same day, *ABC* announced the foundation of a rival, the *Círculo Monárquico Independiente*, 'to serve as a link between the elements wishing to work for the substantive ideals of Monarchy'.

The cause of Alfonsine Monarchism was at a very low ebb. The King's first message to his followers from a London hotel did nothing to relieve their gloom, for in it he did not even counsel stoicism in the face of the Republic. Monarchists were not to put obstacles in the way of the new government, which Alfonso himself accepted as 'the government of Spain'; in fact they ought to support it in the defence of order and national integrity. Military rebellion was specifically condemned. The Monarchy would only return if the electorate wanted it. Alfonso was not against Monarchists organising as Monarchists provided that they worked openly for the elections in a legal manner and followed his advice on the attitude to the government. The King's lack of enthusiasm was further emphasised when the editor of *ABC* was told in the language of *El Debate*: 'above the formal ideas of Republic or Monarchy is Spain'.[45]

Although *ABC* continued to sponsor the CMI and to attack *Acción Nacional* for its 'ambiguous and confused' tactics, it now advocated that the two groups should work together. The ideals of *Acción Nacional*, claimed *ABC*, were its own, 'those of Monarchist Spain'.[46] But first it was necessary to elect an executive committee. Members of the CMI, with the permission of the Director-General of Security, met on 10 May to do this in the former offices of *Reacción Ciudadana* at Alcalá, 67.[47] Afterwards some members celebrated by playing the *Marcha Real* on a gramophone at the busiest hour of the Sunday morning and cheered for King and Monarchy on the balcony. A hostile crowd gathered and threatened to storm the building. The Monarchists telephoned for the

Civil Guard, who took most of them into custody amid scuffling and car-burning.

The Minister of the Interior, Miguel Maura, returned from an excursion to El Pardo on the afternoon of the 10th in time to order Civil Guards to prevent an angry crowd, under the false impression that Luca de Tena (editor of *ABC*) had killed a taxi-driver, from storming the *ABC* building—which they did at the cost of two lives. The result was a meeting of the government in the Ministry of the Interior that night while a crowd outside called for Maura's resignation. Maura was determined that the Second Republic should not degenerate into the anarchy of the First and wanted to make full use of the Civil Guard. Outside, young members of the *Ateneo* distributed lists of religious buildings to be burnt the following day, while other members spoke from the Ministry's windows of the need for 'rapid and exemplary action'. The President of the *Ateneo*, Azaña, the War Minister, refused to use his influence with his fellow *Ateneístas*, and led the opposition within the government to the use of the Civil Guard. With nothing decided the Ministers adjourned until 9 am on the 11th.

Then came the news that the first Jesuit Residence was alight. Maura threatened to resign if no action were taken. An embarrassed Alcalá-Zamora said the trouble would soon be over: 'some little boys' were just 'playing at revolution'. Azaña thought that all the *conventos* in Madrid were not worth the life of one Republican, and said he would resign if action were taken. A vote showed that Maura alone was in favour of action. The Socialists abstained: they saw the need to intervene but would not take responsibility for the use of the Civil Guard. When the government received a delegation of incendiarists, Maura went home to write his letter of resignation. He was pressed not to resign by the Nuncio, who argued that his continued presence in the government might prevent a repetition in the provinces the next day. Maura remained adamant until about midnight, when he withdrew his resignation in exchange for a free hand. The government had called out the Army in the afternoon rather than use the Civil Guard.

Despite strict orders to provincial Governors, a repetition of the events in Madrid on the 11th was not avoided on 12 May in parts of Andalusia and the Levante. The worst outbreak occurred in Málaga, where the Military Governor sent a telegram to the War

Minister reading: 'The burning of churches has begun. Tomorrow it will continue.' Maura dismissed the Director-General of Security and various provincial Governors. *ABC*, *El Debate* and the Communist *Mundo Obrero* were suspended.

The buildings burnt in Madrid included two colleges in which free education was given to 800 working-class children, and one of the few Institutes in Spain capable of providing good technical education.[48] In all, eleven buildings of a religious character were burnt or sacked in Madrid, forty-one in Málaga, twenty-one in the capital and province of Valencia, thirteen in Alicante, five in Jerez de la Frontera, four each in Cádiz, Murcia and Seville and two each in Algeciras and Sanlúcar de Barrameda.[49] *El Debate* was suspended until 20 May, and *ABC* until 5 June.

The fires of 11 and 12 May did not, perhaps surprisingly, cause any change in the attitude of the Vatican towards the Republic. The Holy See had declared itself untroubled by the change of régime. Although the separation of Church and State was expected, it was hoped that Republican declarations of respect for the Church would be maintained.[50] From 15 April until 9 May the Nuncio, Mgr Tedeschini, an exponent of co-operation with the Republic, had been negotiating with a team of three Ministers, led by Alcalá-Zamora, on the civil status of the Church. The moderate Republicans wanted their position strengthened by the Nuncio's influence, in the Republic's favour, with Bishops and the Catholic opposition. The Nuncio wished to maintain amicable relations with the Republic so as to protect the Church's interests and weaken the anti-clerical case. No specific agreements could be made before the Constitution was drawn up, but Tedeschini received the promise of Alcalá-Zamora and Lerroux that they would oppose extremism. The Socialist Los Ríos promised nothing.[51]

The Nuncio's policy prevailed. Archbishops and Bishops issued statements pointing to Leonine texts on the question of forms of government and obedience to the constituted power.[52] On 2 May, however, the government decreed that the sale or transfer of ecclesiastical property was forbidden, despite the assurances that the Church's possessions would not be confiscated. On the 6th, compulsory religious instruction in State schools was made voluntary. On the 22nd a decree established freedom of religion, as the Juridical Statute had promised. Although the Concordat had been broken the two latter decrees produced only what Tedeschini called 'a very moderate little note'. The burnings themselves led to a moderate protest, and the Vatican refused its *placet* to the Republican Ambassador.[53]

A real cause of tension in Church-State relations was the Primate, Cardinal Segura, Archbishop of Toledo, a man of irascible intransigence who once called *El Debate* 'a liberal sheet'.[54] Segura was generally expected to take a hostile stand against the Republic with its freedom of religion. Almost at once a campaign against him began. The Left alleged that he had said: 'May the wrath of God and the curse of the Heavens fall upon Spain, if the Republic takes root!'[55] When his Pastoral appeared it was termed by the government 'eminently political' and of 'concealed bellicosity', showing 'opposition, when not hostility, to the Republican régime'.[56] The Vatican was asked to remove the offending Prelate.

The Pastoral began, in fact, by reminding Catholics that the Church was not tied to any particular type of earthly institution, and continued, controversially, with a glowing tribute to Alfonso XIII and the Monarchy. After again stressing Papal doctrines on obedience to the constituted power, the Primate declared the Church to be in danger. Catholics were urged to bestir themselves and, in accordance with Papal teaching, to take an active part in politics to defend religion. The document ended by explaining that, since the form of government was a secondary matter, it was the duty of all Catholics to unite for the elections in defence of religion and the social order.[57]

On 13 May, after the burning of the *conventos*, the Cardinal-Primate left Spain for consultations in Rome. On 11 June he re-crossed the Pyrenees, but was arrested near Guadalajara and escorted back to the frontier, which he again crossed on the 15th without having received an explanation for his expulsion.

According to Miguel Maura's subsequent account, Segura had spent a week in Rome and then stayed at a village on the French side of the Pyrenees, while his secretary made daily journeys with a suspicious brief-case to San Sebastián. Searched one day at the frontier, the case was found to contain documents ordering parish priests to sell certain ecclesiastical possessions with a view to sending the money obtained to a safe place outside Spain. Other documents sought to justify this with legal arguments based on the

Concordat. Clearly the proposition violated the Decree of 2 May, which presumably had prompted the idea. Maura showed the captured papers to the Nuncio, who was shocked and promised to use his influence in Rome to prevent these orders being carried out, as well as to arrange a fixed place of residence for Segura. When the Primate crossed the frontier unexpectedly, Maura had him arrested and expelled. Only then did Maura inform his colleagues, leaving Alcalá-Zamora to explain things away. Thus was one cause of tension removed. The Nuncio delivered a formal protest from the Vatican.[58]

The Minister of the Interior had earlier removed another strong-willed cleric while the Right's press was suspended, and again on his own initiative. The Bishop of Vitoria had arranged his diocesan tour on 1 April, and the fervent Catholics of Bilbao made plans to hold a major demonstration on his arrival there, a demonstration which the Socialists of Bilbao said they could not permit. The Bishop refused to cancel his visit and was expelled.[59]

Yet despite the Bishop's expulsion and the burning of the *conventos*, *El Debate* on its reappearance printed no detailed account of the events of 10–12 May, although, like the Metropolitans, it protested at what had happened. The paper's aim was to allow the atmosphere to clear; as a Young Propagandist of *Acción Nacional* explained, the Constituent Cortes could do more harm to the Church than could hooligans.[60]

Although such views were uncommon among Catholics, the policy of the Vatican remained constant. When Urquijo Ibarra, representing the Integrist Catholics of the north, sought approval in Rome for a policy of outright opposition by every means to the Republic and all its works, the Vatican chose to endorse the passive resistance of *ralliement* advocated by Herrera and pursued by the Nuncio.[61] Thus the summary expulsion of the Primate of the Spains drew no more than a formal protest. Church-State relations now depended on the composition and actions of the Constituent Cortes. The Metropolitans therefore told Catholics that they had 'the strictest duty to take part as actively as possible' in the elections and to 'unite circumstantially' for the defence of religion. They repeated their own 'sincere desire not to create difficulties for the Republic'.[62]

With the CMI closed from 10 May, Herrera's *Acción Nacional* was left as the principal electoral organisation for those who were not Republicans. It was therefore thought wise after the burnings to issue a second manifesto 'to avoid possible erroneous interpretations'. It explicitly stated that *Acción Nacional* was 'not a Monarchist organisation'. The Seville branch in its manifesto announced that 'the consolidation of the *de facto* régime in Spain is a patriotic imperative for all Spaniards even at the cost of sacrificing individual preferences'.[63] Candidates fighting under the aegis of the organisation had to accept its basic principles— Religion, Country, Family, Order, Work, Property and the implicit one of inhibition regarding forms of government—but were otherwise independent.[64]

Although its founder constantly stressed legality, condemned violence and appealed to the conservative classes to accept the social teaching of the Church so as to bring about 'a real ideological revolution in the world of labour ... which will often coincide with Socialist solutions',[65] there were other candidates who fitted poorly the image of the social-Catholic indifferent to the form of government. Goicoechea, its interim leader, who was incapable of being anything but a Monarchist, was a candidate in Madrid with Herrera. The Conde de Vallellano, the Dictator's Mayor of Madrid who stood in Jaén, had in May been involved in the first Monarchist conspiracy.[66] As was to be expected, the candidates were a motley assortment. Many were Young Propagandists or connected with *El Debate*. Some were priests. A few were ex-Conservatives like the Marqués de Lema and Marín Lázaro. Also included were a Traditionalist and the poet José María Pemán.[67]

Acción Nacional conducted its campaign on the religious issue and also on unemployment and rural discontent. The actual details of the programme were filled in to suit their constituencies by the candidates themselves. The provincial committees of 'elements of order' were often created by Young Propagandists sent out from Madrid for the purpose. Sometimes the work of organisation was hindered by the local authorities.[68] In the first few days, it was reported that committees had been formed in Cádiz, Palencia, Jerez, Seville, Huelva, Valladolid and León, the latter using the offices of the *Círculo de la Juventud Monárquica*.[69] Doubtless in other areas the new organisation was based on the skeleton of a former grouping, but in Valladolid most of the work was done by

students who preferred campaigning to examinations.[70] A good
example of the improvised committee was that of Córdoba: the
President was the editor of the local Catholic newspaper and its
members were three engineers, three lawyers, two landowners and
two traders.[71] Committees were set up in many places, but it seems
likely that organisation did not progress much beyond this stage
before the elections in the majority of cases.

In a few areas *Acción Nacional* was able to link itself with similar
organisations already in existence. In Salamanca, an organisation
founded in June 1930 for farmers with a Rightist outlook now had
a hundred local committees in the province. *Acción Castellana*, as
it was called, did not abandon its Monarchist convictions, but set
them aside for the election. Thus it was able to enter into alliance
with two Right Republicans on a programme of 'agro-social
reform': better credit facilities, the creation of smallholdings and
the defence of property.[72] In Palma de Mallorca the *Derecha
Social* was founded and included Integrists.[73]

The most important of such local groups was the *Derecha
Regional Valenciana*, founded by the ex-Jaimist editor of the *Diario
de Valencia*, Luis Lucía, in December 1929. This confessional
party had declared forms of government to be of secondary importance before the fall of the Monarchy. Its principles were Religion,
Society, Country and Christian Public Law. In social policy it
adopted Papal doctrines as a basis. It put first priority on the
renovation of local government and local services with a view to
making the three provinces of the old Kingdom of Valencia an
autonomous and autarchic region 'within the unity of Spain'. On
this regionalist foundation Lucía planned to build a national
Catholic party with a similar ideology, which would be a federation
of regional parties. The DRV was composed in the main of former
Jaimists who had made the transition from Traditional Monarchy
to Christian Democracy. As Lucía explained: 'It does not matter
to us whether the vessel is of clay or gold: what is important is
the content.'[74]

Traditionalists who had not, like Lucía, evolved, remained
divided into Jaimists and Integrists. The strength of Jaimism lay
as ever in Navarre, though the Communion still had pockets of
adherents elsewhere, principally in Aragón, Catalonia and the
province of Castellón. It had no great figures and no daily in

Madrid to compete with the Integrist *El Siglo Futuro*. The only Traditionalist orator of importance, Víctor Pradera, now wrote articles for the Alfonsine *ABC*. The advent of the Republic, however, left all Traditionalists in agreement that the prophecies had been fulfilled: Monarchies associating themselves with liberalism were doomed to perish by reason of their inner contradictions.

In the new situation, Traditionalists prepared to resist laicism to the death. To mark the Republic's decree ending obligatory religious instruction, the Jaimists of Aragón telegraphed Cardinal Segura to offer him their lives in defence of the Catholic Church.[75] The coming of the Republic had also the practical result of healing the old divisions. Jaime issued a manifesto on 23 April calling for the formation of a single, federative, Legitimist party beneath the banner of anti-Communism. His experience of Russia convinced him that Marxist revolution followed quickly upon the fall of a throne.[76] The Integrists were returning to the fold: at a rally in Pamplona on 14 June an Integrist made a speech while the Delegate of the Communion, the Marqués de Villores, presided.[77] Indeed with the Republic triumphant, plans for Monarchist unity went still further. Representatives of the two Bourbon exiles met in St Jean-de-Luz to form, at least as a first step, a single anti-revolutionary front inspired by Traditionalist principles.[78]

Jaime's followers were not content with mere words. In June, Young Jaimists in Pamplona founded *La Esperanza*, a journal bidding Navarrese not simply to live on the memory of the glories of the Carlist past, but to surpass them in the present. Any thought of obedience to the heathen Republic was totally rejected. At Leiza on 14 June, delegates from Navarre, Logroño, Guipúzcoa and Biscay reached agreement on the first plans for an uprising and then submitted them to Jaime in Paris. Jaime gave his permission. In the meantime *Decurias* of *Requetés* were formed with the immediate assignment of guarding religious buildings. These duties were performed with the advice of a committee of parish priests.[79] The coming elections were not to be overlooked, and for these a tactical alliance was to be negotiated with the Basque Nationalists. Traditionalists did not, however, put much trust in such things. A leading Jaimist explained the nature of elections as follows: 'If they are not sincere, fraud triumphs; if they are sincere, they are wont to be the triumph of cultural inferiority, that is to say, of the greater number.'[80]

In the three Basque provinces (Biscay, Guipúzcoa and Álava) a three-cornered fight had taken place on 12 April. The Basque Nationalists opposed the Monarchist and Republican-Socialist coalitions with sufficient success, at least outside the main towns, to allow the young Mayor of Guecho, José Antonio de Aguirre, to get most of the councils of Biscay to accept the idea of a Basque Republic within a Federation of Spanish Republics on 14 April. An assembly was to meet on 17 April at Guernica, at which, 'in the name of Almighty God and the Biscayan people', the Mayors were to call on their colleagues in Álava, Guipúzcoa and Navarre, to join in the creation of a Basque State. Although the government did not allow the assembly to take place, the Biscayan Mayors persevered; rural municipalities were generally favourable, but Leftist councils remained hostile. A set-back was the government's appointment of temporary committees for the Basque Deputations. The elected Mayors therefore changed their plans to use these bodies, and entrusted the drafting of a Statute to a cultural body, the *Sociedad de Estudios Vascos*.

The Statute was to be passed by a grand assembly in Pamplona and then to be used as the electoral programme. It was drafted by Nationalists and Alfonsine and Jaimist Monarchists and was ready by 1 June. The Navarrese had collaborated to obtain 'complete restitution of *fueros* and recognition of the sovereign rights of Navarre'. On the eve of the Grand Assembly, political attitudes were still confused. In general, the Nationalist press was in favour, and Urquijo Ibarra's influential *La Gaceta del Norte* lent its support, whereas the Republican, Socialist, Alfonsine, Integrist and Jaimist press came out against it. In the opinion of the Basque Nationalist Party (PNV), the draft did not give Euzkadi its full sovereignty. Representatives of the Traditionalist Communion who met at San Sebastián were in favour if, as the PNV also desired, it were amended to ensure regional control of education and Church-State relations. Socialists were generally hostile, but there was some vacillation. In the event, it was a strong section of the Traditionalists of Navarre whose opposition disrupted plans. They organised their own Catholic-*fuerista* rally for 14 June in Pamplona, the same date and place as that scheduled for the Grand Assembly, which now had to be held in Estella.

At Estella, the draft was duly amended to include provision for a Basque concordat with Rome and linguistic parity in education and the administration of justice. To this 'General Statute of the Basque State' the Traditionalists of Pamplona then adhered, and on this basis they negotiated a coalition for the elections with Aguirre. The circumstantial nature of this alliance is clear from the interpretations of the two parties. For Aguirre's PNV, the elections were to be a plebiscite for or against the Basque State, autonomous within the Republic. The Navarrese, on the other hand, saw the agreement as a 'Catholic-*fuerista* coalition for the defence of the lofty interests of the Church, full restitution of *fueros* and the Statute which Navarre may approve'.[81] It was a rather negative alliance for religion and against centralisation; the PNV and Traditionalists held incompatible views on where sovereignty should reside.

In contrast to the Basque situation in 1931, the forces of Catalan nationalism were firmly in the Republican camp. On 14 April the Republic was proclaimed by the non-separatist Companys. Less than three hours later his colleague in the *Esquerra*, Maciá, leader of the separatists of *Estat Català*, proclaimed the Catalan Republic within an Iberian Federation. Although the position was regularised on 18 April when Maciá agreed to a *Generalidad*, the Spanish Right had been provided with the emotive weapon of 'anti-separatist' propaganda.[82]

Inside Catalonia, the conservative regionalists of the *Lliga* found themselves without their two leaders, Cambó and Ventosa Calvell, who had compromised themselves with the Monarchy and left for a spell abroad. The party was now led by Abadal, who on 17 April told Maciá that the *Lliga* would support him in the defence of Catalanist aspirations 'within the Spanish State'. On 21 April the Catalan Regional Committee of Traditionalists also offered Maciá their collaboration, but on condition that his actions were not hostile to their ideals or the Christian tradition of the people.[83] Relations with the *Esquerra*, however, were troubled. *Lliga* councillors often found themselves removed by the *Generalidad* because they had been elected as Monarchists. The *Lliga* appointed a new committee under Abadal, excluding Cambó, Ventosa

D

Calvell and Durán Ventosa, to demonstrate its wish to become a party of the Republican Right.[84]

The first political event in the rule of the *Generalidad* was the election, on 24 May, of the Provisional Deputation, which was to draft the Statute of Autonomy. For the sake of solidarity, the parties in Catalonia made a pact allocating the number of seats proportionately. By the terms of the agreement the *Lliga* was allotted six seats, compared with twenty-one for the *Esquerra* and ten for *Acció Catalana Republicana*.[85] The *Lliga*, however, claimed that the *Esquerra* had broken the pact by putting up candidates where seats had not been allotted to it. The *Lliga* and other parties therefore withdrew from the elections.

It was made clear at the same time that the party would support the Statute to be drafted if it were 'in accord with the needs, not only of Catalonia, but of Spain, insofar as it can be copied by all the regions which so desire'. On the other hand, with a view doubtless to the economic interests of the party leadership as well as to the non-Catalan vote, Abadal said that the *Lliga* would oppose it if it were 'restrictive, parochial, narrow, incompatible with the complete life of Spain'. The party's attitude was, as usual, carefully opportunist. Officially it now stood for autonomy within the Republic: 'Great Catalonia within a great Spain is our text.'[86]

The attitude of former leaders of factions under the Monarchy was similar. The Constitutionalists accepted the Republic and the idea of change, though convinced that concessions should be made as slowly as possible. On the question of the form of government, Sánchez Guerra described his position as follows: 'I, a Monarchist, want the Republic to consolidate itself and take root, because before being a Monarchist I am a Spaniard, and consequently I say that there is no other solution for Spain but the Republic.'[87] Melquíades Álvarez, whose main support lay in Asturias, went back on his previous acceptance of the Monarchy. His Reformists became the Liberal-Democrat Republicans, a 'party of conservation and social progress'. They wanted a Republic of order, liberty and justice, neither revolutionary nor reactionary, laicist but with respect for religion.[88]

Santiago Alba declared himself 'for Spain, with the Republic', the keynotes of which should be order and gradual reform. Thirty years should be taken to revise the status of the Church, and an unspecified period to create the half-million smallholders needed as a barrier against Communism.[89] Typical of this vague liberal reformist-conservative mentality of the 'Republicans of 14 April' was the list of candidates entitled 'Support for the Republic' in Madrid. Its organiser was Monticl, the ex-*Ciervista* President of the *Círculo de la Unión Mercantil*. The other three on the list were Sánchez Guerra, Ossorio (now a 'Monarchist without a King in the service of the Republic') and M. Álvarez.[90]

Within the government coalition, the Right—in an economic rather than a religious sense—advocated a similar version of the Republic. It was the Radical Republicans of Lerroux, more than the Liberal Republican Right of Alcalá-Zamora and Miguel Maura, who now began to win praise in the columns of *ABC* as the anti-Socialist champions. Both parties, in fact, produced the same vague, conservative, opportunist phraseology as the ex-Constitutionalists. Miguel Maura called for an 'evolutionary revolution . . . of slow but constant rhythm', with tolerance for Catholics in a State separated from the Church. Regarding Catalonia, the Pact of San Sebastián was to be strictly adhered to; the Cortes should pass a statute of autonomy, but the 'blasphemy' of separatism must be eschewed.[91]

Lerroux, like Maura, took his stand on the Pact of San Sebastián. He also tried to justify his political evolution from the radical Left to the conservative Centre, if not Right. This he did by pointing to the change of régime: with the Republic installed, revolutionary violence was unnecessary. The way to consolidate the Republic lay in tolerance towards religious and economic interests.[92] His views were in marked contrast to those of the Republican Left who thought that the Republic was by definition a radical régime with no obligation to conserve anything.

As in the municipal elections of 12 April, the Republicans were to a very considerable extent dependent upon Socialist organisation for the success of their candidates. Co-operation was forthcoming from the Socialist leadership, but the Liberal Right, which at first had hoped for some 150 seats to compare with perhaps 50 for the Socialists, soon discovered that its position within the coalition in the provinces had been eroded. A case in point was the province of Seville: there two Liberal Rightists found that the ambitions of local Socialists had swollen the number of candidates.

Lists of coalition candidates were then circulated by them, on which the Liberal Rightists did not appear.[93]

Another weapon which Liberal Rightists could use was what remained of the old parties' *caciquismo*. This they and the Radicals did, at the cost of antagonising the Socialists, who considered such 'neo-Republicans' worse than Monarchists. The latter at least could not 'disfigure' the Republic from within.[94] Thus the Liberal Right was at a considerable disadvantage compared with the fiery Radical-Socialists, whose *caciques* the Socialists were prepared to overlook as long as both had the same ideal of making the anti-clerical, bourgeois revolution. The Radicals were not as badly affected, as they had some organisation of their own on which to rely. But such were the internal tensions within the Republican-Socialist coalition that only 115 candidates actually fought under the coalition label.[95]

Caciquismo was a perennial topic of controversy in elections during the Republic, but its significance would seem to have been much exaggerated for obvious purposes of propaganda. In subsequent elections, the Left was to ascribe the Right's voting strength almost entirely to the machinations of local *caciques*, just as the Right was to attribute much of the Left's strength to the *caciquismo* of Socialist union-leaders using the old trick of making future employment dependent on the appropriate vote being cast.

In 1931, with the Right in disarray, the situation could not fit the pattern. According to *El Socialista*, the coming of the Republic caused the old local bosses of the Monarchy to turn Republican in order to preserve their influence.[96] The paper denounced the entry of *caciques* into the Right Republican parties. However, judging from later recriminations in the Cortes, it would seem that *caciques* offered their services to all the parties of the new régime. It was a general belief in the ensuing months that *caciques* of the *Unión Patriótica* had in the main been employed by the Radical-Socialists, and some by the Socialists themselves. Those who were not mere time-servers remained loyal to the Right. Their fate was illuminated by the case of Priego (Córdoba), which before 1923 had been the 'fief' of Alcalá-Zamora. Primo de Rivera had turned out Alcalá-Zamora's men and on 12 April 1931 they had been defeated by the Dictator's supporters. The new régime soon removed these Monarchists and the President's friends returned to office. On the basis of a whole series of such dismissals, the press of the Right attacked the government for its 'caciquista policy' in the coming elections.[97]

The evidence concerning the Provisional Government's conduct with regard to municipal councils is incomplete and confused. Maura announced on 17 April that he would appoint temporary committees in municipalities where malpractice was alleged. He later annulled 5 per cent of the 2,700 cases which he looked into, and the positions thus left vacant were filled by partial elections on 31 May.[98] Allowing for the good intentions of the Minister of the Interior, it would seem that in many areas the actions of local Republicans prevented Monarchists from taking their posts. In any case, 'Republicanisation' of local councils took place on a large scale; possibly this was as much the result of voluntary changes of allegiance by the elected councillors themselves as of arbitrary measures.[99]

Another electoral practice taken over by the Republicans was the 'instruction' of Mayors by provincial Governors—with or without the permission of the Minister of the Interior.[100] Given the Monarchist nature of the rural councils elected on 12 April, it would seem unlikely that the Republican authorities at some level did not take steps to change the character of local government in the great majority of cases. In any event, it can be said that caciquismo in June and July 1931 worked in favour of parties represented in the Provisional Government and the Generalidad.

A crucial step, however, was taken to undermine the system of caciquismo in the sense of the influence of political bosses over a small area or pueblo. The Decree of 8 May abolished the former small constituencies and created new ones on the basis of provincial boundaries, except for urban centres of over 100,000 inhabitants, which formed separate constituencies. Within these new constituencies, the number of deputies elected corresponded to the size of the population: one deputy for each 50,000 people. Candidates, who could now be women or priests, had to obtain over 20 per cent of the vote to be elected, vacancies being filled in a second contest a fortnight later. The electorate was composed of all males of twenty-three and over.[101] The decree therefore largely submerged pockets of influence, and gave the advantage to well-organised mass parties with sizable financial resources or auxiliary organisations. In 1931, there existed two of the latter type, although they were of a regional nature: the Socialist UGT, strong in Madrid, Bilbao, Extremadura and eastern Andalusia; and the CNCA, concentrated in the Castiles and León. According to Largo Caballero after the event, Socialist success was the result of good organisation, *caciquismo* having been largely destroyed by the new electoral system.[102]

Apart from changes in local councils, the conversion of local bosses into Republicans and the 'instruction' of provincial Governors, the principal disadvantages from which the Right suffered were the almost total lack of organisation and the frequent lack of juridical guarantees. With the closure of the CMI, *ABC* counselled abstention because the government had made opposition impossible.[103] In contrast, *El Debate*—supported by *La Nación* (*Primoderriverista*), *El Siglo Futuro* (Traditionalist) and *La Época* (conservative), and by the Bishops—campaigned against such defeatism. The maximum effort should be made in elections for Cortes which would decide vital matters of religion, education and national unity. It admitted that abstention was justifiable where no meetings could be held, no papers published and where the police were employed for partisan purposes; even so, it was not recommended.[104] On the eve of the election, *ABC* modified its attitude and advised Monarchists to vote for conservative candidates, preferably for those of *Acción Nacional*.[105] Notable withdrawals due to lack of guarantees were the DRV and the Liberal-Democrats of Asturias, whose first meeting was broken up by a mob of Socialists and Republicans.[106]

Autopsies by candidates of *Acción Nacional* revealed the weakness of the new Right: ignorance of the social teaching of the Church among all classes of society. Other factors contributed to defeat. Intervention by the authorities on behalf of government candidates was noted in Toledo, Guadalajara and in Cuenca, where the Governor instructed all 291 Mayors to see that coalition candidates were returned. Violence by the Left, making Rightist propaganda difficult, was noted in Córdoba and Jaén, while in Cuenca the Catholic paper was suspended and only one meeting was held; a second was prevented by the Governor who told the Mayor that the Right's list had been withdrawn. Abstention by the classes of order was recorded in Toledo. In Cuenca it was attributed to disapproval of *Acción Nacional*'s passivity regarding the burning of the *conventos*, while in Jaén, Córdoba and Guadalajara, fear of violence was believed to be the reason.

In Toledo, the two successful candidates attributed their victory to the 30,000 votes of Catholic farmers: Dimas de Madariaga was a native of Corral de Almaguer and therefore known in one part of the province as a social-Catholic worker, while Fr Molina picked up protest votes against the expulsion of the Cardinal-Archbishop. In Cuenca, votes came from the small *pueblos* influenced by the local notables. In Jaén and Córdoba, defeat was seen as the inevitable consequence of the desperation of the masses who voted Socialist after fifty years' suppression by *caciques* because of the lack of popular Catholicism. In Jaén, all *caciques* were defeated except Alcalá-Zamora, while in Córdoba the callousness of employers could be gauged by the fact that Canon Gallegos Rocafull, founder of a small workers' union, was almost run out of the province as a revolutionary. In Guadalajara, fragmentation brought defeat: Rightist voters had a choice between Romanones, the Liberal Right, independent conservatives, *Acción Nacional*, and Agrarian Republicans. The Agrarians represented a Catholic peasants' league, and campaigned against the rural proletariat of the CNCA, represented by *Acción Nacional*. The lack of organisation was apparent, if not glaring, in all provinces.[107]

The elections for the single chamber of the Constituent Cortes were held on 28 June, with second contests on 12 July. Polling-day produced no serious disturbances, although some irregularities occurred.[108] The government parties, in particular the Socialists, did well. Abstention was blamed for the poor performance of the Liberal Right and the other Rightist groups, although 70 per cent of the electorate voted. The Radicals emerged as the main conservative force of the Republic. In Madrid, Lerroux topped the poll with 133,425 votes, compared with 117,993 for the first Socialist. Herrera, who obtained 27,481 to Goicoechea's 26,744, just missed election, being beaten by the list giving 'Support for the Republic'.[109] In Barcelona, the *Esquerra*, supported by the CNT, won easily.

The resultant composition of the Cortes was as follows: Socialists, 113; Radicals, 89; Radical-Socialists, 50; *Esquerra*, 43; *Acción Republicana*, 24; Agrarians, 24; Liberal Right, 23; Federals, 16;

ORGA, 16; Basque-Navarrese coalition, 15; 'In the Service of the Republic', 11; Catalan Regionalists (*Lliga*), 3; Liberal Democrats, 2; Social Revolutionary (later Communist), 1. There were also 26 independents.[110]

In the Basque provinces and Navarre, the Catholic Rightist coalition was victorious, although in Bilbao Prieto's Republican-Socialist list won. At San Sebastián on 5 July, the Basque-Navarrese electoral coalition was renewed by the 'Pact of the Hotel de Londres': the question of régime was omitted, and a minimum programme for the defence of religion and the restoration of ancient local rights was approved. The parliamentary minority was to be led by the Jaimist Joaquín Beúnza, with the Nationalist chief Aguirre as secretary.[111] On 12 July a rally was held in celebration at Guernica. The atmosphere was one of aggressive euphoria. The Lectoral Canon of Vitoria announced: 'We are the Ireland of the West, and we now have our O'Connell [Aguirre] to rouse us.' Aguirre threatened that the Basques would seize the autonomy they wanted if it were not given to them.

Yet although one Traditionalist considered Aguirre 'providential', the old differences could be detected. The Conde de Rodezno concentrated on religious issues though he referred to 'the traditional liberties of the *Fueros*, consubstantial with these provinces and the Kingdom of Navarre'. The Statute was implicitly rejected.[112] The minority consisted of six Traditionalists, six Basque Nationalists, two independents from Guipúzcoa closely allied to the PNV, and an ex-*Maurista*. Socialists described the minority as 'the Beúnza tribe' of 'cavemen' and 'troglodytes'.

In Catalonia, the popularity of the *Lliga* was at a low ebb. The veterans Abadal and Rahola represented Barcelona-capital, while Estelrich won a seat in Gerona in coalition with the Liberal Right. The Liberal Republican Right itself, although the largest single Catholic group in the Cortes, had not proved a success. With the rest of the Right disorganised, only twenty-four of its hundred and twenty-four candidates were elected; its most favourable moment had passed without glory. The group's deputies were scattered over constituencies as far apart as Almería and Lugo, Cádiz and Castellón: no indication of potential strength could be observed in any particular locality.

The new Right Republicans also recorded little success. M.

Álvarez was elected in Madrid with Ossorio and Sánchez Guerra, and, thanks to Lerroux, in Valencia; his only Liberal Democrat colleague, Villalobos, owed his place to the Agrarian coalition in Salamanca. Among the miscellany of independents could be found Santiago Alba, in Zamora; also, on home ground in the Balearics, two 'Centre Republicans' revealed themselves as Juan March Ordinas and an associate, but they announced their spiritual home in Madrid as the Radical minority. The only deputy actually elected as a Monarchist was the independent liberal Romanones in his usual *habitat* of Guadalajara. Also a known Monarchist, though of a different kind, was the independent Deputy for Orense, José Calvo Sotelo; he was not, however, permitted to take his seat in the Cortes and so stayed in exile in Portugal, later moving to France.[113]

The Agrarian minority, as General Fanjul explained, was a gathering of Deputies of conflicting ideologies who had coalesced to comply with parliamentary regulations stipulating the minimum size for a minority in order to qualify for representation on parliamentary committees. The leader of the minority was the last Under-Secretary of Grace and Justice of the Monarchy, José Martínez de Velasco, an *Albista* Liberal. Its secretary was a former Conservative Senator, Ramón de la Cuesta, also elected for Burgos.[114] The minority's members came almost entirely from the Castiles and León: 22 of its 24 Deputies were elected for constituencies in this region, six for Burgos alone, and three for Salamanca.

That such should be the case was not pure chance. The CNCA and other farmers' organisations were strong in this area where smallholdings predominated. Furthermore, wheat-growing was the area's principal occupation. A Republican-Socialist government, with its real strength in the towns, was likely to favour cheaper bread for the urban worker: this could be achieved only by the import of cheaper foreign wheat at the expense of the Castilian peasant's livelihood. This underlying economic factor, combined with the fact that Catholicism had not been seriously challenged here by Socialist or Anarchist propaganda, explains this regional phenomenon, apparent in 1931 if quite obvious in later elections.

If geographically homogeneous, the Agrarian minority was cer-

tainly politically heterogeneous. Two main types were discernible:
the liberal—liberal in politics, conservative with regard to the
agrarian *status quo*—and the Catholic—putting first priority on
defence of the Church, while being interested in agrarian matters.
The liberal trend found its focus in the ex-*Albistas*: Royo Villanova, Martínez de Velasco and Cid.[115] Half the minority was
liberal, and the clearest example of its connection with the 'old
politics' was the ex-Conservative Minister Abilio Calderón, who
had represented Palencia since 1890. The Catholic trend, on the
other hand, was in general composed of younger men. The
minority included four priests (one a Traditionalist), the worker
Dimas de Madariaga, the Alfonsine academic Sáinz Rodríguez,
and a disciple of Herrera, José María Gil Robles.

Thus the disarray of the Right in 1931 produced some alliances
which would at other times have been thought infamous. Heterogeneous in their political pasts, the minority's members remained
so: of the twenty-four, eleven were simply Agrarians and six men
of *Acción Nacional*; three were Traditionalist and one Alfonsine
Monarchists. The number was made up by a lawyer from the
Canaries and a priest from Santander who had no marked political
loyalties. Though officially led by the fifty-six-year-old Martínez
de Velasco, the thirty-two-year-old Gil Robles immediately
eclipsed him as the minority's real leader with a maiden speech in
defence of the purity of the Agrarian coalition of Salamanca's
electoral victory. The leading Republican intellectual declared
that the Right, as always, had found a great parliamentarian to
lead it.[116]

Notes to this chapter are on pages 296–305.

Chapter 2 LEGALITY AND CONSPIRACY
July 1931–September 1932

THE FUTURE of the Republic was in the hands of the deputies elected in June. If the new régime were to take permanent root in Spain it had to have a constitution acceptable not only to the Socialists and Left Republicans but also to Catholic opinion, which events were to show was under-represented in the Constituent Cortes. The driving-force behind the Constitution came from the 'Jacobin' Left Republicans whose first priority was the subjugation of the Church. They were loyally supported by the Socialists who wanted them to carry through the 'bourgeois revolution'. The anti-clerical Constitution which resulted from this alliance offended Catholic Spain and ominously identified the régime with the particular type of Republicanism epitomised by Azaña. The first President of the Republic, Alcalá-Zamora, found to his dismay that the violent spirit of the incendiarists of May had been clothed in legality: the Constitution was a standing invitation to civil war.[1]

Moderate Republicans saw that the survival of the régime depended on its ability to retain the loyalty of the 'neutral masses' who had voted against Alfonso and to reassure and attract as many as possible of those who had voted for him in April. The chances of rebuilding in modified form the bridge between the two Spains constructed by Cánovas rapidly disappeared. The constant factor in the Republic's history was to be the increasing polarisation of politics around Right and Left: parties in the Centre kept collapsing. This process began with the resignation of Alcalá-Zamora and Maura in October 1931: anti-clerical intransigence torpedoed

59

liberal-Catholic Republicanism. The gap was widened in December when Azaña formed a coalition with the Socialists. Lerroux was excluded because he wanted to attract conservatives into the Republic through his own party.

The Socialists were clearly the key to the Republic's history. Their position seemed paradoxical. They provided the government with mass support and proclaimed themselves defenders of the régime while admitting that for them the Republic was accidental and Socialism fundamental. They refused to accept the idea of a Republic ruled by conservatives like Lerroux. In fact they were keeping their eyes on the main chance and using Azaña's Republic as a means of eliminating conservative obstacles to their future progress as well as a tool for crushing their old rivals in the CNT. Their social-democratic reformism was therefore tactical. Azaña and his colleagues were forced to ally with the Socialists because progressive politicians without masses could not do otherwise.[2]

In a sense the Left Republicans and the Socialists played into the hands of their opponents. The anti-clerical content of the Constitution provoked a nationwide Catholic reaction which took them by surprise, while moderate opinion wary of this reaction rallied to Lerroux for protection. The cardinal error of Azaña and his supporters was to launch a frontal attack on the Church first, for this enabled opponents of social reform and of decentralisation to hitch their interests to the cause of religion. At the same time the government's delay in implementing social changes, notably agrarian reform, led disillusioned workers into the revolutionary paths of the CNT, now controlled by the extremists of the FAI. Its constant violence, which the government seemed unable to eradicate,[3] contributed to the conservative revival, as did fear of Socialism and increasing economic difficulties for which the world depression was not mainly responsible. The Defence Law of the Republic also had the effect of helping the Right. The government's use of its dictatorial powers caused anger, bitterness and inconvenience; capricious discrimination stiffened the resolve of its opponents, only a minority of whom resorted to arms, thereby playing into the hands of the government.

The Constituent Cortes of the Second Spanish Republic met on Bastille Day, 1931. The Socialist academic Besteiro was elected its

President, and confidence in the government was quickly ratified. The Republican-Socialist coalition remained in being, forming a solid majority in the Chamber.[4] Debates on the Constitution did not begin, however, until late in August.

The first draft produced by the Advisory Juridical Committee, under Ossorio, had been rejected by the principal government party, the Socialists, as confused, reactionary and inadequate.[5] Ossorio's draft was an attempt to adapt the Constitution of 1876 to a Republican framework, with some admixture of ideas from the social Encyclicals. Its religious provisions reflected the liberal-Catholic views of Right Republcans.i Freedom of conscience and religion was proclaimed, while Church and State were to be separated by the Church becoming an 'institution of public law'. Religious instruction in schools was guaranteed, though freedom to start private schools was also granted.[6] The Episcopacy, however, objected to this subordination of the Church to 'the absolute laicism of the State'. Catholic deputies were told that they must defend the Church. All Catholics ought to implore the Virgin for help in keeping Spain 'the Catholic nation *par excellence*' and oppose a document which denied that the State had a religion and that all power proceeded from God.[7]

Relations between Church and State became strained even though the Vatican continued to be conciliatory. Cardinal Segura, from his exile in France, continued to protest about his unjust expulsion and asked Alcalá-Zamora to allow him to return. He still counselled resistance in matters where the interests of the Church were threatened, but reaffirmed his obedience to the constituted power.[8] The climax came when the Vicar-General of Vitoria was arrested at the frontier on 14 August. He was found to be the bearer of a plan for disguising the fact that the Church owned property.[9] Segura denied that the documents concerned the sale of ecclesiastical property and the investment of the proceeds abroad and said that the intention was simply to prevent the confiscation of diocesan reserve funds.[10] Nevertheless, the government suspended the temporalities of the Cardinal-Archbishop of Toledo and his fellow exile, Bishop Múgica of Vitoria.[11] When Segura's renunciation of the archiepiscopal see was announced on 26 September Los Ríos saw it as a great victory for the State and proof that, in the Vatican, liberal views had prevailed over integrist pressures.[12] These events added fuel to the flames during the debates on the religious clauses of the Constitution.

After the rejection of Ossorio's draft, a new constitutional committee was set up under the Socialist Jiménez de Asúa. Debates on the new draft began in the second half of August.[13] For the Socialists, the Constitution of the bourgeois Republic was the first stage on the road to Socialism. They wanted the Church to be firmly under the control of the laicist Republic. The expulsion of the Orders, confiscation of their possessions and cancellation of the ecclesiastical budget were 'elementary aspirations of democracy'.[14]

Catholics naturally considered the religious question the most important. Gil Robles warned that the future of the Republic would depend largely on the solution found.[15] *El Debate* exhorted Catholics to be resolute and so prevent victory for the opponents of the Church.[16] Compromise was from the first unlikely; Catholic deputies were often shouted down. For the Agrarians, Sáinz Rodríguez put forward a basis for compromise. He suggested that the Right would accept the most advanced social legislation of the Left, if the Left would accept the national spiritual tradition. If the Left did not accept it, the Republic could abandon hope for a legal existence. The Socialists, however, walked out of the Chamber at the start of his speech.[17]

Before the religious clauses were discussed, the regional issue and the rights of property were debated. The Republic was defined as 'an integral State compatible with the autonomy of Municipalities and Regions'.[18] Articles 11 to 20 of the draft defined in general terms what functions should be kept by the State and what should be conceded to the regions, as well as the procedure for obtaining a statute of autonomy. Here, as in general on regional questions, the Right was split. The Basque-Navarrese advocated wider powers for the regions, as did the *Lliga*, whereas the Agrarians favoured the minimum power for regions, being obsessed by fears of separatism. Their main spokesman was a staunch liberal, Antonio Royo Villanova, and the liberal element in the minority took the lead in opposing regional aspirations. The Catholic element adhered to traditionalist theories. Thus while the Basque Leizaola sought more regional control over Church-State relations, the judiciary and the Army, Royo and the Agrarians concentrated on 'the preservation of national unity and integrity'.[19]

Passions were aroused, but Catalans and Castilians alike treated the debates as a preliminary skirmish. Article 22 of the Constitution, allowing provinces to opt out of a constituted region if they wished, was notable in being the sole Agrarian amendment accepted.[20]

The Articles concerning property and labour which caused friction were numbered 42 and 44. Article 42 stated that all sources of national wealth were really owned by the State in the name of the Nation. Private property rights would be recognised until gradual socialisation took place. The State virtually had the right to do what it liked with private property; compensation need not be paid in all cases. Public services and undertakings of national interest were to be nationalised as soon as possible. Confiscation of possessions could not be imposed as a legal or political penalty.

Agrarians, Catholics and all conservative Republicans protested against this 'sword of Damocles suspended over property rights'.[21] Gil Robles and Leizaola opposed the social-Catholic view to the Socialist: property was a natural, but not absolute, right. The State should only take over property for reasons of social utility after 'previous just compensation'. They rejected the classical view of *jus utendi, fruendi et abutendi* as anti-Christian.[22] The liberal Agrarians, however, thought expropriation justifiable with full compensation only if the courts could prove unlawful ownership. One of them noted that it was little consolation for an owner to be told that he had been expropriated without compensation, though assured that the penalty of confiscation had not been imposed.[23] Eventually the original text of Article 42 was amended by anti-Socialist Republicans, so that Article 44 of the Constitution, as it became, permitted expropriation for reasons of social utility, or socialisation, with adequate compensation, unless an absolute majority voted against compensation. The penalty of confiscation was strictly forbidden. Thus, although blunted a little, the sword of Damocles remained in position.

Article 44 of the draft, which became Article 46 of the Constitution, defined work as 'a social obligation'. Social legislation was to cover social securities, child and female labour, the length of the working day, minimum and family wages, annual holidays with pay, the rights of the Spanish worker abroad, co-operative societies, workers' participation in the management, administration and profits of firms, and the economic and juridical relationship between the factors of production. This enumeration of social aims was modified and extended in an amendment presented by the Catholic worker Dimas de Madariaga. Work ought to be redefined as 'an ethical duty which is binding on everybody'. The worker, in addition to the aforesaid, should have the right to cheap and healthy housing and rest-homes. Legislation should also deal with savings and insurance societies. The economic and juridical relationship between the factors of production ought to be institutionalised in corporative bodies with equal representation for both sides. Madariaga's amendment was, in fact, an unsuccessful attempt to pour into Article 44 the most comprehensive statement possible of social-Catholic aims.[24]

The religious clauses were recognised by all to be the most important in the Constitution. They formed, claimed Catholics, the *leit-motiv* of this 'laicist, anti-religious, atheist' document designed to rob Spain of her faith.[25] The Alfonsine Sáinz Rodríguez pointed out that such anachronistic Jacobinism was to be found in no other post-war constitution.[26] Other Catholic Agrarians were at pains to avoid accusations of Monarchism: 'We are not idolisers of the person, but servants of the principle . . . of discipline, of order, of subordination, of obedience to the legitimate power, whatever it be called, in whatever person it be incarnate, whether Charles V or Alcalá-Zamora.'[27]

Article 3 of the draft read simply: 'There is no state religion.' This the Catholics found unacceptable. They wanted the Article omitted because there was only one religion in Spain, that of the vast majority, namely Catholicism.[28] The Article was, in fact, rephrased so that it read: 'The Spanish State has no official religion.' This text was passed on 13 October against the opposition of Agrarians, Basques, Navarrese and various Catholic Republicans, including Alcalá-Zamora. It remained for such as Fr Guallar the epitome of 'integral laicism'.[29] There was also friction over part of Article 1, which stated that all power emanated from the people. Catholics wanted some recognition that all power in the last resort proceeded from God, but the majority remained unmoved when told that the Constitution of the Polish Republic made reference to the Almighty.[30]

The religious provisions abrogated the Concordat of 1851 and represented the vengeance which anti-clericals, the most voluble of whom were the Radical-Socialists, wished to take on the Church. Article 25 of the draft proclaimed freedom of religion, but allowed it to be practised only inside churches, thus implicitly forbidding religious processions. This article Gil Robles and Leizaola again wanted suppressed. The liberal Royo Villanova joined with Right Republicans in pointing out that if it were not omitted, the Constitution would automatically lead to rioting over the banning of traditional processions.[31] Article 41 permitted divorce by mutual consent, and equal rights in the family for legitimate and illegitimate children. The Catholics also wanted this provision suppressed. Instead, they asked for state support for large families.[32] Article 46 of the draft stated that primary education would be obligatory, free and laicist in a 'single school' system; religious instruction was allowed only in the Church's own establishments. This article has to be seen together with the most controversial, Article 24 of the draft, which declared all religions 'Associations subject to the general laws of the country'. The State was under no circumstances to favour or give material aid to any religious body, and it was stated that all religious orders would be dissolved and their property nationalised. It was around Article 24, and its consequences upon Article 46, that the battle really raged.

Gil Robles and Leizaola suggested an alternative Article 24: Church-State relations should be regulated by a new concordat with the Holy See. The liberal Agrarians and Right Republicans asked for no more than that the Orders be allowed to continue.[33] Regarding education, amendments were put forward to permit parents to decide about religious instruction, to permit the foundation of local religious schools, to allow the Orders to go on teaching in institutions where workers received free education, and to suggest that state aid be given to all educational establishments.[34] Article 24 also brought to an end the ecclesiastical budget which the State paid under the terms of the Concordat as compensation for the disentailment of Church lands in the nineteenth century. Fr Guallar demanded that the budget continue as long as there was no other compensation, while Beúnza and the Basque-Navarrese argued that it must continue unless the lands of the Church were returned.[35]

From 8 to 13 October the battle was waged in the Cortes with

E

increasing intensity. Whilst Traditionalists fought against separation, social-Catholics like Gil Robles demanded the 'absolute separation of Church and State as two perfect societies' in their own spheres. From this Gil Robles deduced that the Church must have complete independence in its own sphere. This the draft did not permit because the religious articles violated the general precepts of other articles already passed concerning individual liberties, the right of association and the principle of equality. The draft was therefore 'a plan for religious persecution'. From the liberal-Catholic standpoint, Martínez de Velasco denounced the laicist 'single school' system as 'tyrannical'.[36] Catholics who were declared Republicans pleaded with the majority to avoid identifying the Republic with anti-Catholicism by being intolerant. If the articles were passed, warned the Premier, Catholics would have to move into opposition: better, therefore, a negotiated settlement than the resuscitation of the policy of Combes.[37] Catholic opposition, in its impotence in the Cortes, resorted to warnings and threats. Alcalá-Zamora advocated opposition within the Republic. Gil Robles spoke of a Spanish *Kulturkampf*, a passionate but legal campaign for revision. The Traditionalist answer, however, was more radical: Beúnza warned that persecution would force them to resort to 'the dignity of free men against tyranny'[38]—a veiled threat of violence.

Under pressure from Alcalá-Zamora, a new draft of Article 24, drawn up by the Constitutional Committee without the knowledge of Gil Robles and Leizaola, was put to the Cortes. The new draft called for the ending of the ecclesiastical budget within two years. Religious Orders taking a fourth vow (the Jesuits) were to be dissolved and their property nationalised. Other Orders were to be subject to a special law permitting their dissolution if they constituted 'a danger for the security of the State'; they were not to engage in industry, commerce nor education, and provision was made for the nationalisation of their property. Alcalá-Zamora persuaded all the Ministers except Prieto to accept a relatively harmonious solution.[39]

The session of 13 October was passionate and lengthy. The Catholics continued to present amendments against the new draft, and the Radical-Socialists in favour of the old; when the latter were rejected, the Radical-Socialists, including two Ministers, walked out. The anti-clerical Azaña proclaimed that Spain had ceased to be Catholic because its intellectual *élite* was now laicist; measures taken against the Orders were necessary for public safety and the defence of the Republic. In reply, the Catholic Catalan nationalist Carrasco Formiguera denounced Azaña's 'Fascist concept of the State'. Gil Robles asked how the State was going to replace the teaching of the Orders without at least temporarily depriving 60,000 children in Madrid alone of education: no answer was given.[40] Alcalá-Zamora pleaded for tolerance, but the ministerial promises of his colleagues were not kept. Article 24— Article 26 of the Constitution—was passed by 178 votes to 59. The session ended at 7.35 am on 14 October amid cries of 'Long live the Republic' from the Left and 'Long live freedom' from the Basque-Navarrese. Leizaola was assaulted by an anti-clerical deputy. The Basque-Navarrese, the Agrarians and the Right Republican deputy Ayats now withdrew from the Cortes for the remaining constitutional debates;[41] the exception in the two Rightist minorities was Royo Villanova.

On 14 October Alcalá-Zamora and Miguel Maura, who had voted against Article 26, resigned, and a second provisional government was formed by Manuel Azaña, the *bête noire* of the Right.[42] With only Royo Villanova present from the Rightist minorities, the remaining articles, mainly concerned with the balance of constitutional powers, were the subject of controversy between Republicans. Prior to 13 October, however, the Catholics had, with the Socialists, voted for female suffrage and won in the face of opposition from the bourgeois Republicans.[43] The Catholics' ideas on other constitutional matters were contained in amendments they had earlier presented. Like Alcalá-Zamora, they wanted a second chamber to put a brake on extremism. Gil Robles and Leizaola envisaged a bi-cameral system with equal powers for Senate and Congress. Congress, the lower house, was to be elected on the individualist basis of proportional representation; the Senate was to be organic and corporative. They also sought provision for a referendum on important pieces of legislation if a tenth of the electorate or a third of Parliament should demand one. The Court of Constitutional Guarantees was to have power to decide whether or not laws were constitutional.[44] The second chamber and the referendum were rejected.

Royo Villanova took a different view from the Catholics on such questions. As a liberal, he defended to the utmost the supremacy of Parliament against plebiscitary or presidentialist tendencies: 'For me the ideal Republic, like the ideal Monarchy (for the form of government is accidental), is parliamentary; the essential thing in the world is liberty and democracy, and the essential thing in politics is Parliament.'[45]

The Constitution was passed on 9 December 1931 by 368 votes, including those of Alcalá-Zamora and Maura. Although its controversial religious provisions were soon put into effect, in the sphere of civil rights it long remained a paper constitution. Though Spain had officially ceased to be Catholic, Azaña immediately took steps to defend the Republican creation against the Catholic revisionist campaign. An enabling law, the Defence Law of the Republic, was introduced on 20 October and quickly approved. The law defined as 'acts of aggression against the Republic' incitement to resist legislation, incitement of the armed forces, spreading news which could be harmful to public peace, political and unjustifiable strikes, use of Monarchist emblems and verbal defence of the Monarchy, lack of zeal in carrying out orders by civil servants and, indeed, 'any action or expression which redounds to the discredit of the Institutions and organs of the State'. The Minister of the Interior was to decide when and by whom the law had been contravened, and could sanction confinement of the alleged offender, impose a fine of up to 10,000 pesetas and suspend any meeting, association or publication at will.[46] The government, in fact, voted itself dictatorial powers.

The Cortes also passed a bill of attainder against Alfonso XIII. The King was found guilty by acclamation of high treason, and sentenced to perpetual banishment. His property was confiscated.[47] *ABC* described the bill as 'an act of spiteful and unnecessary persecution', for which it was fined and suspended for three days.[48] On 10 December 1931 the Cortes elected Alcalá-Zamora the first President of the Republic.[49] The first government was formed by Azaña, who chose to rely on Socialist support instead of the Radical alternative.[50]

The government went ahead quickly with legislation to implement the religious clauses of the Constitution. On 23 January 1932 President Alcalá-Zamora signed a decree dissolving the Society of

Jesus in Spain; the process was to be completed within ten days and steps were taken to nationalise its property.[51] The Traditionalist Agrarian Lamamié de Clairac immediately demanded a debate. He argued that, since the fourth vow was taken by only 10 per cent of Jesuits, who thereby made explicit for missionary work their obedience to the Pope, Article 26 could not properly be applied to all Jesuits. Moreover, the Jesuits were not enemies of the Republic, and their religious activities did not concern the State. The decree, he said, contravened Article 44, forbidding confiscation of property and permitting expropriation only with adequate compensation. He lamented that the Court of Constitutional Guarantees was not in being so that such matters could be submitted to it. The closing of Jesuit colleges violated the government's promise to let children complete their education in religious institutions.

Traditionalists saw in such legislation the sinister influence of a Masonic International bent on the destruction of the Church. Beúnza, leader of the Basque-Navarrese, defending the Order founded by the Basque St Ignatius of Loyola, challenged Masonic deputies to declare their affiliations so that Traditionalist suspicions could be proved or disproved.[52] The Nuncio protested that the decree was an insult to the Church, but on 4 February the debate was guillotined by 189 votes to 45.[53] The Jesuits were therefore dissolved, their schools and institutes closed and preparations made to confiscate their reputedly great riches. Though some remained in Spain, most of them went to the Low Countries.[54]

In January 1932, a law was passed confirming the Decree of 9 July for the secularisation of cemeteries. Church burials were permitted if requested in the deceased's will, but as nine-tenths of Spaniards made no will, surviving relatives were allowed to decide. In practice an anti-clerical municipality could do much to hinder the survivors' wishes.[55] In Madrid during the preceding twenty years, 346,970 Catholic burials had been recorded, compared with 2,343 civil ceremonies; in the last six months of 1931, with the anti-clericals in full cry, the figures were 7,859 to 134 in favour of Catholic funerals.[56]

Catholic opposition was based on the principle of 'one faith, one cemetery'. Aguirre argued that the law violated the spirit of the

League of Nations, and contrasted the Spanish Republicans' attitude with Greek respect for Moslem cemeteries and Turkish
respect for Christian and Jewish cemeteries.[57] The law in fact
provided an outlet for the unsatisfied passions of anti-clerical town
councillors: if it were more difficult to laicise the living, at least the
dead could be secularised. Cemeteries were taken over, and many
municipalities prohibited the appearance of the Cross at burials;
in some municipalities taking the Viaticum through the streets, as
well as use of the Cross at burials, was banned by a strict interpretation of Article 27 as public demonstrations of religion which
only the government could authorise.[58] In Barcelona, Ventosa
Calvell reported, anti-clericals actually put up a barrier between
Catholic and non-Catholic graves so that they could symbolically
knock it down.[59]

The divorce law, implementing Article 43, was called by Catholics 'one insult more to the Church'.[60] The Basque Nationalist
Leizaola marshalled statistics to demonstrate that the crime rate
among divorced and widowed Germans was double the average.
Divorce, he concluded, stimulated crime, juvenile delinquency
and suicide. Therefore, if divorce were introduced into Spain, the
majority in the Cortes would be responsible for 4,500 deaths a
year. The majority, however, was not deterred and passed the law
on 25 February by 260 votes to 23.[61]

The temporalities of the Bishop of Segovia were suspended
following his Pastoral of 30 March, in which he condemned civil
marriage as blatant concubinage. Fr Guallar here found further
proof that in Spain there existed, 'not the free Church in the free
State, but the oppressed Church in the oppressor-State'. Bishop
Pérez Platero had been denied the right to defend marriage as a
Sacrament, while the propagation of other views went unhin-
dered.[62] The reduction of the ecclesiastical budget from sixty-six
to twenty-nine million pesetas was also strongly opposed by the
Catholics.[63]

The Episcopacy bewailed the 'absolute laicism' of the Constitution, that 'juridical outrage against the Church'. The Bishops
protested against the unilateral termination of the Concordat by
the Republic, towards which they had carefully avoided any act of
hostility. The grievances against each religious clause were listed.
Catholics were urged to obey the constituted power, but to do

their utmost to bring about a change in the laws. Catholic Action
was to be reinvigorated and Catholics were to found schools.
'Religious reconquest' was to be 'the totalitarian ideal' of the
faithful. While the Church could not identify itself with any
political party, *a priori* abstention and opposition were declared
'irreconcilable with love of Religion and Country': it was 'almost
treason' to upset the social order in the hope that something better
might follow. In such times 'union, or at least common practical
action, is an unavoidable obligation for all Catholics, whatever be
the party to which they belong'.[64] Within this framework Catholics
embarked on a determined and passionate revisionist campaign:
'Purify us by persecution and the victory is ours!'[65]

The results of the elections of June 1931 were considered by the
leaders of *Acción Nacional* sufficiently encouraging to justify the
electoral organisation being turned into a permanent body.
Monthly subscriptions were demanded to cover the expenses of
offices, electoral organisation and propaganda.[66] The new phase
was inaugurated with a dinner on 12 July at which its founder,
Herrera, outlined his plans. The general aim was the creation of
'a great, profoundly Christian nation', to be achieved by winning
the working-class to the social-Catholic programme by legal
means. Military victories never solved any political problem.

Acción Nacional was not a political party, though it could be the
midwife for one. Meanwhile its candidates, when elected, retained
their independence within the framework of its fundamental principles. Herrera took as his model the Belgian *Union Catholique*, an
amalgam of trade unions, agrarians, bourgeois and Catholic associations which formed one parliamentary bloc although each section independently defended its particular interests. In Spain, the
agrarian wing already existed, as did the Catholic associations. The
election of Dimas de Madariaga, he hoped, would mark the beginning of a Catholic workers' movement created by the workers
themselves. Conservatives could help in this indispensable task by
atoning for the sins of injustice they had committed.[67] Territorially
the first priority was consolidation in the Castiles to give *Acción
Nacional* a solid basis.[68]

It was not until October 1931 that *Acción Nacional* really got
under way with the passing of the anti-clerical clauses of the
Constitution and the withdrawal of the Catholic deputies; Article

26 was the turning-point. The movement for withdrawal from the
Cortes was initiated by the Basque-Navarrese, whom *El Debate*
originally publicly asked not to withdraw.[69] At a meeting of the
Basque-Navarrese and Agrarian minorities at which some other
Catholic deputies were present, Gil Robles argued in favour of
staying, as did Royo Villanova and Martínez de Velasco.[70] A
majority of Agrarians, however, favoured withdrawal while the
Constitution was being debated, and only Royo Villanova actually
stayed on in the Cortes. The Alfonsine Sáinz Rodríguez and the
Traditionalist Lamamié de Clairac claimed credit for the withdrawal.[71]

The manifesto issued by the deputies who retired declared that
the views of the country and the Cortes had diverged: the 'neutral
masses' who had voted for the Republic in April and June had not
voted for anti-clericalism. The deputies took no responsibility for
the Constitution and raised the standard of revision within the law
even before it was passed. The Basque-Navarrese withdrew to a
man, while the recalcitrance of Royo Villanova among the
Agrarians was compensated by the withdrawal of Ayats, elected
as a Liberal Rightist for Gerona. Royo Villanova nevertheless
signed the manifesto, as did the Catalan nationalist Carrasco, the
Lliga deputies, four Catholic Regionalists from Galicia and the
Right Republican Gregorio Arranz.[72]

The effect of this on the organisation of *Acción Nacional* was
immediate. In July the provisional statutes had been drawn up for
this 'politico-social organisation' for 'the defence of the principles
of Religion, Country, Family, Order, Work and Property'. Its task
was twofold: to set up branches and to be the link between regional
and provincial groups accepting its fundamental principles. Local
groups were semi-autonomous: the central body controlled the
choice of candidates, electoral alliances and national policy. A
deliberative assembly was to be elected by all members to approve
the political programme and elect a finance and an executive
committee, the latter being the initiator of policy.[73]

Elections were held in July and August for the deliberative
assembly. Those elected included Gil Robles, Madariaga and
others with a similar political outlook, the liberal Agrarian Martínez
de Velasco, and Alfonsines with a *penchant* for conspiracy such as
Vallellano and Juan Pujol.[74] The assembly did not meet to elect

the executive committee until 17 October. Most of its ten members were *Herreristas*; three were prominent Alfonsines, one a Traditionalist and one, Ramón Bergé, had been a co-founder of *Maurismo* in 1913. Gil Robles became its President on 17 November.[75]

Acción Nacional was now ready to undertake the revisionist campaign which *El Debate* announced on 15 October as the answer to Azaña's vision of a laicist State 'with all its consequences'.[76] The first meeting was held at Ledesma on 18 October. 'Many are asking what is happening in Madrid,' said Gil Robles, 'when will a General arise to bring the present state of affairs to an end? And to those who ask the answer must be that salvation lies in the exertions of all, in citizenship. We have to find salvation by ourselves, and not wait for a Messiah who will not come.'[77]

The first of the big rallies which were to be a feature of the campaign took place, despite Socialist disapproval, at Palencia on 8 November: 22,000 people were present at this 'new Covadonga', as were twenty-six deputies. If the meeting proved that the campaign had support, it also drew attention to the heterogeneity of the campaigners. The liberal Martínez de Velasco disclaimed any anti-Republican motives. On the other hand, the Carlist Beúnza believed the government was run by 'a bunch of Masons' against whom 'all means, legal and illegal', were licit.[78] While Gil Robles stressed that the campaign did not involve the question of régime, Sáinz Rodríguez, a member of the same organisation, advocated a programme of anti-parliamentarist 'integral nationalism' inspired by the Golden Century. Traditionalists emphasised that their participation in *Acción Nacional* was circumstantial: God and Country they would defend with others, but they remained 'representative Monarchists'.[79] The *Herrerista* Medina Togores described *Acción Nacional* as a Rightist movement 'within the law and within the Republic'.[80] Clearly an effort had to be made to define *Acción Nacional* more closely.

On 3 December the Deliberative Assembly met, confirmed Gil Robles as leader, and approved a much more detailed programme.[81] *Acción Nacional* was not a political party, nor a federation of groups: it sought 'to establish a formula of comprehension and a bond of union between citizens of diverse ideology, who, whether attached or not to other parties, have the same opinions on some urgent and capital problems and on the solutions to be applied. The programme of *Acción Nacional* is, then, "circumstantial", like the union to which it aspires; "minimal", as it is the product of a real compromise between political ideas and positions . . . ; simply "affirmative" concerning fundamental ideas and "defensive" regarding threatened sentiments and institutions. Finally, *Acción Nacional* reiterates its respect for the prevailing legality and its aim of obedience to the constituted power. *Acción Nacional* respects in its members not only the conviction which each person holds regarding the form of government, but also the freedom to defend his ideal outside its organisation.'

The programme was 'minimal' on religious matters in order to overcome differences between those for and against separation of Church and State. All were to uphold the 'liberty and dignity' of the Church and recognition for its personality, defend the right of the Orders to exist and teach, and agitate for maintenance of the ecclesiastical budget and the principle of settlement by concordat. The Nation, it was believed, was threatened by international Socialism and extremist separatism. Spanish unity was 'perpetual and indestructible'. The Family was the basis of social organisation. The principle of private property was reaffirmed, and extension of ownership to as many people as possible was desirable. The common good was supreme, but any expropriation must be compensated. Economic individualism was declared 'destructive of the sources of wealth, and thus as noxious as true Communism'.

Under the heading of 'Work', Christian spirit was to replace class warfare; the good of all depended on inter-class solidarity. Workers nevertheless had a right to the family wage, shares, social security, cheap housing and technical education. The principle of Authority should be strengthened to keep order, but laws must be equitably applied. With regard to regional autonomy, something more than administrative decentralisation was necessary, although the Constitution was condemned for its federalism. Control over languages, education, public order and the fiscal system ought to be kept in central hands. Liberty of education was demanded because the 'single school' was 'really no more than Communism applied to education': laicist claims for neutrality were hypocrisy. In matters of agrarian reform, utopian demagogy had to be avoided and irrigation was the proper way to create smallholdings. Rural wages ought to be higher than they had been in the past. Finally, the Constitution was, of course, to be revised.[82]

The phraseology of the new programme did not, in fact, settle differences about forms of government. Probably it was only intended as a transitory compromise, for almost immediately Monarchists and 'accidentalists', as those like Herrera and Gil Robles were termed, set about working for the future. Herrera's *El Debate* now called for the formation of a political party and *Acción Nacional* was clearly intended to develop into that party: 'The political and social doctrines of this party must be derived from the fundamental principles of the doctrine of the Church. . . . We speak of a party analogous to the Belgian Catholic Union, to the German Centre, to the Czechoslovak People's Party, to the Christian Social Party of Austria, or to the Catholic parties of Holland or Switzerland. All this, clearly, with the necessary adaptation to Spanish needs.' The Encyclicals were to become more than the mere expressions of pious sentiments.[83]

The leadership of *Acción Nacional* began to lay increasing stress on the concept of 'accidentalism', whereas previously the emphasis had been upon 'inhibition' of convictions regarding forms of government. In practice, accidentalism meant that the movement or party would be in the Republic, but not of it. Herrera found an 'infallible guide: the great Leo XIII'. The situation in France in the 1890s, he argued, was 'identical' with that in Spain in the 1930s. Catholics must therefore 'fight to improve the legislation within the established Constitution', although he himself was very critical of this Constitution.[84] Herrera and Gil Robles found their blueprint for future development in Lucía's *Derecha Regional Valenciana*, which the *caudillo* of the revisionists proclaimed a model for the rest of Spain.[85]

As part of the organisation of the Right at a local level, which was stimulated by *Acción Nacional*'s campaign, the opportunity was taken to form women's organisations, a youth movement and a workers' party. The first women's organisation was founded in Salamanca in October 1931.[86] The central organisation (*Asociación Femenina de Acción Nacional*) formed its first general purposes' committee in Madrid on 17 December under the presidency of Mercedes Fernández Villaverde. Membership was for those over eighteen, and was divided into three categories: honorary (appointed by the committee), active and followers who gave moral support. The monthly subscription was 25 céntimos, but the executive committee could excuse working-class women from payment.

The general procedure for the formation of provincial organisations was as follows. First, an organising committee was created, which then drew up the statutes defining the organisation as political, though not necessarily as Catholic. Links were then to be forged with the local male organisation, and branches set up in the *pueblos*. Women's organisations were divided into functional sections for cultural activities, checking of the electoral roll and propaganda. Close links were established with Madrid,[87] which would seem to indicate that the accidentalists planned to tie provincial organisation as much as possible to the centre in case the politically heterogeneous male organisations should choose to be dissident.

The decision to create a youth movement was taken in mid-October 1931, and the first *Juventud de Acción Nacional* appeared a month later in Cuenca.[88] The central organisation of the same name was formed in February 1932 under the presidency of José María Valiente. Membership was open to those between the ages of sixteen and thirty-five. The movement was described as having 'autonomy within the superior organism' of *Acción Nacional*.[89]

Its manifesto elaborated the programme of the parent organisation, but conveyed an impression of urgency and energy, a dynamism tending to extremism. 'We are the future and we must prevent the materialist civilisation of Moscow from replacing a spiritual civilisation twenty centuries old. . . . We go forth to preach the justice and the love which flow from the Gospel and the Encyclicals of the Popes, convinced that Catholic social doctrine alone can mollify frenzy below and bridle egoism above. We want the true spirit of Christ to renovate completely the present society, certain that only thus will a better world be attained. . . . We are men of the Right. . . . We shall obey the legitimate orders of authority; but we shall not tolerate the impositions of the irresponsible rabble. The valour necessary to assure ourselves respect will never be wanting. We declare war on Communism, as on Masonry, . . . now allied with a sectarian and exploiting bourgeoisie which, in denying the traditions of Spain, denies Spain itself.' The group expressed the desire to be the vanguard of the Right in fraternal union with other youth movements defending the same ideals.[90] 'We must forge new men,' said Valiente, 'a new authentic youth, happy, optimistic, in short, Spanish, and not like that other youth, sad and sour, stuffed with Russian novels and fitting offspring of the anarchic Generation of Ninety-Eight.'[91]

Whereas the youth and women's organisations soon flourished, the workers' party made little headway. Since 1927 Dimas de Madariaga had wanted to add a political wing to the CNSCO but had been opposed by those who believed Catholic unionism should be outside politics. His idea was given new life by Herrera on 12 July when he stressed the need for a workers' component for *Acción Nacional*. In December 1931 a committee was set up by Madariaga with a railwayman and a priest. Social propaganda was a prominent feature of *Acción Nacional*'s campaign in early 1932, but progress was hardly spectacular; not until 30 June was *Acción Obrerista* properly constituted as an autonomous 'Christian Social Workers' Party'.[92]

There was indeed little that could be done, given the semi-revolutionary situation exploited by the CNT and the monopolistic tendencies of the UGT with Largo Caballero at the Ministry of Labour. Catholic social doctrine permitted no appeals to violence or immoderate solutions. As Madariaga himself said: 'The mass of the workers is separated from us.' A verbal onslaught was nevertheless launched on the *conservaduros* (social reactionaries). Herrera saw the contemporary situation as a just punishment for past injustices by employers and called for 'the redemption of the proletariat'.[93] Fr Guallar, a scourge of the *conservaduros*, hoped for 'the embrace of worker and employer in the arms of the first worker, Jesus Christ'.[94] Gil Robles himself attacked the selfishness of the conservative classes, 'who passed the time idly warming themselves in the rays of the sun of prosperity, without a thought for their other brothers in Christ who endured hunger and were forsaken'.[95]

While these efforts were being made to develop *Acción Nacional*, which on 29 April 1932 had to change its name to *Acción Popular*,[96] the Monarchists of both dynastic branches were not inactive. Though it was clear from the first that Jaimists were active in *Acción Nacional* solely for the defence of religion and society,[97] the case of the Alfonsines, who had no organisation of their own, was rather more confusing. *Acción Nacional* demanded of its members inhibition regarding forms of government, but it did not become clear for some time whether Alfonsines had really accepted accidentalism or were using that organisation for their own purposes. The programme of 3 December gave rise to a paradoxical situation: Monarchists, who, as members of *Acción Nacional*, were bound to obey the Republic as the constituted power, could also, as Monarchists, make speeches against the established régime. Similarly, although *Acción Nacional* declared its *raison d'être* to be the organisation of a legal revisionist campaign, some of its fervently Monarchist members at the same time indulged in conspiracy.

As a result of meetings between Traditionalists and Alfonsines in France, the two exiled Monarchs, Jaime III and Alfonso XIII, decided upon joint action. In September 1931, they agreed in a pact that new Constituent Cortes should decide who was to be King. It was also agreed that Alfonsines and Traditionalists should work together for Religion and Country against the Republic. Jaime, however, died early in October, and was succeeded by his octogenarian uncle Alfonso, who, to avoid confusion, took the title of Alfonso Carlos I. He decided that co-operation between Alfonsines and Carlists should continue, but, although retaining dynastic union as an objective, he would have no truck with the 'liberal' pact made by his nephew with Alfonso. Apart from the question of persons, the acceptance of Carlist-Traditionalist principles was the issue at stake. The two branches remained distinct, if on amicable terms; the only positive result was the decision to combine their forces of propaganda.[98]

The outcome of these contacts and negotiations was to be seen in two manifestos. On 6 January Alfonso Carlos issued his attack on the 'atheist Republic' with its 'illegitimate' Constitution. Freedom of religion and the anti-religious clauses were denounced and the Carlist *credo* re-stated: traditional Cortes, regionalism, agricultural protection, industrial harmony, public works. His cousin Alfonso could succeed him as King, as he ought under the law of hereditary succession, but only if he first accepted Traditionalist principles.[99] Alfonso XIII's manifesto appeared on 23 January. In it, he called upon all Monarchists to unite and work for new

Constituent Cortes. While stating that the 'fundamental principles' of Alfonso Carlos and himself were the same, he once again offered to be King if asked by the national will.[100] In Spain in early 1932, prominent Traditionalists campaigned jointly with prominent Alfonsines.[101]

Probably the most important repercussion was the apparent conversion of Alfonsine leaders to a neo-Traditionalist doctrinal position. On 15 December 1931 there appeared in Madrid the first number of *Acción Española*, a fortnightly review of culture, economics and politics defending 'the most substantive and traditional concepts of our Country'. Its contributors included Alfonsines like Calvo Sotelo and Maeztu, who with the Integrist Pradera was its leading figure, and well-known names from *Acción Nacional*— Pemán, Goicoechea, Sáinz Rodríguez, the Marqués de Lozoya.[102]

Maeztu's first editorial sketched the neo-Traditionalist ideology now adopted by most Alfonsines. He chose Balmes, Donoso and Menéndez Pelayo as its spiritual ancestors, and outlined the Traditionalist interpretation of Spanish history. The 'symphony' of the 'Hispanic ideal' of the Golden Age had been interrupted in 1700 by 'two hundred years of the Revolution', a period of 'foreignisation' during which the 'Anti-Country' prevailed over Spanish Tradition. Since 1900, however, the failure of 'pagan humanism and naturalism' had become apparent. 'The world has come full circle and is now with us, for its better spirits are everywhere seeking principles analogous to or identical with those which we upheld in our great centuries.' The Thomist common good had ousted theories of the popular will. Spain must therefore take up its half-completed historical mission in these propitious times.[103] In February 1932, there developed from the review a 'cultural society absolutely free from all political parties, past and present', the intellectual manifestation of the Alfonsine-Carlist rapprochement.[104]

Monarchists within *Acción Nacional* began to air views very different from the accidentalism of Herrera and Gil Robles. 'I was and am a Monarchist,' declared Sáinz Rodríguez; 'the Republic is a régime of denationalisation incompatible with the tradition and future of Spain. . . . Today the State is our enemy, and if the Right does not change its mentality we are lost. . . . Either Russia or a just society founded upon traditional doctrines.'[105] Beúnza

declared that Traditionalists were 'abolitionists', not 'revisionists';
when other countries were adopting corporativism, Spain must
return to its traditional system and abandon 'the French system
adopted in the Cortes of Cádiz'.[106] Monarchists of both lines
preached counter-revolution, basing their programme on Spanish
Traditionalism and encouraged by other 'counter-revolutionary'
successes abroad. Luca de Tena (editor of *ABC*) was exceptional
in declaring himself 'more liberal than ever'.[107]

Despite the formula of 3 December, it was becoming increasingly difficult to fit such authoritarian Monarchism into the accidentalist, legalist framework of *Acción Nacional*. Goicoechea attempted to do so by defining it as 'a federation of parties respecting
the autonomy of each one of them for the defence of its respective
ideals'. He envisaged *Acción Nacional*, *Acción Española*, independents and old-style Monarchists, all forming one grand coalition:
'into the vast national ambit all can be fitted, as all the colours of
the rainbow are found in a single sunbeam'.[108] The inner contradictions of *Acción Nacional*'s programme, however, proved too
much. The divergence increased until the government issued
summonses against Goicoechea and Vallellano for attacks on the
régime at the *Acción Popular* meeting at Gijón on 16 July.[109]

Gil Robles continued to develop the accidentalist viewpoint.
The authoritarian Monarchism of the Dictatorship he denounced
as a façade behind which no problems had been solved, so that on
12 April, not only the Spanish Monarchy fell, but a whole social
and political system whose foundations had rotted away and which
had no vitality left. The only sure way to re-make Catholic Spain
was by a lengthy civil struggle, the maxims for which were 'first,
elimination of the problem relating to the form of government;
second, obedience to the constituted power; and third, fight within
legality'. Gil Robles remained convinced of the correctness of the
Kulturkampf tactics: 'If examination of one year's activity shows
us the splendid results of the present moment, what else must we
do but follow the same road?'[110]

The revisionist campaign had in fact provided the stimulus for
the creation of a nationwide and increasingly strong political
organisation under the banner of *Acción Nacional*, even though the
campaign was often suspended. The real bugbear of the revisionists was the Defence Law of the Republic, called by Herrera 'a law

of defence against the legitimate manifestations of public opinion'.[111] The campaign was suspended almost as soon as it had started until the Constitution had been passed. It was suspended again while the Jesuits were dissolved, a ban lifted on 4 February by the Minister of the Interior, Casares Quiroga, subject to authorisation of meetings by provincial Governors.[112] In mid-June, Gil Robles said 61 meetings had been banned, while the DRV, which planned 44 meetings on 26 June, had 19 of them banned.[113] Provincial branches of *Acción Popular* were closed from time to time, often on slender grounds.[114]

Much of the pressure against the campaign came from the Socialists, the largest group in Azaña's government. They originally said it would be a failure because Catholics were in a minority and because the Civil Guard would no longer protect Rightist speakers. Their attitude changed when events belied the prophecy. They then advocated strike action to sabotage a religious campaign 'distracting' the proletariat from its material aims. They also denounced it as a Monarchist campaign in preparation for an armed rising. The Socialist Youth declared itself the vanguard of the Republic and proclaimed violence obligatory. Those who had collaborated with the Dictator—except for the Socialists—had no right to claim Republican liberty.[115] Violence frequently occurred at meetings. *El Debate* was suspended for sixty-six days for criticising the doings of the Cortes and the prevalence of disorder; Royo Villanova, an opponent of the Dictatorship, noted that Primo de Rivera had never imposed such a penalty. Gil Robles asked why the law was applied one-sidedly: 'is it that the government has one standard for its political friends and another for political enemies?' 'Obviously!' was Azaña's truculent reply.[116]

Despite these difficulties *Acción Popular* extended its organisation at a rapid pace. The DRV was chosen as the model because it was the best organised and most dynamic of the provincial groups. It was democratically run and had sections to look after legal matters, to found Catholic schools and to foster local culture. It had many working-class members and was therefore a good advertisement for social-Catholic ideals; workers and employers appeared side by side on its platforms. It also admirably represented traditional theories of regionalism: members were busy drawing up a statute of autonomy for the Valencian region which would

F

give parity to Valencia and make Catholicism the official religion
of a Valencian State 'within the unity of Spain'.[117] Lucía's DRV
rejected separatist nationalism, but in other respects it was similar
to the PNV and to Carrasco's small *Unió Democràtica de Catalunya*.

Elsewhere in Spain a marked acceleration in the creation of local
Rightist groups was noticeable once the revisionist campaign got
under way. More and more politically heterogeneous organisations
appeared. In one province Alfonsine and Carlist Monarchists
combined with Catholic farm-workers; in another 'accidentalist'
social-Catholics joined forces with farmers and provincial notables
who represented the 'old politics'. These subsidiary bodies of
Acción Popular flourished in Old Castile and León, where the CNCA
was strongest, though they also made progress in Galicia, Asturias,
New Castile, Aragón and to a lesser extent in the south. By the
summer of 1932 there were autonomous Rightist groups adhering
to the 'fundamental principles' of *Acción Popular* in nearly every
province outside Catalonia and the Basque Country.[118] Thanks to
the initiative of Herrera, the stimulus of anti-clericalism and the
seemingly boundless energy of Gil Robles, the Right was better
organised than ever before.

Azaña's government had the support of the Socialists but not
of their Anarcho-Syndicalist rivals who declared that 'not one
minute's truce' was possible with Republicans and Socialists who
had abandoned revolutionary methods. The CNT provided a backcloth of disorder for the Republic which alienated conservative
sections of society. Agitation by deed was constant, though violence was also used by local Socialists. Sporadic and particularly
violent outbreaks brought notoriety to some hitherto remote and
scarcely known *pueblos*. Notable in the first year of the Republic
were the Anarchist rising in Seville in July 1931, and in 1932 the
episodes at Castilblanco, in the Llobregat valley and at Villa de
Don Fadrique. Not even deportation to Africa could still the
turbulence.[119] The first eighteen months of the Republic provided
a total of 400 dead, 3,000 injured, 30 general and 3,600 partial
strikes.[120] These disorders were mainly the work of Anarcho-
Syndicalists carrying on a vendetta with the Socialists.

The Socialists were in fact the kingpin of the Republic: they had
the largest parliamentary minority and they had the UGT behind
them as a powerful bargaining-counter with the Republicans.

Their dilemma was whether to satisfy their revolutionary aspirations directly, or to consolidate the Republic and risk losing face with the revolutionary masses. The dilemma was resolved in favour of evolutionary tactics by the party's congress in July 1931.[121] The PSOE was to be the axis of the Republic, the consolidation of which was to be achieved by a social-democratic programme to carry through the bourgeois revolution from above.[122] The ultimate aim of full Socialism was not forgotten: no steps backward were permissible on the evolutionary road. The disorders of the CNT were condemned: parliamentary democracy was the means for the time being.[123]

The Socialists in the government were to stay there to keep the Republic to the Left and protect it against the conservative forces led by Lerroux.[124] All means were justifiable to keep the 'historic' Republicans out of power or to prevent a dissolution of the Cortes. Largo Caballero in November 1931 announced that the Socialist Party would switch to revolutionary methods if excluded from power; a dissolution would oblige it 'to proceed to civil war'.[125] 'Rightist domination' of the Republic would mean frustration of the revolution.[126] The Republic, for the Socialists, was no more than a means to their end. Largo Caballero warned the proletariat not to be dazzled by its myth; Socialists aided the Republic solely for their own interests.[127] As Cordero said, 'the Republic is accidental and Socialism fundamental'.[128]

Perennial disorder and the promise of progressive socialisation did at least as much in the first year of the Republic to bring about economic crisis as the longer-term effects of the world depression. The worsening of the situation in May 1931 was not, as the government claimed, solely due to the withdrawal of capital by anti-Republicans, which totalled only some 70,000,000 pesetas.[129] Carner, Minister of Finance in 1932, admitted that early Republican measures had produced a partial economic collapse and a fall in the revenue.[130] On the London market the peseta fell from $45\frac{1}{4}$ to the £ in March to 54 in September 1931.[131] The cost of living index rose from 171·6 in 1930 to 175 in 1931, while industrial shares fell.[132]

The main attack on the government was made by Ventosa Calvell of the *Lliga* who voiced the discontents of industry. He painted a gloomy picture of everything falling: the peseta, gold reserves, savings, bank accounts, the volume of credit, the amount of trade. The assets of the Bank of Spain had fallen by a quarter, mortgages by a fifth; building in Madrid was down by a half, while an insurance company which paid out 362,000 pesetas in 1930, paid out 618,000 in 1931. The root cause was disorder.[133] Calvo Sotelo noted from exile that trade figures showed a fall in imports reflecting industrial collapse, since industry was dependent on foreign raw materials. Public expenditure had risen, but the bureaucracy swallowed up the rise while public works remained strangled and unemployment rose. Wages were rising fast, but the national cake was diminishing.[134] Gil Robles noted 60,000 unemployed in Madrid, increasing at the rate of 500 a day.[135] While the government blamed the world crisis and the work of Calvo Sotelo the Right blamed disorder and lack of confidence brought about by incompetence and threats of socialisation.

Such a situation led many who had voted for the Republic to complain that 'it is not this'.[136] Ortega Gasset spoke of the need to 'rectify' the Republic which after seven months had turned 'sad and sour'. He suggested the formation of a 'party of national breadth' to help 'nationalise' the new régime. The ideal of 'the Nation' was necessary to stir the masses, so 'Nation and Labour' was put forward as the slogan for a new democracy. The idea was, however, still-born.[137]

Nor was the Liberal Republican Right successful in exploiting the wave of disillusion. It became in August 1931 the Progressive Republican Party with a liberal-conservative programme.[138] Miguel Maura, who had left the group in July, also wanted a conservative Republic and revision of the Constitution, though he attacked *Acción Nacional*'s campaign as dangerous for the Republic. He was in fact trying to re-create the old Conservative Party within the Republic but, though he gained the adherence of some Progressives, the Catholic masses were hostile to the man who, they believed, had let the *conventos* burn. Possibly he could lead a group of economic interests, but not the 'authentic' Catholic Right.[139]

Ortega, Maura, and the President's friends were in fact crushed between *Acción Nacional* and Lerroux's Radicals who sought to persuade the 'neutral masses' that they were the best hope for moderation. Lerroux opposed Socialist participation in the government, wanted a dissolution and preached tolerance, especially in religious matters.[140] He expected to succeed Alcalá-Zamora in October, but Socialists, Left Republicans and the *Esquerra* presented a united front against him. In December his ambition was again thwarted when Azaña chose Socialist partners, thereby rejecting Lerroux's view that conservatives could be attracted into the Republic if the Socialists were dropped.[141] His policy was one of opposition within the Republic which he hoped soon to govern.

If the 'authentic' Right shunned representation of industrial interests, it was certainly eager to defend agriculture: 'the idea of God', said Royo Villanova, 'is something consubstantial with the peasant'.[142] The Castilian Agrarians were stalwart defenders of the wheat interest and complained that the cost of production had risen 30 per cent due to higher wages and shorter hours, while the minimum price-level was 47 pesetas per quintal compared with 54/55 pesetas for the cost of production. For Agrarians the wheat price was the main agricultural problem; they wanted it raised with government aid. Higher wages and land re-distribution were farcical if produce had to be sold at less than cost price. Tariffs should be maintained so that cheap foreign wheat would not undercut the livelihood of Castile. In this respect, Catalonia must not be allowed to disturb its traditional economic interdependence with Castile: Castilian wheat for Catalonia, Catalan manufactures for Castile.

If necessary urban food prices should be raised: 10 céntimos on bread, calculated their chief spokesman Pedro Martín, would make another peseta a day possible for the landworker. Without such measures, however, a 40–50 per cent increase in rural wages and the import of 2,924,122 quintals of foreign wheat in 1932 were ridiculous, they argued, because higher wages and lower prices would cause a decrease in the area cultivated, and the bankruptcy of smallholders who could not pay their debts nor obtain credit. The result was an increase in unemployment—70 per cent of the unemployed were on the land—as public works schemes were inadequate to cope with this problem.[143]

The causes of unemployment were seen by the Right as a combination of the reduction of irrigation and public works schemes, the effects of the Law of Municipal Boundaries, the consequence of depressed prices for agricultural produce, the

threat of Socialist legislation which caused uncertainty, falling
land values and the virtual extinction of credit, and revolutionary
demagogy which stirred up the rural masses with utopian promises. The 600,000 unemployed were the result of retrenchment
by the Berenguer government, which abandoned the Dictatorship's plans for irrigation and road and rail development; in
September 1931, under 2,000 were employed by the *Confederación
del Ebro*, compared with 24,000 under the Dictator.[144]

The Law of Municipal Boundaries was an attempt by Largo
Caballero to prevent the payment of starvation wages by rural
employers who brought in outside labour to swamp the local
market. Though the intention was excellent, in practice it was not
a great success. In municipalities where there was little labour,
farm-hands had to be taken on who knew nothing of agriculture;
in municipalities with a big labour force, surplus numbers were
billeted unofficially on farmers who often went bankrupt as a
result. With the use of machinery strictly limited, the harvest was
often held up because the traditional migration of labourers from
Galicia to Castile and from the Levante to Andalusia was now
prohibited.[145] In Seville it had the effect of reducing dramatically
the amount of land cultivated by owners by January 1932.[146]

Apart from Anarchist agitation, great uncertainty was caused by
Socialist actions. Decrees on 29 April and 6 August 1931 halted
evictions of tenants—leases were notoriously short—while tenants
could propose the immediate revision of leases and reduction of
rents pending legislation.[147] Legislation did not come, so uncertainty upset the rural economic structure, as did the delay in
drafting an agrarian reform law. Credit dried up and cultivation
decreased when Ministers said that nationalisation of the land was
the only solution to the agrarian problem.[148] At a local level
Socialists encouraged the landless to adopt their own solutions.[149]

The solutions proposed by the Right to the agrarian problem
were of a non-revolutionary, long-term nature. Faith was generally
placed in irrigation as a solution, not only for the temporary
absorption of the unemployed, but also to provide new viable
smallholdings. Calvo Sotelo thought that the irrigation of a million
and a half hectares was the answer. Maeztu also developed the
ideas of Guadalhorce: the unirrigated land of the *latifundios* was
suitable only for large-scale mechanised farming, while irrigated

land was to be used to settle the landless and at the same time help the urban unemployment problem by expanding the internal market.[150] As for re-distribution, the model was that of the CNCA, which between 1917 and 1931 had bought and parcelled out 29,859 hectares among 9,849 smallholders: a modest achievement, but the only initiative of its kind at the time.[151]

Alongside such measures, concentration should be fixed upon price-maintenance, advantageous foreign trade treaties to assure export markets, maintenance of the closed economy in general, the abolition of the Law of Municipal Boundaries, the settlement of rent disputes by mixed juries, better credit facilities, and the organisation of co-operatives for marketing and the mutual aid of smallholders and workers.[152] In general, the Right seemed much more concerned with the smallholder society of the northern half of Spain than with the thornier problems of the south. Furthermore, the more vocal sections of the Right tended to be the more socially minded; behind them lurked large numbers of defenders of the *status quo*.

Debates on the fourth draft of the Law of Bases for Agrarian Reform began in May 1932, simultaneously with debates on the Catalan Statute. The aim of the Minister of Agriculture, Marcelino Domingo, was to alleviate rural unemployment by the re-distribution of property and the rationalisation of Spanish agriculture. *El Debate* pointed to ILO statistics showing that such re-parcellation led to increased unemployment, but at the same time condemned the draft as the only agrarian reform in Europe, except for Russia, to reject the idea of the smallholding.[153] The debates dragged on at a very slow pace. The Agrarians were accused of obstruction, though Domingo himself thought their amendments justifiable.[154]

The law was to apply to Andalusia, Extremadura, and the provinces of Albacete, Ciudad Real, Salamanca and Toledo—the dry south—as well as to *señorios* all over Spain. The Agrarians were in broad agreement as to the area of application, although Lamamié de Clairac and Casanueva, landowners in Salamanca, pleaded for the exclusion of their province.[155] The State was to give the Institute of Agrarian Reform 50,000,000 pesetas annually to carry out the reform; original hopes of settling 75,000 before the end of the year had been reduced to 25,000. Casanueva calculated that it would cost some 200,000,000 pesetas to create so many viable settlements in the remaining nine months, an amount which could not be spared from the unbalanced budget.[156]

Much heat was generated over the question of the *señorios* which were to be expropriated without compensation; compensation was to be given for uncultivated or badly cultivated land, land capable of rapid irrigation, lands leased for more than twelve years and various estates of more than a given area. Agrarians opposed wholesale expropriation of *señorios*, which had legally ceased to exist in 1811, seeing in the proposal a political act aimed at the economic destruction of the Monarchist aristocracy. *Señorios* cultivated in a model manner ought to be excluded, they argued. Similarly, size was no criterion for expropriation, as the quality of land varied. There was no provision for owners to cultivate leased lands to avoid expropriation, and landlords who had not increased the rent for thirty years were to be hard done by. The law was seen as a sop to revolutionary violence stirred up by electoral propaganda.[157] Methods of compensation were also attacked, objection being made to the idea of special agrarian debt bonds, disposable only at the rate of a tenth a year.[158] Particular annoyance was caused by the assessment of compensation according to the declared net taxable profit, always well below the real figure: Agrarians wanted expert valuation with recourse to the Supreme Court if necessary.[159] Common lands were to be reclaimed by 'simple presumption of their former existence': Agrarians preferred municipalities to prove their claims in the courts.[160]

The main objection of Agrarians was, however, to the law's 'Socialism'. This was common ground upon which the minority could unite, keeping a divergence of views latent. There were two concepts of property: that of the social-Catholics who advocated the smallholder ideal as conducive to the common good, and who were prepared to accept expropriation with compensation if necessary,[161] and whose aim was the law's technical amelioration and its approximation to their ideal; and that of the liberal Agrarians, who would use any argument to safeguard the unmolested enjoyment of private property. The law provided for the settlement of poor workers and peasants, who were to form a community on each estate and themselves decide whether to work it collectively or individually. The land was to be held in perpetuity, those settled paying an annual land-tax to the State. The formula was, in fact, a compromise between the bourgeois Republican preference for smallholdings and the Socialist collective ideal.[162] The Agrarian position was based on the creation of smallholdings pure and simple. The law, they argued, made the beneficiaries of reform 'serfs in the service of a feudal lord—the State'.[163]

Yet despite efforts to turn the law into social-Catholic channels, the Agrarians in the last resort rejected it as impracticable. Their leading spokesman, Cándido Casanueva, told the majority in the Cortes that it was 'a very well-outlined scheme on paper, but with the inconvenience of being completely removed from the life of the Spanish countryside. . . . You must bear in mind that [agrarian reform] is not the work of a day, nor of a year, but of generations; to carry it out in haste is to take a leap into space.'[164] The law was at last passed by 318 votes to 19 on 9 September.[165]

The debates on the Catalan Statute, alternating with those on agrarian reform, provoked a reaction inside and outside the Cortes comparable with that against religious legislation. Since 14 April, the guardians of Spanish unity and Castilian nationalists had been on the alert; their ranks included not only the Right, but also Socialists, Radicals and Right Republicans who were bound by the Pact of San Sebastián to support a statute of autonomy.[166] The Statute was drafted by the *Esquerra* at Nuria and approved overwhelmingly in the plebiscite of 2 August 1931.[167] Immediately emotions were roused. Maciá declared Catalans free at last: no human power could oppose the will of the Catalans, who had 'deprived themselves for a short time of a modicum of that sovereignty which is theirs by right. . . . If the fruits of our plebiscite are denied to us we will fight to the death to achieve our aspirations to freedom.'[168] His aim was to obtain the maximum concessions from Madrid by brinkmanship and present the Statute as a pact between two sovereign powers.[169]

In Castile and Aragón such language provoked equally strong passions. For Goicoechea the Statute contained 'not the maximum programme of the autonomists, but the minimum programme of separatism'.[170] *El Debate* described it as an insult to the Constitution, the Cortes and the entire Spanish people, a piece of camouflaged separatism.[171] The editor of *ABC* considered it equivalent

to 'the dismemberment of the Country'.[172] Students demonstrated against it,[173] and a leading Radical urged that the struggle
against separatism be taken into the streets: 'In Parliament nothing
can be achieved . . . Spaniards! Let us perish if perish we must;
but may the Country be saved!'[174]

Behind the strong language, however, the Right was divided
into liberal centralisers and traditional regionalists. Royo Villanova, the most vehement anti-Catalanist, said that it was not
'reactionary' to oppose the Statute, but 'liberal and progressive'.
Attacks on Spanish unity were more shocking for him than attacks
on religion.[175] The Traditionalist Lamamié de Clairac, on the
other hand, believed the Carlist doctrine of 'infra-sovereignty' the
only one capable of pleasing both Catalonia and Castile: full
regionalism could be enjoyed by Catalonia without endangering
the unity of the nation only when the highest representatives of
region and nation were one and the same person.[176] *El Debate* also
advocated 'sound, legitimate, traditional regionalism' in opposition to the revolutionary federalism of a Statute pushed through
the Cortes by 'a conglomeration of Masons, separatists and
Socialists'.[177] Centralisers and de-centralisers could nevertheless
present a common front in defence of the integrity of the Spanish
nation against covert separatism. 'We want liberty for that region',
said Gil Robles, 'but we do not want to hand it over to the
Esquerra.'[178] *ABC* took the lead in the campaign against the
Statute, while inside the Cortes Catalans were exasperated by the
unending amendments persistently defended by Royo Villanova
to the point of obstruction.[179]

Apart from the questions of sovereignty and linguistic parity,
opposition centred around the division of powers between the
Generalidad and the State, with particular regard to finance, public
order and education. Basic objections were to the head of the
region, the representative of the central State, being appointed by
Catalonia, and to Catalan control of the police.[180] To give Catalans
charge of the police, quite apart from the danger of separatism,
would be to deliver public order into the hands of a régime
dependent on the revolution in the form of the CNT, which the
Generalidad had not shown itself capable of mastering.[181] Yet at
the same time Royo defended immigrant workers against the fate
of 'Catalanisation' by the *Esquerra*. Justice and education he

thought should be controlled from Madrid; the young ought not to be indoctrinated with 'anti-Spanish nationalism'. The University must remain Castilian.[182]

Regarding finance, the State was to retain control of indirect taxation, but surrender direct taxation to Barcelona. Aside from the question of fiscal sovereignty, it was argued that provinces of Spain should contribute to the Treasury according to their wealth. The idea of Catalonia contributing solely in proportion to its population was preposterous since Catalans were collectively wealthier than other Spaniards as the result of protection of their industries behind national tariffs which ensured them 90 per cent of the home market.[183] It was argued that the rest of Spain would be financing a privileged status for the richest region: taxes ceded to the *Generalidad* were valued at 282,759,741 pesetas, while the services to be transferred would cost the region only 79,735,000 pesetas.[184] Yet in its final form the Statute was not as favourable to Catalonia as the 'economic arrangement' was to the Basques.[185] The Statute, in a more moderate form than that voted by Catalans, was eventually passed by 314 votes to 24 in September.[186]

The *Lliga* had decided to support the Statute of Nuria before the plebiscite of 2 August.[187] In the Cortes, its three deputies supported the *Esquerra* because the *Lliga* had always worked for 'the autonomy of Catalonia within the Spanish State'. Abadal claimed that autonomous regions represented the true structure of Spain. The *Generalidad* was part of the 'integral State' of Article 1 of the Constitution: therefore there was no division of sovereignty. Furthermore, like the Constitution, the Statute was not immutable.[188] Estelrich took a traditionalist line. His Catalan nationalism was not that sired by the French revolution; a State containing distinct nations was therefore quite possible. His ideal was the internal re-establishment, resurgence and restoration of the 'collective personality' of Catalonia, with the ultimate ideal of union with Portugal in Iberian harmony.[189]

Ventosa Calvell's championship of Spanish industry, however, showed that the facts of economic interdependence between Catalonia and Castile were still very much present in *Lliga* minds, even if no agreement could be reached with *Acción Popular*.[190] Cambó, still in exile, counselled compromise on both sides.[191] Durán Ventosa went further and in July blamed the difficulties encountered by the Statute in the Cortes on the *Esquerra* because it had not adopted the more moderate draft of 1919 which bore the signatures of Lerroux and Largo Caballero.[192]

An effort to form a Basque-Navarrese-Catalan front in the summer of 1931 came to nothing, but the Basques voted with the Catalans on the regional clauses of the Constitution. Aguirre and two deputies visited Barcelona in October to reaffirm their solidarity with Maciá.[193] In August 1931, Maura had noted in Biscay 'great effervescence on account of the religious question' and had suspended thirteen newspapers.[194] Typical of the Traditionalist attitude was the counsel of the *Heraldo Alavés*: ' "Obey your authorities", says the Scripture. But it adds, in another place: "It is necessary to obey God, before men." '[195]

Despite all this the Traditionalist alliance with the Republican PNV continued. The Statute of Estella, approved by the Navarrese town councils, was presented to a non-committal Alcalá-Zamora in September.[196] But by the beginning of October at the latest, Aguirre had decided that the Traditionalist alliance was a drawback to the aspirations of the PNV. He persuaded the Temporary Committees to accept the Statute of the SEV before amendment at Estella. When in December the government decreed that the Temporary Committees should draw up a Statute to be approved by the town councils before a plebiscite could take place, a mixed committee of ten was soon formed by the Committees, the Nationalist Mayors and the Socialists. By 31 January 1932 a single Statute for the four provinces had been agreed upon, the provisions of which omitted those aspects of the Statute of Estella which had appealed to the Traditionalists. The possibility of a regional concordat was excluded and the region conceded greater powers to the State in the spheres of education, public order and justice.[197]

This 'Single Statute' was strongly attacked by the Integrist leader Juan de Olazábal, who lamented: 'Oh, if St. Peter the Apostle were living in these times, what epistles he would write against certain Catholics!' The Bishop of Vitoria, in exile near Poitiers, refused, however, to take sides. In Navarre, Traditionalists came out strongly against the new 'Single Statute' because it would subject their province to a new centralism. When all the councillors assembled in Pamplona on 19 June for the Great

Assembly of Basque Municipalities, they encountered such slogans as 'Do not vote for the laicist Statute' and *'Fueros*, yes! Statute, no!' There was confusion at the Assembly, but the town councils of Álava, Guipúzcoa and Biscay voted for the 'Single Statute' while the Navarrese rejected it. Oriol Urigüen, Traditionalist deputy for Álava, now began to campaign against the Statute since, without Navarre, Álava would be a satellite of industrial Biscay.[198]

The PNV-Traditionalist alliance broke down over the provisions of the 'Single Statute'. The Navarrese had only agreed to the alliance after the amendments made at Estella permitting a regional concordat, and they differed from the PNV on the definition of *fueros*. A contributory factor was also the change which began to take place within Traditionalism after the accession of Alfonso Carlos. At a meeting in Pamplona on 6 January 1932, at which Integrists and *Mellistas* were officially accepted back into the fold, the new title of *Comunión Tradicionalista Carlista* was adopted instead of the former *Comunión Católico-Monárquica*.[199] Alfonso Carlos reappointed as his Delegate the Valencian Marqués de Villores, but with schemes afoot for joint action with Alfonsines any lingering ideas of co-operation with Basque Nationalism as a lesser evil soon disappeared.

A supreme national committee of seven was created in January 1932 and when Villores died in May the Navarrese Rodezno became the principal leader.[200] Alfonso Carlos moved to Ascain, arms were smuggled across the frontier, shooting affrays occurred with Socialists and recruiting of youths in the mountains for training by a retired Colonel, Sanz de Lerín, got under way.[201] The Basque-Navarrese parliamentary minority was therefore dissolved in July 1932, and the Basques began to take a more active part in the Cortes in support of the Catalan Statute. The breaking of the alliance was in any case inevitable because, although the PNV was a confessional party of 'virile and integral Catholicism', its leader openly proclaimed his separatist aspirations: 'In the political sphere, we seek the full sovereignty of Euzkadi over itself.'[202]

On the whole, the Army had avoided compromising itself with Monarchy or Republic before 14 April and after the change of régime its attitude continued to be 'accidentalist'. Typical perhaps of the Generals' view was the attitude of Francisco Franco, com-

manding the General Military Academy at Saragossa. Orders for
15 April 1931 emphasised discipline and the duty of sacrificing all
personal opinions for the good of the Country and for civil peace.
On 18 April, dispelling rumours that he was to be given an important appointment in Morocco, Franco explained that he had been
loyal to the Monarchy until its fall, but now that the new régime
was installed he was equally obedient to it. When the War Minister,
Azaña, abruptly closed the Academy, Franco's farewell speech in
July again stressed discipline and loyalty to Spain.[203]

Many officers, however, decided, despite Alfonso's parting
message to the armed forces bidding them to serve Spain, that the
oath of loyalty to the Republic was too much, especially when
accompanied by a change in the national flag. By the Decree of
25 April, officers were permitted to retire on full pay if they so
wished; some 11,000 of the 21,000 availed themselves of the
opportunity.[204]

From one standpoint, Azaña's military reforms were no more
radical than the plans of Primo de Rivera, save that the former put
his into practice. There was general agreement that the top-heavy
bureaucracy which was the military establishment, with its one
officer to every six men and its 800 Generals on the active and
reserve lists, was in urgent need of pruning. Azaña in fact reduced
the number of Infantry Divisions from sixteen to eight, and
Cavalry Divisions from eight to three. What needled military
feelings were the accompanying aspects of the reforms, carried out
by an anti-militarist who boasted that his aim was to 'mash' the
Army. Captains-General, the Law of Jurisdictions, the Supreme
Army and Navy Council and Courts of Honour were all abolished,
thereby placing the Army under the civilian jurisdiction of the
Minister's personal 'Military Cabinet' packed, it was alleged, with
discontents out to settle old grudges.

Azaña, some military men complained, was undermining military discipline and morale and showing unwarranted distrust of
officers who had sworn loyalty to the Republic. He had ignored the
advice of the technical departments of his Ministry, and had
broken his promise not to interfere with promotions. Officers
expelled from the Army under the Dictatorship were being reinstated regardless of the reason for their expulsion. Discrimination in appointments in favour of chairborne *Junteros*, who had

intrigued while others had risked their lives in Morocco, was much resented; the moral integrity of the officer corps could no longer be guaranteed. Azaña's 'policy of persecution' disregarded military criteria: the best Academy had been closed, and the Moroccan establishment cut so heavily that Mola doubted whether it could withstand a native rising. If the Minister had found Infantry Regiments of eighty men and Cavalry Regiments without horses, he had not been sufficiently energetic in re-equipping the armed forces. Azaña's 'Republicanisation' was altogether most distasteful, not to say unpatriotic.[205]

Conspirators against the government could therefore play upon the internal dissatisfactions of the Army and could draw on an ample fund of retired officers. The first attempt at conspiracy was led by General Luis Orgaz who, with General Ponte, had been involved since May 1931 with the Alfonsine group (including Vallellano, Pujol and Fuentes Pila) meeting at Quintanar's house.[206] The conspiracy, however, never progressed very far. Some funds were collected from Monarchists and efforts were aimed chiefly at bringing together retired officers, but the plotters never got beyond the talking stage.[207]

Before Orgaz's arrest and banishment to the Canaries, unsuccessful contact was made with the Basque Nationalists after a march-past of thousands of *Mendigoixales* (Basque Nationalist youths) at a rally at Deva at the end of August 1931. Accounts of the episode differ. According to Aguirre, a meeting was requested by Orgaz, then involved with circles in Bilbao in a military conspiracy. Orgaz told Aguirre that his aim was to overthrow the Provisional Government so that elections could be held for new Constituent Cortes to decide upon the form of régime. It was a movement for Spain: 'We are not attempting restoration of the Monarchy.' The Alfonsine General wanted to hear Aguirre's views and promised the Basques 'extensive powers of autonomy' excluding the possibility of secession. Orgaz, on the other hand, said that the meeting, which took place at Lequeitio at the beginning of September, was requested by Aguirre, who was in search of officers to train his *Mendigoixales* for an uprising in the Basque Country which he wished the General to lead. Whatever actually took place, the interview had no repercussions and no agreement proved possible.[208] The General's plot came to nothing.

By November 1931 the ex-Constitutionalists had become thoroughly alarmed at the progress of the Republic. Burgos Mazo discussed the situation with the Director-General of the Civil Guard, General José Sanjurjo, whom he found to be in general agreement with him; both agreed that they were conservatives and Republicans.[209] In January, Sanjurjo's views became apparent when he saw the mutilated bodies of four of his Civil Guards in Castilblanco; he was pressed to rise there and then by Civil Guard officers, but decided not to act precipitately.[210] General Goded, Chief of the General Staff, visited Burgos Mazo, however, to offer his services in case of a rising. Burgos Mazo, who had abandoned hope of Azaña's government being toppled by Lerroux, went ahead with his preparations: the capable Goded was to be the master-mind of the movement, while the brave but not very intelligent Sanjurjo was to be the figure-head. A manifesto drawn up in July by Burgos Mazo was approved by Melquíades Álvarez and Santiago Alba, also ex-Constitutionalists: it spoke of maintaining and purifying the Republic, not of a Monarchist restoration.[211]

Meanwhile Sanjurjo vacillated. In January he saw his old friend Lerroux, who sympathised with his views but would not agree to rise against the Republican government.[212] In February Sanjurjo was demoted to the Directorate-General of Customs Guards because of his forthright speech at the funeral of the four Civil Guards; he declined Azaña's offer to become Marshal of Spain and tour the Americas for a couple of years with an annual salary of 125,000 pesetas.[213] The debates on the Catalan Statute, however, pushed him towards a decision. He again visited Lerroux, who again refused to join in a rising although it was clear that the Statute could not be stopped in the Cortes. Early in July 1932 Sanjurjo made his preparations, linking up with a Monarchist conspiracy already in existence.[214]

The strands of the Monarchist conspiracy disrupted by the removal of Orgaz to the Canaries in 1931 were taken up in 1932 by his associate General Ponte from France. In the spring, Pujol asked the Alfonsine General Emilio Barrera to head a *junta* to prepare a revolt; some 300,000 pesetas had already been collected for the purpose.[215] In April, an intrepid aviator, the retired Major Juan Antonio Ansaldo, was sent to Rome by Ponte to seek Italian aid; agreement was reached with the Air Minister, Marshal Balbo, but there were in the event no practical consequences.[216] Monarchist security, however, was poor, for on 15 June various conspirators, including Barrera and Orgaz, were arrested. Although the Director-General of Security announced the existence of a Monarchist plot, they were nevertheless released within a few days.[217]

The incident helped to worsen relations between the military and the government. Officers were incensed when a Minister declared that the Generals were wrong to believe that they could have influence under the Republic, and added: 'the Generals think the régime is going to waver because they sneeze'.[218] Addressing infantry officers at a dinner at Carabanchel on 27 June, Goded spoke on the theme of national unity, ending: 'Long live Spain and nothing more!' Thereupon the ex-*Juntero* Colonel Mangada made it plain that he was not amused by this slight on the government. Mangada was put in military prison, but Generals Villegas and Caballero were removed from their posts. Goded resigned in protest at this.[219] Such was the situation at the beginning of July 1932 when Sanjurjo finally made up his mind to join military colleagues in the preparation of a *pronunciamiento*, which had civilian support from Monarchists, the JONS in Valladolid and some disillusioned Republicans of conservative opinions like Joaquín del Moral.[220]

Among Alfonsine Monarchists, La Cierva and the ex-Ministers of the Dictatorship were involved, as were leading members of *Acción Española* such as Vallellano, Sáinz Rodríguez and Goicoechea (also members of *Acción Popular*).[221] The military *junta* for the rising was headed by the Alfonsine Barrera, who insisted that the 'single and exclusive aim' of the movement was the overthrow of Azaña's government. The question of the régime was secondary; the provisional *junta* was simply to guarantee order.[222] Alfonso XIII was not himself involved, but the plan fitted well with his manifesto of 23 January, drawn up by Vallellano: if he were to return, it should be at the request of new Cortes convoked by a provisional government. Although he did not go back on his earlier statements forbidding violence on behalf of his person, the last sentence seemed to suggest the overthrow of the government: 'Act suitably before the labour of destruction is fully consummated

G

and with it the ruin of our dear Country.'[223] Alfonsine Monarchists took part, therefore, in order to weaken the Republic, and with the secondary hope that success could be the first step towards an eventual restoration.[224] Thus there was sufficient common ground to allow joint action with Sanjurjo, who looked upon his action as for the good of Spain but not against the Republican régime.[225] The Carlists were doubtful about the character of the movement. At the Assembly of the Communion at the Château de Mondonville, near Toulouse, it was decided that the Communion as such could not participate because the conspirators' programme was so imprecise, but individual members could take part if they wished.[226]

Civilian support was far from being the prime consideration of the military conspirators, but their plans incorporated the use of Albiñana's PNE and the JONS in Valladolid as auxiliaries. With the arrival of the Republic, Albiñana was detained without trial and the Madrid offices of the PNE sacked by Republican enthusiasts. Albiñana was released in December 1931, to be re-arrested in May 1932 and deported to Las Hurdes. During his spell of freedom he took the opportunity to re-found the PNE as the Spanish equivalent of the movements of Hitler and Mussolini. Nationalism must be based on native traditions: therefore in Spain the programme must be founded on religion, Monarchy and the red and gold flag. Masonry was not to be tolerated; only God could take precedence over the Country. With Albiñana again detained, the small PNE was drawn into the orbit of *Acción Española*.[227]

Ledesma's *La Conquista del Estado*, the other radical Rightist group of pre-Republican days, fared equally badly: government seizures of the paper and lack of financial support had killed it by 24 October.[228] Before its termination, however, Ledesma fused what remained of his group with a similar grouping in Valladolid, led by Onésimo Redondo, to form the *Juntas de Ofensiva Nacional-Sindicalista* (JONS) on 13 October 1931. The Sixteen Points of the new amalgam stressed national unity, respect for the national Catholic tradition, recovery of Gibraltar, imperial expansion in North Africa, and the end of parliamentarism. The JONS pledged themselves to 'direct action in the service of the Country' and the dissolution and extermination of all Marxist and anti-national parties. The new National-Syndicalist State, to be ruled by the under-forties, was to be based on the National-Syndicalist Militia.[229] *Jonsistas* wore black shirts and red ties, the colours of the Anarchists, while adopting as their device the yoked arrows of the Catholic Kings with the motto 'Spain One, Great and Free!'[230]

The two leaders of the JONS, Ledesma and Redondo, came of similar backgrounds. Both were born in 1905 in Old Castile of peasant stock and both took state employment to help their university studies. Their political views coincided on the need for revolutionary violence to implant an authoritarian National-Syndicalist State, yet their basic ideological approaches differed. Ledesma was influenced by Unamuno, Nietzsche and Ortega Gasset. His writings, though illiberal and extremist, bore a certain resemblance to Ortega's—both found inspiration in German thought. *La Conquista del Estado* had a Germanic tone with its theatrical generalisations: the *Zeitgeist* was collectivist, therefore 'the individual is dead'. Ledesma as a social radical declared his hatred of the mediocre, decadent, liberal, bourgeois spirit, although the first enemy was Communism. Any who hindered the advance of Syndicalist organisation were 'enemies of the Country'. The two supreme aims ought to be 'to subvert the present Masonic anti-Spanish system' and 'to impose by violence the strictest fidelity to the spirit of the Country'. Support was sought among the students, who were tiring of the monopoly of representation given to the Republican FUE. The immediate issue to be exploited was Castilian opposition to Catalanism.[231]

With the termination of *La Conquista del Estado*, the centre of activity of the JONS in 1932 was Valladolid rather than Madrid. There Onésimo Redondo, a Catholic activist who had lectured in Germany, had founded a union for beet-growers in 1930.[232] In May 1931 he had been one of the young founders of *Acción Nacional* in the province. On 13 June the first issue of his own paper, *Libertad*, appeared in defence of the rural population and against Catalanism; *La Conquista del Estado* was admired for its fighting spirit and 'Hispanic vehemence' but criticised for its excessive anti-Semitism.[233] In August, the *Juntas Castellanas de Actuación Hispánica* appeared as a political group with the slogan 'Castile, save Spain!' Their programme was traditional and nationalistic and aimed at renovating Castile by better agricultural methods, afforestation and modernisation of villages. A compul-

sory corporative syndical organisation, protected and regulated by
the State to unify 'the national interests of production', was
advocated.[234]

Like Ledesma, Redondo concentrated on anti-Catalanism. The
JONS of Valladolid during 1932 drew off members of the *Juventud
de Acción Popular* who had despaired of the passivity of that
organisation. At first, Redondo's group was little different from the
JAP, but, perhaps under Ledesma's influence, all relations were
severed between the local JAP and the non-confessional JONS.[235]
Unlike Ledesma, who was unenthusiastic about conservative
Generals, Redondo supported the military conspiracy as a means
towards a dictatorship. *Libertad* was frequently seized and fined,
suffering twenty lawsuits before suspension in August 1932.[236]
Despite the fusion the JONS of Valladolid and Madrid tended to
exist as separate units. The direction of the movement was officially
in the hands of a triumvirate of Ledesma, Redondo and Bermúdez
Cañete,[237] a young journalist ideologically of a type with the
authoritarian Catholic Redondo rather than with the secular
nationalist Ledesma. The JONS was as yet insignificant in national
politics.

The support of Rightist political groups was a tertiary consideration for the Generals; apart from soldiers on active service,
they planned to use numerous retired officers as auxiliaries where
necessary, notably in Madrid. The success of the movement depended on the attitude of the garrisons once the cry of revolt had
been raised in the classic tradition of the nineteenth-century *pronunciamiento*. Sanjurjo's aide-de-camp explained that 'it was never
thought that the moment to fight would arrive. The real strength
of the insurrection consisted in avoiding it.'[238] The broad plan of
the plotters was for simultaneous take-overs in various cities: in
Madrid, General Barrera was to be in command as Head of the
Junta; Sanjurjo was to rise in Seville, Colonel Varela in Cádiz,
General González Carrasco in Granada and General Ponte in
Valladolid, seconded by the JONS. Other garrisons were expected
to follow suit, but their commanders had not positively compromised themselves with the movement.[239] Perhaps several adopted
the attitude of Franco, commanding the garrison at Corunna, who
told Sanjurjo that he would not rise—though he promised not to
lead troops against those who did rise, if ordered to do so.[240]

Preparations went ahead for the rising in July as the debates on the Catalan Statute dragged on. The imminence of a military move to be led by Sanjurjo was an open secret. After Lerroux's meeting with Sanjurjo at Montemayor in June, Azaña had been informed of a military movement by Martínez Barrio.[241] Azaña had in fact known of the conspiracy for some time, but decided to play a waiting game, believing the movement doomed to failure; before the rising he only closed the offices of the PNE and *Acción Española*.[242]

The Generals were aware that possibilities of surprise were not good; the danger of preventive action against the conspirators appeared to be increasing. Many conspirators, too, were beginning to despair of the military ever rising and began to leave for their summer holidays. Sanjurjo, at a meeting of the *Junta* on 8 August at the estate near Madrid of the Duque del Infantado, demanded further postponement on the grounds that the time was not propitious, but was apparently overruled by Barrera and other colleagues.[243] Another motive for urgency was presumably the announcement of the government's intention shortly to guillotine debates on the Statute and agrarian reform.[244] News that the rising would commence early on 10 August reached the government as quickly as it did some of the conspirators.[245]

In Madrid the rising began at 4 am on 10 August as scheduled. Generals Barrera, Cavalcanti and Fernández Pérez were the leaders. Azaña was to be detained in the War Ministry by a band composed mainly of retired officers, who were to gain entry with the complicity of the Civil Guards on duty; from there the good news was to be telephoned to the rebel Generals, the garrisons and the Captaincy-General, the commanding officers of which were expected to rally to the cause. Azaña, forewarned, had, however, put ninety trusted Assault Guards in the Ministry garden, and these repulsed the surprised intruders. Firing continued for a while in the Plaza de la Cibeles, but the Post Office was not taken by the rebels, ten of whom were killed. Under the circumstances, conspiratorial promises were not kept: the 31st Infantry Regiment did not leave barracks, and someone turned back the cavalry approaching from Alcalá de Henares. The rising in Madrid proved a fiasco which was over before breakfast.[246] Ansaldo therefore flew the Head of the *Junta*, Barrera, to Pamplona, but no one in

Navarre could be persuaded to rise. The General was accordingly taken on to Biarritz. At La Cierva's house he was persuaded by Calvo Sotelo to fly to Seville with Ansaldo when it was learnt from the radio that the rising there had not been suppressed; but by the time they arrived in Seville, the fleeting reign of Sanjurjo was at an end.[247]

In Seville Sanjurjo won the allegiance of the garrison and took over the city by 7 am on the 10th.[248] Not a shot was fired, and martial law was declared by Sanjurjo as Captain-General of Andalusia. The proclamation ended with the words 'Long live Spain one and immortal!' The full manifesto of the *pronunciamiento* also referred to saving Spain from 'dismemberment'; although it denounced the entire activity of the government and the Cortes, anti-Catalanism and anti-Socialism, together with complaints about anarchy and military policy, appear to have been the dominant motives for the insurrection.[249] Sanjurjo in Seville was, however, alone: in Cádiz, Córdoba and Granada no one stirred, and the momentary success of Civil Guards in Jerez was insignificant.[250] From Madrid, Azaña ordered troop movements and made naval and air preparations;[251] a Moorish unit was landed at Cádiz but was not needed.[252] In the afternoon, the first signs of opposition to the *coup* in Seville came from workers' unions, which organised a strike soon paralysing the city.

By the late hours of the 10th, it was clear that the position of Sanjurjo, isolated and inactive in Seville, was hopeless. Faced with the possibility of having to fight their colleagues, the officers of Seville withdrew their support from the 'Lion of the Riff' who, with the words 'Farewell, loyal veterans! This time we have lost the game,' left the city at 1.30 am on the 11th to give himself up to the authorities at Huelva, where he was arrested by a policeman.[253] The affair had been a sword-stroke in the water, conducted in the best bloodless tradition of the *pronunciamiento*—on the eve of his attempt, Sanjurjo had told friends that, like a good conspirator, he was re-reading the doings of Prim and other Generals of the nineteenth century.[254]

The failure of the movement intended to overthrow the government in fact put Azaña, at least for some time, more firmly in the saddle and gave him an excuse to accelerate implementation of the Left Republican programme. He publicly denounced the rising as an attempt to 'oust the Republican régime' and restore the Monarchy or set up a military dictatorship; its failure represented 'the death-rattle of a parasite within the Republic'.[255] Republican solidarity was at a premium: not only Radicals and ex-Constitutionalists, but also the Agrarian leader hastened to assure the government of their loyalty.[256] Azaña therefore exploited his advantage: 'I do not want to make martyrs, but beggars.'[257] On 16 August a bill was introduced to expropriate without compensation the lands of suspected plotters, in effect all the Grandees, the economic basis of Monarchism.[258] The measure was opposed by Casanueva as 'a juridical enormity' since confiscation was to be approved before the suspects had been tried. He alleged this 'spoliation' was unconstitutional. The State, in breaking the law, was guilty of 'a monstrosity as great as that which a father would commit by violating his daughter. . . . From today . . . the national wealth is at the mercy of any informer.' The bill was passed by 262 votes to 14.[259] The list of Grandees affected totalled 390, and included 127 Dukes, 174 Marquesses and 78 Counts. The measure was incorporated in the Law of Agrarian Reform, which, with the Catalan Statute, now had a much speedier passage through the Cortes.[260] Further 'Republicanisation' of the armed forces, civil service, foreign service and judiciary also took place.[261]

Sanjurjo himself was quickly tried for military rebellion and attempting to overthrow the régime. His lawyer was an ex-Constitutional friend, Bergamín, who argued that the rising was against the government, not the régime, and that bloodshed had been deliberately avoided. The court sentenced him to death, but the sentence was commuted by the government and President to life imprisonment.[262] Conservatives expected leniency for a General who had made a mistake in interpreting the general will and were shocked when he became a common prisoner.[263] Eleven Madrid newspapers were suspended and ninety-eight in the provinces;[264] 145 suspected plotters were deported to Villa Cisneros in the Sahara without trial, in the main retired officers from the upper class.[265] Over 5,000 people were detained.[266] Of these some were local committee members of *Acción Popular*, many of whose branches were closed.

For the legalists like Gil Robles, the affair was a setback; although a few prominent Monarchists within the grouping were clearly involved the organisation as such had not conspired.[267] In Pontevedra, youths of Lis Quiben's *Unión Regional de Derechas* demonstrated in favour of Sanjurjo on the 10th, but they were the exception.[268] Members of the Seville branch were detained although they had explicitly refused to co-operate with Sanjurjo on the 10th, in accordance with instructions from Madrid given four months earlier to keep out of conspiracies.[269] Gil Robles himself had contacts with the Monarchist plotters, but even though he attended a meeting at Biarritz on 7 August, he would not undertake to restore the Monarchy or be a plotter.[270] In June he had already made clear his position and that of *Acción Popular*: 'fight within legality'. He explicitly stated that he was opposed to a resort to arms which was quite unjustifiable because government was not in the gutter.[271] Government action against *Acción Popular* exacerbated internal divisions and led to recriminations and new departures.

Notes to this chapter are on pages 305–20.

Chapter 3 UNITY IN DIVERSITY
September 1932–December 1933

SANJURJO'S UNSUCCESSFUL attempt to revive the *pronunciamiento* as an instrument of political change reinvigorated Azaña's coalition, but only briefly. The high-handedness of its repressive measures, which won Azaña the admiration of Mussolini, gave renewed impetus to the movement of reaction against the government. The shootings at Casas Viejas (January 1933) and the government's failure to tackle social problems more energetically accentuated the growing disillusionment of a section of the working class. Casas Viejas caused the Radicals to go into full opposition and obstruct in the Cortes, though they rallied to the government when laws complementary to the Constitution were debated. The Law concerning Religious Confessions and Congregations, however, only served to strengthen the Catholic opposition still further. The President therefore sought an opportunity to dissolve the Cortes before the reaction against Azaña's rule turned into a reaction against the Republic itself. As expected the elections went against Azaña and the Socialists. Lerroux and Gil Robles were the victors.

The participation of Monarchist members of *Acción Popular* in the abortive *pronunciamiento* precipitated a crisis in the Catholic organisation. The division had been latent since the end of 1931. Gil Robles and his 'accidentalist' supporters wanted the movement to develop into a Catholic political party within the Republic. Monarchists, however, wanted to use the organisation as a front for their own anti-Republican propaganda. This division of opinion coincided with another: the 'accidentalists' stood for legal methods, whereas the Monarchists were prepared to use violence. *Acción Popular* gave birth to the CEDA while the Alfonsines created

Renovación Española, abandoning altogether their traditional liberalism in an attempt to attract Carlists.

Behind the 'accidentalist'-Monarchist schism on the Right lay what was perhaps the most important, if often implicit, issue in the politics of the time: the interpretation of the word 'Republic'. For the lifelong Republican Lerroux it simply meant a form of government open to all provided they did not use violence. For Left Republicans like Azaña, as for the Monarchists, Republicanism was an ideology defined in the Constitution of 1931 and its complementary laws; anyone who did not accept these as final was therefore not truly a Republican. The corollary of this for Monarchists was that Catholics could never accept the Republic. Gil Robles thought otherwise: Catholics could be loyal to the Republic though they could not formally accept it as long as its legislation infringed the rights of the Church. In his view legislation was the essential thing, the form of government was accidental. From their point of view the Socialists Prieto and Largo Caballero also considered the legislative content of the Republic more important than the Republic as a mere form of government. Thus the word 'Republic' meant different things to different people.

The views of Azaña and the Socialists on one side and of Lerroux and the CEDA on the other proved mutually exclusive. However, the vital difference between the two most important political groups, the Socialists and the CEDA, was one of methods. The 'possibilism' of Gil Robles signified evolution towards an ideal Catholic régime by legal means; violence could be used only in reply to the violence of others. The Socialists adopted evolutionary tactics, but only for opportunistic reasons. When in 1933 opinion started to turn against them they spoke of revolutionary methods for the defence of their gains and the furtherance of Socialist ideals. The Socialists and the CEDA both had ideals incompatible with liberal-democracy, but whereas the evolutionary tactic was dogma for the CEDA it was not for the Socialists. The latter accused the former of being Fascist in 1933, but whereas Largo Caballero had threatened to use violence since the autumn of 1931, Gil Robles did not make counter-threats until the autumn of 1933. It was the Socialists, not the CEDA, who turned against the democratic system.

The repressive measures taken by the government after 10

August included the closure of many branches of *Acción Popular* which had not been involved in the military movement. The participation in it of prominent Alfonsine politicians brought on a crisis within *Acción Popular* which was inevitable sooner or later. Gil Robles seized his opportunity: the conglomeration of individuals and groups whose leadership he had taken over in the autumn of 1931 could now be transformed into a homogeneous political party with the aim of obtaining power by legal means.[1] Now was the moment to make a reality of the counsels of *El Debate*: the members of *Acción Popular* should be 'the paladins of the legal struggle and of obedience to the constituted powers'.[2] The moment was particularly propitious as Goicoechea was in gaol, Vallellano was still in France and *ABC* was still suspended.[3] Five hundred delegates, claiming to represent 619,000 members of *Acción Popular* and allied entities, therefore journeyed to Madrid for the First Assembly of the movement, which opened on 22 October 1932.[4]

The political debate revolved around the paradoxical formula of the programme of December 1931 which, although making no mention explicitly of forms of government, had reaffirmed the obedience of *Acción Popular* to the constituted power while permitting members to defend their own ideals as they saw fit. This formula was now discussed in the light of the *pronunciamiento* and the growing tension between Alfonsines and 'accidentalists' in the preceding months.

The debate on 22 October began with speakers defending the *status quo*. Fernández Ruano from Málaga asked: 'Declaration of Republican faith? Never. (*Applause*.) This, as well as being an act of folly as great as that of making an affirmation of Monarchism, would be at this juncture an act of cowardice and meanness.' Fernández-Ladreda, the Dictator's Mayor of Oviedo and leader of the strong Asturian group, also wished to avoid the expulsion of Monarchists: 'Within *Acción Popular* there are men who believe that the Republic in Spain is not a régime, but a revolutionary doctrine; men who, faced with the government's anti-religious campaign, believe that they cannot collaborate with a régime which assists and defends this system. There are others, too, who are Catholics and enter *Acción Popular* to fight against those who oppose their religious ideas, but who are in political communion with the Republic. . . . Those who hold Republican opinions cannot ask us to support the work of consolidation of the Republican régime; we have nothing to consolidate.' His speech brought the first exchanges over the formula of December 1931, and fears that the movement would now break up prompted Fr Guallar to ask that the issue be shelved and that *Acción Popular* continue as originally conceived, as a union in defence of Religion and Country, not a political party.

Convinced accidentalists, however, were determined that the issue should be squarely faced and resolved. Medina Togores, a leader-writer for *El Debate*, took up the cudgels: 'It is disloyal to lend obedience to the régime at one moment and appear later as a Monarchist. (*Protests. A voice*: "Why is it disloyal?") It is disloyal because one cannot talk of obedience and then pick up a rifle and rush into the street. . . . This obedience must be converted into a postulate. . . . With regard to the régime, obedience pure and simple. (*Applause*.)' Now that battle had been joined, Cimas Leal, editor of *La Gaceta Regional* of Salamanca, the organ of Gil Robles, carried the accidentalist thesis a stage further: 'Obedience means acceptance. (*Voices*: "No! No!") . . . Obedience means acceptance, or it means nothing more than an external formula demanded by the law. And this would be cowardice.' The Monarchists were now incensed and the division clear. Moutas from Oviedo attempted at this point to move a round of applause for the absent Goicoechea, but found himself overruled by the chair. Ceballos drew the conclusion from Cimas Leal's speech that Monarchists would have to leave if *Acción Popular* could not permit freedom in this matter to the individual member; but, as Medina Togores remarked, on joining members accepted the programme: 'obedience cannot be a fiction'.

Now that it was obvious that the accidentalists would not give way, the debate broadened out. The Alfonsine deputy Sáinz Rodríguez, leader of the *Agrupación Regional Independiente* of Santander, argued that the problem had been raised solely as a consequence of '10 August'; the issue was being introduced under pressure of the government's actions. He wished Monarchists to remain, denying that the *ralliement* was a valid parallel since in Spain the legislation was consubstantial with the régime—precisely the view of Azaña. Valiente, leader of the JAP, therefore introduced a compromise solution which was to have the effect of splitting the Monarchists: the issue should be shelved on condition that the leaders of *Acción Popular* did not indulge in Republican or Monarchist propaganda.

While it later became apparent that Monarchists such as Fernández-Ladreda were prepared to accept this condition, ardent Alfonsines could not. Tornos not only continued to resist the transformation of *Acción Popular* into a political party led by accidentalists, but claimed that it had already 'failed in its methods'. The Young Propagandist Moreno Dávila was quick to avail himself of a golden opportunity and replied that 'all that has been lost is the fault of 10 August; our [legal] tactic led us on to victory and other tactics caused us to lose what had been gained. Let us, then, follow the tactic of yesterday.'

Fr Guallar added a corollary to the legal tactic, the need for an advanced social programme. He believed that violence was incompatible with the 'Christian redemption of society'; such methods were used only by selfish materialists. Lucía, leader of the important DRV, agreed: schools and the workers' bread were the issues, and the slow, hard task was to recover the ground lost by a century of 'Christian abandonment'. *Acción Popular* must become a disciplined political party to overcome its great defect: the lack of a cut-and-dried political programme.[5]

The outcome of the debate was victory for the accidentalists: violence and membership of *Acción Popular* were incompatible and its leaders could not be active members of other parties. Respect for opinions concerning the form of government was, however, reiterated.[6] The accidentalists wished to dissociate themselves from Monarchism, but not to press their case too strongly and so drive out such important organisations as that in Asturias with 29,000 members, the Monarchist leaders of which were willing to accept compromises. Closing the Assembly, Gil Robles emphasised the need for constitutional revision to liberate the Church and for a social policy 'to consolidate the just social advances'; the question of the form of régime was less important than the struggle against atheist materialism.[7]

Plans for the creation of a political party to succeed *Acción Popular* developed in November 1932 when Gil Robles attended the Third Assembly of the DRV in Valencia. Lucía's blueprint of

1930 for a nationwide, confederal, Catholic party fitted well with
his aims and Lucía, in charge of *Acción Popular*'s organisation,
became his source of inspiration. Their mission was 'to recover
what has been lost, not the institutions, which pass away, but the
principles which cannot die'.[8] The Right must await events and
prepare itself for the task of government. The immediate rise of
the Right to power would be 'a catastrophe' because persecution
was too recent to allow serenity of judgment. The target should
be the election of 120 or 150 deputies to the Cortes to put an end
to this persecution and press for revision of the Constitution.
'These truths may not be to the liking of the partisans of "all or
nothing", who, by wanting all, will most probably achieve nothing.
. . . The Right must be prepared for the occupation of power.
When? At any time. Under what régime? Under any régime. Let
us not get bogged down over what is accidental. The essential
thing is the defence of Religion and Country. . . . I am going to
defend these wherever necessary and however possible; not to do
this will be to put what is accidental before what is essential.'[9]

Although Goicoechea's resignation from *Acción Popular* was
not made public until January 1933,[10] it was clear from the
October Assembly that Monarchist activists could no longer continue within *Acción Popular*. If, to ease tender Monarchist consciences, Gil Robles maintained the theory that 'each member
remains at liberty to uphold his convictions in their entirety and
can defend them outside the organisation',[11] in practice the programme of December 1931, in which Goicoechea had been responsible for the clause proclaiming 'the necessity for a discreet
silence on the problem of the form of government',[12] was now a
dead letter.

As soon as he was released from gaol in November 1932
Goicoechea began to work for a new *Federación de Derechas* which
would take a stand on forms of government.[13] He hoped to attract
into this new formation Monarchists within *Acción Popular* who
felt uneasy about 'twisting their hearts round' in order to accept
the new discipline of the group.[14] He also hoped that the Traditionalists would join, and at the invitation of some Traditionalists
he addressed them on his programme, the basis of which he
claimed was 'one symbol-word: tradition'. He explicitly rejected
'possibilism' and outlined a common policy founded upon Re-

ligion, Nation and 'unity of command'. He followed Vázquez de Mella in recommending separation of Church and State in conjunction with a concordat. Individual rights were to be guaranteed by a strong and independent judiciary. His new Monarchy was also to have a 'parliamentary institution': Traditionalists were uneasy about his exact meaning on this point.[15]

The opportunity for Carlist-Alfonsine co-operation once again offered itself after the new turn taken by *Acción Popular*. In the autumn of 1932, on the initiative of Calvo Sotelo, another effort was made in Paris to end the dynastic schism. Alfonso XIII, accompanied by Calvo Sotelo and Vallellano among others, discussed matters with the Carlists Rodezno, Lamamié de Clairac, Oriol and Olazábal. As usual, the theoretical solution was that Alfonso's son Juan should succeed Alfonso Carlos after having accepted the principles of Traditionalism; since he would succeed Alfonso XIII, the two branches of the dynasty would thus be reunited. In practice, however, mutual distrust made matters difficult. Lamamié de Clairac suggested that Alfonso should renounce his claims in favour of his son, with the proviso that the renunciation would become invalid if Alfonso Carlos did not also renounce his rights in favour of Juan before an agreed time-limit should expire. Similarly, to reassure Carlists, Juan must go to live with Alfonso Carlos so that he could be immersed in the Traditionalist *credo* to which he would have to subscribe. The efforts failed in 1932 as they had in 1931: this time Alfonso XIII declined to accept the proposition after consultation with the old party-leaders La Cierva, Lema and Romanones. This failure, which led to renewed exchanges in Madrid between *ABC* and *El Siglo Futuro* in December,[16] put paid to Goicoechea's hopes for a *Federación de Derechas*. The letter of 10 January 1933, asking him to found a new grouping to be based on his speech on 'Traditionalism', was signed only by Alfonsines.[17]

Goicoechea announced the party's programme in another letter, which began by criticising his former colleagues in *Acción Popular* for their undignified and deceitful accidentalist ideas. The aim of his own Monarchist party was to be 'nationalisation of our institutions . . . and at the same time a total change in the organisation and life of the State'—both impossible 'if we consider as indifferent problems described as being those of form, but which, in reality,

are those of régime. . . . We want a renovated Spain, but one which
does not cease to be Spain. Spanish Renovation: such is our ideal
and such must also be our device. . . . For us the State is not form
without content, but activity and thought consciously directed to
the achievement of ends. . . . The movement of redemptive reaction
which we represent does not propose as its objective the pure and
simple resurrection of the past prior to 14 April.

'In the religious sphere, we are Catholics; in the political sphere,
Monarchists; in the juridical sphere, constitutionalists and legalists; and in the social sphere, democrats.' Elaborating upon this
statement of belief, Goicoechea explained that Church and State
were to be separate. On the subject of politics he was emphatic:
'We are not Monarchists without a King, nor Monarchists without
a Monarchy, nor Monarchists of a Monarchy silently buried in our
breasts, but convinced and active Monarchists, who see in the
Monarchy the keystone of the constitutional arch and the essential
principle irreplaceable in a new order.' Nevertheless he saw the
need for 'popular intervention in government' through an 'organised suffrage' and strong municipal liberties. He called for 'the
submission of the State to Law', not in a parliament, but in 'a
system of guarantees, of petitions; in a word, in what the English
were wont to call "remedies" and Spanish political history called
"fueros". . . . The centre of gravity of the constitutional edifice of
the future will be removed from the parliamentary organ to the
monarchical power and the judicial power.'

His social programme was vaguely Thomist. It spoke of responsibility for the mighty and aid for the weak and poor, thus
obviating the class struggle by building a society in which the
State regained 'its natural function of giving to each one his own,
in default of spontaneous agreement between the parts'.[18] Some
days later Pemán spoke of reincorporating in the Monarchist
programme 'the postulates of social renovation. . . . Socially, such
has been our behaviour that we have given grounds for the people
to believe that capitalism and Catholicism are twin ideas, or at
least that they have a non-aggression pact signed between them.
And this is to bring Christ into disrepute and sterilise the Blood
of the Cross.'[19] The programme of Goicoechea did not provide
incontrovertible proof of a volte-face.

Renovación Española was officially constituted on 23 February

1933.[20] Goicoechea continued to woo the Traditionalists: 'Of Traditionalism I shall say that in the past much has separated us; in the present almost nothing separates us, and in the future nothing will separate us.'[21] The Traditionalists, however, were not convinced of Alfonsine sincerity: Traditionalists remained Traditionalists and though circumstantial alliances could be concluded, they were determined to retain their identity and ideas intact.[22] The meagre result of all Goicoechea's labours was the creation in March of a joint electoral office, TYRE.[23]

The dynastic conundrum remained unsolved. The very thought of alliance with Alfonsine usurpers led to the foundation of a dissident *Círculo Carlista* in Madrid.[24] Within the Communion the *El Cruzado Español* group refused to countenance possible usurpation and pressed the senile Alfonso Carlos to convoke a grand assembly of Carlists to choose a successor.[25] Although Alfonso Carlos rejected such impertinence, comparing the scheme to an election for a President of the Republic, he remained firm in his contention that his rights could 'only be entrusted to that person who promises and swears to preserve intact the traditional principles, which . . . are above persons'. He did not actually exclude Juan provided that all the required conditions were fulfilled.[26] In June 1933 Juan formally became Alfonso XIII's heir, but his father remained adamant: 'Even though the Monarchy is absent, I am and I shall be as long as I live the King of Spain. I have not renounced my rights nor am I thinking of doing so. . . . I shall not abdicate in exile.'[27]

While these developments had been taking place within the Monarchist Right, Gil Robles and Lucía had been active in the formation of a confederal Catholic party incorporating as far as was possible all the former groups adhering to *Acción Popular*. The new formation was to conclude electoral alliances with other Rightist groups as circumstances demanded. Gil Robles was an opponent of any 'permanent organisation of union for Rightist forces'.[28] Members could be Republican or Monarchist at home, but must adhere publicly only to the principles of *Acción Popular*.[29] A congress of the various groups interested opened in Madrid on 28 February 1933. It was attended by delegates representing 735,058 members, thus constituting the biggest-ever Spanish political party.[30] On 4 March the *Confederación Española de*

H

Derechas Autónomas (CEDA) was officially founded on the initiative of the DRV, whose leader had originally conceived the idea. Immediately the party passed as three general points of its programme its affirmation of Christian civilisation, the need for constitutional revision to help attain this ideal, and obedience to the precepts of the Collective Declaration of the Episcopacy of December 1931.[31]

The social policies of the new party followed closely the Encyclicals of Leo XIII and Pius XI. The principles on which its social policy was based were rejection of the class struggle, the limited intervention of the State in social and economic affairs, a directed economy regulated, not by the State, but by means of its own corporative organisation, a juster distribution of wealth and the spread of small-scale property-owning, and the right to work for all workers, manual and intellectual. From these principles, the party programme formulated certain practical deductions. Free choice was allowed in respect of membership of unions, but membership of corporations was to be obligatory. The system of mixed juries was to be retained to settle work-contracts and resolve labour disputes, but the members of the juries were to be elected on a system of proportional representation and presidents were to be 'social magistrates' uncommitted to either side. There was to be a just minimum wage, profit-sharing and co-management in firms within the framework of the Encyclicals, as well as a compulsory system of social insurance to be financed jointly by the State, employers and workers. The length of the working-day was to depend on the nature of the work. Workers were to receive training in skills, while in general industries were to be 'Hispanicised' and workers given the best deal possible, subject to the exigencies of the national economy in relation to the international economy.[32]

Thus the Congress decided against 'an anti-Christian social régime, based upon egoism, which has failed', and against 'the suicidal class struggle, which ruins the economy, and, therefore, the working class'. The motion for a corporative state based on such a policy was put forward by the DRV, *Acción Obrerista* and the JAP of Madrid.[33] The result was a formulation of social and economic corporativism in line with the Encyclical *Quadragesimo Anno* (1931). The political superstructure to be built on this socio-economic basis was left an open question by the Congress, though a motion put down by the JAP condemning universal inorganic suffrage and calling for an Italian-style corporative régime was rejected.[34] In the CEDA's system, unions were to cease to be purely organisations for resistance and were to become organs for collaboration in 'a Christian conception of the corporative organisation of the State'.[35] The party sought a third way between economic individualism and the 'fetishism' of socialism, nationalism or communism.[36] Gil Robles proclaimed that 'one does not fight against Marxism with Hitlerian militias or Fascist legions, but with an advanced social programme'.[37]

The CEDA, like *Acción Popular*, with its autonomous ally *Acción Obrerista*, before it, took great care to project its image as a party of social reform, and as such, an alternative to Socialism. In the process, strong attacks were made on selfish property-owners and employers whose sole ambition lay 'in the maintenance of an order guaranteed by the rifles of the Civil Guard' and who intended 'the priests to fulfil the shameful function of keeping order by preaching to the people resignation and obedience and not revealing to them their rights'.[38] The time had come for a change: 'we live in times of terrible truths; we want nothing to do with the Red Star of Moscow; but we declare war on black capitalism, exploiter of the poor. . . . More religion and less Pharisaism; more justice and less liturgy.'[39] For those like Herrera, who lamented that *Rerum Novarum* had not penetrated the minds of Spanish Catholics,[40] this was a source of encouragement. The new wave of enthusiasm led Fr Guallar to quote Bakunin with approval: 'Let us go to the people!'[41] The social-Catholic cry was taken up throughout the CEDA; even the millionaire notary and absentee landlord Casanueva asked: 'What concept of property have the propertied upheld? Ninety per cent of them do not know the Encyclicals of Leo XIII and Pius XI save by name. What has the upper class done? It has forgotten its tradition and played polo and golf. And the youth? Cut class and played billiards.'[42] Self-criticism was fashionable; it remained to be seen whether it would lead to practical consequences.

The policy of the CEDA also emphasised decentralisation in accordance with Papal doctrines of pluralism, although for some members of the party its programme tended towards centralism. If the party's ideology subscribed to traditional theories of regionalism, the importance of the *rôle* of the region was perhaps undermined by the stress put on the *rôle* of the municipality as a natural entity to be recognised by law. Municipal government was seen as a 'school for citizenship' and must therefore be freed from *caciquismo* and be granted wide powers of administrative autonomy. In this respect, the party programme was consciously indebted to *Maurismo*.[43]

Policy reflected perhaps the regional strength of the CEDA: the local patriotism of the Meseta tended to identify itself with national patriotism and its 'regionalism' was 'anti-regionalist', for the Meseta was the heart of Spain, not simply one region among many. Regionalism was kept fully alive in 'peripheral' Spain by the DRV, which held fast to its vision of 'an autonomous and autarchic Valencia with capacity and power to govern itself and prescribe the laws by which it must be ruled, within the sphere of its regional ends'. This liberty was for Lucía a *sine qua non* for participation in the Catholic political confederation, which he carefully emphasised was based on a pact and was not the product of simple amalgamation. He saw the DRV as forming the link between the CEDA and other Catholic regional parties—the *Lliga* and the PNV—although his grand design was never realised.[44]

In general, the policies and structure of the CEDA bore quite close resemblance to the Christian Democrat parties of Western Europe. Like them, it was a confederation of regions and social classes, even if the working-class element was not very considerable in the towns. The backbone of its membership was the farming community, particularly the peasant society of León and the two Castiles. It believed in 'localism' subject to the greater organism represented by the nation, and its policies followed carefully the social teaching of the Church.[45] First and foremost it was profoundly Catholic: 'the essence, the marrow and the heart of *Acción Popular* and, consequently, of the CEDA, is its religious confessionalism'.[46] 'We are proud of our confessionalism', said Lucía, 'but . . . those responsible for our political acts are ourselves. . . . We wish to be of service to the Church, not to use the Church in our service.' 'Let us defend God and Spain and leave in His hands the form of government,' said Gil Robles. 'They [the Monarchists] tell us that we are cowards because we do not commit ourselves in favour of one or other form of government. . . . But is it we who

allowed the Monarchy to fall? . . . From the Crown that perished
I could only pluck a Cross and I clasped it to me and with it I began
the Reconquest of the Spanish Right. . . . Before form we defend
content; before the perishable we defend the eternal; before men,
we defend God.'[47]

The formation of rival Catholic-accidentalist and Alfonsine
parties brought division and a new alignment to the Right. The
CEDA, successor to *Acción Popular* and *Acción Nacional,* was not in
the event weakened significantly by the departure of Alfonsines
who could not bring themselves to remain Monarchists *in foro
interno.* Of the two groups which had opposed the virtual expulsion
of the Monarchists at the October Assembly, the *Agrupación
Regional Independiente* (Santander) retained its independence as a
local coalition of all Rightists, while *Acción Popular* in Asturias
accepted the discipline of the CEDA. Alfonsines, like Carlists, left
the original provincial coalitions, but only one of these, *Acción
Ciudadana* of Cádiz, cast off from the parent organisation.[48]

Goicoechea's hopes of drawing off large numbers of Alfonsines
were dashed. *Renovación Española* proved such a disappointment
that by June 1933 its leaders were pressing for use of the ultimate
weapon: a declaration by Alfonso XIII that membership of the
CEDA was incompatible with Monarchist convictions. Alfonso saw
Gil Robles in Paris, but although the latter told him that he would
be loyal to the Republic, the King chose not to make difficulties
for the CEDA.[49] The division of the 'authentic' Right into three
parts—accidentalist, Alfonsine, Carlist—was now clear and polemics frequent. To opponents, however, the Right still appeared
as a Traditionalist had envisaged it: three corps of the same army
separated only by tactical considerations.[50]

The immediate concern of the Right when the Cortes reopened
in October 1932 was to mitigate the repressive measures taken by
the government after 10 August. Of the main newspapers suspended, *El Debate* was allowed to reappear on 8 October and *La
Nación* and *El Imparcial* on 22 October, but it was not until
30 November that the 'civic death' of *ABC* came to an end after
three and a half months which had cost the Monarchist daily
2,391,438 pesetas.[51] Gil Robles, who had supported the government on 10 August, protested that people were still detained after
two months although government-appointed special judges had

acquitted them, and newspapers remained suspended even though no charge could be brought against them under the Defence Law.[52]

On 23 November Agrarians, Basque-Navarrese and Federal Republicans demanded the immediate discussion of the law creating the Court of Constitutional Guarantees, or alternatively the setting up of a Cortes committee to deal with complaints concerning detentions and deportations. The motion was rejected but it gave rise to an interesting confrontation between Azaña and Gil Robles. '*Sr. Azaña*: Independence of the judicial power? It depends! Independence from what? (*Sr. Gil Robles*: From the government.) Exactly. Independence of the judicial power from what? (*Sr. Gil Robles*: From the meddlings of the government.— *Murmurs*) Then I do not believe in the independence of the judicial power. (*Sr. Gil Robles*: But the Constitution says so.) The Constitution may say what it likes, what I say. . . . (*Sr. Gil Robles*: Article 94 of the Constitution.) Calm yourself, Sr. Gil Robles. What I say, Señores Diputados, is that neither the judicial power, nor the legislative power, nor the executive power can be independent of the national public spirit.'[53]

The deportations without trial or time-limit to Villa Cisneros were not debated until the end of December, though Lamamié de Clairac had been pressing for a debate since 7 October. They were, he said, quite unconstitutional; he made an issue of the government's choice of vessel, *España núm. 5*, an old cattle-transport, unsafe, insanitary and overcrowded. [54] Apart from deportations, detentions and closure of political offices, the constant complaint of the Right in 1933, as in 1932, was the use made of the Defence Law of the Republic. Priests were fined or imprisoned for sermons against civil marriage and divorce; one of their number claimed that 'any attack, not on the régime, but on the laws emanating from the powers of the Republic, is considered an attack on the régime'.[55] Local authorities in the hands of the government's friends were accused of *caciquismo*.[56] The arch-liberal Royo Villanova said that 'a government which calls itself liberal and democratic cannot govern with the Defence Law of the Republic'. The new régime had become 'a Fascist Republic. . . . You have had the effrontery to say: "Long live the Republic and death to liberty".'[57] During 1932 *Acción Popular* held 695 meetings, but had 172 suspended;[58]

this situation continued into 1933 and was seen by Gil Robles as an effort by Azaña to tempt the party to abandon legal methods.[59]

Whether or not the Right was correct in maintaining that measures against its propaganda were motivated by fear of publicity of the government's shortcomings, the economic situation continued to worsen as a consequence of disorder and now of the world depression. The volume of trade decreased, while imports continued to exceed exports. The crisis continued in the metallurgical and mining industries, the chief employers of non-agricultural labour, and agricultural exports fell by half during the biennium.[60] With falling revenue and increased expenditure, the budget deficit increased.[61] The peseta also continued to fall: the exchange-rate with the French franc, 37·05 per 100 in April 1931, was 48·05 in September 1932.[62] While, in general, the government presented economic difficulties in the light of the world depression, the Right blamed it for its incompetence, its chronic inability to keep order and its socialising tendencies which destroyed internal and external business confidence. Industrial unrest was perhaps at its worst in the first half of 1933, being largely the consequence of the revolutionary *émeutes* of the CNT. It was calculated that 102 persons were killed and 140 hurt as a result of social crimes in the first six months of 1933.[63] It was against such a background that the budget for 1933 was severely criticised in the Cortes.

The main lines of the Agrarian attack on Carner's budget were that expenditure had been increased in non-productive sectors, while it was inadequate for the things that really mattered. Frequent criticisms were voiced concerning the wasteful expansion of the bureaucracy at the expense of the productive sector, notably public works; *enchufismo* was something which scandalised all Agrarians.[64] Under the Monarchy, some 2,000,000,000 pesetas had been spent on public works; Carner had increased this item to the inadequate extent of 143,000,000, despite the termination of the royal and ecclesiastical budgets and a cut of 170,000,000 in Moroccan expenditure—and this at a time when there were more than half a million unemployed. On the other hand, expenditure on the bureaucracy had soared by 1,000,000,000 pesetas.[65] The Republic of workers of every class had become, in Unamuno's phrase, the Republic of functionaries.

On the Ministry of Labour's budget, Largo Caballero found

himself under fire from Fr Guallar from the Right and Balbontín from his Left; 1,000,000 pesetas had been allocated for relief of the unemployed, just one four-hundredth of the total budget. Fr Guallar demanded a fortyfold increase, though agreeing with the Minister that preparation of a compulsory insurance system by the State was an urgent necessity. In the short run, more relief and more public works were the answers, together with the restoration of order necessary to attract capital and get the economy moving again. He also attacked Largo Caballero's mixed juries: although the principle was good, partisan presidents were not. Yet the boycott by the CNT often made them pointless; in some areas Governors and employers negotiated directly with the Anarcho-Syndicalists, and this must either be stopped or the juries disbanded.[66] Social-Catholics complained that the theory and practice of social legislation diverged widely for political reasons. The system had been turned into 'a weapon in the service of the new *caciquismos*' of the Socialists.[67]

Spirited attacks were also directed against the agricultural budget; unemployment was mostly rural. Only 0·45 per cent of the total budget was devoted to agriculture, and bureaucrats accounted for much of this at the expense of the need for credit, electricity and reafforestation.[68] The condition of the countryside in 1933 remained much as it had been in 1932; here again anarchy and government incompetence were the charges levelled by the Right.[69] In the 'stable' area of the Meseta the problem was one of wheat prices. In the provinces of Burgos and Palencia, it was said, prices had fallen to a pre-1914 level; in Valladolid wheat was being sold at 40 pesetas, instead of the official minimum 46 pesetas. There was a surplus in 1933, but Agrarians could not persuade Domingo to raise the minimum price-level, give more credit-facilities to farmers and millers, build silos for storage or tie wages to prices.[70]

In the Cortes a cerealist group was formed under Royo Villanova which included Agrarians, Conservatives, Radicals and Progressives.[71] The National Cerealist Assembly held in May 1933 demanded the resignations of Domingo and Largo Caballero, a minimum price-level of 53 pesetas, lower rail-charges, better credit-facilities, an end to disorder and the Law of Municipal Boundaries, a total ban on importation of cereals and a reform of

the mixed juries to give the deciding voice to judges and agrono-
mists.[72] According to Gil Robles, 3,140,000 rural workers were
being sacrificed to please 1,860,000 urban workers; an increase of
the wheat price, at least to cover the cost of production, was
imperative. The consequent rise in the price of bread could be
borne by townsmen if they spent less on luxuries.[73]

In the 'unstable' countryside of Andalusia and Extremadura,
where unemployment was worst, government policies (or lack of
them) and disorder were denounced by the Right as the root-
causes of the trouble. The government's promises of agrarian
reform did not materialise; by February 1933, 1,325 properties of
16,082 hectares had been expropriated by the Institute,[74] but
Domingo seemed to be able to do nothing except create confusion
and disillusionment.[75] Disillusionment led to extra-legal methods
and the Decree for the Intensification of Farming (1 November
1932) which was used to legalise as temporary occupations the
illegal seizure of land, notably in Extremadura.[76] In Extremadura,
it was reported, 'a state of veritable anarchy' existed, with daily
violence and invasions of estates organised by the Socialist *Casas
del Pueblo* without the interference of the Civil Guard which had
orders to turn a blind eye.[77] According to the conservative *ABC*
'the atmosphere of violence, of anarchic indiscipline, which con-
tinues unabated like an incurable madness from end to end of
Spain, goes on providing its daily list of killings, of outrages, of
pillagings, of all kind of rebelliousness and abuse. The break-up
of the State . . . is not a rhetorical image.'[78]

Apart from violence the actions of the Socialist-controlled
mixed juries caused trouble. The jury of Salamanca province
permitted employment of UGT members only and forbade dismissals. Reapers were to be paid 12 pesetas for an eight-hour day,
and since overtime was inevitable at harvest-time the daily wage
rose to 19·65 pesetas, more than was earned by a skilled urban
worker. With prices depressed, smallholders simply could not pay
these sums and joined the ranks of unemployed labourers. The
area under cultivation fell, and Gil Robles noted unprecedented
unemployment in Salamanca in spite of the ban on Portuguese and
Gallego migrant labour.[79] The farmers reacted by disregarding the
jury's orders. Clashes and arrests followed.[80] In the province of
Seville the picture was also one of decreasing cultivation, falling

production, low prices, starvation, anarchy and economic collapse.[81]

It was in this atmosphere of desperation and collapse in the countryside that one of the periodic Anarchist *jacqueries* took place in January 1933. One of the places affected was an insignificant *pueblo* in the backward province of Cádiz called Casas Viejas, where on 11 January 'Libertarian Communism' was proclaimed by 'Sixfingers', a man with ideas. The government sought to put down the Anarchist outbreaks as speedily as possible, and Assault Guards were sent to Casas Viejas with orders to be tough which came from the impulsive Minister of the Interior, Casares Quiroga.[82] In Casas Viejas the resistance of 'Sixfingers' was overcome; the officer in charge then rounded up twelve of the inhabitants and shot them. When this became known, Azaña and his government came under severe attack from the extreme Left and from the Radicals, who saw a chance to bring down the government and who had a reputation for favouring local Anarchists as a way of worsting their common Socialist enemy.

The debates in the Cortes were prolonged and heated, and revolved around whether or not the government had given the order 'No wounded, no prisoners. Shoot in the belly.' The Right did not lead the attack in the Cortes but allowed the Radicals to do the work so that the gap between the Republican parties would widen. Lerroux's lieutenant Martínez Barrio launched a fierce attack on the government: 'I believe that there is something worse than a régime being lost, and that is that this régime should fall spattered with mud, cursed by History, surrounded by disgrace, tears and blood.'[83] From these words the Right as well as the Radicals were to gain great profit; henceforth Azaña's régime was widely known as 'the government of Casas Viejas'.[84]

After the Casas Viejas affair, which caused a fall in Azaña's popularity in Republican circles, debate began in earnest on the Law concerning Religious Confessions and Congregations, already denounced by *El Debate* when introduced in the previous autumn as 'an act of aggression against the Catholic Church ... a declaration of war on a most important sector of Spanish society; we believe the most numerous one'. Government policy seemed to be to force Catholics into opposition to the Republic.[85] The law was designed to give effect to Articles 26 and 27 of the Constitution and said that all ecclesiastical property belonged to the State, though the Church could go on using the buildings. Religious Orders and Congregations were forbidden to engage directly or indirectly in commerce, industry, agriculture or education. The activities of the Orders were thus drastically curtailed and brought under close supervision by the State.[86]

According to Catholic statistics, the educational and welfare work of the Orders affected 1,312,770 people. The Orders gave primary education to 601,950 pupils in comparison with the 1,774,400 in state schools, while they provided secondary schooling for 27,000, compared with the State's 25,000.[87] All this was to come to an end. Gil Robles declared Catholics' 'implacable hostility' to the bill, and warned that if it ever came into force they would have to disobey it.[88] The Radicals, who had said that they would obstruct in the Cortes until the Socialists left power, now dissociated themselves from the Catholics on the grounds that this was an exceptional case of a law complementary to the Constitution.[89] For the Socialists, the law meant 'simply a deprivation of privileges which nobody can claim when the State wishes to be truly sovereign'.[90]

Agrarian deputies opposed the law with claims that it exceeded the terms of Article 26 and contradicted other articles of the Constitution; the State ownership of Church property was confiscation clearly contrary to the Constitution. For Gil Robles, opposition was a 'duty of conscience' since he recognised that the Catholics had no hope of modifying the Draft or even of submitting it to the Court of Constitutional Guarantees because this still had to be created. To replace the Orders' education would cost the debilitated Treasury another 200,000,000 pesetas annually. He saw the law as an expedient to hold together Azaña's creaking coalition, 'an injection of anti-clericalism to give life to the corpse which occupies the Blue Bench'; even though the price was spiritual civil war. He warned the government that it was opening an abyss between Catholics and non-Catholics: 'Sedition is not licit, but passive resistance is when the law is contrary to the principles of justice, which are above legal formalism.'[91]

Basque Nationalists considered the law an attack on Basque liberty as well as on their consciences. The government's bill reflected the educational concepts of Gentile and the *étatisme* of

Mussolini and was therefore 'pure Fascism'.[92] From the liberal-Catholic standpoint, Estelrich of the *Lliga* thought it an 'act of war' while Royo Villanova found it contradictory: Church and State were separate, yet this was intervention by the State in the province of the Church.[93] Meanwhile Fr Guallar examined the government's motives: 'Anti-clericalism is the cream-tart which is given to people when there is nothing else to give them. . . . Just as the Roman Emperors distracted the people with the cruel and brutish games of the amphitheatre so that it should not be mindful of its servitude, so today they distract it with the parish priests and the monks. These are the *circenses* of our times.'[94]

Yet despite all the passion engendered, the articles of the law were passed one by one. Encouraged by the victory they claimed in the municipal elections of 23 April, the Agrarians and Basque-Navarrese began systematic obstruction of the measure at the end of April, when the additional provisions of Radical-Socialists and Left Republicans that the Orders' education should end by 1 October (except for primary education which could continue until 31 December 1933) were accepted by the government.[95] To obviate lengthy discussion of amendments demanding the exclusion of each Order from the effects of the law, the government decided to guillotine the debates. The law was finally passed on 17 May by 278 votes to 50.[96] Catholics saw the 'Law against Religious Congregations and Communities' as the fruit of the labour of the five Ministers and sixty-two deputies who were Masons; but 'the Masonic lodges can press their victory too far'.[97]

Now it was up to Alcalá-Zamora, for the Constitution allowed the President to send laws back to the Cortes for reconsideration. Catholic organisations lobbied him relentlessly for the statutory fortnight, but Alcalá-Zamora merely made the token gesture of postponing his signature for as long as constitutionally permissible.[98] He signed on 2 June. The next day the Catholic deputies issued their manifesto to the country. In it, Alcalá-Zamora was criticised for not having made full use of his constitutional powers. The deputies called for the repeal of all anti-religious legislation, appealing to 'all citizens of good faith who view with deep sadness the ruin of their Country, irresponsibly managed by the foreign powers of the Masonic sects and the Socialist International'.[99]

Alcalá-Zamora's signature also prompted the publication of a collective declaration by the Bishops protesting against the laicist attack on the Church but stressing that the Church was not anti-Republican. The law had infringed the right of fathers to educate their children and disregarded the Church's inviolable right to instruct. The Declaration reminded the faithful that attendance at lay schools was contrary to canon law and that there were canonical penalties for persecutors of the Church. The Bishops spoke of the 'lack of legal force of all enacted in opposition to the integral rights of the Church' and exhorted the faithful to see to it that the offending sections were removed from the law of the land.[100]

Similarly Pius XI's Encyclical *Dilectissimi Nobis* (3 June) referred to 'the unjust situation created for the Church in Spain. . . . We have frequently made known to the present Spanish rulers how erroneous is the path embarked upon.' The Pope nevertheless emphasised that 'Our Word is not directed against forms of government'. Catholics ought to oppose the latest law by 'all the legitimate means which Natural Law and [Republican] legislation allow them'. Religious education must be fostered, unity must be the watchword and Catholic Action must be strengthened 'for the defence of the Faith and to ward off the dangers which threaten civil society itself'.[101] Rightist personalities therefore united to start a company to found Catholic private schools,[102] while Catholic Action was reinvigorated by Herrera. *El Debate* recommended a boycott of lay schools, following the precedent of Belgium.[103]

During the acrimonious debates on the Law concerning Religious Confessions and Congregations, partial municipal elections were held on 23 April to replace the temporary committees appointed by Maura in 1931. Although Martínez de Velasco suggested that the Right should boycott the elections if the Defence Law were not suspended, it was the contrary view of Gil Robles which prevailed. Abstention by Rightists would be wrong; they should form part of a 'single anti-Marxist front'.[104] The Agrarian minority reached agreement with the Republicans in opposition— Radicals, Conservatives, Liberal-Democrats—and alliances were concluded according to local needs.[105]

The elections were important, not only as a sounding of opinion, but because Mayors controlled local life by their command over rural police and labour-exchanges.[106] During the campaign there were many violent incidents and some irregularities, in which the Left would seem to have been mainly at fault.[107] The Ministry of the Interior's figures showed that 5,048 councillors had been elected for the government parties, 4,954 for the parties of the Right, 4,206 for the Republicans in opposition, 548 for other Republicans, and 1,272 for various other groups.[108] The Right and the Republicans in opposition had together elected almost twice as many councillors as the government parties. The former therefore claimed a popular mandate for their policies of obstruction. On the other hand, these municipalities had in most cases elected Monarchists on 12 April 1931; Azaña contemptuously dismissed the results as insignificant because these were 'rotten boroughs'.[109] Time was soon to tell who was right.

A combination of the results of the municipal elections, his own dislike of the Law concerning Religious Confessions and Congregations, the obstruction in the Cortes of Radicals, Conservatives, Progressives, Federals, Independent Republicans and some Radical-Socialists, together with the approval of the Law setting up the Court of Constitutional Guarantees,[110] prompted Alcalá-Zamora to force a government crisis on 8 June even though Azaña had not been defeated in the Cortes. The President's intention was to broaden the governing coalition, but efforts to achieve this broke against the rocks of the Radical demand for exclusion of the Socialists and the Socialist veto on Radical participation. The outcome of the 'crisis of the five days' was the formation on 13 June of a new government by Azaña similar to the last.[111]

All the parties in opposition were infuriated. Gil Robles complained that the new government prolonged 'a dictatorship supported by a [parliamentary] majority which does not represent the country'; he warned that such prolongation would undo his careful work of organising the Right for evolutionary, democratic methods.[112] The strongest reaction came, however, from Miguel Maura, who saw a chance to regain lost ground. He demanded a dissolution and the fourteen Conservatives withdrew from the Cortes after the 'manifest fraud' perpetrated on opinion by the government parties ganging up on the President. The Conservative Republicans would permit themselves 'neither dialogue nor relations with this dictatorial government nor with these Cortes

which represent the exact opposite of the true opinion of Spain.
... We find ourselves before a dictatorship.'[113]

The three months which the new Azaña government lasted were
little more than a slow death-agony. Legislation was made almost
impossible by determined obstruction by the parties in opposition,
obstruction which Azaña termed 'parliamentary terrorism'.[114]
During July, a law was passed to permit legal action to be taken
for non-payment of rent by tenants, but prohibiting evictions for
any other reason, and also the Law concerning Public Order,
which gave elaborate constitutional validity to the powers of the
Defence Law.[115]

The crucial battle, however, was fought over the Draft of the
Law on Rural Leases, a subject that Agrarians had wanted to
include as an extra item in the Law of Bases for Agrarian Reform
of 1932.[116] The Draft forbade sub-letting and its Article 7 pegged
rents at a maximum of two-thirds of the tax-assessment or, where
it existed, at the property-census figure; mixed juries were to
regulate this and reductions in rent were to be enforced in the case
of natural disaster. Leases were to run for a minimum six years,
and the lessee had the right to renew the lease at the end of each
six years unless the owner wished himself to farm the land.
Article 17 permitted tenants or their close kin who had leased land
for twenty years to convert their tenure into a 'reserved annuity'
(*censo reservativo*). All necessary repairs were to be carried out by
the owner. Eviction could take place for non-payment of rent, at
the end of six years if the owner wanted to farm the land himself,
if the tenant sub-let any of the land, or for bad farming as decided
by the mixed juries. Mixed juries for rural property were to keep
watch on leases and settle disputes. A fourth additional provision
stated that conversion of tenure into 'reserved annuities' was to
apply to lands leased already.[117]

Agrarians objected to the law for several reasons, but their
opposition centred on Articles 7 and 17 and the fourth additional
provision. According to *El Debate*, owners would no longer make
long leases and would evict tenants before the twenty years were
up; if they did not, they would neglect their property. The Draft
meant in the last analysis 'the death of the rural lease as a juridical
institution'.[118] In the Cortes, it was argued that annuities were
usurious and in any case did not provide owners with adequate

compensation. In Galicia, with its *minifundios*, application of the law would bring chaos, and deputies of the ORGA also moved into the ranks of the opposition. Liberal Agrarians maintained that the law was unfair to landlords and was far removed from their ideal of *laissez faire*, while social-Catholics protested that 'reserved annuities' were not the smallholdings recommended by Leo XIII.[119]

The Agrarians had in fact decided to obstruct from the first, and the initial batch of 250 amendments was justified by Royo Villanova on the grounds that the law was inopportune; also a respectable liberal precedent could be found in the Liberal and Republican obstruction of Maura's local government bill in 1907.[120] Compromise appeared possible on 4 August when the Committee agreed to consider an amendment to Article 17 by Gil Robles which, in fulfilment of Article 47 of the Constitution, would create 'family patrimonies' that could not be distrained, divided or alienated. After negotiation in the Committee agreement was reached, but in the Cortes the Socialists opposed the Committee's new draft. They were heatedly accused of breach of faith by the Agrarians and Basque-Navarrese, who were now joined in their obstruction by the Radicals and the ORGA.[121] Progress on the law now came to a standstill under the weight of amendments and the resulting frequent lack of a quorum.[122]

With obstruction in full swing in the Cortes, elections were held on 3 September for the Court of Constitutional Guarantees. Its members were elected by the councillors of the municipalities—in Catalonia by the Parliament of the *Generalidad*—and by the universities and colleges of lawyers. The results showed the defeat of the government's candidates in ten of the fifteen regions as well as in the universities and colleges of lawyers. The parties in opposition polled 34,193 municipal votes to the 12,910 of the ruling parties. For the regions seven Radicals were elected, six *Cedistas*, three Socialists, two members each for the Traditionalists, the Basque Nationalists, *Acción Republicana*, the *Esquerra*, the ORGA and the Centre Republicans of Juan March, and one each for the Radical-Socialists and the Federals. The universities and colleges of lawyers gave victory to the Right; the election of such figures as the exiled Monarchist Calvo Sotelo reflected a marked swing to the Right among the professional bourgeoisie.[123]

Faced with this new blow, and mindful of the disintegration of his coalition, Azaña finally resigned on 8 September.[124] On 12 September 1933 a new Republican coalition was formed under Lerroux. The Socialists, ousted from office, announced the opening of 'a new revolutionary phase' now that the Republic with the 'historic' Republican at the helm had become 'much less Republican'.[125]

In October 1932 the Socialist Party held its Congress in Madrid. The PSOE, like its affiliated union, the UGT, could claim a great increase in its numbers since the installation of the Republic, an increase due at least in some cases to the advantages of office as much as to spontaneous conversion.[126] At the Congress, personalities and policies were, as usual, intertwined. As in December 1930, Besteiro, a convinced reformist, took a stand against collaboration in the government, and was opposed by Prieto and Largo Caballero, Ministers under Azaña. The Congress approved a motion put forward by Prieto justifying Socialist participation in order to keep out the Radicals of Lerroux. Socialists in government must pursue 'a possibilist policy' leading towards 'the redemptive light of the ideal' of true Socialism. Thus the party adopted the evolutionary tactics of furthering the Socialist cause from within the government, a policy which safeguarded its widespread control of local government. Largo Caballero was elected President of the Executive Committee, ousting Besteiro and his supporters.[127]

The Congress of the party was closely followed by that of the UGT, at which Besteiro and his ally Saborit were elected President and Vice-President; Largo Caballero was elected Secretary-General, but declined to take up the office.[128] El Socialista summed up the position in the autumn of 1932 thus: 'After the Republic Socialism will be imposed. The Republic is the surest bridge for the historical transition. Therefore we Socialists defend it and, up to a point, consider it ours.'[129]

Apart from the bogey of Freemasonry, the Right's propaganda had from the first denounced Socialism as its real opponent. While Gil Robles found in the failure of '10 August' proof that the democratic method was the way to meet the Socialist threat, avowed Monarchists, enemies of the Republic in any case, found in Socialist participation, if not dominance, in government an added incentive for violent counter-revolutionary action. The

I

possibility of Spain becoming a Socialist State, together with
contemporary events elsewhere in Europe, persuaded them of the
need for a 'Fascist reaction' in Spain. Goicoechea discovered two
ways of putting an end to class-warfare, the Russian and the
Italian, and he came down decidedly in favour of the latter.[130]
According to another of its leaders, the new Alfonsine party was
'anti-Marxist, anti-liberal, anti-democratic and anti-parliamen-
tary. *Renovación Española* is the spirit of tradition, adapted to the
fashions of present-day life'.[131] Such fashions were deemed to
include corporative organisation on Italian lines.[132] Goicoechea
asked himself: 'What is my position? That of a Traditionalist?
That of a Fascist? A bit of each, why deny it.'[133] Nor did the
ideological review *Acción Española* ignore the practical example of
Italy, though its doctrines remained firmly rooted in Spanish
tradition.[134]

While *Renovación Española* propagated the counter-revolution
in Spain, Monarchists conspired anew north of the Pyrenees. In
September 1932 a group of Alfonsines—Vegas Latapié, Ansaldo,
Vigón, the Marqués de la Eliseda—made preparations in Biarritz
for a *coup d'état*. Ansaldo was entrusted with the collection of
funds and some 3,000,000 pesetas were soon collected or promised.[135] In the autumn the aid of Alfonso XIII was enlisted; he
assured the plotters of his full support and gave permission for his
name to be used in procuring funds, though reserving the right to
decide himself when the moment for action should arrive.[136] It was
intended that Sanjurjo be the nominal leader, but since he was
still imprisoned, the plotters approached Martínez Anido; the
ex-Minister, however, declined the offer and so the conspiracy had
no official head.[137]

The original plan conceived by Vegas envisaged the surprise
seizure of key-points in Madrid and the arrest of Ministers, but
this scheme was soon broadened to include action by the military
in conjunction with retired officers and civilian auxiliaries.[138] The
modified scheme demanded infiltration of the officer corps, which
did not prove easy as soldiers were often discovered to value their
pay more than their lives, as well as to be imbued with an irritating
respect for discipline. Nevertheless the help of two well-placed
men was acquired: one Martín Báguenas, chief of police in the
Directorate-General of Security, the other Colonel Galarza ('*El*

Técnico'), a member of the Army General Staff, who co-ordinated conspiratorial activities among officers.[139] The only positive action taken inside Spain seems to have been to contribute to the funds of Anarcho-Syndicalist revolutionaries.[140]

Other activities of the conspirators in Biarritz were the selection and grooming of a civilian leader for the coming counter-revolution, and the quest for external aid. Calvo Sotelo's *rôle* on 10 August in persuading Barrera to fly back to Seville drew the attention of the conspirators to the ex-Minister's change of heart: he had now overcome his susceptibilities concerning the use of violence. The task was therefore to give this former *Maurista* a proper counter-revolutionary education. The means were to hand in the person of a half-Colombian member of the *Action Française*, Armand Magescas, who was known to the plotters and who was able to arrange frequent meetings between Calvo Sotelo and the leaders of the French Monarchist movement.[141] Soon the works of Maurras appeared in pride of place in Calvo Sotelo's room in Paris, and he expressed admiration for Fascism and the belief that the spirit of the age was irrevocably authoritarian.[142] In February 1933 he visited Rome for talks with Fascist leaders, but no agreement could be reached with the Italians, who did not wish at this time to enter into any clandestine commitments with Spanish Rightists.[143]

The Alfonsine military conspiracy was not a great success, and the success of *Renovación Española* also proved to be marginal: membership never extended beyond a minority of the aristocracy and a section of the bourgeoisie with a sentimental attachment to Alfonso XIII.[144] Such drawing-room Monarchists were unlikely to take on the Socialists in the streets. It was necessary therefore to find some shock-troops. The PNE was still to hand, but it was a *quantité négligeable*; except for the detention of its leader, its only distinction was to have its offices raided by the police in March 1933.[145] Also in March, an attempt was made to launch a publication entitled *El Fascio*, advocating a strong State to guarantee the 'internal unity of Spain and its expansion in the world'.[146]

The moving spirit was Delgado Barreto, editor of *La Nación* (the daily founded by the Dictator). His editorial board for the propagation of Fascist ideas comprised an array of dissimilar personalities, including the Dictator's eldest son José Antonio, the wandering intellectual Giménez Caballero, Ledesma Ramos of the JONS, the adventurous airman Ruiz de Alda, García Valdecasas, a deputy and disciple of Ortega Gasset, and Rodríguez Tarduchy, who led a more or less Traditionalist combat-group. There was disagreement between José Antonio, then pro-Italian in outlook, and the Germanophil Ledesma, but such differences proved irrelevant, for the first issue—due to appear on 16 March, the day of the Dictator's death—was banned by the government at Socialist prompting.[147]

The result of this abortive little affair, however, was indirectly to attract national attention at last to the JONS. Already, though Redondo was in Portugal, a transport-workers' union had been started in Valladolid in January which by July claimed 3,000 members. In Madrid, though Ledesma was in gaol, a clash occurred on 10 March in the university between *Jonsistas* and members of the increasingly unpopular official FUE, after which 400 students formed the first *Jonsista* union. The anti-FUE protest movement spread to other universities and other *Jonsista* groups were formed.[148]

The Monarchist conspirators, however, pinned their hopes less on the JONS of the little-known Ledesma than on the prestigious figure of José Antonio Primo de Rivera, once an under-secretary of the UMN. Apart from unsuccessfully contesting a by-election in Madrid in October 1931 simply to win 'a seat in the Cortes to defend the memory of my father',[149] José Antonio kept out of politics until late in 1932. Then he saw the Dictator's Ministers in Paris and agreed that an authoritarian régime was needed to save Spain and that foreign aid should be procured with a view to installing this.[150] After the *El Fascio* episode, he began to plan a Fascist movement with Julio Ruiz de Alda whose thoughts turned to a violent movement of workers and intellectuals unencumbered by the defence of capitalism—and to nationalisation of the virtually non-existent aircraft industry.[151]

For José Antonio Fascism meant unity. The Country could not allow class-warfare, the product of the relativist, liberal State which made 'a dogma of the anti-dogma'. In place of liberalism there was to be, not a transitory dictatorship like that of his father, but permanent conquest of the State by the upholders of 'an integrative, totalitarian, national principle'. Violence was justifiable in defence of justice or against Socialist domination.[152] In October 1933 he paid Mussolini a visit, and returned to declare that Fascism was 'a total, universal, interpretation of life . . . Fascism is "essentially traditionalist". In Italy it seeks the tradition of the [Roman] Empire. In Spain it will seek the tradition of our Empire.'[153] In the autumn he and Ruiz de Alda visited Ansaldo in St Jean-de-Luz, and the latter arranged the necessary financial backing for the foundation of the *Falange Española*, seen by the conspirators as just one more group to be co-ordinated with the PNE and the Traditionalists in Alfonsine plans.[154]

On 29 October 1933 the *Falange Española* was founded at a meeting of 'Spanish affirmation' in Madrid at which the speakers were Ruiz de Alda, García Valdecasas and Primo de Rivera.[155] José Antonio denounced Rousseau for his wrong-headed individualism and the liberal State for its inability to believe in a mission of its own. Socialism was the necessary reaction to the inhuman consequences of economic liberalism, but Socialism aimed, not at a return to justice, but at the creation of a new form of oppression. It was destructive of social and spiritual unity and was materialist. The proper solution therefore lay in 'a lord who does not die', one above interests and parties; thus the State would acquire its primary need, unity, as well as the pre-condition for true social justice. To achieve this state of political salvation, 'a poetic movement' was required, an anti-party of neither Left nor Right which was prepared to make use of 'the dialectic of fists and pistols' and not put its faith in the ballot-box.[156] Despite the poetic phraseology, the speech was not particularly original; as the Traditionalist Pradera pointed out, with the exception of one or two ideas on social policy, it was merely a recital of the ideas of Traditionalism.[157]

Thus Fascism in Spain was patronised by Alfonsine Monarchists. The government and the Socialists might reasonably be expected to have been alarmed at its growth, and measures were accordingly taken. *El Fascio* did not appear and in July hundreds of suspected Fascists were arrested; they were soon released when the government was satisfied that there was no real threat from this quarter.[158] Socialists kept an eye on *Jonsistas* and headstrong Monarchists, but were not unduly alarmed; Goicoechea, leader of the counter-revolutionaries of *Renovación Española*, was dismissed as a figure of fun unworthy of serious attention.[159] The Socialists turned their fire instead on their two main opponents: the Radicals of Lerroux, whose accession to power they had seen as justifying civil strife as early as 1931, and the CEDA of Gil Robles, which ousted Lerroux from his place as first enemy of Socialism in 1933.

Socialist attacks on their political enemies were always couched in strong terms. In January 1932 *El Socialista* denounced the liberal-democrat Lerroux as the Mussolini of the upholders of order.[160] When the Radicals went into full opposition to the government over Casas Viejas, the charges were equally spirited: Lerroux's Republicanism was 'purely nominal' because he was now the 'patron-saint of the landowners and devoted defender of the plutocracy, which is certainly Monarchist'. For the party's organ 'the Monarchist-clerical-Anarchist alliance against the re-volution' was a fact.[161] During 1933, however, the CEDA became the *bête noire*. The policies of Gil Robles meant 'the enslavement, in Mussoliniesque style, of the proletariat'; as for the slogan of *Acción Popular*—'Before all, Religion and Spain'—'it is the Fascist device'.[162] With Hitler's rise to power the tone of *El Socialista* became more strident: illiberal means should be employed and liberty sacrificed in face of the Fascist threat, principally coming from the CEDA. Spanish Socialists must be prepared to fight, heeding the words of Otto Braun from Germany: 'May our comrades in Spain not fall into our own errors!'[163]

To what extent were the charges and fears of the Socialists with regard to Gil Robles justified? The CEDA Congress had formulated a programme of socio-economic corporativism in tune with Papal doctrines and had rejected a *Japista* motion for Italian-style cor-porativism, but had left political aims unclear. Shortly afterwards Gil Robles formally denounced Fascism. Identification of the Nation with the State, fusion of the State with a political party and 'total nullification of the individual personality' were inadmissible doctrines for Catholics. Fascism was a heresy, 'the last phase of a politico-philosophical revolution beginning with the criterio-logical [sic] individualism and the psychological subjectivism of Descartes and ending with the pantheist monism of Hegel. . . . Catholic Doctrine defines political society as a moral entity, . . . a system which exalts and dignifies the personality of the individual in opposition to the absorbent and pagan *étatisme* of the modern

Fascist doctrines.' Violence was inseparable from Fascism, whereas the CEDA's tactic was 'legal struggle. . . . Evolution instead of revolution.' Gil Robles followed in the footsteps of Windthorst, not Mussolini.[164]

Clearly the CEDA leadership did not regard itself as Fascist; but for Socialists the internal doctrinal niceties of the Right were unimportant. The negative critique of pure Fascism was for them irrelevant; the real question was, what were the positive intentions of Gil Robles? He had, in practice, accepted the Republic and constantly advocated the legal, democratic method of attaining power, the path of evolution; but in power, what would he do?

Before the autumn of 1933 statements of intent were few. In a speech at Salamanca in December 1932 made with local political considerations in mind, he stressed his family's Carlist tradition and declared: 'The Traditionalist Party has ten basic fundamental principles. . . . We have no more than nine fundamental and one accidental. Here lies the difference.'[165] The policy of the CEDA, he later explained, was motivated by the Encyclicals and reality. Its programme was not 'maximalist' but 'possibilist': it would be implemented gradually as circumstances permitted, but it did not include a change in the form of government.[166] Though pronouncements were few and imprecise, the basic points were by now clear. The ultimate goal of the CEDA was a State based on Catholic corporative principles. This State would be the result of a process of gradual transformation of the liberal-democratic structure by constitutional and democratic means. The pace of change would depend on the extent and profundity of the conversion of Spanish society by propaganda to Catholic social and political doctrines. Force was ruled out, as the impatient young men of the JAP were told: 'Today the first thing the Right must do is to incorporate the masses of the people to make the true revolution, crucifix in hand. We are not partisans of universal suffrage, but for good or ill this is the only weapon and it must be used well.'[167]

The Socialists, however, were not inclined to draw a distinction between Fascism and evolutionary Catholic corporativism, which, if it were attained, would mean the end of Socialism just as the attainment of Socialism would mean suppression of political Catholicism. Their attitude to the political rallies of *Acción Popular*

in 1933 was the same as it had been in 1932; but whereas before
10 August they could point to prominent Monarchists in *Acción
Popular* who were bent on overthrowing the Republic, by late 1932
the argument no longer held good because the party had rid itself
of those who would not forswear violence or agree to obey the
established form of government. In 1933 Socialists called for
prohibition of the meetings of *Acción Popular* on the grounds that
they were 'Fascist demonstrations', and they were sometimes
successful, as in the case of the meeting to be held in Valladolid
in May.

Agrarians and *Acción Popular* obtained the permission of the
Governor to hold a rally, at which Gil Robles and Royo Villanova
were to speak, in celebration of the electoral success of 23 April;
they hoped that up to 40,000 people would attend from Castile,
León and Asturias. The Socialist railwaymen of the city, alleging
that the JONS had associated itself with this 'Monarchistic' meeting, decided that the rally should not take place. They duly got the
Governor's permission to stage a counter-demonstration on the
same day, and announced a strike to sabotage the Right's plans—a
political strike forbidden by Article 1 of the Defence Law. When
the Socialists seemed to have persuaded the Governor to ban the
Right's rally to avert bloodshed, the affair took on national significance. Gil Robles saw Casares Quiroga, the Minister of the Interior, who told him that the Socialist attitude represented compulsion which he was not prepared to tolerate. *El Socialista*
denounced the anti-Republican 'Fascist mobilisation' and warned:
'If the State folds its arms before the challenging meeting of
Valladolid, the workers will know how to replace the State and
show it its duties.' After meeting the Socialist Ministers, Casares
Quiroga decided to suspend the rally.[168] From such episodes
Rightists concluded that the Socialists had the whip hand in the
government.

The anti-Fascist campaign of the Socialists had two faces. If,
negatively, it were necessary to halt the Right's propaganda, the
other lesson from Germany was that Fascism could only be
thwarted if Socialists themselves took charge of the State. The
'accidentalism' of *Acción Popular*, according to *El Socialista*, was
just a method for 'knocking out all the revolutionary content which
the Republic has, without overthrowing the Republic. . . . We

[Socialists] defend it and support it for what it contains.'[169] Prieto said that it was all the same to him whether the Right intended to overthrow the Republic or whether it intended to revise the laws of the Republic: 'The names of things matter little to me; what certainly matters to me are the things themselves.' Socialists could be loyal to the Republic only so long as it progressed along the same path as hitherto.[170] Los Ríos declared that Socialists, whether inside or outside the government, would not yield an inch of the ground gained.[171] The party's organ denied suggestions that Spanish Socialism was losing momentum and members, and continued: 'It is with this strength and with this enthusiasm that we propose to act. In Parliament? Outside Parliament? As the others wish. We should prefer it to be in Parliament; but it does not seem to be there that we must make our victory legitimate. The paths of democracy are denied us. But such a refusal binds us to nothing. . . .'[172]

How, in fact, had the paths of democracy been denied to the Socialists? They had not—unless denial of greater ministerial representation by their Republican partners, or the possibility of an electoral defeat interrupting their inevitable progress towards the ultimate goal of Socialism, be called undemocratic.

The speech which spread real alarm on the Right was made by Largo Caballero to an ILO conference in Geneva. There he asked Lenin's question, 'liberty for what? . . . Liberty to undermine the foundations of the State and demolish it on the first suitable occasion? That would be an act of ingenuousness that the true Republicans and we Socialists are not prepared to commit. We shall not desert our duty and we shall carry the Spanish revolution to the ends that the people's will indicates, by all the means which may be necessary for this.'[173] This line of thought was opposed by Besteiro, an admirer of MacDonald and leader of a diminishing section of Spanish Socialist opinion. He begged his colleagues to accept democracy, because revolutionary tactics would lead to a powerful anti-Socialist reaction. Salvation lay in revitalising bourgeois democracy: 'With the Republic installed, to think of dictatorship is false reasoning. I declare myself an enemy of the dictatorship of the proletariat.'[174]

Largo Caballero's reply was that the Republic depended on the PSOE and the UGT for its defence: 'Being Socialists, we are Republi-

cans. . . . We are proceeding to the conquest of power within the
Constitution and the laws. . . . We have worked for flexible
legislation that allows us to achieve power without great violence,
without great bloodshed, legally if possible. But if because we are
workers we are put outside the Constitution, we shall conquer
power in another manner.' He told the Socialist Youth later:
'Today I am convinced that to carry out Socialist work within a
bourgeois democracy is impossible.'[175] Other Socialist deputies
were equally outspoken. 'Let those who want to fight for the
revolution follow us; but if they [the enemies of Socialism] cross
our path, blocking the way, we shall sweep them aside even though
it cost blood!'[176]

Thus by mid-September 1933 there existed a certain parallelism
between the attitudes of the two mass groupings, the Socialists and
the CEDA, on the Left and Right of the Republic. Both wanted to
transform the Republic of Azaña into a State to their own tastes,
Socialist or corporativist. While the Socialists boasted of being the
bulwark of Republican defence, their position was really similar
to the official accidentalism of the CEDA: what mattered to both was
the legislative content of the Republic. There was, however, a
crucial difference between their pronouncements. Whereas the
CEDA sought to achieve its aims by evolutionary, democratic
means, the Socialists, while declaring their preferences for this
method, added the proviso that they would use other, revolutionary, means if the paths of democracy should prove fruitless
for them.

Doubtless fear of Fascism in the Europe of 1933 was genuine,
but this was not the only factor influencing Socialist attitudes.
El Debate saw the labelling of the legalist Right as Fascist as a ploy
to obscure the CEDA's position of legality. *ABC* suggested that the
anti-Fascist campaign was a convenient way of covering up for the
government's failings, a red herring produced as a distraction from
the stench of Casas Viejas.[177] The Socialists, who demanded to be
in the government to keep Lerroux out of it, found that they had
to share in its growing unpopularity; desperation attracted
workers to the chronic revolutionism of the CNT. The anti-
Fascist campaign was a smokescreen for the Socialist change of
tactics.

In mid-September 1933 Azaña's two years of power came to an

end and Lerroux formed a new Republican coalition. His aims were 'to give battle to the Socialists and to contain an avalanche from the inflamed Right' caused by the deeds of the previous government. His ideal Republic was 'neither conservative, nor revolutionary, neither Right-wing, nor Left-wing, but equidistant from all extremism . . . ; a tolerant, progressive, reforming Republic without violence, strictly just without vengeance'. He became Premier, he believed, with the President's tacit authorisation for a dissolution which would lead to 'rectification' of the policies of the Republic.[178] He told the Cortes that he wanted to put through a budget first; his general policy would be to modify the practice of existing laws without repealing the work of the Constituent Cortes. Such a policy would consolidate the Republic, which to be stable must be orderly and possess a moderate Right to balance the Left. The new Right that he hoped to tie to the Republic was the CEDA, which he did not mention by name, referring instead to 'a great legion of men full of goodwill, who are convinced of the impossibility of a Monarchist restoration'.[179]

The Socialists were in opposition from the first. Outside the Cortes Largo Caballero declared that power had been given to 'the saboteurs of the Republic. . . . The Republic is in danger. . . . Our party, ideologically, tactically, is a revolutionary party . . . and aspires to a complete transformation of society. . . . To do this it is necessary to create a revolutionary spirit in the masses . . . to exchange this Republic for a social Republic.'[180] In the Cortes Prieto moved a motion of no confidence: all Socialist compromises with all Republicans were at an end. According to Azaña, Lerroux's overtures to the Right were a betrayal of the Republic, since such elements were incompatible with the Constitution and the spirit of the régime; Lerroux's was a policy which aimed at 'attracting to the Republic Monarchists who still remain hostile to the régime'. *Acción Republicana*, the *Esquerra*, the Radical-Socialists and the ORGA, all represented in the government, withdrew their support and their Ministers, and Lerroux's first government fell on 3 October.[181] Alcalá-Zamora was anxious for a dissolution lest the reaction against Azaña's rule should turn into a reaction against the Republic.[182] After some unsuccessful attempts to find a Premier, another Republican coalition was formed on 8 October by Lerroux's lieutenant Martínez Barrio, who did not risk meeting the Cortes. General elections were announced for 19 November, with second contests where necessary on 3 December.[183]

The election campaign was conducted in a pre-revolutionary atmosphere dominated by the rival figures of Largo Caballero and Gil Robles. Gil Robles was more explicit about his conception of the future State and imitated the bellicose language of Socialists. The tone of the Right's campaign was set by the JAP, whose manifestos said that it was debatable 'whether parliamentarism is or is not the fit means for ruling peoples . . . but it is the only way that we now have for succeeding in restoring Spain. . . . The JAP does not expect the solution of Spain's problems from the possible result of a parliamentary victory in a worn-out inorganic system.'[184] *Japistas* would use violence in the elections only by way of legitimate self-defence.

Gil Robles, speaking in Madrid on 15 October, outlined his policies. Violence as a means he ruled out, for the April and September elections proved that the Right could win a democratic contest. Once again he dissociated himself from Fascism: 'In the way we have heard voices which spoke to us of exotic novelties; but I ask myself if they are not mad, for we find the unifying principle for a totalitarian policy in our glorious Tradition. We need not take as our unifying principle that of other countries, which seek it in the glories of the Roman Empire, in the fetishism of the State, in the idolatry of the race.' His vision of the future was a great Spain, purged of Freemasons and 'Judaisers', and 'in harmony with the spiritual currents which are springing up anew in the world'. The State would respect individual liberties, but impose unity and social justice. 'We must proceed to a new State. . . . What does it matter if it costs us bloodshed! We need complete power and this is what we demand. . . . Democracy is for us not an end, but a means for proceeding to the conquest of a new State. When the time comes Parliament either agrees or we make it disappear.'[185]

On 2 November Gil Robles spoke in Valladolid. He warned Leftists not to use illegal methods or turn against democracy. If they did, then his party would also turn against democracy and install its own system of government.[186] Back in Madrid on 5 November, he repeated that it was up to the Socialists to choose the battleground: 'If they want the law, the law; if they want violence, violence.'

The following Sunday he further explained the nature of the new State: 'We do not want a dictatorship that destroys the rights of the individual; but neither do we want excess of individual liberty to destroy collective rights. We do not want a personal power that never ends: but neither do we want a dissolvent parliamentarism. We seek a revision of the Constitution in its dogmatic part, which is repugnant to our consciences, and in its organic part, representing a Parliament that is the most active agent in the dissolution of the Spanish people. To do this we shall not resort to foreign patrons, very worthy people, who have arisen the day before yesterday. In Tradition I find everything relating to the limitation of power, justice and corporations. Let us return to our old traditions, which is to return to Spain, to return to our own life.'[187] His speech on film, shown in the capital from a mobile cinema, had, however, a more demagogic ring: 'We want a new policy to put an end to this sterile parliamentarism. . . . We are about to put democracy to the test, perhaps for the last time. It does not matter to us. We are going to Parliament to defend our ideals, but if tomorrow Parliament is against our ideals, we shall go against Parliament, because in politics, not the forms, but the content is what interests us.'[188]

From this plethora of words spoken during the campaign, what now emerged concerning the intentions of Gil Robles? With regard to his eventual aim, the rather vague Catholic corporativism of the summer had taken on a new dimension. Whether he was prompted by the fear that many of his followers and his impatient youth movement would go over to the 'maximalist' Right, with its Fascist tendencies, or whether he yearned for the Integrism of his youth, he had now committed himself to a new State inspired by Traditionalist principles. With regard to the means by which this State was to be attained, he still adhered to the evolutionary method, though the violent tone of his speeches and their sometimes ambiguous phraseology gave the impression that he was perhaps less firmly wedded to this course. While it was inherent in his declared aims that liberal-parliamentarism would be abolished at some time, the bald manner in which he had now stated this conveyed the impression that it might be sooner rather than later. Possibly the ambiguities were deliberate and aimed at curbing impatient followers with words without compromising his principles; yet perhaps these ambiguities reflected an inner vacillation between the Christian-Democrat influence of Herrera on the one hand, and on the other a combination of the influences of his Carlist upbringing and the rising tide of authoritarianism outside Spain.

Gil Robles's language at this stage was similar to that of his Monarchist ally Calvo Sotelo, who thought it important for the Right to win seats in Parliament to stop the Left winning them, not because Parliament was important in itself. European trends showed that 'the hour of inorganic parliamentarism has passed'.[189] If Gil Robles and Calvo Sotelo agreed on this point, they were still at odds as to the pace and means of transformation, the form of government and their attitudes to Fascism. In exile Calvo Sotelo announced: 'More than a century ago we allowed ourselves to be carried away by the Encyclopedist cry, and we think in the French manner. We shall not now be able to escape the corporative and Fascist tide. With the difference that then we de-Hispanicised ourselves and now we are re-Hispanicising ourselves.'[190]

Whether or not Gil Robles was clear in his mind about his intentions, his Socialist opponents were clear in theirs. His recent speeches, starting with the 'authentic Fascist harangue'[191] of 15 October, provided evidence for the charges they had been making against the CEDA in previous months. Largo Caballero told Socialists: 'First in the voting-urns . . . then in the street. . . . The enemies have already begun the war, and say through the mouth of Gil Robles that if Parliament does not serve their purpose they will go against it. All right. We reply: "We are proceeding legally toward the evolution of society. But if you do not want this, we shall make the revolution violently." "This", the enemies will say, "is to stir up civil war." Let us be realistic. . . . We are in [a] full-scale civil war [although] this war has not yet taken on the bloody character that, for good or ill, it will inexorably assume.' 'The leader of *Acción Popular* said . . . that the Socialists accept democracy when it suits them; but when it does not suit them, they take the shortest path. All right; I must say with frankness that this is the truth. If legality is of no use to us, if it hinders our advance, we shall bypass bourgeois democracy and proceed to the revolutionary conquest of power.'[192]

The party's intellectuals, mindful of Germany, found themselves in agreement with Largo Caballero's course. Fascism was 'inevitable' where Socialism was not revolutionary, 'but it will not be inevitable where Socialism is animated by a revolutionary spirit; it has not been so in Russia'.[193] Socialists would make no electoral alliances with Republicans who had failed to keep 80 per cent of their promises; when Azaña fell agrarian reform existed only on paper and laicist education was a myth in the eyes of Largo Caballero.[194]

While Azaña and his former Socialist allies went to the polls separately, the opposition presented to the electorate the united front which had proved successful in the municipal elections in April. The parties of the Right had from the first expected to fight in alliance; the call of *Dilectissimi Nobis* for Catholic unity provided an added stimulant. For the CEDA, the Monarchist split was seen not as 'a division, which does not exist, but a differentiation. . . . There will not just be union with only one or two parties, but with all those groups which coincide on the reform of the Constitution and its complementary laws. . . . These unions will be circumstantial and dependent upon what the situation in national politics demands' though the local groupings were to make the arrangements. Lamamié de Clairac for the Carlists had long maintained that it was necessary 'to go to the elections united, although we do not much believe in them'. Goicoechea for the Alfonsines was anxious not to be left out and so made the concession of 'sacrificing momentarily our Monarchist ideal. The ideal now can be none other than revision of the Constitution.'[195]

It was therefore no surprise when a central committee was set up in Madrid to facilitate agreement on the Right. It consisted of Agrarian deputies representing the various strains in the minority —*Cedista*, Alfonsine, Carlist and Agrarian—under the presidency of Martínez de Velasco.[196] The Right's electoral unity was based on the following pact:[197]

> Common aspirations, without detriment to the particular ideology of each organisation, will be:
> A) Revision of the laicist and socialistic legislation set out in the constitutional text as in other laws.

B) A rigorous defence in the future Parliament of the economic interests of the country, with recognition of the legitimate preponderance of agriculture as the basis of national wealth.

C) Absolute amnesty for all political offences as soon as the Cortes are constituted, with the same generosity with which it was conceded to those responsible for the revolutionary movement of August 1917.

Although the co-ordinating committee was soon functioning, the drafting of lists of candidates did not proceed very smoothly. Local rivalries had to be dealt with and each party jockeyed for the greatest possible representation. The Right was also divided on who should be included in the coalitions. Gil Robles wanted not only circumstantial alliance with other Rightists, but also a purely electoral anti-Marxist front with Republicans of the Centre in areas where this was necessary to defeat the Socialists; in this, he was supported by liberal Agrarians.[198] Alfonsines strongly objected to this, preferring to set the bounds of the coalition no wider than the Agrarian minority. For *ABC*, anti-Marxism was not the best of ideas; all the parties in the original Republican coalition of 1931 were enemies.[199] Carlists felt that they could unite with fellow Catholics but, like *ABC*, jibbed at the thought of alliance with any Republicans.[200]

Gil Robles, however, was adamant about his broad anti-Marxist front and carried the day. The Right formed anti-Marxist lists for 19 November with Republicans of the Centre and Centre-Right in thirteen provinces outside Catalonia and the Basque Country.[201] The Radicals had earlier announced that there would be no government lists: they would ally with Right or Left according to the particular local situation.[202] To make co-operation with Republicans easier and so as not to frighten the 'neutral masses', Gil Robles exerted his party's numerical predominance within the Right to eliminate, especially from the list in the capital, names associated with violence or dictatorship.[203]

In Catalonia, the situation was different. After the passage of the Statute, elections were held for the Parliament of the *Generalidad* on 20 November 1932. The contest proved to be between the *Esquerra*, which received the votes of 40 per cent of the total electorate and obtained 69 seats, and the *Lliga*, now again led by Cambó, which got 18 seats with 35 per cent. In December Maciá was elected President of the *Generalidad*, with Companys as President of the Parliament; the rule of the *Esquerra* continued.[204] The *Lliga* had improved its position with the return of many of its supporters to their old allegiance, a process that continued during 1933.[205] The party set about reorganising itself within the new political framework, and its assembly in February 1933 changed the name from the *Lliga Regionalista* to *Lliga Catalana*.[206] The party sought to recover its pre-Republican strength from the general reaction to Azaña's government and the defects of the *Esquerra*'s administration. Now that the CNT and the *Esquerra* had fallen out, turbulence mounted in Barcelona under the direction of the FAI. The conservative press claimed that 'unbridled anarchy' ruled in the capital.[207]

In the Catalan countryside the *Lliga* also looked to a reaction from conservative elements. Under the Dictatorship Companys had built himself firm political support in the *Unió de Rabassaires* —*rabassaires* being leaseholders who had put down a lump sum initially and held the land for the duration of the vine, paying the landowner perhaps a third or a half of each harvest. Now they wanted to become the owners themselves.[208] Maciá promised legislation to give them land and thus stave off violence, a promise of dubious constitutional validity. His plans, however, were held up in Parliament and this led to a crisis in the *Generalidad* in October when Aragay, Secretary of the *Unió*, resigned in protest from the Catalan government.[209] While the *Lliga* sought to rally the owners and other farmers exasperated by lawlessness, Companys decided to renew his pledges to the *Unió*, a good source of electoral support.[210] In November 1933, as in November 1932, the struggle was therefore between the Catalanist forces of the *Lliga* and the *Esquerra*; in Barcelona, the Monarchists and anti-Catalanists tried to get an alliance with the *Lliga*, but found the latter's terms impossible.[211]

In the Basque Country, too, peculiar factors were present. The gap between the PNV and the Traditionalists grew wider. The strength of Aguirre's party came from the countryside, where people were much under the tutelage of pro-Nationalist parish priests, from younger members of the bourgeoisie, and from the workers of the *Solidaridad de Obreros Vascos*, the rival in the area of the UGT.[212] Apart from the resurgence of Carlism in Álava, the

K

great disappointment for the PNV was Navarre, which continued to be their Ulster.[213] Following the break-up of the Basque-Navarrese minority, Monarchists in August 1932 produced a pamphlet revealing a startling Nationalist-Communist-Jewish-Masonic plot; the PNV, however, enlisted the aid of the Nuncio and the Bishops of Vitoria and Pamplona against this libel. While warding off the Right, Aguirre continued to work for a Statute. Hopes were raised when the President signed the Catalan Statute in San Sebastián on 15 September 1932; on this occasion, Prieto, the leader of the Socialists of Bilbao, privately told Nationalists that he favoured a Statute for the three Basque provinces. In October the PNV deputies met in Madrid to speed up operations, and on 19 October a new committee to draft a Statute was formed with Socialists and Traditionalists, both of whom, however, soon sabotaged the plan.[214]

In the municipal elections of April 1933 the PNV stood alone and won twice as many seats as all the other groups together. In May, therefore, the visit of the President was coolly received and accompanied by clashes and a general strike by the SOV. On 6 August a meeting of town councils and temporary committees took place in Vitoria; disagreement between the PNV and the Traditionalists was again rife, the latter defending provincial rights. Nevertheless a Statute was accepted by 249 town councils and rejected by only 28; a Committee of Eighteen was set up to organise a plebiscite as the Constitution demanded. The plebiscite was arranged in the three provinces for 5 November.

The PNV approached the Socialists for their support, but this Prieto, who wanted the plebiscite to be held after the general election (19 November), refused. Also with a view to the elections, the Traditionalist José María Urquijo offered to help Aguirre by calling off Oriol's Traditionalist propaganda campaign in Álava in exchange for a united Catholic list with the PNV in the general election; this Aguirre refused. The Traditionalists, as usual, vacillated before the plebiscite; the matter was left to individual consciences though Alfonso Carlos was himself against the Statute and Oriol pressed the government to suspend the plebiscite. The Socialists advised abstention. The result of the plebiscite of 5 November, in which women voted, showed that 88·44 per cent of the inhabitants of Biscay and 89·52 per cent of those of Guipúzcoa were in favour of the Statute; in Álava, however, only 46·4 per cent were in favour of it.[215] The PNV again approached the Socialists for a joint 'pro-Statute' list for the elections, but was again rebuffed; the PNV once again fought alone.[216]

The national campaign, dominated by the verbal contest between Gil Robles and Largo Caballero, was naturally fought around the performance of the first Republican biennium. The propaganda of the Right was, by Spanish standards, massive; the shortcomings of Azaña and the evils of Masonry and Marxism were brought home to the electorate by thousands of posters, over the radio and, initially, by aerial means.[217] The precise sources of the funds for this expensive campaign were not revealed, but the cash available for the Right would seem to have been something approaching 1,000,000 pesetas.[218] The posters of *Acción Popular* denounced two years which had seen burning churches, Casas Viejas, deportations, the Defence Law, separatism, laicism, *enchufismo, pistolerismo*, the ruin of the countryside, hunger, unemployment, blood and tears: 'Vote for the Right! Vote against Marxism!' One poster pictured a luxurious official limousine beside an impoverished workman, with the comment that 14,000,000 pesetas had been spent on official cars and 1,000,000 on the unemployed. Another poster took 'anti-national policy' to task with a blood-stained map of Spain rent by the three daggers of Masonry, Socialism and separatism; over it passed a red line indicative of a Moscow-Mexico axis.

ABC contrasted the utopias of Marxism with the realities of anti-Marxism, such as denial of God with true religion, class war with social peace, free love with the sanctity of marriage and exaltation of force with the rule of law.[219] *Cedistas* appealed to the disillusioned and whipped up their supporters to renewed enthusiasm: 'For two years in Spain we have endured the class struggle and there has never been so much hunger. . . . Religion, Country, Family . . . all that is most fundamental for a civilised people turns to enter into battle. Spain will not pardon deserters!'[220] Calvo Sotelo's recorded voice called on electors 'to choose between three hosts: Socialists, Republicans and Rightists. . . . Demagogy. . . . Democracy. . . . Hierarchy and Authority. . . . Three names: Marx, Rousseau, Christ. Three symbols: the hammer and sickle, the triangle and the Cross.'[221]

The elections of 19 November were held in accordance with the Electoral Law of 27 July 1933. This law was in principle the same as the decree of 1931: each province formed a constituency, but provincial capitals with over 150,000 inhabitants formed distinct constituencies. The number of deputies allotted to each constituency in relation to its population was divided into a majority and a minority: to gain election in the first round, one candidate at least had to obtain 40 per cent of the poll. If a second ballot had to be held, only candidates who had obtained over 8 per cent of the votes in the previous round could seek election. The real innovation since 1931 was the introduction of female suffrage. The system of majorities and minorities put the premium on mass parties and the formation of alliances, since representation was weighted in favour of the majorities[222]—a factor in the formation of alliances between the Right and the Centre in areas where the Socialists were strong. Gil Robles, in fact, had wanted abolition of majorities and minorities, foreseeing violent changes in the composition of the Cortes and the need for moderate parties to ally with the political extremes, but the government of Azaña had rejected his plea.[223]

On Sunday 19 November voters went to the polls; the electorate at this time numbered 13,187,311—6,337,885 men and 6,849,426 women.[224] A swing to the Right was evident, but second contests had to be held on 3 December to elect some 95 deputies.[225]

The intervening fortnight gave time for realignment of forces. *El Debate* noted the success of the Centre-Right coalition in keeping out the Socialists. In the four provinces of Badajoz, Cáceres, Granada and Jaén, strongholds of rural Socialism, the representation of the PSOE had been cut from 38 seats to 11.[226] Gil Robles had on the eve of the poll made it plain that his party did not seek to govern, but would lend outside support to a Centre government. The Secretary-General of the CEDA now said that Gil Robles had got more seats than he wanted.[227] The bait was thus clearly dangled before Lerroux who took it. He rejected a plea from the Radical-Socialist Minister Palomo for a Socialist-Radical-Left Republican alliance on 3 December on the grounds that this would be a betrayal of the votes cast on 19 November; instead, he repeated that Radicals would ally with anyone but Socialists and Monarchists.[228] In practice, this meant alliance between the laicist Radicals and the Catholic CEDA against the common Socialist enemy to the chagrin of the Monarchists, who had to be squeezed off the lists. In the two Madrid constituencies, the latter apparently refused to budge, and so the Radical and Conservative candidates simply withdrew.[229] In the marginal constituencies of Murcia (capital and province), Málaga (capital and province), Alicante and Córdoba, Centre-Right coalitions were negotiated for 3 December; in Alicante and Córdoba Monarchists had to withdraw.[230] In five of the six constituencies the new combination won.[231]

The final results of the general election gave a new look to the first ordinary Cortes of the Republic. On the Left, the Socialists had 58 seats, the *Esquerra* 22, *Acción Republicana* 5, the ORGA 5, the Federals 2, the Independent Radical-Socialists 2, the Radical-Socialists 2, the Communists one. In the Centre, the Radicals had 104 seats, the *Lliga* 24, the Conservatives 17, the Basque Nationalists 12, the Liberal-Democrats 9, the Progressives 3, the Centre Republicans 2; there were also 5 independent Republicans and one Balearic Regionalist. On the Right, the CEDA had 117 seats, the Agrarians 29, the Traditionalists 21, *Renovación Española* 14, the PNE one; in addition, there were 19 independents, among them José Antonio Primo de Rivera.

In comparison with the Constituent Cortes, the Left had fallen from 247 to 97, the Centre had risen from 152 to 177, while the Right had soared from 41 to 201.[232] The parties of Azaña's former coalition were now very much in a minority; 62·9 per cent of the electorate had voted, the CNT having abstained. The Right—CEDA, Agrarians and Monarchists—obtained 3,085,676 votes, compared with the Radicals 1,351,100 and the 321,754 of the Conservatives. On the Left, the Socialists obtained 1,673,648 votes to the 636,705 of the parties of the Republican Left, excluding the *Esquerra*. The Basque Nationalists polled 183,190 votes, the Progressives 58,477, and the Communists 171,040. In Catalonia, the *Lliga*, with 24 seats, obtained 307,730 votes, while the *Esquerra* got 372,932 votes but only 22 seats. The election revealed a sharp swing to the Right, and the decimation of the Republican Left, tendencies accentuated by the quirks of the electoral system. The Right alone had won 28 constituencies, the Centre and the Centre and Right in alliance 27 more; the Left had carried only 5.[233]

The Socialists attempted to explain away their defeat by accus-

ing the anti-Marxists of corrupt practices; thus, according to
Araquistáin, the party's defeat was the result of the Radicals' old
political methods.[234] In some provinces, it would seem, Radicals
and other Ministers did try to use governmental machinery in their
favour, against both Left and Right, though apparently to little
effect.[235] The most turbulent areas were Granada, Badajoz and
Valencia: in the former provinces violence came from both sides,
and the Right claimed that Socialist local authorities intimidated
voters and influenced them by their control over employment.[236]
Electoral malpractice seems to have occurred in Galicia, and there
was something possibly awry in Valencia, in this case to the
disadvantage of the Right.[237] Since local government was still
largely in Leftist hands, it is difficult to believe that any *caciquismo*
by anti-Marxists was not cancelled out on a national scale by the
neo-*caciquismo* of the Socialist Left.[238] Though six people were
killed on 19 November, the Right successfully got its voters,
including nuns and the aged and infirm, to the polls; in some areas
they were escorted by *Japistas* carrying pistols. The JAP lost eight
dead in the campaign, but apparently carried out no reprisals.[239]
A clandestine activity of the Right was payment of money to
Anarchists in some areas; Rightists were haunted by the fear that
the CNT might vote for the Left, but it seems certain that their
decision to abstain was not just the result of Rightist bribery.[240]

The reasons for the Right's victory were less intriguing than the
Left suggested. The Right was now well organised with a mass
following, and went to the polls in some areas with the Centre. The
Socialists refused to ally with the Republican Left, in any case
weak, and were defeated by the wave of disillusionment which the
preceding biennium had provoked. The electoral law drawn up
and passed by the Left proved under the circumstances disadvan-
tageous to itself, leaving it proportionally under-represented. The
CNT's decision to abstain deprived the Left of perhaps 800,000
proletarian votes.

The elections revealed the political geography of Spain. In León
and the Castiles, the Catholic Right held sway, if elements of the
'old politics', now styled Agrarians, retained a certain influence
among cereal-growers. In Extremadura, Upper Andalusia, Murcia, Asturias, Madrid and Bilbao, the Socialists were strong, but
they were counterbalanced by the forces of the Right and Centre

in the south and the capital, by the PNV in Bilbao, and by the Catholics and Liberal-Democrats in Asturias. Biscay and Guipúzcoa formed the fortress of the PNV, while Navarre and Álava were the Traditionalist bastion. Right and Left were roughly balanced in Galicia, and in Catalonia the *Lliga* balanced the *Esquerra*, in Valencia the DRV the *Blasquista* Radicals. The CNT was an unpredictable counterweight to conservative forces in Lower Andalusia and Aragón, and could tip the balance against them in Barcelona, Asturias and perhaps parts of the Levante. Off the mainland, the Canaries were a Radical preserve; the men of Juan March were a key factor in the Balearics. Nothing can be said about the one-deputy *presidios* of Ceuta and Melilla. Thus Right and Left were more or less evenly balanced. Given the nature of the electoral system, marginal movements of opinion could lead to marked changes in the composition of the Cortes. In 1933, the trend of opinion was clearly against the Left; therefore for the Right, as a French observer noted, the outcome was a 'triumph surpassing the most optimistic forecasts'.[241]

Notes to this chapter are on pages 320–37.

Chapter 4 THE REPUBLIC AND THE REVOLUTION
December 1933–October 1934

From December 1933 until October 1934 Spain was ruled by Republican coalitions based on Lerroux's Radical Party and supported from outside by the CEDA. This arrangement was made possible by Lerroux and Gil Robles. Lerroux wanted to rectify the Leftist policies pursued by governments in the previous two years and move the centre of gravity of the régime from the Left to the Centre. Such a policy was acceptable to Gil Robles who had announced on the eve of the elections that he did not want his party to govern for some time. Collaboration in the elections between Radicals and *Cedistas* cemented this alliance of convenience.

Lerroux wanted to open the Republic to the Right in order to consolidate the régime, but owing to the composition of the new Cortes and to the hostility towards him of Socialists and Left Republicans he now had no alternative but to rely on Rightist allies. *Cedista* and Agrarian benevolence in turn made government possible and perhaps saved the country from civil war at this stage. For Lerroux the CEDA's willingness to support his government with the Constitution still unreformed was proof that Gil Robles had really accepted the Republic: the CEDA, to the fury of Monarchists, was now a Republican party in all but name. Lerroux's opinion was not shared by Left Republicans or Socialists because they had their own conceptions of what the Republic ought to be. Most Socialists flatly refused to accept the verdict of the polls for government by conservatives; nor did Azaña and his colleagues renounce their narrow conception of Republicanism even though the results demonstrated that theirs was a Republic almost without Republicans except in Catalonia.

According to Prieto *Cedistas* were 'enemies of the Republic' and repeal of the work of the Constituent Cortes—the 'essence' of the régime—would be tantamount to a *coup d'état*, which in turn would justify and necessitate revolution. For Left Republicans revision of their policies was equivalent to putting the clock back to the pre-Republican days of 1930 and this justified revolutionary action to restore their 'true' Republic. Except for the *Esquerra*, they did not take part in the new revolutionary movement because its motive-power was represented by Largo Caballero, whose views were incompatible with their own. The majority of Socialists in 1934 sought to install the dictatorship of the proletariat, not to restore the progressive bourgeois régime. 'In 1934 the liberal Republic had failed in Spain, as it had failed in Russia in October 1917.'[1] Hence Azaña was caught between the Scylla of a conservative Republic with *Cedista* participation in government and the Charybdis of proletarian revolution. Though he advised Catalan Leftists not to rise at the last minute, Azaña did not set his face against violence during 1934 in the same way as Gil Robles had in 1932.

Gil Robles took up the challenge of Prieto: the entry of the CEDA into the government, given the views of the Left on the nature of the régime, would indeed represent a *coup d'état*, even without violence. As leader of the biggest parliamentary group, which undertook to serve and defend the Republic with complete loyalty, his democratic right to claim at least a share in government could not be denied him. In the tradition of Balmes he followed the path of 'possibilism' and rejected the 'catastrophist' solutions of the Monarchists, from whom he dissociated his party even more clearly after the elections than before. While trying to restrain the impatience of his followers (especially the JAP), he saw that his legal 'tactic' must produce results if the Right's masses were not to desert him. Even so there were signs that he was becoming less insistent on introducing his new State during 1934; but in any case his dogmatic adherence to constitutional means meant that the electorate would have to consent to any changes.[2]

The largest group in the new Cortes was led by Gil Robles and composed of those who had stood as candidates of the branches of the CEDA and of many who technically had been representatives of farmers' organisations: it was therefore officially called the *Minoria Popular Agraria*.[3] On the eve of the poll Gil Robles had announced that his party did not intend to govern immediately. The parties of the Centre would reform Azaña's handiwork because they would be unable to govern without the Right's support.[4] After the poll he repeated this view, which he had first expressed in Valencia in November 1932. The CEDA was unfit to govern immediately because Catholic feelings were still upset by Azaña's persecution.[5]

Cedistas were conscious of their strength and commanding position: government was impossible without their support. There would be a period of government by the Centre after which the Right would take over.[6] Gil Robles warned those Rightists who disliked this policy that, given the incompatibility of Lerroux and the Socialists, the alternative was 'a solution of the Left' which would be 'the brief preface to an essay in the dictatorship of the proletariat'.[7] Monarchist pressure to use his strength to wreck the Republic was ignored though he made it plain to the Radicals that his support was conditional on implementation of policies which they had in common.[8] Gil Robles stated his intentions simply and clearly: 'Today I shall facilitate the formation of governments of the Centre; tomorrow, when the time comes, I shall call for power and carry out constitutional reform. If they do not hand over power to us, if events show that there is no room for Rightist political evolution within the Republic, it will pay the consequences. This is not a threat; it is a warning.'[9]

The size of the CEDA's parliamentary group reflected the success of the leadership in attracting and keeping the allegiance of a large proportion of the representatives of agricultural organisations. It betokened, in fact, victory over the liberal Agrarians in the discreet battle waged behind the scenes since the municipal elections of April 1933 for the support of discontented rural interests. At the end of November 1933, Martínez de Velasco, leader of the old Agrarian minority, expected 40 to 50 deputies to form a new Agrarian group which, said Royo Villanova, would act as a third force on the Right alongside the CEDA and the Monarchists, but would participate in government to make the Republic more liberal, more conservative, more unitary and altogether less

Socialist.[10] A preliminary meeting held on 1 December, was attended by 41 deputies: present were the liberal wing of the old Agrarian minority—figures such as Cid, Calderón and Martín Martín; other survivors from the 'old politics', such as Romanones and the Conservative ex-Minister Rodríguez de Viguri; and, by invitation, some conservative *Cedistas* like Casanueva.

This attempt to attract *Cedistas* failed. The new Agrarian minority had only 29 members, the majority of whom favoured the personal participation of one of their number in the government.[11] The leader, Martínez de Velasco, nevertheless set out to create a national party with the immediate objective of repealing the existing agrarian and educational laws. On 23 January he announced the unanimous decision of Agrarians 'to accept the legally constituted régime' (a formal declaration of Republicanism).[12] It quickly transpired, however, that there had been no unanimous decision: within a week eight deputies, including Romanones, Calderón and Fanjul, left in protest at this piece of sharp practice. A clique of ex-*Albistas*—Martínez de Velasco, Cid, Royo Villanova, and Velayos—were now in clear control of the rump.[13]

The manifesto of Martínez de Velasco's *Partido Agrario Español* appeared on 31 January 1934. The party declared that it would support and participate in Republican governments, and that it stood for order at home and peace abroad, the reform of the anti-clerical and 'socialistic' parts of the Constitution and the creation of a second chamber. It pledged itself always to defend national unity, though not to the exclusion of some administrative decentralisation, as well as to procure reductions in government expenditure. Its prime concern was protection for agriculture, as for industry, by means of tariffs fixed by bodies beyond ministerial control. Inside the tariff-walls, however, the party was strongly in favour of the principle of *laissez faire*. The exception here was the need for intervention by the State to ensure rural prosperity: thus, if there were to be price-levels for produce, these must be fully adequate. The State ought to organise better credit-facilities and improve rural life with more roads, electricity, technical education and reafforestation. The party did not approve of the redistribution of landed property, though it conceded that some *latifundios* could be broken up if full compensation were paid to the owners.[14]

The manifesto was typical of the programme of a rural party defending political and economic liberalism and social conservatism, an accurate reflection of those who composed it. The new Agrarian Party of the ex-*Albista* Liberals, though Republican, had more in common with the world of the liberal Monarchy than with the new Right of the 1930s. Though its membership was not confined to Castile and it did not defend the wheat interest alone, it was nevertheless, in essence, a party of the Castilian well-to-do; as such, it incorporated many elements of the 'old politics'.

The decisions of the CEDA and the Agrarians to support government by the Centre dismayed the Monarchists, who wanted the electoral coalition to be maintained in the Cortes. Their spokesman Calvo Sotelo advised from France that the Right should make their support available only for revision of the Constitution by the Radicals. If they would not do this, then the Right should obstruct to a man. In contrast to the 'possibilism' of Gil Robles, this exponent of 'catastrophism' opposed any Rightist participation in Republican government. The unstable Centre would not long be able to postpone the fated clash of Left and Right. Parliament was incapable of coping with revolution. The answer was a totalitarian State incorporating the masses, because the imminent choice before Spain lay between 'collectivist tyranny (or, as Caillaux says of Russia, "a State capitalism founded upon bondage") and a State with an authoritarian basis, with a parliament, but not parliamentary, and, of course, with a corporative system'.[15]

However, since Gil Robles had decided not to torpedo the Centre, it was necessary to prepare for parliamentary activity. Goicoechea and the Alfonsines declared their 'irreducible' hostility to the Republican régime, but decided to co-operate in carrying out the electoral mandate.[16] The Traditionalists also announced their support for implementation of the electoral pact, but their leader, Rodezno, informed deputies that they would at all times make clear their 'absolute, resolute and categorical incompatibility with the established régime, as Catholics and as Spaniards'.[17] The Monarchists were joined in their hostility by the independent snipers Albiñana and Primo de Rivera.[18]

While these various attitudes were being clarified on the Right, Lerroux, as leader of the biggest Republican minority, had to decide how best to insure the Republic which he at last had within his grasp. He announced that he would govern with anyone 'within the Republican orbit'.[19] The Republicans alone did not have sufficient deputies to maintain a government. The Socialists were now, because of their revolutionary position, 'outside Republican orthodoxy' and a coalition with them was thus impossible. The only possible solution, he argued, was a minority government with the attendant risks of dependence on outside support from the Right. When Gil Robles and the Agrarians offered him their aid, he therefore accepted it: an open agreement with accidentalists he thought certainly no worse than the pacts made with 'separatists', 'Communists' and ex-Monarchists such as the President himself, in order to bring in the Republic. Gil Robles and Martínez de Velasco made the continuance of the Republic possible.[20]

Time was given for Lerroux to put the finishing touches to his government by the outbreak on 8 December of the most serious uprising yet by the CNT. The caretaker government of Martínez Barrio proclaimed a 'state of alarm' and was supported by all Rightists against the threat of Libertarian Communism.[21] It was not until 19 December that Lerroux presented to the Cortes a government of seven other Radicals allied with four Centre Republicans and an Agrarian.[22]

In his ministerial declaration, Lerroux said he would govern so as to reconcile all Spaniards: Azaña's legislation would be modified where necessary by constitutional means, order would be kept, expenditure curbed and the amnesty promised in the electoral programme would not be introduced immediately. Keeping his side of the bargain, Gil Robles interpreted the electoral victory as a vote against the Constituent Cortes but not against the Republic; he would press the Centre to reform religious legislation, grant an amnesty, reform agrarian and labour legislation and pass an unemployment measure. The CEDA would act 'with complete and absolute loyalty to a régime which the Spanish people has willed. ... We should never use the means placed in our hands to proceed against the political system placed in our hands.' Reform was necessary, but he explicitly rejected a dictatorship of Right or Left, as he did the 'integral, authoritarian' solution proposed by José Antonio.

The Socialist spokesman, Prieto, was not convinced of *Cedista* sincerity and brushed aside these protestations of loyalty. The

danger of 'the seizure of the Republic by the Right hostile to it'
remained: 'Deep down, Sr. Gil Robles, you hanker after a dictatorial régime.' Lerroux's collaboration with the CEDA, he claimed,
was a betrayal of the Pact of San Sebastián. He solemnly announced that the Socialists would defend 'by every means' the
'essential postulates of the Republic' (ie the work of the Constituent Cortes): 'the revolution will be found facing the *coup d'état.
. . .* The Socialist Party publicly commits itself to unleashing the
revolution in this event.' The Socialists and the Left Republicans
voted against the government, which easily survived with the
support of the Centre, the CEDA and the Agrarians by 265 votes to
53; the Monarchists abstained.[23]

The attitude of revolutionary opposition to the CEDA assumed
by Socialists during 1933 was intensified by the electoral defeat of
the Left—'the unjust result of November' which, as one Socialist
put it, 'created a revolutionary situation in Spain'.[24] The leaders'
attitude to the second contests on 3 December clearly showed that
they were unwilling to accept the verdict of the ballot-boxes.
Prieto urged Socialists to go to the polls 'as a prologue to other
revolutionary days which, in my view, are in Spain inevitable'.
According to Largo Caballero, 'the working class recognises that
it is not incompatible to go to the polls on the 3rd and to the
revolutionary battle on any other day'. The latter declared that the
Communist Party was 'no more Communist than we': the coming
revolution would give the PSOE full power to achieve the transition
to integral Socialism.[25]

During January 1934, *El Socialista* continued its enthusiastic
advocacy of revolution. 'Concord? No. Class war! Hatred to the
death of the criminal bourgeoisie. Concord? Yes; but between
proletarians of all opinions who want to gain salvation and free
Spain from derision. Come what may, watch the red signal!' Some
days later, the newspaper again subjected itself to interrogation:
'Anti-democrats? Yes. Completely. But not enemies of the true
democracy, ours, Socialist democracy, the birth of which will not
be brought about by the art of magic, just as bourgeois democracy
was not born by magic means.'[26] Since the elections had put
legality on the side of Gil Robles, Largo Caballero adopted the
theory that 'legality is created by whoever is in power. Therefore,
should the workers conquer power, the legality they would create

would be just as legal as that which the present government creates.' Amid shouts of 'Long live the machine-guns!' the 'Spanish Lenin' appealed for a single workers' front.[27]

It was against this troubled background that Lerroux's lieutenant, Martínez Barrio, took over the Ministry of the Interior on 23 January from the inexperienced hands of Rico Avello.[28] On 7 February, however, Gil Robles voiced the discontent of his party with Martínez Barrio, whose inactivity in a pre-revolutionary situation was much resented. It soon became clear, too, that Martínez Barrio did not approve of Lerroux's policy of dependence on the accidentalist Right.[29] The distaste of the Grand Master of the Spanish Grand Orient for Lerroux's Giolittian scheme for 'transforming' the CEDA into the conservative party of the Republic was brought irrevocably into the open in an interview with a Monarchist magazine on 11 February.[30]

By the end of that month, Gil Robles had decided that it was time to oust the Minister by ceasing to support this 'completely exhausted government'. He told Cedistas, however, that the time for government by the Right was not yet at hand: 'it is still necessary to exhaust intermediate solutions, analogous to the present one'. This speech brought the crisis within the Radical Party to a head, and Martínez Barrio resigned from the government. Alcalá-Zamora, whose relations with Lerroux were somewhat strained, took the opportunity to withdraw Presidential confidence, thus precipitating the first in a weary succession of government crises.[31] Later, in May, Martínez Barrio, the outgoing Minister of Finance Lara, and twelve other deputies left the Radical Party to become Radical-Democrats, giving as their reason belief that the CEDA ought not to be allowed to govern since it was not an explicitly Republican party and was likely to betray the régime.[32]

Lerroux re-formed his government on 3 March.[33] It was called upon to deal with the question of an amnesty, which had troubled its predecessor. Gil Robles and Lerroux had agreed in December not to press the issue for the moment, but the Monarchists were mindful that Calvo Sotelo and Guadalhorce, elected to the Cortes, were still in exile. With Agrarian support, Monarchists put down a motion that they should be legally proclaimed deputies immediately, a motion embarrassing for the CEDA. In the debate on

24 January, Goicoechea, who reminded the Right and the Radicals that the amnesty was part of both their electoral programmes, was stalled by the Minister of Justice, who promised instead a general amnesty in due course. Gil Robles and Martínez de Velasco declared that they were satisfied with the Minister's pledge, and Goicoechea's motion was accordingly defeated.[34]

In April the government's bill appeared, providing amnesty for those who had committed offences prior to 3 December 1933.[35] For the Socialists, Prieto argued that the measure should also apply to those detained for the post-electoral uprising of the CNT, while at the same time maintaining that the Republic was not strong enough to be able to concede any amnesty. Álvarez Valdés, the Liberal-Democrat Minister of Justice, stood firm in his belief that the election results were a mandate to amnesty the men of '10 August', while insisting that he was opposed to violence in politics. The skilled parliamentarian Prieto seized upon this statement and challenged the Minister to apply his maxim to the Jaca rising of December 1930. Álvarez Valdés said he did not condone that episode, adding that the Republic owed its existence to the elections of 12 April. Politically, however, the damage was done; Prieto made much capital from rhetoric in praise of the Republican martyrs of Jaca disowned by a Minister of the Republic. So great was the scandal that Álvarez Valdés was forced to resign.[36]

In mid-April, the intellectual diplomat Madariaga took over the Ministry of Justice and found the measure blocked by a host of Socialist amendments. He accepted some of them, so that the measure now applied to offences committed up to 14 April 1934. He argued that the amnesty was an act of generosity, not of justice, but Monarchists who wanted reinstatement of the military in their former posts were left unsatisfied. In the face of their opposition the measure was finally passed on 20 April.[37] Yet this was not the end of the matter, for the President, lobbied by the Left, was reluctant to give his consent and wished to send it back to the Cortes as Article 83 of the Constitution permitted. Article 84 stipulated that such a decision must be countersigned by a Minister. No Minister would oblige, and Alcalá-Zamora even failed to persuade his Progressive colleague Del Río to resign. He therefore agreed to promulgate the amnesty, but insisted on issuing a note to demonstrate his dislike for it—a course which

Rightists were quick to note that he had omitted to follow when confronted with Azaña's religious legislation. The government was opposed to the Presidential note. Don Niceto and Don Alejandro were again at loggerheads and another crisis ensued.[38]

Apart from the amnesty, the outgoing government had achieved a minor but very controversial 'rectification' of the Republic in the religious sphere by passing a law regulating the incomes of parish priests. A bill had been introduced in January to pay two-thirds of their stipends to priests over forty in areas with a population of under 3,000; this was justified on the grounds that such priests had rendered services to the State under the Concordat of 1851 and the Constitution of 1876.[39] The Socialists obstructed the measure with a flood of amendments and were supported by the *Esquerra* and other Left Republicans. They argued, rightly, that Article 26 of the Constitution expressly forbade the State to give financial aid to religious bodies, and the same article said that the clerical budget was to end before December 1933. To evade Article 26, the government insisted that the impoverished rural clergy were public servants under the terms of the Constitution of 1876; the bill merely rewarded them. The Left retorted that ecclesiastical services could not be equated with public services.[40] A gesture of compromise by the Radicals to limit the annual sum payable to 16,500,000 pesetas was accepted by Gil Robles as the current 'possible good', but obstruction continued from the Left until debate was finally guillotined and the law passed on 4 April.[41]

A more important modification was the suspension of the Law concerning Religious Confessions and Congregations with regard to the replacement of religious by lay schools. Lerroux realised that the CEDA would make its support conditional on cancellation of this part of the law, but was justified in saying that replacement by January 1934 was in any case impossible.[42] Suspension of the offending clauses was decreed on 30 December 1933.[43]

The crisis provoked by Alcalá-Zamora over the amnesty exasperated the Right. Rodezno and Royo Villanova demanded the resignation of this 'Alfonso in paperback'.[44] The Left called for new elections, while Gil Robles put the CEDA at the President's disposal as 'an instrument of government loyally serving the Republic'.[45] The President declined the offer. During the political manœuvring Gil Robles and Casanueva offered the votes of the

L

CEDA to Lerroux should the latter wish to censure Alcalá-Zamora in the Cortes. This offer was declined by the Radical leader. The outcome of the crisis was, on 28 April, a government headed by Ricardo Samper, a little-known *Blasquista* Radical from Valencia more amenable to Presidential advice than Lerroux. Neither Lerroux himself nor the CEDA participated in the new Ministry, though the energetic young Radical Salazar Alonso remained at the Interior.[46] With the continuing support of the accidentalist Right, the new Centre coalition turned to the vexed question of the repeal of the Law of Municipal Boundaries of 1931.

The debates on agrarian matters in the new Cortes revealed divisions on the Right. In general, Agrarians and Monarchists saw the electoral victory as a mandate for the restoration of order in the countryside, the reduction of wages, the maintenance of the inviolability of property rights and repeal of the laws of the first Republican biennium to permit a return to the *status quo ante* 1931. Similar views were held by many within the CEDA. Within the Right as a whole, the social-Christian wing of the CEDA, while accepting the need for order, opposed as best they could the *revanchisme* of their colleagues. These internal differences became apparent early in 1934 when debates began on a measure introduced by the Progressive Minister of Agriculture, Cirilo del Río. He proposed that, since they had already sown for 1934, the ploughmen (*yunteros*) of Extremadura should be allowed to stay on the land which they had occupied under the aegis of Domingo's Decree for the Intensification of Farming, at least until the end of 1934. The Institute of Agrarian Reform ought to be left to decide on the rent which they would then pay the owners.[47] The Minister argued that to turn the *yunteros* off the land would simply re-create the situation of 1932, and there would be renewed attacks on and invasions of property. Surely a peaceful solution, which legalised the facts of life in Extremadura, was preferable to this for all concerned.[48]

Conservaduros, including the *Cedistas* Casanueva and Azpeitia, did not agree. They pointed out that the seizure of land by the *yunteros* was not provided for in the Law of Agrarian Reform. The *yunteros* were in possession only because Azaña's Governor-General, Peña Novo, had made spurious use of a decree to condone illegal acts. The Minister's scheme was therefore as revolutionary as Domingo's decree of November 1932. Furthermore, the pastures of Extremadura were being ruined by attempts to grow cereals, an activity for which the unirrigated soil was unsuited. The *yunteros* must leave as soon as they had harvested at the latest, and should pay a 'just' rent to the owners as well as compensation for damage done.[49] The Minister was supported by *Cedista* deputies who represented Extremadura. One, Manuel Giménez Fernández, Professor of Canon Law at Seville, stated that this was clearly a case in which moral consideration of the plight of the *yunteros* took precedence over the rights of property. On 9 February Del Río's law was passed by the Cortes.[50] Gil Robles persuaded *Cedistas* to vote with the Centre and Left in favour of the measure, much to the chagrin of Agrarian and Monarchist opponents.[51]

The Samper government was called upon to deal with the Law of Municipal Boundaries, which, since it affected all Spain, the Right was even more anxious to repeal. A bill to this effect was introduced in January, but it was not until 24 May, after determined Socialist obstruction, that debates were guillotined. The law repealing that of 9 September 1931 stipulated that employers hiring hands from other areas must pay wages equivalent to those fixed by the mixed juries in their own district.[52] *Acción Popular* quickly issued a statement saying that it would expel any of its members who slashed the wages of employees,[53] but it may be doubted how strictly provincial organisations adhered to this directive.

The repeal of the law had been debated against a background of Socialist accusations that wage-levels were being ignored, mixed juries were no longer functioning and employers were discriminating against Socialists when hiring labour. The deputies of *Acción Obrerista* claimed, on the other hand, that the State's labour-exchanges were still in the grip of *caciques* of the *Casas del Pueblo* and were run for political purposes.[54] In fact *Acción Popular*'s Secretariat for Social Questions was a network of labour-exchanges parallel to the State organisation which the Socialists had appropriated when in power.[55] After the repeal of the Law of Municipal Boundaries it was rightly said that the onus for 'the pacification of spirits' now rested upon employers rather than workers. In general, however, such appeals for moderation went unheeded.[56]

It was from the social discontent engendered by such 'rectifica-
tions' of the Republic that the Socialists sought to draw support
for their political revolution against the CEDA and its 'compliant
slaves' the Radicals. They were seconded 'unconditionally' by the
Esquerra.[57] They explained their position by contending that the
CEDA was not Republican. Yet, as the Liberal-Democrat leader
argued, such people overlooked the fact that, 'by virtue of the
number of deputies they have in Parliament, it would follow that
the country had elected a Monarchist majority. . . . All those
parties that declared themselves custodians of the Republic . . . say
that they are going to restore true Republicanism, but I ask in
whose name they are going to do it. If they are really democratic,
they must resign themselves to the privation and begin again to
win over the people with propaganda.'[58] The Left strongly objected to the deeds of the new Cortes. A veteran parliamentarian
asked 'if we are to proclaim and come to the absurd conclusion
that these Cortes do not possess the same sovereignty as the
Constituent Cortes to alter laws?' If this were the case, it 'would
be contrary to the very essence of the parliamentary régime'.[59]

The Socialists, however, had already enunciated their own
theory of democracy which had nothing to do with numerical
majorities. The Left Republicans approved neither of Radical
practice nor of Socialist theory and were thus in a quandary—apart
from Domingo, who fell back on the Jacobin formula that 'when
a policy that benefits the people is found not to be wanted by the
people, it must be imposed even against the people's will'.[60] The
former members of Azaña's coalition confused the Republic as a
form of government with their own ideological predilections.
Those who had remained Monarchists could console themselves
with the thought that the Republic was not proving to be the
system of government which divided Spaniards least.

From the advent of the Republic internal disputes on the Right
centred on the rights and wrongs of 'accidentalism' as a political
doctrine. The argument started in April 1931 as a dialogue between the leader-writers of *ABC* and *El Debate* and in 1932
brought about the schism in *Acción Popular*. The controversy was
at its fiercest in 1933 and 1934, but it was no longer simply a
question of whether or not Rightist parties should 'inhibit' themselves with regard to forms of government. New dimensions were

added. Was it licit for Catholics to serve, support or even accept a Republic with an anti-Catholic Constitution? Was Republican legislation so harmful to the Church as to justify or even necessitate the use of armed force against the Republic according to Catholic doctrine?

Herrera and Gil Robles, with the support of the Nuncio, based their policy on the precedents of the *ralliement* in France in the 1890s and on the German Centre's acceptance of the Weimar Republic.[61] Alfonsine Monarchists like Vegas argued that Leo XIII's policy had failed in France and should not therefore be repeated in Spain. The *ralliement* had weakened the powers of resistance of French Catholics by dividing them into *ralliés* and Monarchists. The Republicans had been able to intensify religious persecution, separate Church and State and expel the Orders. As in France, so in Spain, the Republic was consubstantial with irreligion and Freemasonry; its Constitution enshrined doctrines condemned by the Church. Appeasement did not pay: the *ralliement* was 'sterile and . . . prejudicial to the interests of France and also of the Church'. The French Jesuit Fr de la Taille had written that it was licit for citizens of a *de facto* régime to prepare for the restoration of the *de jure* government 'even by a *coup de force*, if this *coup de force* has the approval of the legitimate prince and has real possibilities of success'.[62]

Another contributor to *Acción Española*, Canon Castro Albarrán, reached similar conclusions. He argued that Leo XIII's *Au milieu des sollicitudes* applied only to France because it was not written in Latin. Moreover the circumstances in Spain were different from those in France, where the Republic had become the legitimate régime because it had taken root by the 1890s. In Spain in the 1930s the Republic was still a *de facto* régime which could not demand obedience from Catholics because it trampled on the rights of the Church and did not exercise power for the common good. Even Leo XIII had made respect for the liberty of the Church and good government preconditions for obedience. Gil Robles and Herrera were therefore in error: 'obedience to the constituted power' could only be an external and transitory formula for Catholics under an illegitimate régime. Accidentalism was licit in theory, but in practice each country must adopt the form of government most suited to its character and history.

Ecclesiastical authority could not be used for political ends; Papal advice on matters other than faith and morals was not binding. The laws of the Republic were contrary to Divine Law and therefore, as Suárez had written, it was licit to rise up against tyranny and restore the legitimate power. 'Do not seek to lull the Spanish soul to sleep with the drug of false acquiescence. Do not put out the fire of holy disobedience.'[63]

Complete Monarchist disillusionment with the CEDA set in after the elections. Monarchists hoped that Gil Robles would continue his electoral alliance with them so as to wreck the Republic as a prelude to restoration of the Monarchy.[64] However, *El Debate*'s editorial 'Catholics and the Republic' on 15 December 1933 was welcomed by politicians of the Centre. The paper argued that, although opposition to some of the existing laws would have to be maintained until repeal, Catholicism and Republicanism were not incompatible: 'always saving the rights of God and the Christian conscience, Spanish Catholics, as such, can find no difficulty . . . in reconciling themselves with the Republican institutions'.

The Monarchist press was appalled. The Carlist *El Siglo Futuro* claimed that *El Debate* had proclaimed a new and curious 'obligation of conscience' for Catholics, namely to become Republicans. Like the Carlist organ, the Alfonsine *ABC* reminded readers that the Church left Spanish Catholics a free choice between Monarchism and Republicanism and went on to accuse the CEDA of 'treachery' to those who had voted for it because it was not a Republican party.[65] *El Debate* and Gil Robles replied that the CEDA was merely drawing the logical conclusion from its adherence to accidentalism. It was defending religion, property and the family under the established régime, which Spain had given itself thanks to 'the action of some and the omissions of others'. The *Minoría Popular Agraria* declared its complete solidarity with its leader.[66] The ideologues of *Acción Española* nevertheless persisted in their criticism. The Republic was the political incarnation of 'the principles of the Revolution'. The 'essence of the Republican régime is precisely this: laicism, absolute popular sovereignty and, consequently, liberalism'; since these principles were 'condemned in their entirety by the Church' Catholicism and Republicanism were mutually exclusive.[67]

Certain Monarchist accusations were more difficult to answer.

On 27 September 1933 the *Cedista* leader spoke of having made a vow when Article 26 was passed 'never to accept, never, pacts or compromises of any kind' with those who had voted for it until it had been repealed.[68] Yet within three months of this statement he reached agreement with Lerroux's Radicals. Gil Robles answered such accusations of insincerity by invoking a higher morality: 'everything I am doing is to save the Church'.[69] Monarchists drew the conclusion that accidentalism was motivated only by 'the pontifical obstinacy of Herrera and the cowardly ambition of Gil Robles'. The *Cedista* leader was in their opinion the marionette of that *éminence grise* Herrera, 'the apostle of "the lesser evil", which he has now re-christened "the possible good" '.[70]

The CEDA was also attacked by Monarchists for its 'tactic' of 'possibilism'. They complained that this method of defending religion contributed to the consolidation of the Republic and that root-cause of Spain's ruin, parliamentarism. The 'tactic' was sapping the morale of the Right's masses and in practice put the victors at the polls 'in the service of the vanquished'.[71] *Cedistas* were not being very patriotic in trying to evangelise the enemy; they were 'people who are always dreaming of entering Attila's tent to draw him to the truth. And if they can, they stay there.'[72] According to *ABC*, however, they were unlikely to be admitted. The trend of events showed that Alcalá-Zamora was determined to keep the CEDA out of power whether or not Gil Robles edged closer to a declaration of outright Republicanism. The paper confidently prophesied 'the failure of a tactic'.[73]

Gil Robles was unabashed. He defended the CEDA's accidentalist and strictly legal policies against critics from the Right, while at the same time issuing warnings to Republicans. Legal activity had brought success at the polls; similarly, 'when legality is on our side, the right to power cannot be denied us. . . . Should this happen, we who lead the Right should consider ourselves failures. . . . The Rightist masses, with their organisations, would follow another road, thereby constituting a grave source of perturbation for the country.'[74] Meanwhile the party did edge closer to outright Republicanism. Its leader promised in December 1933 that it would behave 'with complete loyalty regarding the régime that the people has willed'—thus accepting the Republican interpretation

of the elections of April 1931. In May 1934 the party and its
deputies proclaimed themselves 'ready to serve and defend the
Republic so as to serve and defend Spain'.[75]

In the controversy about accidentalism neither *Cedistas* nor
Monarchists could demonstrate conclusively from Papal texts that
either were in the right. This was partly explicable by the general
vagueness of Papal declarations, and partly owing to the preference
of *Cedistas* for the texts of Leo XIII and Pius XI in contrast to
the Monarchist preference for the more conservative pronouncements of Pius IX and St Pius X. The debate therefore moved to
Rome, where from February to August 1934 the Republican
Minister Pita Romero, to the horror of Monarchists, negotiated
unsuccessfully with the Vatican for a *modus vivendi*.[76]

The pro-*Cedista* lobby in Rome included the Nuncio, Herrera
(now head of Spanish Catholic Action), Cardinal Vidal Barraquer
(Archbishop of Tarragona) and Mgr Pizzardo (Papal Pro-
Secretary). The opposing lobby included the exiled Segura, and
his successor as Primate, Archbishop Gomá.[77] *Cedistas* failed to
get Castro Albarrán's *El derecho a la rebeldía* condemned as
heretical, but otherwise their views prevailed.[78] An Alfonsine
visitor to the Vatican was told that he ought not to think in terms
of a Monarchist restoration, but of making the Republic more
conservative.[79] When Gomá and Segura met at Anglet in July 1934
they agreed that the pro-Republican policy of the cold and cal-
culating Pius XI stemmed from his desire to be on good terms with
all governments.[80] Papal support for *Cedista* views enraged Traditionalists. The Communion's bulletin accused the CEDA of 'playing
Masonry's game' by caring more for liberalism than for religion,
and it hinted darkly at apostasy.[81]

Renovación Española made as little headway against the CEDA in
Spain as it did in Rome. Membership remained stationary and
only one *Cedista* deputy deserted to the Alfonsines although most
of the *Minoría Popular Agraria* were, like their leader, Monarchist
in foro interno.[82] *Renovación Española*'s only hope lay in persuading
Alfonso XIII to declare membership of the CEDA incompatible
with Monarchist convictions. Valiente, the President of the JAP,
went secretly to Fontainebleau with Gil Robles's knowledge early
in June 1934 to see Alfonso and argue against any such development. Much to Gil Robles's embarrassment news of the visit

appeared in *ABC* and Valiente was forced to resign his offices in the party.[83] Nevertheless *Renovación Española* gained no benefit from the episode. Alfonso still saw success for the CEDA as a pre-condition for his return by peaceful means; Monarchists should therefore stay under its umbrella until the Republican storm abated. He reminded the leader of his 'drawing-room Monarchists' that his cause was 'accidental and transient' compared with 'the supreme good', the unity and survival of Spain.[84]

Gil Robles stuck to the 'tactic' of achieving a new Catholic corporative State by evolutionary means. The CEDA would put its programme into effect stage by stage and then, 'when the time is ripe, entirely'. After a long period of government by the Centre it would take power despite the hostility of the Left: 'power for us, why deny it, would be a *coup d'état*'.[85] Monarchist dissatisfaction with the 'tactic' was a less important factor for him than the pressure of the JAP for quick authoritarian solutions. Gil Robles was obliged to give *Japistas* a measure of independence to retain their allegiance even though their youthful exuberance provided the Left with ammunition for their accusations of 'Fascism'. Gil Robles himself sought to rebut the charge by likening the CEDA to Sturzo's party which had opposed Fascism: 'I am not a Fascist nor do I sympathise with that system of government.'[86]

The nature of the JAP was accurately reflected in the telegraphic style of its 'Nineteen Points':[87]

1. To think of Spain, to work for Spain, to die for Spain.
2. Discipline. The leaders do not make mistakes.
3. Youth, faith, boldness, purpose, young spirit in the new politics.
4. Repeal of sectarian, socialistic and anti-Spanish legislation.
5. Christian family in opposition to pagan modernism.
6. Valour of the race, pre-military education, abolition of the *soldado de cuota*.
7. Freedom of education. Children do not belong to the State.
8. Love for the region the basis of love for Spain.
9. Specialisation, more preparation and fewer speeches.
10. Our revolution is social justice, neither egoistic capitalism nor destructive Marxism.
11. More property-owners and a juster distribution of wealth.
12. War on decadent *señoritismo* and professional vagrancy, re-

cognition for all activities, work for all; he who does not work shall not eat.

13. Anti-parliamentarianism, anti-dictatorship, the people incorporated in government in an organic and hierarchic manner, not by degenerate democracy.

14. Reconstruction of Spain, war on the class-struggle, the economy in the service of the nation.

15. Spain strong, respected in the world.

16. First: Reason, and faced with violence, reason and force.

17. Prestige of authority, strong executive power, to prevent better than to repress.

18. In the presence of the martyrs of our ideal, present and forward.

19. Above all Spain, and above Spain God.

The *Japista* programme perhaps reflected the ideals preached during the Dictatorship when many of its members had been at school or university.

José María Pérez de Laborda, its leader from June 1934, said the movement was not Fascist because it could not accept 'the God-State' or 'violence as a system'. Nevertheless Fascism was respected as a system for others and *Japistas* who visited Italy in 1933 were impressed by the régime although they found its educational policies quite unacceptable. The JAP's flags and rallies might be reminiscent of Fascism, but they were in fact inspired by the example of the Socialist Youth. Its *Movilización Civil* was not a force of storm-troopers but a young citizens' organisation to help the authorities run essential services during a revolutionary general strike.[88]

Japistas saw themselves as the vanguard of the CEDA in both the social and political fields. They wanted 'to inject a young spirit into Spanish politics' and 'to be rebels faced with an unjust and anti-Christian society'. They considered themselves the antithesis of the 'Generation of '98'; the JAP was to be a patriotic national movement for renovation 'guided by a providential man', a movement neither of Right nor Left which would incorporate all Spaniards.[89] Some *Japistas* dreamed of a new Catholic totalitarian State with 'only one national party carrying out a genuinely Spanish policy'.[90] At their congress in April 1934, however, they failed to agree on the nature of the future State and this matter was left an open question. Their indecision on this point gave the 'infallible leader' a free hand, as did their decision not to insist on making the various local youth groups into a single autonomous body within the party.[91]

The first of a series of big *Japista* rallies was held in front of the Monastery of El Escorial on 22 April amid snow showers, while the Socialists protested by staging a general strike in Madrid.[92] The crowd of around 20,000 was told by Gil Robles after Mass that *Cedistas* were 'the staunchest defenders of established legality' and the only force capable of effectively opposing social revolution. 'We are an army of citizens, not an army that needs uniforms and martial parades.' The *Japistas* then took an oath of complete obedience to their leader, raised their right hands to their left shoulders in salute and sang their anthem:[93]

> Forward, with faith in victory,
> For the Country and for God,
> To conquer or to die;
> The laurel of Glory awaits us,
> For History is with us,
> The future is on our side.

Gil Robles was determined that *Japistas* should not be seduced by Fascist ideas. 'We must not have recourse to pagan Rome nor to the diseased exaltation of race. The more Catholic, the more Spanish. The more Spanish, the more Catholic.'[94] Advocates of 'excessive haste' within the CEDA should stop and study Spanish history and traditions instead of seeking non-Spanish patrons; to introduce the 'foreignising prurience' of Fascism into Spain would be as calamitous as was the introduction of liberalism. 'Hysterical enthusiasm' and 'external theatricality' should be shunned. The JAP would not, like the *Falange*, form bands of gunmen: 'to send lads of eighteen to avenge deaths with deaths is a treasonable crime'.[95] Gil Robles was nevertheless subjected to 'Fascistic' adulation. *Japistas* considered him a gift from God and chanted '¡ *Jefe*! ¡ *Jefe*! ¡ *Jefe*!' at their rallies. Nor was adulation confined to the young: the wealthy landowner Casanueva thought that cleaning out latrines would be enjoyable with a leader like Gil Robles.[96]

Socialists concluded that if Gil Robles were not the Spanish

Mussolini he was the Spanish Dollfuss. Certainly *Cedistas* found the Austrian Chancellor a 'very suggestive figure, the quintessence of Christian nationalism'.[97] *El Debate* praised his new régime in principle, but suspended definitive judgment until the practical working of its constitution could be observed. The leaders of the CEDA watched the Austrian experiment closely and sympathetically,[98] but they did not set out to imitate. The leadership was concerned, not with introducing a dictatorship, but with evolution towards a Catholic corporative State inspired by Spanish traditions, adapted to current Spanish needs and in line with *Quadragesimo Anno*. The new State must not be 'a tree without roots, a danger to those going near it'; it must have a solid socio-economic basis. The CEDA's 'national solution' demanded working-class support; Gil Robles echoed Pius XI: 'so long as we do not incorporate labouring masses in our movement, we shall have built our victory on sand'.[99]

While the CEDA's corporativism presupposed a 'revolution from below', that of the Alfonsines, many of whom had been *Mauristas*, put greater emphasis on a 'revolution from above'. National regeneration would be primarily the work of the State and an *élite* in contrast to the social evolution preached by *Cedistas*. The intellectual dynamo of Monarchism was *Acción Española*, whose offices, closed on 5 August 1932, reopened on 3 May 1934. The aim of this 'politico-cultural' body, led by Pemán but still including some *Cedistas*, was to undo the work of the 'Generation of '98' by converting the intelligentsia to Rightist doctrines.[100] Once this intellectual reconquest had been achieved, the right ideas would filter down to the masses.

With the failure of *Renovación Española* under Goicoechea's leadership the Alfonsines of *Acción Española* were anxious to make the most of the return from exile of Calvo Sotelo at the beginning of May 1934. At a dinner given for him on 20 May Sáinz Rodríguez outlined Monarchist plans. All those who had not gone to the polls in November as Republicans—Alfonsines, Carlists, *Cedistas*, *Falangistas*—should join together in a 'national bloc' under Calvo Sotelo's leadership. To facilitate this new union of the Right the Monarchists would 'not make a precondition of the presence of a king on the throne'.[101] Calvo Sotelo, accepting the task, made it clear that he did not agree with the 'tactic' of Gil Robles.

Monarchists stood for the dogmatic straight line in politics which led to 'integral possession' of power; the CEDA's tactical curve could never achieve what the Right and Spain desired.[102]

Calvo Sotelo spent the summer of 1934 criticising the policies of Gil Robles and outlining his own solution for Spanish problems. Though a member of the minority of *Renovación Española*, outside the Cortes he declined to join any party so that he could be 'cementing material' for a new '*Bloque Hispano Nacional*'. He admired the work done by Gil Robles up to the elections, but believed the *Cedista* leader was now pursuing mistaken policies despite his patriotic intentions. It would be just as easy for Gil Robles to scrap the whole Constitution as it would be to revise Article 26. The 'possibilism' of the CEDA meant that its energy was being frittered away in parliamentary manœuvring and it would lose sight of the ideal of its new State. Calvo Sotelo thought him too timid. 'Gil Robles wants power; we, the State. Gil Robles, within the régime; we, over and above the régime. Gil Robles, partial revision [of the Constitution]; we, total.'

Calvo Sotelo said his difference with Gil Robles on the form of government was 'substantive', but he nevertheless hoped that the CEDA would join his Rightist bloc to carry through a common minimal programme, namely 'the complete conquest of the State'. For Calvo Sotelo the new State meant in the economic field 'a new economic structure' built around the corporative organisation of labour and a modified form of capitalism: in short, 'a directed economy'. In the political sphere there would be plebiscites and a parliament of interest-groups; people would vote separately for ideas and interests, not (as in the existing system) for parties and personalities. This new State had to be set up immediately, but the Monarchy would only return at a later stage. It would be a Monarchy different in every respect from that which collapsed in 1931; there would be an 'installation (*instauración*)' not a 'restoration (*restauración*)'.[103]

Gil Robles, however, would have nothing to do with Calvo Sotelo's 'dictatorial' schemes and stuck to his evolutionary policy. He thought that the parliamentary system of representation could certainly be improved but he made it quite clear, borrowing a phrase from Cavour, that he preferred 'a bad Chamber (*Cámara*) to a good *camarilla*'.[104] Gil Robles believed the political structure must be reformed piecemeal as a result of popular pressure; Calvo Sotelo saw the State as the instrument of total reform from above.

Monarchists still dreamed of the overthrow of the Republic. In March 1934 the Alfonsines Goicoechea and General Barrera, and the Carlists Rafael de Olazábal and Lizarza, visited Rome for talks with Marshal Balbo. On 31 March, after a meeting with the *Duce* himself, agreements were signed between the Spanish Monarchists and the Italian leaders. The Italians undertook to 'support the two parties in opposition to the present régime in Spain with assistance and necessary means in the work of overthrowing it and substituting a Regency which would prepare the complete restoration of the Monarchy'. As an initial gesture of good faith, the Italians promised an immediate gift of a quantity of arms and 1,500,000 pesetas in cash. More aid would be supplied 'as the work realised justified it and circumstances rendered it necessary'. It was agreed that Olazábal should take charge of the money—a third of which was handed over on 1 April—and he would hand it over in Spain to Goicoechea and Rodezno, who were also to see to the importation and distribution of the arms, which Barrera and Balbo had agreed should be collected in Tripoli. Some young Spaniards were also to be given weapon-training in Italy.

A political agreement was also signed, providing for an Italo-Spanish treaty of friendship and neutrality when the new régime had been installed. The *status quo* respecting Spanish territorial rights in the western Mediterranean was to be guaranteed by Italy. Italy and Spain would conclude a commercial treaty to co-ordinate exports of certain products, and would generally forge close economic links. Such treaties, however, were dependent upon prior 'denunciation and abrogation of the secret Franco-Spanish treaty' which the Italians and the Monarchists both wrongly believed that Azaña had made with Herriot in 1932 to allow passage of French troops through Spain and French occupation of the Balearics in wartime. These political provisions were to take effect within a month of the new régime's foundation; Italy would help it obtain recognition 'insofar as it is internationally possible'.[105] From the Italian viewpoint, the pact was another move in their rivalry with France for influence in the Mediterranean, while the Monarchists could congratulate themselves on enlisting a powerful ally.

The Monarchists, however, could not agree on whom the King should be. When Mussolini asked the delegation whether Alfonso XIII were to be restored, all gave a negative reply; but when Goicoechea said Juan could be the new King, the Carlists disagreed. Similarly there was a dispute over the distribution of arms: Goicoechea demanded that they be shared equally between the two parties, but Lizarza pointed out that the Alfonsines had no troops whereas the Carlists had their *Requetés*.[106]

Until May 1934, the Communion was led by Rodezno, known to Carlists as the champion of dynastic fusion in the person of Juan. Rodezno, like Pradera a collaborator in *Acción Española*, had no faith in Carlist violence and thought that Carlism had now completed its mission of preserving Traditionalist principles. Rodezno, who had remained a Jaimist, had a rival within the Communion in the person of a young ex-Integrist lawyer from Seville, Manuel Fal Conde, an advocate of armed action as opposed to the 'diplomatic way' of Rodezno, and one who had shown energy and resource in organising the Communion in Andalusia virtually from scratch since 1931. Though he did not completely reject the *Juanista* solution, he was suspicious of close relations with Alfonsines. On this score, he had circumstantial allies within the Communion in the *ultras* who, while loath to forgive him for his disloyalty to Jaime, were totally opposed to Rodezno's passive and 'pro-Alfonsine' policies.[107] The views of Fal Conde and the *ultras* were shared by the youth of Navarre, whose organ declared: 'Are we always going to be hard-hearted ombre-players, assiduous frequenters of cafés? No, no and no. . . . We want to be like them, like the Carlists of the last century.'[108] Victory would be achieved, not by the skills of incorrigible politicians, but with the bayonets of the *Requetés*.[109]

On 20 April 1934 a meeting of regional leaders took place, and they recommended that 'new orientations' be given to the Communion without changing 'the immutable principles of our ideology'. On 3 May Alfonso Carlos granted their request with the appointment of Fal Conde as Royal Secretary General, with instructions to carry out a complete reorganisation of the Communion. Rodezno and his advisory committee therefore resigned.[110]

The new orientation of the Communion with regard to the

Alfonsines quickly became apparent. On 6 May Alfonso Carlos issued orders to the former leader, Rodezno, that 'TYRE must be suppressed. . . . There must be no union nor any affiliation with those of *Renovación*.'[111] Thus Alfonso Carlos reflected the views of Navarrese youth, who saw Goicoechea's party as the 'refuge of *caciques* and riff-raff of the Alfonsine Monarchy, which has adopted the name of *Renovación Española*, as if we did not know that the renovation with which they entice us is the return of a régime of iniquity repugnant to every honourable conscience'.[112]

Nevertheless, the neo-Traditionalist Alfonsines of *Acción Española*, whose daily organ was *La Época*, were anxious for agreement on the dynastic question so as to give the projected *Bloque Hispano Nacional* some chance of success. On 14 June, in his interview with *ABC*, Calvo Sotelo had spoken of the 'installation' of the Monarchy, not its 'restoration'. *La Época* accordingly sought to calm Carlist fears: 'We cannot restore the liberal, democratic Monarchy that fell on 14 April, nor the absolute Monarchy of Carlos III and Fernando VII.' It was a question, as St Pius X had said, of 'restoring the organisms destroyed by the revolution, adapting them to present needs'. Rodezno declared himself in agreement with these views, but not with the conclusion that Alfonso XIII or Juan could be King in such a Monarchy. *La Época* therefore recalled the words of the Comte de Chambord: 'My person is nothing; my principle is everything.' The paper continued to advocate dynastic union in the person of Juan, and reminded Carlists that Alfonso Carlos was himself the son of a liberal skeleton in their cupboard, Juan III.[113]

The Carlist die-hards in Navarre, however, were not open to persuasion by *La Época*: the succession of Juan signified 'usurpation'.[114] The official Carlist reply to Alfonsine overtures was contained in Alfonso Carlos's manifesto of 29 June. Monarchy, he wrote, needs continuity, and hence there was a law of succession; but it also requires legitimacy—legitimacy of origin by the law of succession and 'legitimacy of exercise, according to which the King remains subject to the inviolable prescriptions of Natural Law and to the corpus of those fundamental laws that, consecrated by tradition and promulgated prior to the revolutions, constitute, with respect for the spiritual sovereignty of the Church, the insuperable limit of their own sovereignty'. This 'double legitimacy' he and his line represented 'in opposition to all Monarchist or Republican illegitimacies'. Since he had no direct heir, his successor would have to swear to these principles and recognise the legitimacy of the Carlist line; 'legitimacy of exercise' was considered more important than 'legitimacy of origin'. If he should return to Spain he would convoke Cortes-General of the Kingdom and proclaim his successor. Should he die in exile without having named a successor, Carlists must not be dismayed: 'even though all possible legitimacies be extinct', there remained the sacred right of peoples 'to give themselves the prince who knows how to represent with dignity the cause of the Country'.[115]

Juan was not therefore totally excluded, but the Carlist terms proved unacceptable to Alfonso XIII, who still hoped to be restored by electoral means and remained at heart a liberal.[116] *ABC* therefore replied: 'The succession in the dynasty has been reduced to only one line, represented by the last King, Don Alfonso XIII, and his heirs. The dissidence cannot last because, after the venerable old man who today maintains it, there will be no one left in his branch to invoke the titles that he uselessly upheld. . . . If the restoration of the Spanish Monarchy takes place, it will be exclusively the work of the national will . . . and it alone can . . . give [the Monarchy] form and content.'[117]

The 'fundamental bases' which the Communion upheld 'in permanent protest against all illegitimacies enthroned by the liberal revolution' were definitively restated by Alfonso Carlos in his manifesto of 29 June 1934:

First. Religious unity, which is to say the close and everlasting moral union of Church and State, and the complete affirmation of the rights that, in its internal as in the external order, belong to the former by reason of its indisputable sovereignty.

Second. The political affirmation, or the re-establishment of the traditional Monarchy with its key notes: Catholic, moderated, federative, hereditary and legitimate, and, therefore, fundamentally opposed to the liberal, democratic, parliamentary, centralistic and constitutionalist Monarchy.

Third. The organic affirmation, which, repudiating the individualist, atomic and disorganising spirit of liberal systems, establishes society upon a harmonious mass of organisms, ordered with regard to the hierarchy of their ends and endowed with the

M

autarchy necessary for their fulfilment, with their own organs, Councils, Juntas and regional Cortes, commencing with the family, the first of all social activities, restored to the plenitude of its natural rights.

Fourth. The federative affirmation, which entails the restoration of the regions with all their *Fueros*, liberties, franchises, good uses and customs, exemptions and rights that belong to them and with the guarantee of the *pase foral*, a condition necessary for their integrity, not only compatible with, but moreover inseparable from the indissoluble unity of the Spanish nation.

Fifth. The affirmation of the Monarchy, moderated by its councils, necessary organs for its consultation, and the Cortes, authentic instrument of the national will. No fundamental law of the kingdom may be changed or altered save in Cortes convoked for this purpose and with the assistance of the *procuradores*, subject to the authoritative mandate of the organisms and activities represented by them.

Sixth. The dynastic affirmation, which originated with what was inappropriately called the Salic Law—because it does not absolutely exclude females, called to the succession by the failure of the male line—as Felipe V promulgated it in 1713.

After seeking the aid and benediction of the Sacred Heart of Jesus, to which the Banner of National Tradition had been consecrated, the manifesto ended with the words: 'Long live Christ the King! Long live Spain!'[118]

Carlists remained 'quixotic idealists of the Revolution. . . . Reaction is to return to the situation immediately preceding the present one. Revolution is the tendency to re-establish a much older situation, which means the traditional régime . . . the sixteenth century.'[119] Their ideal social order lay even further in the past. The railwayman Ginés Martínez Rubio, deputy for Seville, had expressed the Traditionalist outlook before the elections: 'When people talk of advances in the social laws, I recall that in the fifteenth century there was in Spain an organisation of labour superior to all present gains.'[120]

The appointment of Fal Conde led to a complete overhaul of the Communion and to increased enthusiasm for military preparations. During the summer of 1934 new regional and local leaders were appointed and special delegacies set up for propaganda, the youth and the press. A cultural council was also created under

Pradera.[121] In the previous year, Lamamié de Clairac had organised *Unidades de Acción* to counter disorder and anarchy,[122] and the *Decurias* of Navarrese *Requetés* had been re-formed into five-man Patrols. By 1934, these *Requetés* were militarily organised and went about the *pueblos* dressed in their khaki uniforms and red berets. Arms were purchased and bombs locally manufactured.[123] Fal Conde organised a series of *aplechs* (rallies) in all parts of Spain, beginning with one in Seville province on 15 April; *Requetés* attended in their uniforms and in military formations.[124] These *aplechs* served the purpose of drawing attention to the *Requetés* as 'the true national counter-revolutionary militia'.[125] The hopes of Fal Conde were clearly expressed at the *aplech* at Potes. 'A historical bridge stretches between the seventy thousand volunteers who fought in the past epic and these youths of today.... Peoples have a right to rise up against tyrants. ... Let us proceed to the third reconquest, but to a reconquest lasting not eight centuries, but eight days, eight hours.'[126]

While the Carlists could count on their own *Requetés*, the Alfonsines hoped to rely on Primo de Rivera's *Falange*, the foundation of which they had financed; but they were to be disappointed, and thus left without a force of shock-troops. Within a month of its creation, *Falange Española* claimed over a thousand members, drawn in the main from the FUE and revolutionary Republican elements.[127] Its success boded ill for Ledesma's JONS, which began to stagnate; the two groups therefore merged on 13 February 1934 into the *Falange Española de las* JONS, led by the triumvirate of José Antonio, Ledesma and Ruiz de Alda.[128] The new formation retained the old *Jonsista* slogans and now attracted some Rightists interested in Fascism.[129]

The 'initial points' of the *Falange* had declared Spain, in terms borrowed from Ortega, 'a unit of destiny in the universal' superior to all individuals, classes and groups. The State ought to be in the service of this unit, and should banish separatism, the class struggle, parties and Parliament. The *Falangista* totalitarian State was to be based on the family, the municipality and the guild or union; social justice was to be its prime aim, on a basis of 'Authority, Hierarchy, Order'. This State would be Catholic but not clerical. Until its installation, 'violence can be licit when used for a justifiable ideal'.[130] José Antonio claimed to have integrated

'Country and social justice, and . . . upon these two unshakable principles we wish to carry out our revolution . . . the true revolution'. The *leit-motiv* of his policy was a fusion of Castilian nationalism with a brand of un-Marxian and pre-Marxian Socialism— Socialism, he believed, had ceased to be a redemptive movement when Marx introduced the primacy of economics. The new group could be styled Fascist, since Fascism meant for José Antonio the turning inward of each nation upon its own essence. Finally, he insisted that his grouping was not a party: 'it is a militia'.[131]

Early in 1934 several Monarchists, notably Ansaldo, joined the *Falange* and set about making it a Monarchist instrument for street-warfare and a *coup de main*.[132] The Alfonsines hoped to bring the new group into their plans for a national Rightist bloc, but such hopes were frustrated by the acute dislike of José Antonio for Calvo Sotelo.[133] José Antonio refused to declare himself a Monarchist: '14 April . . . is a historical fact that must be accepted'.[134] Alfonsines nevertheless continued to subsidise the FE *de las* JONS in the hope of bringing it under their control, but their efforts came to nothing because its leader was determined that his group should not be employed as 'a voluntary *gendarmerie* for the defence of what is conservative'.[135] Towards the end of July 1934, relations between José Antonio and the Monarchist *Falangistas* became strained to breaking-point; Ansaldo was expelled and those with similar opinions then left. Goicoechea, however, persisted in his attempts to gain some hold on José Antonio by financial means, but his efforts were in vain. The headstrong son of the Dictator had decided to go his own way.[136]

From its foundation the *Falange*, like the JONS, had declared itself explicitly in favour of violence. Young Socialists from the first took the *Falange* at its word, and during 1934 the list of *Falangista* 'martyrs' grew steadily longer. José Antonio, 'more a poet than a politician',[137] disliked the practice of violence, but by April 1934 he had conceded the need to observe 'the law of reprisal' under pressure from his followers. Counter-terrorism was carried out by the '*Falange de la Sangre*' which Ansaldo had started to organise in February as 'Chief of Objectives for the Militias'.[138] Such activities placed the *Falange* beyond the law, and the Minister of the Interior kept a watchful eye on it. A surprise concentration of *Falangistas* on an airfield near Madrid in June was dispersed by the Civil Guard and heavy fines imposed on the leaders. In July 65 *Falangistas* were arrested for possessing arms and explosives.[139]

The *Falange* relied for its membership mainly on students opposed to the FUE, and these were enrolled in the SEU, founded in November 1933 with a double aim: 'Syndical professional action. Revolutionary political action.'[140] In the summer of 1934 a union was created called the CONS which taxi-drivers found attractive.[141] *Falangistas* hoped that a decline in Gil Robles's popularity among *Japistas* would boost their numbers in the future. Meanwhile, the polemic between the two accidentalist parties was heated. Gil Robles said *Falangistas* were *señoritos* incapable of achieving anything; José Antonio likened the CEDA to sterilised milk, containing neither microbes nor vitamins.[142]

After the elections of 1933 the Socialist leadership was, in fact, divided as to the course of action to be followed. Besteiro and reformists in the UGT still favoured a peaceful and democratic transformation of Spain and emphasised the need to introduce a second corporative chamber which would open the way to a revolution allegedly more profound than that achieved by violent methods in Russia. Besteiro argued that, whereas *Cedista* corporativism was 'static', his Socialist corporativism was 'dynamic'.[143] Provincial Socialist leaders, on the other hand, favoured the revolutionary path indicated by Largo Caballero. The executives of the PSOE and the UGT met in January 1934 and came to a decision in favour of the revolutionary method, and a committee was set up to supervise the purchase and distribution of arms. Besteiro and the reformists resigned from leadership of the UGT, thus leaving the union in revolutionary hands. Prieto adhered to the revolutionary group with a programme that included the socialisation of land, some socialisation of industry, abolition of religious Orders, the disbanding of the existing army and Civil Guard, reform of taxation and a purge of civil servants, all of which was to be implemented by decree and endorsed by the people's legislative organs; the President was to accept these decrees or be ousted. Following the decision in favour of revolution, the Socialists of Madrid demanded a united front 'so that a start may be made on the revolutionary movement giving us the conquest of political power as soon as possible'.[144]

A sense of urgency was given to the Socialists by Dollfuss's suppression of the Austrian Socialist rising in February 1934. The Spanish party's organ noted: 'the fight that the Austrian workers are putting up is, like ours, a struggle for existence itself against clerical Fascism; but the outbreak in Austria has come with some delay. Let this fault be a lesson for us and its dangers be a warning.' The Austrian Christian-Socials were 'almost identical' to the CEDA, and Dollfuss was an 'agent of the Vatican, like Gil Robles'. While *El Socialista* drew the conclusion that it was fatal to remain within legality too long, *El Debate* discovered a different 'lesson for all': revolution against a government prepared to quell it was useless and left behind only a futile wake of corpses.[145] The Socialists persisted in their view that the CEDA was the Fascist menace in Spain.[146]

After the Austrian rising the tone of *El Socialista* became even more strident and uncompromising: 'there is only one solution: the revolutionary dictatorship of the Socialist Party with the proletariat that is prepared to emancipate itself'. Socialists had now become disillusioned with the Republic, the keenest defenders of which they had claimed to be: 'Another 14 April? Much better something else: a Spanish October. The difference is this: April, frustrated hope, lost illusion; October, firm eagerness, sure solution. . . . April, citizens with ballot-papers; October, workers with rifles.'[147] Largo Caballero continued meanwhile to rouse the Socialist masses: 'Comrades! Organise the final struggle. And in this struggle, abnegation, sacrifice, heroism. The battle will be cruel and long. But if we enter it with the will to win, then we shall be able to frustrate the coercive apparatus of the bourgeois State.'[148]

The reaction of the Left Republicans to Socialist revolutionary plans was at first one of disapproval. Azaña said privately that the electoral defeat could only be undone by electoral means, and that a Socialist revolution would be a disaster whether or not it was successful: 'no Republican . . . accepts power from a victorious proletarian insurrection'.[149] Yet he did not exclude the possibility of a basically Republican revolutionary movement: 'A Republican barrier must be formed; a victorious Republic. In short, the revolution must be made. Long live the revolution! . . . We are not prepared to support a Republic imbued with Monarchism. . . . Rather than the Republic converted into the ugliness of Fascism or Monarchism . . . we prefer any catastrophe, even though it be our lot to lose.'[150] Azaña wanted to oppose to the 'elements which . . . have set out to destroy the Republic' a social-democratic coalition of Left Republicans and moderate Socialists, including Besteiro and Prieto. Although he still believed in 'a parliamentary government as the medium through which to achieve revolution . . ., the day may come when we will have no other remedy but to take up the carbine'.[151]

The Left Republicans were left in a quandary, for the revolutionary Socialists were not interested in reviving the first biennium. They now believed that 'the Republic is lost. . . . We say this: Let it die. And let us do this: Prepare ourselves for the new conquest.' Any union with Republicans was explicitly rejected: the workers would act alone.[152] 'We fight the Monarchists better without middle-men. We want no obstructions in our path.'[153] *El Socialista* stated Azaña's dilemma: 'Tied to the Socialists . . . the Republic cannot live. Separated from the Socialists the Republic is dead. Strange paradox!'[154]

Largo Caballero and the Socialists preferred a united front with the extreme Left to a revived Republican-Socialist coalition. To this end, *Alianzas Obreras* were set up to unite beneath a single executive committee all workers' parties and unions in the various areas of Spain. The Russian *soviet* was taken consciously as the model.[155] The CNT, dominated by the inflexible Anarchism of the FAI, had since 1931 opposed the Socialists in power, but in February 1934 there was a change of policy with a call for united action against Fascism in response to Largo Caballero's overtures. In many areas the CNT in fact continued to hold itself aloof from the Socialists. In March, however, the important Asturian section of the Anarcho-Syndicalists agreed to a revolutionary alliance based upon federal and Socialist principles.[156] The Communists of the PCE had also been opposed to the Socialists since 1931, dubbing their leaders 'social-Fascists'; they had also been on poor terms with the CNT. However, during 1934 the PCE too came round to the view that Fascism was the main enemy, and in September it agreed to join the *Alianzas Obreras*. The Socialist and Communist Youths had already begun to co-operate and the new alliance was consummated by a joint youth rally in Madrid on 14 September.[157]

On 7 March 1934 a 'state of alarm' was proclaimed under the Law of Public Order, and 'states of alarm and prevention' remained in force until October. They permitted the Minister of the Interior, Salazar Alonso, to deal with the strike activities of the UGT and the CNT, and with revolutionary preparations in general. The most serious threat faced by the government was the rural strike movement launched by the Socialists on 5 June with the aim of sabotaging the harvest. Salazar Alonso declared the harvest a 'national service', and only a fifth of the rural workers in fifteen provinces went on strike: the areas most affected were the Socialist strongholds of Extremadura and Jaén. The harvest collected proved to be the second best of the century.[158]

Many strikes took place in Spanish cities during 1934, but it was noticeable that two of the more important—a builders' strike in Madrid and one in the metallurgical industry—were halted by the government, which upheld the workers' claim for a 44-hour week against the employers' plans to cut wages and stage a lock-out.[159] The month of March saw a strike over the question of the use of non-UGT labour by the Alfonsine daily *ABC*; a general printers' strike ensued in the capital. The real issue at stake was whether the UGT should maintain a closed-shop in the printing industry, and with it the power to halt publication of the non-Socialist press when it suited Socialist plans. *El Debate*, which did not use Socialist labour, and *El Socialista* were the only papers to appear for a fortnight, and the strike then ended. Salazar Alonso was determined not to allow the growth of a Socialist State within the existing State.[160]

His actions, none of which contravened the Law of Public Order passed by Azaña's Republican-Socialist coalition, made him the *bête noire* of the Socialists. His aim was to uphold the authority of the State against all, be they of Left or Right. 'We shall maintain the prestige of authority', he said, 'with serenity and energy . . . because we know that without this serenity and this energy the dissolution of society would be a fact. . . . There exists a government determined to defend the State and Spain against any who desire to oppose them. . . . For me, Right and Left are the same. The law is the same for all, and I shall do my duty. . . . Neither Italy nor Russia. Spain!' Extremism could only triumph if the Republic failed to face up to its responsibility for keeping order.[161]

The Socialists attacked him for partiality to the Right, but by and large he seems to have been impartial. *Falangista* offices were closed and issues of Rightist dailies seized, though the brunt of his activity fell upon the Socialists who were openly preparing for revolution.[162] The official figures for the number of youths killed or arrested for political crimes showed that the Left had been more to blame than the Right.[163] The number of town councils dismissed for disobedience or irregularities was no greater than the number dismissed by Casares Quiroga.[164] The government and the CEDA voted for proceedings to be taken against José Antonio, as well as two Socialist deputies, for illegal possession of arms.[165] Salazar Alonso indeed continued to be energetic in seizing Socialist arms, whether in Madrid or Asturias.[166] Some people on the Right, however, remained dissatisfied with governmental unwillingness to use extra-legal methods. In September *ABC* again asked whether the State and the country could passively await the revolution threatening them.[167]

After the elections of 1933 the Basque Nationalists were confident that at last they would obtain a statute of autonomy. In December the Draft Statute was presented to the President and Lerroux, who virtually promised to support the Statute in exchange for the PNV's support for the government.[168] In February 1934 a Cortes committee was set up to examine the Statute, but already opposition to it had begun to form. The Traditionalist deputy for Álava, Oriol Urigüen, backed by 57 of the 77 town councils of the province, demanded that Álava be excluded on the grounds that the voting in November had clearly gone against the PNV.[169]

The Cortes committee, with a Rightist majority, proposed that another plebiscite be held in Álava, but Aguirre and the PNV opposed this.[170] For the CEDA, Salmón pointed out that in the original plebiscite in Álava the Statute had not obtained the two-thirds majority required by the Constitution. The Traditionalists said that they favoured autonomy on a provincial basis, but not a single statute entailing Álava's domination by the two other provinces; anyhow, the Draft Statute endangered national unity. Aguirre and the PNV argued that abstention in the plebiscite meant approval of the Statute. Álava was an integral part of the Basque region for geographical and economic reasons. The Statute's progress was blocked by early April 1934 by Rightist support for the claims of Álava. The PNV was frustrated and the Monarchists delighted.[171] Having failed to enlist *Cedista* support, the PNV now began to drift towards the Left.[172] When the *Esquerra* withdrew from the Cortes in June, the PNV also withdrew at the request of the *Generalidad*.[173]

The PNV now found that it had to defend Basque economic privileges, all that had remained of Basque liberties since 1876. The central government, at the request of many deputies, wished to reduce the tariffs on wines, upon which the local finances of the Basque Country happened to depend; it also wanted to negotiate the inclusion of an income-tax into the 'economic arrangement'. However, the Basque negotiating body, the Temporary Provincial Committees, were staffed by Radicals at odds with the Nationalist town councils, and so the PNV asked the government to be allowed to hold elections on 12 August for 'the executive committee in defence of the economic arrangement and municipal autonomy in each Basque region'—a plan which Velarde, the Radical Governor, declared illegal.[174] The government said that it would not break the 'economic arrangement' and that elections could be held in due course, but stood firm on the illegality of a locally organised poll on 12 August.[175]

Aguirre, perhaps under pressure from his extremists, went ahead with the scheme, though in fact elections were held only by a minority of town councils. Many mayors were arrested and fines imposed.[176] Samper now tried to do a deal with the PNV, promising to give way over the elections if Basques would oppose the threatened revolution; neither the PNV nor Samper's colleagues accepted the plan. Instead, the PNV held a joint rally with the *Esquerra* and the Socialists at Zumárraga on 2 September, at which Prieto was the main speaker; there followed clashes with the police and many arrests. The Socialists then tried to bring the PNV into its revolutionary plans, but the PNV declined to rise save against a dictatorship or a restoration. Aguirre still pursued a policy of sacred egoism and held aloof from non-Basque causes: 'I conceive of my people fighting for its liberty and if necessary going to the ultimate consequences. But for foreign flags, no.'[177]

On Christmas Day 1933 President Maciá died and in January the Catalan Parliament elected Companys, leader of the *Esquerra*, as the next President of Catalonia.[178] In January also, the *Lliga* withdrew from the regional parliament in protest against the *Esquerra*'s use of the police and its *Escamots* (youth movement) against the *Lliga* in the local election campaign, as well as against the lack of proportional representation.[179] In the elections on 14 January the *Esquerra* won comfortably, the *Lliga* having control of 420 of the 1,069 town councils of Catalonia.[180] Catalonia therefore remained in the eyes of the Left 'the bulwark of the Republic'.[181]

With the *Lliga* absent from parliament and with its victory at the polls behind it, the *Esquerra* now set about fulfilling its pledges to the *rabassaires*. The Law of Farming Leases stipulated that leases were to be for a minimum six-year period, with the tenant having the option of renewing it. If the owner wanted to farm the land himself, he was to pay the tenant a sum of money. Rents were to be fixed at 4 per cent of land value, and tenants could buy the land, if necessary by instalments, if they had farmed it for eighteen years.[182] This law was passed by the Catalan Parliament on 11 April; the *Lliga* protested that it attacked 'the most elementary principles of contract-law' and was not in tune with Catalan law.[183] Catalan landowners of the *Instituto Agrícola Catalán de San Isidro* visited Madrid to win support for their view that the law was illegal, and in April the *Lliga* and the CEDA brought up the matter in the Cortes and it was referred to the Court of Constitutional Guarantees.[184]

On 8 June the Court announced its verdict: the Catalan Parliament, by passing the law, had violated Article 15 of the Constitution and the Law of Agrarian Reform of 1932, and the law was therefore null and void.[185] On 12 June the *Esquerra* withdrew from the Cortes, its spokesman declaring the verdict and the slowness in transferring services 'acts of aggression' against Catalonia, which would play its historic *rôle* as 'the last defender of Spanish liberties'.[186]

The Monarchists pressed for a debate to embarrass the government and the CEDA, upon which it was dependent.[187] In the debate on 25 June, Samper announced the government's intention of reaching 'a harmonious solution based on obedience to the verdict'. Cambó and Martínez de Velasco emphasised that the Constitution and verdict had to be upheld, while Goicoechea denounced the

government for its inaction and appeasement of open rebellion
which was leading to the Balkanisation of Spain. Gil Robles was
also emphatic on enforcement of the verdict, though he explained
that his aim was not an offensive against Catalonia and its Statute.
Prieto, however, declared that Catalonia could count on the
Spanish proletariat in its battle, while Azaña said that the *Generalidad* was the last bastion of Republicanism left in Spain.[188] In the
very stormy session on 4 July, during which fist-fights broke out
and pistols were brandished, the government succeeded in ad-
journing the Cortes so as to reach a solution in accord with the
Constitution and the Statute. The CEDA voted for the government
on this condition.[189]

From July to October Companys stood his ground, offering at
most minor amendments that did not affect the content or illegality
of the law.[190] Tension was increased by an order to ban imports
of wheat from the rest of Spain, and by a meeting of Catalan
farmers in Madrid on 8 September, held under the auspices of the
Right.[191] Nevertheless Samper continued to try and negotiate with
Companys and services were still handed over to the intransigent
Generalidad.[192] In Catalonia the Councillor for the Interior, the
separatist Dencás, made military preparations.[193] On the Right,
the Alfonsines were the most ardent partisans of immediate action
against the Catalan rebels.[194] Gil Robles, for his part, hoped that
the government would solve the thorny problem satisfactorily and
went abroad for his honeymoon. In mid-August he returned, and,
after talks at San Sebastián with Lucía, Aizpún and Martínez de
Velasco, it was decided that the CEDA would not support the
government when the Cortes reopened in October if the matter
remained unsolved—a decision probably hastened by pressure
from within the party.[195]

This promise to topple the government if it produced no satisfactory results Gil Robles officially announced to cheering *Japistas*
at Covadonga on 9 September.[196] Indeed, the idea was now canvassed that a majority government, including the CEDA, should be
installed before the Cortes met, but nothing came of this owing
to some Radical opposition.[197] The Cortes was due to assemble in
October, and in late September people throughout Spain were
certain that the government would fall, but not so certain of the
consequences. *El Socialista*, perhaps still hoping that the President

would yield to pressure and keep the CEDA out of office, wrote: 'The clouds move laden towards October. What is going to happen? The truth is that no one knows. The workers must always be ready for everything. . . . Watch the red signal!'[198]

When the Cortes met on 1 October, Samper began by saying that he had found a formula for solving the Catalan question: the *Generalidad* could modify the text of its law if the Cortes were to pass a law allowing the former to legislate on the issue. Gil Robles then rose to say that this would be legalisation of rebellion and the flouting of the Court of Constitutional Guarantees—in short, capitulation. Samper had performed 'the service of showing that the ways of concord and accommodation are impossible when the same desire and the same good faith are not to be found in both parties'. Now a new policy was necessary, for which Samper was not the man; he demanded a majority government or elections. Samper next asked for other leaders to express their views, but none rose. The Agrarian Minister Cid then left the government bench amid applause. The session was suspended at 6.40 pm and the government resigned at 7.05 pm.[199]

On 2 October Lerroux was entrusted by the President to form a government, the composition of which was finally announced on 4 October. It included three *Cedistas*—Aizpún at Justice, Giménez Fernández at Agriculture, Anguera de Sojo at Labour—and Lerroux guaranteed its 'absolute obedience to the Constitution'.[200] On the same day the Left Republicans and Miguel Maura formally broke with the existing régime,[201] and the Socialist general strike began. On 6 October, with Barcelona in revolt, Lerroux declared a 'state of war' at 10 pm.[202]

In Madrid the general strike turned out to be political rather than revolutionary and lasted about ten days. The Socialists suffered from lack of arms, and no soldiers came over to them as they had hoped. A police raid on their headquarters on 4 October dealt a crucial blow to their plans. There was sporadic shooting for eight days, but the position of the government was never threatened. Young men of the JAP's *Movilización Civil* saw to it that essential services continued to operate.[203] The revolution had coincided with a meeting of the National Council of the *Falange*, at which José Antonio was elected 'National Chief'. The *Falange* demonstrated in favour of the government and offered its services to clean up the capital if given arms. This offer Lerroux refused, just as he declined to address the *Falangista* demonstrators, answering their cries of 'Long live Spain' with shouts of 'long live the Republic'.[204]

In Barcelona there was at first vacillation in the *Generalidad*. Azaña, who happened to be in Barcelona, advised the Catalans not to use violent methods.[205] However, Companys gave way to the pressure of the separatists of *Estat Català*, led by Dencás, and to a much lesser extent to the wishes of the *Alianza Obreras*, from which the all-important CNT held itself aloof. At 8 pm on 6 October Companys declared that 'Monarchistic and Fascist forces' had taken power in Madrid and that true Republicans and other Leftists had taken up arms as a result; he therefore proclaimed 'the Catalan State in the Federal Spanish Republic' and invited the formation of a provisional Republican government in Catalonia. The military commander, General Batet, remained loyal to Madrid and, after little resistance, he brought about the surrender of Companys and the *Generalidad* at 6.30 am on 7 October. Dencás escaped down a sewer.[206] The *Lliga* was in no way implicated in the rising, and its municipal councillors openly opposed the decision to revolt.[207]

The most serious revolt occurred in Asturias, commencing with the seizure of Mieres by revolutionary miners on the night of 4 October. In Asturias the Socialists and Communists of the *Sindicato Minero* had formed a united proletarian front with the Anarcho-Syndicalists of the *Confederación Regional del Trabajo*; perhaps 8,000 of their number entered Oviedo on the night of 5 October. In the province there were, according to Salazar Alonso, 1,493 soldiers, 650 Civil Guards, 490 Assault Guards and 64 policemen; these government forces had to face the larger and more determined body of miners armed with the dynamite, rifles and machine-guns they had captured from arms factories. With Asturias virtually overrun by the revolutionaries and land communications cut, the War Minister, Hidalgo, called in General Franco, whom he esteemed the ablest officer in the army. It was soon decided that the rebellion could only be crushed by experienced, professional troops. The other areas of Spain could not be denuded of their garrisons in case there were other revolutionary outbreaks. Franco therefore called upon Colonel Yagüe to lead a force of Moorish regulars to help reconquer the province from the rebels. The men of General López de Ochoa finally retook Oviedo on 12 October, but mopping-up operations went on until at least 19 October.[208]

In the Basque provinces there were risings in Socialist areas such as the mining district of Biscay. At Mondragón the revolutionaries murdered the Traditionalist deputy Oreja Elósegui. The attitude of Aguirre and the PNV was one of 'absolute abstention': the Nationalists told Radicals on 3 October that they would not rise, but neither would they lift a finger to help the government if others did. Despite this official neutrality members of the SOV, the PNV's union, did take part in the general strike in several places.[209] As a result of their attitude Aguirre and his fellow Nationalists were greeted with shouts of 'Out! Out!' when they entered the Cortes on 9 October, and Traditionalist deputies had to intervene to separate Aguirre and Calvo Sotelo, who came to blows. The Basque Nationalist deputies sat impassively while other deputies shouted 'Long live Spain!'[210]

The Cortes met on 9 October in an atmosphere charged with emotion. Gil Robles, after calling recent events a disgrace to a civilised country, said that the CEDA recognised that 'the representation of the Republic is the very incarnation of Spain'. Goicoechea, Lamamié de Clairac and Romanones, speaking for their various brands of Monarchism, were more cautious but, horrified at the revolutionary outbreaks, they all supported Lerroux to the hilt for the preservation of public order and national unity. The staunch liberal Royo Villanova solemnly declared: 'I have learnt from Castelar that the Country comes first, Liberty second and the Republic third; and because for me the Country comes first, I tell the government not to be afraid to sacrifice Liberty, if this sacrifice must be made to save the Country.' José Antonio, for his part, thanked Lerroux for releasing Spanish youth from its pessimism and for restoring to many faith in Spain. A jubilant Lerroux ended the session, from which Socialists and Left Republicans had absented themselves, with a cry of 'Long live Spain! Long live the Republic!'[211] It was the moment of triumph for Lerroux and the conservative Republic for which he stood, but if the defeated Left were silent, there were still discordant notes struck on the Right.

Monarchists preferred to give thanks for their salvation to the Army; 'not the Republican nor the Monarchist Army, but the Army of Spain'.[212]

Notes to this chapter are on pages 337–53.

Chapter 5 THE CEDA-RADICAL PARTNERSHIP
October 1934–December 1935

THE SOCIALIST and Catalan Leftist rebellions of October 1934 against the legal government, and the severance of relations by other Republicans with the system which they themselves created simply because they no longer controlled it, represented a watershed in the history of the Republic. Those who had proclaimed themselves the stoutest champions of democracy in theory rejected it in practice. A fateful precedent had been set for the future.

After the rebellion Lerroux, as the historic Republican, sought to re-establish the Republic as the régime for all Spaniards. He hoped that the defeat of the revolution would persuade Left Republicans and Socialists to form themselves into a democratic party of the Left which could play the parliamentary game against the democratic party of the Right, the CEDA. Though he had no success with the Left, the 'pact of Salamanca' with Gil Robles signified the consolidation of the régime: the reformist Catholic Right definitively accepted it to the chagrin of Monarchists. The intransigence of the Left, the President's suspicion of Lerroux and Gil Robles and, above all, the disintegration of the Radical Party in the autumn of 1935 under the weight of financial scandals, destroyed Lerroux's vision of a peaceful future. The collapse of his party was the penultimate stage in the process of eradicating the Centre. The Radical buffer between Left and Right disappeared and only the President remained trying to hold apart the two Spains and prevent full-scale civil war.

The real political debate after October 1934 took place within

the Right and concerned the methods to be used to defeat the
Left. Gil Robles remained true to his 'tactic' of possibilism and
refused to seize the chance presented by the disarray of the Left
to take possession of the State with the help of the military and
the Monarchists. He believed that dictatorship would merely make
things worse in the long run and thus sought to overcome 'the
Revolution' with advanced social measures as a preliminary to
constitutional reform. His hopes for social reform were, however,
dashed by the opposition of members of his own party and others
on the Right, as well as by the pressure of economic circumstances
and recurrent political crises. Even so, governments which his
party supported or in which it participated introduced the first law
against unemployment and achieved more in the realm of agrarian
reform than their predecessors. Gil Robles considered liberal-
democracy a lesser evil than *étatisme* even though he wanted
eventually to get a mandate to set up corporative institutions
inspired by Traditionalist ideas.

His Monarchist opponents, led by Calvo Sotelo, preferred the
solutions of Donoso to the tactics of Balmes. The October rebellion
proved to them that the 'other' Spain was not prepared to accept
a parliamentary system which allowed the Right to govern. The
golden opportunity to take full possession of the State before the
Left had time to recover must be seized. The Army was the
guarantee for the nation's future, which ought not to be gambled
away in more elections. The Left had chosen violence and was
unrepentant; many Socialists saw the rebellion as the Spanish
equivalent of the Russian revolution of 1905. Spain was therefore
in a state of civil war and the Right must get its blow in first while
conditions were favourable if catastrophe were to be averted.

From October 1934 until the fall of the first Radical-CEDA coalition government in March 1935, the principal political issue was
the repression of the revolution. The government announced that
the revolutionaries would be treated with 'neither cruelty nor
impunity'. *El Debate* subscribed to this view, but emphasised that
full use must be made of the law to punish the guilty lest they be
tempted to repeat the attempt to seize power.[1] Gil Robles said that
death-sentences should be carried out right away so that the
government could not be accused of cruelty and so that the necessary example might be set.[2] *ABC* demanded that the law be obeyed

since Spain's ills sprang from the failure of citizens and governments to heed the law. Lerroux must therefore apply the law inflexibly to the culprits: the real culprits were the promoters and leaders of the rebellion.[3]

The government tried to act calmly, but it had to contend with the emotional and vengeful atmosphere created by the events of October which had so terrified the Spanish bourgeoisie. A *Cedista* deputy said that the events were comparable to the burning of Rome by Nero and the invasion of Spain by the barbarians of the north.[4] The horror felt by Rightists was epitomised by the assertion that a monk had been burnt alive by the revolutionaries after they had cut off his legs.[5]

Gil Robles and the CEDA found themselves caught between demands for vengeance from the Right and demands for a conciliatory policy from the President. Certain Monarchist and military elements attempted to seize the opportunity presented by the abortive revolution for a *coup d'état*, but their plans were thwarted by the opposition of General Franco.[6] Monarchists really wanted the installation of an authoritarian régime based upon the Army, and Gil Robles was pressed to take action when the first death-sentences came before the cabinet at the beginning of November. Twenty-three such sentences had been passed by military courts. Article 102 of the Constitution empowered the President to commute these sentences only if the government proposed that this be done. The government opposed commutation until Lerroux, who was not thirsty for blood, allowed Alcalá-Zamora to persuade him to propose commutation of twenty-one of the sentences. Two minor revolutionaries were executed because of the 'especial ferocity' of their crimes.[7] The Monarchists wanted Gil Robles to bring down the government by withdrawing his Ministers. Gil Robles, however, feared that if he did this Alcalá-Zamora would appoint Martínez Barrio as Premier, in which case all would be lost. Generals Goded and Fanjul told Gil Robles that they would stage a *coup*, but this idea was abandoned after the garrison commanders had been consulted.[8]

In the Cortes Lerroux sought to justify his action. Those responsible for the 'wind of criminal folly [that had] passed over the whole Peninsula' in October must face the legal consequences, but the Republic, like the Monarchy before it, ought also to exercise the prerogative of mercy. Calvo Sotelo wanted officially to accuse Alcalá-Zamora of acting unconstitutionally in usurping the government's function of proposing commutation, but he failed to collect the necessary fifty deputies' signatures for his motion. Instead, he reminded Lerroux of the words of Quevedo: 'He who orders what he does not do, undoes what he orders.' The key to the survival of the Third French Republic, he said, was the stern repression of the Paris Commune. Lerroux must be as tough as Thiers if the Spanish Republic were to survive.[9] Up to the present, Calvo Sotelo argued, the Republic had only succeeded in inverting the maxim of Bishop Antonio de Guevara: 'It is the custom of Castilian kings to pardon the people and behead the leaders.'[10]

While Monarchists accused Lerroux and the CEDA of weakness, the Left began to protest at the severity of repression in Asturias. It was said that innocent people had been shot and prisoners brutally tortured by the agents of authority.[11] Until December 1934 the work of repression was carried out by Major Doval of the Civil Guard, a man with a reputation for severity, as Special Delegate of the War Ministry in Asturias.[12] The government denied that the Left's atrocity propaganda was true, and forbade publication of the charges; the Left therefore publicised its case abroad.[13]

Inside the government there was always tension. The CEDA was concerned lest the revolutionaries escape lightly and sought to increase its share of portfolios so as to be able to force Lerroux to carry out its wishes. Lerroux, Martínez de Velasco and M. Álvarez, the leaders of the other parties in the coalition, were anxious to keep their existing representation, if not to increase it. Between November 1934 and January 1935 ministerial adjustments did occur, but the government's complexion remained the same.[14]

Breaking-point was reached in March 1935 when the cabinet considered the death-sentences passed on the Socialist Deputies González Peña and T. Menéndez for their parts in the Asturian revolt. Pressed by his followers to take a firmer line than he had in November, Gil Robles demanded the liquidation of the revolution 'without vacillations, with energy, with a spirit of justice, without making distinctions between delinquents'.[15] A government crisis seemed inevitable, so he announced that the existing coalition should be maintained with portfolios distributed rather differently.[16] In an attempt to make the most of the opportunity, the CEDA on 26 March sent a public memorandum to Lerroux on how to reduce unemployment.[17] Alcalá-Zamora again urged Lerroux to commute the death-sentences and the Radical majority in the cabinet agreed to do this. On 27 March *El Debate*'s editorial suggested that the crisis could be averted if Lerroux agreed to implement the unemployment proposal; by implication, the CEDA would turn a blind eye to commutation of the death-sentences. Gil Robles and the CEDA, however, for once dissociated themselves from *El Debate*. When the cabinet next met, on 29 March, the seven Radicals voted against the sentences. The *Cedista*, Agrarian and Liberal-Democrat Ministers immediately resigned.[18]

The President entrusted the formation of a new government to Lerroux, but he failed to reconcile the conflicting demands of his coalition partners. Martínez de Velasco failed for the same reason. The basic clash was between the CEDA, demanding six portfolios, and the Agrarians, demanding four; both parties wanted the Ministries of War and the Interior. Neither Lerroux nor Alcalá-Zamora would accept these terms. Lerroux finally formed an interim government with some of the President's friends on 3 April. Since it could not hope to secure a parliamentary majority, the President suspended the Cortes for a month.[19] Monarchists were delighted at the CEDA's apparent failure; Calvo Sotelo's organ announced that the tactic had failed completely,[20] while Goicoechea hoped for a reunited Right.[21]

However, Lerroux was determined to reconstitute the governmental bloc while the Cortes were suspended.[22] This was also Gil Robles's aim: armed with another vote of confidence from the CEDA's National Council, he asked for more portfolios or elections.[23] By the end of April Gil Robles, Lerroux, Martínez de Velasco and M. Álvarez—'the Four'—had reached agreement among themselves.[24] Alcalá-Zamora was still something of a stumbling-block. He distrusted Gil Robles and was hostile to the CEDA because he considered it insufficiently Republican and because he had ambitions of his own. He also wanted to be the recognised leader of the Republican Right.[25] He tried to break up the CEDA with the same technique that he had used to part Martínez Barrio from Lerroux. He made tempting propositions to Giménez

Fernández, to Lucía and to Gil Robles himself, but without success.[26] He therefore had to accept on 6 May a government led by Lerroux which included five *Cedistas*, one of whom was Gil Robles at the War Ministry.[27]

The question of how to deal with the active revolutionaries was not the only problem that the Radical-CEDA government faced after October 1934. There was also the problem posed by the passive revolutionaries—the Republicans who had publicly severed relations with those in power. The government quickly introduced censorship of speeches made in the Cortes. Despite this, Besteiro advised the reformist Socialists who, like himself, had taken no part in the rebellion, to return to the Cortes. The majority of the Socialist deputies, however, rejected his counsel. *Izquierda Republicana*, the *Esquerra*, *Unión Republicana* and the Conservatives also boycotted the Cortes. When the government lifted this form of censorship in mid-November 1934, the deputies of the Left and M. Maura again began to attend sessions.[28]

Their return was welcomed by Lerroux, but was not to the liking of Monarchists and many *Cedistas*. The Right therefore made efforts to eliminate Azaña from the political scene. It was widely believed among Rightists that he had encouraged the rising in Barcelona, but it soon transpired that the evidence for this was lacking. The Monarchists therefore demanded that both Azaña and Casares Quiroga stand trial for providing Portuguese revolutionaries with arms during the first biennium; these arms had been sent to Asturias in 1934.[29] The Court of Constitutional Guarantees in fact acquitted Azaña on 6 April 1935. A Monarchist motion to reopen the matter in July failed to obtain the requisite number of votes in the Cortes.[30] The Court did condemn Companys and the former Councillors of the *Generalidad* to thirty years in prison and exclusion from public office.[31]

The Catalan Statute was also an important political issue after October 1934. On the eve of the rising in Barcelona Gil Robles had declared that he favoured revision of the Statute and 're-stricted autonomy'.[32] When the Cortes met on 9 October the Monarchists, as expected, proposed its abolition. Lerroux opposed this, though he conceded that it could be modified by constitutional means. Ventosa for the *Lliga* announced that his party intended to defend the Statute in its existing form and pointed out that the *Lliga* had 'practised respect for the integrity of Spain' by opposing the rising of 6 October.[33] The Monarchists nevertheless still aimed to do away with the Statute. The *Lliga*, they claimed, really did not differ from the *Esquerra* in its aims; its methods were more subtle. They were anxious lest this golden opportunity to correct past mistakes should be missed.[34] *ABC* wrote that Catalonia could legitimately aspire only to 'purely administrative local and provincial autonomy', which entailed the 'pure and simple repeal' of the Statute.[35] Gil Robles restated the quasi-Traditionalist view of the CEDA. The Traditionalists themselves, like the Alfonsines, Agrarians, Liberal-Democrats and José Antonio, called for its abolition.[36] On 11 December the Monarchist motion for its abolition suffered defeat although many of the government's usual supporters abstained. Lerroux, buttressed by Gil Robles, held firm to the principle of autonomy: 'we have no right to chastise a [whole] people'.[37]

The Radical-CEDA alternative to abolition was suspension of the Statute until the Cortes, at the suggestion of the government, should vote for the gradual restoration of the powers of the *Generalidad*. In the meantime a Governor-General was to preside over the *Generalidad*'s executive council. The government undertook to set up a committee to decide on the transfer of services within three months; a special law was to deal with the controversial services of public order, justice and education. Such were the terms of the Law of 2 January 1935 establishing a provisional régime in Catalonia.[38]

Portela Valladares, a prominent Freemason whom the CEDA disliked, was appointed Governor-General.[39] In April 1935 Pich Pon, the leader of the Catalan Radicals, became President of the *Generalidad* and Lerroux's interim government decreed the return to Barcelona of all services previously transferred, with the exception of public order.[40]

The leaders of the Right held different views on Catalan autonomy, as on most subjects. Gil Robles believed that Catalonia was 'a region with distinguishable characteristics and has a right to an autonomy . . . that does not bring Catalonia and Spain into conflict'.[41] Calvo Sotelo, however, interpreted the 'definitive dogma' of the motto of the Catholic Kings, 'Spain united and in order', as permitting only administrative variety. Political auto-

nomy in the hands of the *Lliga* was for him no better than rule
by the *Esquerra*: 'The Statute is a vehicle for disintegration. . . .
Political autonomy leads to secessionism. As has happened in
Ireland.'[42]

The Radical-CEDA governments had to face also the legacy of
Azaña's biennium in matters of agrarian reform, labour legislation
and education. From April 1934 until September 1935 the
Ministry of Public Instruction was almost continuously in the
care of Liberal-Democrats. This was probably more by design
than by accident, for their tenure provided an assurance to both
Catholics and laicists that neither educational system would be
destroyed. In general terms, the cautious laicisers Villalobos and
Dualde continued to build up state schools, albeit at a slower rate
than that of the first biennium. Catholic and private educational
establishments were left to their own devices. This compromise
satisfied the partners in the coalition, although in December 1934
Villalobos resigned after *Cedistas* had sharply criticised his plans
for the organisation of secondary education.[43] During 1935 the
expansion of laicist education fell a victim to the general policy of
economic retrenchment, which was not a cause for gloom among
Cedistas. The laicising policies of Azaña's governments were then
considerably diluted and eventually came to a virtual halt, but it
cannot be said that any effort was made to turn back the clock
during the second biennium. The CEDA respected the Constitution.[44]

Giménez Fernández's first task as Minister of Agriculture was
to draft a law for the protection of *yunteros* and small farmers. The
purpose of the law was to remedy unemployment in Extremadura
by ensuring that those with little or no land who owned ploughs
or other implements should have sufficient land to make a living.
In general, the idea was to extend until 31 July 1935 the occupations that had taken place under Domingo's decree of November
1932 and Del Río's law of February 1934, except where the land
was unsuitable for sowing. Landowners were told that occupation
did not mean expropriation, while those *yunteros* likely to be
evicted in 1935 were promised that their names would be put on
the Institute of Agrarian Reform's waiting-list.[45]

Giménez Fernández was determined to take action 'that redounds to the benefit of Spain and the Republic. . . . I cannot

forget that I am a professor of canon law and I uphold a canonical concept of property. That is to say that since all property must be based on the concept that possessions have been given to us as a means of aiding human nature, all use of possessions that exceeds what is necessary for covering those needs for which property was created may be abusive, and certainly is abusive when coinciding with a state of extreme need in our brethren.' The Minister obeyed the dictates of his conscience: 'I do things because I must do them.'[46] Agrarians and Monarchists complained that the hopes of Extremeño landowners and stock-breeders had been dashed by a 'revolutionary' and 'demagogic' law that, like Domingo's decree, ignored the rights of property. Redistribution of land was not to be equated with social justice and would not prevent Marxist revolution: 'let us not abandon the Civil Guard and let us arm ourselves to the teeth'.[47] Some landed *Cedistas* opposed their colleague's law though Gil Robles supported it.[48] It was passed on 20 December 1934 by 203 votes to 30.[49]

Giménez Fernández next brought before the Cortes a law on rural leases which he had inherited from Del Río. Its purpose was to assure tenants of long leases, compensation for improvements done by them, rents fixed by arbitration tribunals and eviction only for non-payment of rent. At the same time he introduced his own law allowing tenants to acquire the land they farmed from the owners after twelve or sixteen years (depending on the nature of the land) for a sum agreed between them or fixed by independent arbitration.[50] The Minister's plans caused a storm of protest from landowners, represented in the Cortes by Agrarians, Monarchists and conservative *Cedistas* like Casanueva and Rodríguez Jurado. They said that these laws would subvert tenancy-agreements, for many tenants would, in effect, be immune from eviction, which would make the possibility of their buying the land a certainty. Landlords under this system were sure to get controlled rents unfair to the landlord. The two laws would lead to owners being relieved of their property without even the guarantee of proper compensation.[51] For Rodríguez Jurado, President of the Landowners' Association, irrigation was the only permissible way of creating new smallholdings.[52] The Minister's opponents were not impressed by his appeals to the teaching of the Church. Lamamié de Clairac even declared: 'If the Minister of Agriculture goes on quoting Papal Encyclicals to defend his drafts, you can be sure that we shall end up by becoming Greek schismatics.'[53]

Giménez Fernández's ideal was that those who farmed the land should also own it. The only way to create a large number of smallholdings, he argued, was to transfer the ownership of rented land, because the State could not afford to spend vast sums on irrigation or compensation for expropriation. He wanted the minimum duration of a lease to be six years, but he thought it fair that owners should be able to farm one of their holdings themselves.[54] In the debates in the Cortes his main supporters were his predecessor in the Ministry Del Río, the Radical landowner Álvarez Mendizábal and a *Cedista* deputy for León, Álvarez Robles.[55] Outside the Cortes the JAP made the Minister their hero, 'genuine representative of the spirit of *Acción Popular*'.[56]

However, some other *Cedistas* saw him in a different light and dubbed him a 'white Bolshevik'. Gil Robles had to mediate between the social-Catholic and conservative wings of his party in order to avoid a split which would put his political aims in jeopardy.[57] As a result a modified law on rural leases was passed on 14 March which reduced the minimum duration of leases to four years, left arbitration to the courts and permitted buyers of land to evict tenants and farm it themselves.[58] For the time being the law for the acquisition of land by tenants fell by the wayside. Giménez Fernández and the conservative wing of the CEDA were at loggerheads. Although Gil Robles himself favoured the Minister's laws, as leader of the party he had to keep it in one piece.[59] The price of unity soon became known: Giménez Fernández was not reappointed as Minister of Agriculture when the CEDA re-entered the government in May 1935 even though his work was clearly unfinished.

That 'dynamism' in the Ministry of Agriculture, which Calvo Sotelo had seen as the only redeeming feature of the first Radical-CEDA government,[60] disappeared with the appointment of the conservative Agrarian Velayos in May 1935. The law on rural leases proved in practice to be a boon for *conservaduros*. By July 1935 many evictions had taken place and a mass of notices to quit had been given by landlords, who everywhere made unscrupulous use of the provision that allowed tenants to be evicted so that the owners could farm the land directly. In most cases the landlords had no intention of doing this and simply took advantage of their tenants' ignorance of their legal rights. Velayos refused to intervene to stop these abuses.[61] The modified law passed in March 1935 did not serve the intentions of its original sponsors. Though its wording prompted attempts to evict tenants, the real trouble was that local authorities of all political persuasions neither enforced its provisions nor made any effort to inform tenants of their rights. In any case, tenants were unlikely to be able to afford litigation. After Velayos's declaration that he would not intervene, the number of evictions soared into tens of thousands.[62]

Almost the sole concern of Velayos, as of Monarchists and his fellow Agrarians, was the repeal of the Law of Agrarian Reform of 1932. Del Río had continued to enforce the law in 1934 and Giménez Fernández did the same, though by a decree of January 1935 he halted expropriations of Grandees' estates while continuing, to the distress of Monarchists, to carry out confiscations already ordered.[63] Although the actions of Del Río and Giménez Fernández were not exactly spectacular, they achieved more in the realm of land redistribution than their predecessors.[64] Agrarian reform ground to a halt under Velayos; more had not previously been achieved owing to the inefficiency of the Institute.[65]

Various drafts modifying the law of 1932 were discussed in committee and debates did not begin in the Cortes until July 1935. The aim of Velayos's draft was to reform the law of 15 September 1932 and thus to promote a return to normality in the countryside and a rise in property-values. Its main feature was to abolish any expropriation of land without compensation. The method of valuing land for purchase, like the method of compensation, was modified to the landowners' advantage. Certain types of estates were exempted from the provisions of the law, and the type of settlement to be adopted was the smallholding. The Cortes committee made it clear that lands hitherto expropriated were to be considered as temporarily occupied. If after six years the settler had shown himself to be a capable farmer, he would be able to buy the land over a period at a price fixed by the Institute.[66]

While some Monarchists and Agrarians grumbled that the draft should simply have stated that the law of 1932 had been abolished in its entirety, others on the Right were less happy. Giménez Fernández and Álvarez Robles clearly did not like the draft, and eventually gained sufficient support among *Cedistas*, Radicals and Progressives for the inclusion of clauses on the accession of tenant-farmers to property and the tax-free family patrimony. The main opposition to the draft in the Cortes came from Del Río, José Antonio and, for the Left Republicans, Sánchez-Albornoz. They all argued that agrarian reform, in the form of land redistribution, was an urgent necessity in Spain, and that Velayos's law was merely a disguise for its nullification. The State could not afford to buy estates at their full market-value. Settlers could not be expected to purchase their holdings without falling completely into the hands of usurers. Sánchez-Albornoz warned conservatives that if there were no legal reform, revolution would quickly follow. José Antonio calculated that with the Institute's expenditure limited as it was to 50,000,000 pesetas a year, it would take 160 years to buy up the land scheduled for redistribution. He also advocated collective settlements on unirrigated land. Velayos, however, stuck to his view that 'a liberal Republic cannot proceed against one social class'. The Left Republicans therefore withdrew from the Cortes on 25 July. This reform of agrarian reform, promulgated on 1 August 1935, represented a triumph for the conservatives, and, in the atmosphere of general economic re-trenchment, brought the redistribution of land to a standstill.[67]

In the realm of social policy, the *Cedista* Ministers made little or no headway. Before October 1934 many mixed juries had ceased to function; the confusion was increased thereafter by the action taken against members of the UGT for revolutionary activities. In December 1934 the conservative *Cedista* Anguera de Sojo suspended the juries' activities for a month so that they could be re-staffed with non-revolutionary workers' representatives,[68] but it would seem that the system of labour arbitration to a large extent collapsed.[69] The building and metallurgical industries went back to a 48-hour week and the dismissal of workers for having taken part in revolutionary strikes was fairly general despite ministerial exhortations to employers not to do this.[70] When D. de Madariaga protested against the vengeful attitude of employers, Anguera de Sojo replied that he would not fight 'Red Socialism' with 'White Socialism'.[71] In the countryside in particular, employers took their revenge by slashing wages. The Ministry of Labour was flooded with petitions about infringements of wage-agreements by employers. Federico Salmón, the social-Catholic who became Minister in May 1935, made a brave attempt to stem the tide of reaction, but was swamped by the sheer volume of complaints.[72]

Salmón's aim was to make the mixed juries into institutions of social harmony and social justice by appointing civil servants with a legal training as their presidents, but this was a mere paper reform: the UGT boycotted elections for new juries. The Minister virtually admitted that, in so far as they still existed, the juries had been turned into instruments for social exploitation.[73] He also introduced a law to counter unemployment which stipulated that 200,000,000 pesetas would be spent on public works, social insurance and bounties for firms undertaking public works, and that committees would be set up to direct long-term policies.[74] Such plans were, however, subject to the overall economic situation, which was far from healthy. The law aided recovery in the building industry, but, on the whole, little impression was made on the level of unemployment, statistics about which were in any case suspect. Government grants tended to end up in the pockets of town councillors.[75]

The social ideas of the CEDA, such as the family wage, remained utopian theories. Salmón sadly commented that 'if the doctrines of St. Thomas were to be applied in all their purity they would lead to anarchy'.[76] Gil Robles still castigated *conservadurismo* with words,[77] but these were not matched by actions. The CEDA was failing to live up to its promises of killing revolution by kindness.

After October 1934 the government of the Republic was still dependent on collaboration between Radicals and *Cedistas*. Though Lerroux and Gil Robles had different views about the purpose of the coalition, the two parties worked together quite smoothly until the demise of the Radicals in the autumn of 1935. Both leaders had to defend the arrangement against attacks from their opponents. The three stages of the CEDA's tactic were: firstly, to support Lerroux; then to collaborate with him; and eventually to supplant him in power.[78] Gil Robles pointed out to Monarchists that, since he had not enough deputies to govern alone, his party had to unite with groups outside the Right in order to serve Spain: 'It is said that we are working with Masons. . . . Christ ate with sinners.'[79] He would not allow his party to adopt 'the catastrophic tactic' of others, for 'after the Dictatorship . . . came political revolution. A new dictatorship could produce, after a period of tranquillity, social revolution, a Communist Republic.' The main-tenance of the governmental bloc was therefore the only solution; its ends were 'to make social revolution impossible, to undertake a work of national reconstruction, to plan the reform of the Constitution'.[80]

For his part, Lerroux was willing to co-operate with the CEDA and promised it the 'loyal collaboration' of Radicals, if it should take power, on the understanding that it kept 'within Republican legality'.[81] While he still believed that the CEDA should be the conservative party of the Republic, he also thought that Spain needed the formation of 'a great party of the Left' which could take power on suitable occasions.[82] Lerroux's ideal was then that the Radicals should hold the balance between Right and Left. When both had been brought within the Republican fold Lerroux could retire from the scene with dignity.[83]

On 23 June 1935 Lerroux and Gil Robles put their relationship on a firm basis by concluding the 'governmental pact of Sala-manca'. Gil Robles said that the CEDA had not renounced its ideals, but would realise its programme 'with a healthy possi-bilism'. He and Lerroux would continue to work together 'for a long time', and when the moment came to part they would go their own ways 'not as enemies, nor even as adversaries, but as faithful friends'. Lerroux recalled that he had offered his party's friendship to Left and Right, but the Left had spurned his offer. He had been a revolutionary, but now declared his incompatibility with those who appealed to violence. The union with the CEDA had been of use in 'laying the foundations for the new institutions, for saving society'. He solemnly swore not to abandon the coalition as long as the CEDA also supported it.[84]

Lerroux and the Monarchists were agreed that Gil Robles had definitely committed himself to the Republic, thereby finally con-solidating it.[85] Lerroux tried to raise his standing with the Left by drawing attention to his achievements. His work of 'widening the base of the Republic' was proving successful. The régime was now 'definitively constituted' with the CEDA's adherence to it: 'Let them tell me upon what I have had to compromise. . . . Who have evolved? They [ie the CEDA] or we? . . . They.'[86] Lerroux and Gil Robles reaffirmed their pact at a dinner in Madrid on 9 October.[87] Monarchists observed how the claws of an old lion were slowly crushing the delicate young bones of a simple guileless dove.[88]

Gil Robles's intention was to govern with the Radicals, implement some of the CEDA's social policies, prepare a generally acceptable draft for constitutional reform, and then, after 9 December 1935, go to the country to get the draft approved.[89] Preparations for reform began in January 1935 when the President advocated moderate changes, such as a second chamber and the toning down of the clauses on religion and the socialisation of property. There was much argument between the partners in the coalition and it was not until July that a draft prepared by the Liberal-Democrat Dualde was ready. It proposed the revision of 44 of the 125 Articles of the Constitution.[90] Since it was the function of the next Cortes to draft the new texts, Dualde's proposal only provided general guide-lines.

The more important features of his draft included rectification of the articles about regional autonomy to keep public order in the sphere of the central power and prevent statutes endangering national unity. The religious clauses (notably Article 26) were to be modified to permit a concordat, to soften the rigidity of provisions on religious matters and to disentangle ordinary legislation from the Constitution. The text of Article 44, allowing expropriation without compensation, was to be thoroughly revised, as was the article on state education. A senate which could censure the government was to be created, and it, with the lower chamber, would elect the President of the Republic. The President's powers were to be re-defined, so that he might have more freedom regarding dissolution of the Cortes, but less opportunity to meddle in day-to-day government. The Senate would take over many of the functions of the Court of Constitutional Guarantees. The articles concerning amnesties, pardons, budgets and the procedure for constitutional reform were to be amended. This document satisfied the coalition partners and the President, but the Left flatly refused to consider any revision of its constitution.[91]

Gil Robles spoke freely after October 1934 about his policies and his ideas for Spain's future. In his pronouncements he showed himself to be a reformist; he adopted a tone different from that of the electoral campaign of 1933. Yet, despite this important change of emphasis, his long-term aims remained unchanged: the complete transformation of existing institutions.[92] His thinking was based upon a traditionalist view of history. He expressed nostalgia for pre-liberal corporative life dominated by 'the religious sentiment of Catholicity', and he desired a return to its principles. However, for reasons of human imperfection, the old organic society had been undermined by eighteenth-century rationalism and given the *coup de grâce* by the French revolution. The consequence had been the atomisation of society and political life. Political parties and associations for class-warfare had become the only realities. Rationalism and revolutionary individualism had produced the fruit of liberal-democracy, which, by virtue of its origins, was unacceptable to Catholic philosophy. Although English constitutionalism was not for export, since it did not accord with continental traditions, one must nevertheless recognise that democracy, defined as the incorporation of the people into the governance of the State, was 'a definitive conquest of modern times'. However desirable a return to medieval political organisation might be in theory, in practice one had to reckon with reality; and the reality was that liberalism, as the variety of political parties demonstrated, had shattered the old consensus upon which corporativism had been based.

The excesses of political liberalism had provoked a doctrinal reaction which had resulted in the absorption by the State of all individual and social activities. The philosophy behind this phenomenon could be termed 'Hegelian pantheism'. The practical result of such doctrines was 'the exacerbation of nationalist sentiments', leading to 'pagan nationalism' and 'divinisation of the State'. An inevitable consequence of this was a system of State Socialism with the unrestricted growth of the powers of the central organs of government and 'nullification, not only of the individual personality, but of the natural societies anterior and even superior to the State'. This totalitarian phenomenon was epitomised by the Fascist formula: 'Everything in the State, nothing outside the State, nothing against the State.' It was just as necessary to react against this political trend, which was likely to appeal to the young and also conflicted with Catholic orthodoxy, as it was to react against decadent nineteenth-century liberalism. He told Calvo

Sotelo in the Cortes that he feared the excesses of individualism but he feared much more the excesses of *étatisme*.[93]

Some form of corporativism was then desirable, but any political evolution must start out from the reality of parliamentarianism with its political parties. The suppression of political parties, however noble the motives for doing this, would merely bring about the absolute predominance of one party, whose programme and principles would be identified with those of the State itself. The legal existence of other parties would be thus terminated, but the ideological divisions which they reflected would not die with them. A dictatorship would not create a national consensus. The political transformation of a people could not be decreed from above: this was 'a dangerous illusion'. Bottai had recognised that Italian corporativism, despite favourable circumstances, had made little real progress in this field. Fascist corporativism was the artificial creation of a dictatorial power; were this power to be removed, the whole edifice would probably collapse. The same criticism applied to the German régime. In short, to conquer the State and impose corporativism on a society unprepared for it was no solution. Such an *étatiste* reaction to the anarchy of liberal individualism was understandable, but was likely to degenerate into mere tyranny without effecting any real change in society.

Therefore 'the problem, which we could call post-democratic, is not one of conquest, but of organisation. . . . I am a decided partisan of deliberative assemblies. More than once I have recalled the famous phrase that "a bad chamber is worth more than a good *camarilla*". . . . The excesses of parliamentarism and the abuses of so-called popular assemblies have brought down upon the representative principle the discredit which ought, in justice, only to fall upon parliamentarist errors. . . . A parliamentarist? . . . I am not such in the derogatory sense of a parliament which neither governs nor permits government, which neither administers nor permits administration. But I am a partisan of political representation, of deliberative chambers with popular representation. . . . I am aware of the multitude of its defects, but I am not liable to the madness of trying to overthrow Parliament. It is very easy to undermine the foundations of institutions, and difficult afterwards to replace efficiently the function that they fulfilled.'

In the near future, he thought that the executive power should

o

be strengthened; popular assemblies should be reduced 'to their specific legislative function and limited criticism of governmental work'; subsidiary social bodies should share in the work of government, and administration and services should be decentralised. 'Alongside parliaments of ideology, which will be necessary while parties exist, and parties will exist while there are differences of opinion among men, it is necessary to create the representation of interests.' One way of doing this would be to resurrect the defunct National Economic Council with representatives of economic interests, workers and employers. The Council could legislate on economic matters, the laws being voted without debate by Parliament 'because parliamentarians have no economic competence'. It would therefore become 'a co-legislative organ', a second chamber.

Gil Robles's long-term aim was a corporative system based upon the principles of Christian public law. 'I am not attempting to create a new State right away. I want to take existing reality, with its indubitable errors, and transform it. . . . I do not want to have recourse under any circumstances to foreign, dramatic and exotic visions.' A strong State was necessary to enforce the law and as a pre-condition for economic development; it must also be above interests. It must be neither tyrannical nor absorbent, but must protect, stimulate and co-ordinate the efforts of different social forces in the collective interest. The goal was a *via media* between totalitarian excess and unrestrained individualism, a State in harmony with society. The State could encourage the growth of, and indeed give the 'initial impulse' to the re-creation of subsidiary social bodies. However, to be fecund and lasting, changes in the political structure must be the work principally of society, and secondarily of the State: 'The political transformation of a people has to be the product of evolution.' Such evolution would be gradual because the new order had to be created from below, by society itself. 'We seek something more organic. . . . But first it is necessary for collective and syndical feeling to be strengthened. It is a very slow business, which sometimes takes centuries.'[94]

The new State's structure and the ideal society of the distant future would be true to Catholic principles and Spanish traditions. Their precise details could only be the product of experience gained during the long process of evolution by a society prepared to renew itself and which put its faith 'in a glorious destiny' and not 'in messianic human hopes'. Having accepted the Christian concept of the State in principle, Gil Robles admitted that 'difficulties arise when one comes down to earth' to apply the concept. Nevertheless, in general, 'true corporativism is a complete system. It embraces the economic, the social and the political order; it has as its basis men grouped according to the community of their natural interests and social functions; and it aspires to the public and distinct representation of such organisms, as the coping and pinnacle of the system.'

The great keynotes of Gil Robles's policy were 'possibilism' and gradualism: all depended on the pace at which the Spanish people could be schooled in the idea of the great enterprise. The ultimate goal was clearly quite different from liberal-democracy; democracy, indeed, was only 'a transitory means' to the corporative end. In the final analysis, however, it was up to the electorate to accept or reject this blue-print for the future. 'Will the peoples return to those immutable and eternal principles, unifiers of consciences, without loss of liberty? I do not know, though I hope so. . . . Meanwhile, we do not deceive ourselves. In Spain there is in the political sphere no reality other than parties.'

Gil Robles was trying to adapt Traditionalism to the age of democracy. His debt to the Carlist heritage was perhaps most obvious with regard to regionalism. Gil Robles believed that the region and the municipality were 'natural personalities' within the nation, which could include several races. 'The region, within the sovereign State, is a public personality perfectly defined by tradition and history. It has the faculty for self-government, which I call autarchy, with two limitations: the capacity to rule itself and the collective interest of the nation, which is above all regional interests. . . . Regional languages must be respected and, furthermore, be lovingly preserved.' He was firmly opposed to anything smacking of separatism.[95]

Gil Robles's regionalism, like that of the Traditionalists, was anachronistic. Anything more than administrative autonomy conceded to the regions was bound to resemble federalism, which, since it would imply the regions' right to sovereignty, he rejected. During 1934 and 1935 relations between the Basque Nationalists and the Right deteriorated still further. The PNV's Draft Statute made no progress in the Cortes, and the party remained essentially separatist.[96] There was no common ground. In October 1934 the CEDA opened branches in San Sebastián and Bilbao to try and draw support away from the PNV.[97] However, in so far as the PNV was in decline in 1935, it was to the Left that it lost followers.[98]

October 1934 also saw the foundation of *Acción Popular Catalana* under the leadership of Cirera Voltá. Its manifesto proclaimed 'the consubstantial union of Catalonia with the rest of Spain'—hostility to separatism but not to autonomy.[99] The group quickly absorbed a local agrarian party, but it was weakened almost from the start by internal dissension. In essence, it was a group representing conservative interests in the countryside who saw their best chance for protection in the minimum of autonomy for their region.[100] It attracted politicians from other Catalan parties but, despite its participation in the government of the *Generalidad* in 1935, it made no real headway.[101] The only achievement attributable to the CEDA in regional affairs was the law of December 1934 re-establishing the *Diputación foral* in Navarre, a law introduced at the behest of Aizpún and Traditionalists.[102]

During 1935 Gil Robles continued to experience difficulties with his youth movement, Pérez de Laborda's JAP. These young men in a hurry were liable to be seduced by the simpler authoritarian policies of Calvo Sotelo, José Antonio and the Traditionalists. In order to keep their allegiance, Gil Robles was constrained to allow them a certain independence,[103] even though this sometimes led to some discrepancy between the pronouncements of the CEDA and the JAP. The Left seized on *Japista* deviations to justify its continuing distrust of Gil Robles 'the anti-Republic . . ., a Catholic Fascist' pursuing a course 'exactly the same as Dollfuss in Austria'.[104]

Gil Robles tried to cover up differences by saying that the JAP was the vanguard of the CEDA, which moved in the same direction at a slower and surer pace.[105] Embarrassing statements were dismissed as 'young people's business which is of no importance'.[106] In November 1935, however, he decided to talk seriously to wayward spirits. The JAP's views were being used by others as 'a battering-ram' against himself and the party. He declared his solidarity with the JAP, though not with its 'juvenile paroxysms', understandable and even desirable though these might be. *Japistas* must guard against 'accidental indiscipline which could disturb the spiritual communion of our ideals. . . . Sometimes you do not seem to see the way clearly; sometimes external aspects of other apparently more gaudy attitudes seem to seduce you. . . . To do great things you do not need to extend your arms. . . . You do not need to have a uniform, which is often no more than an external covering for internal deformity.'[107]

The JAP continually affirmed its loyalty and obedience to 'the political genius and virile energy' of Gil Robles in extravagant terms: 'Providence has presented us with the vigorous personality of a great *caudillo* and guide: the *Jefe*, our *Jefe*, the *Jefe* of Spain; he is one of those men whom God gives to nations every two or three hundred years to devise their happiness.'[108] For all that, *Japistas* thought that their 'intrepid mission in the van' allowed them loudly to demand the 'new State'. There was henceforth to be no thought of rotation in power with Azaña and the Socialists, nor would they permit 'shameful' revision of some parts of the Constitution: 'we want all power for the *Jefe*' and 'a total reform of the Constitution . . ., another Constitution!'[109] The CEDA could never be 'a party in the style of the German Centre and the Italian People's parties'; it was 'a National Movement' for 'moral and material regeneration'. It was the JAP's function to counteract any tendency to return to the old politics of rotation of parties in power; Pérez de Laborda said he would resign if this were to happen.[110]

The JAP's enemies were 'Spain's enemies: Marxism, egoistic capitalism, *caciquismo*, separatism and Masonry'. Within the CEDA, the JAP's duty was to oppose 'those who imagined that our movement was to be in the service of employers, firms, vested interests. . . . Let them stay outside, the Pharisees, the usurers who call themselves Rightists because they beat their breasts at the one o'clock mass!'[111] Spain's salvation would come from the 'workers of the countryside, hardened by the sun', who ate 'simple foods', and not from the university students of the *Falange*.[112]

Though it maintained that 'the Spanish Fascists have no *raison d'être*', the JAP shared some of the *Falange*'s views, but objected to its violence, the allegedly Marxist implications of its economic policies and the 'connection of its leaders with the anti-traditional "Generation of '98" '. The *Falange* had no masses and 'a surfeit of pedantic intellectuality'; José Antonio was 'an intelligent lad, qualified, a good lawyer. But nothing more.'[113] Traditionalism was also inadequate: 'We do not stagnate in the past or mourn for the return of our magnificent sixteenth century. . . . Drawing inspiration from our traditional spirit we think of the twenty-first century.' With Calvo Sotelo's programme they were in basic agreement and at times seem to have preferred it to the CEDA's; ideally, however, 'the illustrious Spaniard' ought to be the *Jefe*'s Minister of Finance. The men of *Renovación Española*, on the other hand, suffered from 'monarchical thrombosis'.[114]

Loyal to the *Jefe*, the JAP intended to uphold its own intensely Catholic position; yet it flirted with *Falangista* slogans. 'Imperialism' was invoked by *Japistas*, as were the heady slogans '¡ *Arriba España!*' and the scarcely grammatical '¡ *A por los 300!*'[115] Their manifesto in December 1935 showed that they were still at odds with Gil Robles's views, and the document hinted that *Japistas*' faith and enthusiasm would evaporate if the CEDA did not stop behaving like any other parliamentarist party.[116] *Falangistas* and *Requetés*, however, had only contempt for the legalism of the 'soft' young men of the JAP.[117]

Most of the CEDA's mass following came from the peasantry of Castile and León, where Catholic agrarian organisations were strongest.[118] Catholics agreed that the failure of the revolution and the action taken against Socialist *Casas del Pueblo* provided a great opportunity for winning over the proletariat.[119] Catholic and other non-revolutionary unions therefore formed the *Frente Nacional del Trabajo* in October 1934 as an independent non-political grouping to defend workers against employers, Marxism and anarchy, under the leadership of the metal-worker Incháusti. The FNT claimed to have won over in the autumn of 1934 several unions in Andalusia hitherto affiliated to the UGT.[120]

Catholic working-class leaders, however, did not see eye to eye on what ought to be done. In November 1934 Ruiz Alonso resigned from *Acción Obrerista* because he believed that all efforts should be concentrated on the creation of professional and Catholic unions not affiliated to any political party. In his opinion, it was a mistake to try and build up a national, anti-Marxist workers' party. *Acción Obrerista* nevertheless continued to campaign under D. de Madariaga's leadership and extended its organisation in the south.[121] A parallel attempt was made to spread a social-Christian outlook among employers with the foundation in November 1934 of the *Asociación Patronal Católica de España*,[122] but it did not prove successful.

In December 1935 the FNT held its congress in Madrid. It was attended by representatives of 276,389 members of the Catholic CNSCO, the *Falange*'s CONS, the CET, the FET and other local free unions. The outcome was the creation of the *Confederación Española de Sindicatos Obreros*, from which the CONS held itself aloof.[123] The CESO was affiliated to no political party and was a purely professional organisation with an aversion to political strikes. Although its programme was based upon Christian ethico-religious principles and it was affiliated to the Utrecht International of Christian Trade Unions, it rejected confessionalism.[124]

Catholic and professional trade-unionism remained, however, a delicate bloom in Spain. Probably most of those who joined after October 1934 did so, not from conviction, but simply to find employment. As the CEDA's Minister of Labour remarked, 'the unions hostile to the class-struggle have not yet generated in workers the conviction that they are honestly going to defend their rights and interests with independence and truth'.[125] Madariaga's and Ruiz Alonso's demands in the Cortes for energetic measures against unemployment and injustices apparently found few determined supporters. In October 1935 Madariaga came near to withdrawing *Acción Obrerista* from the CEDA because the latter was not living up to its social programme.[126] The CEDA was not producing those social and economic results for the workers that were so necessary if it were to gain their confidence for its programme of political reform.[127] José Antonio's prophecy that the Right's electoral triumph would prove a 'wingless victory' seemed to be being fulfilled.[128]

For Monarchists, the events of October and Gil Robles's failure to seize his chance to take over the State underlined the need to give Calvo Sotelo a broadly based political movement. In the Cortes, Calvo Sotelo explained that Parliament was a dialogue dependent upon a basic measure of agreement between all political groups. Recent events demonstrated conclusively that there was now no such consensus of opinion: 'The possibility of parliamentary dialogue in Spain has disappeared. . . . Let us have no

illusions.' Furthermore, the liberal State had shown itself incapable of suppressing class-warfare: 'Liberties based upon sub-
jective prerogatives, upon individual affirmations of absolute
rights, are now no use whatsoever.' Prerogative must be replaced
by function, right by duty, profit by service.[129] In short, the
liberal State was 'a genuine ruin' and must be succeeded by a
totalitarian, corporative State.

Though a declared Monarchist, he realised that the fundamental
problem was not the immediate installation of the 'institution' of
Monarchy, but the infusion into the State of 'Monarchist essences,
that is to say single command, continuity, tradition, authority.
Each hour has its task.' He would therefore found the *Bloque
Nacional*, 'a patriotic front to coordinate . . . existing forces.
Objective? The conquest of the State. Programme? . . . In economic
matters, Leftism; in political matters, Rightism. That is to say,
social justice and authority.'[130] The need to swing the Right's
masses behind Calvo Sotelo was pressing, for 'it seems that it is
the historic Republicans who have taken possession of the CEDA's
leader, rather than he of them'.[131]

The manifesto of the *Bloque Nacional* finally appeared early in
December 1934, but the censors permitted only extracts to appear
in the press.[132] The document declared that 'the Revolution is
still unbeaten since it has been the natural fruit of political causes
which persist and whose necessary extirpation is a desire beyond
the reach of the present rulers'. There remained 'doleful memorials
to the Constituent spirit, without whose disappearance the recovery of the country, subjected for a long period to deadly
Marxist and anti-Spanish poisoning, will be a chimera'. Both
State and society had to be reformed and existing institutions
destroyed. The government had wasted its opportunities and all
the Republican parties had failed. The new political grouping
wanted a Catholic Spain and adopted the motto of Fernando the
Catholic: 'Spain united and in order.' It demanded 'an authentic
Spain, faithful to its history and its own image: one and indivi-
sible'. 'Defence to the death and frenzied exaltation of Spanish
unity' and the 'singular political sovereignty of the State' were its
slogans. The 'integrative State' of the future would guarantee
'natural rights, inherent in the human personality', and impose
moral, political and economic unity upon all classes by intervention

to ban strikes, lock-outs and 'the trade-unionist anti-State' and by enforcement of 'a distributive social justice'.

Just as economic life would be corporatively organised, so the parliamentary constitutional system, 'anti-Spanish in spirit and letter', would make way for 'organic Cortes'. The manifesto demanded a referendum, which, though forbidden by the Constitution, 'no democracy can refuse', in order to let Spain decide whether it accepted or rejected laicism, and whether it did or did not want the suppression of the class struggle, the restoration of the old flag and the abolition of the Catalan Statute. 'A few weeks of implacable action' by a strong, patriotic government would set things right, while 'the backbone of the Country', the Army, 'school of citizenship, purified by its Courts of Honour, will spread discipline and the civic virtues, forging in its barracks a youth filled with patriotic spirit and beyond the reach of all Marxist and separatist venom'.

The signatories, 'trembling with emotion and burning with faith', therefore called for 'the organisation of a sweeping *Bloque Nacional*' to conquer completely the existing State, and to replace it by 'a new State' with 'unity of command and traditional historical continuity'. The movement was open to 'all citizens who share our ideas', be they Republican, Monarchist or neither. Nearly all the signatories were, in fact, Monarchists who refused to hide their convictions. The 'substantive' question of the form of government was to be postponed for the present because the hour demanded a State based on 'the principles of unity, continuity, hierarchy, competence, corporation and spirituality'. They would act simply 'for the sake of Spain' as part of 'a social, national, nationalist and nationalising force' at a 'difficult, most grave, dolorous' time.

The manifesto was signed by nearly all the deputies of *Renovación Española* and the Traditionalist Communion, and by two Independents and one *Cedista* in the Cortes.[133] Other signatories included Ministers of the Dictatorship, ex-*Mauristas* and contributors to *Acción Española*.[134] A number of lawyers, academics and authors, including the playwright Benavente, signed the document, as did some engineers, businessmen, bankers and propertyowners. The aim of the movement was to gather as many parties and individuals as possible beneath one umbrella. Before the manifesto appeared, Albiñana's PNE announced that it would join, but the *Falange* said that it would not.[135] The Traditionalist Communion adhered to the *Bloque Nacional* because the latter was a patriotic grouping.[136] *Renovación Española* officially adhered on 27 December 1934. The *Bloque* was to be a link between the Communion and *Renovación Española* in provinces where both existed; in provinces where there was as yet no Monarchist organisation, Monarchists were to unite to found branches of the *Bloque Nacional*.[137] The movement therefore did little more than officially unite Monarchists behind Calvo Sotelo in opposition to the Republic and liberal-democracy.

There was never any chance of the CEDA adhering to the *Bloque*; indeed, Calvo Sotelo complained that a government supported by Gil Robles was using the press censorship to suffocate the new movement.[138] The offices of the *Bloque* and TYRE were closed for a time in January 1935.[139] During the course of 1935, Calvo Sotelo tried hard to attract *Cedistas* away from Gil Robles. In March he suggested that the *Bloque* and the CEDA might unite to reform the Constitution, after which the *Bloque* would pursue its own Monarchist ideal. Yet in the same breath he strongly attacked 'the theory of the possible good' and its 'dangerous synthesis in the formula "may it be as it may be". . . . We oppose to it another [formula] more juridical and Christian . . .: "may it be as it ought to be". Accidentalism is . . . politically sleight of hand; spiritually, inelegance; morally, mutilation, when not lameness.'[140]

When in May the CEDA obtained five portfolios, Calvo Sotelo said that he still thought the 'tactic' would fail, but he seemed less sure: 'If our forebodings do not come to pass, Spain will have been saved; if they do come to pass, we shall have to save her. . . . We are an army in reserve.' However, in August he defined the *Bloque*'s attitude as one of 'deep affinity with the [*Cedista*] masses. Serious discrepancy with the lines that their leaders are taking. I make mine the cry of the JAP: "Another Constitution".' By November he was speaking confidently of the CEDA's counter-revolution that failed.[141] Yet, despite his constant criticism of the 'tactic' and despite the CEDA's setbacks, the *Bloque*'s gains at its rival's expense were negligible.[142]

During 1935 Calvo Sotelo continued to define his own views as well as to criticise the inadequacy of Gil Robles's policy. The basic difference between the two leaders lay in the means by which the 'new State' was to come into being: Gil Robles saw it as the product of gradual evolution, Calvo Sotelo as a creation imposed from above by a strong government at the first opportunity. In the latter's opinion, the future of Spain could not be left to the whims of electors. The counting of heads was 'more suitable for Zulus than for civilised men':[143] democracy was 'the supreme inanity leading Spain to chaos'.[144] The Spanish situation had to be seen 'in its intimate reality. Either Marxism is extirpated, or Marxism destroys Spain. . . . The reality is that Spain is living in [a state of] civil war.'[145] The rotation of parties in power was possible only when they agreed on essentials and differed on inessentials, 'but now the debate is between being or not being, between Christ and anti-Christ, between civilisation and non-civilisation'.[146] No one could remain neutral, not even the President of the Republic: 'he who is not against the revolution is with the revolution'.[147] The Centre was doomed to 'pulverisation, atomisation, nothingness'.[148] The plans for constitutional reform were pointless, since it was a question 'not of revision, but of substitution . . ., of foundations, not of architecture'.[149] Regional nationalism had also to be extirpated, because 'a broken Spain (*España rota*)' would be even worse than 'a Red Spain (*España roja*)'.[150]

According to Calvo Sotelo, the 'integrative State' which should be installed immediately was 'authoritarian', but not 'absolutist' nor 'pantheist. . . . We say . . .: "Nothing within the State against the State; but the State in the service of the Nation". . . . The people's interest does not lie in governing, but in being governed well.' Yet 'the single command . . . requires a double complement: the suffrage of social interests or corporativism, and the suffrage of guiding ideas or plebiscite'.[151] Calvo Sotelo therefore denied that his ideas were pantheistic. He also denied that he wanted to be a dictator: 'I am a man firmly convinced that governments need parliamentary control' by a chamber elected by organic suffrage.[152] He could not imagine a counter-revolution being carried out with the Republican tricolour and anthem, yet the Monarchy was only to return at the end of an indefinite 'evolutionary cycle'.[153]

Although the immediate need was a State 'capable of saving Christian civilisation',[154] he nevertheless maintained his uncompromising allegiance to 'the ideal . . ., the installation of a Monarchy... which has the essences but none of the dross of that which fell, with the Crown and the Cross as its symbol, the red and gold flag as its ensign, and as its content tradition'.[155] He believed that 'Tradition is not an unfruitfully mummified past, but a profound, life-giving spirit. Tradition is the sap in the tree of the Country. Because we love Tradition, we are progressives. The Spain of the future must be based upon its Tradition and to it we must give our labours, our exertions and, when they may be needed, our lives.'[156] Calvo Sotelo's pronouncements were sometimes rather contradictory, but his 'new State' seemed to imply some form of dictatorship, at least in its initial stages.[157]

Within the general framework of the programme of the *Bloque Nacional*, the Alfonsines of *La Época* continued to propound hereditary Monarchy as 'the best form of government'. Dictators like Porfirio Díaz and Pilsudski were not enough: 'the *caudillo* dies; a dynasty does not'. Kings were 'for the kingdom, for the people, not *vice versa*', but they must govern as well as reign. 'The Catholic Monarchy' could not be 'a crowned Republic' like that in Spain before 1923, nor 'a democratic Republic with an hereditary crowned President' like the Britain of George V. 'The new State' would be the first step towards eradicating 'the revolutionary ideology' whose 'origin and source may be placed around the name of Rousseau, Marx and Marxism being no more than a stage, an anticipated milestone on the route toward chaos'. Dollfuss in Austria had demonstrated that 'truth can be imposed by force'. Such was the true doctrine of counter-revolution.[158]

Acción Española's leading Alfonsine intellectual, the Anglo-Basque Maeztu, saw the Spanish problem as part of an international one. The roots of 'the Revolution' lay in the Enlightenment's subversion of traditional values and its anthropological naturalism. From this rejection of the dogma of original sin stemmed all evils: anti-Christian laicism, relativism, Republicanism, democracy, class-warfare, nationalism (though not Spanish nationalism), Catalanism, liberalism, Socialism, Communism, and, of course, Freemasonry, 'the world organisation of the Revolution . . . in the service of the race of Israel'. Revolutionary aggression, however, had provoked an equally international counter-revolutionary movement to restore, not the *status quo*, but the 'essences' of Tradition. In the battle to the death between the

Cross and the hammer and sickle, no quarter could be given: 'with the Revolution no pacts are possible'. It could not be killed by kindness. Good was certain to triumph over evil, for 'the winds of the world, adverse for so many centuries, are now blowing in our favour'.

He stressed that the counter-revolutionary State must suppress class-warfare and pursue an advanced social programme based on 'the Thomist principle' within a 'directed economy', but it must assert the primacy of the spirit over instinct and materialism. Maeztu's twin themes were 'the Counter-Revolution' and 'Hispanity'. The Hispanic peoples of Europe and America, 'threatened by Communist revolution on one side, and by Nordic financial imperialism on the other', must reaffirm their consciousness of common ideals and form 'a confraternity'. 'Hispanity' was a spiritual, not a racial or territorial concept. 'Liberty, Equality, Fraternity' must be replaced by 'Service, Hierarchy and Brotherhood'. Only a return to 'the old Catholic Monarchy' and its Hispanic mission could save Spain. Only a return to Spanish medieval values could preserve the West against the awakening East: '*ex praeterito spes in futurum*'.[159]

Another Alfonsine intellectual, Sáinz Rodríguez, argued that 'the totalitarian State', far from being foreign, was 'something that springs from the very substratum of the Spanish soul' and was to be found in the sixteenth-century Monarchy, when 'State and Nation formed a single moral concept'. The State of the future must be true to the Catholicism of the Counter-Reformation and the 'theological concept of freedom. . . . We are not enemies of freedom; what we are enemies of is the liberal interpretation of freedom', which, by imposing no restraint on human passions, made men slaves of these passions. The State ought to have a municipal basis, no political parties, and Cortes to vote money and to censure bad government. In short, the traditional Monarchy had to be reinstalled.[160]

Yet another variation on the counter-revolutionary theme was written by Aunós, the Dictator's Minister of Labour, who appealed to the young. He wanted 'a great *caudillo*', supported by Socialist masses and aided by an 'ardent, disinterested, young militia, a sort of order of chivalry'. This mass movement 'absolutely free from capitalist servitude' would install a national, functional, corporative State, the motor of which would be social justice. This State would surpass Fascism, dominated as it was by Sorelian Syndicalism and Socialist *étatisme*, by drawing inspiration from La Tour du Pin's traditionalism. Aunós's State would therefore be 'organic' and 'pluralist', not 'absorbent'. The corporations would have a certain autonomy within a directed economy, and have a legislative function. There was to be no State-party. The Monarchy would be restored only if it were fully corporativist in spirit. The future would see 'the imperial unity of Europe' on a corporative basis, inspired by Christianity like the empires of Charlemagne and Charles V.[161]

The Alfonsines wanted to install a Monarchy similar to that of the Carlists, and efforts to end the dynastic schism continued during 1935. The Traditionalists conceded that Juan was Alfonso Carlos's successor by the laws of heredity, but this was not enough. They could accept him as king only if he embraced Traditionalism.[162] The aim of the Alfonsines of the *Bloque Nacional* was to persuade Alfonso XIII to renounce his rights in favour of Juan, so as to expedite complete union with the Traditionalists. Alfonso, however, refused to abdicate and opposed the idea of premature union with the Traditionalists, because he would in any case become Head of the House of Bourbon when Alfonso Carlos died. Juan rejected any suggestion that he should act independently of his father.[163] Thus the dynastic deadlock continued. Alfonso also refused his followers' requests to condemn the CEDA, although in October 1935 he made his first public criticism of it.[164]

The sort of State which Carlists seeking the *Juanista* solution hoped that Alfonso's heir would agree to was described by Pradera. His 'New State' was broadly similar to that of the Alfonsine Neo-Traditionalists with whom he collaborated, though he adhered more rigidly to the ideas of Vázquez de Mella. The new State must be a good State subject to God's laws and based upon Tradition, 'the past that survives and has the virtue to make itself future'. The true rights of man were 'rights of Nature', and 'public law ... must of necessity be Catholic. ... Society ... implies plurality. ... The nation does not consume its components, for personality and sovereignty are two different things.' The nation was the aggregate unit for achieving a common destiny: 'without Tradition there is no nation'. Church and State were dual societies, but, in the final analysis, the spiritual sphere took precedence over the temporal.

Civil society was composed of four basic 'infra-sovereign societies': domestic, municipal, regional, national. While sovereignty resided in the nation, the minor societies should each enjoy 'autarchy, which is the government peculiar to the particular social ends'. This Catholic conception of society 'removes the apparent antinomies which arise in the human order and, at the same time, it destroys the opposite errors of individualism, nationalism and socialism'. Social classes were not to be defined horizontally by birth or wealth, but by the vertical functional divisions in society. Such classes were naturally organised in corporations whose various indispensable functions were in harmony with the national interest. There was no place for political parties or Rousseauist monism; society was 'organic', not 'mechanical', in composition.

Authority, as Leo XIII had said, was necessary 'to reduce plurality to a certain unity'. The source of authority was God. The prince of the new State which would replace ramshackle liberalism was the representative organ of the nation. Pradera argued from Leo XIII's statements that the Church inhibited itself regarding forms of government. He himself was sure that Spain's 'internal constitution propounds . . . the representative Monarchy as a national form of government. Science points to it as the most perfect of all political forms,' because one man could best represent national sovereignty and a dynasty secured independence and continuity for this 'most eminent organ'. The King was restrained from absolutism by the Church, 'the autarchies belonging to the sub-sovereign societies' and by the Cortes and councils through which he must act—in fact, by the 'objective juridical principle' derived from natural laws. The State's function was to be 'the juridical regulator of social cooperation . . ., the integrator of the diverse social interests in the general interest'. Corporative Cortes would legislate, while executive power would be exercised separately by a government nominated by the King. The judiciary, also nominated by the King, would be totally independent of executive and legislature. In general, wealth 'must be the object of distribution among those who in social solidarity produce it'. Liberal and socialist economic views were false. Paradoxically, therefore, 'the

New State is no other than the Spanish State of the Catholic Kings'.[165]

Pradera's was then an aesthetic vision of the beauty of order, stability, harmony and unity. In the terminology of European Catholic thought, the Spanish Monarchists of the 1930s were social-romantics, the *Cedistas* social-reformists.

Not all Traditionalists, however, were as enthusiastic about the *Juanista* solution as the likes of Pradera. The Communion retained its distinctive position, despite patriotic adherence to the *Bloque Nacional*.[166] The CEDA's policy of consolidating the Republic was bitterly criticised by Traditionalists. Catholics ought to prefer the equally 'licit and holy' aim of the Communion, with its tactic of outright hostility towards all liberalism, parties and 'illegitimate powers'.[167] Spanish Fascism was also denounced, because it was 'a materialist monster, lacking in Christian supernaturalism'.[168] The Communion still refused to compromise with anyone, but there was the consolation that 'the way of the Cross is hard and painful'.[169] The process of internal reorganisation continued into 1935. Efforts were made to spread the gospel in Andalusia and Aragón.[170] The *Requetés* were reorganised with Colonel Varela's help, more arms were distributed, and some two hundred young Carlists went to Italy for training.[171] An atmosphere of expectancy was generated at *aplechs*, where the faithful were told that 'the hour of sacrifice is at hand. *Requetés*, be ready ... to fight, to fight, to fight, and to conquer, to conquer, to conquer!'[172]

One of the main purposes of the *Bloque* was to attract José Antonio into the Monarchist camp, although in 1934 convinced Alfonsines had left the *Falange*. In January 1935 Monarchists started giving money to the *Bloque* instead of to José Antonio. The consequent shortage of funds tempted José Antonio to join, but he was dissuaded by Ruiz de Alda.[173] Monarchists were incensed by José Antonio's attitude to Monarchy: 'we feel no nostalgia for the dead institutions; we want to renovate the revolutionary aspiration of 14 April'.[174] His group remained apart from Monarchist or Catholic 'reaction', belonged neither to the Right, nor to the Left, nor to the Centre, and was 'implacably anti-capitalist, implacably anti-Communist'.[175] To make the *Falange*'s position absolutely unique, he added that it was 'not a Fascist movement'.[176]

The *Falange* represented, in fact, the regenerationist outlook of older Spanish intellectuals, adapted to a post-liberal age. The leaders of the 'Generation of '98', however, felt themselves too old to readjust to youthful authoritarianism.[177] *Falangista* ideology stemmed less from the 'Tradition' of Monarchists and *Cedistas* than from liberal regenerationism, which José Antonio transformed into authoritarian regenerationism. Typical of this outlook were such phrases as, 'we love Spain because we do not like it', and the need to change completely the Spaniards' 'mode of being'.[178]

Just as José Antonio's references to 'dead institutions' shocked Monarchists, so his attacks on 'the Bolshevism of the privileged' and his desire to 'clear away' capitalism, abolish the payment of rent and expropriate estates without compensation scandalised the wealthy and conservative,[179] even though Ledesma and his radical friends left the *Falange* in January 1935.[180] The 'Twenty-Seven Points' of November 1934 declared Spain, in Ortega's phrase, 'a unit of destiny in the universal' and proclaimed the *Falangista* 'will to Empire'. The State was to be 'a totalitarian instrument' founded upon family, municipality and syndicate. Though private enterprise was not to disappear, Spain was to become 'one gigantic syndicate of producers' corporatively organised by branches of production in vertical syndicates. Banking was to be nationalised.

Agrarian reform would be carried out: bad land would be planted with trees; land in the dry zone would be redistributed for collective mechanised farming; smallholdings in the wet zone would be reorganised so that each would be of viable size. Although 'the Catholic sentiment' was to play its part in national reconstruction, the State would have control of education and the Church would be strictly confined to its own sphere by a concordat. Such was to be the *Falangista* 'new order' after 'the national revolution', which would be carried out in 'direct, ardent and combative' style because 'life is warfare'. Point 27 expressed the hope that the *Falange* would triumph with its own forces; any pacts made with others would be on the basis of its predominance.[181] Meanwhile, the government kept its eye on the movement, which still consisted mainly of students under voting age.[182]

Apart from the drilling of *Requetés*, the only illegal action taken by the Right in 1935 was the work of *Falangistas*.[183] In June, José Antonio's political committee met at the Parador de Gredos to

P

discuss tactics and the possibility of making an armed 'gesture'. They agreed that the *Falange* should rise alone if necessary, though they hoped to have military support. Since it was a *carbonaro*-type group without masses, its leaders decided to try to infiltrate the garrisons by means of the *Unión Militar Española*.[184] The UME was a clandestine organisation founded by Captain Barba Hernández in 1934 which circulated anonymous leaflets in garrisons all over Spain. Its aims were rather vague, but the general idea was to bind together junior officers in a sort of Rightist underground to preserve the Army from harmful influences. Barba persuaded General Goded to become its mentor. José Antonio's aim was to make the UME a dependency of the *Falange* and a source of supply for arms.[185]

Meanwhile, Colonel Galarza linked the UME with Alfonsines who tried to make it a dependency of the *Bloque Nacional*.[186] Some officers were also in touch with Sanjurjo in Estoril, who was in turn in touch with Carlists. Sanjurjo at first disapproved of the UME, but eventually agreed to become its nominal head.[187] All in all, the conspiratorial activities of 1935 were really not to be taken seriously.

When Gil Robles became Minister of War in May 1935, the Left feared that dictatorship was at hand. Leftist fears, however, proved unfounded. Gil Robles told his supporters: 'What ignorance of what our party stands for to suppose that we were going to station ourselves on ground different from the law! . . . Why should I have wanted to go to the War Ministry to carry out a *coup d'état*? What need had I of the Army to triumph? . . . A *coup d'état* is carried out by one who is in a minority; but he who, like us, has honest Spain [behind him], has sufficient with the force of citizenship, with ballot-papers.'[188]

Calvo Sotelo, who, since he lacked masses, wished to win over the military, spoke of the Army as 'much more than the arm of the Country; I shall not say that it is the brain, because it ought not to be, but . . . it is the backbone, and if it is broken . . . Spain is broken'.[189] Gil Robles objected to such a definition: 'The Army is not the backbone, but the weaponed arm of the Country. The backbone is the people itself.' Politicians ought not to woo the Army, nor try to use it for party political ends: 'the Army is above politics, it is in the service of all Spaniards'.[190] Gil Robles's appointment as Minister of War reassured conservatives and the officer corps, and thus dealt a crucial blow to the hopes of the *Bloque Nacional*.[191]

The policy of Radical War Ministers had been to soothe military feelings ruffled by Azaña and give the Army satisfaction, for Lerroux believed that it was still liberal at heart.[192] Gil Robles's aim was also to 'restore internal satisfaction' after Azaña's 'mashing'; to 'give the Army confidence in its own strength, faith in the destinies of the Country' by 'the creation and development of the organs necessary to assure the continuity of a military policy entrusted always to responsible technical organisms; a policy that will have to be above the fluctuations that conflicting parties may cause'—in short, 'to take this Army and give it the material and moral benefits that it needs to live with dignity and to fulfil its mission'.[193] Gil Robles insisted that 'the Spanish Army, faithful to its tradition, has to be completely removed from anything that is not the supreme national interest within the régime that Spain itself has resolved to bestow on itself. . . . The Army's purpose is not to carry out any *coups d'état* nor to intervene in politics. The Army is the guaranty for independence and security in the external sphere; it is also the guaranty in the internal sphere, when disturbances arise that could end up with power having been abandoned in the street.'[194]

Thus the tacit *quid pro quo* was that the Army would be loyal to the civil authorities in exchange for a certain internal autonomy and outward prestige. Gil Robles wanted to make the Spanish Army strong like that of the French Republic in order to safeguard Spanish neutrality and prevent humiliation in international affairs, but it was not to dream of 'imperialist labours', nor of 'mad adventures'.[195]

Gil Robles set about restoring 'internal satisfaction' in the Army by promising to re-equip it and by promoting popular officers. He appointed the former Agrarian General Fanjul as his undersecretary and, on 17 May, General Franco, who shared his ideas on the Army's function, as Chief of the General Staff.[196] A Supreme War Council was created under the Minister's presidency. Some forty officers known for their *Azañista* sympathies were dismissed for 'technical reasons', while among those promoted were Generals Goded and Mola and the pro-Carlist Colonel Varela because they were 'excellent soldiers'.[197] Gil Robles said that he would not tolerate military *juntas*, and he dismissed the UME as a retired officers' group with little support within the Army.[198] He made no preparations for a *coup*, and refused to countenance any suggestions for one.[199] The Supreme War Council set about reorganising and re-equipping the Army, which was in rather a parlous condition. Existing divisions were reorganised. Two new brigades were created. New aircraft were ordered. The code of military justice was revised. Steps were taken to boost recruiting. Munitions workers were forbidden to join political organisations. Production of armaments was increased. The defences of the Balearics and Cartagena were strengthened. A three-year plan for national defence and rearmament was drawn up.[200] However, implementation of this long-term programme depended upon the government's economic policy, as well as on political developments.

The principal political issue in the second half of 1935 was the economic situation, which continued to worsen. The economic crisis was more Spanish in origin than a consequence of the world depression. The budgetary situation was chaotic. In 1931 the Republicans had simply taken over the Monarchy's budget. Carner's budget of 1932 was the Republic's only budget, which was subsequently extended again and again. Between 1931 and 1935 expenditure had risen by some 1,000,000,000 pesetas, but revenue had increased only by about 150,000,000. A rise in expenditure was inevitable, but much of it was unproductive: no less than 39 per cent of it went on the bureaucracy, which swallowed 300,000,000 more than in 1931. The floating debt stood at some 1,690,000,000 pesetas in January 1935.[201] The budget deficit had risen steadily to reach 811,800,000 pesetas in 1934.[202] The volume of foreign trade diminished by around a third between 1931 and 1934, and the trade deficit continued to rise dangerously.[203] The widening trade gap had by 1935 led to talk of devaluation of the peseta.

The Right was divided as to the remedies to be applied. Chapaprieta and the bankers and businessmen of the *Lliga* believed in the strictest financial orthodoxy and the virtues of *laissez faire*, while Calvo Sotelo believed in a directed economy and was willing to borrow ideas from the Roosevelt administration.[204] Gil Robles also favoured a mixed economy and State intervention when necessary. All were agreed, however, on the need for political stability and the maintenance of public order.

The most controversial economist on the Right was Calvo Sotelo. He argued that the 'surplus value'—the difference between the cost of labour and the value of the product—was 'the cornerstone of the present economic system . . . and of any other economic system that implies State organisation', including Soviet 'State-capitalism'. In any economic system, expansion depended on the utilisation of this surplus value. In practice, Soviet collectivism had not improved conditions of production and had lowered workers' living standards, while the State had absorbed the surplus value. The capitalist system had the advantage of allowing social mobility. However, primitive capitalism, based on saving, had given way to speculative capitalism, based on credit. The growth in the size of firms and the importance of the stock-exchange had led to the concentration of financial power in a few hands, as Pius XI had observed. The banker had ousted the manufacturer. Trusts and cartels were not in themselves evil, but they must be controlled in the interests of the consumer, just as the State must control banking policy. Laws must be passed to stop the abuses of unbridled capitalism, for it was the abuses of finance-capitalism that had led to crisis. Capitalism was good in so far as it satisfied a natural desire for property, and its productive capacity was beyond question. What had to be changed was the system of distribution of the wealth.

Irresponsible speculation on the stock-exchange would have to be prohibited and, as in Italy and Germany, a limit would have to be placed on dividends. The worker must be made to feel part of the firm. The 'integrative State' above class would administer social justice as it did civil or criminal justice. There could be no return to the liberal or individualistic capitalism of the nineteenth century. The State would control the stock company by means of independent experts, who would see that shareholders were protected and that national and social interests were served. Banks were not to be allowed to share in the running of stock companies, and directors' salaries were to be limited. Calvo Sotelo favoured a mixed economy with public corporations for such things as irrigation and cheap housing. 'The State must assume a tutelary mission of vigilance and prevention over the creation and circulation of capital.' His 'new capitalism' was to have none of the failings of the old capitalism, whose anti-social consequences were to be replaced by a just distribution of wealth. Such a system demanded 'a diligent State, imbued with holy Christian spirituality and capable of carrying it into the very marrow of economic life'.[205] Therefore Spain must decide once and for all between a socialist, a liberal and a directed economy; the latter was the only one suitable. Economic and political liberalism must be abolished in order to get to grips with the problem of unemployment.[206]

Calvo Sotelo's economic ideas, like his political ideas, necessitated sweeping changes. He still thought in terms of a balanced ordinary budget, with a parallel extraordinary budget for public works, as he had under the Dictatorship, though now he invoked the example of the American 'New Deal'.[207] All this, of course, was anathema to the liberal economists of the *Lliga*, who rejected 'the so-called directed economy, which constitutes a concealed and attenuated form of Socialism'. Intervention by the State meant 'the disturbed economy, not the directed economy'.[208]

Gil Robles's economic ideas were a little vague, but, like Calvo Sotelo, he envisaged a mixed economy.[209] His short-term solutions were also not unlike those of Calvo Sotelo, although he was more chary of deficit-finance. The government ought to take special powers to circumvent parliamentary procedures and reduce budget expenditure, rationalise administration and make economies in the bureaucracy. The income-tax introduced by Carner should be developed at the expense of the wealthy and over-privileged. At the root of the unemployment problem, he argued, lay the evil of under-consumption. Prices of agricultural produce should be raised to provide purchasing-power among the rural masses for Spanish industrial products. Public works' schemes and subsidies for industry would also help to cure unemployment. A lower bank-rate would stimulate expansion.[210]

The politician to whom the task of leading Spain out of her economic difficulties fell was Joaquín Chapaprieta, a former Minister of the Monarchy now an independent Republican, and a firm believer in retrenchment.[211] On becoming Minister of Finance in May 1935, he drafted a law authorising the government to restrict expenditure. The bureaucracy was to be reorganised to achieve economies; expenditure on personnel was to be reduced and those not properly qualified were to be dismissed. The number of Ministries and their employees was to be reduced by decree. Special funds and quasi-legal levies were to be suppressed. Pensions were to be revised and cut. Grants to bodies like the Institute of Agrarian Reform were also to be cut, and all government spending generally curbed.[212] He intended to eliminate corruption and balance the budget for normal expenditure by the end of 1936. He would reduce the deficit in 1935 by a third by his economies and by the reform of taxation and the harrying of tax-dodgers.

Calvo Sotelo and Ventosa thought these proposals all right as far as they went. Ventosa saw balanced budgeting as soon as possible as the only way to restore confidence and rejected Calvo Sotelo's suggestions. For the latter, the fundamental problem was monetary. Only his own permanent political solution could guarantee public order, the key to economic recovery. Only thus could foreign capital be attracted for long-term investment and the currency be stabilised. Meanwhile, the peseta should be allowed to float between minimum and maximum limits, like the currencies of Belgium and the United States.[213]

Gil Robles fully approved of these economies, but warned Chapaprieta not to get too carried away by the vision of a balanced budget: there must be no economies on defence, unemployment or 'the development of the national wealth'.[214] Chapaprieta's law was expected to take effect on 23 September, and the next day the government was to be quietly reorganised with fewer Ministers. Six Ministries were to become three. The CEDA expected the Radicals, the Agrarians and itself each to renounce a portfolio.[215]

No such smooth transition, however, took place. On 20 September, the two Agrarian Ministers resigned and another governmental crisis ensued. The Minister of the Navy, Royo Villanova, who always, in Lerroux's phrase, 'lost his equanimity' where Catalan affairs were concerned, resigned in protest against his colleagues' transfer of public works to the *Generalidad*. Velayos, whose inactivity at the Ministry of Agriculture was criticised by *Cedistas*, declared his solidarity with his fellow Agrarian.[216] Alcalá-Zamora wanted a coalition government to include the PNV and reformist Socialists, but the CEDA vetoed this idea. He entrusted formation of a government first to Alba and then to Chapaprieta, both ex-Monarchist Ministers like himself. 'The Four' agreed to support the latter, whose government included three *Cedistas*, Martínez de Velasco and Rahola (*Lliga*), although the Agrarians had previously said they would not serve with the *Lliga*.[217] The new government intended to balance the budget in 1936.[218]

Lerroux did not press his claims to the Premiership in September because he knew that a scandal implicating leading Radicals was about to break. One Daniel Strauss, of uncertain nationality, had in 1934 bribed Radical politicians to introduce into Spain the '*straperlo*', a roulette-wheel which allegedly eliminated the element of chance. Socialists had got to hear about it, and so the then Minister of the Interior, Salazar Alonso, had put a stop to this illegal gambling. During 1935 Strauss had written to Lerroux (whose adopted son Aurelio had been involved) seeking compensation for the losses he had incurred when the government had revoked his concession. Later a French lawyer visited Lerroux and threatened to provoke a scandal if the matter were not settled privately. Lerroux ignored these attempts at blackmail. Strauss next wrote to Alcalá-Zamora, who insisted on making it a cabinet issue.

The matter was brought into the open on 18 October, when Chapaprieta said that Strauss's accusation had been handed over to the Attorney-General. The Cortes then debated the issue. The government wanted the courts to deal with it, and Gil Robles and Lerroux accused the Left of collusion with Strauss in withholding the matter until it could be used to the best political advantage. Gil Robles, however, gave way to Monarchist demands for a committee of the Cortes, even though Monarchists were using the issue to discredit the Republican régime. On 28 October the Cortes exonerated Salazar Alonso, but found Aurelio Lerroux and three leading Radicals guilty.[219]

Lerroux's Radical Republicans had enjoyed a reputation for corruption from their foundation, and all opposition groups were now determined to make the most of the '*straperlo*' affair. The Left found in it proof that the Radicals were unprincipled and unfit to govern, and hinted that the CEDA-Radical alliance depended on a tacit deal: Gil Robles would turn a blind eye to corruption if Lerroux went along with the CEDA's ambitions. Monarchists took the chance to try and equate the régime with corruption, and attacked Gil Robles's alliance with rogues. The Radical Party itself began to disintegrate, and Lerroux and Rocha left the government on 29 October.[220] José Antonio saw the affair as typical of parliamentary politics, while a Communist said it was 'a symptom of the decomposition of the capitalist system'.[221]

Only a month later, a 'second wave of asphyxiating gases'[222] known as 'the Nombela affair' gave the Radicals the *coup de grâce*. Lerroux's Under-Secretary had agreed to compensate a shipping-line out of government funds to the tune of 3,033,318 pesetas for certain losses. The Inspector-General of Colonies, Nombela, had been sacked and then alleged irregularities. He was now appealing against wrongful dismissal. Monarchists wanted the Cortes to accuse Lerroux himself, but in the voting he was exonerated and his Under-Secretary found guilty.[223] The scandals destroyed the Republic's Radical Centre. The Socialist and Catholic masses now had no buffer between them.

If the scandals lowered their prestige indirectly, the reputation of the CEDA and the Agrarians sank in the eyes of their most loyal supporters as a result of their handling of the wheat surplus, called by *El Debate* 'the most serious economic conflict that has faced any government since the proclamation of the Republic'.[224] The average annual demand for wheat in Spain was 40,000,000 quintals, but the bumper crop of 1934 had produced over 50,000,000. Unless the surplus was somehow withdrawn from the market, the farmers would suffer as much as in a bad year.[225] By January 1935, the position was serious: smallholders were unable to sell their crops and were falling more and more heavily into debt. Giménez Fernández at first resisted demands for State buying because the State could not afford it and a precedent would be set for other produce. The most that he could do would be to set up storage depots and prevent more land being used for wheat-growing.[226] However, pressure from the farmers led to legislation in February and June authorising the withdrawal of about 6,000,000 quintals.[227] Wheat-growers continued to complain that the official price-levels were being ignored by their *bêtes noires*, the millers. When the 1935 crop was harvested, the situation became even worse. By September, the peasants' cry was: 'We have no money, we are not selling wheat, we are being ruined.'[228]

Gil Robles now intervened himself. The War Ministry was to buy a large amount of wheat; the State was immediately to pur-

chase 'defective wheat' and pay millers to grind it; credit was to
be extended to farmers, and one organisation per province was to
be designated to buy wheat for the State.[229] In the Cortes, *Cedista*
deputies launched strong attacks on the incompetence of successive Ministers of Agriculture: the Agrarians Velayos and
Martínez de Velasco and the Radical Usabiaga. They said that the
law was not being enforced. In Toledo, the company designated
to buy wheat was in league with the millers and was forcing the
smaller growers to sell at prices well below the official level. In
Guadalajara, millers refused to buy at the official price, which the
Governor declined to enforce. In Zamora and in Andalusia, the
Minister had failed even to authorise buying. In Valladolid, the
1935 crop was being bought; the official buying organisation told
small growers to sell the 1934 crop privately at low prices, and the
price-levels had disappeared. Everywhere there was corruption.[230]
The thirty ministerial decrees of 1935 added to the confusion.
After the Agrarians torpedoed plans for a national agrarian bank,
the government in October authorised loans to farmers, but once
again the law was not enforced.[231] The small wheat-growers
suffered much hardship. Late in 1935 an expert, Larraz, was
appointed Commissary for Wheat, and he drew up plans for a
long-term solution.[232]

When the Cortes was not discussing scandals or surplus wheat
in the autumn of 1935, Chapaprieta's budget for 1936 was debated.
He estimated that he would reduce expenditure by more than
400,000,000 pesetas as a result of his economies and the conversion
of debts. He would introduce no new taxes, but would look into
exemptions and energetically pursue tax-dodgers. He would reform the taxes on alcohol and lower the starting-level for the
graduated income-tax. The land-tax would be graduated and payment of death-duties would be made universal. Thus he estimated
a rise of some 500,000,000 pesetas in revenue. Allowing for defence
and public works needs, he even hoped for a surplus of perhaps
50,000,000 pesetas. A balanced budget ought to restore confidence
and get the economy moving again.[233] He rejected devaluation as
a means of boosting exports.[234]

Lerroux and Gil Robles both supported Chapaprieta's view
that the wealthy would have to make sacrifices, though not all
their followers agreed with them.[235] For Chapaprieta a balanced

budget was dogma. Although on 27 January 1935 he had said it would take three years to balance it, on 19 November he announced that it would be balanced in six months. 'One cannot have a sound economic policy when the budget is not sound. Our economy must be invigorated by balancing the budget.' A balanced budget was the essential pre-condition for economic reconstruction and progress; it must precede any such schemes.[236]

Gil Robles, however, had rather different ideas. He thought that the government should put through a legislative programme as well as the budget. When indispensable laws had been passed, the government ought to propose constitutional reform; the Cortes would then automatically be dissolved and elections could be held under an absolutely impartial government.[237] Drafts of these 'indispensable' laws were now ready. Lucía produced a five-year plan for modernising rural life: roads were to be built to remote villages; *pueblos* were to be provided with sanitation and a water-supply; irrigation was to go ahead. Salmón planned more public buildings and a cheap housing programme. Gil Robles himself tried to spur the Institute of Agrarian Reform into action.[238] Such plans, if implemented, would be of more use to the CEDA in an election than a balanced budget. Then, on 2 December, Larraz said he wanted the government to lend farmers more money. Since these costly measures were incompatible with a balanced budget in 1936, Gil Robles asked Chapaprieta to think again.[239] Chapaprieta, however, refused to cancel his budget and took his stand on his proposals for death-duties, to which the conservative *Cedista* Azpeitia had put forward amendments. The result was that on 9 December Spain faced yet another governmental crisis. If its immediate cause was death-duties, its real origin lay in the clash between the priorities of Gil Robles and Chapaprieta.[240]

The Left demanded a dissolution to avert constitutional reform, which now required only an absolute majority in the Cortes. Gil Robles demanded another government based on 'the Four' with himself as Premier.[241] The President, however, wanted either a coalition including both Right and Left, or a government of the Centre. The formation of such a government was first entrusted to his friend Martínez de Velasco. When he failed, *El Debate* suggested an all-*Cedista* government. Alcalá-Zamora, however, now entrusted the task to Miguel Maura and then to Chapaprieta, but their efforts were thwarted by opposition from 'the Four'. On 14 December, a government was at last formed by Portela Valla-dares, a leading Freemason and a *cacique* in Galicia, who was not a deputy. The Right disliked him for his conduct at the Ministry of the Interior during 1935, which had won him some sympathy on the Left. Portela's government included Martínez de Velasco, a Liberal-Democrat, two Radicals whom Lerroux disowned, and Rahola of the *Lliga*.[242] 'The Four' were no longer united. *Cedistas* were angry at their exclusion from power. One of them commented: 'Total, two years lost for Spain.'[243]

When Gil Robles asked to be made Premier, Alcalá-Zamora persuaded Pablo-Blanco (Minister of the Interior) to surround the War Ministry with Civil Guards because he feared a *coup*. Generals Fanjul and Varela, indeed, wanted to seize the President of the Republic, but Gil Robles warned them that a *pronunciamiento* would only result in civil war. He refused to countenance a *coup* on his behalf, but left the Generals to decide whether or not they ought to rise. General Franco again vetoed a rising.[244] Gil Robles therefore bade the Army farewell at a tearful ceremony. Franco declared that 'honour, discipline, all the basic concepts of the Army have been restored and given substance by your excellency'. Gil Robles replied that he was sure that he would return to the War Ministry, but repeated that the Army must always remain outside party conflicts.[245]

The politicians of the Right now indulged in mutual recrimina-tions as to who had provoked the crisis and why 'the Four' had broken up.[246] The CEDA's main attack was on the President, who had supported a Minister without followers (ie Chapaprieta) against the rest of the government. Furthermore, the President had brushed aside the legitimate claims of the biggest parlia-mentary group: 'At bottom what won the day was a revolutionary threat that, before the possibility of the reform of the Constitution, demanded the elimination of the CEDA from power and the dis-solution of the Cortes.' However, 'the injustice that has been perpetrated against us does not shift us from our position nor from our tactic'.[247] Alcalá-Zamora, indeed, wanted the CEDA out of power because it was not sufficiently Republican. He also wished to be rid of the 'Fernandine Cortes'.[248] Ironically, the four main posts in the régime were now held by former Liberal Ministers of the King.[249] Those who were still Monarchists thought that their prophecies had been fulfilled: 'the tactic has realised all the suspicions that we, its adversaries, harboured and none of the hopes that its partisans cherished'.[250] In fact, for the CEDA, as for Spain, all depended on the outcome of the elections.

Notes to this chapter are on pages 353–76.

Chapter 6 'DESCENSUS IN AVERNO'
December 1935–July 1936

ALCALÁ-ZAMORA'S REFUSAL to entrust Gil Robles with power in December 1935 did not mark, as Monarchists claimed, the definitive failure of the CEDA's 'tactic'. If he could win the election Gil Robles would retain the loyalty of the Right's masses and thus take the wind out of the sails of his critics. But when the Leftist coalition won the majority of seats, though not of votes, and revolution again seemed to threaten, his followers began to desert and put their faith in the violence he could not sanction. 'Possibilism' only yielded to 'catastrophism' after the elections.

The election campaign was fought in an atmosphere of civil war and was the continuation of the violent events of October 1934 by other means. Right and Left both saw the supreme significance of this election and each feared the victory of the other. Rightists saw the battle as one between revolution and counter-revolution, between Spain and 'anti-Spain'; Socialists believed the choice lay between 'Rome and Moscow, between the black banner of Fascism and the red flag of Socialism'.[1] The efforts of Alcalá-Zamora and Portela to create a new buffer between the two Spains by reverting to the corrupt means of the 'old politics' came to nothing. Left and Right came face to face and fear bred aggression.

The events of February to July 1936 were the prelude to civil war. On the Left most Socialists, spurred on as ever by fear of gains by the CNT among the working class, prepared for the advent of the dictatorship of the proletariat. On the Right the *Falange* met the sporadic violence of the Left with counter-terrorism while military leaders and Monarchists prepared to do battle with 'the

Revolution'. Largo Caballero and Calvo Sotelo emerged as the symbolic leaders of the two Spains.

The moderates, Azaña (now again Premier), Prieto (now the advocate of evolutionary Socialism) and the legalist Gil Robles, were pessimistic but tried to avert the disaster which they clearly saw ahead. The only chance of avoiding full-scale civil war lay in the formation of a national coalition government with full powers and including Socialists and *Cedistas*. When Azaña became President of the Republic in May the opportunity for realignment occurred. However, Prieto realised that Largo Caballero would split the Popular Front and the Socialist movement rather than allow him to become Premier, and this would mean the collapse of the Left before the Right and the Army. The possibility of a national coalition was torpedoed by Largo Caballero because he was trying to unite all the proletarian forces for the violent seizure of power. In a sense therefore, 'what made the Spanish Civil War inevitable was the civil war within the Socialist Party'.[2] As in Italy in the early 1920s violence accompanied by talk of revolution drove the bourgeoisie to 'Fascism'.

The two months of government by Casares Quiroga (May–July) represented the death-agony of the Republic of 1931. He enraged the Right without giving satisfaction to the Marxist Left. Lacking a mass following, the Left Republican government could only walk the tight-rope between the Army and the revolutionary working class while the tide of anarchy rose. Survival depended on neither turning openly against the régime. When the murder of Calvo Sotelo presented the military[3] with the psychological moment for action to restore order and save the Country from the revolutionary threat, the Republic of 1931 only remained as a pathetic façade for the revolutionaries.

With the formation of Portela's government, it was assumed by both Left and Right that the President had given his Premier the decree for dissolution. This was not, in fact, the case, but the election campaign nevertheless began immediately. Gil Robles sought to form 'a national front against the revolution and its accomplices', to launch 'a great Spanish spiritual crusade' to win the elections.[4] Portela, however, wanted not only to act as umpire, but to create a new Centre under his own and Alcalá-Zamora's leadership so as to hold the balance between Right and Left. He hoped to achieve this by the old means of using government machinery in support of his nominees. New Governors were appointed and he began 'packing' provincial committees with his men.[5]

If Portela were to persevere with his plans, the anti-Leftist vote would be split. Gil Robles therefore set about disrupting the government. Inside the government Chapaprieta, Martínez de Velasco and Pablo-Blanco were believed to favour a Centre-Rightist 'anti-revolutionary bloc' and the CEDA's inclusion in the government, while Portela and Del Río wanted separate government lists of candidates. Gil Robles exerted pressure on two fronts. Firstly, he said that it would be illegal to extend the budget that expired on 31 December by decree. Therefore either the Cortes must meet, in which case Portela would fall, or the decree of dissolution must appear very soon. Secondly, the CEDA would not ally with the Agrarians, the Liberal-Democrats or Chapaprieta if they were still in the government when the decree of dissolution appeared. Therefore they must either leave the government or be prepared to commit electoral suicide.[6]

Portela's first government duly broke up on 30 December. By 10 pm on the same day, however, he had formed another, consisting entirely of independents amenable to his and the President's wishes.[7] Portela needed time to attract politicians to the new Centre that he believed essential because Left and Right were so hostile towards each other. Alcalá-Zamora therefore signed a decree on 1 January suspending the Cortes until the end of the month. However, the President of the Cortes, Alba, said that this was an unconstitutional act upon which the Cortes would have to pass judgment. On 2 January, the Alfonsine Vallellano presented Alba with a document signed by the necessary one-tenth of the deputies (Monarchists and *Cedistas*) demanding that the Cortes meet immediately. Gil Robles declared that 'the suspension of sessions by the government implied a manifest violation of the present Constitution, was equivalent to a *coup d'état* and put the President of the Republic and the government outside the law'. He demanded a meeting of the Permanent Deputation of the Cortes to consider the matter. Portela agreed to its meeting on 7 January.[8] Since he could not hope for a majority, he published the decree of dissolution, drawn up on 30 December, only hours before it met.[9] The electoral campaign now officially began. Polling-day was to be 16 February, with second contests where necessary on 1 March.

Portela's confidence, however, had not yet been shaken. He continued to 'pack' local government posts with his friends.[10] At Lugo, Gil Robles launched a violent attack on the government, whose candidates without a programme merely sought 'to put themselves on the side of the hottest sun. . . . Previously only Heads of State were untouchable; now the magnificent precious Governors are also untouchable. . . . I am not offended because they call me a Catholic, so neither can Señor Portela be offended because they say that he is a Mason, and Grade 33.' He appealed to the electors of Galicia, where Portela's *caciquismo* was most in evidence, to show that they would not be corrupted.[11]

The Socialists and Left Republicans were also outraged, and threatened to boycott the elections if Portela did not act more fairly.[12] The Right's press continued to report a whole stream of abuses committed by the government and its agents.[13] During January, however, it would seem that Portela and his Ministers began to lose confidence in the possibilities of managing the election. Though the *Portelista* Centre's manifesto again appealed to electors to vote for it as the only way of avoiding the civil war that Left and Right both threatened to unleash, its candidates were encouraged to enter coalitions, at first with anyone from Besteiro to the CEDA, and later with anyone.[14]

Both Left and Right, then, disapproved of what Largo Caballero called Portela's 'political hermaphroditism'.[15] On 7 February, Portela announced that his candidates would ally with the Right in constituencies where the Left refused to give them a place on its lists.[16] In fact, the Left rebuffed Portela everywhere, except in Lugo and Cuenca, where alliances were made. Although Monarchists disapproved, Gil Robles was more receptive to Portela's suggestions, despite his recent bitter attacks on the Premier, because the CEDA expected the Left to win in the south.[17] Both Portela and Gil Robles stressed that no pact between the government and the CEDA had been made: it was simply a question of local tactical alliances.[18] *Portelistas* were indeed included in the 'counter-revolutionary' coalition in a dozen provinces in the south. Here, therefore, the CEDA had the marginal advantage of the

Q

support of the authorities.[19] Elsewhere, *Portelista* candidates fought alone—for example, the Progressive Del Río in Ciudad Real, Pita Romero (ex-ORGA) in Corunna and Portela himself in Pontevedra. In Valencia, the *Blasquistas* were the government's candidates. Efforts to reach agreement with the PNV failed: it fought on its own again.[20]

Local alliances between the CEDA and elements of the Republican Right were general. In Catalonia the *Lliga* went to the polls with Radicals, Traditionalists and *Cedistas* in the 'Catalan Front of Order'. Lerroux and those Radicals that remained loyal to him, such as Salazar Alonso, Velarde and Pérez Madrigal, took up a clear Rightist position: Spain's problem was 'not one of régime, but of being or not being'.[21] The 'counter-revolutionary' coalitions often included Radicals, Agrarians, independent local notables, a few Conservatives, and (mostly in Asturias) Liberal-Democrats. The Conservative leaders M. Maura and Arranz fought alone in Soria, though Maura announced that his party would ally with the Right. Like Gil Robles, he demanded that the next Cortes judge the President's conduct.[22] Local notables with whom the CEDA allied included Romanones in Guadalajara, March in the Balearics and Calderón in Palencia. Agrarians formed part of the coalition in many provinces, but not in Burgos, where the CEDA, Traditionalists and Albiñana set out to trounce Martínez de Velasco and his fellow *caciques*.[23]

Gil Robles sought the widest possible coalition. The CEDA's alliances were 'most varied. . . . For us, the counter-revolutionary front begins where that formed by the defenders of the revolution ends. . . . Our compromises, with whatever party or forces they may be, are entirely electoral; they will not last a day longer than the electoral agreement. . . . We are united because thus we are going to beat the revolution.'[24]

Agreement with the Monarchists, however, was not so easy. Calvo Sotelo proclaimed the need for 'a great anti-revolutionary front' based on a pact for unity during and after the elections until its provisions were implemented. This pact should stipulate prohibition of separatist parties and revolutionary Marxism, strict arbitration in labour disputes, strict maintenance of public order, crucifixes in the schools, a big unemployment programme and higher agricultural prices. It was 'ingenuousness' to hope to transform the régime from within. An alliance of Monarchists, *Cedistas* and independents—all Radicals were excluded—should judge the President, install a new constitution and set up a dictatorship: 'If two years from our victory we have to engage in a new life-and-death battle, like this one, it will not be worth the trouble to win now.'[25] The *Falange* also said that it was in favour of a 'national front' in principle. Calvo Sotelo therefore asked for its inclusion in his projected Rightist coalition.[26]

Gil Robles, however, was not going to be stampeded into any entangling commitments. The 'tactic' had not failed: an electoral victory would indeed assure its success. The CEDA would keep its personality as the 'axis' of a counter-revolutionary front made up of local, tactical, circumstantial, purely electoral coalitions.[27] Calvo Sotelo, who had said that the next Cortes would be constituent, had to announce that this was only a personal opinion.[28] Monarchists continued to demand a joint Rightist pact or manifesto, ostensibly because a definite programme would arouse more enthusiasm.[29] What they really sought was an agreement binding the CEDA to the *Bloque Nacional* and thus making Centre-Rightist alliances impossible. If, as they hoped, the Right won a marginal majority, Gil Robles would then have to rely on the Monarchists to govern and there would be many opportunities for political blackmail. Gil Robles, however, refused Monarchist and *Falangista* demands for large numbers of places on anti-Leftist lists.[30]

The *Falange*'s failure to get places and its disapproval of Gil Robles's type of national front soon led it to break with the Right. It put up candidates of its own in eleven constituencies; José Antonio himself stood in eight.[31] As usual, he advocated his own blend of social-nationalism. He denounced the Centre-Right's 'sterile and melancholy biennium', and stated that the *Falange* would not respect the verdict of the polls if it proved 'dangerously contrary to the eternal destinies of Spain'.[32]

Calvo Sotelo agreed to support the CEDA on 20 January, but earlier in the day Gil Robles had agreed with Radicals, Conservatives and Agrarians that their aim was to defend the Republic and ensure the proper functioning of Parliament. No pact was made with the Monarchists, who campaigned separately.[33] Monarchists appeared on the anti-revolutionary lists in most constituencies, though many were excluded by the CEDA when places had to be found for Republicans.[34] As a result, some lone Alfonsine candidates appeared in some provinces—for instance, the Dictator's Minister Yanguas in Ávila. The Traditionalists put up separate lists in Castellón and Santander.[35] The 'National Counter-Revolutionary Front' list for the capital, including Monarchists and Republicans, was not agreed upon until 4 February.[36] Monarchists disliked having to accept alliances with Republicans, but grudgingly conceded that this was a cruel necessity. Monarchists saw themselves as upright gentlemen, Gil Robles as a scheming politician whom they had to assist with their money and their votes, even though they knew that he would again betray them, because Largo Caballero was the only alternative.[37]

The *Bloque Nacional*'s campaign was not just anti-Leftist, but anti-Republican and anti-democratic. For Calvo Sotelo, 'the Revolution' could not simply be beaten at the polls; this was only a preliminary skirmish. The Right would have to make it legally impossible for revolutionary parties to operate as they were now in the Leftist coalition, which was merely 'the Revolution . . . in the sheep's clothing of legality'. He also made what he called 'an indirect invocation to force': the Army, 'the Nation in arms', was expected to rise when legality was used by the government against 'the Country'—a clear reference to the course to be taken if the Left were to win. Such disobedience, he believed, was fully justified according to St Thomas and Fr Mariana. He agreed with Pradera that 'the Republic is the Revolution'. The next Cortes must be constituent and abolish elections.[38] The main point, then, in Monarchist propaganda in 1936 was the same as it had been in 1933: 'Let us vote so that some day we can stop voting.'[39]

As usual, the Right's campaign fund was bigger than the Left's, and surpassed the amount of money raised in 1933.[40] The CEDA's propaganda, in the care of the JAP, concentrated on the fear of revolution, but it also made as much as possible of its Ministers' achievements, of the plans that its exclusion from power had prevented from being carried out, and of the personality of the *Jefe*.[41]

Japistas were rather unruly. Since the autumn they had been preparing for an electoral victory which would end the liberal State, universal suffrage and the revolutionary threat once and for all. In December they still talked of 'annihilating the revolution', of 'dictating another Constitution', of 'conquering all power' and of 'the decisive victory'. At the same time they tried to goad the apathetic into action.[42] In January the JAP's pronouncements were curbed from above.[43] However, it was perhaps pressure from his youth movement that led Gil Robles to make an important change in policy in the last week of the campaign: in Seville he announced that the new Cortes would revise the Constitution.[44] He nevertheless continued to reject dictatorship.[45] On the eve of the poll he declared his intention of governing in energetic and determined fashion, but without this signifying 'the smashing of the adversary, destruction of the enemy, annihilation of he who is opposed to us'. To try to steal the Left's thunder, he promised an amnesty for 'all those dragged along or deceived' by revolutionaries.[46]

The Leftist coalition gave an impression of greater cohesion than the Rightist, but it too had its divisions. Azaña's *Izquierda Republicana*, Martínez Barrio's *Unión Republicana* and Sánchez Román's group of National Republicans had worked together closely in 1935 for a return to the first biennium. The Socialists were divided: Besteiro's reformists rejected revolution and a Republican alliance; Prieto's centrists wanted a repetition of the first biennium; Largo Caballero and the party's Youth wanted an all-Socialist government to follow a short Republican interlude.[47] The PSOE opened negotiations with the Left Republicans on 14 November at the latter's request. Within the PSOE, the collaborationist views of Prieto carried the day. His rival, Largo Caballero, therefore resigned from the party's executive committee on 18 December.[48] However, he and his followers, the *Caballeristas*, accepted the need for unity at the polls in order to defeat the Right. The PCE, the orthodox Communist party, also favoured collaboration, in obedience to the Comintern's decision in August 1935 to create 'anti-Fascist' Popular Fronts.[49]

The Popular Front's pact, signed by *Izquierda Republicana*, *Unión Republicana*, the PSOE, the UGT, the Socialist Youth, the PCE, Pestaña's small Syndicalist Party and Maurín's POUM, appeared in mid-January. It was an electoral pact which set out an eight-point programme to be implemented by the Left Republicans with the support of the rest of the Left. All those arrested since the last election were to be amnestied, and workers and civil servants dismissed since then were to be reinstated. The provisions of the

Constitution were to be properly enforced. Agrarian legislation would be revised to help the peasant and smallholder; it was recorded that the Socialists had wanted nationalisation of the land, but the Republicans had not accepted this. Industry was to be protected. A public works' programme was to be implemented; the workers' parties' demand for aid for the unemployed was noted, as was the Republicans' belief that this would be rendered superfluous by the rest of the programme. The social legislation of 1931–3 was to be reintroduced, though the Republicans rejected Socialist ideas of workers' control: 'The Republic conceived by the Republican parties is not a Republic directed by social or economic class motives, but a régime of political liberty, driven by considerations of public interest and social progress.' State laicist education would be developed, as would regional autonomy and support for the League of Nations.[50]

Just as Monarchists saw their alliance with the CEDA as a tactical necessity in order to defeat the other side, so the *Caballeristas* saw the Popular Front in similar terms. It was 'an intermediate stage of common labour, in which the Republicans dissolve the Fascist centres and purge the armed forces, so that the Socialists may soon install the dictatorship of the proletariat'.[51] Largo Caballero himself declared 'that, before the Republic, our duty was to bring it about; but, with the Republic established, our duty is to bring about Socialism. And when I speak of Socialism, I do not speak of Socialism alone; I speak of Marxist Socialism. And in speaking of Marxist Socialism, I speak of revolutionary Socialism. . . . We are Socialists, but revolutionary Marxist Socialists. . . . Our aspiration is the conquest of political power. Method? That which we are able to use! . . . Let it be well understood that by going with the Left Republicans we are not mortgaging anything in our ideology and action. . . . It is a circumstantial coalition, for which a programme is being produced that is certainly not going to satisfy us.'[52]

If the Right were to win the elections, then 'we shall have to proceed to declared civil war. And this is not a threat, it is a warning. . . . I desire a Republic without class warfare; but for this it is necessary for one class to disappear.'[53] Young Socialists proclaimed their disagreement with 'the democratic way-out', but accepted it for the moment in order to bar Fascism's path, free prisoners and exact responsibilities for the repression. They wanted no ministerial portfolios: 'The only thing that we long for is to be allowed freedom to prepare our revolutionary army and conquer power.'[54]

Socialists of all persuasions took the initiative in making the repression in Asturias the main issue in the campaign.[55] They also dwelt on the Centre-Right's biennium as a whole: 'Hunger. Unemployment. Tyranny. Fraud. Exploitation. Robbery. Nepotism. Ineptitude. Negligence. Immorality. Mire. Slime. Such is, in synthesis, the work of these two years of Fernandine reaction, of Inquisition.'[56] They appealed for the support of the CNT in order to get their prisoners released,[57] since they knew that they needed Anarchist votes to be sure of winning in the south, the Levante, Saragossa and Catalonia. The FAI-CNT scorned the Popular Front's programme because it was a 'profoundly conservative document', but advised its followers to vote for the Left so as to get prisoners released and also because a Rightist victory would be more prejudicial to the Anarcho-Syndicalist cause.[58]

According to *El Socialista*, Spanish politics were now polarised: the Right advocated clerical-Fascism, the Left wished to draw out 'the natural consequences' from the Republic. The Left was terrified of 'Fascism', the Right of 'Revolution'. Both sides were fully conscious of the vital importance of this election. Only victory could ensure survival.[59]

The campaign was conducted by both sides in an atmosphere of civil war, and there were the usual violent incidents in the streets.[60] Tension mounted not only because of the nature of the issues at stake, but also because no one was really confident of success.[61] Leaders on both sides naturally planned for victory, but nothing illustrated the uncertainty better than the declarations of José Antonio, Largo Caballero and Calvo Sotelo that they would take to violence if defeated. *El Debate*, which sought to avoid violence, made anguished appeals for everyone to vote: 'To abstain is a crime, which in this case is committed against the rights of God and the sacred interests of Spain.'[62]

On Sunday 16 February, some 70 per cent of the electorate went to the polling-booths to select 472 Deputies from 987 candidates.[63] The elections resulted in a victory for the Left.[64] Of the partise of the Popular Front, the Socialists won 88 seats, *Izquierda*

Republicana 79, *Unión Republicana* 32, *Esquerra de Catalunya* 20, Communists 15, *Acció Catalana* 5, *Unió Socialista de Catalunya* 4, *Galleguistas* 3, Federals, Catalan Nationalist Republicans and *Unió de Rabassaires* two each, and Left Agrarians, *Esquerra Valenciana*, *Frente Català Proletari* and the POUM one each; there were also eight independents, among them the Syndicalist Pestaña. In the Centre, *Portelistas* won 19 seats, *Lliga* 11, PNV 9, Radicals 8, Progressives 6, Conservatives 3 and Liberal-Democrats one; there were also seven independents. On the Right, the CEDA won 96 seats, Traditionalists 14, *Renovación Española* 12, Agrarians 11 and the PNE one; there were also ten independents, including Romanones and his son. Thus, in comparison with the position in 1933, the Left had risen from 97 to 264, the Centre had declined from 177 to 64 and the Right from 201 to 144 seats.[65]

Although, as usual, the Cortes were conceived of as composed of three segments, many of the deputies of the Centre had been on the Right in the elections. Paradoxically, the candidates of the Popular Front obtained some 4,356,559 votes, while the 'antirevolutionary' candidates polled 4,570,744. The *Portelistas*, Progressives and odd independents of the Centre received 340,073, and the Basque Nationalists 141,137 votes.[66] Thus the opponents of the Popular Front, excluding the non-aligned Centre and PNV, got more votes than the Left. The quirks of the electoral system worked in favour of the latter, because it won in 34 constituencies, whereas the Right retained only 24 and the PNV two.[67] Portela had made the mistake of believing that Spain was electorally more corrupt than it was.

The results of the voting on 16 February showed that the Right—principally the CEDA—was unshakable in León and the Castiles. In 1936 there were more abstentions in these regions than in 1933, probably because some wheat-growers did not vote in protest against the mishandling of the wheat surplus. The Right held some areas bordering the Castilian heartland: Albacete, Teruel, Saragossa province, Álava and, of course, Navarre. Madrid province, however, was lost to the Left—perhaps a special case, as it was more open to the influences of the capital. All the big cities went to the Left: Madrid, Barcelona, Saragossa, Bilbao, Seville, Málaga, Valencia, Murcia.[68] In areas where the CNT was strong, its intervention assured the Left of victory and the level of abstentions was lower than in 1933, as was the case in Lower Andalusia, the Levante, Catalonia and Huesca. Possibly its followers voted for Left Republicans rather than Socialists. In provinces where Socialists and anti-Socialists were fairly evenly balanced, there was a swing to the Left—in Extremadura, Upper Andalusia and Asturias.[69] In Galicia, the Right retained Orense, but the Left gained the coastal provinces. Here Anarchist intervention may possibly have helped the Left, but the situation was confused by the attitude of the *Portelista* Governors, for Galicia was the region where *caciquismo* seems still to have been a significant factor. Off the mainland, the Balearics remained March's preserve, whilst Ceuta and Melilla went to the Left. In the Canaries Las Palmas went to the Left and Tenerife to the Right, though *caciquismo* perhaps played a part in both results.

In general, then, there was a marginal movement of opinion to the Left, reinforced by Anarchist support. In 1933 the Left had been divided and the electoral system had accentuated the swing to the Centre-Right; in 1936 the opposite happened, though numerically the Popular Front was in a minority. The demise of the old liberal-conservative Centre was symbolised by the defeat of Lerroux, Cambó and Martínez de Velasco.[70]

Voting on 16 February took place in a general atmosphere of order and calm. There were only a few incidents.[71] Although the Rightist press was slow to concede defeat, politicians realised by late on the 16th that the Popular Front had won.[72] On the night of the 16th, rioting broke out in parts of the country, apparently instigated by supporters of the CNT who wanted to release their prisoners immediately, and by young Leftists eager for the immediate transfer of power to the Popular Front. The rioting spread in the next couple of days, even though Portela declared a 'state of alarm' on the 17th. Several Civil Governors threw in the sponge and simply deserted their posts.[73] Against this background of growing disorder, Rightist and military leaders pressed Portela to call out the Army and hold the Left at bay.

During the night of 16–17 February, José Antonio asked Portela in vain for rifles. He offered the Premier the services of the *Falange* in the event of a Leftist *coup*.[74] In the early hours of the 17th Gil Robles, who had just angrily rejected Monarchist appeals for a Rightist *coup*, also called on Portela at the Ministry of the Interior.

He asked for a 'state of war' to be proclaimed immediately, and told Portela to associate him with the government, be it as 'a Minister, or your secretary, or a stenographer, or whatever you like', so as to allay Rightist fears. Portela refused both these requests.[75]

Next, the Chief of Staff, Franco, telephoned the War Minister to ask for the proclamation of a 'state of war', but General Molero replied that he would not do this without the authority of Portela. Franco also telephoned General Pozas, who was in command of the Civil Guard, and was given the same answer. Franco and other Generals nevertheless made ready for such a proclamation, and, in the process, were informed by officers that they would not lead troops on to the streets unless the support of the Civil and Assault Guards were assured. Franco therefore next pressed the Premier to declare a 'state of war'. Portela apparently suggested such a course when the cabinet met, but the President advised against it because it would be an act of provocation in the eyes of the Left.[76]

On the evening of the 17th—the day on which Portela declared a 'state of alarm'—a meeting between Portela and Franco was arranged by Natalio Rivas, a *Portelista* candidate in the elections. Franco again pressed the Premier to proclaim a 'state of war', if necessary in defiance of the President's wishes. The Army, Franco explained, could not act on its own because 'it has not now the moral unity needed for carrying out this undertaking'. The legal sanction of a proclamation by the Premier would overcome internal military differences and ensure the necessary police support from Pozas. Portela, however, said that he was too old for such strong measures, but he nevertheless promised to sleep on it.[77]

By this stage, the Socialists were demanding power for the Popular Front immediately; the alternative was a general strike. Gil Robles, on the other hand, publicly asked Portela to follow Martínez Barrio's example in 1933: he should keep order and stay in power until the new Cortes met on 16 March.[78] However, on the morning of the 18th Portela contacted Azaña because he thought that the disorders could only be halted by the latter taking power immediately; but Azaña wanted Portela to stay on until the Cortes met.[79] In the evening Portela conferred with Martínez Barrio in an effort to persuade him either to take power himself or to get Azaña to change his mind. During the meeting Pozas spoke of preparations being made by the military. When Portela told Franco of his intention to give power to the Left and assured him that the situation was not really so bad, Franco tried hard to dissuade him.[80]

A last effort to persuade Portela not to hand over power to the Left was made later that night by Calvo Sotelo at a prearranged meeting in the Hotel Palace. He asked Portela to use the Army to save Spain from anarchy, crush the Left and entrust government to stronger hands than his own. When Portela refused, Calvo Sotelo declared that all was lost.[81] On the morning of the 19th, Portela again asked Azaña to become Premier, but he again refused. In Portela's opinion, only Azaña could restore order and avert a general strike. He therefore resigned in order to precipitate Azaña's assumption of power. The President, who had wanted Portela to remain in power at least until the votes had been scrutinised on 20 February, had now to ask Azaña to form a government. The latter felt bound to accept power in the circumstances, and a new government was announced by him at 9 pm on the 19th. Spain was now ruled by Left Republicans in the name of the Popular Front.[82]

The parties of the Right now sought to explain why it was that they had lost the elections. Gil Robles tried to put the defeat in proportion: the CEDA, with its 96 seats, was still the biggest single parliamentary group, and it alone on the Right had increased its vote since 1933. There was therefore no cause for despair. Various factors, in his opinion, accounted for the defeat. In 1935 the party had not had time to put its programme into effect. Portela's attempt to create his own 'Centre' had confused conservative voters. The Left had been united and had been able to exploit Catalanist feeling as well as the emotional issue of an amnesty; in 1933 Casas Viejas had worked in favour of the Right, in 1936 the Asturian repression had worked against it, since 'Spain is a country that always takes the side of him whom it believes [to have been] persecuted'.

In some provinces the allies of the CEDA had been in league with the Governors and had been disloyal. In others, he said, the Left had used force or threats, and thus had caused the crucial abstention of some conservative voters. In four or five provinces, he went on, the Right had lost thirty to thirty-five seats because Leftists

had falsified the results during the 'anarchy' of 17–20 February.
The votes of the CNT and the lack of martyrs on the CEDA's part
had also been factors. Lastly, all capitalists and property owners
ought not to be blamed, yet there were 'very many who, as soon
as the Right attained a share in government, with suicidal egoism
lowered wages, put up rents, started unjust evictions and forgot
the sad experience of the years 1930–1933. Therefore in many
provinces the Left's vote increased among humble farmers and
agricultural workers, who, with a just social policy, would always
be on our side.'[83]

The *Cedistas* of León added that Socialist organisation was
superior to the CEDA's. Opinion was fickle, and the Right had lost
votes by mishandling the wheat problem and by pruning the
bureaucracy. Nevertheless, the key factor had been the non-
implementation of social and agrarian legislation: 'We must be
more generous than we have been in social policy. The behaviour
of certain Rightist elements has not been in harmony with the
doctrines that we preach, and owing to certain abuses, . . . the
Right in effect has appeared as defender of these in the eyes of the
proletariat.'[84] *El Debate* came to the general conclusion that there
were three Spains: the towns, the stable countryside and the
unstable countryside. The first was Leftist, the second Rightist,
while the fickle third (Extremadura, Andalusia, etc) held the
balance: it had voted against the Left in 1933, but against the
Right in 1936.[85]

Monarchists, however, put forward different explanations.
Calvo Sotelo held the CEDA responsible for the defeat because it
had called the tune during the campaign. Goicoechea blamed the
policy of appeasement in 1934–5, and attributed abstentions to the
CEDA's refusal to adopt an offensive counter-revolutionary programme with Monarchists against the régime. Rightists had lacked
enthusiasm and conviction: 'the tactic and its defenders will be
answerable to the Rightist masses'. Fal Conde spoke of 'a defeat
for lack of programme, unity of thought and tactic. As always,
those who subordinate the substantive to the tactical end up by
losing the tactical and the substantive.'[86] It remained to be seen
whether these internal divisions on the Right would or would not
disappear in opposition to government by the Popular Front.

When he assumed power again on 19 February 1936, Azaña was

a man fully conscious of his great responsibilities in a delicate situation. His address to the nation was notable for the absence of his old partisan bitterness: 'No persecution is to be feared from the government, as long as everyone keeps within the law. . . . Prosperity, liberty and justice . . .: let us all unite under this banner, beneath which there is room for Republicans and non-Republicans, for all who feel love of Country, discipline and respect for constituted authority.'[87] The CEDA's leaders responded by saying that they would put no obstacles in the way of a Republican government which acted with moderation and kept order. They were very critical of Rightists who panicked.[88] Azaña began by repealing by decree Chapaprieta's economic measures, restoring the town councillors of 1931 to their posts and appointing new provincial Governors to replace those who had deserted their posts. The Right saw that it must help Azaña if the extreme Left were to be brought under control and order restored. In the Permanent Deputation of the Cortes Rightists voted for decrees freeing the Basque Mayors and all others held for political or social crimes, and allowing the Catalan Parliament to meet right away so that it could give the *Generalidad* a government led by Companys.[89]

El Debate outlined the CEDA's terms for co-operation with the government: dissolution of all militias as in France, a programme of economic reconstruction that the Right could support and no full-scale campaign against Catholic schools.[90] Gil Robles thought that Azaña would keep his head above water for a time, but sooner or later the Socialists would turn against him and his position would become perilous.[91] After a meeting of his party's National Council on 4 March, he defined the CEDA's attitude to the government more precisely: 'At its side without hesitation concerning the maintenance of public order, seriously endangered by great masses of the Popular Front. In other matters, most firm maintenance of our party's ideas and position in the face of the government's plans. In Parliament, firm, reasoned, unruffled opposition to all that conflicts with what we are and represent, with no systematic obstruction, sterile when not self-defeating. . . . Our party is not changing its tactic, neither does it think vaguely of solutions by force. It knows how to win and it knows how to lose. . . . Could a moment of anarchy arrive when the legal struggle would become impossible? In the first place, I just do not believe that the government will allow itself to be overrun, and we are all ready to aid it in this undertaking. But, in the last resort, action in moments of anarchy is not the function of political parties. And we, in the final analysis, are a party.'[92]

While Gil Robles wanted to bolster Azaña's position *vis-à-vis* his Socialist allies, other Rightist leaders in February decided to give Azaña a breathing-space for tactical reasons. Goicoechea conceded that Azaña would act legally, but the decisive factor would be the activity of the Leftist masses. Alfonsines would support any government that seriously meant to keep order, but he said that he could find no evidence that Azaña had the firm intention of becoming 'a barrier against the uncontrolled revolutionary torrent'.[93] Even Fal Conde spoke of supporting the government if necessary in the interests of Spain. Calvo Sotelo publicly declared that, in his opinion, Azaña would try to keep order for reasons of *amour-propre*, but his honeymoon with the Leftist extremists could not last long.[94] José Antonio also instructed his followers for the moment to wait and see. He advised Azaña to break with his Marxist and separatist allies, broaden his government and carry out the 'national revolution'. If this did not happen, then *Falangistas* themselves would begin to carry out this revolution.[95]

In early March, however, the Monarchist Right decided that any hope of compromise had vanished. The government had not quelled the disorders and the streets were still in the hands of uniformed Socialist and Communist militiamen chanting revolutionary slogans. The CEDA was impenitent and, according to Monarchists, was refusing to recognise the revolutionary realities of the situation.[96] For its part, the *Falange* again took to a policy of physical reprisals, which led to the imprisonment of José Antonio in mid-March and, in mid-April, to the proscription of the movement. Nevertheless it continued its activities as a clandestine militia.[97] The *Falange*'s counter-terrorist violence from late February onwards attracted into its ranks *Japistas* and other young Rightists in considerable numbers. So great was the influx that José Antonio was worried lest his movement lose its identity.[98] The JAP under the leadership of Pérez de Laborda remained loyal to the *Jefe* despite the decline in numbers, and the Catholic student body refused to amalgamate with *Falangistas*.[99] The CEDA firmly denied Socialist accusations that it was harbouring gunmen, but it warned that people would lose faith in legality if there were no return to normal.[100]

Gil Robles was not to be deflected from his course: 'We must rely on the patriotic [good] sense of Señor Azaña to turn the government towards the Centre, breaking its links with Socialism and Communism. . . . It is necessary to reinforce Azaña's authority so that, strengthened, he can face up to the situation of public order that confronts him. The resources of government are very great, and when they are well used there is nothing to fear.' Conservatives must accept an advanced social programme as the *quid pro quo*; indeed, 'the Spanish privileged classes need cudgelling to make them see reason'.[101]

Hopes of compromise suffered something of a setback in late March when a committee of the Cortes began to examine various certificates of election (*actas*). As usual, each side accused the other of malpractice and corruption. According to the Right, Leftists had taken advantage of the anarchic situation between polling-day and the official provincial scrutiny (20 February) to falsify returns, thus robbing the Right of victory in Cáceres, Corunna, Lugo, Pontevedra and Valencia province. The Left denied these charges and accused the Right of winning by foul means in the Balearics, Cuenca, Granada, Orense, Salamanca and Saragossa province, which, of course, the Right denied. Were the Popular Front, which had majorities in both the committee and the chamber, to act in a partisan spirit of unity, Gil Robles, Calvo Sotelo and Goicoechea would all be unseated. For the intransigent Left (*Caballeristas* and Communists) this was a tempting solution. The Popular Front was also aware that, although it already had a majority in the Cortes, it did not have sufficient deputies on its own to ensure the quorum necessary for approving legislation. It is impossible to reach any definitive judgment on the validity of the evidence presented, but it would seem that odd things had been happening, particularly in Cáceres, Cuenca, Granada and Galicia.[102]

In the committee on the *actas*, the Right accused the Left of acting from partisan motives and refusing to study the evidence impartially. On 27 March the Right withdrew from the committee, leaving Calderón as an observer, after rejecting a political compromise giving the Right the Balearics and Saragossa province and the Left Cuenca and Granada. Then, on 30 March, Prieto, chairman of the committee, resigned because he said that he could not be sure of agreeing with one of the decisions about to be made.[103] On 31 March, the CEDA and the Monarchists withdrew temporarily from the Cortes. Giménez Fernández declared that the CEDA could not be party to 'the substitution of the popular will, basis of a democratic régime, by the absolute command of a disputable majority, essence of totalitarian régimes. . . . Your path is free. Constitute Parliament as you please. . . . We leave in your hands, gentlemen of the majority, the fate of the parliamentary system.' Goicoechea said that coexistence was now impossible in the Cortes, while Lamamié de Clairac in effect announced that rebellion was now licit. Ventosa (*Lliga*) and Cid (Agrarian) said that their parties would not withdraw, but they appealed to the Left not to light the fires of civil war for the sake of a few extra seats.[104]

The moderates of the Popular Front saved the day: the Republicans of the Left and Centre outvoted Socialists and Communists and so upheld the results in Orense and Salamanca, which had respectively elected Calvo Sotelo and Gil Robles. The elections in Granada and Cuenca (Goicoechea's constituency) were annulled,[105] but no other changes were made, save that four Rightists were unseated for 'incompatibilities'.[106]

New elections were to be held in Cuenca and Granada on 3 May. In both provinces the Right formed a 'National Front'. That in Granada contained four *Falangistas*, General Varela and *Cedistas* (including Pérez de Laborda and the worker Ruiz Alonso). On 29 April the Right withdrew from the contest as the Governor denied its candidates the freedom to campaign and took no action against the violence of Leftists. Gil Robles refused a Socialist offer of three seats for the CEDA on condition that Ruiz Alonso withdrew. All thirteen candidates of the Popular Front were returned.[107]

In Cuenca the Right's list consisted initially of a local *Cedista*, an ex-Agrarian independent, Goicoechea, General Franco and José Antonio. As Prieto pointed out, the list cast doubts on the legalism of the Right. Franco soon withdrew because the imprisoned José Antonio refused for personal reasons to appear on the list with him. The government next changed its mind and insisted that this election was, in fact, the second round of the contest of 16 February, thus disqualifying José Antonio because he had not then been a candidate in Cuenca. The Governor arrested Rightists during the campaign and closed many of their offices, while the Socialists brought in gunmen from the capital. Some returns were falsified. Three Leftist candidates, the *Portelista* Álvarez Mendizábal, the *Cedista* and the ex-Agrarian were declared elected. José Antonio obtained the highest Rightist poll but was disqualified.[108] The final composition of the Cortes was: Left, 277; Centre, 60; Right, 131. The Socialists emerged as the biggest single group.

After this blow to the cause of compromise, Azaña made another attempt to appease Right and Left. He asked Socialists to be patient: he intended to carry out the Popular Front's programme without omissions and without additions. He explained to the Right that on 19 February he had inherited 'a country abandoned by the authorities', with scarcely a provincial Governor doing his duty. Time would be needed to overcome disorder and re-establish the power of the State.

The government, however, decided that there was no more time available for Alcalá-Zamora. The President was at odds with the government because it seemed to him to be doing nothing to restore order, although it was armed with 'draconian censorship'; it was letting itself be overawed by the Leftist extremists in the streets. The last straw for both President and Premier came at the end of March over the question of dismissing inept Governors.[109] On 3 April, at Prieto's bidding, the Cortes decided that Alcalá-Zamora's powers of dissolution of the Cortes were exhausted according to Article 81 of the Constitution. This was not Alcalá-Zamora's opinion. If, as the Cortes had decided, the dissolution in January represented the President's second use of his powers, then the Cortes were bound by Article 81 to examine whether the last dissolution had been justified. The Left now went back on its earlier pronouncements and decided it had not been justified, although it had resulted in a victory for the Left. Gil Robles, who had also previously called for judgment of the President by the Cortes, now wanted the Court of Constitutional Guarantees to settle the matter. Nevertheless, on 7 April Alcalá-Zamora was

R

dismissed by the Cortes, the President of which, Martínez Barrio, became the interim President of the Republic.[110]

There was, indeed, a rising tide of lawlessness which the government failed to stem. Censorship prevented the Rightist press from reporting what was happening in full, but the more sensational incidents could not be suppressed. The impression consequently emerged of gang-warfare carried on mainly in the capital between extremist gunmen. In March, unsuccessful attempts were made to kill the Socialist Jiménez de Asúa and to burn down Largo Caballero's house by *Falangistas*, while in Oviedo the Liberal-Democrat ex-Minister Martínez was killed by the extreme Left. In April, a judge in Madrid who had passed sentence on a *Falangista* gunman was shot by the *Falange*; in Seville, a parallel attempt on the life of a judge who had sentenced a Communist for killing a *Falangista* was made by the extreme Left. On 14 April, Lieutenant Los Reyes of the Civil Guard was shot, apparently by a Socialist. The funeral two days later was attended by such Rightists as Gil Robles, Calvo Sotelo and Pradera, and ended with a gun-battle between *Falangistas* and Young Socialists, an abortive attempt by some of the mourners to march on the Cortes and mutiny in a Civil Guard barracks. On 8 May, Captain Faraudo, who drilled Socialist militiamen, was shot, possibly by the UME. His funeral, in turn, was made into a big demonstration, with Prieto and Sra Ibárruri (the Communist 'La Pasionaria') among the mourners. A few days earlier, a rumour, denounced by the government as 'absolutely false', had been spread in working-class districts of Madrid that monks had given children poisoned sweets. Monks and nuns were attacked and churches burnt as a consequence.[111]

Not all of Spain was convulsed by violence all the time: the 'Catalan oasis' under Companys was normally quiet, and the Holy Week processions in Seville passed off without incident.[112] Socialists and Rightists, however, were agreed that there existed a general state of disorder; the former talked of Rightist 'provocation', the latter blamed the Left. Since publication of parliamentary debates went uncensored in the press, Rightist leaders used the Cortes to state their complaints at length. Indeed, for Calvo Sotelo this was the only use for the Cortes, and the Right saw to it that public disorder was an issue regularly aired.

The first of what was to be a series of great and dramatic debates took place on 15 April. Calvo Sotelo noted that the government appealed for calm, but he asked how people could possibly keep calm when 'security of life is non-existent in the street, when everywhere stalks the threat of social disintegration. . . . Since 16 February it could be said that a storm of fire and fury has raged over Spain,' and he presented detailed statistics of the damage. He admitted that Azaña had faced a difficult situation on 19 February, but this could not explain why the Church of San Luis, only two hundred paces from the Ministry of the Interior, had been allowed to burn on 13 March: 'If a State does not know how to guarantee order, peace, the rights of all its citizens . . ., [then] let the representatives of this State resign!' If the government's inaction were to leave the path clear for the seizure of power by Bolshevised Socialists, then 'we must stand up here and cry that we are prepared to resist with every means, saying that the precedent of extermination, of tragic destruction, that the bourgeois and conservative classes of Russia experienced will not be repeated in Spain'.[113]

For Gil Robles, the Cortes also provided a platform from which to address the country; but whereas Calvo Sotelo's speeches were purely denunciatory and propagandistic in intention, Gil Robles also hoped that his speeches would persuade the government of the error of its ways before all were engulfed by violence. He pleaded with Azaña to restore order and either discipline or break with his extremist allies, because the alternative was civil war: the Rightist half of Spain could not and would not resign itself to extinction. If the government really believed that *agents provocateurs* were behind the disorders as it claimed, why then, he asked, was the government not taking action against them? He would not object to strong measures provided that the government treated Rightist and Leftist offenders in the same way. 'We condemn all violence, from whatever quarter it may come.' However, the disorders and the unjust 'implacable persecution' of Rightists was leading to a situation in which 'we, the parties that act within legality, begin to lose control of our masses, we begin to appear failures in their eyes; the idea of violence to fight against persecution starts to germinate among our people; we, men with firm convictions, cannot change course so easily; but a time will come

when, as a citizenly obligation of conscience, we shall have to turn
to our masses and tell them: "Within legality you have no protection, because the law, which is the supreme guarantee of [the
rights of] citizenship, does not enjoy the government's support;
in our party we cannot defend you; with anguish we must tell you
to go to other organisations, to other political nuclei that offer you
at least the attraction of revenge." '[114]

Azaña gave an assurance to the Right that he had not taken
power 'to preside over a civil war. . . . The Popular Front does
not signify social revolution, nor does it signify the business of
enthroning Communism . . .: it signifies the reinstallation of the
Republic on [the plinth of] its Constitution and the Republican
parties.'[115] The emphasis of his Minister of the Interior, Casares
Quiroga, was, however, rather different: when asked by Calvo
Sotelo to disarm everyone, he replied that he would concentrate
his energies on 'Fascism' and added: 'social revolution does not
worry me'.[116]

According to *Caballeristas*, 'all incidents, all, have been provoked by the Right. Every one.'[117] However, this myth was destroyed from within the Socialist ranks by Prieto: 'What no country
can endure is the constant blood-letting of public disorder without
an immediate revolutionary end; what no nation can bear is the
attrition of its public authority and its own economic vitality
through the continuance of uneasiness, anxiety and restlessness.'
In Prieto's opinion, the Socialists' task was 'to proceed intelli-
gently to the destruction of privileges, to destroy the foundation
on which these privileges rest; but this is not done by means of
isolated, sporadic excesses that leave behind as evidence of the
people's exertions some charred images, some burnt altars or some
church-doors blackened by flames. I tell you that this is not the
revolution.' Indeed, he continued, such actions simply created a
situation in which 'Fascism' could prosper: 'that way does not
lead to Socialism, nor does that way lead to the consolidation of
the democratic Republic, which I believe is in our interest . . .;
it leads to an utterly hopeless anarchy that is not even in the
Libertarian ideology; it leads to an economic mess that may finish
the country'.[118] Thus Prieto put the main burden of responsibility
for disorder on the extreme Left—where it properly belonged.

The division within the Socialist Party was perhaps the most important factor in Spanish politics in 1936. In part, the division was one of personalities: there had been recriminations over the Asturian revolt, and Prieto, from comfortable exile, had accused the imprisoned Largo Caballero of having been half-hearted about the rising. In part, it was a question of analysis and beliefs: Prieto drew the conclusion that the Socialists were not strong or mature enough to stage a successful revolution, while Largo Caballero decided that Prieto 'did not fit Socialist ideas'. Besteiro was by this time of no consequence. Prieto believed that the political moment was Republican, not Socialist; Largo Caballero saw this as a betrayal of the working class.[119] Prieto thought that the Socialists could not afford to desert the Left Republicans: if they did, Azaña would 'find compensating votes in the Centre and a benevolent attitude on the Right', which would support him 'unconditionally' against revolutionary Socialism.[120] To Largo Caballero, Azaña's idea of social peace without Socialism was anathema.[121] In April he announced: 'The present régime cannot continue, and, although circumstantially we support it, we must declare that this help and this support has not to be prolonged indefinitely.' The proletariat had to be ready to use force, for 'no new régime has been born without bloodshed and violence'.[122]

The Socialist deputies were divided in their allegiances, but Prieto was in control of the PSOE's executive and the party's official organ, *El Socialista*.[123] Largo Caballero's support came principally from the UGT, the Socialist Youth and the *Agrupación Socialista Madrileña*, and he had his own mouthpiece in *Claridad*.[124] The Socialist Youth was the most pro-Communist section of the party, and in March most of its branches agreed to join the Communist Youth in the JSU (*Juventudes Socialistas Unificadas*). It was hoped that this would be the prelude to ideological and organic union between the Socialist and Communist parties.[125] Largo Caballero was not himself a mere puppet of Moscow, but his views at this time coincided with those of the PCE.[126] Largo Caballero's aim was to unite Socialists, Communists and Anarcho-Syndicalists in one proletarian front. In the meantime, there must be no thought of rotation in power with the Right ever again. Socialists had to criticise and bully the government in their own interests[127]—hence the threats of revolution and the need for acts of violence.

Against this backcloth of violence a new President of the Republic was to be elected by the deputies and an equal number of delegates chosen by universal suffrage. The Right decided to boycott the elections for delegates on 26 April,[128] partly because there was little freedom to campaign, partly no doubt to try and accelerate the break-up of the Popular Front. The disputes over *actas* and the inaction of the government did not cause Gil Robles to abandon hope of a national government. He thought that the Popular Front was about to fall apart, while the spirit of violence was increasing on the extreme Left. The choice therefore lay between revolution and strong government. He called for 'a very extensive concentration of non-Marxist forces to oppose the revolution in relentless fashion within the régime' and to put through 'very advanced' social and economic measures: 'in short; either anarchy or [a] government of national understanding, strong and authoritarian. The latter, very quickly.'[129] Calvo Sotelo was not in agreement: the imminent choice lay between 'Communism or [a] national State' and the Right must therefore stick together.[130] The CEDA's leaders saw that the governmental reorganisation necessary when the new President was elected provided a great opportunity for a change of course by the moderates of the Popular Front. *El Debate* therefore told the Catholic masses that their duty remained 'perseverant obedience' to the authorities. Giménez Fernández called on them to 'lend support to the government, for the government is the Republic and the Republic is Spain, and Spain is all of us'.[131]

The national coalition which the CEDA desired was not to be. Azaña suggested Sánchez Román for President because he was a Republican outside the Popular Front, but the extreme Left vetoed his name for this very reason. Some suggested Besteiro or Los Ríos: Largo Caballero vetoed them too, and others were not keen because they were Socialists. *Caballeristas* proposed Albornoz, a convinced anti-clerical who was sure to antagonise the Right. The Popular Front therefore compromised on Azaña himself.[132] On 10 May he was duly elected President, with the *Cedista* deputies casting blank votes to show that they were within the régime but disapproved of such a partisan candidate.[133] Now seemed the moment to broaden the government to Left and to Right under the Premiership of Prieto. However, the *Caballeristas* vetoed any Socialist participation in the government and invoked the terms of the electoral pact.[134] Azaña nevertheless asked Prieto to form a government, but the latter refused, since to do so without the support of his party would have brought about the break-up of the Popular Front and the bifurcation of its mainstay, the PSOE, developments which could only have redounded to the benefit of the Right.[135] Martínez Barrio was Azaña's next choice, but he was apparently thought to be too conservative by Socialists. Therefore the lot fell upon his old colleague, the impetuous consumptive Casares Quiroga, who formed another Left Republican Ministry.[136]

The idea of a national coalition government under Prieto was the product of private conversations at the end of March between M. Maura, Sánchez-Albornoz (*Izquierda Republicana*), the National Republican Sánchez Román, Giménez Fernández, Besteiro, Azaña and Prieto himself. For the CEDA, Gil Robles authorised Giménez Fernández in April to negotiate for a government including Maura and moderate Socialists which would have the positive parliamentary support of the Agrarians and half the Socialist and *Cedista* deputies as well as Republicans of the Centre and Left, notably Martínez Barrio's *Unión Republicana*. Prieto intended to reserve the portfolio of Communications for Lucía. Just after he had declined President Azaña's offer to form a government, Prieto indirectly sounded out Gil Robles on the possibility of *Cedista* participation, but Gil Robles rejected this overture because it was by now clear that Prieto could not be sure of sufficient Socialist support to make such a government viable; besides, more than half the *Cedista* deputies were opposed to supporting one of the revolutionaries of October 1934 and precipitate action would split the legalist Right. Nevertheless Gil Robles authorised Giménez Fernández to continue negotiating for a coalition government without *Cedista* participation and undertook to do his best to prevent *Cedistas* hostile to the idea voting against such a government if it could be formed. Negotiations came to an end by the beginning of June because the necessary support on the Left was lacking.[137]

Azaña as Premier had been pessimistic about the future and was probably thankful for what Calvo Sotelo called his 'withdrawal to the Palatine'.[138] During the crisis the moderates of the Popular Front had allowed themselves to be blackmailed by the *Cabal-*

leristas, who had prevented any 'opening to the Right'. Consequently they had mortgaged the future of their Republic to Largo Caballero, whose declared policy was to destroy liberal-democracy when it suited him. Prieto and some Left Republicans clearly realised that strong government was needed, but Largo Caballero outmanœuvred Prieto as Stalin had outmanœuvred his opponents in the 1920s: he was prepared to risk splitting the party in order to get his own way. Prieto rightly saw that the break-up of the PSOE and its dependent bodies would only benefit the Right. Yet Gil Robles could not hope to keep his Rightists from adopting violent means for very much longer unless the *Caballeristas* were disciplined by a strong government which treated everybody equally. A strong government with which the CEDA could collaborate closely was the only way of taking the wind out of the sails of Monarchist and military conspirators seeking to put an end to anarchy with more drastic remedies. Such a government would have reassured Rightists and removed any justification for unilateral military action or continued *Falangista* reprisals.[139] This failure to form a coalition with elements to the Right of the Popular Front therefore brought civil war much closer. Furthermore, the new Premier's outlook and temperament were not likely to appease the Right.

Casares Quiroga presented his new government to the Cortes on 19 May 1936. He declared that he would adhere to the Popular Front's programme, but that now the pace would be quickened to please Leftist critics. He said that he did not care whether or not his government received the support of deputies outside the Popular Front. He spoke of introducing measures to restrict the independence of the judiciary, and announced that he intended to defend the Republic with the best method known to him, namely with 'the tactic of attack in depth . . . : wherever the enemy presents himself . . . we shall proceed to smash him. . . . When it is a question of Fascism, when it is a question of implanting in Spain a system that is contrary to the democratic Republic and contrary to all those conquests which we have made in company with the proletariat, ah! [then] I cannot remain detached from these struggles and I make it public to you, gentlemen of the Popular Front, that against Fascism the government is a belligerent.'

Casares Quiroga's speech well illustrated the predicament of

Left Republicans: lacking masses, they were doomed to be prisoners either of the Socialists or of the Right. Casares Quiroga clearly resolved this dilemma with the old formula, *'pas d'ennemis à gauche'*. As the liberal-conservative Ventosa pointed out, the new Premier's speech marked the end of the politics of tentative compromise: unlike his predecessor, he had not held out his hand to the Right and he had expressed no intention of trying to govern in a conciliatory manner, rather the reverse. Ventosa wondered whether his method of defending the Republic did not entail persecution of people for their ideas, not just punishment for their actions.[140]

Gil Robles immediately denied that the CEDA was in any way Fascist: 'we can feel neither enthusiasm for nor concomitance with the Fascist ideology. . . . If our party has signified anything in Spanish politics, it has represented a prodigious effort to introduce the Rightist masses to democratic processes.' Yet he thought it undeniable that 'Fascism' was growing in Spain: not the doctrine of Fascism, but 'Fascism' as a state of mind. The blame for this growth, he argued, must be apportioned to the Left since it had disillusioned Rightists with democracy by its behaviour at a time when this system was everywhere in crisis. By persecuting Rightists, the government was driving them into the arms of 'Fascism': Ministers were therefore 'today the best propagandists for Fascism', a phenomenon whose growth in Spain could also be explained as a reaction to the influence of Moscow-inspired Socialists on the government. As usual, Gil Robles appealed for an impartial national government which would effect reforms: the alternative was civil war.[141]

He had recently admitted in the press that many had already deserted the CEDA, though not all had left it for the same reason. There were those who had departed 'for paths of violence, honestly believing that national problems are resolved in this way', and those who had gone because the party could not now distribute offices and sinecures. However, the CEDA would carry on, even though 'heroic remedies seduce many people, because they are quick, and perhaps because they do not require effort from everyone. Slow evolution is always more fruitful.'[142] The leader of the JAP once again pledged the loyalty of himself and those who still served him to the *Jefe* and his policy.[143]

Calvo Sotelo interpreted the new Premier's speech as a declaration of solidarity with the *Caballeristas*, whose leader not only rejected the evolutionary Marxism of Blum but had ideas on property more radical than those of the Secretary of the French Communist Party. He continued: 'The government can never be a belligerent, Sr. Casares Quiroga; the government must apply the law inexorably, and to all.' It was not the government's function to interfere with the judiciary. 'We are living in [a state of] Asiatic cantonalism. . . . Where is authority?' The results of such lack of authority were plain to see: 'economically, impoverishment; spiritually, hatred; morally, indiscipline; politically, sterility; nationally, disintegration'.[144]

Ten days later the leader of the *Bloque Nacional* again attacked 'a government, or rather a few gentlemen who call themselves Ministers and say they govern, but misgovern. . . . In Spain the State . . . is absent from its main functions . . ., [is] humiliated by being supplanted by elements alien to the State's organisation who are putting their own essential beliefs into practice, who are corroding the bases of Spanish life and preparing a fearful future. . . . Parliament is haughtily, pompously presiding over the Spanish anarchy; the legislative power gives an impression of normality, while all the other powers, the whole of Spanish life, are the personification of chaos, disorder and abnormality. This seems to me as grotesque, as absurd, as out of place as would be the holding of a magnificent cabaret amid the cypresses of a magnificent necropolis.' Then he reminded the government of the maxim of Tardieu: ' "If you want to make the Country healthy and preserve liberty, re-establish authority." . . . You are living on anarchy, . . . because to repress it you would have to forfeit the political oxygen which these extreme forces give you. Have the courage to die slaying anarchy and Spain will be saved.'[145]

The Right's principal complaint therefore was that the government could not or would not keep order; when it did take action, it took action only against Rightists whom it often dubbed 'Fascists'. The burning of churches was particularly offensive to Catholics, but the CEDA was not prepared to make of this a separate issue: it was just part of the problem of public order.

The willingness of Azaña's government to proceed cautiously in religious matters was demonstrated on 28 April, when only

Socialists and Communists voted in favour of abolishing the payment of stipends.[146] The new government, however, with Barnés as Minister of Public Instruction, opened old wounds. Azaña's government had on 28 February ordered inspectors to visit schools run by religious congregations. Apparently these inspectors often closed down schools on their own initiative. With the appointment of Barnés, however, it would seem that closure of schools run by the congregations and the illegal confiscation of private schools became, in effect, official policy.[147] *Cedista* spokesmen asked that no schools be closed unless there were places for their pupils in State schools. The Minister replied that Catholics must now suffer for their sins of omission in failing to develop sufficiently the State system since 1933. On 4 June, the CEDA temporarily withdrew from the Cortes because the Minister's insulting language as much as his policy gave 'intolerable offence to the Catholic conscience of the country'.[148] *Cedistas* continued to complain of religious persecution, while the government went ahead with its laicising policies.[149]

The question of regional autonomy also reappeared as a political issue. In Catalonia, the former régime of the *Generalidad* had been restored and the Law on Farming Leases implemented, but Companys, like Azaña, was now more moderate than he had been earlier. In May 1936 he edged the separatists of *Estat Català* out of the *Esquerra*. He stood firm against religious persecution and adopted, in general, an empirical reformist position: the economy was not to be sacrificed to social experimentation. He intended to hold new elections in October, and was in July negotiating with the *Lliga* for a joint 'Front of Order'.[150] The PNV supported the government in order to obtain a Basque statute of autonomy, which came before the Cortes in April. By July the Cortes committee had approved the text despite obstruction from Calvo Sotelo.[151] On 28 June voting took place in Galicia on a statute for that region, but the referendum was marred by corruption and Rightist abstention.[152] There was also talk of statutes being drafted for Aragón, Valencia, Navarre, Asturias, the Balearics and Andalusia.[153]

This potential proliferation of autonomy caused concern on the Right about the unity of the country. In May, however, the ex-*Maurista* Silió put forward the idea of a defensive statute for León and Old Castile. His suggestion was supported by Rightists, though for tactical reasons in the main: the idea was quite soon forgotten. Nevertheless the very suggestion caused misgivings in some Rightist circles. The fierce anti-regionalist Royo Villanova retired from politics in disgust at this attempt by his political friends to play the separatists' game.[154]

Like the question of religious persecution, agrarian and economic matters could not altogether be divorced from the issue of public order. The government of the Popular Front was expected to reintroduce the agrarian legislation of 1932–3, and did so. Landowners were as outraged as ever, but the CEDA's attitude was not one of blind opposition. With some modification the Law of Agrarian Reform of 1932 replaced that of 1935; Giménez Fernández regretted that the sections on accession to property and the family patrimony had not been retained. *Cedistas* abstained when all evictions of tenants since 1 July 1934 were annulled. A new law on rural leases was also introduced, as were plans for a graduated tax on rural property, previously advocated by Giménez Fernández, and, in June, a law for the recovery of common lands.[155]

The latter draft was bitterly attacked by Rightists. They claimed that it would affect some 70 per cent of rural property and would ruin small and medium-sized farmers who were supposed to be the basis of the Republic. The municipalities were not, in any case, competent to farm the land. It was a 'Marxist' scheme to confiscate private property and ruin the peasantry. The social-Catholic Álvarez Robles, however, said that he approved of the idea in principle, but in practice it would 'degenerate into a policy for common misery'. On the other hand, the Socialist Landworkers' leader said that the draft did not go far enough, though it was a step towards socialisation of the land.[156] Yet, despite the controversy that took place over the government's legislation, all recognised that in 1936 the texts of laws were not the most important aspect of the situation. Perhaps only in the case of wheat prices was what the government decreed of some consequence. In April the price-levels were abolished, with the result that prices fell and the small grower ran into difficulties once again.[157]

The Minister of Agriculture, Ruiz Funes, intended to speed up land redistribution and, like Domingo in 1932, he issued decrees authorising the temporary occupation of estates, particularly in

Extremadura. By the end of April he was speaking of tens of thousands having been provided with land, but in most cases the Ministry was merely giving legal recognition to the invasion and seizure of estates that had already taken place under the auspices of local Leftists.[158] The Left claimed that landowners were ceasing to cultivate their lands so as to make the situation worse for the government. According to the Right, smallholders were being forced to give up farming because they simply could not pay the high wages now demanded by the unions. Farmers were also being forced by local union officials to pay unemployed workers billeted on them; if the farmers could not or would not pay up, their land was taken from them and often they were imprisoned. Farmers said that they were being bankrupted by high wages, short hours and low prices. When bad weather was added to these factors, it seemed very probable that the harvest would be meagre and a food-shortage would ensue. *ABC* described the situation as 'tragic, simply tragic'.

In the Cortes on 1 July, the Agrarian Cid painted a picture of rural chaos, especially in Andalusia, where revolutionary committees were in many places the *de facto* authority. There was security neither for persons nor for property. Calvo Sotelo, for his part, conceded that rural wages had been unjust, but the pendulum had already swung so far in the opposite direction that economic collapse in the autumn was now certain: 'people are going to move from wages of starvation to starvation of wages'. Addressing the extreme Left, he said that, if all this were intended as the prelude to the horrors of Soviet collectivisation, then 'you will not get the chance to try out your absurd schemes. We shall not let you!'[159]

Urban as well as rural employers suffered from being forced to keep men who were unemployed on their pay-rolls. The government decreed on 29 February that all workers dismissed for taking part in political strikes since 1 January 1934 were to get their jobs back and be compensated by employers for the wages lost since then.[160] At the end of April, a young *Cedista* said that the consequences of this decree were proving catastrophic: 'the disorganisation of the productive organism will be a reality in this country within a few months'.[161] Unemployment in February 1936 had already risen above the level in 1935. The economic situation was being made worse by continuing disorder and the increasing number of strikes from both economic and political motives which occurred with still greater frequency from May onwards. Some employers began to feel that they had nothing to lose by absolute intransigence.[162]

A by-product of this situation was the elimination of Catholic workers' unions. Leftist unionists insisted on the sacking of Catholic unionists, which meant virtual starvation for them.[163] Urban Catholic unionism therefore collapsed as a result of outside pressures. Yet its general weakness in the 1930s had other causes as well: a dearth of working-class leaders, internal bickering, and a lack of vision and understanding on the part of its ecclesiastical and lay mentors who often had 'an excessively "bourgeois" outlook on life [which] masked [from them] the poignant reality of the Spanish proletariat'.[164]

Leftists maintained that Rightists were sabotaging the economy by taking their money abroad, and on 16 May the government forbade anyone to take more than 500 pesetas out of the country. The Right saw the export of capital and the fall on the stock-exchange as inevitable results of lack of confidence brought about by disorder and the absence of an economic policy on the part of the government. No attempt was being made to draw up a budget, revenue was falling, unemployment was increasing, prices were rising, consumption was decreasing and the peseta was losing ground.[165] Calvo Sotelo advocated a policy like that of Roosevelt to solve the problem of unemployment. However, he believed that the extreme Left was out to wreck the economy as a prelude to Marxist revolution, and that the government was doing nothing to prevent this.[166]

The Right was becoming convinced that continued disorder and the prevalence of strikes were part of a plan to bring about economic collapse as the precondition for revolution: 'History will have to record that the Marxists realised what they planned because you, the Republicans and democrats, neither knew how to nor wished to defend what you said you loved.'[167] On 11 June the *Cedista* Carrascal stated that the Minister of the Interior had simply lost control of the country: Governors were acting independently of the Ministry, Mayors independently of Governors and the masses of the Left were doing as they pleased. A statement from the government the next day suggested that Carrascal's claims were substantially true.[168]

A frightened bourgeoisie took revolutionary phraseology at its face-value. Yet the duality of powers which the extremists of the Left sought was becoming a reality: on the one hand the government and Cortes, and on the other the *Casas del Pueblo* and the *Alianzas Obreras y Campesinas*, which were intended to be Spanish *soviets*.[169]

In fact the situation on the Left was rather more complex than this view would suggest. Largo Caballero did not tie himself to a precise revolutionary time-table, but he made it quite clear that the Socialists would not submit 'directly or indirectly' to 'certain parties that have no strength in Spain'. As a prelude to the political fusion of the organisations of the extreme Left, the proletariat (Socialist, Communist, Anarcho-Syndicalist) was to unite in the *Alianzas Obreras*. Once the proletariat was united, it would be strong enough to overpower the police and the military, and the desired violent revolution could take place.[170] The CNT reacted to such overtures by saying that it would sign a 'revolutionary pact' with the PSOE only if the latter would abandon all parliamentary activities and pledge itself to the complete destruction of the existing régime.[171] *Prietistas*, however, still controlled the PSOE's executive and official newspaper, which continued to praise the policies of Blum and to uphold the evolutionary course.[172] On 26 May, the *Prietista* executive accused the *Caballeristas* of 'revolutionary verbalism' that was helping 'the counter-revolution', and of dividing the party. On 31 May, *Caballeristas* and the JSU replied with a remarkable demonstration against 'rotten reformism and centrism' at Écija: Prieto and two Asturian miners' leaders were forced to flee from the town under a hail of fraternal bullets.[173]

Communists and *Caballeristas* were united in all but name. Relations between *Caballeristas* and the CNT, however, deteriorated. There were disagreements over strike action in Madrid, while in Málaga in June Communists and the UGT tried to settle their differences with the CNT with bullets.[174] Meanwhile, the struggle inside the PSOE continued. In May the *Prietistas* had decided to postpone the party's congress until October. The *Caballeristas* denounced this decision as a *Prietista coup* within the party. They demanded an extraordinary congress for 27 June, at which an inquest would be held on the events of October 1934, the party's programme would be revised, a new executive would be elected and unity with other proletarian parties would be effected. The *Prietista* executive now decided to hold a plebiscite within the party on whether such a congress should meet, but the *Caballeristas* feared gerrymandering and announced in advance that they would not accept the result. The *Prietistas'* plebiscite duly found insufficient support for the convening of a special congress. The *Caballeristas* said the plebiscite had been corrupt, as had the elections for a new executive, on which *Prietistas* were again dominant.[175]

Possibly Prieto hoped that by October Largo Caballero's policies would have been discredited in the eyes of the Socialist rank-and-file and that the congress would then agree to adhere to evolutionary tactics; if so, time was not on his side. Although Largo Caballero did not envisage revolution until he had come to terms with the all-important CNT, which seemed less and less likely to happen, his revolutionary talk and the uncoordinated revolutionary activity and chaos which his words encouraged nevertheless served to advance the cause of counter-revolution, as both Prieto and Gil Robles had prophesied.

In June, attempts were still being made by Miguel Maura to bring about a national coalition government which would act as a 'Republican dictatorship'.[176] However, during the debate on 16 June, it became clear that the time for such efforts had now passed.[177] As usual, Gil Robles complained of inaction, the persecution of Rightists and the lawlessness of local authorities despite the government's special powers: 'You have exercised power arbitrarily, but, moreover, with absolute, with total inefficacy.' He denied that the Right was responsible for the disorder, but added for the sake of argument that 'a government fails just the same by not being able to master subversion whether caused by the Right or created by the Left'.

He then announced an important change in policy. He no longer hoped for the break-up of the Popular Front, whose parties constituted, as far as the CEDA was concerned, the only possible governmental majority in the Cortes. Furthermore, 'as the failure is obvious, as you are going to lead the country to ruin, as your fall is going to be noisy', it was in the CEDA's interest that the

Popular Front should alone be held responsible for the disaster. 'A country can survive as a Monarchy or as a Republic, with a parliamentary system or with a presidential system, with Sovietism or with Fascism; however the one way that it does not survive is in anarchy, and Spain today, unhappily, is living in anarchy'—the prelude to Socialist dictatorship. Gil Robles insisted that it was the government's fault that the deputies were 'attending democracy's funeral'.[178]

Speaking in the same debate, Calvo Sotelo expressed the belief that the propaganda and policies of the Popular Front had provoked 60 per cent of the disorders; the government's inaction had exacerbated the situation. He then made what Socialists took to be a declaration that he was now the leader of Spanish Fascism:[179] 'In opposition to this sterile State, I raise the concept of the integrative State, which administers economic justice and can say with complete authority: "no more strikes, no more lock-outs, no more usurious interest, no more of abusive capitalism's financial formulas, no more starvation wages, no more political salaries gained by a happy accident, no more anarchic liberty, no more criminal loss of production, for national production is above all classes, all parties and all interests." This State many call a Fascist State; well, if this is the Fascist State, I, who agree with the idea of this State, I, who believe in it, declare myself a Fascist.' He also criticised the government's interference in military matters, and concluded that any officer who would rise against the Republic for the Monarchy would be 'a madman'; but so would any officer who would not rise for Spain against anarchy 'if this came to pass'.

Casares Quiroga interpreted these remarks by Calvo Sotelo as an appeal to the Army to rise against the government, an attempt to rouse 'a subversive spirit'. Therefore, said the Premier, 'if anything were to happen, your excellency would be the one responsible, with full responsibility'. According to Casares Quiroga, the disorder was the product of the policies pursued during the 'second biennium'. He spoke of the 'veritable frenzy' of the masses, yet in the same breath claimed that there was 'relative peace' in Spain: this 'state of confusion' was not to be equated with anarchy. Ventosa, for the *Lliga*, accused the Premier of complacency and of encouraging subversion by his declared belligerence and his tampering with the judiciary. For Maurín (POUM), on the

s

other hand, the very fact that Calvo Sotelo was still at large was evidence that the government was insufficiently belligerent: it was allowing 'a pre-Fascist situation' to develop.

Later in the debate, Calvo Sotelo replied to the Premier's challenge: 'My shoulders are broad; I accept with pleasure and I shirk none of the responsibilities that may be derived from acts that I perform, and I also accept others' responsibilities, if they are for the good of my Country (*Exclamations*) and for the glory of Spain. Well, how absurd! I say what St. Dominic of Silos said in reply to a Castilian King: "Sire, life you can take from me, but more you cannot." And it is better to die with glory than to live with contempt. . . . Kerensky represented ignorance; Károlyi, the betrayal of a whole millenary civilisation. Your excellency will not be Kerensky, because he is not witless, he is fully aware of what he says, of what he does not say and what he thinks. God grant that your excellency may never be able to compare himself with Károlyi.'[180]

The tone of the debate on 16 June suggested that positions were being taken up in anticipation of the outbreak of hostilities. As he himself had foreseen, Gil Robles was losing ground to those to his Right.[181] The speeches of the Leftists clearly showed that they knew Calvo Sotelo was a leading figure among Rightist and military conspirators, who were expected to act in the near future. Since April, threats had been made in the Cortes against Gil Robles and Calvo Sotelo.[182] Early in July, Monarchist friends of Calvo Sotelo heard that there were plans afoot to liquidate him. Since his police escort was involved, Calvo Sotelo went to see the Minister of the Interior, Moles, who said that he had given no orders to endanger the life of the leader of the *Bloque Nacional*.[183]

Late on 12 July, Lieutenant Castillo of the Assault Guards was shot by gunmen of the extreme Right.[184] This event produced a longing for revenge among members of his company of Assault Guards, stationed at the barracks next to the Ministry of the Interior. Captain Moreno, their commander, and Captain Condés of the Civil Guard, both collaborators with the extreme Left, took advantage of the situation to organise expeditions to assassinate Calvo Sotelo, Gil Robles and Goicoechea. However, only Calvo Sotelo could be found at home in the early hours of the 13th. He was kidnapped, shot and his corpse left at a cemetery.[185] The government issued a statement deploring both assassinations and the members of Moreno's company were detained.[186] The Socialists and Communists feared imminent action by the Right and announced their support for the régime, but the Premier refused their request for arms.[187]

Calvo Sotelo's funeral took place on the 14th, and was attended by thousands, including representatives of all Monarchist groups, Gil Robles and other *Cedistas*, Liberal-Democrats, *Portelistas*, Agrarians, Radicals, the *Lliga* and the independent intellectual Marañón. Many gave Roman salutes, and Goicoechea delivered a funeral oration which was, in effect, a declaration of civil war: 'Before this flag placed as a relic over your breast, before God who hears us and sees us, we take a solemn oath to devote our lives to this triple labour: to imitate your example, to avenge your death, to save Spain, which is all one and the same thing.' Rightist leaders had to stop the crowd stoning the Republican representatives from the Cortes, and in the ensuing demonstrations the Assault Guards opened fire and seventy arrests were made.[188]

The next morning *El Socialista* printed an article by Prieto, in which he declared that, 'for the honour of all, this cannot go on. . . . Faced with the enemy, union. . . . If reaction dreams of a bloodless *coup d'état* like that of 1923, it is entirely mistaken. If it supposes that it will find the régime defenceless, it is deluding itself. To conquer it will have to surmount the human barrier with which the proletarian masses bar its way. There will be, I have said it many times, a battle to the death, because each side knows that the adversary, if he wins, will give him no quarter. Even if this were the way it had to be, a decisive engagement would be better than this continuous blood-letting.'[189]

Prieto's opinion was echoed in the last session of the Permanent Deputation of the Cortes on 15 July.[190] For the Monarchists, Vallellano announced that Calvo Sotelo's death—a 'crime without precedent in our political history . . ., carried out by authority's own agents'—obliged them to withdraw from the Cortes. The background of Leftist threats and the Premier's speech on 16 June meant that they could 'not coexist a moment longer with the protectors and moral accomplices of this act. We do not want to mislead the country and international opinion by accepting a part in the farce of feigning the existence of a normal civilised State, when, in reality, since 16 February we have been living in complete anarchy, beneath the sway of a monstrous subversion of all moral values that has succeeded in putting authority and justice in the service of violence. . . . He who wishes to save Spain, its moral patrimony as a civilised people, will find us first on the path of duty and sacrifice.'[191]

Gil Robles also attacked the government for failing to keep order: 'Neither the right to life, nor freedom of association, nor freedom of syndication, nor freedom of work, nor the inviolability of the home have enjoyed the least guarantee with this exceptional law in the government's hands, which, on the contrary, has been made into an element of persecution against all those who do not hold the same political ideas as the component elements of the Popular Front.' The CEDA now had as little influence over its masses, who had despaired of legality, as the government had over the workers' organisations of the Popular Front. 'When citizens' lives are at the mercy of the first gunman, when the government is incapable of putting an end to this state of affairs, do not pretend that people believe in either legality or democracy; rest assured that they will turn more and more to paths of violence, and we who are not capable of preaching violence nor of profiting from it will gradually be displaced by others bolder and more violent who will come to harvest this deep national feeling.'

He condemned both murders, but claimed that they were not connected. Calvo Sotelo had been 'assassinated by agents of authority', but he believed the government bore no direct or indirect criminal responsibility. However, it must bear the political and moral responsibility for the crime: the Premier himself had prepared the 'moral climate'. The Minister of the Interior was not responsible, but the organs he controlled had failed to take obvious precautions when Calvo Sotelo had said his life had been threatened. Gil Robles concluded by saying that there was now 'an abyss between the farce that Parliament is performing and the profound and most grave national tragedy. We are not prepared to let this farce continue.' Violence would breed more violence, and the revolution would devour its children. He ended: 'You will soon be in Spain the government of the Popular Front of hunger and misery, as you are now of shame, mud and blood.'[192]

After the 'Spanish Sarajevo' everyone awaited the outbreak of civil war.[193]

One of Azaña's first acts after taking power was to remove two Generals of whom he was suspicious from the Peninsula. On 21 February a decree announced that the Chief of Staff, Franco, was to be posted to the Canaries, and the Chief of the Air Force, Goded, to the Balearics.[194] Both had played leading parts in preparing the Army for action in anticipation of the proclamation of the 'state of war' which they desired. Military opinion was alarmed at the result of the elections and at the ensuing disorders. The two Generals reacted by visiting Alcalá-Zamora and Azaña, apparently to urge them to proclaim the 'state of war' and to assure them of the Army's loyalty in this event, but their counsels were disregarded.[195] The military leaders feared the worst, but were by no means agreed on the course to be taken. Franco discreetly sounded out political opinion.[196] Goded, however, thought of General Pavía's *coup* in 1874 and suggested that the military should arrest all Deputies likely to oppose them when the Cortes opened on 16 March.[197]

In fact, two main schools of thought soon emerged among the Generals. Some were cautious and, impressed by the strength of the Left, wanted careful preparation with civilian support for a nationwide rising, which would only take place *in extremis*. Other more exuberant spirits thought in terms of rapid military action in the capital, believing that the rest of the country would accept a *fait accompli*.

This conflict of opinion became apparent during a five-hour meeting of *Africanistas* on 8 March at the home of the stockbroker Delgado in Madrid. Present were Generals Varela (apparently acting as Sanjurjo's delegate), Franco (who was leaving for the Canaries that night),[198] Fanjul, Villegas, Orgaz and Mola (on his way to Pamplona, having been transferred from Morocco on 28 February),[199] as well as 'The Technician' (Colonel Galarza). Varela announced that he favoured 'a *coup* of audacity and valour' in Madrid, which would achieve success by surprise. Mola, however, was not so optimistic: the time for such a *coup* had passed and the troops could not be relied upon to obey orders. In short, the days of the *pronunciamiento* had gone; civilian support was essential. Franco held a similar view, and he and Mola agreed that military intervention would only be justified if Largo Caballero were given power, or if Spain were to drift into anarchy, or if a civilian rising occurred which entailed the Army being called out into the streets. Franco also got general agreement that any such action would be taken purely and simply 'for Spain' and for no other cause; the old flag would only be restored later. There was also agreement on the distribution of commands if a deterioration in the situation should make a rising necessary. However, Varela and Orgaz, who were to be in charge in Madrid, persisted with their scheme for a military *coup* in the capital, arguing that the *Requetés* and others would rally round afterwards.[200]

Varela and Orgaz believed in audacity. They planned to strike on 19 April, with the Inspector-General of the Army, Rodríguez del Barrio, as nominal head of the movement, as agreed in March. Rodríguez del Barrio was to arrange an interview between Varela and the War Minister, General Masquelet, in the War Ministry. Varela would then arrest the Minister, take over his office and issue orders to the Army. Meanwhile, Orgaz would seize the Captaincy-General with a force of Civil Guards waiting in the Italian Embassy nearby. A retired Admiral, the Marqués de Villapesadilla (an Alfonsine deputy), would also seize the Ministry of the Navy with a plain-clothes force from the Post Office and the Bank of Spain. It seems that they also hoped to stage simultaneous *coups* in Barcelona, Burgos and Tarragona, and to count on certain *Falangista* and even *Japista* elements in Madrid. On 18 April, however, Rodríguez del Barrio said he was ill and could not go through with the plan—perhaps he got cold feet, perhaps more prudent Generals advised him to torpedo the scheme. Varela's plans therefore had to be cancelled. The government, apprehensive after what had happened at Los Reyes's funeral on the 16th, seems to have got wind of the plan and immediately sent Varela to Cádiz and Orgaz to the Canaries.[201]

Mola arrived in Pamplona on 15 March.[202] With the removal of Varela, he now became the principal conspirator. He enjoyed the confidence of Franco and apparently had the approval of Sanjurjo.[203] In mid-April, the Republican General Queipo de Llano offered his services to Mola. He had decided to join the plotters after the deposition by the Popular Front of President Alcalá-Zamora, a relation. He also influenced other Republican

officers to take a similar course—notably the commander in Saragossa, the Radical General Cabanellas. Queipo de Llano, who in
1930 had been on the opposite side to Mola, never enjoyed the
latter's confidence, but as Inspector-General of Customs Guards
he had plenty of freedom to travel. Apparently at Fanjul's suggestion, he began to sound out garrisons in the south; his old-
fashioned method of conspiring openly and on his own account
caused alarm amongst other Generals.[204]

In the second half of April, Mola issued his first confidential
circular, which may be said to have opened a new and more
earnest phase in military conspiracy. He informed fellow officers
that this was not the time for 'unpremeditated high-spirited
adventures', but for 'caution, reflection and quiet audacity. . . .
The most grave circumstances through which the Nation is passing owing to an electoral pact, the immediate consequence of
which has been to make the government prisoner of the revolutionary organisations, is fatefully leading Spain to a chaotic situation that can only be avoided by means of violent action. Therefore, the elements that love the Country must of necessity organise
themselves for rebellion, with the aim of conquering power and
imposing therefrom Order, Peace and Justice.' Power was to be
seized at 'the first favourable opportunity' by the military and
anti-revolutionary civilians. All leaders of revolutionary parties
and unions would be locked up, parallel military and civil authorities would be set up in each province and a military dictatorship
would be installed to restore order and the rule of law. The nation
itself would decide later on the form of government.[205]

Mola, however, by no means had the monopoly of conspiratorial
activity even among the military. Generals like Varela were not yct
convinced of the need for civilian auxiliaries: 'Better ourselves
alone. They will rally round afterwards.'[206] Fanjul and Villegas,
now the leaders of the plot in Madrid, hit upon the idea of a *coup*
on 11 May, when Azaña was to be sworn in as President, but this
plan was abandoned.[207] The exiled Sanjurjo, who was plotting on
his own account, perhaps now realised that Mola was the man who
must be put in control and must negotiate direct with the Carlists
in Pamplona. At the end of May, Sanjurjo agreed to Mola becoming the leader of the conspiracy.[208] This was a victory for Mola's
conception of the movement's aims as well as for his strategy. He

counted on the failure of the rising in the capital, which he would take with four columns converging on it from the north and east.[209]

Sanjurjo in Estoril, as head of the UME and a man in close touch with Carlists for many months, acted as the link between various conspiratorial activities.[210] It would seem that, as in 1932, he kept the threads of various ill-coordinated plots in his own hands. The Traditionalist Communion under Fal Conde was in a permanent state of reorganisation and preparation. On 20 December 1935 Fal Conde had been appointed by Alfonso Carlos Delegate-in-Chief in Spain with an advisory council, which meant that he was now in charge of all Carlist activities, not simply the political, as hitherto.[211] Within the Communion, views on who should succeed Alfonso Carlos were divergent.[212] When, in January 1936, the aged Claimant was taken ill at Guéthary, the selection of a successor became a matter of urgency. On 23 January Alfonso Carlos issued a decree embodying a compromise solution. If no legitimate successor had been chosen before the old man died, Javier of Bourbon-Parma (François Xavier, a son of Duke Robert of Parma and nephew of Alfonso Carlos's wife María de las Nieves) was to become the Carlist Regent. His designation as Regent was not to deprive him of any right to the throne, and as Regent he had of course to swear to the principles of Carlist legitimism.[213]

Dissension in the Carlist ranks had not, however, been eliminated. In general, the Traditionalist deputies still favoured the *Juanista* solution and complete adherence to the *Bloque Nacional*, while the Carlist die-hards, such as Larramendi and Senante, were opposed to this policy. In February, Fal Conde convened a meeting in Barcelona to settle matters. He had his way and the Communion continued officially to form part of the *Bloque*, though the delegates from the regions where Carlism was strongest were not in favour of this.[214] Any hopes for the *Juanista* solution were dashed on 10 March, when Alfonso Carlos informed Javier by letter that all attempts to come to terms with Alfonso had failed. Javier was now charged with the task of finding a successor faithful to Carlist principles, and the old man strongly hinted that Javier was himself the best candidate.[215] Nevertheless the *Cruzadistas*, a group of Carlists excluded from the Traditionalist Communion, continued to uphold the cause of Carlos VII's grandchildren.[216]

In March 1936, the Carlist Supreme Military Junta in St Jean-de-Luz drew up a plan for a Carlist rising. The Carlists felt sure that Sanjurjo was their man, and in March Fal Conde offered him the leadership of the *Requetés*, which he accepted. Sanjurjo now sought to link Carlist plans with the Army's plans, with Varela as his delegate in Spain.[217] The Carlists, however, were anxious to strike soon, because in March the government started threatening to oust the Provincial Deputation elected by the Law of 27 December 1934.[218] A clandestine leaflet announced: 'At last the decisive hour, so longed for by the Carlist *Requetés*, has come. . . . Workers of the Dawn: Open the shutters to the sun, for the sun of Hispanic resurgence is already casting its first rays on the North.'[219] Sanjurjo continued to negotiate with Fal Conde and the Army, and in May Javier himself went to Estoril to complete matters. If the Carlists and the Army rose together, Sanjurjo would head a 'Provisional Government of Monarchist Restoration'; but if the Carlists had to rise alone, Sanjurjo would put Alfonso Carlos on the throne.[220]

Sanjurjo also approved the Carlist Military Junta's plan of campaign drawn up in March. *Requetés* would rise in the mountains of Huelva and Cáceres, next to the Portuguese frontier. While the government was thus distracted, the *Requetés* of Navarre and the Basque Country, under Sanjurjo, would march on Madrid, as would others who were to rise in the Maestrazgo. In the capital, more *Requetés*, disguised as Civil Guards, would seize key buildings. The government, however, soon confiscated these Civil Guard uniforms.[221]

Exactly how these Carlist plans were co-ordinated with Varela's or Fanjul's schemes to take over Madrid is not clear; indeed, it would seem that there was no connection, although Sanjurjo was supposed to act as a link between them. Exactly what was Mola's relationship with the Carlists and Sanjurjo up to the end of May is also not clear. Various Captains of the UME in the Pamplona garrison were in touch with the Carlists from February, and they in turn had contacts with officers in other northern garrisons, but these Captains did not put themselves under Mola's control until 19 April.[222] It would seem that Fal Conde successfully pressed Sanjurjo to appoint Mola as his delegate in Spain after Varela's removal to Cádiz. Javier brought back from Estoril in May a letter asking Mola, if he would make a certain decision, to act as Sanjurjo's delegate, in which case Sanjurjo would only enter Spain

at his request. Mola then sent his emissary 'Garcilaso' to Estoril
to confirm this agreement, and thus at the end of May he became
'The Director' of all conspiratorial activities,[223] upon whom
success or failure now depended.

José Antonio had been in prison in Madrid since 14 March, but
this did not prevent him from issuing orders and instructions to
the *Falange*. In March he said that the *Falange* would assist the
Army if it were asked so to do, but he insisted that his movement
remain an independent force.[224] On 4 May he issued an address
to the military, to be circulated by the UME in the barracks.[225] The
extinction of Spain he believed was now at hand, and he therefore
appealed to the Army, 'guardian of what is permanent', to rise up
and save Spain before it was too late. He reminded officers of
Spengler's dictum: 'In the last resort it has always been a platoon
of soldiers that has saved civilisation.'[226] On 13 May he again told
his followers not to make pacts with other parties.[227] Then, at the
end of May, the *Falange* joined the mainstream of conspiracy.
Through an emissary, José Antonio told Mola that he could offer
him 4,000 *Falangista* shock-troops.[228] He had also been in touch
with Fal Conde for some time, and now told him that, if the
Carlists reached agreement with Mola, he would give the necessary
orders to the *Falange* if forewarned.[229] On 28 May José Antonio
was given a five-month sentence for illegal possession of fire-arms,
and on 5 June the government transferred him to the gaol at
Alicante. His brother Fernando was now left to negotiate with the
military, though José Antonio in fact retained overall control.[230]

Mola was from the end of May the '*de jure*' head of the conspiracy, as it were, though since April he had been its '*de facto*'
leader. His task was not an easy one; as Félix Maíz recorded in
his diary: 'The task of General Mola is two-fold: to organise a
National Movement and to disorganise ill-advised local actions.'[231]
Some officers wanted to rise immediately regardless of the consequences, while others had yet to be won over to the movement.
Decrees in March and June allowed the War Minister to retire
officers at will and replace them with whom he pleased.[232] Conservative military men were perturbed by being thus put at the
mercy of a civilian's whim; new appointments would be 'political',
in the sense that the Minister would choose officers of Leftist
sympathies on whom he could rely absolutely. The effect of these

measures was to exacerbate the feelings of officers: the more hot-headed became more hot-headed, the more cautious became more cautious. A similar effect on military minds, which further increased Mola's difficulties, was produced by incidents between officers and workers' organisations. For example, in May cavalrymen and workers had clashed at Alcalá de Henares. The government decided it would be best to transfer two regiments, but officers were outraged at the government taking the side of the revolutionary Left against them. They mutinied and were duly arrested.[233] Then there was the fear that the War Minister would transfer or remove key conspirators—as nearly happened to Mola and Yagüe.[234]

Mola therefore had constantly to try and assert his authority over both military and civilian conspirators. It would seem that he was in the main successful. For organising the plot in the garrisons Mola now had the network of the UME at his disposal[235]— perhaps more impressive on paper than in practice.[236] In June he provisionally assigned Generals on whom he hoped he could rely to command operations in the various regions.[237] He asked the various garrisons to despatch representatives to Pamplona to receive final instructions.[238] His strategy was still to march on the capital from various points, and on 24 June he signed the plan for the rising in Morocco, where operations were to begin. A coded telegram would be sent from Pamplona to Yagüe telling him when to strike.[239]

However, Mola was still not sure of some garrisons and was having difficulty with civilians. On 1 July, a confidential report from Pamplona informed fellow conspirators that 'the executive of the patriotic movement' believed that 'enthusiasm for the cause has still not reached the degree of exaltation needed to obtain a decisive victory'. Agreement had not been reached with a 'very important national force, indispensable for action in certain provinces', because it was making impossible demands that would make the military its prisoners for the future.[240] The original plan to rise between 24 and 29 June had therefore to be cancelled.[241]

Mola apparently had no dealings with the Carlists until June. It would seem that early in the month local Carlists offered him *Requetés* in connection with opposition to the government's plans to change the personnel of local government in Navarre.[242] Mola

believed Carlist support essential because he did not have many
soldiers in Pamplona, and many of these were Asturians with
Leftist sympathies. The Communion claimed to be able to put
8,400 men into the field at a moment's notice, but its leaders were
not prepared to sacrifice their *Requetés* merely for a *coup* to overthrow the government.[243] In Pamplona on 11 June Mola met
Zamanillo, representing the Communion's leadership, who insisted that the aims must be to abolish the Constitution, parties
and unions, and to make Sanjurjo dictator for the purpose of
creating a corporative State with corporative Cortes and the old
flag.[244] Mola considered these Carlist conditions 'inadmissible',
for they would take away the Generals' freedom to manœuvre as
effectively as the Pact of San Sebastián had that of the Republicans.

On 15 June he gave Fal Conde at Irache a copy of his own
proposals, dated 5 June: a five-man Directory of Generals would
rule with the help of technicians, and they would legislate by
decree. In effect, they would constitute a 'Republican dictatorship'
as they would undertake not to change the form of government.
They would in due course convoke Cortes, but the electoral system
was to be left an open question for the time being. Fal Conde and
Mola agreed to rise in principle, but neither would give an inch
to facilitate agreement. On 2 July Mola was officially told by
Zamanillo that his programme was unacceptable to the Carlists.
Thus there was deadlock.[245]

The *Falange* meanwhile provided headaches for both José
Antonio and Mola. José Antonio, as usual, wanted to run the
Falange personally, even though he was in Alicante gaol. He was
still anxious about the movement's independence: on 24 June he
threatened local leaders with expulsion if they negotiated with
local military conspirators. He did not want his social policy to be
disregarded by the Army in the hour of victory.[246] He was also
anxious that his rival Calvo Sotelo should not emerge as the main
civilian leader.[247] However, even José Antonio soon realised that
the *Falange*'s system of communications was a shambles, and so,
on 29 June, he issued a guide for negotiating with the military:
the *Falange* should retain its independence. At the same time he
wondered, like others, whether the Generals would ever make a
move, and there was apparently a plan for a *Falangista* rising on
10 July to force their hand. This was cancelled, but in the general

confusion Valencian *Falangistas* seized the local radio station on the 11th.[248]

Meanwhile, Mola was more worried about the Carlist impasse. Earlier, he had even thought of retiring to his native Cuba rather than risk failure with a lot of bloodshed,[249] but this phase of extreme pessimism seems to have passed by the beginning of July. On the 4th he wrote to Varela, saying that the rising might take place between the 12th and the 20th.[250] However, owing to the Carlist problem, and perhaps to the San Fermín celebrations in Pamplona, Mola revised this to between the 15th and the 23rd.[251]

Mola now apparently thought that the military conspiracy at least was in as good shape as it was ever likely to be. He had always bargained for failure in Madrid, and seems now to have resigned himself to the possibility of failure in Barcelona, Valencia and Corunna; nor does he seem to have been very sure of how things would go in Saragossa or Andalusia.[252] The question of Carlist participation had to be settled urgently. On 7 July he told Fal Conde that his decision was required immediately, saying that the question of the flag could be settled soon after the rising. Fal Conde replied that the question of the flag had to be settled right away and he must have a guarantee that an anti-democratic régime would be installed. Mola refused to countenance these conditions and accused the Communion of unpatriotic intransigence worthy of the Popular Front.[253]

Two attempts at mediation were now made. Lizarza, on Fal Conde's behalf, went to Estoril to see Sanjurjo, who wrote two copies of a letter on the 9th, one for Fal Conde, one for Mola. This letter suggested that the Carlists should use the old flag, and military units to which they were attached should use none. The military would form a 'purely apolitical' government with advisers from among the civilian conspirators. This government would revise religious and social legislation, end parties and introduce an anti-democratic system. Thus agreement with the Carlists on these terms was possible. Lizarza gave Fal Conde his copy in St Jean-de-Luz on the 11th, firmly believing that Sanjurjo had given his backing to the Carlists.[254]

At about the time Sanjurjo was being consulted, Fal Conde's old rival Rodezno met Mola, who said he wanted some *Requetés* to stiffen his companies, but he did not have arms for the 7,000 or so offered. Rodezno suggested that Mola negotiate with the Regional Junta, who would be less intransigent, though both recognised that St Jean-de-Luz would have to be consulted.[255] Mola received his copy of Sanjurjo's letter on the 12th but did not change his attitude to Fal Conde, who now ordered negotiations with Mola to be broken off. Apparently unbeknown to Lizarza and Fal Conde, Sanjurjo had sent another emissary to Mola to explain that he had only signed the letter to keep the Carlists in the movement; he was not restricting Mola's freedom of action.[256] In fact, Sanjurjo was playing a double game. By this stage his first loyalties were to his military colleagues, not to the Carlists. Meanwhile Mola had taken up Rodezno's suggestion and saw that his best chance lay with the Regional Junta. Thus, when the Regional Junta on the 12th asked Javier for permission to mobilise the *Requetés* and put them under Mola, its members came armed with a promise that they could use the old flag and could staff all the town councils in Navarre. Javier, without consulting Fal Conde, agreed to this.[257] Mola thus assured himself of Carlist support, or so it seemed.

Mola now wanted the matter fully cut and dried with all Carlist leaders, for Calvo Sotelo's death presented an ideal psychological moment for a rising. It appears that he had already agreed with the Regional Junta that the Carlists could use the old flag and the Army the tricolour, and that companies of *Requetés* 'would go together with' his own companies.[258] However, Fal Conde complicated matters on the 13th by ordering Lizarza to get the *Requeté* leaders in Pamplona to swear not to join a rising unless orders came from St Jean-de-Luz *via* Lizarza. Lizarza and the UME Captains now agreed that the latter should tell Mola to accept the terms of Sanjurjo's letter. Mola sent Lizarza a note saying that he did accept its 'orientations', a note which Lizarza immediately took to St Jean-de-Luz. He came back with a note for Mola from Javier and Fal Conde saying the Communion would participate on the basis of Sanjurjo's letter.[259] Before Lizarza gave this note to Mola, it would seem that the General had already despatched Félix Maíz to St Jean-de-Luz to see Fal Conde, who gave him a note identical to the one given to Lizarza, which Félix Maíz duly delivered to Mola on the 16th. Mola could now give the final order for the rising to begin.[260]

It could be said that the *Bloque Nacional* had implicitly relied on military action for the realisation of its programme since its inception in 1934. In 1935 some of its members had been in close touch with the UME. From February 1936 Calvo Sotelo was in touch with military conspirators, and was recognised by many as the civilian leader of the movement. Because he was closely watched by agents of the government, he was unable to take a direct part in the plotting, but he was kept informed by and gave advice to the military through friends.[261] He disagreed with Mola's plan and wanted success in the capital to be assured.[262] Nevertheless, in mid-June he put himself at Mola's disposal, and in early July assured him of the support of his followers.[263] On 10 July his friend Bau met the leading conspirators in Madrid, and reported back that the conspiracy was still not in very good shape. Calvo Sotelo, who had been told on the 8th of the orders given to his police escort, said that his own death could have the effect of giving the plotters the necessary jolt.[264] After his assassination there were demands for immediate action. José Antonio from Alicante sent an emissary to Mola to say that the *Falange* would rise alone if the General did not act by the 18th.[265] In Madrid, officers from a regiment at El Pardo asked for machine-guns with which to kill Azaña, but they were told that all was now in hand.[266] In Estoril, Sanjurjo bemoaned the loss of his future Premier.[267]

For the conspirators in the Peninsula, there remained the mystery of Franco in Tenerife. In early July, Varela asked another conspirator, Kindelán: 'Do you think Franquito will come?' Kindelán replied: 'Mola thinks so.'[268] On 8 March Franco had approved of preparations being made for a rising should the situation deteriorate. He had also apparently agreed that Mola should be in charge of these preparations.[269] On 12 March he arrived in Tenerife.[270] In early May he told a visitor that the Army's intervention was justifiable only when matters 'escape from the political sphere and enter into the orbit of the true supreme interest of the salvation of the country'.[271] In the Canaries he was often visited by Serrano Súñer, but neither he nor the Generals could ascertain Franco's views.[272] Mola's plans were therefore flexible: they envisaged Franco flying to Morocco, but they also envisaged Yagüe bringing forces across the Straits. Franco's sphinx-like attitude may have been simply prompted by caution. On the other hand, his conduct during the Republic suggests that he had a strong respect for legality, and therefore needed to be sure in his own mind whether or not rebellion was justified in the circumstances. His letter of 23 June to Casares Quiroga complaining of interference with promotions can be interpreted either as an attempt to effect a change in policy to avoid a rising, or as an effort to make the conspirators' task easier.[273]

Franco seems to have made his decision to participate in the rising between 10 and 13 July, having received an ultimatum to the effect that the other Generals would go ahead without him if necessary.[274] The conspirators attached great importance to Franco's participation because of his prestige. They had therefore taken the precaution of ordering an aircraft to take him to Morocco. He was able to go from Tenerife to Las Palmas (on Grand Canary) with the government's permission to attend the funeral of General Balmes on the 17th. Early on the 18th he heard that Yagüe had begun to take over in Morocco. He then set off in the hired Dragon Rapide and landed at Tetuán at 7 am on the 19th to take command of the best troops in the Army.[275] On the 17th, Yagüe had taken over in Morocco from his Republican civilian and military superiors. The rising had begun.[276]

During the 18th, military risings took place in Andalusia. The government was not taken by surprise. Ministers knew of military conspiracies, but took no determined action against the suspected leaders. Politically, the Left Republicans were dependent on the Left's masses. They had minimised the disorder caused by the latter when addressing the Right. They took no determined action against the military because the existence of an armed anti-revolutionary force was for them the only hope of preserving a certain independence of action vis-à-vis the workers' organisations. This tight-rope walking was the only course really open to the Left Republicans if they were not to break up the Popular Front: therefore they minimised the doings of the military to the Left as well as the deeds of the extreme Left to the politicians of the Right. Their complacent, optimistic declarations to both sides were dictated by necessity.[277]

Casares Quiroga had tried to insure against military action by putting forward the troops' summer leave in July,[278] but the Left Republicans' policy never really had much hope of success. With the rising in Morocco the policy entered its death-agony. To keep the Socialists at bay, the government throughout the 18th broadcast the news that the military rising had collapsed; on the same day, a telegram was received from Lucía supporting the government's position. The UGT, however, declared a general strike and the Socialists ordered their followers to mobilise for 'victory or death'.[279]

The Left Republicans tried one last throw. In the early hours of the 19th a new government was formed under Martínez Barrio, the least Leftist leader in the Popular Front, and Sánchez Román was one of the Ministers.[280] General Miaja, the new War Minister, telephoned Mola, and discovered that he would rise within hours. Martínez Barrio now telephoned to offer him the War Ministry in a coalition government which would restore order. Mola refused: 'If I were to agree on a compromise with you, we should both be traitors to our ideals and our men, and we should both be strung up by them. . . . Only the Army can now give the country back the peace it needs. . . . Only a military dictatorship can save Spain.'[281] The attempt to disrupt the military movement thus failed, and the Left Republicans were now in the power of the workers' organisations. Within hours the Socialists forced this government's replacement by another weak Left Republican Ministry under Giral. Arms were distributed to the workers, who had been demanding them since the 18th.[282] In Pamplona, Mola proclaimed martial law at 6 am and the *Requetés* flocked to support him.[283]

On 19 and 20 July the movement spread to the rest of the Peninsula. By the 21st it was clear that any hopes of a rapid and complete military take-over had disappeared. The insurgents had gained control of less than half the country: Galicia, León, northern Castile (but not Santander), Aragón, Navarre, Álava, half Cáceres, the Canaries, Morocco and the Balearics (though not Minorca). They also held a pocket around Cádiz, Seville, Córdoba and Oviedo.[284] In general terms, it seemed that where military leaders acted quickly, boldly and with resource, they gained the advantage even in Leftist cities, such as Seville, Oviedo and Saragossa. Where they vacillated, as for instance in Málaga, Valencia and Santander, the Popular Front's forces thwarted their plans.[285] Yet, given the confused and ill-prepared nature of the

T

conspiracy and the risings, the military plotters were lucky to have
done so well.[286] They had to rely on quite small numbers of
soldiers in the Peninsula.[287] Outside Navarre, civilian para-
military help came from small groups of Monarchists, *Falangistas*
and, in some areas, *Japistas*.[288] The acknowledged leader of the
whole movement, Sanjurjo, was killed in an air-crash near Cascais
on the 20th. It seems clear, however, that he had little intention
of putting the movement under Carlist control.[289]

Notes to this chapter are on pages 376–408.

Epilogue

THE POLITICAL aims of the 'National Rising' were somewhat imprecise: it was a movement 'for Spain' but not in favour of the Monarchy. Mola's proclamation of martial law made no mention of the form of government. It merely stated that the military were acting 'to hold Spain back from the very brink of the abyss' because 'Spain, prey to the most fearful anarchy, is bleeding to death'. Franco's proclamation in the Canaries also simply referred to the restoration of order and the quelling of revolution.[1] This 'accidentalist' approach meant that the movement did not aim to end the Republican form of government; indeed, the first proclamation in Melilla said: 'It is a question of re-establishing the rule of order within the Republic', and maintained that the Army was acting to carry out the will of the majority.[2]

This was not perhaps an unjustified claim, bearing in mind the numbers of votes cast in the elections. Though, with the division of the country, outward loyalties tended to be decided geographically, it may be presumed that the attitudes of political leaders still largely reflected the views of their supporters. Following the rising, Gil Robles, Lerroux, Cambó and Ventosa, M. Álvarez, Martínez de Velasco, Portela and, rather ironically, Unamuno, Ortega Gasset and Marañón, all showed support for it.[3] The PNV, to the anger of the insurgents, sided with the Popular Front because the Basques had been promised a statute of autonomy.[4]

The military conspirators rose principally because they believed an unpatriotic government was not keeping order, and Socialist or Communist revolution would be the eventual outcome if they did not intervene. The more conspiratorially minded among the insurgents perhaps believed in a 'Red plot'.[5] Military motives have perhaps been best expressed by General González Mendoza, who has written of a rising against 'anti-Spain' by 'the party in the

Army [that] maintained the concept of National Honour, and the internal mission pertaining to the Army within the definition of this principle when a depraved and anti-national State seeks to lead the country against its proper destiny'.[6]

Conservative-minded Republicans like Lerroux thought the rising was justified because citizens had no obligation to obey a government which could not guarantee their safety. Calvo Sotelo's death demonstrated, for them, that legality and the State had ceased to exist in practice. Therefore it fell to the Army to fill the vacuum and supply the necessary authority.[7] The great majority of Catholic opinion—lay and ecclesiastical—endorsed the rising on similar grounds and because the Popular Front was seen as the enemy of religion. (The Church could not, of course, initiate such a rising.) The Catholic viewpoint was summarised by Gil Robles: 'The Leftist government lacked legitimacy of origin and of execution. Its action was not directed to the common good but to the destruction of society. It was no longer a duty to obey a power which was habitually and seriously unjust. The Spanish Rightists found themselves faced by a situation uniting all the conditions which, according to the traditional doctrine of Catholic political ethics, justified resistance to oppression, not only passively, but actively, through the use of armed force.'[8]

Gil Robles, true to his belief in remaining within legality, took no active part in the preparation of the military rising. However, he knew that preparations were being made and that the CEDA was disintegrating: typical of what took place was the case of the DRV, many of whose members started to prepare for violence after the elections even though their leader, Lucía, always kept firmly within Republican legality.[9] *Cedistas* who despaired of legality and asked Gil Robles's advice were told to follow their consciences and act as individuals; they should not form autonomous militias but should make contact with the military and obey their orders.[10] Gil Robles rejected a suggestion made by Mola that all Rightist deputies should assemble in Burgos on 17 July and show their solidarity with the insurgents, but at the beginning of July he did authorise the transfer of 500,000 pesetas of his party's funds to the General.[11] In July he was also present at meetings of Monarchist conspirators in France as an observer rather than as an active participant.[12]

The failure of the military conspirators to achieve complete success meant civil war. Mola had earlier prophesied: 'the campaign will be long and costly. . . . In Madrid there will be another Commune.'[13] What began, at least so far as the military insurgents were concerned, as a rising within the existing Republican framework, soon took on a different political aspect, if only because the Popular Front's forces had already monopolised the adjective 'Republican'.[14] In the 'National' zone, all political groups were amalgamated on the basis of the *Falange*'s programme into the FET *y de las* JONS on 19 April 1937. The leader of this 'single political entity of a national character' was General Franco, since September 1936 the 'Head of the Government of the Spanish State'. Thus the parties of the Spanish Right were united from without.[15]

During the civil war the 'Nationals' received foreign aid— German, Italian and Portuguese. Certainly attempts were made by the conspirators to buy arms from abroad before the rising, but they bought from private sources. The pact of 1934 with the Italians seems to have been virtually dead until immediately after the rising. Aid from Germany and Portugal was also negotiated after the war had started. The plotters, however, expected sympathy from these quarters when they rose.[16]

For three years the 'Nationals' with their foreign auxiliaries fought the 'Republicans' with their foreign auxiliaries. The outcome of this battle without quarter between the two Spains was the extinction of the Second Republic. The 'National Rising' that led to this had begun just five years to the day after the most eminent Republican had declared: 'If the Spanish Republic goes under, ours will be the blame. If we do not know how to govern, the blame will be ours.'[17]

Notes are on pages 408–10.

References

INTRODUCTION

1 J. Donoso Cortés, *Textos políticos* (Madrid, 1954), 127.
2 R. Menéndez Pidal, *The Spaniards in Their History* (London, 1950), esp 207–44; F. de Figueiredo, *As duas Espanhas* (4th ed, Lisbon, 1959).
3 Text of manifesto in V. Marrero (ed), *El tradicionalismo español del siglo XIX* (Madrid, 1955), 1–68. See also R. Carr, *Spain 1808–1939* (Oxford, 1966), 45–8, 60–72, 80, 92–101 & 115–19.
4 Carr, *Spain*, 120–1, 137–43, 146–54, 156–7 & 172–6.
5 Carr, *Spain*, 184–93.
6 Carr, *Spain*, 175 & 193–4; F. Melgar, *El noble final de la escisión dinástica* (Madrid, 1964), 85–101.
7 C. Silió, *Trayectoria y significación de España* (Madrid, 1939), 107–23; C. Cardó, *Histoire spirituelle des Espagnes* (Paris, 1946), 127–32 & 147; S. Aznar, *Estudios religioso-sociales* (Madrid, 1949), 131–8; S. Galindo Herrero, *Breve historia del tradicionalismo español* (Madrid, 1956), 201–4; & Marrero, *Tradicionalismo*, 119–20.
8 E. A. Peers, *Spain, the Church and the Orders* (London, 1939), 81–6; J. M. Sánchez, *Reform and Reaction* (Chapel Hill, 1964), 28–30 & 34; Carr, *Spain*, 234–5.
9 Donoso Cortés, *Textos políticos*; also F. Suárez, *Introducción a Donoso Cortés* (Madrid, 1964).
10 Carr, *Spain*, 194–5 & 285; Galindo, *Tradicionalismo*, 211–23; Marrero, *Tradicionalismo*, 121–83.
11 Quoted in J. N. Schumacher, 'Integrism', *Catholic Historical Review*, XLVIII (1962), 344.
12 Carr, *Spain*, 337–41.
13 For the work of Cánovas see Carr, *Spain*, 347–79; cf J. M. García Escudero, *De Cánovas a la República* (2nd ed, Madrid, 1953), 21–102.
14 Schumacher, 'Integrism', 345–6; Melgar, *Escisión dinástica*, 98–100; F. J. Montalbán, B. Llorca & R. García Villoslada, *Historia de la Iglesia Católica, tomo IV* (3rd ed, Madrid, 1963), 569–70.
15 M. Menéndez Pelayo, *Textos sobre España* (2nd ed, Madrid, 1962); also P. Sáinz Rodríguez, *Evolución de las ideas sobre la decadencia española y otros estudios de crítica literaria* (Madrid, 1962), 430–572, & A. Herrera Oria, *Obras selectas* (Madrid, 1963), 266–311.

16 Schumacher, 'Integrism', 348–63; R. Oyarzun, *Historia del carlismo* (2nd ed, Madrid, 1944), 430–5; Marrero, *Tradicionalismo*, 315–42; Galindo, *Tradicionalismo*, 225–6.

17 J. Vázquez de Mella, *Regionalismo y Monarquía* (Madrid, 1957); L. Aguirre Prado, *Vázquez de Mella* (2nd ed, Madrid, 1959); L. Legaz Lacambra & R. Buide Laverde, *Cátedra Vázquez de Mella: conferencias* (Santiago de Compostela, 1945); and Carlos VII's political testament in *El Correo Español*, 24 July 1909.

18 Oyarzun, *Carlismo*, 445–51; Melgar, *Escisión dinástica*, 44–5 & 61–72.

19 Duque de Maura & M. Fernández Almagro, *Por qué cayó Alfonso XIII* (Madrid, 1948), 345.

20 A. de Foxá, *Madrid de Corte a Cheka* (n. pl., 1938), 62–3—a novel, but politically accurate and well informed.

21 M. García Venero, *Historia del nacionalismo catalán* (Madrid, 1944), passim; E. A. Peers, *Catalonia Infelix* (London, 1937), esp 123–76; J. Torras Bages, J. Maragall & F. Cambó, *La actitud tradicional en Cataluña* (Madrid, 1961); A. Ramos Oliveira, *Politics, Economics and Men of Modern Spain* (London, 1946), 381–98; & Carr, *Spain*, 538–56.

22 M. García Venero, *Historia del nacionalismo vasco* (Madrid, 1945), passim; R. Sierra Bustamente, *Euzkadi* (Madrid, 1941), 22–110; J. de Iturralde, *El catolicismo y la cruzada de Franco* (Vienne, 1955–65), I, 302–10; Ramos Oliveira, *Politics*, 406–21; & Carr, *Spain*, 192, 221 & 556–8.

23 Ramos Oliveira, *Politics*, 278.

24 On the years 1898–1923 see Carr, *Spain*, chaps xi–xiii; cf García Escudero, *De Cánovas*, 135–235.

25 J. Vicens Vives, *Historia social y económica de España y América*, IV–2 (Barcelona, 1959), 145–8.

26 F. del Valle, *El P. Antonio Vicent, S.J., y la acción social católica española* (Madrid, 1947); A. Osorio García, 'El sindicalismo español anterior a 1936', *A.C.N. de P.*, 15 May 1961.

27 Osorio García, ibid; J. N. García-Nieto, *El sindicalismo cristiano en España* (Bilbao, 1960), 63–178; J. Gómez Acebo, *Origen, desarrollo y trascendencia del movimiento sindicalista obrero* (Madrid, 1915), passim; and Cardó, *Histoire spirituelle*, 144–5.

28 A. Monedero Martín, *La Confederación Nacional Católico-Agraria en 1920* (Madrid, 1921).

29 D. Sevilla Andrés, *Antonio Maura* (Barcelona, 1954), esp 190–5; Carr, *Spain*, 477–87.

30 J. Gutiérrez-Ravé, *Yo fuí un joven maurista* (Madrid, 1945); Sevilla Andrés, *Maura*, 444ff; A. Ossorio Gallardo, *La guerra de España y los católicos* (Buenos Aires, 1942), 62–73; M. Pi Navarro, *Los primeros veinticinco años de la vida de José Calvo Sotelo* (Saragossa, 1961), 124–31.

31 See A. Boissel, *Un chef: Gil Robles* (Paris, 1934), 24 & 37–9; Gutiér-

rez-Ravé, *Joven maurista*, 256–63; and J. M. Gil Robles, *No fue posible la paz* (Barcelona, 1968), 29.

32 Carr, *Spain*, esp 124–6, 129, 214–19 & 336–7; cf S. G. Payne, *Politics and the Military in Modern Spain* (London, 1967), 1–43.

33 Carr, *Spain*, 500–6, 516–23 & 558–64; Vicens Vives, *Historia social*, IV–2, 184–5; García Escudero, *De Cánovas*, 184–5, 217–28 & 238–9; Payne, *The Military*, 44–205.

34 On the Dictatorship see Carr, *Spain*, 564–91; Payne, *The Military*, 205–55; D. F. Ratcliff, *Prelude to Franco* (New York, 1957); M. Tuñón de Lara, *La España del siglo XX* (Paris, 1966), 121–88; and articles by Primo de Rivera in *El Debate*, 21, 22, 23 & 25 March 1930.

35 Sáinz Rodríguez (conversation), who attended the Assembly as a loyal critic of the Dictator, says that had Prieto's arguments not prevailed with Largo Caballero and the UGT, the Assembly would have been truly representative and could have resulted in the Belgian-style democratic Monarchy which he and Besteiro both wanted.

CHAPTER 1

1   For the fall of the Monarchy see Carr, *Spain*, 591–602. Cf García Escudero, *De Cánovas*, 289–317; S. Galindo Herrero, *Los partidos monárquicos bajo la segunda República* (2nd ed, Madrid, 1956), 40–70, & Tuñón de Lara, *España*, 189–227.

2   Sáinz Rodríguez (conversation), who was a member of the abortive Constitutional Centre.

3   He added that his cat had more advanced views—it had already become a Republican.

4   Goicoechea, speech in Madrid, 20 Apr 1930, quoted in *Historia de la Cruzada española* (ed J. Arrarás Iribarren), (Madrid, 1939–43), I–2, 218.

5   Monarchist confidence is reflected in the report of the local Governor, describing the meeting as 'of no importance'. (A. Alcalá Galiano, *The Fall of a Throne* [London, 1933], 29.)

6   Largo Caballero, *El Socialista*, 7 Apr 1931.

7   Speech at Valencia, 15 Apr 1930, quoted in *HCE* I–2, 217.

8   Quoted by A. Mendizábal, *The Martyrdom of Spain* (London, 1938), 94.

9   M. Maura, *Así cayó Alfonso XIII* . . . (Mexico City, 1962), 50 & 82.

10 Quoted by Sánchez, *Reform and Reaction*, 74.

11 Quoted by Alcalá Galiano, *Fall of a Throne*, 106.

12 *HCE* I–2, 223–4; & Galindo, *Los partidos*, 49. The ex-Minister of Labour, Aunós, set out to found his own Labour Party.

13 Interviewed in *The Spectator*, 21 Mar 1931, 453–4.

14 Marqués de Hoyos, *Mi testimonio* (Madrid, 1962), 108. Alfonso's failure to attend Primo de Rivera's funeral caused resentment among UMN Monarchists.

15 *ABC*, 2 & 3 Apr 1931.

16 Galindo, *Los partidos*, 61–2.
17 E. Vegas Latapié, 'Maeztu y *Acción Española*', *ABC*, 2 Nov 1952.
18 *ABC*, 7 Apr 1931.
19 Hoyos, *Testimonio*, 106–7 & 217.
20 Galindo, *Los partidos*, 50; Alcalá Galiano, *Fall of a Throne*, 58–9. *El Socialista*, 1 Apr 1931, reported that a man in Córdoba who displayed a placard reading 'Long live the King' on his balcony had been ordered to take it down.
21 R. Ledesma Ramos, *Antología* (Barcelona, 1940), 33–7 & 42; S. G. Payne, *Falange* (London, 1962), 13.
22 E. Mola Vidal, *Obras completas* (Valladolid, 1940), 1038–42.
23 D. Berenguer, *De la Dictadura a la República* (Madrid, 1946), 223. Col Varela, approached unsuccessfully in 1930 by Lerroux, noted in his diary: 'I believe that the Army must remain on the touchline in political struggles.' (J. M. Pemán, *Un soldado en la Historia* [Cádiz, 1954], 100.) In the autumn of 1930 the ex-*Maurista* Gen Fanjul politely but firmly declined Alcalá-Zamora's request to work for the Republic (M. García Venero, *El general Fanjul* [Madrid, 1967], 152). The Navy's lack of enthusiasm was reflected in Alfonso's later lament to Lord Londonderry: 'Charlie, even the Navy turned against me!' (R. Sencourt, *King Alfonso* [London, 1942], 231.)
24 Sánchez, *Reform and Reaction*, 68–9 & 75.
25 S. Aznar, *Impresiones de un demócrata cristiano* (2nd ed, Madrid, 1950), 223–30 & 237.
26 Herrera, *Obras*, 11–24 (speech of 11 June 1930).
27 *El Debate*, 8 Apr 1931.
28 Hoyos, *Testimonio*, 67. Romanones also testifies to the complete 'inhibition' of the government in this election (Conde de Romanones, *Obras completas*, III [Madrid, 1949], 441).
29 Hoyos, *Testimonio*, 68, 109 & 206–7.
30 Hoyos, *Testimonio*, 183–6; 14,216 Monarchist and 1,747 Anti-Monarchist councillors were proclaimed unopposed under Article 29 of the electoral law. The 9 capitals won by the Monarchists were Ávila, Burgos, Cádiz, Gerona, Lugo, Palma de Mallorca, Pamplona, Soria and Vitoria. The full results were never published and a request to see the returns was refused by the Republicans later. (E. A. Peers, *The Spanish Tragedy* [3rd ed, London, 1936], 233.) M. Maura concedes victory to the Monarchists in the countryside, where the Republicans had not campaigned (*Así cayó Alfonso*, 141 & 147).
31 Romanones and La Cierva were shaken by Republican victories in their 'fiefs' of Guadalajara and Murcia, and Hoyos by the loss of Toledo with its ecclesiastical, military and rural electorate. In Madrid the Republicans won the upper-class district of Buenavista, and 30 seats in all to the 20 Monarchists. In Barcelona the Catalan Left beat the *Lliga*, thanks to a pact with the CNT made after an optimistic Cambó refused the request of a pessimistic Maciá for a coalition.

(Hoyos, *Testimonio*, 51, 110–11, 121 & 125; Romanones, *Obras* III, 442–3; Maura, *Así cayó Alfonso*, 147.)

32 See Maura, *Así cayó Alfonso*, 164.

33 Galindo, *Los partidos*, 73–4 & 77–8. The Premier, Aznar, said that Spain had gone to bed Monarchist and awoken Republican.

34 Romanones, *Obras* III, 443–4. Sanjurjo's unhelpful attitude was perhaps prompted by Alfonso's shabby treatment of Primo de Rivera, a close friend. A. Lerroux, *La pequeña historia* (Buenos Aires, 1945), 83–4, describes Sanjurjo's position as that of a benevolent neutral. He did not offer his services to the Republicans until after he knew of the King's decision to leave. (Maura, *Así cayó Alfonso*, 164–6.)

35 Maura, *Así cayó Alfonso*, 152–3 & 188; he excludes himself from the pessimism.

36 Texts in *Habla el Rey* (ed J. Gutiérrez-Ravé), (Madrid, 1955), 330–1. On reaching Marseilles, his first question was whether a reaction had yet begun in Spain in his favour; he was clearly disappointed when told that it had not. (J. Arrarás, *Historia de la segunda República española* [Madrid, 1956–68], I, 47.)

37 E. Vegas Latapié, *El pensamiento político de Calvo Sotelo* (Madrid, 1941), 88–92.

38 *ABC*, 14, 18 & 19 Apr 1931.

39 *El Debate*, 14 & 15 Apr 1931.

40 Text in Arrarás, *HSRE* I, 27–9. The Provisional Government was composed of two Liberal Rightists (Alcalá-Zamora, President; M. Maura, Interior); two Radicals (Lerroux, Foreign Affairs; Martínez Barrio, Communications); three Socialists (Largo Caballero, Labour; Prieto, Finance; Los Ríos, Justice); two Radical-Socialists (Domingo, Public Instruction; Albornoz, Public Works); and one representative each of the Left Republican groups *Acción Republicana*, *Acció Catalana* and the ORGA (Azaña, War; Nicoláu d'Olwer, Industry and Commerce; Casares Quiroga, Navy, respectively).

41 J. Monge Bernal, *Acción Popular* (Madrid, 1936), 128; & Galindo, *Los partidos*, 101.

42 *El Debate*, 21 & 23 Apr 1931.

43 *ABC*, 22 & 26 Apr 1931. Monarchists attributed Herrera's coolness towards the Monarchy to the failure of his 'Great Social Campaign' in 1922 when Alfonso refused to give 125,000 pesetas. (J. Cortés Cavanillas, *Gil Robles, ¿ monárquico?* [Madrid, 1935], 39–47.)

44 Monge Bernal, *AP*, 129–32. *Acción Nacional* was sponsored by the Nuncio and Cardinals Vidal Barraquer and Ilundáin (Archbishops of Tarragona and Seville respectively) (Cardó, *Histoire spirituelle*, 208).

45 *ABC*, 5 May 1931. Alfonso's view was also expressed in a private letter to Honorio Maura, offering overt collaboration with the government (H. Vallotton, *Alphonse XIII* [Lausanne, 1943], 192).

46 *ABC*, 8 & 10 May 1931.

47 It was decided that the leadership should not include figures prominently associated with the liberal or *Primoderriverista* groups. Lesser-known men were therefore chosen: the Conde de Gamazo, E. Cobián, A. Bernabéu, J. Danvila Rivera, the Duque de la Seo de Urgel, F. Santander, L. Garrido Juaristi.

48 This account is based principally on Maura, *Así cayó Alfonso*, 240-64; Arrarás, *HSRE* I, 74-100; *El Sol*, 12 May 1931; and F. Narbona, *La quema de conventos* (2nd ed, Madrid, 1959). Maura's account presumably shows himself in the best light. No mention is made of the later statement by Casares Quiroga that Maura had been informed of plans to burn *conventos* forty-eight hours earlier and chose to disregard the information (*Memorias íntimas de Azaña* [ed J. Arrarás], [5th ed, Madrid, 1939], 132). The moving spirits of the outbreak in Madrid were *Ateneístas*, at this time in touch with two opposition groups on the Left, the CNT and the Communists. Certainly the burnings occurred in areas where the CNT was strong. Exceptions were Saragossa, where Maura records the energetic action of the Governor, and Barcelona, where the CNT was dissuaded from burning *conventos* by Companys (J. Plá, *Historia de la segunda República española* [Barcelona, 1940-1], I, 145).

49 A. Montero Moreno, *Historia de la persecución religiosa en España* (Madrid, 1961), 25.

50 *El Debate*, 16 Apr 1931.

51 Sánchez, *Reform and Reaction*, 81-4. J. de la Cierva, *Notas de mi vida* (Madrid, 1955), 330-4, refers to a pact between Tedeschini and Alcalá-Zamora prior to 12 April which was negotiated in the German Embassy; Plá, *IISRE* I, 72, refers to an interview.

52 For the texts, see *El Debate*, 19 Apr-26 May 1931. There were hesitations: the Bishop of Segovia on 15 April thought of renouncing his position (J. F. Huerta, *Defensa de España*, [Biarritz, 1964], 207).

53 *El Debate*, 10, 23, 25 & 30 May 1931. The removal of crucifixes from schools produced an outcry from Catholic parents. It was the view of the Socialist Director-General of Primary Education, Llopis, that education should be a 'revolutionary' weapon to transform society. (*El Socialista*, 19 Apr 1931.)

54 H. Buckley, *Life and Death of the Spanish Republic*, [London, 1940], 107.

55 *El Socialista*, 23 Apr 1931. His biographer claims Segura said: 'The Spanish Church is sad and troubled.' (J. Requejo San Román, *El cardenal Segura*, [Toledo, 1932], 130-1.) The Socialist A. Ramos Oliveira (*Politics, Economics and Men of Modern Spain* [London, 1946], 438) describes the Cardinal-Primate as 'a type which the Church no longer produces, a man whose piety seemed eccentric to modern eyes, who thought a bath was the invention of the heathen, if not of the devil himself, and who wore the hair-shirt like a monk of old'.

56 Quoted in *Bulletin of Spanish Studies*, VIII (1931), 140.

57 In *El Debate*, 7 May 1931.

58 Maura, *Así cayó Alfonso*, 299–304. The almost contemporary account by Requejo San Román (*Segura*, 150–63) did not, obviously, include the then secret activities of Maura; the accounts also differ on certain facts, eg where Segura crossed the frontier and how. Cortés Cavanillas (*Gil Robles*, 80) suggests that Herrera was involved; Maura mentions only that Herrera arranged the passport for Segura's first departure. The Nuncio and Segura had been on very bad terms since 1929 (Iturralde, *Catolicismo*, I, 371–2). Gil Robles (*No fue posible*, 422) denies that he or Herrera had any part in the expulsion.

59 Maura, *Así cayó Alfonso*, 294–6; & *El Debate*, 20 & 22 May 1931. *El Socialista*, 10 Apr 1931, called the Bishop 'the Negus of the diocese of Vitoria'.

60 *El Debate*, 20 May & 2 June 1931.

61 Cortés Cavanillas, *Gil Robles*, 65–7.

62 Collective Pastoral of the Metropolitans, *El Debate*, 12 June 1931.

63 *El Debate*, 20 & 27 May 1931 respectively. The first manifesto (*El Debate*, 7 May 1931) was a compendium of *El Debate*'s ideas. The Executive Committee of *Acción Nacional* was composed of: Pres, A. Herrera Oria; Vice-President, J. M. Valiente Soriano; Sec, A. López; Undersec, J. Martín-Sánchez Juliá; Treasurer, J. Martín Artajo; Undersec, J. Moreno Dávila; Members, J. M. Sagüés Irujo, M. Senante, F. Eliso and M. Serrano Mendicute. The key posts were held by Young Propagandists; one member, Senante, was an Integrist. The ex-*Maurista* Antonio Goicoechea was the movement's interim leader; he emphasised 'inhibition' rather than 'accidentalism' regarding the form of government (Gil Robles, *No fue posible*, 77; J. Gutiérrez-Ravé, *Gil Robles* [Madrid, 1967], 26–7).

64 *El Debate*, 11 June 1931. The label 'Republican of *Acción Nacional*' was forbidden (ibid, 15 June).

65 *El Debate*, 2 & 13 June 1931.

66 *HCE* I–4, 486. A discussion took place in Quintanar's house, but the idea of action was vetoed by the ex-Ministers in Biarritz. Also involved was the journalist Pujol, at this time an *Acción Nacional* speaker.

67 *El Debate*, 23 June 1931, mentioned 39 candidates in 19 constituencies; the accompanying list, however, named 44 in 18 constituencies (after subtraction of 3 who later dropped out).

68 Eg in Murcia, when the Propagandists Valiente and Sánchez Miranda arrived to hold talks in the Catholic Workingmen's Club, the Governor took them for agents of a Basque plot. (Monge Bernal, *AP*, 1034.) In Cádiz, some 2,000 wanted to join in the first two days, but the Governor would not approve the branch's statutes. (*El Debate*, 9 June.) In Madrid, 2,361 joined in the first three days (*El Debate*, 6 May).

69 *El Debate*, 6 May 1931.

70 Monge Bernal, *AP*, 1118.

71   *El Debate*, 8 May 1931.
72   *El Debate*, 9 & 13 June 1931.
73   *El Debate*, 8 May 1931.
74   Quotation from *El Debate*, 31 May 1931. The programme is set out in L. Lucía Lucía, *En estas horas de transición* (Valencia, 1930). Lucía had worked with Fr Vicent.
75   Quoted in *El Debate*, 10 May 1931.
76   A. Lizarza Iribarren, *Memorias de la conspiración* (3rd ed, Pamplona, 1954), 15–16. The manifesto was the work of Bilbao Eguía who had been expelled from the Communion for accepting office under the Dictator (Galindo, *Los partidos*, 103).
77   HCE I–4, 486; & L. Redondo & J. de Zavala, *El Requeté* (2nd ed, Barcelona, 1957), 236. The Integrist was Senante, at this time on the Committee of *Acción Nacional*. The meeting ended with shouts of 'Long live Don Jaime' and 'To Madrid! To Madrid!'
78   Melgar, *Escisión dinástica*, 105–7.
79   Lizarza, *Memorias*, 16–17; Redondo & Zavala, *Requeté*, 235. The atmosphere of religious fervour in the Basque provinces may be deduced from the 'visions of Ezquioga' (Guipúzcoa). Two children claimed to have seen the Virgin, and thousands of people from the Basque provinces, Navarre and Burgos came to pray at the scene in June 1931. Many claimed that they had seen the Virgin and St Michael the Archangel, who held a sword dripping with blood, and that they had been told there would be war between Catholics and non-Catholics: initially the Catholics would suffer heavy losses, but ultimately they would triumph with the aid of the angels and Our Lady. (W. Starkie, 'Spanish kaleidoscope', *The Fortnightly*, Dec 1936, 684.)
80   Electoral manifesto of Larramendi, *El Debate*, 26 June 1931.
81   J. A. de Agire Lekube (= Aguirre Lecube), *Entre la libertad y la revolución* (Bilbao, 1935), 6–92. A PNV delegation had offered its support to the Republican Committee before 12 April on condition that the Republic would be federalist (op cit, 121). Alfonsine Monarchists were advised to join the Basque Nationalists as a tactic while the King remained in exile (op cit, 146–7). The text of the General Statute is in García Venero, *Nacionalismo vasco*, 473–91. The main points were that Spain should retain control over foreign affairs (except with the Vatican), customs, and the monetary system. The *Concierto económico* was to remain until re-negotiated. The Basques were to control nearly everything else, even to the extent of Basque soldiers forming a distinct section of the Army which was to serve only in the Basque provinces. Pradera, the veteran anti-Nationalist, refused to be a candidate in the elections, considering the Statute anti-*fuerista* (Arrarás, *HSRE* I, 178). Prieto, leader of the Bilbao Socialists, at this time called the Statute reactionarily anti-liberal: 'Spain cannot tolerate that territory turning itself into a Vaticanist Gibraltar' (*El Socialista*, 30 June 1931). According to one

source Prieto had got the Provisional Government to agree in 1930 that only Leftist regions should be given autonomy (Iturralde, *Catolicismo*, I, 60).

82 A. Ossorio Gallardo, *Vida y sacrificio de Companys* (Buenos Aires, 1943), 83–7. Maciá now adopted the view that he would swap separatism for a statute of autonomy, but would return to his former separatism if the Cortes voted for a unitary Republic (statement of 29 May in García Venero, *Nacionalismo catalán*, 517). *ABC* (eg 23 Apr) fulminated against 'the separatist threat'. *El Debate* (24 Apr, 12 June) attacked Maciá for his lack of *seny*, while defending administrative decentralisation as opposed to political autonomy.

83 Arrarás, *HSRE* I, 64–5. The Catalan Traditionalists had drafted a statute in 1930.

84 *El Debate*, 10 May 1931.

85 *El Debate*, 20 May 1931.

86 Abadal, *El Sol*, 5 June 1931. The other parties which withdrew from the May elections were: Traditionalists, Liberal Republican Right, Federals, Radicals and UGT-Socialists (*El Debate*, 23 May 1931).

87 *El Debate*, 11 June 1931. Initially he appeared on the *Acción Nacional* list, but soon withdrew.

88 *El Sol*, 26 May 1931.

89 *El Socialista*, 19 May 1931; *El Sol*, 19 June 1931.

90 A. Ossorio, *Mis memorias* (Buenos Aires, 1946), 230.

91 *El Sol*, 16 June 1931.

92 *El Sol*, 9, 14 & 23 June 1931.

93 Fernández Castillejo (conversation).

94 Complaints appeared in *El Socialista* (10, 17 & 21 June 1931). A notable example of the process was Burgos Mazo's decision to join the Radicals in Huelva (*ABC*, 20 June 1931). There was much dissension inside the Liberal Right, aggravated by the appointment of Chapaprieta as organiser. Efforts to incorporate similar groups were not always successful: thus a number of Ossorio's disciples in Saragossa joined the party, but left again when no seats were assured them (*El Sol*, 2 & 21 June).

95 Prieto, *El Socialista*, 27 June 1931.

96 *El Socialista*, 19 Apr 1931, reported this phenomenon with reference to Galicia. On 25 Apr, it was reported in many *pueblos*. On 6 May, the paper stated that rural *caciquismo* was now Republican. A French visitor to Toledo was told that *caciques* were still active, but they now called themselves Republicans (P. Dominique, *Marche, Espagne* [Paris, 1931], 124).

97 *ABC*, 21, 25 & 28 Apr; *El Debate*, 29 Apr 1931. *ABC* on 28 Apr reported M. Maura as saying that if he had followed the example of Cánovas before the Cortes of the Restoration, there would not be one Monarchist council left; to which *ABC* retorted that, had the last government of the King acted in this way, there would not now be

a Republic. *ABC*, 25 Apr, thought Maura worse than Romero Robledo, the Monarchy's most notorious electoral manager.

98   Maura, *Así cayó Alfonso*, 309. Sir G. Young, *The New Spain* (London, 1933), 136, says Maura removed about 7,500 Monarchist councillors. The results of the partial elections of 31 May were: Government coalition, 1,645 councillors; Socialists, 674; Monarchists, 201; Liberal Republican Right, 757; Radical-Socialists, 301; *Gremiales*, 4; Republican-Regionalist coalition, 5; Federals, 89; independent Republicans, 156; Catholics, 47; Radicals, 208; 'In the Service of the Republic', 15; Agrarian Republicans, 91; workers, 13; Liberal-Democrats, 84; *Alianza Republicana*, 141; followers of J. March, 54; *Unión Republicana Autonomista*, 461; Traditionalists, Nationalists, Jaimists, etc, 354 (*El Sol*, 2 June 1931).

99   Fernández Castillejo, appointed Governor of Valencia after the May burnings, says he found local government in chaos, with the province under the sway of the *Blasquistas* (local Radicals). (Conversation with same.)

100 *El Debate*, 23 June 1931, reported this in Zamora and Salamanca. The description of the average provincial Governor given in Maura's memoirs leads one to suppose them capable of anything. Miguel Maura was himself a candidate in Zamora.

101 Arrarás, *HSRE* I, 111–12.

102 *El Socialista*, 30 June & 5 July 1931. He noted that, of three great *caciques*, only Romanones had been elected; Bergamín and Burgos Mazo were defeated in Málaga and Huelva respectively. The CNT had a wide organisation, but, outside Catalonia, it counselled abstention in protest against 'the revolutionary incapacity of the government'. (Quoted, *El Socialista*, 28 May 1931.) *Caciquismo* nevertheless retained its influence in parts of Galicia; in the province of Corunna *caciques* helped the Republicans of Casares Quiroga (D. Quiroga Ríos, *Contra los nuevos oligarcas* [2nd ed, Corunna, 1932], esp 42–3).

103 *ABC*, 7, 17 & 19 June 1931; *ABC* argued that the government coalition would split up if the non-Republican Right abstained.

104 *El Debate*, 3 May 1931.

105 *ABC*, 26 June 1931.

106 The DRV abstained as its meetings were broken up with impunity (*El Debate*, 17 June); Lucía advised his followers to vote for the Jaimists. Events in Asturias were reported in *El Sol*, 20–21 June; the local *Acción Nacional* also withdrew in solidarity (*El Debate*, 23 June). M. Álvarez had earlier been approached by Azaña for a coalition in Asturias, but had refused. (M. García Venero, *Melquíades Alvarez*, [Madrid, 1954], 365.)

107 Reports by Madariaga (Toledo), Marín Lázaro (Cuenca), Tornos (Jaén), Fr Yaben (Guadalajara) and Medina Togores (Córdoba-prov) in *El Debate*, 8, 10, 12, 13 & 16 July 1931 respectively. In Seville-prov, *Acción Nacional* was prevented from holding even one meeting by the Left. (Monge Bernal, *AP*, 1078.)

108   *El Debate*, 30 June 1931. *BSS*, VIII, 194, says that there were no major riots, but there was a toll of 8 dead. A riot occurred in Salamanca, in protest against the Agrarian coalition's success (*El Debate*, 1 July). *El Debate* also reported that in some parts of León province it was not known that elections had taken place (5 July). In some places, old habits were not broken: more votes were recorded than there were voters.

109   *El Debate*, 2 July 1931. According to Prieto, the Socialists had expected 40–50 seats (*El Socialista*, 1 July 1931).

110   Figures compiled from statistics of the *Instituto Geográfico y Estadístico*, in *El Debate*, 5 Dec 1933. Press and books give similar figures for the composition of the chamber, though they rarely agree exactly. The *Instituto*'s figures incorporate the odd by-elections later in 1931. These results did not affect the overall position: in them, the *Lliga* got its third seat and an Agrarian was elected in Logroño, replacing a Liberal Rightist who died. Initially, therefore, the Liberal Right numbered 24 to the Agrarians' 23.

111   Aguirre, *Libertad*, 96–8. The minority initially numbered 14: Aguirre was elected for Navarre and Biscay-prov; in a by-election in the latter, he was replaced by the worker Robles Aránguiz (PNV).

112   Aguirre, *Libertad*, 99–106; García Venero, *Nacionalismo vasco*, 425; Arrarás, *HSRE* I, 179–80. In his opening speech in the Cortes, Beúnza placed religion first as the justification for the minority; on local rights, he explained with great tact that it was a union of Navarrese defending '*Dios y Fueros*' and Basques defending '*Jaungoikoa eta lagi-zarra*' (God and the ancient laws). He then spoke of a separate statute for Navarre. (*Diario de sesiones de las Cortes constituyentes de la República española*, 29 July 1931.)

113   His aim in standing was to be able to defend his work as the Dictator's Minister of Finance, then under strong attack. He told the Lisbon *Diário da Manhã* in May that he did not support the idea of a restoration at the moment; Monarchists should collaborate with the Republican government but not become too closely involved with it. He accepted freedom of religion so long as the Orders remained with permission to teach. As always, he stressed the need for order to keep up confidence in the economy. Although he wanted to return after his election, he could not obtain a guarantee of parliamentary immunity from Alcalá-Zamora. (J. Calvo Sotelo, *En defensa propia*, [Madrid, 1932], 119–29 & 185–90.) In Biarritz, Guadalhorce, on behalf of the ex-Ministers of Primo de Rivera, refused to accept the Republic when asked so to do by an emissary from Herrera (Cortés Cavanillas, *Gil Robles*, 70).

114   Speech, in *DSCC*, 28 July 1931. The minority, as formed on 15 July, numbered nineteen: all from the Castiles and León except Guallar from Aragón (*El Debate*, 16 July 1931).

115   These deputies had planned a National Agrarian Party, which they hoped Alba himself would lead, just before the fall of the Monarchy.

Alba, in fact, was Cid's running mate in Zamora; however, like Velayos, another of his followers elected in Ávila, he did not join the Agrarian minority. (M. García Venero, *Santiago Alba*, [Madrid, 1963], 331 & 333.)

116 Comment of Ortega Gasset (quoted in *El Debate*, 25 July 1931). The complete list of the Agrarian minority was: Burgos, 4 Agrarians & 2 Traditionalists; Cuenca, 2 Agrarians; Logroño, 1 *Acción Riojana*; Palencia, 1 Agrarian & 1 *Unión Castellana Agraria*; Salamanca, 1 Traditionalist & 2 *Acción Nacional*; Sta Cruz de Tenerife, 1 independent Republican; Santander, 2 *Agrupación Regional Independiente*; Saragossa-cap, 1 *Acción Nacional*; Segovia, 1 Agrarian Republican; Toledo, 2 *Acción Nacional*; Valladolid, 2 Agrarians; Zamora, 1 Agrarian Republican.

Based on the professions declared by the deputies themselves, the minority consisted of: Lawyers, 9; priests, 4; engineers, 3; academics, 3; property-owners, 2; worker, 1; Army General, 1; notary, 1. The list provides an indication of the social composition of the minority, though not of its economic interests.

CHAPTER 2

1 N. Alcalá-Zamora, *Los defectos de la Constitución de 1931* (Madrid, 1936), 50 & 91.

2 Azaña insisted that it was 'impossible for a Republican government to exist' without Socialist collaboration (G. Picard-Moch & J. Moch, *L'Espagne républicaine* [Paris, 1933], 48).

3 Asked whether the agitation of the extreme Left worried him, Azaña replied that it did not: 'it fills me with joy' (Dominique, *Marche, Espagne*, 118).

4 *DSCC*, 30 July 1931.

5 *El Socialista*, 3 July 1931.

6 Ossorio, *Mis memorias*, 189–99; R. M. Smith, *The Day of the Liberals in Spain* (London, 1938), 119–34.

7 Collective Pastoral, *El Debate*, 16 Aug 1931. Individually some Bishops were more forthright: the Bishop of Orense protested to Alcalá-Zamora about separation of Church and State in violation of the Concordat, and about the 'legal banishment of all religious emblems and catechist instruction from public schools at the behest of any Bolshevik seeking to convert Spain into a Soviet Russia' (*El Debate*, 13 Aug 1931).

8 Pastoral, and letter to Alcalá-Zamora, in *El Debate*, 31 July & 5 Aug 1931 respectively.

9 Prieto, *El Socialista*, 25 Aug 1931.

10 Sánchez, *Reform and Reaction*, 119.

11 *El Debate*, 23 Aug 1931.

12 *El Debate*, 1 Oct 1931. It was said that Herrera and S. Aznar had earlier counselled Segura's deposition in Rome. Segura, in Paris, was

U

asked by Mgr Maglione (Nuncio in France) on behalf of Pius XI to renounce the see. Segura agreed after argument, but renounced also his office of Cardinal, something for which the Pope had not bargained. When they met in Rome, Pius got Segura to withdraw this to avoid further scandal; but when asked by the Pope to say that he had renounced the see of his own free will, Segura flatly refused, telling Pius that he would not lie even for the Pope (Cortés Cavanillas, *Gil Robles*, 82–5). Segura, whom the Pope officially thanked for the sacrifice he had made in following the example of St Gregory of Nazianzus, was given a post in Rome (*El Debate*, 26 Dec 1931).

13 The Committee consisted of 5 Socialists, 4 Radicals, 3 Radical-Socialists, 2 *Esquerra* and one representative each of *Acción Republicana*, ORGA, the Federals, Alcalá-Zamora's group, those 'in the service of the Republic', the Basque-Navarrese coalition and the Agrarians—the latter two being Leizaola and Gil Robles (Smith, *Day of the Liberals*, 166–7). The new draft is in *DSCC*, 18 Aug 1931, App.

14 *El Socialista*, 11 Aug & 1, 9 & 17 Oct 1931.

15 *ABC*, 4 Oct 1931.

16 *El Debate*, 21 July 1931.

17 *DSCC*, 8 Sept 1931. The Socialists, who had collaborated with the Dictator, left in protest against a speech by one who had attended the Dictator's National Assembly.

18 Unless cited, the sources are the original and final text of the Constitution, respectively in appendices to *DSCC*, 18 Aug & 9 Dec 1931.

19 *DSCC*, 25 Sept 1931; & amdmts of Leizaola to Artics 14 & 15, & Royo to Artic 14, in apps to *DSCC*, 20 & 21 Aug & 11 Sept 1931.

20 Alonso de Armiño, *DSCC*, 25 Sept 1931.

21 Sáinz Rodríguez, *DSCC*, 8 Sept 1931.

22 Gil Robles-Leizaola amdmt to Artic 42, *DSCC*, 20 Aug 1931 App; & Gil Robles, *DSCC*, 6 Oct 1931.

23 Martín Martín, amdmt to Artic 42, *DSCC*, 1 Oct 1931 App; & Alonso de Armiño, *DSCC*, 6 Oct 1931.

24 Madariaga, amdmt to Artic 44, *DSCC*, 23 Sept 1931 App.

25 Molina Nieto, *DSCC*, 27 Aug 1931.

26 *DSCC*, 8 Sept 1931.

27 Molina Nieto, *DSCC*, 27 Aug 1931. The choice of examples by the Canon from Toledo caused considerable amusement in the Cortes.

28 Gil Robles-Leizaola amdmt, *DSCC*, 21 Aug 1931 App.

29 *DSCC*, 13 Oct 1931.

30 Estévanez, *DSCC*, 10 Sept 1931.

31 Amdmts of Gil Robles-Leizaola & Royo Villanova, *DSCC*, 21 Aug & 30 Sept 1931 Apps. Royo and the leader of the minority, Martínez de Velasco, had entered Parliament in 1910 as supporters of freedom of worship under the leadership of Canalejas (T. Ortega, *Presidente: Martínez de Velasco* [Barcelona, 1935], 8 & 68).

32 Amdmts of Gil Robles-Leizaola & Oriol, *DSCC*, 21 Aug & 6 Oct 1931 Apps.

33 Amdmts to Artic 24 of Gil Robles-Leizaola & Royo Villanova, *DSCC*, 21 Aug & 30 Sept 1931 Apps.

34 Amdmts of Gil Robles-Leizaola to Artics 46 & 47; of Madariaga to Artic 46; & of Royo Villanova to Artic 46, in Apps to *DSCC*, 21 Aug, 23 Sept, & 7 Oct 1931 respectively.

35 Amdmts of Guallar to Artic 24, & of Beúnza to Artic 3, *DSCC*, 24 Sept & 15 Sept 1931 Apps respectively.

36 Gil Robles & Martínez de Velasco, *DSCC*, 8 Oct 1931. For Traditionalist opposition to separation, see Estévanez, *DSCC*, 29 July 1931.

37 García Gallego & Alcalá-Zamora, *DSCC*, 9 & 10 Oct 1931. Canon García Gallego was an opponent of Primo de Rivera and *El Debate*; elected as a Catholic Republican Democrat, he worked 'in the service of the Republic'.

38 Gil Robles, *DSCC*, 8 Oct; & Alcalá-Zamora & Beúnza, *DSCC*, 10 Oct 1931. In Beúnza's view, necessities of State could demand a man's life and fortune, but could never lay claim to the souls of the children.

39 The cabinet met on 13 Oct in the Finance Ministry (Alcalá-Zamora, *Los defectos*, 13).

40 *DSCC*, 13 Oct 1931.

41 Ie they attended any sessions during which matters other than the text of the Constitution were debated.

42 *El Socialista*, 15 Oct 1931, rejoiced over their resignation: 'a great difficulty for the development of the Revolution' had been removed. The Government of 14 Oct was: Premier and War Minister, Azaña (*Acción Republicana*); State, Lerroux (Radical); Interior, Casares Quiroga (ORGA); Navy, Giral (*Acción Republicana*); Finance, Prieto (Socialist); Public Instruction, Domingo (Radical-Socialist); Public Works, Albornoz (Radical-Socialist); Labour, Largo Caballero (Socialist); Economy, Nicoláu d'Olwer (*Acció Catalana*); Communications, Martínez Barrio (Radical); & Justice, Los Ríos (Socialist).

43 *DSCC*, 29 & 30 Sept 1931.

44 Amdmts to Artics 49, 50, 80, 81, 118 & 121 in *DSCC*, 20 & 21 Aug 1931 Apps. The Senate was to be composed of 100 representatives of regions, provinces & municipalities; 25 workers; 25 employers; 50 liberal professions; & 50 representatives from universities, cultural institutions and religious bodies. It was to be indissoluble, each group being renewed by election every four years.

45 *DSCC*, 29 Oct 1931; see also his amdmt, 26 Nov 1931 App.

46 Text in Arrarás, *HSRE* I, 197.

47 The original charges, *DSCC*, 12 Nov App, accused Alfonso of *lèse-majesté* and military rebellion. In the debate (*DSCC*, 19 Nov) Romanones defended him on the grounds that he had yielded to

public opinion in 1923 and 1931. Gil Robles and Balbontín (Social Revolutionary) asked why, if the charges were known, Alcalá-Zamora had asked the King to leave Spain on 14 April.

48 *ABC*, 20 & 22 Nov 1931; it was suspended 25–27 Nov and fined 1,000 ptas.

49 *DSCC*, 10 Dec 1931. He got 362 votes, to the 7 of his nearest rival, Pi Arsuaga (Federal). The Basque Nationalists voted for him to reaffirm their Republicanism, while the Navarrese abstained (Aguirre, *Libertad*, 225–6).

50 Govt of 15 Dec: Premier & War, Azaña; State, Zulueta (independent Republican); Justice, Albornoz; Navy, Giral; Finance, Carner (*Acció Catalana*); Interior, Casares Quiroga; Public Instruction, Los Ríos; Public Works, Prieto; Labour, Largo Caballero; Agriculture, Industry & Commerce, Domingo.

51 Text in Arrarás, *HSRE* I, 275–6.

52 Lamamié & Beúnza in *DSCC*, 29 Jan & 2 Feb 1932.

53 Nuncio's protest of 29 Jan, Arrarás, *HSRE* I, 277–80; & *DSCC*, 4 Feb 1932. Lamamié's reply to a government defence was thus not permitted; he claimed that the Minister had misquoted a Bull to prove his case. He also said that a Radical-Socialist had told him that there were 183 Masons in the Chamber that day (*La Época*, 15 Feb 1932).

54 There were 2,987 Jesuits resident in Spain at the time; they gave free primary and technical education to a total of 31,805 in Madrid, and to 26,910 in the rest of Spain, and secondary education to 6,798 children. They ran the ICAI in Madrid and the commercial university of Deusto, as well as two observatories and modern scientific laboratories. Their workers' clubs gave free education to 11,800 workers in Valladolid and Burgos (*El Debate*, 26 March 1932). Their wealth is unknown, though in 4 years property worth 200,000,000 pesetas was confiscated (Ramos Oliveira, *Politics*, 446). Third persons were usually the owners, eg the Iglesia del Flor was owned by a New Yorker (Buckley, *Spanish Republic*, 99). *ABC*, 8 June 1932, said that alleged Jesuit property held by third persons was being seized in violation of the letter of the decree.

55 Sánchez, *Reform and Reaction*, 117–18, & Madariaga, *Spain*, 406; text of the law in *DSCC*, 2 Feb 1932 App. Artic 27 of the Constitution declared civil jurisdiction over cemeteries and forbade separation of burial-grounds for religious reasons.

56 In *DSCC*, 19 Jan 1932. In Salamanca, 13,753 deaths were recorded since 1920, but only 26 civil funerals (*El Debate*, 24 June 1932).

57 Aguirre, *DSCC*, 19 Jan, & Gómez Rojí & Lamamié, *DSCC*, 13 & 15 Jan 1932.

58 Ortiz de Solórzano, *DSCC*, 19 July 1932; *El Debate*, 22 June 1932, cited other examples.

59 J. Camba, *Haciendo de República* (Madrid, 1934), 206–7.

60 Guallar, *DSCC*, 3 Feb 1932.

61 Leizaola, *DSCC*, 8 Sept 1931 & 3 Feb 1932; & *DSCC*, 25 Feb 1932.
62 In *DSCC*, 17 June 1932; & *El Debate*, 12 June 1932.
63 *DSCC*, 30 March 1932.
64 *Declaración colectiva del Episcopado español* (Madrid, 1932). The Declaration was dated 20 Dec 1931.
65 Gil Robles, *DSCC*, 8 Oct 1931.
66 *El Debate*, 4 July 1931. Subscription rates were 1 pta for students, workers & employees; 5 ptas minimum; 10 ptas ordinary; 50 ptas special; & 1,000 for 'guardian members'.
67 *El Debate*, 14 July 1931.
68 Herrera, *El Debate*, 21 July 1931.
69 *El Debate*, 14 Oct 1931.
70 *El Debate*, 15 Oct 1931.
71 *El Debate*, 15 & 17 Oct 1931; Sáinz Rodríguez, *El Debate*, 1 Nov & Lamamié, *El Debate*, 20 Oct & 21 Nov 1931. The latter said that a minority of Agrarians had opposed collaboration from the start, but the majority had only been won over by the passage of Artic 26.
72 *El Debate*, 17 Oct 1931.
73 *El Debate*, 18 July 1931.
74 *El Debate*, 29 July & 7 Aug 1931.
75 *El Debate*, 18 Oct & 18 Nov 1931; & Monge, *AP*, 169. The Executive Committee consisted of: J. M. Gil Robles Quiñones de León, D. de Madariaga Almendros, C. Martín Álvarez, J. Medina Togores, C. Plá, C. Tornos Laffitte, Conde de Vallellano, A. Goicoechea Cosculluela, Conde de Rodezno, R. Bergé. Martínez de Velasco joined in Apr 1932. Herrera stood down because Gil Robles was a deputy whereas he himself had not been elected (according to Monge, *AP*, 165–7). However, Gutiérrez-Ravé (*Gil Robles*, 38) says that Herrera persuaded Goicoechea to relinquish leadership because he was not a deputy; this seems to be confirmed by Gil Robles, *No fue posible*, 78.
76 *El Debate*, 15 Oct 1931.
77 *El Debate*, 20 Oct 1931.
78 *El Debate*, 10 Nov 1931.
79 *El Debate*, 22 Oct (Gil Robles), 12 Nov (Sáinz Rodríguez), & 21 & 29 Nov 1931 (Lamamié & Beúnza).
80 *El Debate*, 1 Dec 1931.
81 Monge, *AP*, 169 & 185.
82 *El Debate*, 6 Dec 1931.
83 *El Debate*, 10 Dec 1931.
84 Herrera, *Obras*, 25–40 (speech in Valencia, 21 Dec 1931); also *El Debate*, 5 Apr 1932.
85 Gil Robles (visiting the DRV) *El Debate*, 5 Apr 1932. Herrera praised the party in his speech of 21 Dec 1931.
86 *El Debate*, 25 Oct 1931.
87 Monge, *AP*, 205–12. The President soon joined the executive committee of *Acción Nacional*.

88 *El Debate*, 20 Oct & 22 Nov 1931. On 2 Dec the paper reported the creation of a *Juventud de Unión Regional de Derechas* at Santiago de Compostela with 400 members, mostly students.

89 *La Época*, 22 Feb 1932, & Monge, *AP*, 223. The executive committee consisted of J. M. Valiente Soriano, J. M. Pérez de Laborda, G. Santiago Castiella, A. Parrondo, J. R. Prieto Noriega, M. Serrano Mendicute, A. Bermúdez Cañete, A. Crespi de Valldaura, L. Doussinague, J. García Val, V. Pérez de Laborda, M. Palacios Amores, the Marqués de Navarrés, T. de la Cerda & J. López Vázquez. Valiente, like Serrano Mendicute a member of the original *Acción Nacional* committee, was President of the *Juventud Española Católica* and the law-partner of Gil Robles. Bermúdez Cañete was at this time also a 'triumvir' of the JONS.

90 *La Época*, 24 Feb 1932.

91 *El Debate*, 28 June 1932.

92 Monge, *AP*, 313–16.

93 Speeches of 21 Dec 1931 (*Obras*, 40) & 21 Feb 1932 (Arrarás, *HSRE* I, 269–70).

94 *El Debate*, 28 June 1932. Guallar was confused by the terminology of Right and Left: if the Left attacked Country, Religion, Family, etc, he was a Rightist; if the Right meant oligarchies of economic interests and plutocrats with souls padlocked against reform, he was a Leftist. The present human condition was the result of 'the pagan Renaissance' and the Reformation which produced capitalism, so that 'modern society is like those old prints of the Last Judgment, in which only a chosen few exulted in Glory while the vast majority vegetated and were lost in the darkness of the tomb and misery. For us to be able to call ourselves civilised, these miseries must disappear . . .' (*DSCC*, 7 Oct 1931).

95 *La Época*, 23 Feb 1932.

96 In accordance with the Decree of 21 April 1932, prohibiting use of the word '*nacional*' by other than State organisations (Monge, *AP*, 183).

97 Rodezno, *El Debate*, 26 July 1931.

98 See Appendix 1.

99 *HCE*, I–4, 460–2. It was drafted by Bilbao Eguía, who was at this time detained at Navia de Suavia under the Defence Law (Galindo, *Los partidos*, 142).

100 *Habla el Rey*, 340–3. It was drawn up by Vallellano, approved by La Cierva and the ex-Ministers of the Dictatorship, and signed at Mürren (*HCE*, I–4, 462). Alfonso himself, questioned later by reporters in the Near East, denied knowledge of it (Arrarás, *HSRE* I, 246).

101 Traditionalists, eg Rodezno, Bilbao, Lamamié, Beúnza, Chicharro; Alfonsines, eg Vallellano, Sáinz Rodríguez (*HCE*, I–4, 463; Galindo, *Los partidos*, 146–8).

102 Advertisement in *El Debate*, 16 Dec 1931. The 'prime mover' was

Vegas Latapié, who had planned to found a cultural review 'with religious and patriotic missionary characteristics'. In 1928–30 he obtained the collaboration of Rodezno, Maeztu, Lozoya and Quintanar, but could get no funds. *Acción Española* was founded on 100,000 ptas originally given by the Marqueses de Pelayo for Orgaz's plot (E. Vegas Latapié, *Escritos políticos* [Madrid, 1940], 8–12; & his 'Maeztu y *Acción Española*', *ABC*, 2 Nov 1952). Vegas had wanted to call the review *Contrarrevolución*; Maeztu preferred *Hispanidad* (L. Aguirre Prado, *Ramiro de Maeztu* [Madrid, 1959], 18).

103 *Acción Española: antología* (XVIII, no 89), (Burgos, 1937), 45–51.
104 *El Debate*, 27 Apr 1932; Aguirre Prado, *Maeztu*, 18; Vegas Latapié (conversation).
105 *ABC*, 29 March 1932.
106 *El Debate*, 5 & 12 Jan 1932.
107 *El Debate*, 5 Apr 1932.
108 *El Debate*, 5 Apr 1932.
109 *La Época*, 5 Aug 1932. At a dinner on 11 June for Goicoechea, Pradera and Sáinz Rodríguez, there was much Monarchist fervour with attacks on the Republic and toasts to the King (L. M. Ansón, *Acción Española* [Saragossa, 1960], 104).
110 *El Debate*, 16 June 1932.
111 *El Debate*, 5 Apr 1932.
112 *El Socialiste*, 14 Nov 1931, & *ABC*, 28 Nov 1931 & 4 Feb 1932.
113 *El Debate*, 14 & 28 June 1932. An *AP* meeting on 22 May was banned while the CNT—the title was now illegal—was allowed to hold meetings to launch a 'week of revolutionary agitation' (*El Debate*, 24 May 1932).
114 The Oviedo branch was closed & fines imposed as members had circulated a sonnet lampooning the Leftist Victoria Kent & had 'subversive postcards' (*El Debate*, 18 June 1932). On 9 July it reported the Ávila branch had been closed for sixty days.
115 *El Socialista*, 20 Oct, 8, 10 & 12 Nov 1931, & 19 & 27 Jan 1932. Leaflets circulated before a meeting in Lugo read: 'The clericals, captained by a group of idle women, are trying to go against the Republic, brought about with the blood of the people; you must not tolerate their wild cavemen's cries. . . . Crush the enemies without hesitation or pity!' (*El Debate*, 3 Jan 1932).
116 *DSCC*, 9 Mar 1932. *El Debate* was suspended 20 Jan–25 Mar 1932.
117 *El Debate*, 17 Nov 1931 (report of DRV assembly).
118 For details of these groups see Appendix 2.
119 104 revolutionaries were deported to Spanish Guinea in Feb 1932 (Plá, *HSRE* II, 37). On the disorders, see Arrarás, *HSRE* I, 120–6, 186–93, 247–64, 293–4, 322–31 & 419–28.
120 Plá, *HSRE* II, 153, & V. Alba, *Historia de la segunda República española* (Mexico City, 1961), 147.
121 Victory of Largo Caballero & Prieto over Besteiro, who wanted the

party out of the government, but not revolution (*El Socialista*, 1, 2, 9, 11 & 12 July 1931).

122   *El Socialista*, 18 July 1931.
123   *El Socialista*, eg 23, 25, 26, 29 July, 6 Sept, 18 Oct, 17 Nov & 1 Dec 1931; & 10 & 22 Jan 1932.
124   *El Socialista*, eg 9, 13, 19, 20 Aug, 21 Oct, 4, 28 Nov & 8 Dec 1931; & 15 July 1932.
125   *El Socialista*, 24 Nov 1931.
126   *El Socialista*, 3 June 1932; Rightist domination signified government by Lerroux.
127   *El Socialista*, 4 Feb 1932.
128   *El Socialista*, 19 Nov 1931. The Socialist Youth demanded 'the conquest of power by the revolutionary action of the masses' if bourgeois democrats should obstruct evolution (*El Socialista*, 16 Feb 1932).
129   S. Canals, *De cómo van las cosas de España* (Madrid, 1933), 243–4.
130   In *The Economist*, 27 Feb 1932.
131   *The Economist*, which noted a further 15 per cent fall when the Jesuits were dissolved.
132   *The Economist*, 13 Feb 1932, & 31 Oct 1931. Base 100 = 1913 level.
133   *ABC*, 17 Jan 1932.
134   J. Calvo Sotelo, *La voz de un perseguido* (Madrid, 1933), I, 55 & 152–5.
135   *La Época*, 15 Mar 1932.
136   Cited in Arrarás, *HSRE* I, 228.
137   Ortega, *El Debate*, 8 Dec 1931 & *La Época*, 5, 6 & 8 Feb 1932. A basic reason for failure was the disdain of the 'Intellectuals in the Service of the Republic' for practical matters of organisation (Conversation with Salvador de Madariaga).
138   *El Debate*, 4 Aug 1931.
139   Maura's speeches in *El Debate*, 25 Oct 1931 & 12 Jan 1932; for criticisms, *El Debate*, 6 Aug, 27 Oct, 19, 20 Dec 1931 & 24 May 1932. Apart from differences of temperament, Maura & Alcalá-Zamora disagreed over the feasibility of trying to create a Republican party from defenders of the Monarchy: only Maura thought it possible (Conversation with Fernández Castillejo).
140   *El Sol*, 11 Feb 1932.
141   Lerroux, *Pequeña historia*, 119–20 & 133–8. He promised: 'I will not die without leading a government, and I make it my life's aim to lead one' (*ABC*, 26 Aug 1931).
142   *El Debate*, 10 Nov 1931.
143   Martín, *DSCC*, 4 Aug & 1 Sept 1931 & 3 May 1932; & *DSCC*, 5, 6 & 7 Aug 1931 (Calderón, Lamamié, Royo), & 6 Oct 1931 (Madariaga). Wages were fixed at $5\frac{1}{2}$ ptas a day by Largo Caballero, & 11 ptas at harvest-time; an 8-hour day was enforced (Ramos Oliveira, *Politics*, 340). Domingo's importation of wheat was largely the result of lobbying by millers and bakers who wanted a good profit-

margin (Canals, *Las cosas*, 267). The wheat crop of 1931 was poor: 36,585,330 quintals compared with 39,925,575 in 1930 (*El Debate*, 3 Dec 1931). *El Socialista* (6 Aug 1931) accused Martín of being a wheat monopolist seeking higher prices to increase his personal profit.

144 J. de Medina Togores, *Un año de Cortes constituyentes* (Madrid, 1932), 67, & F. E. Manuel, *The Politics of Modern Spain* (New York, 1938), 96.

145 Decree of 28 Apr, becoming law of 9 Nov 1931. See *El Socialista*, 10 & 14 June 1932; *El Debate*, 1 July 1932 (& Madariaga on 28 June); & Plá, *HSRE* II, 70 & 73–5: in Seville in 1932 the law had to be set aside to get the crops in.

146 Governor of Seville, *ABC*, 14 Jan 1932.

147 Plá, *HSRE* I, 132; Ramos, *Politics*, 340.

148 Largo Caballero, *El Socialista*, 9 July 1931.

149 Eg in Salamanca in June 1932, 200 people led by their Mayor took over an estate, divided it up and registered the new properties with the government official (Manuel, *Politics*, 99).

150 Calvo Sotelo, *En defensa propia*, 147; R. de Maeztu, *Un ideal sindicalista* (Madrid, 1961), 336–7.

151 Gil Robles—who as its secretary-general had a hand in this—in *ABC*, 23 Apr 1932.

152 Eg the programme of the *Bloque Agrario* of Salamanca, in *El Debate*, 1 Dec 1931; also Álvarez Robles, *El Debate*, 4 May 1932.

153 *El Debate*, 17 June 1932.

154 Quoted in *El Debate*, 5 July 1932. The best summary of the draft's provisions, together with the Agrarians' amendments, set out in tabular form, is given by *El Debate*, 10 May 1932; this, together with the final text, in *DSCC*, 1 Oct 1932 App, is the source of information used here, unless specifically cited.

155 *DSCC*, 5 July & 9 Aug 1932; they said the type of soil was unsuited to intensive cultivation: its silicon content made it suitable only for pasture.

156 *DSCC*, 18 May 1932.

157 Casanueva, *DSCC*, 18 & 24 May 1932; & Rodezno, 19 July, who feared for the family *señorío* in Logroño, bought in the eighteenth century; also Guallar, 28 June & 26 July; Rodezno, 22 July; Casanueva, 5 Aug (all *DSCC*, 1932).

158 Casanueva, *DSCC*, 18 May 1932.

159 Martínez de Velasco, *DSCC*, 2 Sept 1932; & Ramos Oliveira, *Politics*, 341.

160 Martínez de Velasco & Lamamié, *DSCC*, 31 Aug & 1 Sept 1932.

161 Eg Gil Robles, *ABC*, 23 Apr 1932.

162 *El Socialista*, 11 & 24 May 1932, said the law was not Socialist, but the minimum they could support as a start. It was a bourgeois law, whereas their reform would bear 'great similarity to the Russian agrarian revolution' (*El Socialista*, 18 June 1932).

163 Madariaga, *El Debate*, 28 June 1932; also *DSCC*, 17 & 18 May (Fanjul & Casanueva) & 6 July 1932 (Guallar).

164 *DSCC*, 18 May 1932.

165 *DSCC*, 9 Sept 1932. Agrarians were supported by the *Lliga*, Fr García Gallego, two Navarrese and, for quite different reasons, by the Social Revolutionary Balbontín. The Basques did not vote. Final text in *DSCC*, 1 Oct 1932 App.

166 The centrally minded Socialists disliked Maciá's patronage of their CNT rivals. Prieto wanted to resign over the regional clauses of the Constitution (*El Socialista*, 25 & 30 Sept 1931). During the debates on the Statute, there was dissidence in the UGT in Aragón led by the deputy Algora, who was expelled from the party for voting against it (*El Socialista*, 25 & 26 June 1932).

167 The text of the original Statute is in *DSCC*, 18 Aug 1931 App. Of 792,574 voters, 595,205 voted in favour and 3,286 against. Plá, *HSRE* I, 251, says the CNT voted in favour.

168 *The Economist*, 22 Aug 1931; & Peers, *Catalonia Infelix*, 202–3.

169 In 1931 Maciá told Miravitlles that separatism would be the death of Catalonia (F. Jellinek, *The Civil War in Spain* [London, 1938], 127).

170 *El Debate*, 1 June 1932; another ex-*Maurista* saw the Catalans coming to Madrid as victors to dictate terms to the vanquished (Alonso de Armiño, *DSCC*, 12 May).

171 *El Debate*, 3 & 4 May 1932.

172 Luca de Tena, *ABC*, 4 May 1932.

173 Arrarás, *HSRE* I, 340; also *DSCC*, 17 May 1932.

174 Emiliano Iglesias, *ABC*, 14 June 1932.

175 *El Debate*, 28 July 1932 & *DSCC*, 27 May 1932.

176 *DSCC*, 4 Aug 1932.

177 *El Debate*, 2 June & 19 July 1932.

178 *El Debate*, 12 July 1932. He declared himself 'an autonomist' and 'profoundly regionalist', but he could not go against 'the intangible unity of the Country', which is what we are at present defending' (*DSCC*, 10 June 1932).

179 An *Esquerra* deputy caused uproar by calling Royo Villanova an ass; Fanjul then called the Catalans 'traitors' (*DSCC*, 6 July 1932). Royo defended an amendment the next day with a speech devoted to the theme of his past speeches (*DSCC*, 7 July 1932). *El Debate* (8 July 1932) reported that Royo had had to stop speaking when overcome by fatigue.

180 The principal objections of *El Debate*, 12 July & 4 Aug 1932.

181 Royo Villanova, *DSCC*, 5 July & 3 Aug 1932.

182 A. Royo Villanova, *Treinta años de política antiespañola* (Valladolid, 1940), 185–6; & *DSCC*, 29 June, 26 July, 2, 9 & 16 Aug 1932. In Barcelona, pop 1,009,000, there were 634,673 non-Catalans (Arrarás, *HSRE* I, 383).

183 *DSCC*, 1932: Alonso de Armiño, 12 May; Martínez de Velasco,

26 May; Fanjul, 10 June; Calderón, 25 Aug; Royo, 1 & 2 Sept. The average wealth of Spaniards outside Catalonia & the Basque Country being 100, the average in Catalonia was 172 (J. Larraz, *La Hacienda pública y el Estatuto catalán* [Madrid, 1932], 90).

184   *HCE*, I–4, 482.
185   Calvo Sotelo, *La voz de un perseguido*, II, 81–4.
186   *DSCC*, 9 Sept 1932. With the Agrarians voted the Republicans M. Maura & Sánchez Román; Lerroux, like the *Lliga* & the Basques, voted for the Statute, the final text of which is in *DSCC*, 1 Oct 1932 App.
187   *El Debate*, 16 July 1931.
188   Abadal, *DSCC*, 13 May 1932.
189   *DSCC*, 30 June 1932. He defended Catalan control of all education.
190   When debates on the Statute began in the Cortes, a polemic developed between *El Debate*, defending de-centralisation but really no more, and the *Lliga* organ *La Veu de Catalunya*; see eg *El Debate*, 15 May 1932.
191   García Venero, *Nacionalismo catalán*, 532.
192   Arrarás, *HSRE* I, 413.
193   García Venero, *Nacionalismo vasco*, 426, 430 & 434–5. At this stage the Basques thought the *Esquerra* had let down the cause by backing the government so strongly. The *Lliga*, Carrasco Formiguera and others took the PNV view.
194   *ABC*, 22 Aug 1931; *El Debate*, 22, 23 & 25 Aug 1931; *DSCC*, 25 Aug 1931. Gil Robles attacked Maura for stepping outside a legality that did not yet exist, thus encouraging others to follow suit.
195   D. de Arrese, *Bajo la Ley de defensa de la República* (Madrid, 1933), 234.
196   Aguirre, *Libertad*, 112 & 133–9.
197   Aguirre, *Libertad*, 180–9 & 193–215; Madariaga, *Spain*, 404. The new Statute also permitted revision of the 'economic arrangement' to Madrid's advantage. The regional parliament was now to be elected by inorganic suffrage.
198   Aguirre, *Libertad*, 231–301. Olazábal's *La Constancia* fulminated against the new Statute because it was 'Godless' and contaminated with laicism and modernism (Iturralde, *Catolicismo* I, 242).
199   Galindo, *Los partidos*, 130; Oyarzun, *Carlismo*, 461. Alfonso Carlos had not offended *Mellistas* by Francophilia in the Great War, nor did he bear the responsibility of his brother for the Integrist split.
200   The seven were Rodezno, Beúnza, Oriol Urigüen, Lamamié de Clairac, Senante, Roma and Sáenz—the lattermost resigned in Feb (Information from M. Blinkhorn). Secondary sources usually say that Rodezno was advised by a committee of three: Pradera, Oriol and Lamamié de Clairac.
201   *HCE*, I–4, 486 & 489; Lizarza, *Memorias*, 20.

202 Aguirre, *DSCC*, 26 Aug 1931; in this speech he ruled out violence as a way of obtaining his ends, and blamed both the government and the Bilbao plutocracy for creating a violent atmosphere.

203 J. Arrarás, *Francisco Franco* (London, 1938), 120–5. Azaña, however, objected to the tone of the speech (G. Hills, *Franco* [London, 1967], 172). Franco asked Alfonso XIII whether he ought to stay in the Army: the King told him that he must serve Spain. Regarding the matter of the flag, Alfonso suggested that officers should try to think of the new purple band of the Republican tricolour as signifying the Royal Ensign of Castile, which was the same colour (Conversation with Cortés Cavanillas).

204 Ramos Oliveira, *Politics*, 326, states that many Republicans were among those who opted out. General Fanjul, *DSCC*, 2 Aug 1932, claimed that retirements were often the result of pressure; 'voluntary' was a military honorific term.

205 Fanjul, *DSCC*, 2 Aug 1932; Ramos Oliveira, *Politics*, 325–6; Maura, *Así cayó Alfonso*, 226–8; Mola, *Obras*, 946, 950, 992, 1020, 1046–51, 1060–3 & 1113. The rebels of Cuatro Vientos were well rewarded: Queipo de Llano became Military Commander in Madrid and then Head of the President's Military Household, while Ramón Franco was Chief of the re-constituted Air Force until his attempt to lead a social revolutionary movement at Seville in June 1931. Cf Payne, *The Military*, 266–76 on Azaña's reforms; he emphasises that *africanistas* (those who had served in Morocco and gained promotion by merit) were the bitterest opponents.

206 *HCE*, I–4, 486; Galindo, *Los partidos*, 115–16.

207 Conversation with Vegas Latapié, who was one of the conspirators. As noted earlier, 100,000 ptas of the funds were used to found *Acción Española* in Dec 1931. The Carlists refused to become involved (Payne, *The Military*, 280).

208 Aguirre (*Libertad*, 150–4) published his version in 1935, whereupon Orgaz produced a different version and claimed that he had got Aguirre to admit his memory was at fault (see García Venero, *Nacionalismo vasco*, 426–9). According to Iturralde (*Catolicismo* I, 35–6), Aguirre and Orgaz met before the Civil War and discovered that the interview had been arranged by Monarchists: both mistakenly believed the other had taken the initiative. Yet Aguirre repeated his first version in his *Freedom was Flesh and Blood* (London, 1945), 233–4.

209 Burgos Mazo, quoted in Arrarás, *HSRE* I, 435–6. There were rumours that Sanjurjo had earlier in 1931 had contacts with the Alfonsine General Cavalcanti regarding a rising.

210 E. Esteban-Infantes, *General Sanjurjo* (Barcelona, 1957), 177. Sanjurjo said the atrocities were worse than he had seen in the Riff, and blamed the Socialist Deputy Margarita Nelken Amusbergen for stirring up the local population.

211 Burgos Mazo, quoted in Arrarás, *HSRE* I, 437–8.

212 Lerroux, *Pequeña historia*, 143–4. Rumours of the interview were reported in *El Socialista*, 8 Jan 1932.

213 J. Romano, *Sanjurjo* (Madrid, 1940), 120–2.

214 Lerroux, *Pequeña historia*, 145; Arrarás, *HSRE* I, 434 & 487; *HCE*, I-4, 492.

215 *HCE*, I-4, 489–90.

216 J. A. Ansaldo, ¿ *Para qué* . . .? (Buenos Aires, 1951), 31 & 34–5; some machine-guns arrived at Gibraltar, but were not unloaded. V. G. Salmador, *Juan Antonio Ansaldo* (Montevideo, 1962), 74, adds that some aircraft were sent to Portugal, ostensibly on a sales tour; but they were not used either. Italian policy was apparently influenced by two considerations: belief that a secret Franco-Spanish pact existed allowing France to take over the Balearics in case of a Mediterranean conflict; and assistance given to Italian exiles by some Spanish Republicans (R. Guariglia, *Ricordi* [Naples, 1950], 185, 189 & 774–80).

217 *El Debate*, 16–18 & 24 June 1932.

218 Albornoz (at Ávila, 19 June), quoted in *HCE*, I-4, 491.

219 *El Debate*, 28–29 June 1932; Arrarás, *HSRE* I, 430–3; M. Goded, *Un faccioso cien por cien* (Saragossa, 1938), 15–16. The General's son claims that his father's conduct was calculated provocation so that an excuse would be provided for revolt and the seizure of Azaña; Villegas and Caballero failed, however, to act.

220 *HCE*, I-4, 485. Moral had been a Republican since 1914, but was anti-Socialist.

221 Salmador, *Ansaldo*, 78.

222 Barrera, quoted by Arrarás, *HSRE* I, 475.

223 *Habla el Rey*, 343.

224 *HCE*, I-4, 485, & conversations with Sáinz Rodríguez, Cortés Cavanillas & Vegas Latapié. Ansaldo says that the aim was left deliberately vague so that agreement could be reached permitting common action; he himself hoped the outcome would be an authoritarian Monarchy with Alfonso's third son, Juan, as King, thus uniting the two branches of the dynasty (¿ *Para qué?*, 32).

225 His manifesto, drafted by the Alfonsines Pujol and Gen García de la Herrán, said that the aim was not to 'impose a political régime against the Republic' but simply to overthrow the government, hold free elections and allow the national will to choose its course (Text in Arrarás, *HSRE* I, 464–5).

226 Galindo, *Los partidos*, 160. Two Traditionalists were among the dead in Madrid; *Requetés* came out to help Sanjurjo in Seville; Traditionalists in Barcelona conspired (Redondo & Zavala, *Requeté*, 239 & 242).

227 *HCE*, I-3, 290; *El Debate*, 10 Dec 1931 & 29 Mar, 12 & 22 May 1932.

228 Arrarás, *HSRE* I, 238. In a letter to *El Debate*, 30 July 1931, Ledesma complained of the confiscation of five consecutive issues.

229 M. Fernández Almagro, *Historia de la República española* (Madrid, 1940), 211.

230 Arrarás, *HSRE* I, 237. The JONS anthem included the words: 'No more kings of foreign stock and no more men without bread to eat' (Ledesma, *Antología*, 16).

231 Fernández Almagro, *República*, 210; Ledesma, *Antología*, esp 17, 45–8, 56, 60–1, 148, 159 & 252; & H. R. Southworth, *Antifalange* (Paris, 1967), 64–70, who stresses Ortega's influence on Ledesma and Giménez Caballero.

232 Arrarás, *HSRE* I, 237.

233 Monge, *AP*, 1118; O. Redondo, *Obras completas* (Madrid, 1954–5), I, 9.

234 Redondo, *Obras*, I, 247–9; Arrarás, *HSRE* I, 237; Fernández Almagro, *República*, 211.

235 Monge, *AP*, 1127. *Libertad*, 28 Dec 1931, praised Herrera, but found his policy lacking in youthful frenzy; on 22 Feb 1932, nationalism was defined as 'neither Monarchist nor anti-Monarchist. Nor is it confessional, though in no way anti-religious' (Redondo, *Obras*, I, 405–7, & II, 27).

236 Payne, *Falange*, 19; N. García Sánchez, *Onésimo Redondo* (Madrid, 1956), 17.

237 Arrarás, *HSRE* I, 238. Antonio Bermúdez Cañete signed the manifesto of *La Conquista del Estado* (Feb 1931) as well as the JONS manifesto; meanwhile he wrote odd editorials on economic affairs for *El Debate* (eg 2 May 1931), was elected a member of the *Acción Nacional* deliberative assembly (July 1931), and in Feb 1932 was a member of the executive committee of *Juventud de Acción Nacional*.

238 E. Esteban-Infantes, *La sublevación del general Sanjurjo* (2nd ed, Madrid, 1933), 31–2.

239 *HCE* I–4, 493; Galindo, *Los partidos*, 158. According to one source, Goded was to have led the rising in Madrid, but Barrera kept him in the dark (M. García Venero, *La Falange en la guerra de España* [Paris, 1967], 20).

240 Interview between Sanjurjo & Franco in a Madrid café, arranged by Sáinz Rodríguez, who was present (Sáinz Rodríguez, conversation). Gil Robles, *No fue posible*, 235, notes that Franco said at a dinner in July 1932 that he was against the rising because it would not succeed; but on p 779 he says Franco came to Madrid to persuade officers not to participate because the military should not interfere in politics. In 1931 Franco had refused to conspire when approached by Monarchists (Iturralde, *Catolicismo* I, 57).

241 Lerroux, *Pequeña historia*, 146.

242 *Memorias íntimas de Azaña*, 186. In his speech in the Cortes on 10 Aug (*DSCC*), he said he had known of the plot's existence for 3 or 4 months. The closure of offices & some arrests on 5 Aug were reported in *El Debate*, 7 Aug & *La Época*, 9 Aug 1932, which noted closure of PNE branches at Burgos, Vigo and Bilbao.

243 Esteban-Infantes, *Sanjurjo*, 191; Arrarás, *HSRE* I, 443; Vegas Latapié, conversation.

244 *El Debate*, 2 Aug 1932.

245 *Memorias íntimas de Azaña*, 187; the Director-General of Security knew that the rising was for that night from the mistress of one of the officers in the plot. The Alfonsine Lequerica said his *sereno* told him that same night (Ansaldo, *¿ Para Qué?*, 35).

246 Ansaldo, *¿ Para qué?*, 38–40; *Memorias íntimas de Azaña*, 188 & 192–3; Arrarás, *HSRE* I, 449–54; & J. del Moral, *Lo del 10 de Agosto y la justicia* (Madrid, 1933), 31–6, who said that the commanding officer in Madrid failed to keep his promise, as did a Colonel of the Civil Guard who had been bribed 6,000 ptas. The ten dead were all military men, apart from the Traditionalist student Triana.

247 Ansaldo, *¿ Para qué?*, 41–5; Salmador, *Ansaldo*, 74–5 & 77; Vegas, *Calvo Sotelo*, 101–2. Esteban-Infantes, *La sublevación*, 31, claimed that the rising in Madrid was diversionary, to give time for the provincial garrisons to march on the capital; a similar view is given by Salmador, but this would seem to be a retrospective explanation. Barrera himself (Arrarás, *HSRE* I, 475) blamed broken promises for the failure.

248 Esteban-Infantes, *La sublevación*, 43.

249 Texts of proclamation and manifesto in Arrarás, *HSRE* I, 464–5; pp 463–74 provide perhaps the best account of the day in Seville.

250 *HCE*, I–4, 516. In Cádiz, Varela did not rise as he did not judge the atmosphere suitable; however, he refused to obey Azaña's orders to march on Seville (F. J. Mariñas, *General Varela* [Barcelona, 1956], 57–9).

251 Arrarás, *HSRE* I, 457.

252 J. J. Calleja, *Yagüe* (Barcelona, 1963), 57.

253 Esteban-Infantes, *La sublevación*, 65, 67, 77 & 91.

254 Esteban-Infantes, *Sanjurjo*, 191.

255 Azaña, *DSCC*, 10 & 11 Aug 1932. In his diary (22 July) he noted the existence of a plot against his government and the Cortes, but not against the régime (*Memorias íntimas*, 184).

256 Martínez de Velasco, *DSCC*, 10 Aug 1932.

257 Quoted in *HCE*, I–4, 530.

258 Text in *DSCC*, 17 Aug 1932 App. The lands were to be used for agrarian reform.

259 *DSCC*, 18 Aug 1932. Para 2 of Artic 44 permitted expropriation 'by reason of social utility with adequate compensation, unless a law approved by the votes of the absolute majority of the Cortes should resolve otherwise'. The measure got an absolute majority, but Para 6 of Artic 44 read: 'In no case will the penalty of confiscation of property be imposed.'

260 Prior to 10 Aug, 5 of the 24 Bases of Agrarian Reform, and only half of the sections of the Statute had been approved. Both were finally

passed on 9 Sept, thanks to the failure of the *pronunciamiento* (Plá, *HSRE*, II, 142–3 & 145).

261 Arrarás, *HSRE* I, 502–8. By the Decree of 8 Sept, Albornoz dismissed a hundred judges and magistrates whom he considered did not 'sense Republican justice'. Thus it was said that Para 3 of Artic 94 was infringed: 'Judges are independent regarding the discharge of their duties. They are subject only to the law' (Moral, *10 de Agosto*, 130–2).

262 *La Época*, 24–26 Aug 1932. Sanjurjo did not wish to appeal, and told Bergamín: 'I played and lost; I am prepared to pay' (*La Época*, 30 Aug 1932). Generals Barrera and González Carrasco went into hiding for a month and then escaped across the frontier into France.

263 R. Carr, 'Spain: rule by Generals', *Soldiers & Governments* (ed M. Howard), (London, 1957), 146.

264 List in J. Cortés Cavanillas, *Acta de acusación* (Madrid, 1933), 744–6; 5 papers were already suspended, making 114 in all.

265 Arrarás, *HSRE* I, 510–11.

266 Estado Mayor Central del Ejército, *Historia de la guerra de liberación* (Madrid, 1945), 289.

267 Gil Robles, *La Época*, 1 Sept 1932.

268 *La Época*, 23 Aug 1932.

269 Arrarás, *HSRE* I, 506.

270 Cortés Cavanillas, *Gil Robles*, 145–6, & conversation with same.

271 *El Debate*, 16 June 1932. A leader of the Zamora branch describes the attitude of *Acción Popular* as one of 'inhibition' (Conversation with Carrascal).

CHAPTER 3

1 This had been his real aim from the time he took over (J. M. Gil Robles, *Spain in Chains* [New York, 1937], 1).

2 *El Debate*, 8 Oct 1932.

3 Goicoechea returned from Hendaye when his wife died, his return being arranged by Gil Robles on condition that he surrendered to the authorities to face charges for verbal attacks on the régime made at Gijón in July. This he did; he was released in November (*El Debate*, 8 & 12 Oct & 12 Nov 1932). Vallellano came back to give himself up and spend a while in gaol in the last week in November (*El Debate*, 30 Nov 1932).

4 *El Debate*, 23 Oct 1932.

5 The debate was fully reported in *El Debate*, 23 Oct 1932.

6 *El Debate*, 23 Oct 1932.

7 *El Debate*, 25 Oct 1932.

8 *El Debate*, 29 Nov 1932; for a summary of Lucía's *En estas horas de transición*, see p 46.

9 Gil Robles, *El Debate*, 30 Nov 1932. Medina Togores reported that

the speech had caused much surprise. The headline read: 'The *Confederación española de las Derechas Autónomas* approved.'

10 Goicoechea's letter of 8 Jan said that he had told Gil Robles in October of his intention to leave after the prohibition of other political activities, and that he had delayed his resignation at the request of Gil Robles. Gil Robles's letter of 9 Jan accepted his resignation and expressed hope for future co-operation (*El Debate*, 11 Jan 1933).

11 *El Nervión* (Bilbao), 5 Jan 1933, cited in Arrarás, *HSRE* II, 138.

12 Arrarás, *HSRE* II, 134–5.

13 Goicoechea, *ABC*, 25 Dec 1932.

14 Conversations with Cortés Cavanillas and Vegas Latapié. Gil Robles, himself a Monarchist *in foro interno*, writes that 'the immense majority' of *Acción Popular*'s members were Monarchists at heart, though many were less keen than others; 90 per cent of members would have opposed a declaration of Republicanism (*No fue posible*, 79).

15 *ABC*, 20 Dec 1932. A Traditionalist advocate of Monarchist unity had the week before emphasised the pre-condition of a traditional, not a parliamentary, Monarchy (Bilbao, *ABC*, 13 Dec 1932). Goicoechea's phraseology did not remove Traditionalist doubts.

16 Galindo Herrero, *Los partidos*, 173–5.

17 *ABC*, 13 Jan 1933. Signatories included ex-*Mauristas* like Silió, ex-members of the UMN like Maeztu, 'historic' Conservative, Liberal and independent Monarchists, Albiñana of the PNE, and two leaders of the *Agrupación Autónoma Asturiana de Acción Popular*, Fernández-Ladreda and Moutas, who had defended the Monarchist presence at the October Assembly, but who in fact chose to follow Gil Robles instead of Goicoechea. La Cierva had declined to lead a new party because he was too old (*HCE*, I–5, 573).

18 *ABC*, 13 Jan 1933.

19 *ABC*, 24 Jan 1933.

20 *ABC*, 24 Feb 1933. The first entry in the party's minute-book is dated 9 Feb. The executive committee was: A. Goicoechea Coscul-luela; Conde de Vallellano; S. Fuentes Pila, J. Danvila Rivera, A. Serrano Jover (all ex-*Mauristas* save one). Sec: J. Layús.

21 *ABC*, 31 Jan 1933; the sentence was a regular feature of subsequent speeches.

22 Lamamié de Clairac, *ABC*, 31 Jan 1933.

23 First mentioned in *ABC*, 26 Mar 1933. Abbreviation of *Tradicionalistas y Renovación Española*.

24 One of its leaders even wrote to *El Socialista* (11 Jan 1933) to explain that the descendants of nineteenth-century veterans opposed Integrists who, 'covering themselves with the name of Traditionalists, which they have usurped from us, and under the pretext of a *Federación de Derechas*, with electoral aims—each time we understand less what the word "Right" means—now seek to create

x

a comic-opera Traditionalism. . . . Never must we Traditionalists accept the person entitled "Alfonso XIII" nor any of his descendants without our faces blushing with shame and the blood shed by our martyrs weighing on our consciences.'

25 Galindo, *Los partidos*, 185–6. The group was led by Gen Díez de la Cortina, José de Cora Lira and Lorenzo Sáenz.

26 *Documentos de D. Alfonso Carlos de Borbón y de Austria-Este* (ed M. Ferrer), (Madrid, 1950), 178, 194, 200, 203–6 & 215–17.

27 J. Cortés Cavanillas, *Confesiones y muerte de Alfonso XIII* (2nd ed, Madrid, 1951), 51 (23 July 1933). Texts of the renunciations of Alfonso and Jaime, the eldest sons, in Melgar, *Escisión dinástica*, 184–5.

28 *El Debate*, 23 Dec 1932.

29 Gil Robles, *El Debate*, 27 Dec 1932.

30 *El Debate*, 2 Mar 1933.

31 *El Debate*, 5 Mar 1933. Lucía explicitly claimed to be the initiator of the CEDA at the DRV Assembly of Nov 1932 (*El Debate*, 8 Jan & 7 Mar 1933). The National Council of the CEDA comprised: Pres: Gil Robles. Vicepres: Lucía (DRV) & Madariaga (*Acción Obrerista*). Sec: F. Salmón Amorín (Murcia). Vice-sec: Srta Velasco (*Asociación Femenina*, Madrid). Treas: Valiente (JAP). Members: Fernández Ruano & Pabón (Andalusia); Mañueco (León); Sánchez Miranda (Extremadura); Ruiz del Castillo (Galicia); Sancho Izquierdo (Aragón); Marqués de Verger (Balearics); Pérez Valero (Canaries); Fernández-Ladreda (Asturias); Ortiz de Solórzano & Cirujano (Castiles); Sra Arroyo & Srta Bohigas (*Asociaciones Femeninas*); & Serrano Rodríguez (*Acción Obrerista*).

32 *El Debate*, 5 Mar 1933. Other points included repeal of anti-clerical legislation and a concordat, the strengthening of the executive, regionalism, full municipal autonomy, freedom of education, neutrality in external affairs, closer links with Spanish America and the Holy See and modernisation of the Army (Arrarás, *HSRE* II, 147).

33 *El Debate*, 4 Mar 1933.

34 *El Debate*, 3 Mar 1933.

35 *El Debate*, 3 Jan 1933 (also 23 Dec 1932).

36 Salmón, *El Debate*, 16 May 1933.

37 *El Debate*, 7 Mar 1933.

38 Fr Guallar, *El Debate*, 19 Nov 1932.

39 The words of a young lawyer addressing the Congress of Catholic Youths, *El Debate*, 20 Dec 1932.

40 *El Debate*, 27 June 1933.

41 *El Debate*, 19 Nov 1932.

42 *El Debate*, 11 Apr 1933. Valiente got a mixed reception at a Monarchist dinner when he said that 'the revolution surprised the aristocracy of lineage playing bridge' (*El Debate*, 24 Feb 1933). Gil Robles himself recommended 'little *casino* life and much going out to the villages and *pueblos* of Spain. Less toasting in champagne and

more going to see the needs of the farmers who cannot make a living' (*El Debate*, 20 June 1933).

43 *El Debate*, 4 & 5 Mar 1933; Monge Bernal, *AP*, 640–61.

44 L. Lucía, *La Confederación Española de Derechas Autónomas* (Valencia, 1933), 13–14; & *El Debate*, 8 Jan 1933, which reported his visit to Barcelona for talks with Cambó. Gil Robles had previously refused to take part in Cambó's plan for a *Derecha Republicana*, to be led by Cambó and to be composed of the *Lliga, Acción Popular* and the Conservative Republicans of Miguel Maura (*ABC*, 30 Dec 1932).

45 Cf M. P. Fogarty, *Christian Democracy in Western Europe* (London, 1957), esp 78, 86 & 101.

46 Monge Bernal, *AP*, 470.

47 *El Debate*, 7 Mar 1933.

48 *Acción Ciudadana* was led by the ex-UMN Alfonsines Pemán and the Marqués de Villapesadilla and the Traditionalist Martínez de Pinillos (*El Debate*, 19 Feb 1933).

49 They met secretly at the Conde de Aybar's flat on 19 June. Gil Robles said: 'I am a Monarchist; but I am prepared to govern under the Republic in defence of the highest interests, and if I govern under the Republic I shall be completely loyal to it, because a Monarchy brought in by anyone disloyal would not last three months in Spain. If I can serve Spain within the Republic I shall do so, even though it be to the detriment of the restoration of the Monarchy.' He argued that the CEDA would not compromise the Monarchist cause if its tactics failed, which he thought probable. Alfonso accepted this and told Gil Robles: 'Your task is immense. I shall do nothing to hinder you.' No condemnation of the CEDA was issued. Another interview, with Casanueva also present, took place a fortnight later to confirm both sides' points of view (Gutiérrez-Ravé, *Gil Robles*, 76–7; Gil Robles, *No fue posible*, 87–9).

50 Lamamié de Clairac, *ABC*, 7 Feb 1933.

51 *ABC* paid its Madrid and Seville staffs during the period; it cited editorials from before 10 August to show that it had not been implicated, and said the government had never given any reason for the suspension: 'Never . . . during all the governments of six reigns and two Republics was there applied to a newspaper a governmental sanction so severe as it was lacking in legal justification' (*ABC*, 30 Nov 1932).

52 *DSCC*, 18 Oct 1932. He said that 5,000 people were still detained, of whom only 137 had been tried (*DSCC*, 9 Nov 1932).

53 *DSCC*, 23 Nov 1932.

54 *DSCC*, 28 Dec 1932. Casares Quiroga called the accusations exaggerated.

55 Guallar, *DSCC*, 11 Nov 1932.

56 In Villafranca de los Caballeros the town-council hired a band and billeted the musicians on their political enemies instead of paying

them (Madariaga, *DSCC*, 31 Mar 1933). In El Redal it was said that a man who had voted for the Right had committed suicide after failing to gain admission to a hospital through the machinations of *caciques* of *Acción Republicana* (Ortiz de Solórzano, *DSCC*, 18 May 1933). Rightists were keen to reveal the origins of government agents: the Mayor of Las Navalmorales, now a self-styled 'Marxist', was formerly President of the local *Unión Patriótica* (Madariaga, *DSCC*, 7 July 1933).

57 *DSCC*, 15 Feb, 15 Mar & 16 May 1933.

58 *El Debate*, 1 Jan 1933.

59 Gil Robles, *Spain in Chains*, 2. Under Azaña, 150 papers were suspended, 320 branches of *Acción Popular* were closed, 3,000 fines levied on Rightists, 470 political activists and publicists imprisoned or deported, 280 meetings banned and 80 members' houses damaged by mobs—all by the arbitrary decision or non-intervention of the authorities.

60 F. G. Bruguera, *Histoire contemporaine d'Espagne* (n.pl., 1954), 391. The index of industrial production fell from 84·5 in March 1931 to 67 in June 1932 (100 = 1928): *DSCC*, 18 Oct 1932. Export markets for the Valencian orange, an important item, shrank in Germany and Britain, in the latter case as a consequence of protection after the Ottawa Conference.

61 Madariaga, *Spain*, 441.

62 Carner, *DSCC*, 18 Oct 1932.

63 Arrarás, *HSRE* II, 157–62 & 164–6.

64 Eg Calderón, *DSCC*, 25 Nov 1932; liberal Agrarians were at heart opposed to any new expenditure and longed for a balanced budget.

65 Pildáin, *DSCC*, 3 & 4 Nov 1932. The Canon of Vitoria stressed the need for work-creation schemes on lines planned by the German Ministry of Labour and the Belgian Socialists. The official figure for unemployment—probably an under-estimate—was around 600–700,000; eg in Aug 1933 there were 285,898 totally unemployed and 258,000 working a 3/4 day week (quoted in *El Debate*, 18 Aug 1933).

66 *DSCC*, 8 & 9 Dec 1932. Guallar pointed out that the juries were a continuation of the Dictator's arbitration committees, if now 'perverted'. Likewise Largo's *Caja especial para el paro forzoso* was the *Instituto Nacional de Previsión* of 1928 under another name.

67 Madariaga, *DSCC*, 8 Dec 1932.

68 Fanjul, *DSCC*, 16 Dec 1932.

69 Eg *El Debate*, 1 Feb 1933.

70 Martín, *DSCC*, 4 May 1933. Domingo thought the surplus exceptionally large.

71 *El Debate*, 17 Mar 1933.

72 *El Debate*, 17 & 18 May 1933. Speakers noted with suspicion that the trade with Catalonia had fallen from 300 to 30 wagons per week.

73 *DSCC*, 18 Oct 1932.

74 *El Debate*, 2 Feb 1933.

75 *Memorias íntimas de Azaña*, 90–3, notes that nothing had been done by the summer of 1933. Azaña portrays Domingo as quite ignorant of agriculture and having little idea of what he was doing; land reform was held up by the 'little parliament' of the Institute.

76 *El Debate*, 2 Feb 1933. The Governor sanctioned occupations with slips of paper (Ventosa, *ABC*, 9 May 1933).

77 Arrarás, *HSRE* II, 50.

78 *ABC*, 21 May 1933.

79 *DSCC*, 18 Oct 1932.

80 *El Debate*, 22 June–11 July 1933. The leader of the *Bloque Agrario* had been imprisoned for advising farmers not to sow or pay taxes. The situation in Jaén had been similar (*El Socialista*, 1 & 4 Oct 1932).

81 Protest of 2,000 Sevillano farmers to Alcalá-Zamora, *El Debate*, 9 May 1933.

82 Entry in Azaña's diary, 11 Jan 1933 (*Memorias íntimas*, 208).

83 *DSCC*, 23 Feb 1933; the phrase in fact became telescoped into: 'a régime of mud, blood and tears'.

84 The Rightist opposition at the time is freely termed 'Pharisaism' by Sáinz Rodríguez (conversation). The affair also destroyed the image of the Assault Guards, a creation of Miguel Maura in 1931; henceforth these armed police had the same prestige as the tricorn-hats of the Civil Guard. On the affair see Arrarás, *HSRE* II, 81–105; cf G. Jackson, *The Spanish Republic and the Civil War* (Princeton, 1965), 101–2 & 513–14.

85 *El Debate*, 15 Oct & 2 Dec 1932.

86 Text of the law in *DSCC*, 2 June 1933 App.

87 *El Debate*, 26 Feb 1933, citing the Church survey of 1931; there were 4,804 religious houses in Spain—998 male and 3,806 female. Los Ríos, who admitted that his figures were deficient, said the Orders had 351,937 primary and 17,098 secondary pupils (Arrarás, *HSRE* II, 122). Among welfare services were help given to 669,982 of the poor, hospital treatment for 82,386, care for 30,784 children, meals for 190,460, shelter for 39,077 and care for 15,320 cases of leprosy and 18,073 mental cases (*El Debate*, 30 Apr 1933).

88 *El Debate*, 21 Feb 1933.

89 Lerroux, *El Debate*, 19 & 23 Feb 1933.

90 *El Socialista*, 7 Feb 1933.

91 Cid & Gil Robles, *DSCC*, 9 Feb 1933.

92 Aguirre & Leizaola, *DSCC*, 10 Feb & 29 Mar 1933; also the Traditionalist Oreja Elósegui, *DSCC*, 22 Feb 1933.

93 Estelrich, *DSCC*, 6 Apr 1933; Royo Villanova, *DSCC*, 15 & 17 Mar 1933.

94 Guallar, *DSCC*, 10 Feb 1933. Canon Pildáin failed to convince Socialists to abandon anti-clericalism and to join Catholics in the quest for social justice (*DSCC*, 10 Feb & 1 Mar 1933).

95 *El Debate*, 28 Apr 1933. Fanjul called for the withdrawal of the law

after the elections, and Gil Robles for the government's resignation (*DSCC*, 26 Apr 1933).

96 *DSCC*, 17 May 1933. Those voting against the law were the Agrarians, the Basque-Navarrese, the *Lliga*, Right Republicans including S. Alba, and Gallego Catholics.

97 *El Debate* & *ABC*, 18 May 1933.

98 It seems very unlikely that Alcalá-Zamora seriously thought of withholding his signature. The Italian Ambassador notes that he sent for the Nuncio, but greeted Tedeschini with the words, 'Excellency, look what they're making me do!' (Guariglia, *Ricordi*, 207).

99 The manifesto was signed by all Agrarians, Basques and Navarrese, and by the Independent Republican Canon García Gallego and Blanco-Rajoy, a Gallego Catholic. *Renovación Española* demanded a referendum (*El Debate*, 4, 5 & 6 June 1933).

100 *El Debate*, 3 June 1933. The Declaration was dated 25 May 1933.

101 *El Debate*, 4 June 1933.

102 The board of the *Sociedad Anónima de Enseñanza Libre* included the liberal Martínez de Velasco, the Alfonsine Sáinz Rodríguez, the Carlist Lamamié de Clairac, Gil Robles, and the wealthy Marqués de la Vega de Anzo (*ABC*, 4 July 1933). Buckley (*Spanish Republic*, 100) says that though there was always a lay headmaster, teachers were often monks or nuns in ordinary dress.

103 *El Debate*, 1 July 1933. Herrera had resigned as editor in February 1933 to take over Catholic Action.

104 Martínez de Velasco & Gil Robles, *El Debate*, 8 & 14 Mar 1933 respectively.

105 *El Debate*, 5 & 8 Apr 1933; the PNV declined to join, not wishing to involve itself in 'Spanish' problems. In some areas, Gil Robles claimed, Radicals and Conservatives allied with Socialists (*El Debate*, 18 Apr 1933).

106 Gil Robles, *El Debate*, 18 Apr 1933.

107 Eg at Reinosa (Santander) on 31 Mar Sáinz Rodríguez & Fernández were addressing local sympathisers with the permission of the Socialist Mayor when Socialists fired on the building and set fire to it. One Rightist was killed, but neither the Mayor nor the Civil Guard would intervene (*El Debate*, 1 & 2 Apr 1933). At Garcirrey (Salamanca) the local Socialist leader, ex-President of the UP, proclaimed himself elected and forbade presentation of the Agrarian candidates. In Guadalajara there were disorders after leaflets were circulated reading: 'Comrades: Let no one dare to take tolerance for weakness. We have already had enough of tolerance!' (*El Debate*, 18 Apr 1933). In Badajoz, the Civil Governor resigned because he had too few Civil Guards to check Socialist intimidation. In Carmona (Seville) 11 members of *Acción Popular* were fined 500 ptas apiece for saying preference for jobs should be given to party members (*El Debate*, 23 Apr 1933).

108 Results from 2,192 of the 2,478 *pueblos*, *El Debate*, 25 Apr 1933. The

532 Basque Nationalists were included with the Right. The figures showed 2,964 'agrarians' among the Right (cf 395 *Acción Popular*); these 'agrarians' were claimed as theirs by M. Maura, Gil Robles & Martínez de Velasco, who saw them as a basis for an Agrarian Party which he did not found for the time being (*El Debate*, 25–26 Apr).

109 Arrarás, *HSRE* II, 118. According to Casares Quiroga 'more sincere elections' were impossible (*ABC*, 25 Apr 1933). Against Azaña's view may be set the earlier claims by the Right that *caciques*, especially those of the UP, had gone over to the government parties *en masse* (Madariaga & Gil Robles, *DSCC*, 14 Oct 1932).

110 Among the provisions of this law was the exclusion of legislation passed by the Constituent Cortes from appeals against its constitutional validity. Text in *DSCC*, 14 June 1933 App.

111 *El Debate*, 9–13 June 1933; *El Socialista* (6 June) said that the Socialists would refuse to leave power, and (13 June) congratulated itself for achieving this. However, Besteiro was not of quite the same opinion; nor was Prieto, according to F. Largo Caballero, *Mis recuerdos* (Mexico City, 1954), 128 & 145. The new government was: Premier & War, Azaña (*Acción Republicana*); State, Los Ríos (Socialist); Justice, Albornoz (Radical-Socialist); Navy, Companys (*Esquerra*); Interior, Casares Quiroga (ORGA); Finance, Viñuales (*Acción Republicana*); Public Instruction, F. Barnés (Radical-Socialist); Labour, Largo Caballero (Socialist); Agriculture, Domingo (Radical-Socialist); Public Works, Prieto (Socialist); & Industry & Commerce, Franchy Roca (Federal). The Federals joined on condition that the Defence Law was lifted; the small Federal minority split when this did not occur.

112 *DSCC*, 14 June 1933.

113 *El Debate*, 14 June 1933. The Progressives, ie the President's friends, decided to stay in the Cortes to vote against a government which had betrayed the Republic and become the 'steering committee of the revolution' (*El Debate*, 17 June 1933).

114 *DSCC*, 25 Aug 1933.

115 The texts of these laws are in *DSCC*, 27 & 28 July 1933 Apps. The Law concerning Public Order, like the Defence Law of the Republic before it, had a clear parallel in Article 48 of the Weimar Constitution; the Law gave wide powers to the government by means of the proclamation of graded states of prevention, alarm and war.

116 This was suggested by Gil Robles at the prompting of the *Bloque Agrario* of Salamanca (*El Debate*, 9 July 1932).

117 The text of the Agriculture Committee's Draft is in *DSCC*, 23 June 1933.

118 *El Debate*, 23 July 1933.

119 Eg *DSCC*, 27 July (Casanueva, Cid, Martín, Cornide Quiroga), 28 July (Blanco-Rajoy, Royo Villanova) & Guallar, 2 Aug 1933.

120 *DSCC*, 28 July & 2 Aug 1933. The Agrarians' intention to obstruct the Draft was reported in *El Debate*, 15 July 1933.

121   *DSCC*, 4 Aug & *El Debate*, 5, 6 & 10 Aug 1933.

122   Eg Guallar put down 125 amendments to Article 8 & Cid 94 to
      Article 16 (*DSCC*, 11 & 25 Aug Apps). Since deputies knew that
      nothing was being done save talk, attendance dropped to a very low
      level; hence the failure to obtain a quorum which was usually
      demanded when the time came to vote. The Radical-Socialists, who
      had an eye to property now that religious legislation had been
      exhausted, refused to help facilitate a quorum for the government
      to which they were committed (*El Debate*, 4 Aug 1933).

123   *El Debate*, 5 & 12 Sept & *ABC*, 6 Sept 1933. The votes recorded
      were: Radicals, 15,868; CEDA, 13,515; Socialists, 9,006; Tradi-
      tionalists, 1,966; PNV, 1,156; Centre, 1,277; *Acción Republicana*,
      497; ORGA, 1,821; Radical-Socialists, 1,586; Liberal-Democrats,
      411.

124   Los Ríos informed the US Ambassador that disintegration of the
      coalition prompted the resignation (C. G. Bowers, *My Mission to
      Spain* [London, 1954], 35). The Radical-Socialists were by now in
      complete chaos and divided into two main factions on whether or
      not Socialists were acceptable as partners in government.

125   *El Socialista*, 14 Sept 1933. The new government consisted of:
      Premier, Lerroux (Radical); State, Sánchez-Albornoz (*Acción Re-
      publicana*); Justice, Botella Asensi (Radical-Socialist Left); War,
      Rocha (Radical); Navy, Iranzo (Independent Republican); Finance,
      Lara (Radical); Interior, Martínez Barrio (Radical); Public In-
      struction, D. Barnés (Radical-Socialist); Public Works, Guerra del
      Río (Radical); Labour, Samper (Radical); Industry & Commerce,
      Gómez Paratcha (ORGA); Communications, Santaló (*Esquerra*);
      Agriculture, Feced (Radical-Socialist).

126   Membership of the PSOE went up from 16,878 in June 1930 to
      75,133 in June 1932. In the same period the UGT expanded from
      277,011 to 1,041,539; 445,414 of these were rural workers (Picard-
      Moch & Moch, *L'Espagne*, 279–81 & 286). *El Debate*, 14 Oct 1932,
      reported an admission by Largo Caballero that Socialists in some
      areas had used the Law of Municipal Boundaries as a weapon of
      caciquismo—ie preference for employment was given to UGT mem-
      bers.

127   *El Socialista* & *El Debate*, 8–13 Oct 1932.

128   *El Socialista*, 23 Oct 1932.

129   *El Socialista*, 9 Nov 1932.

130   *ABC*, 2 Mar 1933.

131   Vallellano, *ABC*, 20 June 1933.

132   Fuentes Pila, *ABC*, 30 Aug 1933.

133   *ABC*, 22 Sept 1933. *Renovación Española* was in fact a party com-
      prising various ideological positions united in defence of the Alfon-
      sine dynasty. The dominant foreign influence on the leadership was
      the practical example of Mussolini's Italy and not—as sometimes
      suggested—the ideas of Maurras's *Action Française* (Conversation

with Cortés Cavanillas, later Secretary-General of *Renovación Española*).

134 *Acción Española*, 16 May 1933, carried an article on the general theory of the corporative state by the Italian academic Costamagna (*Antología*, 101–14). The historian Gaxotte (*Action Française*) was also a contributor in 1933. Yet the review still defined Spanish nationalism as service to Catholicism and the Church by quoting Menéndez Pelayo (16 Aug 1933: *Antología*, 71). Vegas found hope for his cause because 'the Traditionalist doctrine [had been] purified in the crucible of adversity' and secondly because 'the world [is] today pervaded by a "Fascist" atmosphere, which in its main bases retains great similarity to the postulates of Traditionalism' (16 Sept 1933: *Antología*, 157). Vegas (conversation) says that *Acción Española*'s ideology was based on Christian public law and Traditionalism, particularly Menéndez Pelayo. The agnostic Maurras was used only as an additional source for arguments for Monarchy; Mussolini was admired as a 'man of order' though Fascist doctrine was 'laughable'.

135 Ansaldo, ¿ *Para qué?*, 47–8; Salmador, *Ansaldo*, 87, mentions aristocrats as the main contributors.

136 Ansaldo, ¿ *Para qué?*, 48–50. Alfonso would seem to have pursued two policies. On the one hand he declined to make difficulties for Gil Robles, while on the other he sanctioned preparations for violent action should circumstances demand it. He had not been party to '10 August', though he gave money to officers who lost their positions and livelihood (Sáinz Rodríguez, conversation). In the autumn of 1932 Alfonso told Vallellano: 'no acts of force, deaths or violence of any kind for my cause. If God has disposed that I must return to reign, it will be because the Spaniards have decided anew to call for me' (*Habla el Rey*, 362). Perhaps Alfonso drew a distinction between conspiracy on Spain's behalf and conspiracy on behalf of his person.

137 Ansaldo, ¿ *Para qué?*, 51. Salmador, *Ansaldo*, 90, notes that the offer to Martínez Anido was supported by a letter signed by the King.

138 Salmador, *Ansaldo*, 85–6.

139 Ansaldo, ¿ *Para qué?*, 50–1; Salmador, *Ansaldo*, 86.

140 Ansaldo, ¿ *Para qué?*, 51, writes: 'Daring contacts were not lacking with certain Syndicalist sectors, who on some occasions were used to make life difficult for successive Republican governments.' It is impossible to believe, however, that Anarchist disturbances during 1933 were dependent simply on Monarchist money.

141 Vegas Latapié, *Calvo Sotelo*, 104–10.

142 Aunós, *Calvo Sotelo* (Madrid, 1941), 125, 136, 145 & 152. Calvo now thought Tardieu too moderate. Italian Fascism was 'a political régime [which] attracted him with especial warmth'. Calvo saw Hitler's accession to power (30 Jan 1933) as an event that 'announces the fatal triumph of the totalitarian system'.

143   Ansaldo, *? Para qué?*, 58, says that Calvo went because Aunós would
       not, and that he had a cordial interview with Balbo. Salmador,
       Ansaldo, 91, says that he saw Balbo and Cardinal Segura. According
       to the ex-Minister Yanguas Messía, he saw Mussolini (E. del Corral,
       Calvo Sotelo [2nd ed, Madrid, 1956], 18). Guariglia, who became
       Italian Ambassador in Sept 1932, had instructions to repair the
       damage done to Italo-Spanish relations by the contacts with the
       '10 August' plotters, about which Azaña knew. The *Duce* saw the
       failure of 10 August as the entrenchment of Azaña, a possible
       dictator—'he has used my own methods' was his comment on
       Azaña's repressive measures. Mussolini now sought to woo Azaña
       as a diplomatic ally against France (Guariglia, *Ricordi*, 185, 190–9
       & 773–4).

144   Conversation with Cortés Cavanillas; there was a courageous but
       tiny youth movement, *Juventud de Renovación Española*, whose
       members wore green berets.

145   The police seized 101 blue shirts emblazoned with the cross of
       Santiago, and the list of subscribers, with aristocrats in the van, who
       paid the PNE only 6,456·55 ptas a month. Albiñana himself was
       moved from Las Hurdes to Almería, to receive a short sentence for
       insulting the régime, and then to his native Enguera (*El Debate*, 15,
       18, 23 & 29 Mar 1933).

146   *El Debate*, 7 Mar 1933.

147   *HCE* I–5, 593–4; Arrarás, *HSRE* II, 148–54; Payne, *Falange*,
       30–1. Ortega had dissolved his group 'in the service of the Re-
       public' in Oct 1932, since the Republic had proved a disillusion-
       ing reversion to the previous century and had failed to create 'a
       new ideology and politico-social philosophy' (Arrarás, *HSRE* II,
       35–6).

148   Arrarás, *HSRE* II, 154; *HCE*, I–5, 593. The Madrid group's mani-
       festo said: 'The JONS are a Spanish national party which embraces
       the deepest interests of the university and working-class youths: the
       right to a Country, the affirmation of the eternal values of one's land
       and the creation of an economy that guarantees the vigour and
       might of the Spanish people.' *El Debate*, 11 Mar 1933, noted that
       Jonsistas sang *La Giovinezza*.

149   Text of the electoral manifesto is in J. A. Primo de Rivera, *Obras
       completas* (Madrid, 1942), 785–8.

150   Yanguas Messía, quoted by Corral, *Calvo Sotelo*, 18.

151   L. Aguirre Prado, *Ruiz de Alda* (Madrid, 1955), 19–20; Payne,
       Falange, 34.

152   Primo de Rivera, *O.c.*, 531–4, 536–40, 601–5 & 1057–8.

153   J. A. Primo de Rivera, *Textos inéditos y epistolario* (Madrid, 1956),
       140–1. His impressions of his interview with the *Duce* are in *O.c.*,
       522–3. Guariglia, *Ricordi*, 203–4, says that he arranged the visit to
       counter the designs of the German Ambassador, who was trying to
       bring the nascent movement within the Nazi orbit. José Antonio had

been offended by Mussolini's derision for Spanish 'Fascism' and Guariglia wished to keep out Nazi competition.

154 Salmador, *Ansaldo*, 99; & Ansaldo, ¿ *Para qué?*, 63. The minute-book of *Renovación Española* records that 100,000 ptas of party funds were allocated for the foundation of the *Falange*.

155 See Payne, *Falange*, 38–41. García Valdecasas had been an opponent of the Dictatorship.

156 The text of his speech is in his *O.c.*, 17–28.

157 *Acción Española*, 16 Dec 1933 (*Antología*, 210–18).

158 Payne, *Falange*, 35.

159 *El Socialista*, 17 Jan 1933.

160 *El Socialista*, 1 Jan 1932.

161 *El Socialista*, 15, 17 & 22 Feb 1933.

162 *El Socialista*, 21 Jan 1933.

163 *El Socialista*, 18, 21 & 24 Mar 1933. The party's intellectuals were perhaps the most perturbed by events abroad. Araquistáin, the Republic's Ambassador in Berlin, witnessed the Nazi victory, from which he drew the unshakable conclusion that the passive tactics and optimistic fatalism of German Marxists regarding Nazism were quite wrong: the Left must strike first.

164 *El Debate*, 22 Mar 1933. The paper reported that only half his audience in Barcelona approved of his speech, the purpose of which was to bring to their senses 'those stupid people who, by their action, are going to give the government grounds for taking measures against the Right'.

165 *El Debate*, 27 Dec 1932. Political difficulties had arisen in Salamanca within the Rightist coalition grouping after the October Assembly of *Acción Popular*. The Traditionalist Lamamié de Clairac was a key figure, and in fact took the local Carlists out of *Acción Popular*'s subsidiary (*ABC*, 28 Dec 1932).

166 Gil Robles at Murcia, *El Debate*, 14 Mar 1933.

167 Valiente, *El Debate*, 18 Feb 1933. Gil Robles told *Japistas* ('the Youth of 12 April, the Youth of the Revolution') how hard it was to advise young men to desist from force and violence: 'But bear in mind that violence and firmness are distinct' (*El Debate*, 17 Feb 1933).

168 *El Socialista*, 24 May & *El Debate*, 25 May 1933; J. Arrabal, *José María Gil Robles* (Madrid, 1933), 231–47. This example has been chosen as it is the best documented, although the extraneous factor of the JONS is present. The JONS had formed part of the Right's electoral alliance in Valladolid, and local Socialists pledged them-selves to a campaign of disorder as long as the alliance lasted (*El Debate*, 19 & 29 Mar 1933). However, many meetings before and afterwards were suspended under Socialist pressure in areas where there was no JONS, eg that of *Acción Popular* in Badajoz just a few days later (*El Debate*, 27 May 1933). Socialists were also determined that no 'yellow' unions should flourish, eg a strike-threat by the UGT

procured the dismissal of 20 members of the *Federación Española de Trabajadores* working on the same site in the University City (*El Debate*, 29 Aug 1933).

169 *El Socialista*, 25 Oct 1932.
170 *El Socialista*, 14 Mar & 11 Apr 1933.
171 *El Socialista*, 2 May 1933.
172 *El Socialista*, 17 May 1933.
173 *El Socialista* & *El Debate*, 25 June 1933.
174 *El Socialista*, 4 July 1933; Arrarás, *HSRE* II, 190.
175 He added: 'since I have been in the government . . . I have become, if possible, much redder than when I went in: but much redder!' (*El Socialista*, 13 Aug 1933).
176 B. Alonso, *El Socialista*, 29 Aug 1933.
177 *El Debate* & *ABC*, 19 Mar 1933.
178 Lerroux, *Pequeña historia*, 151–2, 163, 168–9 & 173–4.
179 *DSCC*, 2 Oct 1933.
180 *El Socialista*, 3 Oct 1933.
181 *DSCC*, 2–3 Oct 1933. *El Debate*, 10 Sept 1933, had seen the government as an improvement on Azaña's but it had to be opposed as it was laicist. Lerroux was defeated by 187 votes to 91; the Right abstained and he was supported only by his Radicals and some dissident Radical-Socialists and Federals.
182 Alcalá-Zamora, *Los defectos*, 172.
183 *El Debate*, 6–10 Oct 1933. *El Socialista*, 8 Oct 1933, reported the party's refusal to participate. The government was: Premier, Martínez Barrio (Radical); State, Sánchez-Albornoz (*Acción Republicana*); Justice, Botella Asensi (Radical-Socialist Left); War, Iranzo (Independent Republican); Navy, Pita Romero (ORGA); Finance, Lara (Radical); Interior, Rico Avello (Independent Republican); Public Instruction, Barnés (Radical-Socialist); Public Works, Guerra del Río (Radical); Agriculture, Del Río (Progressive); Industry & Commerce, Gordón Ordás (Radical-Socialist); Communications, Palomo (Independent Radical-Socialist); Labour, Pi Súñer (*Esquerra*).
184 *El Debate*, 12 Oct 1933.
185 *El Debate*, 17 Oct 1933. José Antonio wrote that Gil Robles was now proclaiming 'Fascist' principles: 'he does not express himself as the *caudillo* of a Christian-Democrat party' (*Textos inéditos*, 142).
186 *El Debate*, 3 Nov 1933.
187 *El Debate*, 7 & 14 Nov 1933.
188 *El Debate*, 18 Nov 1933.
189 Speech on a gramophone record by Calvo Sotelo, *ABC*, 19 Nov 1933.
190 *ABC*, 10 Oct 1933.
191 Thus it was described by *El Socialista*, 17 Oct 1933.
192 *El Socialista*, 9 & 14 Nov 1933.
193 Araquistáin, *El Socialista*, 31 Oct 1933.

194 Largo Caballero, *El Socialista*, 24 Sept & 20 Oct 1933. Los Ríos told the US Ambassador that he foresaw a Rightist victory (Bowers, *My Mission*, 42).

195 Gil Robles, *El Debate*, 20 June 1933; Lamamié, *El Debate*, 31 Jan 1933; Goicoechea, *ABC*, 18 June 1933.

196 The committee was: Martínez de Velasco, Royo Villanova & Cid (ex-Liberal Agrarians); Gil Robles & Casanueva (CEDA); Lamamié de Clairac (Carlist); Sáinz Rodríguez (Alfonsine); Calderón (ex-Conservative Agrarian).

197 *ABC*, 15 Oct 1933.

198 Gil Robles, Royo Villanova, Cid, in *El Debate*, 28 Sept, 5 & 7 Oct 1933.

199 *ABC*, 30 Sept 1933; also Vallellano, *ABC*, 13 Oct 1933.

200 *El Debate*, 11 Oct 1933.

201 From the press, it would seem that the following alliances were made by the Right: Alicante (with Chapaprieta); Asturias (Liberal-Democrats); Badajoz (Radicals and Conservatives); Balearics (Centre Republicans of March); Cáceres (Radicals); Ceuta (Radicals); Ciudad Real (Conservatives); Granada (Radicals); Huelva (Conservatives); Jaén (Radicals and Conservatives); Lugo (Conservatives); Murcia-prov (Liberal-Democrats); Zamora (S. Alba, now a Radical). In Guadalajara the Right was in alliance with Romanones.

202 Martínez Barrio, *El Debate*, 12 Oct 1933. Left Republicans were very disappointed to hear this. The Radicals fought alone where they were strong, eg Madrid, Valencia, the Canaries, and allied with Left Republicans, eg with Radical-Socialists in Alicante, with *Acción Republicana* in Almería and Ávila.

203 He wanted a Radical-Right alliance in Madrid-cap. The Monarchists would not permit this, but he got José Antonio relegated to Cádiz, Delgado Barreto to the Canaries, Albiñana to Burgos & Sanjurjo to Melilla—where he was not allowed to stand (*El Debate*, 10, 17 & 26 Oct 1933; *HCE*, I–5, 655; F. Casares, *La CEDA va a gobernar* [Madrid, 1934], 38 & 45–6). Redondo had to withdraw in Valladolid and García Valdecasas in Granada. Disputes were legion: one of the more heated was over Madrid-prov, where, as in Valencia, the views of the CEDA prevailed over those of *Renovación Española*.

204 Arrarás, *HSRE* II, 20–5. The *Esquerra* got 192,000 votes to the *Lliga*'s 129,000; the Monarchist Right polled 15,300, the Catalan Communists 10,900.

205 J. M. de Nadal, *Seis años con D. Francisco Cambó* (Barcelona, 1957), 144.

206 M. García Venero, *Vida de Cambó* (Barcelona, 1952), 364. Its policy remained the achievement 'by all legal means' of the 'greatest degree of moral and material progress for the Catalan people' through the region's 'consciousness of its personality and the persistent action of its own endeavour'.

207 *La Vanguardia*, 12 July 1933. Textile men thought it better to emigrate than 'to live under the constant terrorist threat' (Arrarás, *HSRE* II, 165 & 195).

208 Peers, *Catalonia*, 224–5; Ramos Oliveira, *Politics*, 221.

209 Peers, *Catalonia*, 225; Arrarás, *HSRE* II, 219.

210 Farmers in March 1933 had threatened to destroy their crops if the *Generalidad* did not afford them protection (Arrarás, *HSRE* II, 165). Companys, renewing his solidarity with the *Unió*, said: 'I am what I am thanks to the *rabassaires*' (Ossorio, *Companys*, 79).

211 The *Lliga* stood alone in Barcelona, negotiations with the Radicals and the Right having failed, in the latter case because the *Lliga* demanded all the candidates on the list. Monarchists, Agrarians and the like formed their own list under the title *Bloque Nacional de Derechas* in Barcelona, on which Gil Robles refused to appear, ostensibly because of his regionalist convictions. In Lérida, the *Lliga* formed a list with Traditionalists, Radicals and Liberal-Democrats.

212 Sierra Bustamente, *Euzkadi*, 237, 240 & 270; Aguirre, *Libertad*, 315. Aguirre gives the sov over 50,000 members, the Alfonsine Sierra 35,000. In 1932 a priest wrote to Aguirre to assure him that 'there is no other redemption save Nationalism'; another wrote: 'You must not abandon your leadership of the Basque Israel for which God has appointed you.' Support came also from the farmers' organisation *Euzko-Nekazarien Alkartasuna* (Iturralde, *Catolicismo*, I, 426).

213 Letter from Irujo to Aguirre, 5 May 1932, cited by Arrarás, *HSRE* I, 387.

214 Aguirre, *Libertad*, 308–14, 318–31 & 338–42. *El Debate*, 30 Oct 1932, reported that the Traditionalist committees of the 3 provinces had decided on restitution of *fueros* rather than a Statute. Aguirre, *DSCC*, 9 Nov 1932, pointedly said, 'my Country is Euzkadi' when other deputies held that it could only be Spain.

215 Aguirre, *Libertad*, 351–3, 364–80 & 388–404. In Álava, there was widespread abstention by Traditionalists: 26,015 voted in favour, 6,695 against. Alfonso Carlos expressed his opinion in a letter to Olazábal (*Documentos de Alfonso Carlos*, 229). Prieto's organ *El Liberal* suspected gerrymandering, asking how 88 per cent of Biscayans could have voted in favour when the Socialists had counselled abstention. (Quoted in Arrarás, *HSRE* II, 263–4.) The Bishop of Vitoria, who had been allowed to return from exile in April 1933, had said that it was licit for Catholics to vote for the Statute if they so desired (García Venero, *Nacionalismo vasco*, 445).

216 *ABC*, 12 Nov 1933. *El Socialista* (8 Aug 1933) thought it as necessary to 'smother' separatist nationalism as it was 'Fascism'.

217 The government banned aerial propaganda on 4 Nov, as only the Right had aeroplanes; the CEDA had eight, and one autogiro.

218 Many of the gifts were anonymous. *ABC*, 22 Oct 1933, said that

Acción Popular had received 500,000 ptas in gifts, 150,000 from one family alone; *ABC*, 27 Oct, reported another anonymous gift of 100,000 ptas. Cortés Cavanillas (conversation) mentions the names Urquijo and Vega de Anzo among the many members of the plutocracy who made donations. Gil Robles (conversation) says that the CEDA was financed by the monthly subscriptions of members, though there were 'extraordinary subscriptions' for elections.

219 *El Debate*, 27 Oct 1933 & *ABC*, 12 Nov 1933. Catholics used the slogan: 'Save the souls of the little children!' (Manuel, *Politics*, 106).

220 *El Debate*, 3 & 10 Oct 1933.

221 *ABC*, 19 Nov 1933; 'he who votes for the Socialists, votes openly for Marx; but no less so does he who votes for Lerroux . . . because the Centre always fumbles before the Left'.

222 J. Bécarud, *La deuxième République espagnole* (Paris, 1962), 49–50.

223 *DSCC*, 4 July 1933.

224 All electoral statistics, unless otherwise stated, are based on the detailed information, based on official figures, in *El Debate*, 5 Dec 1933 & 2 Feb 1936.

225 *ABC*, 2 Dec 1933.

226 *El Debate*, 23 Nov 1933. In Badajoz the Centre-Right polled 141,316 votes to the Socialists' 136,603, obtaining 11 and 3 seats respectively under the majority-minority system. The other results were similar, viz Cáceres: Centre-Right 7 seats (116,094 votes), Socialists 2 (67,058). Granada: Centre-Right 10 (121,945), Socialists 3 (96,649). Jaén: Centre-Right 10 (140,997), Socialists 3 (112,459).

227 *El Debate*, 19 Nov 1933; Salmón (at Murcia, 25 Nov), cited in Arrarás, *HSRE* II, 240.

228 *ABC*, 22 & 23 Nov 1933.

229 In Madrid-cap in the first contest the Right polled 133,366 votes, the Centre 72,299, Socialists 141,796, Left Republicans 22,177, Communists 12,685. In the second, in a straight fight, Socialists 177,331, the Right 171,757; 13 seats to 4. In Madrid-prov, the Socialists got 58,854, the Right 52,165, the Centre 27,174 in the first; in the second, the Socialists lost to the Right in a straight fight, 2 seats to 6.

230 Córdoba provided a *cause célèbre*: Gil Robles forced out the Alfonsine Valverde, Alcalá-Zamora's personal rival in Priego, to make room on the list for the Progressives, the President's friends (Cortés Cavanillas, *Gil Robles*, 157–60).

231 In Córdoba the Right alone would have beaten the Socialists alone, but a Socialist-Communist alliance—the PCE here polled 25,693— would have defeated the Right and the Centre separately. In Alicante, Murcia and Málaga-prov, the Socialists could only be overcome by a Centre-Right alliance. In Málaga-cap, a Socialist-Communist alliance defeated the Centre-Right: Bolívar of the PCE just topped the poll with 12,901. It may be noted that in Oviedo, the

Socialists were beaten by a CEDA-Liberal-Democrat list, while in Huelva the Socialists won because the Radicals had a separate list from the Conservative-CEDA coalition; both these constituencies were decided on 19 Nov.

232 Dividing the parties in the Constituent Cortes on the same lines as here used for 1933, except that the Basque Nationalists, included in the Right in 1931, have been included with the Centre in 1933. Also, of the 26 independents of 1931, 24 have been included with the Centre, two—Calvo Sotelo and Romanones—with the Right.

233 Viz Barcelona-prov, Gerona, Huelva, Madrid-cap and Málaga-cap.

234 *El Socialista*, 25 Nov 1933; in general, Socialists' complaints involved Radicals more often than Rightists.

235 Socialists spoke of Radical *caciquismo* in Badajoz, Granada, Jaén & Pontevedra, saying the Governors were Radical partisans. *El Debate*, 16 Nov 1933, mentioned *caciquismo* by the Governor of Cuenca, by Radicals in Madrid-prov, and in Toledo where the Minister Palomo was standing: here propagandists were arrested, as was D. de Madariaga for a time. *ABC*, 18 Nov 1933, printed a letter from the Minister Sánchez-Albornoz to a *cacique* in Ávila, requesting his aid.

236 *El Debate*, 21 Nov 1933, reported Socialist breaking of voting-urns in Badajoz. On 26 Oct it reported that Rightists had been fired at in Vigo, Toledo & Madrid-prov. On 14 Nov it reported shots at the audience of Pemán & José Antonio in Cádiz-prov.

237 *Caciquismo* seems still to have flourished in Galicia, possibly because of the great dependence of *minifundistas* on municipal whims. Possibly the Right here inherited the old Conservative organisation, the Left that of the Liberals. Corunna, returning 12 of the Centre & Right, & the 5 ORGA men, was the only province where scrutiny of votes did not take place; *El Debate*, 16 Nov, reported a request by the Governor for the return of blank papers—to allow him to fill them in as he thought fit. Valencia (*Memorias íntimas de Azaña*, 173) was the most corrupt region in Spain under the *Blasquistas* (Radicals). The DRV complained of violence—one of their poll-supervisors was killed. According to Cortés Cavanillas (*Gil Robles*, 160–1) the DRV really won, but Lerroux & Blasco threatened to burn churches, whereupon the Archbishop, Lucía & Gil Robles conferred & agreed to a Radical victory. (The official result in both constituencies of Valencia shows a marginal Radical win over the DRV-Carlist coalition.)

238 Lerroux, *Pequeña historia*, 192–4, says the Interior Minister, Rico, himself defeated in Oviedo, was scrupulously fair and implies that a more 'experienced' man would have produced a Radical majority. Botella, Leftist Justice Minister, resigned because the government's 'inhibition' had let in too many Rightists (*El Socialista*, 30 Nov 1933).

239 *El Debate*, 21 Nov 1933; Monge Bernal, *AP*, 217 & 360–1.

240 Sáinz Rodríguez (conversation) says money was given to Anarchists in the Ebro Valley, Cádiz and other parts of Andalusia. *El Socialista*, 21 Jan 1934, quoted the comment of Guerra del Río (Radical) on the CNT rising of Dec 1933: 'Now they have to justify the money they received in the elections for not voting.' F. Bravo, *José Antonio* (2nd ed, Madrid, 1940), 31–2, says that in Cádiz money went to a CNT leader to accentuate the inhibitionist tendency. The FAI-CNT's whole attitude of violence against the Republican-Socialist régime would seem to indicate a spontaneous decision to abstain; the Right and the Radicals were in a sense, for Anarchists in 1933, allies: they had condemned Casas Viejas and both promised amnesty for political offences in their programmes in November—many Anarchists were detained. B. Bolloten, *The Grand Camouflage* (London, 1961), 150, cites the Anarchist *Tierra y Libertad*, 10 Nov 1933: 'Workers! Do not vote! . . . All politicians are our enemies. . . . The CNT . . . is not interested in Parliament, which is a filthy house of prostitution. . . . Destroy the ballots! Destroy the ballot boxes! Crack the heads of the ballot supervisers as well as those of the candidates!'

241 Nicolas, *Revue des Deux Mondes*, 15 Dec 1933, 918.

CHAPTER 4

1 Ramos Oliveira, *Politics*, 506.
2 Article 125 of the Constitution (concerning its reform) stipulated that the existing Cortes had to be dissolved and proposed changes submitted to the electorate.
3 The minority initially numbered 114—7 Dec 1933—with J. Martín Artajo as Secretary. By June 1934 the number had risen to 117. In April, G. Carrascal Martín took over as Secretary (*El Debate*, 8 Dec 1933, 7 Apr & 1 June 1934).
4 *El Debate*, 19 Nov 1933.
5 *Diario de las sesiones de Cortes*, 19 Dec 1933.
6 *El Debate*, 3 Dec 1933.
7 *El Debate*, 17 Dec 1933.
8 *ABC*, 21 Dec 1933.
9 *El Debate*, 22 Dec 1933.
10 Royo, *El Debate*, 22 & 24 Nov 1933; Martínez de Velasco, *El Debate*, 1 Dec 1933.
11 *El Debate*, 2 Dec 1933. Calderón was Vice-President, J. Romero Radigales Sec. The 29 were divided as to the merits of collaboration: Romanones argued in favour, the ex-Conservatives Calderón and Rodríguez de Viguri against it.
12 *El Debate*, 8 & 15 Dec 1933, & 24 Jan 1934.
13 *ABC* & *El Debate*, 26–27 Jan 1934; & Calderón in *Blanco y Negro*, 4 Feb 1934. *ABC*, which saw the decision as a collective betrayal of the electors, seems to have been instrumental, by its glare of publicity, in securing the resignation of some deputies. Apparently only

four members of the group had declared their preferences in the elections—Romanones as a liberal Monarchist, Royo Villanova, Cid and Velayos as Republicans. Martínez de Velasco defended his announcement by saying that the tactics to be adopted in the defence of agriculture were his personal concern as leader: 'I have chosen the path of serving the régime so as the better to serve Spain' (Arrarás, *HSRE* II, 281).

14 *El Debate*, 1 Feb 1934. Of the 27 signatories, 10 had been deputies in the Constituent Cortes—8 in the old Agrarian minority, and two Right Republicans: Velayos and Lazcano.

15 *ABC*, 21 & 28 Nov & 6 Dec 1933.

16 *ABC* & *El Debate*, 8 Dec 1933. Sec of the minority was S. Fuentes Pila. Goicoechea had tried to create a 'National Agrarian Bloc' with the Agrarians as a rival to the CEDA, but the Agrarians would not join without the CEDA (*El Debate*, 14 Dec 1933).

17 *ABC* & *El Debate*, 16 Dec 1933; *DSC*, 20 Dec 1933. The Sec of the minority was R. de Toledo Robles.

18 Albiñana declared himself simply 'anti-Republican' (*DSC*, 19 Dec 1933) though later on he joined up with *Renovación Española*. Asked where he would sit in the Chamber, he replied: 'The place does not matter. What I want is to be between Casares Quiroga and Azaña, so as to have the same company as Christ on the Cross' (*El Debate*, 8 Dec 1933). Among the Rightist deputies for Cádiz, José Antonio and the Alfonsine Marqués de la Eliseda formed a *Falangista* duo, while Pemán was initially independent though in collaboration with both Monarchist minorities. He and Eliseda joined up with their fellow Alfonsines in due course.

19 *El Debate*, 3 Dec 1933.

20 Lerroux, *Pequeña historia*, 211–12, 231 & 273. Possibly Lerroux and the CEDA came to their agreement while negotiating alliances for the second electoral contests. On 21 Nov, Casanueva visited Lerroux, though it was officially denied that they had been discussing a political solution (*El Debate*, 22 & 26 Nov 1933).

21 *DSC*, 12 Dec 1933; *El Debate*, 9–13 Dec 1933; Arrarás, *HSRE* II, 251–7; J. Peirats, *La CNT en la revolución española*, I (Toulouse, 1951), 64–8. Aragón was the centre of the outbreak, though churches were burned in various places and 19 were killed when the Barcelona–Seville express was derailed. The official toll was 89 dead in 9 provinces, with 160 hurt (*El Debate*, 28 Jan 1934).

22 The government was: Premier, Lerroux (Radical); State, Pita Romero (ORGA-independent); Interior, Rico Avello (independent); War, Martínez Barrio (Radical); Navy, Rocha (Radical); Finance, Lara (Radical); Justice, Álvarez Valdés (Liberal-Democrat); Public Works, Guerra del Río (Radical); Industry & Commerce, Samper (Radical); Public Instruction, Pareja Yébenes (Radical); Labour, Estadella (Radical); Agriculture, Del Río (Progressive); Communications, Cid (Agrarian). In a reshuffle on 23 Jan 1934, Martínez

Barrio moved to the Interior in place of Rico, who became High Commissioner in Morocco; the new War Minister was Hidalgo (Radical).

23 *DSC*, 19 & 20 Dec 1933.
24 A. Ramos Oliveira, *La revolución de octubre* (Madrid, 1935), 19.
25 *El Socialista*, 26 & 30 Nov 1933.
26 *El Socialista*, 3 & 17 Jan 1934.
27 *El Socialista*, 23 Jan 1934.
28 Of the Socialists, Martínez Barrio said: 'After having lived within the law and at the government's side, they now suffer from I know not what dictatorial impulses as if they only want the Republic when it is at their service. They are behaving like real enemies of the Republic' (*El Debate*, 23 Jan 1934).
29 *DSC*, 7 Feb 1934.
30 Lerroux, *Pequeña historia*, 221–2 & 232–6; Martínez Barrio did not agree with Lerroux that, by voting for his government, the CEDA 'had already realised an act of recognition of the régime'—the first stage towards full incorporation in the Republic.
31 *El Debate*, 27 Feb & 1–3 Mar 1934.
32 *El Debate*, 3 & 10 Apr & 17 May 1934. García Venero, *Santiago Alba*, 348–9, says the two younger candidates—Martínez Barrio & Lara—for the Radical leadership were upset by Lerroux's elevation of Alba, who had just joined the party, to the Presidency of the Cortes, a sign that Lerroux had thus chosen a successor. Lerroux himself wrote of the shock of being betrayed by his favourite and ascribed his dissidence to intrigue by Alcalá-Zamora, bent on creating a Republican Right of his own, a plan necessitating destruction of the Radical Party. Lerroux also notes that all the dissidents were militant Freemasons (*Pequeña historia*, 186–8, 216–18, 220, 277–87 & 325–6).
33 The government was: Premier, Lerroux (Radical); State, Pita Romero (independent Republican); Interior, Salazar Alonso (Radical); War, Hidalgo (Radical); Navy, Rocha (Radical); Finance, Marraco (Radical); Agriculture, Del Río (Progressive); Industry & Commerce, Samper (Radical); Labour, Estadella (Radical); Communications, Cid (Agrarian); Public Works, Guerra del Río (Radical); Justice, Álvarez Valdés (Liberal-Democrat); Public Instruction, S. de Madariaga (independent Republican). The latter became interim Minister of Justice as well as on 17 April.
34 *DSC*, 24 Jan 1934. The motion was defeated by 186 to 54: the Left and Centre voted against; Agrarians, Monarchists and four *Cedistas* —Adánez, García Guijarro, Moutas, Serrano Súñer—in favour. Gil Robles said he had allowed them to vote for personal reasons (*El Debate*, 26 Jan 1934). A Radical motion for amnesty in due course was passed by 167 votes (Centre & CEDA) to 54 (Socialists).
35 *DSC*, 6 Apr 1934 App. According to the Director-General of Prisons, the bill would apply to 8,000 inmates, 6,000 of whom were

classified as of the extreme Left, ie chiefly Anarcho-Syndicalists (Arrarás, *HSRE* II, 326).

36 *DSC*, 11, 12 & 13 Apr 1934.

37 *DSC*, 17–20 Apr 1934.

38 Lerroux, *Pequeña historia*, 247–51; *El Debate*, 25–26 Apr 1934.

39 *DSC*, 12 Jan 1934.

40 *DSC*, 14 Mar 1934. *DSC*, 9 Feb 1934 App alone contained 107 Socialist amendments.

41 *DSC*, 22 Mar & 4 Apr 1934. The law was passed by 281 to 6: Socialists and Left Republicans abstained, opponents including some anti-clerical Radicals. Text of the law in *DSC*, 6 Apr 1934 App.

42 Lerroux added that to trouble the consciences of the majority was not in the national interest; he would 'treat the Church with the same consideration as other bodies no less worthy of respect' (*El Debate*, 21 Dec 1933). Gil Robles said his party would flatly refuse to vote credits for substitution and would obstruct any such attempt to the limit (*El Debate*, 22 Dec 1933).

43 Sánchez, *Reform and Reaction*, 181. The official figures claimed the creation of 7,000 schools in 1931; 2,580 in 1932; 3,990 in 1933 (Ramos Oliveira, *Politics*, 457). Madariaga, who became Minister in Mar 1934, writes that of the 7,000 created on paper in 1931, about 3,000 actually existed; he inherited a chaotic situation in which there were 'about 10,500 schoolmasters without a school, and about 10,500 schools without a schoolmaster' (*Spain*, 413). His Radical predecessor declared substitution a flop, and said Los Ríos and Barnés had in fact lacked statistics (Pareja Yébenes, *El Debate*, 16 Mar 1934). The figure of 7,000 for 1931 is probably an embellishment on the claim of Los Ríos that the Republic created 6,280 schools in its first ten months (*El Socialista*, 2 Mar 1932).

44 *ABC*, 26 Apr 1934. This nickname was used by both Republicans and Monarchists to liken Alcalá-Zamora's conduct to the alleged political meddling of Alfonso XIII.

45 *El Debate*, 26 Apr 1934.

46 Lerroux (*Pequeña historia*, 257–62) said that Alcalá-Zamora wanted Samper as Premier; Lerroux agreed, despite opposition from Radical ranks, on condition that Salazar Alonso, on poor terms with the President, was retained. He also said that Casanueva offered him the CEDA's support for the Presidency of the Republic should a vote of censure lead to Alcalá-Zamora's deposition. Alcalá-Zamora wrote (*Los defectos*, 150) that Lerroux's governments never told him more than he had to know—much to the President's displeasure. Lerroux (op cit, 241) complained that Alcalá-Zamora had wanted to 'inspire, draw up, correct and intervene in the discussion of all bills and afterwards make up the decrees and rules for enforcement'. Lerroux twice refused the CEDA's offer because he could not be sure of getting the requisite number of votes and in any case jibbed at

Monarchist support. He also feared that the President would give power to the Left if an unsuccessful attempt were made to depose him. Alcalá-Zamora heard about the episode and liked to remind Gil Robles and Lerroux of it (Gil Robles, *No fue posible*, 121-2). The government was composed of: Premier, Samper (Radical); State, Pita Romero (independent Republican); Interior, Salazar Alonso (Radical); Finance, Marraco (Radical); War, Hidalgo (Radical); Navy, Rocha (Radical); Justice, Cantos (Radical); Public Instruction, Villalobos (Liberal-Democrat); Public Works, Guerra del Río (Radical); Agriculture, Del Río (Progressive); Industry & Commerce, Iranzo (independent Republican); Labour, Estadella (Radical); Communications, Cid (Agrarian).

47 Text in *DSC*, 29 Dec 1933.

48 *DSC*, 1 & 2 Feb 1934—the *yunteros* occupied land because, being unemployed, there was no other means of existence.

49 Azpcitia, Rodríguez Jurado, Casanueva, *DSC*, 31 Jan, 1 & 6 Feb 1934.

50 The law was passed by 147 votes to 41. Giménez Fernández (CEDA, Badajoz) said that 'the *status quo* of what has been termed *juridicidad* and what we call legality cannot continue; at the bottom of juridical problems there exists a moral content—others say it is an economic basis—which we cannot lose sight of, and all recognise that in the case of extreme necessity one must override private property-rights'. Vega Bermejo (CEDA, Cáceres), the son of a cattle-breeder, appealed to deputies to aid 'the efficacious labour of the Minister with some solution . . . so that the means to live, at the least, may be made possible for these thousands of Extremeño peasants who have no land wherein to stick a plough' (*DSC*, 7 & 9 Feb 1934).

51 Gil Robles incurred the wrath of most of the landowners of Cáceres for supporting this law (Romero Solano, *DSC*, 28 Mar 1934). The view of the absentee Monarchist landowner concerning the electoral result is well captured by Foxá: 'The old Duque drank the health of Gil Robles, saviour of Spain and future Regent of the Kingdom. He thought of his pastures in Extremadura saved from agrarian reform. But he confined himself to saying, "Religion has been saved" ' (*Madrid de Corte a Cheka*, 181).

52 *DSC*, 11 Jan & 24 May 1934; the voting was 218 to 18. Text in *DSC*, 29 May 1934 App.

53 *El Debate*, 26 May 1934. Earlier *Acción Popular* in Seville had said that it would expel vengeful employers who disregarded wage-levels. *Acción Popular* in Saragossa asked workers to denounce unjust employers so that they could be expelled. From Granada it was reported that *Acción Popular* had actually expelled an employer for cutting wages (*El Debate*, 16 & 17 Dec 1933, 11 & 20 Feb 1934). The case of the Marqués de Oquendo, leader of the Cáceres branch, was probably exceptional: his workers said they would not take less

than 8 ptas a day, but he thought 10 ptas a fairer wage and paid them accordingly (*El Debate*, 5 June 1934).

54   Eg *DSC*, 10 May 1934. Blázquez (Socialist) said it was necessary to be a *Cedista* to get work: in Albarreal del Tajo (Toledo) only 12 workers had not voted Socialist and these were the only ones employed. D. de Madariaga denied such accusations and charged the Socialists with *caciquismo*. The Radical Minister, Estadella, accepted the veracity of Blázquez's evidence, but added that there were still many *pueblos* where only UGT workers could get a job. There were three workers in the *Minoría Popular Agraria*: D. de Madariaga (Toledo), Ruiz Alonso (Granada) & Martí Olucha (Castellón).

55   Socialists said employers were by-passing the State system. *Acción Popular* denied that its Secretariat was a labour-exchange, but explained that employers seeking labour could enquire and the Secretariat would pass on the request to Catholic unions (*El Debate*, 16 May & 6 June 1934).

56   Eg *El Correo de Zamora* (cited by *El Debate*, 25 May 1934). Though workers were given food and lodgings, Fr Gafo, a pioneer of Catholic unionism, asked how their families could be kept on money-payments as low as 1·80 ptas a day: 'plutocrats, rich men, you who call yourselves Christians, who say it repeatedly with your lips and deny it with your hearts ... the time has come to abandon your positions and your liberal individualism, which is extremism in opposition to this Socialism' (*DSC*, 18 May 1934). *El Debate*, 26 Aug 1934, reported cases of *conservadurismo* which 'indict a social class ... an attitude as suicidal as it is indicative of a conscience devoid of the most elementary principles of justice and charity'.

57   Prieto & Santaló, *DSC*, 2 May 1934.

58   M. Álvarez, *El Debate*, 29 May & 4 Sept 1934.

59   Ventosa Calvell, *DSC*, 7 Feb 1934.

60   Quoted by Casares, *La CEDA*, 162.

61   Gil Robles said *Acción Popular* was comparable to the German Centre: 'Monarchy? Republic? What does it matter!' (Cortés Cavanillas, *Gil Robles*, 93).

62   E. Vegas Latapié, *Catolicismo y República* (Madrid, 1932).

63   A. de Castro Albarrán, *El derecho a la rebeldía* (Madrid, 1934). Cf Pradera: 'If the laws of the State are in opposition to Divine Law, resistance is a duty and obedience a crime' (*HCE*, I–5, 590).

64   Cf Monarchist euphoria after the election in Foxá, *Madrid de Corte a Cheka*, 180: 'The revolution is over'; 'We'll have the King in Madrid in a couple of months'.

65   *ABC*, 16 Dec 1933; & *El Siglo Futuro*, 16 Dec 1933, in Arrarás, *HSRE* II, 275.

66   *El Debate*, 17, 19 & 20 Dec 1933.

67   *La Época*, 29 Dec 1933 (in J. I. Escobar, J. Vigón & E. Vegas Latapié, *Escritos sobre la instauración monárquica* [Madrid, 1955], 38–40).

68 Quoted in Cortés Cavanillas, *Gil Robles*, 125.
69 Quoted in Sánchez, *Reform and Reaction*, 178.
70 Cortés Cavanillas, *Gil Robles*, 38 & 99. Gil Robles himself and Martín Artajo and Carrascal (secretaries of the minority) say Herrera played no part in the party after 1931; decisions were made by Gil Robles, the party executive and the minority. Cortés Cavanillas sticks to the contemporary Monarchist view. (Conversations with all the above.)
71 Lamamié de Clairac, Goicoechea, Pradera in *ABC*, 30 Jan, 6 Feb & 22 May 1934 respectively.
72 Lequerica, *ABC*, 12 May 1934.
73 *ABC*, 16 May & 5 June 1934.
74 *El Debate*, 8 Apr 1934.
75 *El Debate*, 17 Dec 1933 & 13 & 18 May 1934. Casanueva, spokesman of conservative *Cedistas*, said they served the régime 'with no mental reservations' (*El Debate*, 2 Feb 1934).
76 Sánchez, *Reform and Reaction*, 187; Cortés Cavanillas, *Gil Robles*, 23–4; Arrarás, *HSRE* II, 438–9. Pita initially hoped for a concordat, but Cardinal Pacelli insisted on prior revision of Article 26. The Vatican broke off talks in the hope of resuming them with a Rightist government later.
77 Arrarás, *HSRE* II, 310. Gomá was translated from the see of Tarazona in Apr 1933. Both he and the Nuncio were made Cardinals in 1935.
78 Galindo, *Los partidos*, 223–4; Arrarás, *HSRE* II, 276. *El Debate* (10 July 1934) warned Spanish Monarchists against putting politics before religion as the condemned *Action Française* had done. In 1935 Cortés Cavanillas (conversation) cancelled a second edition of his *Gil Robles* at the personal request of the Nuncio; the book had been termed defamatory by *Cedistas* who declined to go to the courts when challenged.
79 Cortés Cavanillas, *Gil Robles*, 27.
80 Iturralde, *Catolicismo* I, 367–8.
81 *Boletín de Orientación Tradicionalista*, 9 & 16 Sept 1934. A Monarchist conspirator, Fr Segarra, said the Vatican had written off the Traditionalists as an insignificant anachronism. He thought *Acción Popular* 'most pernicious', the Nuncio 'a veritable calamity' and *El Debate* 'economically enslaved by the Jews' (Iturralde, *Catolicismo* I, 323–7).
82 *Renovación Española*'s membership in Madrid was constantly around 12,000 (Cortés Cavanillas, conversation). Lis Quiben, a prominent Gallego *Cedista*, went over to the Alfonsines in July 1934. Carrascal, secretary of the minority (conversation), says the majority 'had Monarchist convictions'; the number of those wanting an overt 'opening to the Republic' was always 'very small'.
83 *ABC*, 7–9 June & *El Debate*, 8 & 12 June 1934; Arrarás, *HSRE* II, 350; *HCE*, II–6, 81. Valiente says he was Gil Robles's delegate, but

Gil Robles (*No fue posible*, 89–90) says only that he gave Valiente detailed instructions.
84 Arrarás, loc cit; Cortés Cavanillas, *Confesiones*, 82; *Habla el Rey*, 344.
85 *El Debate*, 27 Feb & 20 Mar 1934.
86 *ABC*, 13 Dec 1933.
87 *El Debate*, 15 Mar 1934. The *soldado de cuota* system permitted the wealthy to buy exemption from military service. *Señoritismo* is a pejorative term for the idleness and egoism of the sons of the rich.
88 *El Debate*, 17 & 23 Jan 1934. It was significant that *Japistas* should visit Italy while travellers sponsored by the Christian-Democrat DRV went to the Low Countries and Denmark. *El Socialista* (21 Dec 1933) saw the *Movilización* as evidence of preparation for a *coup*.
89 Pérez de Laborda & Ceballos, *El Debate*, 23 Jan 1934.
90 La Calzada, *ABC* & *El Debate*, 27 Feb 1934.
91 *El Debate*, 21–22 Apr 1934. Socialists shot a *Japista* on the eve of the Congress, bringing the total of 'martyrs' to 14.
92 *El Debate*, 24 Apr 1934; Buckley, *Spanish Republic*, 126–7. It was to have been held on 8 Apr but the Socialist Youth threatened to break it up by holding a counter-demonstration. Salazar Alonso therefore postponed it until the 22nd and banned a march-past (*El Debate*, 3 & 18 Apr & *El Socialista*, 19 Jan & 20 Mar 1934).
93 Lyric by Pemán (Monge, *AP*, 245); the tune was a march by Grieg. *El Socialista* (16 Mar 1934) reported that Sevillano *Japistas* were told to wear 'uniform', ie gaiters or high boots, breeches, and bright-coloured shirts with the JAP emblem.
94 *El Debate*, 24 Apr 1934.
95 *El Debate*, 2 & 28 June 1934. On 5 July the paper reported the creation, mainly by *Cedistas*, of an *Agrupación Menéndez y Pelayo* to propagate 'the authentic values of immortal Spain'.
96 Valiente, *El Debate*, 21 Apr 1934; Casanueva quoted by Cortés Cavanillas, *Gil Robles*, 151. In 1933 Gil Robles's biographer Arrabal caused unintentional amusement by likening him to the Maid of Orléans in the preface.
97 Martín Artajo (conversation).
98 *El Debate*, 4 May & 26–29 July 1934. The paper lamented Dollfuss's death and saw him as a man who had become a dictator against his wishes in order to defend Austria from Marxism and Nazism.
99 *El Debate*, 7 & 31 Dec 1933 & 24 May 1934.
100 Galindo, *Los partidos*, 229–30. The vice-presidents were Pradera, Sáinz Rodríguez and the *Cedista* Ruiz del Castillo. Of the ten committee members, two were *Cedistas* (Lozoya and Ibáñez Martín) and two of the Alfonsines were in the *Falange* (Ansaldo & Eliseda). Serrano Súñer (*Cedista*) was one of its speakers.
101 *ABC*, 22 May 1934; *HCE*, II–6, 59.
102 *Acción Española*, 1 June 1934 (*Antología*, 244–53). He ended his

speech with a strong attack on Alcalá-Zamora which could not be printed at the time.

103 Calvo Sotelo in *ABC*, 14 June & 24, 29 & 31 July 1934.

104 *ABC*, 26 Sept 1934.

105 The *procès-verbal* and the political agreement found among Italian documents after the Second World War are in W. C. Askew, 'Italian intervention in Spain', *Journal of Modern History*, vol XXIV, no 2 (1952), 182. Lizarza, *Memorias*, 24–7, gives an account in agreement with the documents, though he mentions figures of 20,000 rifles, 20,000 grenades and 200 machine-guns, while the Italian source says 10,000 rifles, 10,000 grenades and 200 machine-guns. For the alleged Franco-Spanish pact, see Arrarás, *HSRE* II, 45–8, & Plá, *HSRE* II, 160. Lizarza writes that the visit was arranged by Olazábal, but Cortés Cavanillas (conversation) says that Alfonso XIII himself, a friend of the *Duce* since his state visit to Italy in 1923, was really responsible for the agreement. The documents were signed by Balbo, but not by Mussolini—Balbo had received Alfonsine visitors in 1932 and 1933.

106 Lizarza, *Memorias*, 25 & 28; Gen Barrera agreed with the Carlists as there was no alternative from the military angle.

107 Lizarza, *Memorias*, 29–33; *HCE*, II–8, 285–6. The *ultras* wanted Alfonso Carlos to be succeeded by Carlos VII's grandsons (Jaime's cousins), though the succession would have to pass through a female (their mother Blanca).

108 *AET* (Pamplona), 2 Feb 1934, quoted by Redondo & Zavala, *Requeté*, 250. *AET* first appeared on 26 Jan 1934; edited by Jaime del Burgo, it succeeded *La Esperanza*.

109 *AET*, 9 Apr 1934, in J. del Burgo, *Requetés en Navarra antes del Alzamiento* (San Sebastián, 1939), 98.

110 *Documentos de Alfonso Carlos*, 240–1; *HCE*, II–8, 285–6.

111 *Documentos de Alfonso Carlos*, 243.

112 *AET*, 9 Mar 1934, in Del Burgo, *Requetés*, 76.

113 *La Época*, 16 & 21 June 1934 (Escobar, *Escritos*, 43–5 & 48–52). Juan III was the Carlist claimant (1861–8) who was more liberal than Isabel II.

114 *AET*, 18 May 1934 (Del Burgo, *Requetés*, 125–8).

115 *Documentos de Alfonso Carlos*, 255–60.

116 Melgar, *Escisión dinástica*, 127, says Alfonso was constantly influenced by defenders of the liberal Monarchy. Fr Segarra thought the Alfonsines would set up a temporary dictatorship, and then revert to liberalism (Iturralde, *Catolicismo* I, 332).

117 *ABC*, 11 July 1934. *ABC* was still liberal and criticised *La Época* for advocating violence and absorption of the individual by the State (23 & 28 Mar 1934); but in August Luca de Tena spoke of a constitutional, parliamentary Monarchy without universal suffrage, though not the Monarchy of 1876 (*ABC*, 16 Aug 1934).

118 A literal and rather clumsy translation has been made in an attempt

to give the 'flavour' of the original. Text in *Documentos de Alfonso Carlos*, 255–60. *Procuradores* was the old term for representatives attending the Cortes. The *pase foral* was the region's right to accept or reject central legislation.

119 *AET*, 16 Feb 1934 (Del Burgo, *Requetés*, 52–3).

120 *ABC*, 14 Nov 1933; he was the only worker in the Traditionalist minority.

121 *Documentos de Alfonso Carlos*, 244–54; *BOT*, 23 Sept 1934. Lamamié de Clairac was in charge of propaganda, González-Quevedo of the press, and Arellano Dihinx of youth, including the student organisation AET (*Agrupación Escolar Tradicionalista*). *BOT*, 9 Sept 1934, listed ten Traditionalist dailies in Barcelona, Jaén, Jérez, Madrid, Pamplona, San Sebastián, Seville, Tortosa, Vich and Vitoria.

122 Redondo & Zavala, *Requeté*, 245.

123 Del Burgo, *Requetés*, 9; Lizarza, *Memorias*, 22–3. Lizarza was the chief organiser in Navarre.

124 For an account of this *aplech* on the estate of El Quintillo, see M. Ferrer, *'Veinticinco años atrás . . .' el Requeté vela las armas* (Seville, 1959).

125 *BOT*, 16 Sept 1934.

126 *HCE*, II–8, 286. There the colours of the *Requeté Cántabro* were blessed by the Abbot of Cóbreces (*Documentos de Alfonso Carlos*, 263). In 1934 the Communion claimed a membership of 700,000 (Redondo & Zavala, *Requeté*, 254)—this seems an exaggeration. Arellano suggests a figure of 500,000 for 1935 (Information from M. Blinkhorn).

127 José Antonio's interview with André Nicolas on 24 Nov (*Revue des Deux Mondes*, 15 Dec 1933, 923).

128 *HCE*, II–6, 22; Payne, *Falange*, 45–7.

129 F. Bravo, *Historia de Falange Española de las JONS* (2nd ed, Madrid, 1943), 23–4; the slogans were 'Spain One, Great and Free' and 'Country, Bread and Justice'.

130 *FE*, 7 Dec 1933 (*O.c.*, 553–63).

131 *O.c.*, 29–40. His ardour for foreign régimes cooled in 1934. He went to Rome (*ABC*, 22 Mar 1934) but was snubbed by Mussolini, who said Largo Caballero was the only leader of masses in Spain (Buckley, *Spanish Republic*, 130). He went to Germany in May and met minor Nazi dignitaries, but returned disillusioned by the internal politics of Nazism (Ansaldo, *¿ Para qué?*, 78; Payne, *Falange*, 77; F. Ximénez de Sandoval, *José Antonio* [2nd ed, Madrid, 1949], 290).

132 Ansaldo, *¿ Para qué?*, 71–2; & Payne, *Falange*, 42, who notes that García Valdecasas left the group when Monarchists and *pistolero* elements of Albiñana's PNE joined it.

133 Ximénez, *JA*, 284 & 565–72; Ansaldo, *¿ Para qué?*, 56 & 76. *ABC* (Seville), 13 Mar 1934, reported that José Antonio had visited Calvo Sotelo in Paris. The two had never been friends. Ansaldo and Ruiz de Alda wanted Calvo Sotelo to join, but José Antonio would not

hear of it as he maintained that Calvo should have defended the Dictator in the Cortes in 1931—ignoring the fact that he would have been arrested upon entering Spain. José Antonio also disliked Calvo's contacts with the financial world and his realism, as opposed to José Antonio's idealism; he thought Calvo 'a man who understood only figures and did not know even one piece of poetry'. In Calvo's view 'numbers also have their poetry' (J. Calvo Sotelo, *El Estado que queremos* [Madrid, 1958], 50).

134 Bravo, *José Antonio*, 69; & *Ultimos hallazgos de escritos y cartas de José Antonio* (Madrid, 1962), 74. Cortés Cavanillas (conversation) thinks he might have remained a Monarchist had the *Juanista* solution been agreed upon, for he was among the first to suggest Juan as a possible King in 1931.

135 Bravo, *José Antonio*, 68. Financial aid was provided by the Alfonsine Lequerica at this time (Ximénez, *JA*, 264–5).

136 *Textos inéditos*, 433–4; Ansaldo, *¿ Para qué?*, 87 & 89; Salmador, *Ansaldo*, 100; Payne, *Falange*, 60–3 & 86. Ansaldo was expelled mainly on the grounds that he was plotting to oust José Antonio and make the group Monarchist. José Antonio and Sáinz Rodríguez drew up 'The Ten Points of El Escorial' in the summer on the content of 'the new Spanish State', and this was written into the agreement signed in Madrid on 20 Aug by Goicoechea and José Antonio. By this seven-point agreement José Antonio undertook not to attack the Alfonsines or Monarchism; in exchange the Alfonsines were to pay the *Falange* at least 10,000 ptas a month and provide a technical adviser on 'military' matters. The agreement soon lapsed because the Alfonsines had not the funds to keep their side of the bargain (Texts in Gil Robles, *No fue posible*, 442–3). The *Juventud de Renovación Española* continued to work closely with the *Falange* (Cortés Cavanillas, conversation).

137 In the words of Bravo, *José Antonio*, 27. He was not a very good poet.

138 Ansaldo, *¿ Para qué?*, 72–3; Salmador, *Ansaldo*, 101; Payne, *Falange*, 54 & 57–8. An attempt was made on José Antonio's life in March.

139 José Antonio, Ledesma, Ruiz de Alda, Ansaldo and Fernández Cuesta were each fined 10,000 ptas (*HCE*, II–6, 75; Bravo, *Falange*, 48). The 65 arrested in July included Ansaldo, José Antonio and the Marqués de la Eliseda; the latter two were released immediately as they enjoyed parliamentary immunity (*El Debate*, 11 July 1934).

140 D. Jato, *La rebelión de los estudiantes* (Madrid, 1953), 10, 61, 70–1 & 102–3. Recruits to the SEU included Monarchists and Communists. Typical of their doings was an assault on the offices of the FUE with the reigning wrestling champion in the van.

141 *HGL*, 336; Payne, *Falange*, 63.

142 Bravo, *Falange*, 24 & 33–5. José Antonio respected only the Traditionalists on the Right, but he considered them old-fashioned. He said that the CEDA could not remove the causes of revolution; only

the *Falange* could by combining a national ideal with social justice (*O.c.*, 853–4).

143 Besteiro, *El Debate*, 31 Jan 1934. In Dec 1933 he said that there was no danger of Fascism in Spain (D. Ibárruri, *El único camino* [2nd ed, Paris, 1965], 176).

144 Largo Caballero, *Recuerdos*, 132–5; Arrarás, *HSRE* II, 296. Largo Caballero became Secretary-General of the UGT. Besteiro had the support of the reformist union-leaders A. Saborit and T. Gómez. It would seem that Prieto hesitated to join the revolutionaries until his programme had been accepted. The programme later appeared in *El Liberal* (Bilbao), 11 Jan 1936 (cited in Peirats, *La CNT*, I, 88–90). Reformists were ousted from the Socialist landworkers' union in Jan 1934 by Zabalza, who advocated revolution as the prelude to socialisation of the land (E. E. Malefakis, *Land Tenure, Agrarian Reform and Peasant Revolution in Twentieth Century Spain* [unpublished thesis, Columbia Univ, 1965], part II, chapter viii).

145 *El Socialista*, 14 Feb & *El Debate*, 16 Feb 1934.

146 *El Socialista*, 5 May 1934, said it did not matter whether or not Gil Robles declared himself a Republican, for Hitler, Dollfuss, Mussolini, Carmona and Juan Vicente Gómez, 'the hangman of Venezuela', were all Republicans. According to the Socialist intellectual Ramos Oliveira (*La revolución*, 103–4), 'the great Spanish Fascist movement is that of *Acción Popular* . . ., agrarian and Vaticanist, twin-brother of the Austrian. . . . An anti-Marxist front is a Fascist front.'

147 *El Socialista*, 29 Apr 1934. The disillusionment was thus expressed in March 1934 by Araquistáin: 'It was thought that a bourgeois, liberal, democratic Republic, like that installed in 1931, would permit the working class to gain power peacefully, in order gradually to realise the Socialist revolution from power. . . . Less than three years' Republican experience has convinced us that the attempt . . . is a chimera.' (Quoted in C. M. Rama, *La crisis española del siglo XX* [Mexico City, 1960], 165–6.)

148 *El Socialista*, 21 Apr 1934.

149 Azaña's papers (2 Jan 1934), cited in Arrarás, *HSRE* II, 300. Azaña believed that 'in these Cortes one cannot govern as a Republican' (*El Debate*, 17 Dec 1933).

150 Speeches, in *El Socialista*, 17 Apr & 3 July 1934; he thought that the result of the Nov 1933 elections had put back the clock to the time before 12 Apr 1931. On 1 Apr 1934 Azaña became leader of *Izquierda Republicana*, a fusion of his *Acción Republicana* with Casares Quiroga's ORGA and Domingo's Independent Radical-Socialists (*El Debate*, 3 Apr 1934).

151 Interview in the summer of 1934 with L. Fernsworth, *Spain's Struggle for Freedom* (Boston, 1957), 156–61.

152 *El Socialista*, 25, 27 & 28 July 1934.

153 *El Socialista*, 25 Sept 1934.

154   *El Socialista*, 29 Sept 1934.
155   J. Maurín, *Hacia la segunda revolución* (2nd ed, Barcelona, 1935), 107–9.
156   Maurín, *Segunda revolución*, 82–9 & 112–14; Peirats, *La CNT*, I, 78–80.
157   Maurín, *Segunda revolución*, 94–104 & 112–14; Rama, *Crisis*, 169; Arrarás, *HSRE* II, 410–11; H. Thomas, *The Spanish Civil War* (2nd ed, Harmondsworth, 1965), 102 & 106–10; J. A. Balbontín, *La España de mi experiencia* (Mexico City, 1952), 274–5; Ibárruri, *Único camino*, 177. The PCE's policy had been to win over the CNT and UGT rank-and-file; by Dec 1933 it had perhaps 25,000 members. Its union, the CGTU, joined with the UGT in 1934. The party's lone Deputy, Bolívar, said: 'I am not going to come out in defence of this parliamentary régime; I am an enemy of it. . . . The time has come for all Spanish workers and peasants to launch themselves into the street. . . . Only there can the working people gain respect and achieve their total emancipation.' The PCE stood for 'the liberation of the oppressed peoples of Catalonia, Vasconia and Galicia' and for 'the Union of Soviet Republics of Spain' (*DSC*, 4 Apr & 26 June 1934). At the rally of 14 Sept, a Young Socialist said the Spanish Socialists had broken with the Second International, and a Communist said the assembled youths were 'the phalanxes that are going to take power in Spain by assault' (*El Socialista*, 15 Sept 1934).
158   *El Debate*, 30 May, 19 & 23 June 1934; *DSC*, 30 May & 7 June 1934; *BSS*, XI, 209. The Socialists attempted to channel economic discontent into political unrest. *El Debate*, 14 & 23 June 1934, reported that Socialists in Badajoz used funds provided by the State for agrarian reform to finance the strike: people were paid 5 or 6 ptas to fight for the strike and hinder harvesting. A printed appeal to rural workers referred to the strike's political purpose in opposing 'the government of hangmen, with its savage, blood-thirsty dog, Salazar Alonso, this odious and wretched Spanish Dollfuss', and against the threat of 'Fascist dictatorship, under the inspiration of the Fascist Catholic Gil Robles, the representative of the big capitalists, bankers and usurers' (quoted in Fernández Almagro, *República*, 104–5).
159   *El Debate*, 13, 17, 21 & 27 Feb, 7 & 20 Mar, 1 & 17 June 1934; & R. Salazar Alonso, *Bajo el signo de la revolución* (Madrid, 1935), 50–1.
160   *DSC*, 13 Mar 1934; *El Debate*, 1, 11 & 15 Mar 1934; & Salazar Alonso, *Bajo el signo*, 64–71.
161   From Salazar Alonso's speeches, *DSC*, 7 Mar 1934; *El Debate*, 17 Apr & 1 Aug 1934; & *ABC*, 17 Apr 1934.
162   Eg, in March the offices of the PCE, the CNT, the Socialist Youth, *Falange* and PNE were closed, and both Fascist and revolutionary Leftist publications banned (*El Debate*, 8–10 Mar & 22 Apr 1934).

Issues of *Informaciones*, *La Nación*, *El Siglo Futuro* & *La Época* were seized (*El Debate*, 27 & 29 Apr, 23 May & 5 June 1934), but *El Socialista* suffered 104 arraignments between Dec 1933 & Oct 1934, and was fined some 45,000 ptas (*El Socialista*, 3 Aug & 4 Oct 1934).

163 The Directorate-General of Security's figures from 1 Jan to mid-Aug 1934 showed 348 Leftists and 95 Rightists arrested. Similarly the number of those under 21 killed or wounded in Madrid was 43, only 5 of whom were Young Socialists, the great majority being *Falangistas*. (Quoted by *El Debate*, 25 & 29 Aug 1934.)

164 By mid-Aug Salazar Alonso had dismissed 249 councils, compared with the 88 dismissed by Maura, 316 by Casares Quiroga, 6 by Martínez Barrio, 40 by Rico Avello (*El Debate*, 18 Aug 1934). Corruption in local government was normal, and Ministers were perhaps keener to dismiss councils controlled by their political enemies. *El Socialista*, 23 Aug 1934, printed a letter from the Agrarians of Seville province to party leaders in Madrid complaining that the Radicals and the *Cedistas*, to the exclusion of the Agrarians, were sharing out local offices as other councillors were removed.

165 *DSC*, 3–4 July 1934. Socialists and Monarchists voted against removal of parliamentary immunity, as did certain *Cedistas* sympathetic to José Antonio, viz Serrano Súñer, Ibáñez Martín, La Calzada, Sierra Pomares, Núñez Manso, García Atance.

166 For details see *El Debate*, 15–16 & 20 Sept 1934; Arrarás, *HSRE* II, 412–17; J. Álvarez del Vayo, *The Last Optimist* (London, 1950), 261–2.

167 *ABC*, 13 Sept 1934.

168 Aguirre, *Libertad*, 410–11; *El Debate*, 17 Dec 1933; *DSC*, 20 Dec 1933.

169 Aguirre, *Libertad*, 416 & 447–8; Arrarás, *HSRE* II, 265; Oriol, *DSC*, 29 Dec 1933. In the elections the Traditionalists had polled 20,718 votes, the PNV 11,524 and the Left 7,445 in Álava (Sierra, *Euzkadi*, 216).

170 *DSC*, 8 & 9 Feb 1934 Apps.

171 *DSC*, 27 & 28 Feb & 5 Apr 1934. The *Lliga* and the *Esquerra* supported the PNV. The figures for the plebiscite in Álava were, it will be recalled, 46 per cent in favour, 11 per cent against, with 43 per cent abstaining.

172 Gil Robles and Aguirre had met at the end of 1933. Aguirre said the PNV gave the Statute absolute priority, and would prefer it to be conceded by the Right, though the Left had promised to grant it. Gil Robles, however, held to the *Cedista* policy of administrative autonomy, as opposed to the political autonomy of the Statute. Negotiations were broken off, and the Basques said they were willing to seek a Leftist alliance (J. M. Gil Robles, 'The Spanish Republic and Basque independence', *The Tablet*, 19 June 1937, 876–7).

173 *DSC*, 12 June 1934; Aguirre, *Libertad*, 454. Aguirre believed that the cause of Catalan liberty was the cause of Basque liberty. He told

ABC, 13 June 1934: 'We are neither with the Left nor the Right: we are absolutely autonomist.'

174 Aguirre, *Libertad*, 459–71.

175 Aguirre, *Libertad*, 479. Samper was less adamant than Velarde and Salazar Alonso; the latter threatened resignation unless a firm line was taken (Salazar Alonso, *Bajo el signo*, 201–3). The Navarrese opposed the PNV's plan (*El Debate*, 11 Aug 1934) while the Socialists backed it (*El Socialista*, 4 Aug 1934). The government and the CEDA wanted to reform the electoral law before any more elections (*DSC*, 31 Jan 1934).

176 Aguirre, *Libertad*, 481–7. *El Debate*, 14 Aug 1934, reported that elections were held by stratagem by 4 councils in Biscay, 27 in Guipúzcoa, and one in Álava; no attempt was made to hold them in 68 of the 120 councils in Biscay, nor in 43 of the councils in Guipúzcoa. Basque Nationalism was divided into two groups: the moderates (*comunionistas*) such as Leizaola and other deputies who wanted negotiated solutions, and the ultra-separatists (*aberrianos*) led by Gallástegui who refused to stand as a candidate for a 'foreign' parliament in Madrid. The young and the *Mendigoixales* were under his influence and had orders to be ready to proclaim the Basque Republic at any moment, though they were not properly armed (*El Socialista*, 3 Jan & 27 Feb 1934).

177 Aguirre, *Libertad*, 492–6, 500–20, 523–5 & 534–7.

178 *BSS*, XI, 90.

179 *ABC*, 18 & 20 Jan 1934; Nadal, *6 años*, 169–71.

180 *ABC*, 27 Jan 1934. The *Esquerra* polled 162,616 votes, the *Lliga* 132,942, the Radicals 21,088, the Communists 1,504 (Arrarás, *HSRE* II, 271).

181 Prieto, speaking in Barcelona, *El Socialista*, 9 Jan 1934.

182 Ramos Oliveira, *Politics*, 351–2.

183 Arrarás, *HSRE* II, 366.

184 *El Debate*, 24 Mar, 15, 20 & 25 Apr 1934; the paper claimed that Casanueva was mainly responsible for the motion, and he had negotiated with the landlords via the Marqués de Verger, *Cedista* leader in the Balearics. Nadal (*6 años*, 176) claims most of the credit for Cambó.

185 *El Debate*, 9 June 1934; *HCE*, II–6, 67. The attitudes of the Catalan parties were opportunistic: the *Esquerra*, which now upheld the Catalan right to pass the law, had in 1932–3 demanded that the question of the *rabassaires* be dealt with in national legislation; the *Lliga*, now opposing the *Esquerra*'s view, had in 1932 wished to reserve such matters for the Catalan Parliament (Ventosa, *DSC*, 12 June 1934).

186 *DSC*, 12 June 1934. The transfer of services under the Statute had broken down when Cid, Minister of Communications, refused to hand over broadcasting to the *Generalidad* and threatened to resign (*ABC*, 1 June, & *El Debate*, 5 June 1934).

187 *DSC*, 21 June 1934.
188 *DSC*, 25 June 1934.
189 *DSC*, 4 July 1934. The Socialist Tirado fought with the *Cedista* Oriol de la Puerta, and Prieto and another Socialist waved pistols.
190 *El Debate*, 20 July, 10 Aug & 19 Sept 1934.
191 *El Debate*, 21 & 23 Aug & 7–9 Sept 1934. The UGT organised a strike against the meeting, which resulted in clashes with 6 dead and 46 hurt.
192 *El Debate*, 31 July & 13 Sept 1934.
193 Arrarás, *HSRE* II, 374–5.
194 *ABC*, 21 Aug 1934. *El Socialista*, 8 July 1934, published the Alfonsine Marqués de Villapesadilla's plan to change the commander in Catalonia, send warships and put divisions at the ready on the Ebro, form volunteer bands from the loyal 45 provinces and get the government to arm them, and even transfer the Catalan population if necessary.
195 *El Debate*, 15 & 17 Aug 1934. *ABC* (16 Aug 1934) reported discontent within the CEDA over Catalonia; *El Socialista* (8 Sept 1934) reported that 40 *Cedista* deputies were expected to go over to Calvo Sotelo if nothing was done.
196 *El Debate*, 11 Sept 1934.
197 *El Debate*, 13, 14 & 28 Sept 1934. Samper and Guerra del Río were the Radical opponents; Samper was very much a puppet of the President. Cf Gil Robles, *No fue posible*, 131–2.
198 *El Socialista*, 27 Sept 1934; the paper prophesied a choice between the Holy Office and the Red Flag.
199 *DSC*, 1 Oct 1934; Bowers, *My Mission*, 96; *El Debate*, 2 Oct 1934.
200 *El Debate*, 3–5 Oct 1934. There were difficulties in the negotiations. *El Debate* said that the CEDA had wanted Anguera de Sojo, the Catalan and former Republican Attorney-General, at the Interior, but the *Lliga* had objected to this. Gil Robles (*No fue posible*, 137–9) says that he insisted on Anguera de Sojo as Minister of Labour against pressure on the President from the *Esquerra*. He had wanted Lucía at Agriculture but he was excluded since Samper, his local political rival in Valencia, was included. Lerroux (*Pequeña historia*, 295 & 301–2) noted that Alcalá-Zamora intensely disliked Gil Robles and wanted no *Cedista* Ministers; he was persuaded to accept three in exchange for the dropping of his other enemy, Salazar Alonso. The government was: Premier, Lerroux (Radical); State, Samper (Radical); Justice, Aizpún Santafé (CEDA); Finance, Marraco (Radical); War, Hidalgo (Radical); Navy, Rocha (Radical); Agriculture, Giménez Fernández (CEDA); Communications, Jalón (Radical); Industry & Commerce, Orozco (Radical); Interior, Vaquero (Radical); Labour, Anguera de Sojo (CEDA); Public Instruction, Villalobos (Liberal-Democrat); without portfolios, Martínez de Velasco (Agrarian) & Pita Romero (independent Republican).
201 For texts of the notes issued by *Unión Republicana* (a fusion of

Radical-Socialists with Radical-Democrats under Martínez Barrio), *Izquierda Republicana*, the Federals, the Radical-Socialist Left and Maura's Conservatives, see Ramos Oliveira, *La revolución*, 59–61. Maura, by his Leftist orientation during 1934, had shed many of his deputies and provincial branches, and his minority had to be dissolved.

202 *El Debate*, 5–7 Oct 1934. After the fall of Samper's government Alcalá-Zamora sent a message to the Socialist leaders to say that he would not give power to the CEDA, but on 4 Oct he sent them another message begging them not to make a move because he could discredit and bring down the CEDA in a few months (Gil Robles, *No fue posible*, 578).

203 Accounts of events in Madrid are given by Ramos Oliveira, *La revolución*, 77–99; Buckley, *Spanish Republic*, 147–8; & *HCE*, II–7 150–1.

204 *HCE*, II–7, 142–3 & 150; Bravo, *Falange*, 65–70; Lerroux, *Pequeña historia*, 314–16. Fal Conde offered the Traditionalists' services to the government on 7 October (*BOT*, 14 Oct 1934).

205 Reported in *ABC*, 4 Oct 1934—of interest in view of subsequent Rightist accusations against Azaña.

206 Accounts of the Catalan rising are given by Arrarás, *HSRE* II, 469–514; Jackson, *Spanish Republic*, 149–53; Maurín, *Segunda revolución*, 123–43. See also Ossorio, *Companys*, 123–7, & D. Hidalgo, *¿ Por qué fuí lanzado del Ministerio de la Guerra?* (Madrid, 1934), 65–8. The French Ambassador was told in July 1936 by an unnamed member of the Popular Front government that Lerroux paid the CNT 1,600,000 ptas not to rise (*Documents diplomatiques français 1932–1939, 2e série* [Paris, 1963], II, 667–8).

207 *HCE*, II–7, 159.

208 Accounts of the Asturian rising are given by Arrarás, *HSRE* II, 531–641; Jackson, *Spanish Republic*, 153–9; Thomas, *Civil War*, 118–23. See also Ramos Oliveira, *La revolución*, 116–25; Maurín, *Segunda revolución*, 145–66; Mendizábal, *Martyrdom*, 208–13; Hidalgo, *¿ Por qué?*, 77–81, 83–7 & 140–1; Álvarez del Vayo, *Last Optimist*, 268–72. Salazar Alonso, *Bajo el signo*, 299, gives the strength of government forces.

209 Aguirre, *Libertad*, 542–54; García Venero, *Nacionalismo vasco*, 455–6; Sierra, *Euzkadi*, 145.

210 *DSC*, 9 Oct 1934; *El Debate*, 10 Oct 1934.

211 *DSC*, 9 Oct 1934.

212 *ABC*, 16 Oct 1934.

CHAPTER 5

1 *El Debate*, 13, 18, 19 Oct 1934.

2 *ABC*, 26 Oct 1934.

3 *ABC*, 16 Oct 1934.

z

4 Fernández-Ladreda (deputy for Asturias), *DSC*, 7 Nov 1934. According to official figures 1,377 persons died (1,051 being civilians); 2,954 were injured (2,051 being civilians); 7 were missing (quoted in *ABC*, 19 Feb 1935).

5 Cid, *ABC*, 28 Oct 1934. Rightists probably exaggerated the brutality of the rebels; Aizpún told his Navarrese constituents after a visit to Asturias that the rebels' deeds had been magnified (*El Debate*, 28 Oct 1934).

6 Sáinz Rodríguez and Vigón, among others, had agreed to a plan: Ansaldo was to fly Sanjurjo from Portugal to Asturias, where Col Yagüe would put the Army's best troops at his disposal. The operation necessitated the agreement of the overall commander, Franco in Madrid, who refused to co-operate (Ansaldo, ¿ *Para qué?*, 92-3). Sanjurjo and Barrera had previously offered their services to Lerroux, who declined the offers (Royo Villanova, *30 años*, 193).

7 *HCE*, II-8, 275; *El Debate*, 6 Nov 1934; Lerroux, *Pequeña historia*, 326-36 & 363. The two executed were a man who had given an order to fire on women and children and a deserter, Sgt Vázquez, who had used prisoners as a shield in an attack on a barracks (see Arrarás, *HSRE* II, 580 & 591-3).

8 *HCE*, II-8, 277; Gil Robles, *No fue posible*, 141-9. Casanueva was the go-between; military men were particularly perturbed by the commutation of Major Pérez Farrás's sentence. Around this time Fanjul's *Falangista* son acted as go-between for his father, Goded and José Antonio (García Venero, *Fanjul*, 187).

9 *DSC*, 5 & 6 Nov 1934. During the debate, Maeztu interrupted to tell Republicans that it had taken '140,000 shootings' to liquidate the Commune.

10 Quoted by F. Acedo Colunga, *José Calvo Sotelo* (Barcelona, 1957), 279.

11 The Left Republican Miranda (*DSC*, 30 Nov 1934) said 80 innocent persons had been shot. Copious details of alleged atrocities were collected by Los Ríos, Gordón Ordás and Álvarez del Vayo, and were put before British Leftists by L. Manning, *What I Saw in Spain* (London, 1935), 167-221. An army officer later wrote that Civil and Assault Guards each arrested a suspect for the same crime. Both suspects independently confessed their guilt when tortured. Madrid, however, decided that two persons could not be guilty; the two sets of police then got both victims to retract their confessions under torture (J. Martín Blázquez, *I Helped to Build an Army* [London, 1939], 22).

12 In Oct Hidalgo gave Doval the 'necessary autonomy and special jurisdiction' to circumvent normal procedures (Hidalgo, ¿ *Por qué?*, 92). Doval declared he would spare no rebel's life and would 'exterminate the revolutionary seed in the bellies of mothers' (Alba, *HSRE*, 167). Velarde, who became Governor-General in Dec, found 30,000 had been detained; 27,000 of these were released in five

months ('A.S.', 'Comentarios a "La guerra civil española" de Hugh Thomas', *Revista de Estudios Políticos*, no 120 [1961], 246). Trials continued throughout 1935—see Arrarás, *HSRE* III, 74–6, 153–4, 191, 214 & 253–6.

13 If the Left's evidence was as impeccable as it maintained, it seems strange that virtually no action was taken against the alleged offenders in 1936. The Bulgarian Lt Ivanov was given a six-month sentence for shooting the Leftist journalist Sirval (*El Debate*, 5 Sept 1935). Maeztu thought the Left's new '*ferrerada*' just the second half of Nechaev's formula: 'Against bodies, violence; against souls, lies' (*ABC*, 23 Nov 1934). On the campaign abroad, see Arrarás, *HSRE* III, 18–21.

14 On 16 Nov Samper and Hidalgo were ousted to appease the Right, who accused them of having appeased the revolution. They were temporarily replaced by Rocha at State and Lerroux at War. On 27 Dec Villalobos was replaced by Dualde (also a Liberal-Democrat) at Public Instruction after a clash with *Cedistas* (*ABC*, 22 Dec 1934). On 5 Jan Martínez de Velasco and Pita Romero (both without portfolio) resigned. After a wrangle (see *El Debate*, 12–22 Jan 1935), Abad Conde (Radical) became on 23 Jan Minister for the Navy instead of Rocha.

15 *El Debate*, 19 Mar 1935.

16 *El Debate*, 26 Mar 1935.

17 The document called for tax reforms and special legislation and more expenditure to cure unemployment; reafforestation, railway development and the planned expenditure of 150,000,000 ptas before 1 Dec 1936 were advocated (*El Debate*, 27 Mar 1935).

18 *El Debate*, 27–30 Mar 1935; Lerroux, *Pequeña historia*, 369–75. Who wrote this editorial is not known: Bowers (*My Mission*, 132) suggests Herrera. Gil Robles said he was disgusted by the editorial (*ABC*, 28 Mar 1935). The CEDA objected to Alcalá-Zamora's unconstitutional pressure on the government and his reluctance to be tough with revolutionaries (Gil Robles, conversation). This view was expressed also by Martínez de Velasco (*El Debate*, 26 Mar 1935).

19 *El Debate*, 31 Mar & 2–4 Apr 1935. This government consisted of: Premier, Lerroux (Radical); State, Rocha (Radical); Justice, Cantos (Radical); Finance, Zabala (Progressive); War, Gen Masquelet; Navy, Adm Salas; Interior, Portela Valladares (independent); Public Instruction, Prieto Bances (independent); Labour, Vaquero (Radical); Public Works, Guerra del Río (Radical); Agriculture, Benayas (Progressive); Industry, Marraco (Radical); Communications, Jalón (Radical).

20 *La Nación*, 3 Apr 1935 (quoted by *ABC*, 4 Apr 1935).

21 *ABC*, 9 Apr 1935.

22 *El Debate*, 7 Apr 1935.

23 *El Debate*, 10 Apr & Fernández Ruano, *ABC*, 13 Apr 1935.

24 *El Debate*, 28 Apr 1935.

25 Gil Robles, conversation.
26 *HCE*, II–8, 331; C. Seco Serrano, *Historia de España, tomo VI* (Barcelona, 1962), 106.
27 This government consisted of: Premier, Lerroux (Radical); War, Gil Robles (CEDA); Interior, Portela (independent); Labour, Salmón (CEDA); Communications, Lucía (CEDA); Finance, Chapaprieta (Independent Republican); Public Works, Marraco (Radical); State, Rocha (Radical); Industry & Commerce, Aizpún (CEDA); Agriculture, Velayos (Agrarian); Justice, Casanueva (CEDA); Navy, Royo Villanova (Agrarian); Public Instruction, Dualde (Liberal-Democrat). Alcalá-Zamora did not want Gil Robles at War nor so many *Cedistas*; in Lerroux's opinion Gil Robles was 'a gentleman and a loyal fellow' and his party had crossed the Rubicon into the Republic (Lerroux, *Pequeña historia*, 387–90). Giménez Fernández had recently ended a speech with 'Long live the Republic' (*El Debate*, 19 Mar 1935).
28 *El Debate*, 6 Nov & *ABC*, 6, 13 & 14 Nov 1934.
29 *DSC*, 20 & 21 Mar 1935. Gil Robles wanted the Court of Constitutional Guarantees to try Azaña so as to clear up the confusion.
30 *DSC*, 20 July 1935; Jackson, *Spanish Republic*, 168.
31 *El Debate*, 6 June 1935.
32 *ABC*, 2 Oct 1934.
33 *DSC*, 9 Oct 1934.
34 *DSC*, 5 & 29 Nov 1934. The attack was led by Goicoechea and H. Maura. The former found himself accused by Cambó of betraying his political past as a *Maurista* and leader of the abortive Constitutional Centre in 1931 which had proclaimed the principle of autonomy (*DSC*, 6 Dec 1934).
35 *ABC*, 25 Oct & 7 Dec 1934.
36 *DSC*, 30 Nov & 6–7 Dec 1934.
37 *DSC*, 11 Dec 1934; 3 *Cedistas* actually voted for the motion.
38 Text in *DSC*, 23 Jan 1935 App.
39 *El Debate*, 28 Dec 1934; Portela was a Liberal Minister under the Monarchy.
40 *El Debate*, 5 Apr & *ABC*, 18 Apr 1935. The *Lliga* had already complained of the corrupt nature of Pich Pon's men (*DSC*, 6 Feb 1935).
41 *El Debate*, 10 Mar 1935. He complained that when he tried to put into effect the doctrines of Vázquez de Mella the latter's disciples accused him of separatism (*El Debate*, 23 Dec 1934).
42 *ABC*, 30 Apr 1935 (speech at Tarrasa).
43 See speeches of Pabón and Villalobos, *DSC*, 21 Dec 1934.
44 A more critical version, based on laicist sources, is given by Jackson, *Spanish Republic*, 170–1. The law of 16 Sept 1932 stipulated that 50,000,000 ptas would be set aside annually in the budget for new state schools. In fact, 20,000,000 ptas were provided in 1932; 25,000,000 in 1933; 25,000,000 in 1934; and 25,000,000 in 1935, all

of which had been spent by mid-April (Prieto Bances, *ABC*, 17 Apr 1935). The 1935 budget allotted 5,267,000 ptas in aid to the ILE, 2,948,000 more than in 1931 (Galindo, *Los partidos*, 286). According to the Socialist Llopis, only 3,521 new state schools were opened in 1934–5, compared with the 12,988 of 1931–3 (*DSC*, 3 June 1936). *El Debate*, 7 Aug 1935, criticised the 'pedagogical missions' because they had been used to spread political subversion; the paper thought that technical instruction on farming methods would be more useful to the rural population than the declamation of Sophocles. During 1934–5 Catholic schools were built (in accordance with the Constitution) by the *Cruzados de la Enseñanza*, a private company created for the purpose.

45 Giménez Fernández's draft, *DSC*, 5 Nov 1934 App; final text *DSC*, 21 Dec 1934 App. Since Nov 1932 land had been provided for 15,467 peasants in Badajoz and 18,459 in Cáceres.

46 *DSC*, 21 Nov 1934.

47 *DSC*, 21–23 & 28 Nov 1934—speeches of Álvarez Lara, Royo Villanova, Daza and Lamamié de Clairac.

48 Opponents included leaders of the *Entidades Agropecuarias de España*, the *Cedistas* Rodríguez Jurado, Oriol de la Puerta, Sierra Pomares (*ABC*, 28 Nov 1934); such people stayed in the party only to try to restrain the social-reformists (as Rodríguez Jurado admitted, *ABC*, 12 Feb 1935). Gil Robles said this law was an 'urgent necessity' (*ABC*, 4 Dec 1934).

49 *DSC*, 20 Dec 1934. Radicals, *Cedistas*, Progressives, Liberal-Democrats, PNV and *Unión Republicana* voted for it. The Agrarians voted against. The *Lliga* was split. Monarchists abstained. Giménez Fernández thought his main enemies were absentee landlords living in Madrid; landowners in Badajoz were in favour, he claimed (*El Debate*, 1 Jan 1935).

50 Text of law on leases, as modified by Cortes committee, in *DSC*, 15 June 1934 App; text of law on accession to property, *DSC*, 4 Dec 1934 App.

51 See, in particular, speeches of Casanueva, Maroto and Lamamié de Clairac in *DSC*, 5, 11 & 13 Dec 1934 respectively.

52 Rodríguez Jurado, *ABC*, 12 Apr 1935.

53 Quoted in Gil Robles, *No fue posible*, 179. Lamamié de Clairac interpreted Leo XIII's teachings in a very conservative fashion to show that property rights were inviolable. He wanted new smallholdings to be created 'without taking anything from anybody', ie by irrigation (*DSC*, 23 Nov 1934). *El Debate*, 6 Dec 1934, described the drafts as 'the Encyclicals made into laws'.

54 Giménez Fernández, *El Debate*, 5 Dec & *DSC*, 12 Dec 1934.

55 Álvarez Robles, like the Minister, had no faith in an urbanised Spain; he wanted the country to be 're-agrarianised' (*DSC*, 6 Dec 1934).

56 'Manuel Jiménez Fernández! Present and forward! ... The agrarian

laws will go into the *Gaceta*, or *Acción Popular* would cease to be *Acción Popular!*' (*JAP*, 22 Dec 1934). *JAP*, 24 Nov 1934, was not embarrassed when some Deputies referred to the CEDA as 'a confessional Left'.

57 *ABC*, 12 Mar 1935.

58 *DSC*, 14 Mar 1935. This law was passed by 189 votes to 38: Radicals, *Cedistas*, Agrarians, PNV and José Antonio voted for it; Monarchists, Independents and *Lliga* voted against.

59 Giménez Fernández also introduced a bill for the purchase of parts of large estates in Extremadura to increase the size of smallholdings (text, *DSC*, 23 Jan 1935); the Cortes committee rejected it, but the Minister put it forward as a private motion. In the voting the CEDA was completely divided; Gil Robles voted for it. The bill then went back to the committee (*DSC*, 27 Feb & 15 Mar 1935).

60 *ABC*, 23 Apr 1935. Calvo's views on social policies were not typical of the average Alfonsine.

61 *DSC*, 11 & 12 July 1935—debates on a PNV motion, supported by Giménez Fernández, Álvarez Robles, Del Río, some Radicals and *Unión Republicana*. The law permitted tenants to recover land if wrongly evicted. Álvarez Mendizábal estimated that 98 per cent of the notices given were contrary to the law.

62 *DSC*, 29 Apr, 21 May & 1 July 1936: Mije (Communist) said there had been 187,000 evictions, but Giménez Fernández said this figure was ridiculously exaggerated. Azaña put the number at around 80,000. The *yunteros* who had occupied land were evicted or had to pay higher rents after July 1935 (see Malefakis, *Land Tenure* [thesis], Part II, chapter ix).

63 *DSC*, 7 Feb 1935; R. Tamames, *Estructura económica de España* (2nd ed, Madrid, 1964), 44. *ABC*, 1 Dec 1934, thought it intolerable and incredible that the CEDA should allow expropriations to continue.

64 The statistics vary. According to the Institute (in Tamames, *Estructura*, 43), from 1932 to 31 Dec 1934 12,260 settlements had been made on 116,837 hectares. According to a Socialist source, by 31 Dec 1934 18,420 had been made on 128,179 hectares (L. García Palacios, *El segundo bienio* [n.pl., 1936], 32). According to the Ministry of Agriculture, by June 1935 13,471 settlements (ie about 50,000 individuals, as most were families) had been made on 132,160 hectares (quoted in *ABC*, 9 June 1935). By Sept 1935 8,559 labourers had been settled as well as 65,771 persons living in 452 communities leased collectively (according to the *Anuario Estadístico*, quoted by Manuel, *Politics*, 102). Little practical had been achieved before Azaña's fall in 1933. Del Río said he had expropriated 80,000 hectares and settled 10–11,000 families while Minister (*ABC*, 19 Mar 1935); but according to a later Minister, Del Río and Giménez Fernández had settled 7,000 and set up 131 communities (*DSC*, 1 July 1936).

65 The Institute was supposed to receive 50,000,000 ptas pa. In fact in

1932 it got 8,300,000; in 1933 50,000,000; in 1934 50,000,000; in the first half of 1935 25,000,000. Up to 6 June 1935 it had only spent 28,400,000 ptas in all (Ministry of Agriculture report, *ABC*, 9 June 1935). The Institute's personnel, appointed by Domingo, remained unchanged (*ABC*, 13 June 1935). By the end of 1935 the Institute had been given 158,300,000 ptas in all; 95,800,000 remained unspent (Malefakis, *Land Tenure* [thesis], Part II, chapter ix).

66 *DSC*, 28 Mar, 3 & 5 July 1935 Apps.

67 *DSC*, 23–26 July 1935; final text in *DSC*, 24 Sept 1935 App. Giménez Fernández succeeded in getting the principle of expropriation of any farm for reasons of 'social utility' incorporated in the text.

68 *El Debate*, 8 Dec 1934.

69 A subsequent Minister of Labour said that half the mixed juries ceased to exist in 1934–5 (Lluhí, *DSC*, 1 July 1936).

70 *El Debate*, 7 Dec 1934; & Giménez Fernández, *El Debate*, 11 Oct 1934.

71 *DSC*, 12 Feb 1935.

72 Eg Portuguese labourers in Badajoz were paid 3·50–4 ptas a day, when they should have had 9·75; the employers were fined 250 ptas (*El Debate*, 21 May 1935). Wages of 1·25–1·50 ptas a day were paid at Toboso (Bolívar, *DSC*, 2 Oct 1935). The Conde de las Torres was fined 10,000 ptas for paying low wages (*El Debate*, 7 Dec 1934). In Almería wage-rates were cut from 7·50, 8 & 6 ptas a day in 1933 to 4.50, 5 & 3.50 in 1934; in Albuquerque an employer was fined for giving reapers their keep but no wage for a 16-hour day (Mije, *DSC*, 1 July 1936). *El Debate*, 21 June 1935, wrote of constant denunciations of injustice and constant sanctions against employers by Salmón. Lluhí said that in July 1936 there were still 8,000 complaints from Seville province alone waiting to be dealt with (*DSC*, 1 July 1936).

73 *El Debate*, 28 May & 19 Sept 1935; & *DSC*, 11 June 1935 App (text of law).

74 Draft in *DSC*, 15 May 1935 App; final text, *DSC*, 21 June 1935 App.

75 *El Debate*, 8 Nov 1935, said that the law had given work to 20,000 persons, and more building was in progress in Madrid than there had been since 1930. Salmón complained that if he hinted that public works would be started in a municipality, the local returns for the number of unemployed had an uncanny habit of rising steeply; funds stuck to the local politicians' fingers (*DSC*, 12 June & *El Debate*, 4 Dec 1935). Local government was largely the preserve of notoriously corrupt Radicals (*DSC*, 6 Feb 1935; *HCE*, II–8, 361).

76 *DSC*, 12 June 1935. The PNV and D. de Madariaga urged the introduction of the family wage (*DSC*, 18 June & 3 Nov 1935).

77 Eg *El Debate*, 23 Dec 1934, 19 Mar & 4 Sept 1935. He said that

conservatives who would have given half their fortunes in the first
biennium to save the other half, would now not give a tenth of their
wealth to implement a Christian policy. He warned them that social
justice was the only defence against revolution. By September, he
was inviting the rich and hypocritical who claimed to be Catholics
to leave the CEDA.

78 *El Debate*, 18 Nov 1934.

79 *El Debate*, 16 Dec 1934.

80 *El Debate*, 23 Dec 1934.

81 *El Debate*, 18 Dec 1934.

82 *ABC*, 5 Jan 1935. At this time, he said, the CEDA and the Radicals
were the only effective forces 'in the camp of the Republic'.

83 *El Debate*, 27 Aug 1935; Lerroux was by now in old age and
expected younger Radicals to join the party 'whose discipline
satisfies the needs of their consciences'.

84 *El Debate*, 25 June 1935.

85 Lerroux told Guerra del Río: 'With this act . . . the problem of the
Monarchy has been definitively removed' (*ABC*, 25 June 1935).
ABC, 26 & 28 June 1935, complained that the CEDA had sold out to
the Republic and rejected the Right. Romanones commented: 'The
Republican sincerity of Gil Robles leaves no room for doubts. . . .
Sr. Gil Robles, who could have hastened the opportunity for a
restoration after the last elections, has consolidated the Republic. . . .
Acción Popular has turned the insecure and the unripe into the
mature and the stable' (*ABC*, 11 July 1935).

86 Speeches at Valencia and Pontevedra, in *El Debate*, 9 July & 6 Aug
1935, & Fernández Almagro, *República*, 142–3. 'I always prefer a
conservative Republic to a progressive liberal Monarchy.'

87 *El Debate*, 10 Oct 1935; Gil Robles spoke about constitutional
reform, Lerroux again dwelt on the need for a Leftist bloc to give
the Republic stability.

88 Goicoechea, *ABC*, 1 Sept 1935 (Lerroux was the lion, Gil Robles
the dove).

89 Artic 125 allowed the government or a quarter of the deputies to
propose constitutional reforms. These reforms had to be drafted
into a bill which had to obtain an absolute majority after 9 Dec 1935
or a two-thirds majority before that date. If the bill were passed by
the necessary majority, the Cortes were automatically dissolved and
the next Cortes were empowered to decide on the reforms proposed.

90 Alcalá-Zamora, *Los defectos*, 7 & 58 (& passim for his constitutional
ideas). Text of Dualde's draft in *DSC*, 5 July 1935 App.

91 The Left refused to discuss the draft in the Cortes committee (*DSC*,
16 Oct 1935). Azaña came out against reform in April (*El Debate*,
12 Apr 1935). Alcalá-Zamora, *Los defectos*, 60, wrote of the Left's
'unheard-of intransigence' over reform.

92 This paragraph, and those that follow, are a synthesis of Gil Robles's
interview with *La Vanguardia* (Barcelona), reprinted in *ABC*, 22

Nov 1934; speeches reported in *El Debate*, 23 Dec 1934 & 3 Mar 1935; his preface 'on the problem in Spain' (dated 1 May 1935) to A. Tardieu, *La reforma del Estado* (Madrid, 1935), 23–35; & his interview with the *Diario Español* (Buenos Aires), in *El Debate*, 31 May 1936.

93 The Traditionalist Toledo Robles interrupted at this point to exclaim: 'This is Traditionalism.' Gil Robles replied that this was more or less true, but that Traditionalism was not the exclusive property of any one party (*DSC*, 6 Nov 1934).

94 Cf editorial of *El Debate*, 4 Jan 1935: 'It is the State's business to promulgate laws that stimulate and favour the growth of the corporative shoots which the social body itself produces. But these shoots will not spring up if we do not first fashion the corporative social conscience. The individual, the corporative man, must be created before the institutions'—a very slow process.

95 Speech at San Sebastián, *El Debate*, 22 Oct 1935. He criticised the PNV's separatism and said he could not imagine a little parliament beneath the branches of the Tree of Guernica. He suggested the possibility of regional representation in a second chamber.

96 Text of Statute in *DSC*, 4 July 1935 App. At a PNV rally on 24 Nov 1935, Sabino Arana was quoted: 'We want a free and sovereign Country'; independence could be won by stages, the first of which was the Statute. Irujo said: 'It is not a problem of federalism or regionalism; it is a question of Country, and Euzkadi is the Country of the Basques.' In the Cortes, Monzón quoted Pidal to the effect that, if Castile broke the 1839 agreement, the Basques could also consider it void; he believed intransigence in Madrid would lead to separatism as it had in Cuba and the Philippines. Aguirre said: 'I proclaim . . . Basque nationality, Euzkadi, with sovereignty over its own destinies. So as to do what? . . . That depends more on you than on us'—yet 'the essence of nationality is total independence'. (Speeches in *DSC*, 5 Dec 1935.)

97 For details see Appendix 2.

98 García Venero, *Nacionalismo vasco*, 459–60: the PNV kept its hold in the hills.

99 The creation of this group was agreed by Gil Robles, Anguera de Sojo and Cirera at Saragossa (*El Debate*, 29 Sept 1934). Manifesto in *HCE*, II–8, 278. Cirera was head of the *Instituto Agrario Catalán de San Isidro*, the farmers' organisation.

100 Fortuny's *Partit Agrari Catalá* had offices in half the *pueblos* of the region (*El Debate*, 20 Nov 1934). Cirera's men kept control of the *Instituto de San Isidro* against opposition from the *Lliga* (*ABC*, 28 Feb 1935). They wanted little autonomy because a *Generalidad* favourable to the *rabassaires* would adversely affect their interests; there was an economic meaning behind the slogan 'Catalonia will be Spanish or it will die' (*El Debate*, 4 June 1935).

101 Its youth section complained of Catalanist recruits from the *Lliga*,

Acción Catalana and Carrasco's Catholic nationalist *Unió Demo-cràtica de Catalunya*. Anguera de Sojo, one of the latter, left the group within a year (*ABC*, 18 Dec 1934 & 2 Oct 1935). The Catalan deputies Ayats and Mullerat (*Lliga*) joined the CEDA. The *Cedista* Villalonga was Governor-General Nov–Dec 1935.

102 *DSC*, 20 Dec 1934. The elections for this body on 27 Jan 1935 were boycotted by the PNV and the Left; 3 Traditionalists, 1 Radical, 1 independent and 2 members of *Unión Navarra* were elected. *Unión Navarra*, a branch of the CEDA, had 7,000 members and was led by the ex-*Maurista* Aizpún and the ex-Jaimist Gortari (*El Debate*, 11 Dec 1934 & 29 Jan 1935).

103 Martín Artajo (conversation).

104 Gordón Ordás, *DSC*, 30 Oct 1935, who agreed with Monarchists that the Republic was 'not a name, but a content, and there is no other Republic than ours'. Trabal, *DSC*, 7 Nov 1935, believed *Japista* statements represented the real policy of Gil Robles.

105 Speech to JAP rally at Santiago, *El Debate*, 3 Sept 1935; he spoke of 'our aim of total revision' of the Constitution, demanded by the JAP, but took care not to specify when this would occur.

106 *ABC*, 11 Aug 1935. The Ministry of the Interior twice fined the weekly *JAP* 5,000 ptas and banned issues in Aug; Gil Robles himself withdrew the issue of 8 June for 'linguistic excesses' although the censor had passed it (*El Debate*, 14 Apr, 11 June, 18 & 31 Aug 1935).

107 Addressing the Madrid JAP, *El Debate*, 10 Nov 1935. When the group's weekly got into financial difficulties, it had to appeal publicly for funds—something which might not have happened if the JAP's relations with its parent-body had been satisfactory (*JAP*, 5 Oct 1935).

108 'The *Jefe* commands and the JAP obeys. We shall go where he says, how he says and when he says. . . . Any decision of the *Jefe*, for the JAP, is beyond criticism and discussion' (*JAP*, 27 Oct 1934, 19 Jan, 15 May & 19 Oct 1935). Censored columns were filled in with a monotonous '¡ *JEFE!* ¡ *JEFE!* ¡ *JEFE!* ¡ *JEFE!*'

109 *JAP*, 27 Oct 1934, 15 May & 8 June 1935; & *El Debate*, 17 Sept 1935. Pérez de Laborda (*ABC*, 1 Sept 1935) wanted only heads of families to have the vote.

110 *JAP*, 19 Jan, 20 Apr & 22 June 1935; & Pérez de Laborda's interview with *ABC*, 1 Sept 1935. *JAP*, 20 July 1935, recommended study of Portuguese political developments.

111 *JAP*, 27 Oct 1934 & 22 June 1935. Albiñana noticed that half those who went about preaching that people who did not work should not eat (ie *Japistas*) 'have not worked in their lives and continue to eat splendidly' (*ABC*, 26 Mar 1935).

112 Pérez de Laborda, *ABC*, 1 Sept 1935 & *JAP*, 23 Nov 1935.

113 Pérez de Laborda, *ABC*, 1 Sept 1935 & *JAP*, 25 May & 23 Nov 1935. They had in common anti-Marxism, faith in national resurgence

and the cult of youth; both also abhorred use of the 'outdated' terms 'Right' and 'Left' when applied to themselves.

114 *JAP*, 27 Oct, 8 & 22 Dec 1934, 8 June, 17 & 31 Aug, 5 Oct 1935. 'Monarchical thrombosis' was caused by 'bacteriological poisoning by . . . egoism, little passions, morbid anxiety bacilli, worry-insomnia for frivolous exaggerated applause; spectacularism and acute pseudopatriotitis'.

115 *JAP*, 27 Oct & 10 Nov 1934; *ABC*, 1 Sept 1935; *El Debate*, 3 & 17 Sept, 6 & 13 Oct 1935. 'Empire' meant 'spiritual empire', 'faith in Spain's destinies', a big merchant fleet and a voice in international affairs. The Virgin of the Pillar was the JAP's patron-saint— 'Hispanity' was in vogue. The JAP's emblem was a black Cross, from which hung the letters Alpha and Omega, set on a white ground with a red surround—all of which symbolised Pelayo and the Reconquest, and an immaculate ship on a sea of martyrs' blood. 'Menéndez Pelayo is the thinker of the JAP' (*JAP*, 19 Oct 1935).

116 In *El Debate*, 3 Dec 1935.

117 *Requetés* and *Falangistas* usually pronounced the '*j*' in 'JAP' in an excessively guttural manner, thus imitating the sound of expectoration. The SEU leader Jato (*Rebelión*, 99) called *Japistas* 'men without guts'. The JAP numbered tens of thousands to the *Falange*'s thousands. No complete membership figures were given, but its *Movilización Civil* in Madrid alone had 14,217 members (JAP, 2 Feb 1935). The JAP justified its legalism on the grounds that 'with the law . . . we have displaced anti-Spain from the legality that they constructed' (*JAP*, 8 Dec 1934).

118 The CNCA had 200,000 peasant families (about a million individuals) in 39 provinces at the end of 1935; it had redistributed some 50,000 hectares to 10,000 of its members. There were also the *Liga Nacional de Campesinos*, the *Unión Obrera Campesina* with 5,600 members in 29 provinces, and other farmers' organisations. (See the survey in *El Debate*, 14 June 1936.)

119 *El Debate*, 10 & 12 Oct 1934. Ruiz Alonso was to lead a campaign in Marxist-dominated areas. At this time unions were strongest in León and Castile. Catholic workers' unions had 60,000 members and free unions 100,000 (García-Nieto, *Sindicalismo cristiano*, 187–8).

120 *El Debate*, 10, 18, 30 & 31 Oct & 1 & 18 Nov 1934. The FNT affiliates had 12,000 members in Madrid, and made progress among the rural workers of the south. Inspiration was drawn from the example of Vicente Madera, founder of the Catholic miners' union in Asturias in 1922, who held out against the revolutionaries in Oct 1934.

121 Ruiz Alonso, *El Debate*, 18 Nov 1934; *ABC*, 19 Mar 1935.

122 Based on Dutch and Belgian models, it appealed to employers to undertake the noble mission of 'making the horrible scourge of workers' unemployment disappear for ever! Let us not tolerate for

one day more the shame of seeing our brothers, who ask for work, dying of hunger, while we have one peseta paralysed!' (*El Debate*, 18 & 24 Nov 1934).

123   *El Debate*, 20–21 Dec 1935; García-Nieto, *Sindicalismo cristiano*, 189–91; & F. Guillén Salaya, *Historia del sindicalismo español* (Madrid, 1941), 63. The CONS had branches in Madrid and Saragossa.

124   García-Nieto, *Sindicalismo cristiano*, 205, & *El Debate*, 7 Feb 1936. The Madrid *Federación de Sindicatos Católicos* refused to join because it was not confessional. A. de Incháusti was the President of CESO.

125   Salmón, *JAP*, 7 Sept 1935. *Trabajo*, largely circulated free, attacked the abuses of capitalism and its failure to fulfil its social obligations, but defended capitalism in principle (Jellinek, *Civil War*, 52–3).

126   This crack was papered over in the National Council of the CEDA (*ABC*, 18 Oct 1935).

127   Giménez Fernández warned that if the Right did not keep its promises and permitted a return to the *status quo ante* 1931, the sure consequence would be its electoral defeat (*El Debate*, 21 & 22 June 1935).

128   *FE*, 7 Dec 1933 (*O.c.*, 607–10). In *Arriba*, 28 Mar 1935, he prophesied Azaña's return to power within 12 months—unless Gil Robles was converted to the idea of 'the National State' (Arrarás, *HSRE* III, 137).

129   *DSC*, 6 Nov 1934. Calvo said that where there was a consensus—as in Britain, where the Socialists were not revolutionary—Parliament was a fine institution.

130   *ABC*, 11 Nov 1934.

131   *ABC*, 29 Nov 1934. The residual liberalism of *ABC* led it to prefer Gil Robles's conception of the 'new State' to that of Calvo Sotelo. *La Nación* and *La Época* wholeheartedly agreed with Calvo Sotelo's view (*ABC*, 10–11 Nov 1934).

132   Galindo, *Los partidos*, 254. *ABC*, 8 Dec 1934, explained that the manifesto had been ready for some days, and that the censorship had only now consented to its partial publication with one signature (Calvo Sotelo's). *El Debate*, 9 Dec 1934, reported the document's existence, but published no excerpts. Copies printed by *La Nación* were handed out in the streets; what follows is taken from one of these copies, given to me by D. Julián Cortés Cavanillas. The Radical Minister of the Interior forbade publication because the manifesto's aim was to seduce the military (Vaquero, *DSC*, 29 Jan 1935). For a literal translation of the whole document and a consideration of its content see R. A. H. Robinson, 'Calvo Sotelo's *Bloque Nacional* and its manifesto', *University of Birmingham Historical Journal*, vol X, no 2 (1966), 160–84. The manifesto was written by Sáinz Rodríguez (Arrarás, *HSRE* III, 58).

133   The absence may be noted of the Alfonsine Marqués de Villapesa-

dilla and the Traditionalist Bilbao Eguía—for no apparent reason. The *Cedista* was Sierra Pomares, who often seems to have disregarded party discipline. The Independents were Cano López (ex-Conservative Republican) and Fr Gafo (Dominican pioneer of Catholic unionism). The Independent minority in the Cortes was a group of ten led by the ex-Agrarian Calderón, created in Nov 1934.

134 Among the latter, one was Pradera, another Areilza, who was on the *Falange*'s National Council in Oct 1934, and who led *Unión Vascongada*, a Monarchist group in Bilbao, supporting the 'economic arrangement' and 'the integral sovereignty of the State' against separatism (*ABC*, 16 July 1935). The Duque de Alba, a close friend of Alfonso, also signed, as did the disillusioned Republican Del Moral.

135 *ABC*, 16 & 28 Nov 1934. According to Ansaldo (¿ *Para qué?*, 94) one of the main aims was to attract José Antonio. Ansaldo was on the *Bloque*'s executive committee with Calvo Sotelo, Lamamié de Clairac, Sáinz Rodríguez, and Pradera—three Alfonsines and two Carlists. José Antonio scorned the *Bloque* as an attempt by 'the impatient former exile of Paris' to oust other Monarchist leaders (Arrarás, *HSRE* III, 61).

136 *BOT*, 16 Dec 1934.

137 *ABC*, 16 & 28 Dec 1934. From *ABC*, it would seem that *Renovación Española* had opened branches earlier in 1934 in Cáceres, Ciudad Real, Toledo, Valencia, Vigo and Burgos. In 1935 branches of *Renovación Española/Bloque Nacional* were set up in Málaga, Palencia, Salamanca, Ávila, León, Córdoba, Lugo, Murcia, Pontevedra and Lower Aragón.

138 The Alfonsine writer *El Caballero Audaz* was arbitrarily fined 20,000 ptas; an editorial in *La Época* entitled 'The Army, saviour of Spain' was suppressed; it was said that *Cedista* attacks on the Centre in 1933 could not now be quoted (*DSC*, 27 Nov & 5 Dec 1934). The *Bloque* complained of *Japista* attacks as well as the censorship; Gil Robles replied that the *Bloque* attacked him daily, but he would use his influence with the government to see that propaganda aimed at his own party's destruction was not hindered (*El Debate* & *ABC*, 27 Dec 1934).

139 *El Debate*, 16 Jan & *ABC*, 1 Feb 1935.

140 *ABC*, 9 Mar 1935; he believed the theory of the possible good had 'Machiavellian roots'. Goicoechea criticised the 'tactic' with Beatriz de Bobadilla's words to Enrique IV: 'You are buying off uncertain dangers with certain shame' (*ABC*, 28 Dec 1934). In the spring of 1935 Gil Robles secretly met Calvo Sotelo, Goicoechea and Lamamié de Clairac and told them: 'The fact is that today I alone stand between Spain and the Revolution.' He asked them not to make difficulties for him, but silence was the reply (Gutiérrez-Ravé, *Gil Robles*, 139).

141 *ABC*, 11 May, 6 Aug & 12 Nov 1935.

142   Roa de la Vega (CEDA, León) went over to the *Bloque* in Dec 1934; he had, in fact, signed the manifesto. Valiente also left the CEDA in June 1935 as he had not been allowed to speak or hold office for a year; he joined the *Bloque* in Dec and became a Traditionalist. He said that the CEDA was being disfigured by an influx of time-servers (*El Debate*, 2 June 1935; *ABC*, 12 & 15 Dec 1934 & 14 Aug & 11 Dec 1935). Two minor branches joined the Communion: Lagartera (Toledo) and Briones (Logroño) (*BOT*, 3 & 10 Feb 1935). Gil Robles complained that the *Bloque* spent more time and energy attacking his party than it did the advocates of revolution (*El Debate*, 27 Aug 1935).

143   *La Nación*, 1 Nov 1935 (quoted in Vegas, *Calvo Sotelo*, 129).

144   *DSC*, 1 Oct 1935 & *ABC*, 9 Mar 1935.

145   *ABC*, 2 June 1935.

146   *ABC*, 3 Feb 1935. Cf Pemán: 'The *Patria* and the *Sub-Patria* cannot alternate anymore than can life and death; either one is dead or one is alive' (*ABC*, 28 May 1935).

147   *DSC*, 1 Oct 1935.

148   *DSC*, 6 June 1935.

149   *ABC*, 9 Mar 1935, & Vegas, *Calvo Sotelo*, 156 (speech at Tarrasa, 28 Apr 1935). Cf Sangenís (Traditionalist): 'We are abolitionists' (*ABC*, 5 Nov 1935).

150   *ABC*, 12 Nov 1935. His ideas on regionalism were similar to those of Gil Robles, but he wanted the PNV proscribed as a subversive organisation (*DSC*, 5 Dec 1935).

151   *ABC*, 3 Feb 1935. Calvo thought Italy was not 'a perfect model' (Vegas, *Calvo Sotelo*, 139). Goicoechea thought Italy 'the best example on which we can reflect. . . . All for the State. All incorporated in the State, and thus peace and progress' (*ABC*, 13 Aug 1935).

152   *DSC*, 22 Nov 1935. He had previously stated: 'New State, yes. But without dictatorship' (*Alborada*, 6 Oct 1935, in Vegas, *Calvo Sotelo*, 144). However, Comín (Traditionalist) spoke openly of 'National Dictatorship' as the only alternative to 'Red Dictatorship' (*DSC*, 6 June 1935).

153   *ABC*, 23 Apr, & *DSC*, 3 Oct 1935.

154   In *El Estado que queremos*, 73 (speech at Tarrasa, 28 Apr 1935).

155   Vegas, *Calvo Sotelo*, 183 (San Sebastián, 10 Nov 1935); Calvo compared the ideal to the star that guided pilgrims to Compostela.

156   Quoted in *HCE*, II–8, 298.

157   Though he did not commit himself to copying the Italian, Portuguese, Austrian or Hungarian régimes, he thought well of all of them and wanted Spain to adopt something similar (*ABC*, 3 Feb 1935). Cortés Cavanillas (conversation), who signed the *Bloque*'s manifesto, says the movement was not specifically Fascist, but the Italian example was a powerful influence on its style.

158   From the editorials of *La Época*, 1934–5 (collected in Escobar,

Escritos). From some of the phraseology, it would seem that the leader-writers were familiar with the writings of Maurras, as well as the corpus of Spanish Traditionalism.

159 Synthesis of articles by Maeztu, collected under the titles *Frente a la República* (Madrid, 1956), and *El nuevo tradicionalismo y la revolución social* (Madrid, 1959); and R. de Maeztu, *Defensa de la Hispanidad* (Madrid, 1934). He admired Hitler and Mussolini, especially for 'substituting for the class-struggle an authoritarian organisation of social justice'—but he did not like Fascism's 'excess of Italianism'; as for Nazism, 'its racist feeling offends me'. He saw a revival of 'Hispanity' in the Nicaraguan poet Rubén Darío's warnings about the encroachment of the USA; the concept meant that 'the Argentines must be more Argentine', etc.

160 P. Sáinz Rodríguez, *La Tradición nacional y el Estado futuro* (Madrid, 1935).

161 E. Aunós Pérez, *La reforma corporativa del Estado* (Madrid, 1935). His blue-print was worked out in considerable detail, the inspiration coming from the theories of La Tour du Pin and Italian practice, eg he advocated a Grand Council to advise the Head of State. He believed that the Fascist régime was not conservative. His emphasis on the need to get Socialist co-operation derived from his experience as a Minister. He was critical of the artificial corporativism of Dollfuss and Salazar. Spain, of course, was to lead the movement towards European unity.

162 Fal Conde, *Ideal* (Granada), 15 Nov 1934 (quoted in Melgar, *Escisión dinástica*, 180); *HCE*, II-8, 368-9; *HGL*, 398-9. Alfonso's visit to Alfonso Carlos at Puchheim in Aug 1935 was apparently without political significance. The *Círculo Carlista* in Saragossa in May 1935 demanded a national assembly of Carlists to choose a successor; for this, it was disowned by Alfonso Carlos, who stated: 'no one can choose my successor without my assistance' (*ABC*, 19 May & 25 Aug 1935; *Documentos de Alfonso Carlos*, 279 & 287). Some Traditionalists keen on the *Juanista* solution tried to oust Fal Conde and put Rodezno in his place (García Venero, *Falange*, 328).

163 Ansón, *Acción Española*, 155-7; *HCE*, II-8, 307-8; Cortés Cavanillas, *Confesiones*, 121-2; & M. de Almagro San Martín, *Ocaso y fin de un reinado* (Madrid, 1947), 244. There was quite a lot of intrigue to tempt Juan to act alone. The men of *Acción Española* even consulted Maurras, who said that Alfonso XIII ought not to abdicate.

164 In Jan 1935 Alfonso still believed that the 'tactic' was 'a political experiment that must be performed even though it fails'. By June, however, he was lamenting that the chance for a restoration had not been seized in Oct 1934 (Cortés Cavanillas, *Confesiones*, 106 & 113). At Juan's wedding in Rome on 12 Oct 1935, he told Alfonsines that 'sooner or later, the confused, the timorous, the compliant, will have

to follow your example, being persuaded that in Spain Monarchy
and Country continue to be consubstantial' (J. Gutiérrez-Ravé, *El
conde de Barcelona* [Madrid, 1962], 107). *Renovación Española* (entry
in minute-book for 2 July 1935) agreed to ask Alfonso to declare his
disagreement with the methods of *Acción Popular* so that 'things be
made plain and it be known that Monarchists must not and cannot
serve in Republican parties, even though these may call themselves
Rightist'; and secondly, since union with the Traditionalists was
necessary, that 'doubts be cleared up and the situation be explained
for the occasion of Don Juan's marriage, so that an effective
approximation may exist between both branches'.

165 V. Pradera, *The New State* (London, 1939)—first published in
Spain in 1935. The legal code was to be based on the decrees of the
Council of Trent. The organic Cortes were to consist of 400
deputies in eight sections (agriculture, commerce, industry, property, manual labour, professional labour, regions, State bodies)
elected regionally by proportional representation. Another 50 deputies would represent national bodies and corporations. Each section
would meet and debate separately on matters within its own sphere.
The review of the book in *El Debate*, 10 Nov 1935, conceded that
it had its good points, but it provided no really constructive ideas,
since it was not easy to return to the State of the Catholic Kings. In
his speeches, Pradera proclaimed that Spain could be saved by
returning to St Thomas Aquinas (*ABC*, 9 Mar 1935).

166 *BOT*, 24 Mar 1935. Pradera and Rodezno were keener on the
Bloque than was Fal Conde—see Arrarás, *HSRE* III, 133–5.

167 *BOT*, 11 Nov 1934. The CEDA's policy was like that of Christians
who had chosen to accept Moslem law and domination rather than
to crusade; it was a 'Mozarabic and *Muladí* tactic' (*BOT*, 3 Mar
1935).

168 *BOT*, 9 Dec 1934. Fascism could be a very good system abroad, but
'in Spain, no'. González de Amezúa coined the political slogan,
'Neither Moscow nor Rome: Spain' (*BOT*, 25 Aug 1935).

169 *BOT*, 5 & 12 May 1935.

170 From the *Boletín*, it would appear that, apart from the Navarrese
stronghold, Carlist organisation was refurbished in Catalonia,
Valencia, the Basque Country and Santander. Organisations were
springing up in Andalusia and Aragón, but they probably had few
members. In May 1935, the Communion had 11 dailies, 22 weeklies
and 3 reviews.

171 Lizarra, *Memorias*, 35–8, 49 & 55; Oyarzun, *Carlismo*, 464. Varela
(alias 'Don Pepe') from 1934 organised them into battalions
(*Tercios*) of 3 companies (*Requetés*), each of 246 men. He was
replaced as Inspector-General of *Requetés* in June 1935 by Col Rada.
The 200 young Carlists were trained on an airfield near Rome,
where they masqueraded as 'Peruvian officers on a training-mission'.

172 Zamanillo at Montserrat (3 Nov), *ABC*, 5 Nov 1935. The *aplechs* at

Poblet and Montserrat were attended by 30,000 and 50,000 respectively—according to *BOT*, 9 June & 10 Nov 1935.
173 Ansaldo, ¿ *Para qué?*, 94 & 100–1; Ximénez, *JA*, 359–67 & 396. The most notable resignation was that of La Eliseda, who claimed its religious policy was 'frankly heretical' since it gave the political sphere primacy over the religious. José Antonio said he was a 'convinced Catholic', but believed, like Mussolini, that the State should educate the young: 'I am Spain's missionary, not God's missionary.' According to Iturralde, *Catolicismo*, I, 169, José Antonio favoured a more pro-Catholic policy, but gave way to Ledesma, Giménez Caballero and Sánchez Mazas.
174 *Ultimos hallazgos*, 91.
175 *O.c.*, 100–1 & 225. *Falangistas* preferred 'the poetic, tragic, theological, Spanish Christ' of Unamuno to 'the utilitarian, economistic, sociological, Belgian Christ' of the CEDA (Sánchez Mazas, in Bravo, *José Antonio*, 92).
176 Payne, *Falange*, 78. It was said to be a national party coinciding with Fascism. José Antonio did not attend the Montreux 'Fascist International' meeting in 1934, but he did go in 1935 (*HCE*, II–8, 302; Ximénez, *JA*, 407–8).
177 José Antonio was fully conscious of his debt to Ortega's ideas. Sons of Ortega and Marañón were *Falangistas*, and Unamuno's was very interested (Bravo, *José Antonio*, 73). Unamuno himself confessed admiration for José Antonio, but added: 'I must die a liberal. Your affair is for the young' (Bravo, *Falange*, 87). José Antonio's concept of national tradition bore strong resemblance to Unamuno's concept of Spain's eternal '*intrahistoria*'. José Antonio and Ortega had the same Spenglerian end of the nation in athletic form; Ortega's liberal means of doing this with the Republic had failed, hence José Antonio tried Fascist means. (For discussion of the older ideas, see P. Laín Entralgo, *La generación del noventa y ocho* [4th ed, Madrid, 1959], passim.)
178 *O.c.*, 88 & 166.
179 *O.c.*, 92, 122–4 & 619–21. The Rightist paper *Informaciones* in Jan 1935 called the *Falange* 'a legion of people without identity-cards emanating from the Marxist camp' (*Textos inéditos*, 452).
180 Ledesma and a group of ex-*Jonsistas* and ex-Communists left, mainly owing to personal differences with José Antonio, whom they considered too aristocratic and intellectual. They re-started an independent JONS with *La Patria Libre* as its organ. Ledesma wanted greater imitation of Nazism and more emphasis on the workers. He stressed that patriotism and Catholicism were not to be equated (Ximénez, *JA*, 372–3 & 382–6; *HGL*, 336 & 381; Bravo, *Falange*, 85; & R. Ledesma Ramos, *Discurso a las juventudes de España* [4th ed, Madrid, 1942]).
181 Text in F. Díaz-Plaja (ed), *La guerra* (Madrid, 1963), 402–6. Views on agrarian policy in *O.c.*, 119–24. Ideas on a Spanish-American

2A

bloc and agrarian policies were quite close to those of Maeztu—from whom they were possibly derived. José Antonio toned down Ledesma's original draft (Arrarás, *HSRE* III, 62).

182 *El Debate*, 28 Oct 1934, reported arrests after a demonstration in Madrid. The authorities kept a close watch on *Falangista* activities (see García Venero, *Falange*, 75–7). *Arriba* (José Antonio's paper) was suspended from 11 July to 31 Oct 1935 (Bravo, *Falange*, 99). Payne puts membership in 1935 at 5,000: 60–70 per cent were under twenty-one, and students were the biggest single category (*Falange*, 81–2). Shots were often exchanged with revolutionary Leftists (Arrarás, *HSRE* III, 139–41, 190–1 & 238–9).

183 A hundred *Falangistas* raided the SEPU store in Madrid on 16 March to protest against 'Jewish exploitation' of its workers (Bravo, *Falange*, 90). In Dec 1934 Ansaldo put 100 *Guerrillas de España* in grey shirts and legionary caps, but the *Bloque* would only use them for sticking up posters; he was disgusted at such respect for legality and so dissolved them in Feb 1935 (Ansaldo, *¿ Para qué?*, 95–6; Salmador, *Ansaldo*, 108–9).

184 Bravo, *Falange*, 97–8, & his *José Antonio*, 102; *Ultimos hallazgos*, 99–102. José Antonio said that he could count on a General and the supply of 10,000 rifles.

185 A. Cacho Zabalza, *La Unión Militar Española* (Alicante, 1940), 13–21; *HCE*, II–8, 359. Barba and Arredondo ran the network from Madrid with Col Rodríguez Tarduchy, who enlisted the help of officers retired, like himself, by Azaña. José Antonio had four interviews with Barba in 1935, and in Oct saw Goded (*Textos inéditos*, 465).

186 Cacho Zabalza, *UME*, 30; Ansaldo, *¿ Para qué?*, 95.

187 Esteban-Infantes, *Sanjurjo*, 241 & 244. On the UME, cf Payne, *The Military*, 293–4, 300–2 & 306–7: he writes of divisions and confusion among the leaders (among whom he puts Gen Fanjul), but says it made headway after Oct 1934.

188 *El Debate*, 2 July 1935. He addressed 50,000 people at Medina del Campo on the morning of 30 June, and then flew to Valencia to address the biggest rally yet held in Spain: 200,000 were present according to *El Debate*, 125,000 according to *Le Temps*. Gil Robles denied the rumour that he wanted the police forces transferred from the Ministry of the Interior to the War Ministry (*El Debate*, 9 June 1935). He told M. Maura: 'While I hold the portfolio for War, forget any fear of a *coup d'état*. Take no notice of any rumour' (Iturralde, *Catolicismo*, I, 91–2).

189 *DSC*, 6 Nov 1934. Azaña had said that the Army was the Country's arm. Cf Vallellano: 'Soldiers: you are the incarnation of the Spanish people' (quoted in *DSC*, 27 Nov 1934).

190 *El Debate*, 23 Dec 1934.

191 Ansaldo, *¿ Para qué?*, 103–4, who added that the *Bloque*'s financial support dropped when Gil Robles took over, and officers thought of

promotion rather than rebellion. For Ansaldo, the *Bloque* was just the civilian manifestation of Alfonsine military plotting.

192 Lerroux, *Pequeña historia*, 345–7 & 354. During Radical tenure of the Ministry, Gens Goded, Fanjul, Franco, Millán Astray and Queipo de Llano were promoted.

193 *El Debate*, 8 May, 27 Aug & 21 Dec 1935.

194 *El Debate*, 8 May & 10 Nov 1935.

195 *El Debate*, 27 Aug & 10 Nov 1935; *JAP*, 22 Dec 1934.

196 *El Debate*, 18 May 1935. S. de Madariaga (conversation) says that when he met Franco in Oct 1935 he was struck by the latter's conviction that the military ought not to meddle in politics, as well as by his intelligence. Franco had been approached in 1933 to stand as a *Cedista* candidate, but he had refused (Arrarás, *Franco*, 128). Alcalá-Zamora opposed Franco's appointment, but Gil Robles and Lerroux insisted (Gil Robles, *No fue posible*, 141 & 235).

197 Gil Robles, *El Debate*, 21 Dec 1935; Arrarás, *Franco*, 144–5. Alcalá-Zamora disliked the promotion and reinstatement of 'enemies of the Republic'. Varela was made a General, Goded Inspector-General of the Army and later Director-General of the Air Force, Mola Commander-in-Chief in Morocco. Those dismissed included Miaja, Mangada, Riquelme and Hidalgo de Cisneros. Gil Robles (*No fue posible*, 799) says that he did not know of Goded's links with the UME, but he suspected Varela's contacts with the Carlists which he considered unimportant.

198 *El Debate*, 8 Aug, & *ABC*, 28 Aug 1935.

199 Cortés Cavanillas (conversation) says that the majority of officers would have liked a *coup*, which they thought could be legalised in the Cortes by the Right and some Radicals, but Gil Robles and Franco were against the idea. Gil Robles (conversation) says he never asked officers about a *coup*, but officers occasionally approached him to ask his opinion; he always replied by asking them their opinion, and they were never in agreement.

200 Arrarás, *Franco*, 143–4 & 146–8. When Gil Robles took over, the Army had enough munitions for 24 hours of modern warfare, helmets and gas-masks were deficient, and the Air Force's vintage bombers could only carry 5kg bombs. In Oct 1934, soldiers had died of gangrene because they had not even had first-aid kits. A quarter of the troops were said to belong to revolutionary organisations. Gil Robles had intended to re-start a military academy and the Courts of Honour (*El Debate*, 21 Dec 1935).

201 Calvo Sotelo, *DSC*, 5 Jan 1935; & *ABC*, 3 Feb 1935. He argued that public disorder was the fundamental factor in the Spanish situation.

202 The budget deficit rose as follows: 373,400,000 ptas in 1931; 534,900,000 in 1932; 616,300,000 in 1933; 811,800,000 in 1934 (García Palacios, *El segundo bienio*, 24). In 1935, thanks to Chapaprieta, it was to fall to 779,900,000 ptas.

203 The official figures (in *DSC*, 20 Nov 1935) for the trade deficit were as follows: 186,000,000 ptas in 1931; 234,000,000 in 1932; 163,000,000 in 1933; 243,000,000 in 1934. The deficit in 1935 was to be 287,900,000 ptas—quoted by J. Plaza Prieto, 'El desarrollo del comercio exterior español', *Revista de Economía Política*, vol VI, no 2 (May–Aug 1955), 59.

204 For the influence of Roosevelt, see Calvo's speeches in *DSC*, 20 & 30 June 1934.

205 J. Calvo Sotelo, *El capitalismo contemporáneo y su evolución* (Madrid, 1935), being his lecture to the National Academy of Jurisprudence and Legislation on 30 Nov 1935. The footnotes referred to a multitude of sources, including Pope Pius XI, Henri de Man and Sombart.

206 Calvo Sotelo, *DSC*, 30 June 1934. 'The only formula [is] a directed economy, in which the State supplants, is superposed on the conflicting interests of employers and workers, on those of capital, depriving it of usury, and on those of the unions, forbidding them all compulsion, and [in which the State] plans an economic goal to which all the economic activities of the country are subordinated.'

207 *DSC*, 20 June 1934.

208 Ventosa, *DSC*, 9 Jan 1935; Gallart, *DSC*, 12 June 1935.

209 *El Debate*, 4 June 1935.

210 *El Debate*, 3 Mar 1935 (cf Calvo Sotelo, *DSC*, 12 June 1935). Some of these ideas were incorporated in Salmón's unemployment law. Bank-rate had been fixed at 6 per cent in 1932; it was cut to 5½ per cent on 29 Oct 1934, and to 5 per cent on 15 July 1935. D. de Madariaga wanted expenditure on unemployment to take precedence over a balanced budget (*DSC*, 7 Dec 1934).

211 He had been S. Alba's lieutenant and Minister of War, Dec 1922–Sept 1923. In 1931 he had for a time been a leading figure in Alcalá-Zamora's party. In Dec 1934 he set up the Independent Republican minority of ten in the Cortes, which included the Progressives Del Río and Fernández Castillejo; Iranzo, a former follower of Ortega Gasset; and the ex-Radical Iglesias.

212 Text in *DSC*, 29 May 1935 App. The Institute was supposed to get a credit of 50,000,000 ptas a year; in future, it would only be given enough to ensure that it had 50,000,000 at any given time—it had not spent its last grants. Chapaprieta wanted to stop the practice of functionaries drawing a full day's pay for only an afternoon's work, and being paid a salary of 8–10,000 ptas while they drew 60–70,000 ptas for expenses (*ABC*, 1 June 1935).

213 *DSC*, 29 May 1935.

214 *El Debate*, 27 Aug 1935.

215 *El Debate*, 12, 17 & 18 Sept 1935.

216 *El Debate*, 14–21 Sept 1935; Lerroux, *Pequeña historia*, 427–32; Royo Villanova, *30 años*, 218–46. Royo considered the *Lliga* 'enemies of the Country'; he wrote that the cabinet had decided on a decree to transfer road services while he was representing the government

at a memorial service for the Queen of the Belgians in San Sebastián. He first heard of it from the *Gaceta*.

217 *El Debate*, 21–25 Sept 1935; Lerroux, *Pequeña historia*, 432–4. This government of 25 Sept consisted of: Premier & Finance, Chapaprieta (Independent Republican); State, Lerroux (Radical); War, Gil Robles (CEDA); Navy, Rahola (*Lliga*); Interior, Pablo-Blanco (Radical); Public Works & Communications, Lucía (CEDA); Public Instruction, Rocha (Radical); Labour & Justice, Salmón (CEDA); Agriculture & Industry, Martínez de Velasco (Agrarian).

218 *DSC*, 1 Oct 1935. Ventosa said transfer of services to Catalonia was the *Lliga*'s condition for joining the government. Calvo Sotelo attacked the President's handling of the crisis, while Royo compared the ousting of Lerroux to Alfonso's ousting of A. Maura.

219 Lerroux, *Pequeña historia*, 384–7, 399, 411–25 & 446–55; Gil Robles, *No fue posible*, 296–310; *DSC*, 22–28 Oct 1935; Buckley, *Spanish Republic*, 179–80. The three Radicals implicated were Benzo Cano (ex-Under-Sec of the Interior), Pich Pon (leader of the party in Catalonia) and Blasco-Ibáñez (leader of the Valencian Autonomist Radicals). According to Lerroux, Strauss, Prieto and Azaña hatched the plot at the Brussels Exhibition, and Alcalá-Zamora joyfully used it to achieve his aims of destroying the government bloc, the Radical Party and Gil Robles's chances. Bowers refers to Prieto advising Strauss (*My Mission*, 162).

220 *El Debate*, 30 Oct 1935. The Radical Bardají replaced Rocha at Public Instruction; the Radical Usabiaga took over Agriculture & Industry from Martínez de Velasco, who in turn replaced Lerroux as Minister of State.

221 Bolívar, *DSC*, 28 Oct 1935. José Antonio shouted '¡ *Viva straperlo!*' when the vote was taken (Bowers, *My Mission*, 164).

222 Lerroux, *ABC*, 30 Nov 1935.

223 *DSC*, 29 Nov–7 Dec 1935; Lerroux, *Pequeña historia*, 457–76; D. Martínez Barrio, *Orígenes del Frente Popular español* (Buenos Aires, 1943), 66–84; Gil Robles, *No fue posible*, 329–41 & 352–5. The Casa Tayá had a contract, rescinded in 1929, to ply to Spanish Guinea. In fact, Gil Robles and Lucía had prevented payment being made. José Antonio again shouted '¡ *Viva straperlo!*' when the outcome was known (Bowers, *My Mission*, 169).

224 *El Debate*, 19 Sept 1935; 40 per cent of the wheat was grown in León, Old Castile and La Mancha; 30 per cent of the crop was grown by smallholders (J. Larraz, *El ordenamiento del mercado triguero en España* [Madrid, 1935], 34–5).

225 *El Debate*, 1 Feb 1935. Spanish wheat was too dear to compete in foreign markets. Protection since 1922 had led to an increase in the area of wheat cultivation (Larraz, *Mercado triguero*, 10, 29 & 40; Thomas, *Civil War*, 783).

226 *DSC*, 23 & 25 Jan 1935. Smallholders who could not sell their crops were dependent on provincial money-lenders for their existence.

One of the arguments used by opponents of Giménez Fernández's plans to create smallholdings in Extremadura was that the new owners would grow wheat, thus defeating his other object of limiting the area devoted to wheat-growing.

227 Larraz, *Mercado triguero*, 29.

228 *El Debate*, 11 Sept 1935. The wheat-growers of eg Cáceres, said the 1934 crop had not yet been sold; they demanded a tax moratorium, inspection of the port of Barcelona and of flour-mills, and the immediate creation of a consortium and an agrarian bank (*El Debate*, 13 Aug 1935). The four *Cedistas* representing Madrid-prov threatened to renounce their seats in the Cortes if no solution were forthcoming (*ABC*, 23 July 1935). Fixed price-levels had been introduced in 1930, but had often been disregarded, as they were continuously from Sept 1934 (Larraz, *Mercado triguero*, 18, 20 & 27). The 1935 crop was just under 43,000,000 quintals.

229 *El Debate*, 30 Aug, 13, 15 & 19 Sept 1935. The government was to lend some 30,000,000 ptas to farmers to cover urgent payments. The problem was within the Minister of Agriculture's sphere, but a wheat committee was set up on which Gil Robles and Chapaprieta joined Velayos.

230 *DSC*, 4 & 8 Oct, 5 & 6 Dec 1935. The chief critics were Avia and Madariaga (Toledo), La Calzada (Valladolid), Gil Albarellos (Logroño) and Arizcún (Guadalajara)—all *Cedistas*. The respected Agrarian Martín Martín (Valladolid) left his party in disgust at his colleagues' incompetence. The provincial organisations designated were often Catholic farmers' associations who bought their members' crops first, to the detriment of other smallholders (García Palacios, *Segundo bienio*, 60).

231 García Palacios, *Segundo bienio*, 46 & 58; *DSC*, 6 Dec 1935. The decree of 24 Oct stipulated 6-month loans at $4\frac{1}{2}$ per cent on up to two-thirds the value of wheat hypothecated. La Calzada said the farmers could not get the loans promised, certainly not at $4\frac{1}{2}$ per cent; bankers were profiteering unscrupulously. The Agrarian Party to some extent represented provincial money-lenders.

232 He hoped by 1937 to end the free market in wheat, which, even with credits and price-levels, hit the smaller grower hardest. The market would be organised 'on the principle of the single buyer-seller', the *Comunidad Nacional del Trigo*, a corporative organisation for all with an interest in wheat, which would see to prices, credit, etc (*El Debate*, 22 Dec 1935).

233 Chapaprieta, *DSC*, 15 Oct 1935. The lower limit for income-tax was reduced from 100,000 to 80,000 ptas; this the Cortes approved (*DSC*, 12 Nov 1935 App).

234 He supported Cambó's view that devaluation would mean inflation and the destruction of the middle class. Calvo Sotelo argued that Spain ought to abandon the gold standard (only 17 per cent of her trade was with the 'gold bloc'); devaluation would not lead to

inflation. (The *Lliga* opposed devaluation because Catalan industry depended on imports.) Chapaprieta attributed the fall in exports to higher foreign tariffs. He proposed to give legal standing to the quota-system that had grown up. The State was to supervise all importing and exporting, and would encourage exporting bodies and sales propaganda abroad (*DSC*, 15, 20, 22 & 29 Nov [App] 1935).

235 *El Debate*, 7 & 10 Nov 1935.

236 Chapaprieta, in *El Debate*, 3 & 19 Nov & 10 Dec 1935.

237 *El Debate*, 5 Nov 1935.

238 *DSC*, 20 Nov 1935 App; *El Debate*, 23–24 Nov & 1 Dec 1935. There were also plans for rearmament, industrial tariffs, sugar-beet and wheat marketing, railways and fisheries.

239 *ABC*, 3 Dec 1935.

240 *ABC*, 5 & 10 Dec, & *El Debate*, 10 Dec 1935. Gil Robles approved of balanced budgets in principle, but not in practice if they precluded solutions to pressing problems. According to Gil Robles (*No fue posible*, 342–58) Chapaprieta, Cambó and Alcalá-Zamora were really working for a new Centre party. He also says that the Radicals wanted to resign and that Azpeitia and other conservative *Cedistas* were not speaking in the name of his party.

241 *El Debate*, 10 Dec 1935; Seco Serrano, *Historia de España*, VI, 122.

242 *El Debate* & *ABC*, 12–15 Dec 1935. Maura, who had hoped to include the *Lliga* and *Unión Republicana*, refused to join Portela's government 'of the oldest political style'. Maura complained that Alcalá-Zamora had double-crossed him (Bowers, *My Mission*, 170–1). Portela even offered José Antonio Agriculture, but he refused on the advice of Aunós (Ximénez, *JA*, 622). The government of 14 Dec was made up of: Premier & Interior, Portela (independent); State, Martínez de Velasco (Agrarian); Justice & Labour, Martínez (Liberal-Democrat); War, Gen Molero; Navy, Adm Salas; Finance, Chapaprieta (Independent Republican); Public Works, Del Río (Progressive); Public Instruction, Becerra (Radical); Agriculture, Pablo-Blanco (Radical); and without portfolio, Rahola (*Lliga*). Giménez Fernández refused the President's offer to head a Centre coalition (Gil Robles, *No fue posible*, 371).

243 Casanueva, *ABC*, 13 Dec 1935.

244 Gil Robles, *No fue posible*, 364–7. According to Goded, *Un faccioso*, 24–6, Gil Robles would not rise with the Generals and they would not rise without him. Ansaldo was told that the Generals would not rise because they were not sure of their troops (Salmador, *Ansaldo*, 119–20). Franco explained that he had not risen because the Country was 'not yet in imminent danger'. There was therefore no justification for a military rising in support of a political party (Franco's letter to Gil Robles, 4 Feb 1937, in Gil Robles, *No fue posible*, 377–8).

245 *El Debate*, 15 Dec 1935.

246 Gil Robles accused the *Lliga* of plotting for a crisis with Portela. Cambó in turn accused Gil Robles of precipitating it. Gil Robles denied this. Cambó said the *Lliga* had joined Portela's government to prevent a Leftist filling the vacuum. Martínez de Velasco also said he had joined under pressure. Royo Villanova left the Agrarians because of their leader's conduct in the crisis (*El Debate*, 17–19 Dec 1935).

247 Gil Robles, *El Debate*, 17 Dec 1935. Gil Robles (conversation) still maintains that the crisis was engineered by Alcalá-Zamora and the Socialists in order to bring about a dissolution. For Lerroux the crisis proved again that Alcalá-Zamora was eliminating rivals for the leadership of the conservative masses (*Pequeña historia*, 496).

248 Alcalá-Zamora, *Los defectos*, 55, 112 & 163; he wrote of those 'who had not accepted the Republican régime, which a great number of them rejected and many viewed with hostility'.

249 Viz President Alcalá-Zamora; S. Alba, President of the Cortes and hence Vice-President of the Republic; Portela, Premier and Minister of the Interior. (Chapaprieta was Finance Minister in addition.)

250 Calvo Sotelo, *ABC*, 17 Dec 1935. Cf Fal Conde: 'the tactics that failed so many times have failed once more' (*BOT*, 22 Dec 1935).

CHAPTER 6

1 Carrascal (CEDA), *El Debate*, 7 Jan 1936; Zabalza (Socialist), *El Socialista*, 18 Jan 1936.

2 Madariaga, *Spain*, 455.

3 By 'the military' in this context is meant that section of the Army which was prepared to rise against the Popular Front government. Conspirators were, in the main, *africanistas* removed from active commands in late Feb 1936; they had in most cases to get rid of *Azañista* garrison-commanders before 'pronouncing' against the government.

4 *El Debate*, 15 & 17 Dec 1935.

5 *El Debate*, 20, 21 & 29 Dec 1935. Gil Robles said hopes of a Centre bloc of 150 deputies were illusory, since the days of *caciquismo* had gone for ever.

6 *El Debate*, 18, 24, 26–28 Dec, & *ABC*, 28 Dec 1935. Gil Robles (letter of 16 Dec to President of Cortes) took his stand on Artic 110: Parliament, not the executive, must make financial decisions. Alcalá-Zamora (*Los defectos*, 201–6) took his on Artic 107: budgets could be extended by decree if they were not modified. The Liberal-Democrats' only hope for seats was in alliance with the CEDA in Asturias. The CEDA threatened to fight the Agrarians in Martínez de Velasco's own province of Burgos.

7 By 30 Dec the Agrarians, Liberal-Democrats, *Lliga* and Chapaprieta had accepted Gil Robles's demands. The cabinet meeting was stormy: Portela tried to hit Chapaprieta. In the crisis, Agrarians,

Liberal-Democrats, *Lliga*, M. Maura and Calderón all boycotted Portela, whose new government was: Premier & Interior, Portela; State, Urzáiz (ex-Radical); Finance, Rico Avello; Justice & Labour, Becerra (ex-Radical); Public Works, Del Río (Progressive); War, Gen Molero; Navy, Adm Azarola; Agriculture, Álvarez Mendizábal (ex-Radical); Public Instruction, Villalobos (ex-Liberal-Democrat) (*El Debate*, 29 & 31 Dec & *ABC*, 31 Dec 1935; *HCE*, II–8, 407; Bowers, *My Mission*, 175–6).

8 *El Debate*, 1–4 & 7 Jan 1936. The Permanent Deputation was a small group which could meet at any time when the Cortes was suspended; it consisted of representatives of the government and the bigger parliamentary minorities.

9 *El Debate*, 8 Jan 1936; Alcalá-Zamora, *Los defectos*, 175.

10 *El Debate*, & *ABC*, 9–11 Jan 1936. Reports of these activities came from the south, Galicia, Aragón and Valencia. In Daimiel (Ciudad Real) Del Río's men took over. The Radical Tuñón de Lara declared: 'In my province, Almería, where up to now there have only been Socialists, CEDA and Radicals, 15 Progressives have sprung up to form a temporary committee, where from nobody knows.' In Dec, Portela offered the Liberal-Democrats a Governor in Asturias to pack the town councils, if Rico Avello could be on their list. Portela demanded a letter of loyalty from the Governor of Cádiz, otherwise he and all the councillors appointed by him would be sacked. Chapaprieta said the heyday of Romero Robledo had returned. Many appointments were said to be backdated: the Law of 27 July 1933 specifically forbade changes in public personnel in the electoral period.

11 *El Debate*, 7 Jan 1936; his meeting was suspended by the government's observer. His meeting at Guadalajara on 31 Dec was banned, perhaps because he had referred to 'all the illegal acts that are being consummated from the heights of power. . . . The revolution found a redoubt in the heights of power'; Portela was 'an agent of the Masonic Lodges' (*El Debate*, 31 Dec 1935).

12 *El Debate*, 9–10 Jan 1936. Orders were therefore given to reopen *Casas del Pueblo* in the south (*El Debate*, 12 Jan 1936).

13 Eg Velayos protested that the new Governor of Ávila was packing local councils; Portela's friends said Velayos's men were dismissed for peculation. The Gov of Toledo was sacked for not prosecuting Gil Robles. The Gov of Cuenca resigned because the Minister of Agriculture (a candidate there) had dismissed 100 town councils. Pérez de Laborda was detained for pointing out that Del Río had been a Monarchist candidate on 12 Apr 1931. For the first time the government monopolised radio propaganda. Gil Robles said the government was giving public works money to *pueblos* in exchange for their votes (*El Debate*, 19 Jan–13 Feb 1936).

14 *El Debate*, 26 & 29 Jan & *ABC*, 8 Feb 1936. Del Río, who fought alone, said the CEDA and the Socialists were the only forces in Ciudad

Real; he would be lucky if he kept his seat (*El Debate*, 12 Jan 1936).
15 *El Socialista*, 21 Jan 1936.
16 *ABC*, 8 Feb 1936.
17 Bowers was told by a journalist close to Gil Robles that the south,
Catalonia, Saragossa and Bilbao would go to the Left, and a bloody
revolution would follow a Leftist victory. The journalist was sent to
the US, German and British Embassies to get them to press the
President to abandon his policy of creating a Centre—the implication being that if the anti-Leftist vote was split, the Left would win
and threaten foreign investments, etc (*My Mission*, 173–6). Lucía
was the contact between Gil Robles and Portela from 22 Jan (Gil
Robles, *No fue posible*, 413).
18 *El Debate*, 9 Feb & *ABC*, 8 & 9 Feb 1936.
19 Viz Badajoz, Cáceres, Albacete, Alicante, Huelva, Jaén, Granada,
Córdoba, Málaga-prov, Murcia-prov and Tenerife. An interesting
illustration of Portela's efforts was the case of the Progressive
Roldán, whose name first appeared on the Left's list for Málaga-cap,
but was then transferred to the Right's list for Málaga-prov.
20 The PNV's attitude was: 'We want nothing to do with the revolutionaries nor with the counter-revolutionaries' (Monzón, quoted by
Sierra Bustamente, *Euzkadi*, 152). A Basque Nationalist delegation
was told in Rome in January by the Papal Pro-Secretary that the PNV
should unite with the Right since 'the struggle is between Christ and
Lenin'. The Basques reaffirmed their intense Catholicism, but declined to ally with the CEDA (see Iturralde, *Catolicismo*, I, 395–6,
411–16 & 420–1).
21 Lerroux, *ABC*, 4 Feb 1936, echoing Calvo Sotelo's phraseology.
The JAP nevertheless continued to attack him (Bowers, *My Mission*,
181).
22 Maura said that Portela had subverted the Constitution, and the
Republic had been disfigured. Gil Robles, he said, had since 1933
proved himself a loyal servant of the Republic, whereas Azaña was
the revolutionaries' prisoner (*El Debate*, 14 Jan 1936). Gil Robles
called for judgment of the President on 23 Jan (*El Debate*, 24 Jan
1936). Maura's electoral policy was a complete *volte-face* from his
attitude in Oct 1934. Soria had in the past elected Arranz. Some
Conservatives (eg in Salamanca) preferred alliance with *Portelistas*
to joining the Right, which did not like them.
23 There were various reasons for this split. Officially, the Agrarians
refused to stand with Albiñana (*El Debate*, 11 Jan 1936). However,
Cedistas dwelt on Agrarian incompetence over the wheat surplus
and the party's political tergiversations. The local CEDA and Traditionalists represented Catholic farmers and smallholders while Albiñana had a following among farm-labourers. Martínez de Velasco,
on the other hand, represented larger farmers and urban bourgeois
elements, and presumably had the old *Albista* political organisation.
24 Gil Robles, *El Debate*, 6 & 11 Feb 1936.

25 *ABC*, 17, 18 & 24 Dec 1935. Calvo explained: 'England, a model country, excludes from elections the Crown, democracy, legality, religion. . . . We are now gambling on one card everything substantive, discarding the accidental and disputable' (*ABC*, 31 Dec 1935). Traditionalists wanted a national counter-revolutionary front with a definite pact to revise completely the Constitution, citizens' liberties and State organisation (*ABC*, 31 Dec 1935 & 7 Jan 1936; *El Debate*, 20 Dec 1935). Goicoechea demanded 'a Corporative State beneath the guardianship of the Monarchy' (*ABC*, 24 Dec 1935).

26 *El Debate*, 20 Dec 1935; *HCE*, II-9, 415; *ABC*, 31 Dec 1935.

27 *El Debate*, 22 Dec 1935, 3 & 7 Jan 1936. Some *Cedistas* wanted only Monarchist alliances, but Lucía and Giménez Fernández opposed these. Gil Robles wanted Monarchist alliances in 'safe' constituencies, but the broadest possible alliances in others (Gil Robles, *No fue posible*, 405–6; Arrarás, *HSRE* IV, 41).

28 *ABC*, 31 Dec 1935 & 14 Jan 1936; *El Debate*, 23 Jan 1936.

29 *ABC*, 31 Dec 1935, 4, 5 & 14 Jan 1936.

30 An electoral committee of Sáinz Rodríguez, Gil Robles and José Antonio functioned for a time, but Gil Robles rejected big Monarchist claims and vetoed José Antonio's name for the list in the capital (Gutiérrez-Ravé, conversation). Gil Robles (*No fue posible*, 413–14) put a limit of 60 on Monarchist candidates.

31 *El Debate*, 9 Jan 1936; Primo de Rivera, *O.c.*, 1097–102; Bravo, *Falange*, 126, 133–8 & 150; Ximénez, *JA*, 623–5; Payne, *Falange*, 91; García Venero, *Falange*, 89. It would appear that he had wanted 25–30 places. When Gil Robles refused this request, José Antonio said that the Right's front was unacceptably negative. On 14 Jan Gil Robles rejected José Antonio's request for 18 places, but offered him 6, including Salamanca for himself; José Antonio turned down the offer. According to Gil Robles the *Falange* put up lists in 13 constituencies and José Antonio stood in 11 (Gil Robles, *No fue posible*, 444–6, & Gutiérrez-Ravé, *Gil Robles*, 204).

32 *O.c.*, 129–44 (2 Feb 1936) & 181–8 (22 Dec 1935). He thought that the Right's social propaganda was insincere; the Left was unacceptably 'Asiatic' and materialist. *Japistas* tore down *Falangista* posters (Ximénez, *JA*, 657).

33 *HCE*, II-9, 427 & 435. Cf Gil Robles, *No fue posible*, 408–13, who writes that the Duque de Alba and Adm Magaz saw Alfonso XIII on 16 January in Paris and asked him in vain to issue a document critical of the CEDA. On 20 Jan Calvo Sotelo proposed a four-point pact: new constituent Cortes; immediate deposition of Alcalá-Zamora; the setting-up of a provisional government; and a General (probably Sanjurjo) for President—Gil Robles turned down the proposal. Misunderstandings with S. Alba, Cid, M. Maura and Goicoechea were cleared up on the 22nd.

34 *ABC*, 28, 29 Jan, 2, 4, 6, 9, 13, 16 Feb 1936. Eg when 2 Alfonsines in Toledo stood firm, the CEDA threatened to cancel the national

agreement with the Monarchists; the 2 Alfonsines were prevailed
upon to withdraw.

35 In Santander the Traditionalist Zamanillo allied with the *Falangista*
Ruiz de Alda (García Venero, *Falange*, 87 & 92).

36 *El Debate*, 5 Feb 1936. It consisted of Gil Robles and 4 other
Cedistas (one of them Bermúdez Cañete of the JAP, formerly of the
JONS, who had been *El Debate*'s correspondent in Berlin until the
Nazis expelled him in 1935); Calvo Sotelo and 2 other Alfonsines;
2 Radicals; Royo Villanova; a Traditionalist; and Giménez Caballero
(once a *Jonsista*, but now associated with the newly formed
Partido Económico Patronal Español, which demanded abolition of
strikes and revolutionary parties, and a free hand for employers—*El
Debate*, 24 Dec 1935, 21 Jan 1936).

37 The argument of the electoral booklet by 'El Caballero Audaz', *La
revolución y sus cómplices* (Madrid, 1936), 13–15.

38 *ABC*, 14, 21 & 24 Jan 1936; Calvo's speech of 12 Jan, quoted in
J. Pérez Madrigal, *España a dos voces* (Madrid, 1961), 418–20.

39 *Acción Española*, 1 Jan 1936 (*Antología*, 84). *Renovación Española*'s
manifesto said it would obstruct in the Cortes any Rightist government that did not outlaw Socialists and separatists, and depose
Alcalá-Zamora (*ABC*, 15 Feb 1936). Alfonsines and Carlists officially campaigned together in the *Bloque Nacional*, whose meeting
in Madrid on 12 Jan was addressed by Calvo Sotelo, Goicoechea,
Pradera, Rodezno, Fal Conde and Lamamié de Clairac. Alfonso
Carlos ordered his men to put up as many candidates as possible in
defence of Religion and Country, but the Communion must keep
its identity (*Documentos de Alfonso Carlos*, 291). As usual, Fal Conde
refused to be a candidate.

40 Gil Robles, *No fue posible*, 472. *El Socialista*, 19 Jan 1936, said that
March had given 2,000,000 ptas, but Buckley (conversation) says he
was as tight-fisted as ever. *HCE*, II–9, 427, says that *Acción Popular*
raised 1,000,000 ptas in one day.

41 The CEDA claimed credit for the building boom, the fall in unemployment and bank-rate among other things. Others were blamed
for shortcomings in labour legislation and wheat withdrawals (*El
Debate*, 9 Feb 1936). Leaflets were entitled 'Spain and anti-Spain',
'All Spain will be Asturias if the Revolution wins', etc (*El Debate*,
11 Jan 1936). An enormous portrait of the *Jefe* covered a 7-storey
building in the Puerta del Sol (Buckley, *Spanish Republic*, 188–9).
British, French and German electoral techniques were imitated
(*El Debate*, 18 Dec 1935).

42 *JAP*, 5, 12, 19 Oct, 21 & 28 Dec 1935; as usual, they pledged their
obedience to the *Jefe*. They addressed '*señores conservaduros*' as
follows: 'What awaits you if Marxism wins: . . . Arming of the
rabble. Burning of banks and private houses. Sharing out of goods
and lands. Pillaging in earnest. Sharing out of women. Ruin!! Ruin!!
Ruin!! You can go on sleeping if you like!'

43 *El Debate*, 19 & 31 Jan 1936. Gil Robles ordered an issue of the weekly to be withdrawn, and the government banned two others.

44 *El Debate*, 12 Feb 1936.

45 Romanones and Gil Robles were interviewed by the *Diário de Lisboa* (*El Debate*, 13 & 14 Feb 1936). Romanones said he thought a temporary eclipse of parliamentarism inevitable after the elections; Gil Robles would make the transition to a civil dictatorship. Gil Robles, however, denied such rumours as 'impertinence and rubbish to which I have already given the lie in broad daylight for all to see'.

46 *El Debate*, 14 & 16 Feb 1936.

47 Martínez Barrio, *Frente Popular*, 30–61.

48 *El Socialista*, 19 & 26 Dec 1935. The Socialist daily reappeared on 18 Dec, after being suspended for 14 months.

49 Bolloten, *Grand Camouflage*, 93; D. T. Cattell, *Communism and the Spanish Civil War* (Berkeley, 1955), 219; Arrarás, *HSRE* IV, 18–26. After the 7th Congress of the Comintern and the 6th Congress of the Communist Youth International, Socialist Youth members and Communists worked for a single 'Bolshevised' Socialist party with fusion of youth and trade-union movements as first steps.

50 Text in *El Socialista*, 16 Jan 1936. Sánchez Román did not sign because he disapproved of the extreme Left and militias being included in the alliance (*El Debate*, 16 Jan 1936). The *Partido Obrero de Unificación Marxista*, an independent Catalan Communist grouping, later withdrew, but told its followers to vote for the Popular Front even though this was considered a barrier to proletarian revolution (H. Gannes & T. Repard, *Spain in Revolt* [London, 1936], 126). The *Esquerra*, whose leaders were still in prison, was in practice part of the Popular Front. Madariaga (conversation) says that, as delegate to the League, he found Azaña less enthusiastic about it than Lerroux or Chapaprieta; the latter, when Premier, had been prepared to go to war with Italy over Ethiopia if the League had decided on this course. Sánchez Román ironically wrote 90 per cent of the document (Arrarás, *HSRE* IV, 30).

51 Álvarez del Vayo, *ABC*, 3 Jan 1936.

52 *El Socialista*, 14 Jan 1936 (speech in Madrid on 12 Jan, ie before the appearance of the electoral pact).

53 Largo Caballero, *El Socialista*, 28 Jan 1936.

54 Muñoz Lizcano, *El Socialista*, 16 Jan 1936. He and other Leftists talked of over '30,000 prisoners'. According to *HGL*, 424, there were in Feb 1936 only 20,446; just 6,000 of these had been arrested in connection with the events of Oct 1934.

55 Eg Prieto's *El Liberal* printed 18 pages of affidavits on Moorish and Legionary brutality (Bowers, *My Mission*, 181). The Right concentrated instead on the events of 5–13 Oct 1934, which the Left overlooked. Socialists were also accused of using bogus photographs (*El Debate*, 16 Jan 1936).

56 The conclusion of the Socialist election booklet by García Palacios, *El segundo bienio*, 67.

57 Eg *El Socialista*, 25 Dec 1935.

58 Bolloten, *Grand Camouflage*, 151; P. Broué & E. Témime, *La révolution et la guerre d'Espagne* (Paris, 1961), 61. The CNT came out against abstention on 14 Feb (Arrarás, *HSRE* IV, 36–7).

59 *El Socialista*, 19 Dec 1935. The Right was further alarmed by the result of the Socialist poll for their candidates in the capital: *Caballeristas* won, Besteiro was excluded (*El Debate*, 2 Feb 1936; Bowers, *My Mission*, 184–5). The Right thought Republicans in the Popular Front of little account: 'The Girondins helped Robespierre to raise a scaffold that was used to execute them, and Kerensky was ousted and exiled by Lenin. Such is the fate of politicians who, lacking strength of their own, serve only as a mask for revolutionaries!' (Marín Lázaro, *El Debate*, 11 Feb 1936).

60 Between 31 Dec and 21 Jan, 14 people were killed and 19 injured in street incidents (*El Debate*, 22 Jan 1936).

61 Azaña and Gil Robles both confessed in private that they did not expect to win (Madariaga, *Spain*, 484). Azaña told Ossorio (*Memorias*, 215) that he feared the victory of the Popular Front most of all. José Antonio, who had in 1935 gained notoriety for predicting victory for Azaña, now changed his mind and thought Gil Robles would carry the day; hence he saw no need to withdraw the *Falange's* candidates in the interests of defeating the Left (*Ultimos hallazgos*, 116; *Textos inéditos*, 347).

62 *El Debate*, 13 Feb 1936. The Primate's Pastoral referred to the connection in Spain between religion and patriotism and urged all to vote against laicist candidates; but charity must be shown towards opponents: 'Avoid violence. Respect the liberty of those who do not think like you' (*El Debate*, 29 Jan 1936).

63 *ABC*, 10 Feb 1936 for candidates proclaimed. The CEDA had the largest number, 177, followed by the Socialists with 125 and *Izquierda Republicana* with 120. The *Falange* put up 44. According to the calculations of *O Século* (quoted in *El Debate*, 6 Mar 1936), 69·1 per cent of the 13,528,609 electors voted—but these figures apparently excluded the late returns from Las Palmas, and parts of Tenerife and Málaga-cap. Over 4,000,000 electors therefore did not vote. (The poll in 1933 had been 62·9 per cent.)

64 For these elections in general, the studies by the Socialist J. Venegas (*Las elecciones del Frente Popular* [Buenos Aires, 1942]), by C. M. Rama (*Ideología, regiones y clases sociales en la España contemporánea* [Montevideo, 1958]) and by Bécarud (*Deuxième République*, 61–74) have been consulted. The first two, in particular, contain inaccuracies.

65 *El Debate*, 7 Mar 1936. *El Sol*, 3 Mar 1936, classified some deputies in a slightly different way and arrived at totals of: Left, 266; Centre, 65; Right, 142. Both sets of figures took into account the results of

the second round on 1 March in Álava, Castellón, Soria, Biscay-prov and Guipúzcoa. In the lattermost, the Right withdrew in the cause of religion to let the PNV win, as Bishop Múgica of Vitoria had advised (*HCE*, II–9, 463).

66 The totals of the *Juntas del Censo*, in *El Debate*, 26 Feb 1936—these figures excluded returns awaited from Las Palmas and some parts of Tenerife and Málaga-cap. If these returns (details of which did not appear) be included, the gap between Left and Right could not have been narrowed by more than a few thousands. Many works give figures quite different from these and from each other's—often giving the Left a numerical victory—but sources for the figures are never indicated. The figures given here seem, therefore, to be the best available. However, Gil Robles (*No fue posible*, 521) quotes the following figures given by the *Juntas provinciales del Censo* after scrutinisation on 20 Feb: Anti-revolutionary bloc, 4,187,571; Popular Front, 3,912,086; Centre and independents, 325,197; Basque Nationalists, 141,137.

67 The PNV held Biscay-prov and Guipúzcoa. The figure for the Left includes Lugo, won by the Left-*Portelista* list, and that for the Right Albacete, Granada and Tenerife, won by Right-*Portelista* lists, as well as Soria, won by Conservatives.

68 In the capital, the Popular Front got 224,540 votes, the Rightist bloc 186,422, the *Falange* only 4,948 (Venegas, *Elecciones*, 28). The *Falange*'s total national vote was some 40,000 (Payne, *Falange*, 94). Madrid and Málaga had gone to the Left in 1933. Prieto regained Bilbao from the PNV. The CNT vote assured the Left's victory in the other cities.

69 Though sometimes there was not a violent swing: in Cáceres, the Left won with 98,616 votes to the Centre-Right's 95,686; in Jaén, the verdict was 135,823 to 133,991 in the Left's favour; in Granada, where the Left complained of corruption, the Centre-Right got 148,649 votes to the Left's 100,013 (figures from *El Sol*, 3 Mar 1936). In Asturias, the CNT vote swelled the Left's majority. In Catalonia, where the *Esquerra* and its allies won everywhere, the 'Front of Order' obtained some 540,000 votes to the Left's 675,000 (*El Debate*, 29 Feb 1936).

70 Lerroux and Cambó defeated by the Left in Barcelona, Martínez de Velasco by the Right in Burgos.

71 *ABC*, 17 Feb & *El Debate*, 18 Feb 1936 both agreed on this point, though the latter did report some incidents, mostly in Galicia and Seville. Buckley gives a figure of 3 dead and 17 injured (*Spanish Republic*, 192).

72 Bowers, *My Mission*, 189. *ABC*'s special Monday afternoon (17 Feb) edition carried a headline saying that it was impossible to tell yet who had won.

73 Fernández Almagro, *República*, 167; Bowers, *My Mission*, 191–2; Jackson, *Spanish Republic*, 197; Broué & Témime, *La révolution*,

65; N. Alcalá-Zamora, 'Les débuts du *Frente Popular*' in *Journal de Genève*, 17 Jan 1937 (photostat in Ministerio de Justicia, *Causa General* [Madrid, 1944], anexo I). In Alicante, churches were set on fire, whereupon the Military Governor demanded action from the Civil Governor. The latter (who had earlier told a crowd: 'You are free, you are masters of power') informed the Military Governor: 'One ought not to go against the people' (Fernández Almagro, *República*, 169).

74 Ansaldo, *¿ Para qué?*, 114; Jato, *Rebelión*, 208. According to Gil Robles, *No fue posible*, 494, Portela told Socialist visitors later that day that he had told José Antonio that he would be held responsible for disorders; José Antonio replied that it was not the *Falange* which was taking the law into its own hands.

75 *HCE*, II-9, 439; *HGL*, 420-1; Buckley, *Spanish Republic*, 195-6; J. Gutiérrez-Ravé, *Las Cortes errantes del Frente Popular* (Madrid, 1953), 30; & Fernsworth, *Spain's Struggle*, 182-4 (giving Portela's later 'definitive' version). Portela's account refers to Gil Robles's demand for 'dictatorship'—apparently Portela's dramatised version of a 'state of war'. Portela's version, despite the claims made for it, should be treated with caution as it contains obvious chronological errors and was given after he had changed sides in the Civil War. According to *HGL* (loc cit) Portela said he would think over Gil Robles's demands. Gil Robles himself says the meeting took place at 4 am and he persuaded Portela to telephone Alcalá-Zamora, who refused to declare a 'state of war' but promised a 'state of alarm' within a few hours (*No fue posible*, 492-3).

76 *HGL*, 420-2; *HCE*, II-9, 439-40; Arrarás, *Franco*, 164-6; L. Galinsoga, *Centinela de occidente* (Barcelona, 1956), 179. According to Arrarás, *HSRE* IV, 50-1 (an account based on Franco's testimony), Franco telephoned Pozas first to ask for a 'state of war' but Pozas told Franco he was being over-pessimistic—possibly this conversation is the same as that dated 16 February (afternoon) given in Arrarás, *Franco*, 164-5. According to Arrarás, *HSRE* IV (loc cit), Franco rang up Molero in the early hours of the 17th after Fanjul had informed him of intimidation of Rightists; Molero promised Franco that he would ask Portela to declare a 'state of war' and he rang Portela to argue for this. According to Gil Robles (*No fue posible*, 492-3) Franco telephoned Molero after Gil Robles had sent an emissary to tell him what was happening; Franco asked Molero to press for a 'state of war' when the cabinet met and then himself rang up Portela.

Arrarás (*HSRE* IV, 51-2, 58-9 & 61-2) says the cabinet met at 10 am. Portela got a decree for a 'state of alarm' and another decree allowing him to declare a 'state of war' when and where he thought it necessary. Portela had wanted to resign there and then but Alcalá-Zamora dissuaded him. Alcalá-Zamora got Portela to countermand the decree for the 'state of war' on the afternoon of the

17th when the troops were already out in Saragossa, Valencia, Oviedo and Alicante (cf Gil Robles, *No fue posible*, 494–5). *HCE*, II–9, 440, says Alcalá-Zamora vetoed the 'state of war' in the cabinet, but Portela (Fernsworth, loc cit) said he got the decree but did not use it for fear of playing into the hands of the Right. Those involved in preparations for the 'state of war' were Gens Franco, Goded, Fanjul, Rodríguez del Barrio and Col Galarza. According to Goded (*Un faccioso*, 26) the suggestion was conveyed to Portela that he should be neutral if the military decided to make a move. On the eve of the elections Franco had instructed Mola to be ready to send troops from Morocco at a moment's notice (C. Martin, *Franco* [Paris, 1959], 106).

77 *HCE*, II–9, 441; Galinsoga, *Centinela*, 179-'80; Arrarás, *Franco*, 166; *HGL*, 422; & F. de Valdesoto, *Francisco Franco* (Madrid, 1943), 98–9. A UME Captain in Alicante was shot by his Republican Corporals when taking his troops out to restore order (Jellinek, *Civil War*, 219). Portela (Fernsworth, loc cit) claimed that he again resisted a demand for 'dictatorship' outright. Arrarás (in *HSRE* IV, 56–8) says this meeting took place in the Ministry of the Interior at 2 pm on the 18th; only then did Fanjul, Goded, etc press Franco for a military *coup*.

78 *El Socialista*, & *El Debate*, 18 Feb 1936; Bowers, *My Mission*, 191–2.
79 Jackson, *Spanish Republic*, 195 (giving Martínez Barrio's account).
80 Arrarás, *Franco*, 167; *HGL*, 421; Fernsworth, loc cit; Ximénez, *JA*, 676–8. Pozas spoke of Goded and Franco stirring up the garrisons— probably this referred to the soundings among commanders begun on 17 Feb. Jellinek, *Civil War*, 219, writes of officers at Alicante and Saragossa being ready to act, and of the Republican Gens Pozas and Masquelet being told of this. Portela said that Gens Pozas and Núñez del Prado (in command of Assault Guards) had pledged themselves to the Popular Front on the 18th (Arrarás, *HSRE* IV, 60). *ABC*, 19 Feb 1936, reported the rumour that Azaña wanted Martínez Barrio to take power, but the latter thought that Azaña must be Premier. On the 18th it was known in the Ministry of the Interior that the Left was sure of 240 seats—a majority. Martínez Barrio advised the President to transfer power to the Left to prevent the general strike.

81 *HCE*, II–9, 443; *HGL*, 422; Valdesoto, *Franco*, 105–6; F. Bertrán Güell, *Preparación y desarrollo del Alzamiento Nacional* (Valladolid, 1939), 24–5; Junta local del homenaje nacional, *José Calvo Sotelo* (Tarrasa, 1957), 22–3. The meeting was arranged over coffee in the afternoon by Calvo's friend Bau and Portela's secretary. Arrarás (*HSRE* IV, 58) says that Calvo only asked Portela not to hand over power. Gutiérrez-Ravé (*Gil Robles*, 156) says Calvo had telephoned Portela 48 hours previously. Gil Robles (*No fue posible*, 500–1) says he made the last unsuccessful effort to get Portela to stay on till March at 8 am on the 19th.

82 Bowers, *My Mission*, 193–4; *HGL*, 422; Gutiérrez-Ravé, *Las Cortes*, 32; Jackson, *Spanish Republic*, 195; Jellinek, *Civil War*, 220. The government of 19 Feb consisted of: Premier, Azaña; Interior, Salvador; Navy, Giral; Finance, G. Franco; Public Instruction, Domingo; Labour, Ramos; Agriculture, Ruiz Funes; Public Works, Casares Quiroga (all nine of *Izquierda Republicana*); Industry & Commerce, Álvarez-Buylla; Justice, Lara; Communications, Blasco Garzón (all three of *Unión Republicana*); War, Gen Masquelet (interim Gen Miaja). On 16 Apr, owing to the illness of Salvador, Casares Quiroga—also a sick man—took over the Ministry of the Interior. Sánchez Román declined an offer to join the government (Arrarás, *HSRE* IV, 62).

83 Gil Robles, interviewed in *El Debate*, 6 Mar 1936, and quoted by Jellinek, *Civil War*, 217. Timid Rightist voters probably did not go to the polling-booths for fear of Leftist violence. *El Debate*, 25 Feb 1936, explained that the CEDA had spent 1934 trying to win acceptance within the régime, and in 1935 had been hindered by its coalition partners: 'The CEDA, then, had neither the political tranquillity necessary, nor the homogeneity needed, nor the time strictly indispensable, for putting its essential plans into effect.'

84 Speeches of Contreras and Álvarez Robles to *Acción Popular Agraria*, León, in *El Debate*, 25 Feb 1936.

85 *El Debate*, 27 Feb 1936.

86 *ABC*, 19, 21 & 29 Feb 1936.

87 Quoted in *HGL*, 424. He told *Paris-Soir*: 'Before the elections we drew up a minimum reform programme. We intend to carry it out. I want to govern in accordance with the law. No dangerous innovations. We want peace and order, we are moderates' (quoted by Alba, *HSRE*, 178).

88 *El Debate*, 19 & 20 Feb 1936, which criticised those who scuttled abroad and caused a fall on the stock-exchange. Gil Robles, who on 19 Feb took a short rest, leaving the Republican Giménez Fernández in charge of the party, later attacked *Renovación Española*'s behaviour: 'since the Left's victory half the party, seized by an inexplicable panic, has fled abroad' (*ABC*, 22 Mar 1936).

89 *El Debate*, 20 Feb–1 Mar 1936. The Permanent Deputation had a Centre-Rightist majority since it represented the old Cortes. The amnesty was passed unanimously, but Goicoechea voted against the Catalan decree. The Court of Constitutional Guarantees now found the Law of 2 Jan 1935 (concerning Catalonia) to have been unconstitutional (*ABC*, 8 Mar 1936).

90 *El Debate*, 21, 23, 26 Feb & 1 Mar 1936.

91 Jellinek, *Civil War*, 223.

92 *El Debate*, 6 Mar 1936.

93 *ABC*, 29 Feb 1936.

94 *ABC*, 21 Feb 1936.

95 *O.c.*, 1033–7 & 1105–6. In *Arriba*, 5 Mar 1936, he wrote that the

fight was now 'Russia (or Asia) against Europe'; the Socialists and Communists had cast Azaña for the part of Kerensky (*O.c.*, 1039–45).

96 *ABC*, 1 & 10 Mar 1936.

97 All FE offices were closed on 27 Feb. Reprisals then began, and José Antonio soon officially ordered his men to 'go over to the offensive'. The leaders were arrested on 14 Mar, after an attempt on Jiménez de Asúa's life. José Antonio refused suggestions to flee to Portugal. The FE was suspended on 17 Mar and declared illegal on 17 Apr after a general strike by the UGT and CNT (*El Debate*, 28 Feb, 15 & 18 Mar, 18 Apr 1936; Ximénez, *JA*, 698–9 & 709; *Textos inéditos*, 358; Ansaldo, *¿ Para qué?*, 115; Payne, *Falange*, 99–100; Rama, *La crisis española*, 196).

98 Payne, *Falange*, 98 & 104; Jackson, *Spanish Republic*, 216; Bowers, *My Mission*, 253; & E. J. Hughes, *Report from Spain* (New York, 1947), 37, who estimates that 50–75,000 joined the FE between Feb and July 1936. In mid-June José Antonio claimed 10–15,000 *Japistas* had gone over to him and that the FE had 150,000 members (2,000 of them in gaol), being strongest in Valladolid, Madrid, Santander and Asturias (*Ultimos hallazgos*, 127–9). He ordered subordinates to hold firm to *Falangista* ideology and keep newcomers from positions of command; he forbade pacts with other groups (*O.c.*, 1105–6 & 1108).

99 In Mar the SEU and the AET fused in the *Frente Nacional Universitario*, but the Catholics refused to join (Ximénez, *JA*, 706–9). Some young *Cedistas* did co-operate with José Antonio nevertheless: Serrano Súñer, Avia, the Conde de Mayalde and Contreras. José Antonio had assigned the Ministry of Justice to Serrano Súñer in a hypothetical National-Syndicalist government (Gil Robles, *No fue posible*, 470).

100 *El Debate*, 15 Mar 1936; however, Gil Robles admits that some *Cedistas* did work with the *Falange*, but he turned down any suggestion that his party should abandon its legal tactic (*No fue posible*, 574).

101 Gil Robles talking to the Argentine press, in *ABC*, 22 Mar 1936. His gloss that only statements made to the Spanish press were authentic (*ABC*, 24 Mar 1936) seems to indicate that many *Cedistas* were not happy about this policy. In his *No fue posible*, 615–16, Gil Robles says he had constantly to fight against *Cedista* deputies who wanted to withdraw from the Cortes, but only two, Sierra Pomares and Srta Bohigas, actually went over to the *Bloque Nacional*.

102 *El Debate*, 24, 28 & 31 Mar 1936; *HGL*, 425; Plá, *HSRE* IV, 308; *DSC*, 31 Mar & 1 Apr 1936. The evidence presented was very confused: both sides accused the other of lying. The Left seemed to have the better case on Granada, a turbulent area in 1933. The Governor had obstructed the Left's campaign because there was a *Portelista*-Right list. The Right was said to have hired bands of

thugs. Some results were quaint, eg Huéscar de la Sierra: Right, 2,056; Left, o (voters, 2,056). The Right emphasised that 48,000 was a big majority. In the case of Cáceres, the Right claimed to have won by 18,000, basing their figures on municipal returns and the *Junta central del Censo*. The Left upheld the figures of the provincial *junta*, which gave it victory. The Right alleged that the Left had falsified the latter. In Galicia (Gil Robles, *Spain in Chains*, 10), the Governor of Lugo was said to have detained the Right's candidates and requisitioned their cars; in Corunna, the Right's candidates had been locked in the Governor's office and forced to sign a document admitting defeat at gunpoint; in Pontevedra (where Portela was just elected) government agents had seized returns from 230 wards and falsified these to the advantage of Portela and the Left. According to Alcalá-Zamora (cited in *HGL*, 425), the Left falsified the votes in Pontevedra and gave Portela another 22,000—sufficient for him to oust a Rightist from the list of those elected.

103   *El Debate*, 28, 29 & 31 Mar 1936. Prieto maintained a sphinx-like silence, but it was believed that he thought Portela's *acta* invalid.

104   *DSC*, 31 Mar 1936. Whereas Vallellano wanted only a brief withdrawal, Rodezno wanted Monarchists to renounce their seats since it was impossible 'to live with a government and a majority that are the negation of Spain' (*El Socialista*, 1 Apr 1936). According to Alcalá-Zamora (*Journal de Genève*, 17 Jan 1937), the Popular Front and the PNV acted arbitrarily in order to reduce the size of the opposition.

105   *DSC*, 1–3 Apr 1936. The *actas* committee had in fact quickly approved the Salamanca result: the Socialist minority then disagreed with the decision (*El Debate*, 21 Mar 1936). Calvo Sotelo returned to the Cortes to defend his *acta* since he thought it his duty to his electors though Parliament was now quite without significance (Acedo Colunga, *Calvo*, 298). Azaña and the Republicans voted for Calvo to avoid further antagonising the opposition (Duchess of Atholl, *Searchlight on Spain* [3rd ed, Harmondsworth, 1938], 49).

106   Viz 2 Carlists (one Lamamié de Clairac) and 2 *Cedistas* from Salamanca, on the grounds that they held office in agrarian unions that had bought wheat for the State under contract in 1935 (*El Debate*, 20 Mar & 5 Apr 1936). Therefore the relative strengths in the Cortes now were: Left, 261; Centre, 59; Right, 129.

107   *El Debate*, 28–30 Apr & 8 May 1936; *DSC*, 30 Apr & 22 May 1936; Gil Robles, *No fue posible*, 557–61.

108   *El Debate*, 28, 30 Apr, 2 & 12 May 1936; Prieto, *El Socialista*, 2 May 1936; *DSC*, 30 Apr & 2 June 1936; *HGL*, 440–2; *HCE*, II–9, 488; Payne, *Falange*, 106; Bravo, *Falange*, 173–4; Arrarás, *Franco*, 170; B. Félix Maíz, *Alzamiento en España* (Pamplona, 1952), 82. Serrano Súñer suggested Franco so that he could be brought back from the Canaries and be able to conspire with parliamentary immunity. Cortés Cavanillas (conversation) visited José Antonio in gaol but

found him adamant: he hated Franco because the latter had once insulted the Dictator in Morocco. Franco announced his withdrawal ostensibly because 'when the funds of the workers' organisations are devoted to political bribery, the purchase of arms and munitions, and the hiring of gunmen and assassins, democracy, as represented by universal suffrage, has ceased to exist'. The government had at first decreed new elections (the *actas* had been annulled) for 3 May, with a second contest if need be on 17 May. Then the provincial *junta del censo* 'discovered' that no candidate had polled the requisite 40 per cent on 16 Feb. The *Junta central del Censo* said Parliament must decide on the issue, but the government simply upheld the provincial *junta*'s view. José Antonio, if elected, would have been released. Some wards on 3 May recorded more votes cast than there were electors. See also Gil Robles, *No fue posible*, 561–72, & García Venero, *Fanjul*, 208–14 & 226–9.

109 Azaña, *DSC*, 3 Apr 1936; Alcalá-Zamora, *Journal de Genève*, 17 Jan 1937. The government asked him to sign a decree accepting the resignations of the Governors of Cádiz, Murcia, Granada and Logroño, who had allowed churches to burn without ordering the police to intervene. Alcalá-Zamora insisted that the decree say that they had been dismissed, since they had not offered to resign. The government did not agree. According to Gil Robles, *Spain in Chains*, 12, the Governor of Logroño actually led a mob that burnt seven churches in an afternoon. President and Premier had communicated by messenger for three weeks. The cabinet decided to oust the President on 2 Apr (Jellinek, *Civil War*, 237–8, who adds that Alcalá-Zamora was thought to want Sanjurjo as the next President). According to Gil Robles, *No fue posible*, 580–3, Azaña did not hide his contempt for Alcalá-Zamora while the latter, who was said to be thinking of dissolving the Cortes, claimed that his telephone was being tapped on government orders.

110 *DSC*, 3 & 7 Apr, & *El Debate*, 4 & 8 Apr 1936; Lerroux, *Pequeña historia*, 540–50. On 3 Apr the CEDA and Centre-Right voted against Prieto's interpretation; *Portelistas* and Monarchists abstained. On 7 Apr the Right abstained, but 5 *Portelistas* voted against his dismissal. Artic 81 allowed the President to dissolve the Cortes twice only. The decree of 7 Jan referred to dissolution of 'the first ordinary Cortes of the Republic' (*El Socialista*, 8 Jan 1936). *El Socialista*, 18 Dec 1935, openly asked for a dissolution—which indeed had been the Left's aim for the previous two years. Madariaga, *Spain*, 454, calls the episode 'the most glaring denial of logic the history of a free nation can show'. Companys observed that the movement of October 1934 had now been completely successful (*El Debate*, 9 Apr 1936), Calvo Sotelo that here was proof that the Revolution devours its leaders (*ABC*, 8 Apr 1936).

111 *El Debate*, 13, 17, 24, 25 Mar, 15, 17 Apr, 5, 10 May 1936, supplemented by Buckley, *Spanish Republic*, 200–6; *HGL*, 436; Jellinek,

Civil War, 242–5; & R. García, *El bulo de los caramelos* (Madrid, 1953), 3 & 9–12. The UME and *Falangistas* were ordered to attend Los Reyes's funeral armed (Cacho Zabalza, *UME*, 25).

112 Jackson, *Spanish Republic*, 214–15. On 28 Apr Anarchists killed the separatist Badía brothers in Barcelona (*El Debate*, 29 Apr 1936).

113 *DSC*, 15 Apr 1936. Between 16 Feb and 2 Apr the following took place: Assaults and destruction of political offices, 58; of public and private buildings, 72; of private houses, 33; of churches, 36. Burnings of political offices, 12; of public and private buildings, 45; of private houses, 15; of churches, 106 (56 completely destroyed). General strikes, 11. Riots, 169. Shooting affrays, 39. Assaults, 85. Highway robberies, 24. Dead, 74. Injured, 345. Details of each incident were appended to the record of the session. (Highway robberies were usually ascribed to the *Socorro Rojo Internacional*, which officially collected funds for victims of the Asturian repression.)

114 *DSC*, 15 Apr 1936. Ventosa (*Lliga*) also asked Azaña to be firm and told him to beware of a *glissement à gauche*. Since police protection for churches was often not assured, Catholic volunteers guarded them themselves—but often they were arrested for infringing the laws of public assembly (Mendizábal, *Martyrdom*, 259).

115 *DSC*, 15 & 16 Apr 1936.

116 *DSC*, 6 May 1936. In this session Calvo Sotelo presented his statistics for the period 1 Apr–4 May: Dead, 47. Injured, 216 (200 seriously). Strikes, 38. Bombs and petards, 53. Fires, 52 (mostly churches). Robberies, assaults, lootings, etc, 99. Number of 'Fascists' now detained, 8–12,000 (estimated).

117 Llopis, *DSC*, 15 Apr 1936, who said Socialists would support the government so as to implement the Popular Front's programme, but they did not renounce their own aims. Leftist charges of Rightist provocation referred not only to the deeds of *Falangistas* when these could be cited, but also were used to justify *émeutes* on the grounds that these were the inevitable sequel to the Centre-Right's 'black biennium'. Socialists therefore implicitly admitted that the extreme Left was causing disorder.

118 *El Socialista*, 2 May 1936 (Prieto's May Day speech at Cuenca).

119 Largo Caballero, *Recuerdos*, 140–4 & 150.

120 Prieto, quoted in Jellinek, *Civil War*, 230.

121 Largo Caballero, *Recuerdos*, 153–4.

122 Largo's speech on 5 Apr, in *Claridad*, 6 Apr & *El Socialista*, 7 Apr 1936. Interviewed in *L'Intransigeant*, 6 Mar 1936, Largo said that the hour for the Socialist conquest of power had not yet come, but if the government continued to be conservative, the Socialists would stage a revolution, for which undertaking they were adequately armed.

123 Largo Caballero, *Recuerdos*, 148, claimed that Prieto had ousted *Caballeristas* from the executive by sharp practice.

124 *Claridad*, originally a weekly, became an evening daily on 6 April 1936. In March the *Agrupación Madrileña* elections resulted in 1,554 votes for the *Caballeristas* and 474 for González Peña's centrists (*El Debate*, 8 Mar 1936). This influential body declared that the aim was the Socialist conquest of power by any means available in order to install the dictatorship of the proletariat (Broué & Témime, *La révolution*, 67).

125 Cattell, *Communism*, 33; *El Debate*, 27 Mar, *Claridad*, 6 Apr & *El Socialista*, 7 Apr 1936, & Arrarás, *HSRE* IV, 143–7, who says the Socialist Youth had 40,000 members to the Communist Youth's 3,000. Cattell, who says some northern branches under Prieto's influence did not join, gives much higher figures.

126 Sra Ibárruri said the PCE did not think the Cortes very important: 'the struggle in the street to mobilise the masses [is] our essential objective' (*ABC*, 13 Mar 1936). Largo has been described as a 'Titoist before Tito' (by D. Sevilla Andrés, *Historia política de la zona roja* [Madrid, 1954], 178).

127 Largo Caballero, *Claridad*, 11 & 13 Apr 1936.

128 *ABC*, 23 Apr 1936. The *Lliga*, Conservatives and *Portelistas* said that they would take part.

129 *El Debate*, 24 Apr 1936.

130 *ABC*, 26 Apr 1936.

131 *El Debate*, 3 & 5 May 1936.

132 Prieto's account, in *El Socialista*, 29 Apr 1936; & *Claridad*, 22 & 24 Apr 1936, which said that no Socialist could be President save Largo Caballero, whom the Republicans would not accept. Cf Gil Robles, *No fue posible*, 591–600.

133 *El Debate*, 12 May 1936. The Monarchists absented themselves. The voting was: Azaña, 754; González Peña, 2; Largo Caballero, 1; Lerroux, 1; Primo de Rivera, 1; blank, 88.

134 *Claridad*, 6, 7, 9 May & *El Socialista*, 9 May 1936. The JSU and the UGT announced that if a Socialist entered the government, they would go it alone outside the Popular Front.

135 Prieto, *El Socialista*, 26 May 1936; Bolloten, *Grand Camouflage*, 303. The Socialist minority defeated the idea of a *Prietista* government by 49 votes to 19 (M. García Venero, *Historia de las Internacionales en España, tomo II* [Madrid, 1957], 502).

136 *El Debate*, 13 May 1936. Azaña consulted party leaders from the Communists to the CEDA (inclusive). The government of 12 May was: Premier & War, Casares Quiroga; State, Barcia; Interior, Moles; Navy, Giral; Finance, Ramos; Public Instruction, F. Barnés; Public Works, Velao Oñate; Agriculture, Ruiz Funes (all 8 of *Izquierda Republicana*); Justice, Blasco Garzón; Industry & Commerce, Álvarez-Buylla; Communications, Giner de los Ríos (all 3 of *Unión Republicana*); Labour, Lluhí (*Esquerra*).

137 Arrarás, *HSRE* IV, 273–6 (account based on information from Giménez Fernández); Gil Robles, *No fue posible*, 616–23 & 625–6.

Prieto's suggestion of 14 May was conveyed to Gil Robles on the 15th by Larraz. It would seem that about 40 *Cedista* deputies would have actively supported such a government. Loyal supporters of Gil Robles considered Prieto 'a patriot', unlike Largo Caballero (Martín Artajo, conversation). With reference to the negotiations, Gil Robles (conversation) says Prieto 'would not give an inch'. *HGL*, 450, mentions abortive negotiations between Gil Robles and Prieto for a government of seven *Prietistas* with Left Republican and *Cedista* representation—but wrongly puts the episode in late June. According to Araquistáin's later testimony, revolutionary Socialists decided to back Azaña for President and then veto Prieto for Premier to ensure that government remained in weak hands (Gil Robles, *No fue posible*, 599–600).

138   *DSC*, 19 May 1936.
139   Between 16 Feb and 20 May, 40 *Falangistas* were killed and over 100 injured. The *Falange* administered its own form of lynch-law: eg at Carrión de los Condes in May, Socialists shot the local FE leader; the next day, *Falangistas* strung up various local Socialists on trees by the roadside (Bravo, *Falange*, 191).
140   *DSC*, 19 May 1936.
141   *DSC*, 19 May 1936. The party's secretary, Carrascal, said that *Cedistas* were being arrested and imprisoned in all areas simply because they were *Cedistas* (*El Debate*, 16 May 1936).
142   *El Debate*, 10 May 1936.
143   Pérez de Laborda, *El Debate*, 17 May 1936. He emphasised that 'the JAP is where it was, and all rumours circulated concerning its disappearance or fusion with *Falange* are totally false'.
144   *DSC*, 19 May 1936. The Right heatedly opposed the introduction by the government of a bill to set up a 'special court to bring to account judges, magistrates and prosecutors' (*DSC*, 3 June 1936) but the bill became law on 13 June.
145   *DSC*, 29 May 1936.
146   *ABC*, 29 Apr 1936 (the motion was therefore defeated).
147   *El Debate*, 20, 21, 26, 27 May, 2 & 3 June 1936; *DSC*, 3 June 1936.
148   *DSC*, 20 May & 4 June 1936; *El Debate*, 6 June 1936. The *Cedista* deputies said that if Martínez Barrio (President of the Cortes) did not give some assurance to the Right, the *Minoría Popular Agraria* 'would decide on irrevocable separation from a Parliament in which a minimum of coexistence is not decently possible'. Most deputies wanted definitive withdrawal (Gil Robles, *No fue posible*, 699–700).
149   Members of the DRV, in particular, protested against persecution; eg Duato said 100,000 people in the diocese of Valencia had been deprived of spiritual assistance because Mayors had expelled priests and locked churches, quite apart from the fact that 40 churches and 14 rectories had been burnt down in the diocese in 3 months (*DSC*, 17 June 1936). Pabón (CEDA) said that in central Castile in the 25 days up to 15 May, 79 schools (with 5,095 pupils) had been burnt

down or closed by unauthorised persons (*DSC*, 4 June 1936). The government voted 16,500,000 ptas towards building more State schools (*DSC*, 30 June 1936).

150 García Venero, *Nacionalismo catalán*, 540–1; Ossorio, *Companys*, 148–55; Cardó, *Histoire spirituelle*, 245; Peers, *Catalonia*, 241–2.

151 *DSC*, 15 Apr 1936; *ABC*, 16 Apr 1936; Ramos Oliveira, *Politics*, 423. The draft text introduced in Apr bore the signatures of Basque Socialists and Republicans as well as Nationalists. It was sponsored by Prieto and supported by the Popular Front and the *Lliga*.

152 *El Debate*, 26 & 30 June 1936, which reported the official result of voting in Corunna as 36,311 in favour, 82 against, with 52 blank votes. The paper said that a very much smaller proportion of the 39,000 electors had in fact gone to the polls. Complete official figures said 993,531 voted in favour and 6,161 against, out of an electorate of 1,343,335; in reality the poll was much lower (Arrarás, *HSRE* IV, 219–20).

153 According to reports in *El Debate*, 26 & 31 May, & *ABC*, 28 May 1936; see also Arrarás, *HSRE* IV, 218.

154 *El Debate*, 17, 22, 23 & 26 May 1936; Royo Villanova, *30 años*, 273–5. Although *ABC*, 21 May 1936, claimed that Calvo Sotelo had suggested the idea, its main proponents were, apart from Silió, Calderón and the *Cedistas* Cortés and Álvarez Robles. Some were probably sincere in wanting to put into practice, as they saw it, the ideas of Menéndez Pelayo on regionalism. The purpose of the projected statute was to be protection of the region against other regions' claims on the central power by getting adequate economic help for irrigation, etc; also to strengthen municipal government and counteract domination by the capital, and to preserve 'the peculiar vigour of the Castilian spirit'.

155 *DSC*, 17 & 30 Apr, 7 May & 24 June (Apps), & 21–28 May 1936.

156 *DSC*, 26 June & 1 July 1936 (speeches of Berjano, Álvarez Robles, Rebuelta and Zabalza).

157 *El Debate*, 9, 15 Apr, & 5 May 1936; *ABC*, 10 Apr 1936. Abolition of price-levels gave the advantage to the larger grower who could produce more cheaply. Giménez Fernández suggested a multiple answer: co-operatives, dearer bread, State purchasing of wheat and cheaper credit.

158 *DSC*, 15 & 29 Apr 1936; Bolloten, *Grand Camouflage*, 21–2. The Socialist Landworkers' newspaper in February said labourers 'must resolve the agrarian problem by themselves in such a way that the Popular Front government need only give legal form to realities which the peasant organisations have already created'. Seizures of land began in March and were well organised in Extremadura, where 60,000 peasants acted on a single day. About 535,000 hectares had been occupied by 17 July (Malefakis, *Land Tenure*, Part II, ch x).

159 *El Debate*, 29 Mar & 17 & 24 June 1936 (a reaper's wage for a 7-hour

day was now 13·50 ptas); *ABC*, 26 June & 2 July 1936; Bolloten, *Grand Camouflage*, 20; & *DSC*, 1 July 1936. Calvo's speech provoked a near-riot in the Cortes on the part of the extreme Left. Mije (Communist) replied: 'Yes we shall pass: today with the democratic Republic; and tomorrow with something else.' There were as many agricultural strikes between 1 May and 18 July as in the whole of 1932 (Malefakis, loc cit).

160 *ABC*, 29 Feb 1936. This paper on 3 Mar called the decree 'proper to a revolutionary dictatorship'.

161 Bermúdez Cañete, *DSC*, 30 Apr 1936.

162 Bolloten, *Grand Camouflage*, 22–3; Jellinek, *Civil War*, 225; J. Álvarez del Vayo, *Freedom's Battle* (London, 1940), 23. Unemployment on 29 Feb stood at 843,872 (*El Socialista*, 25 Apr 1936). According to Ministry of Labour figures there were 719 industrial strikes between 1 May and 18 July, more than in any previous 12-month period (Malefakis, loc cit). Gil Robles, *Spain in Chains*, 14, writes: 'strikes were not aimed at obtaining economic reforms which were more or less justified'; workers in a *pueblo* in Málaga demanded 30 ptas for a 4-hour day.

163 *El Debate*, 5 Mar, 19 & 24 May 1936; García-Nieto, *Sindicalismo cristiano*, 190–1. In the Cortes, a Socialist said that Catholic workers were 'not workers; they are lackeys in the service of the bosses'. D. de Madariaga replied: 'Your mentality is always the same: a man who does not submit to your yoke is a man who is condemned to die of hunger' (*DSC*, 20 May 1936).

164 García-Nieto, *Sindicalismo cristiano*, 193.

165 *ABC*, 3, 17, 19 May 1936; *DSC*, 15 Apr, 6 & 19 May, 30 June 1936. Socialists said Rightists had taken 500,000,000 ptas out of Spain since 16 Feb, and pointed out that the Bank of Spain was still paying dividends of up to 30 per cent in May. Calvo presented figures to illustrate his case: the value of Spanish securities on the stock-exchange fell by 1,936,000,000 ptas between 14 Feb and 11 Apr; between 14 Feb and 4 Apr the amount of paper-money in circulation rose from 4,850,000,000 to 5,330,000,000 ptas; in the same period the peseta lost 12–14 per cent of its value on the Paris market. *The Economist*, 27 June 1936, quoted the official rate in London as 36·95 ptas to the £, but reported a black-market rate of 45 ptas.

166 *DSC*, 19 May 1936.

167 Ceballos (CEDA), *DSC*, 8 July 1936; *El Debate*, 30 May & 2 July 1936.

168 Carrascal, *DSC*, 11 June 1936; & *El Debate*, 13 June 1936, quoting a cabinet statement publicly appealing to Governors and Mayors to put an end to the usurpation of authority by armed bands. Four Governors were changed on 13 June (*El Debate*, 14 June 1936).

169 E. Conze, *Spain To-Day* (London, 1936), 141–2. Arrarás, *HSRE* IV, 143. The parallel with Russia in 1917 was clear.

170 Largo Caballero, *Claridad*, 11 May 1936. In one speech (*Claridad*, 11 Apr 1936), he talked vaguely of the Cortes lasting four years, but in other speeches he gave the impression that revolution would not be so long delayed.
171 Peirats, *La CNT*, I, 115–16.
172 *El Socialista*, 17, 19, 22 May & 3 June 1936. The paper explained that the French Popular Front stood for a renewal of democracy in the face of Fascism, and for advanced social legislation without full Socialism—ie it had the same aims as had Prieto.
173 *El Socialista*, 2 & 7 June 1936; & Madariaga, *Spain*, 456 (quoting Prieto's account).
174 *El Debate*, 11 June, & *ABC* & *El Socialista*, 12–13 June 1936, on the shooting in Málaga. Largo Caballero and Díaz (Communist) were whistled at by Anarcho-Syndicalists in Saragossa on their visit there, while in Madrid the CNT's building-workers were on strike in defiance of the UGT (*El Debate*, 2 June & *ABC*, 8 & 14 July 1936). CNT offices were closed in Madrid after bomb-attacks were made on bars where waiters were not obeying orders to strike (*ABC*, 30 May 1936).
175 *El Debate*, 26 May & 1 July; *El Socialista*, 1 & 15 July; & *Claridad*, 18 June & 1 July 1936. *Caballeristas* said that their list for the executive had got some 22,000 votes; according to *Prietistas*, their list won by 12,000 votes to the *Caballeristas'* 11,000. In the plebiscite for a special congress, the results given by the *Prietistas* were: in favour, 13,427; votes declared invalid, 10,573 (total party membership, 59,846).
176 Maura, Prieto, Sánchez Román, Los Ríos and others canvassed the idea of a 'government with full powers' in early June, but *Caballeristas* and Casares were against it. Maura wrote six articles in *El Sol* from 18 June (Gil Robles, *No fue posible*, 679–86; Arrarás, *HSRE* IV, 276–82).
177 *DSC*, 16 June 1936.
178 He produced what he said were incomplete figures for disorders between 16 Feb and 15 June: Churches totally destroyed, 160; assaults on and attempted burning or sacking of churches, 251. Dead, 269; injured, 1,287. Attempted assaults on persons, 215. Robberies, 138. Attempted robberies, 138. Private and political offices wrecked, 69; assaulted, 312. General strikes, 113; strikes, 228. Newspaper offices totally wrecked, 10; assaulted and attempts to wreck, 33. Bombs and petards, 146 (plus 78 seized before exploding). Gil Robles had earlier been accused of trying to split the Popular Front when the Right abstained from voting on the Yeste incident (*DSC*, 29 May 1936), in which 17 peasants and 1 Civil Guard had been killed: the Minister ordered an inquiry. For the Right, this was perhaps a test-case to see whether the government would support its servants against Socialists and Communists. *Unión Republicana* had protested against Socialist violence in

Murcia, and the Governor had threatened to resign if the government gave him no support (*El Debate*, 23, 25 Apr & 5 May 1936). Gil Robles's change of policy possibly upset some of his followers: there were reports that Republicans in the CEDA were about to leave it and join the 'conservative sector of the Republic' (*El Socialista*, 17 June 1936); Jellinek (*Civil War*, 252) says that Lucía approached M. Maura.

179   *El Socialista*, 17 June 1936.

180   *DSC*, 16 June 1936. There was obvious personal animosity between the two Gallegos: for Casares, Calvo was a hated 'man of order', a dreaded Fascist; for Calvo, Casares was an opportunist *señorito* demagogue who had once harangued Anarchists.

181   This development may perhaps be illustrated by the poll taken on who should be Head of State by the Madrid Catholic evening paper *Ya*, showing a relative swing away from the moderates, viz José Antonio, 38,496; Calvo Sotelo, 29,522; Gil Robles, 29,201; Lerroux, 27,624; Sanjurjo, 25,874; Alfonso XIII, 25,638; Royo Villanova, 23,887; Martínez Anido, 20,176; D. Juan, 18,502; Ortega Gasset, 16,875 (Bravo, *Falange*, 180).

182   The exact words used are disputed, and only traces of some of the threats appear in the Cortes record. For this, two explanations can be advanced: (*i*) it was usual for the President of the Cortes to order the deletion of 'unparliamentary' remarks from the official record; (*ii*) in the frequent moments of uproar some heated exchanges were probably only heard by some deputies. Rightists allege that the following threats were made: Díaz Ramos (Communist) on 15 Apr: 'I cannot be sure how Sr. Gil Robles will die, but I can affirm that he will die with his boots on.' Calvo's life was threatened on 7 May by Srta Nelken (Socialist); and on 1 July by Sra Ibárruri (who said: 'This man has spoken today for the last time') and by Galarza (Socialist), who said that violence against Calvo would be licit (see A. de Urbina, 'Calvo Sotelo', *Punta Europa*, July–Aug 1958, 111; & Gutiérrez-Ravé, *Las Cortes errantes*, 58). From *DSC*, 15 Apr & 1 July 1936, it seems certain that threats were made by Díaz and Galarza; Ibárruri (*El único camino*, 251) denies making any threat.

183   According to *Causa General*, 6–7, Alonso Mallol (Director-General of Police) changed Calvo's police escort. Then Aguirre Sánchez (i.c. personnel at Madrid Police HQ) told the new escort not to hinder any attempt at assassination, and even to help do the job if an attack should take place outside the city. One of the escort told Bau, a friend of Calvo. Calvo then saw Moles, who did not really believe the story. According to *HGL*, 452–4, Calvo's escort was again changed on 12 July—this source refers to a vague scheme to kill him, without a definite plan, which existed from mid-June and involved the Under-Secretary for the Interior, an ex-Captain, and Condés and Moreno. On 10 July Calvo's friends bought him an armoured Buick which he refused to use because people

would say that he thought he was Mussolini (Bau Nolla, conversation). Cortés Cavanillas (conversation) says he told Calvo on 10 July of a report from a Monarchist spy in the Madrid *Casa del Pueblo* that there was a plot to kill him; Calvo did not take the report seriously.

184 Castillo was a 'known Communist' (Jellinek, *Civil War*, 262). It would seem that he was shot by *Falangistas*—though the UME and Traditionalists have also been suggested (Buckley, *Spanish Republic*, 205; *El Estado que queremos*, 66)—because he had shot a cousin of José Antonio during clashes at Los Reyes's funeral on 16 April (*HGL*, 453). According to Gil Robles, Castillo, Condés, Moreno, González Peña and others had talked of killing Rightist leaders in May after Faraudo's assassination. He also says his own escort was changed in July, but despite his protests it was not changed back until after Calvo's death (*No fue posible*, 639–40 & 747–8).

185 *Causa General*, 8–10; *HGL*, 453–4; Acedo, *Calvo*, 330–42; Jackson, *Spanish Republic*, 229. B. Bentura, 'Hoy hace veinte años', *Ya*, 13 July 1956, gives a different version, according to which Moreno, Condés and Castillo intended to kill Calvo, but Castillo got cold feet, whereupon the other two got rid of Castillo; on 13 July, Castillo's brother said that Assault Guards had killed him. Gil Robles was in Biarritz; an account by a member of the expedition assigned to his house is given by V. Reguengo, *Guerra sin frentes* (3rd ed, Barcelona, 1955), 256. Several accounts say Casares Quiroga sanctioned the expeditions: this seems 'not proven'. See also the accounts in Arrarás, *HSRE* IV, 346–60, & Gil Robles, *No fue posible*, 749–65.

186 *El Debate*, 14 July 1936; Madariaga, *Spain*, 460. *El Socialista*, 14 July 1936, also condemned both murders.

187 *El Socialista*, 14 July 1936; Jellinek, *Civil War*, 263 (Largo Caballero was in London at the time).

188 *El Debate*, 15 July 1936; *El Estado que queremos*, 65; *HCE*, II–9, 543. Cf Gil Robles, *No fue posible*, 760–2.

189 *El Socialista*, 15 July 1936. The article was reprinted from *El Liberal* (Bilbao), 14 July. Prieto later said he knew of the date of the military rising from a Bilbao businessman (Gil Robles, *No fue posible*, 739).

190 On 13 July the President of the Cortes suspended sessions for 8 days, but the Permanent Deputation had to meet to renew the 'state of alarm'. For the official record of this session, see Díaz-Plaja, *La guerra*, 119–48; cf Arrarás, *HSRE* IV, 369–89.

191 Uncensored text of Vallellano's speech in Gutiérrez-Ravé, *Las Cortes errantes*, 99–100. Martínez Barrio caused some remarks about the crime being committed by the government's agents to be deleted from the official record.

192 He produced statistics of events, proved beyond doubt to have taken place, between 16 June and 13 July: Church-burnings, 10; abuse

and expulsion of priests, 9; thefts and confiscations, 11; pulling down of crosses, 5. Dead, 61; injured, 224. Highway robberies, 17. Invasions of and attacks on estates, 32; confiscations and thefts, 16. Offices attacked or burnt, 10. General strikes, 15; strikes, 129. Bombs, 74; petards, 58; bottles of inflammable liquid thrown at persons or things, 7; fires (other than churches), 19. His final words were those which Martínez Barrio had used against Azaña's government after the Casas Viejas affair in 1933.

193 According to Jellinek, *Civil War*, 265, Gil Robles said at the end of the session: 'Right! And now let justice take its course!' Most of the deputies of the Centre and Right left Madrid after the session. Prieto tried to persuade Casares—who had not attended—to arrest the Right's deputies (Gil Robles, *No fue posible*, 768-9).

194 *El Debate*, 22 Feb 1936. According to Gil Robles, these postings were the work of the *Unión Militar Republicana Antifascista*, a rival to the UME founded in 1934 and now influential in the War Ministry. Also, from late 1935 Communist cells were started in the garrisons under the supervision of Líster (*No fue posible*, 706-7 & 719).

195 A. Ruiz Vilaplana, *Burgos Justice* (London, 1938), 79; Arrarás, *Franco*, 168; *HCE*, II-9, 468; *HGL*, 430. Goded was very indignant about being sent to Palma 'to play bridge with the English'.

196 He saw José Antonio, who told him the *Falange*'s strength; the go-between was the *Cedista* Serrano Súñer, an old friend of José Antonio and Franco's brother-in-law (*HCE*, II-9, 467-8; Payne, *Falange*, 281). He also contacted the Carlists through a *Falangista* and was told they would only participate in a Monarchist movement (*HGL*, 430-1).

197 Mariñas, *Varela*, 66; Pemán, *Soldado*, 138.

198 Galinsoga, *Centinela*, 187, who gives the date as 8 March.

199 Date given by Ramos Oliveira, *Politics*, 545.

200 Account based on *HGL*, 429-30; Pemán, *Soldado*, 138-40; Mariñas, *Varela*, 67-8; J. M. Iribarren, *El general Mola* (2nd ed, Madrid, 1945), 43; *HCE*, II-9, 467. There is some disagreement as to who was present: here Delgado's account (in Pemán, loc cit) has been preferred. Franco had earlier exchanged views with Varela. According to Romano, *Sanjurjo*, 188, Sanjurjo had favoured a *coup* before the elections. Sanjurjo, head of the UME, was kept informed of developments in Estoril (Esteban-Infantes, *Sanjurjo*, 251-3).

201 Synthesis of Pemán, *Soldado*, 140-3; Mariñas, *Varela*, 68-70; *HCE*, II-9, 510; *HGL*, 436-7 (the accounts differ on some points—as usual). Fanjul was to raise the garrison in Burgos, Villegas that in Tarragona, González Carrasco that in Barcelona. They presumably counted on a 'negative *pronunciamiento*' elsewhere. When Mola arrived in Pamplona, he told Félix Maíz: 'The organisation of a rising like the one projected, and the conditions in which it is going to be carried out, ... has the minimum of possibilities of success and

the maximum of probabilities of failure' (*Alzamiento*, 54). Cf Payne's account (*The Military*, 319–20) which makes Fanjul the moving spirit behind this attempted *coup*.

202 Iribarren, *Mola*, 41.

203 See *HGL*, 429 & 437; Pemán, *Soldado*, 147; Lizarza, *Memorias*, 79; Félix Maíz, *Alzamiento*, 71; *HCE*, II–9, 511; Esteban-Infantes, *Sanjurjo*, 253; J. Vigón, *General Mola* (Barcelona, 1957), 91. Some versions suggest that Mola was now Sanjurjo's delegate and in full charge of the conspiracy; Vigón's version, that Mola considered himself Sanjurjo's delegate at this stage but had not yet in fact been appointed as such, would seem to be the correct one. Certainly Mola was now fully in charge of military plotting in the north.

204 Félix Maíz, *Alzamiento*, 72 & 100; Esteban-Infantes, *Sanjurjo*, 254; Pemán, *Soldado*, 149 & 154; A. Olmedo Delgado & J. Cuesta Monereo, *General Queipo de Llano* (Barcelona, 1957), 84–9. He specialised in contacting Civil and Assault Guard officers; the garrisons he found unenthusiastic, and was rebuffed by the officers of Granada, Huelva and Málaga. (When Alcalá-Zamora was deposed, the Cortes delegation found him at home with Queipo de Llano and Samper—*ABC*, 8 Apr 1936.) Apparently Queipo, who later claimed to have initiated the conspiracy, first saw Mola on 13 or 15 Apr and found him very guarded. An emissary later contacted Cabanellas and Mola met him near Tudela in June, when he got his promise to rise and the vital assurance that 10–12,000 rifles and ammunition would be sent to Pamplona on the day (Arrarás, *HSRE* IV, 299 & 304–5; Gil Robles, *No fue posible*, 722–5).

205 I. Bernard, *Mola* (Granada, 1938), 83–7; Iribarren, *Mola*, 45–7; Pemán, *Soldado*, 148. Arrarás (conversation) stresses that as far as Mola was concerned, meetings and contacts up to this point were merely exchanges of impressions; now he started to conspire seriously.

206 Pemán, *Soldado*, 149 (quoting Varela). Mola and Franco favoured detailed preparations; Varela and Orgaz continued to urge speed (Pemán, *Soldado*, 157).

207 *HGL*, 443; *HCE*, II–9, 510; Romano, *Sanjurjo*, 202. Payne (*The Military*, 321) refers to a plan by López de Ochoa to persuade Alcalá-Zamora to oust the government at this time, but the deposed President would not co-operate. López de Ochoa is said to have been the UME leader at this time in Madrid, the UME having turned against Fanjul.

208 Vigón, *Mola*, 92; Iribarren, *Mola*, 51; Esteban-Infantes, *Sanjurjo*, 251–4; Félix Maíz, *Alzamiento*, 103. This decision was conveyed by the go-between 'Garcilaso' (R. García, independent Rightist deputy for Navarre and editor of the *Diario de Navarra*), who had been sent to Estoril by Mola to inquire about the position of the Carlists. The date is variously given as 29 or 31 May.

209 Iribarren, *Mola*, 51–2; *HGL*, 447. The four columns were to start out from Valencia, Valladolid, Saragossa and Navarre (the latter being joined by forces from Burgos and Logroño).

210 Esteban-Infantes, *Sanjurjo*, 251–3.

211 *Documentos de Alfonso Carlos*, 293. The Council of the Communion was: J. M. Lamamié de Clairac, L. H. de Larramendi, E. Bilbao Eguía, L. M. Alier and M. Senante, with Fal Conde as president. As Arrarás, *HSRE* IV, 8, notes, there were no Navarrese on the Council—which meant a victory for Fal Conde over his rivals.

212 Some (including Larramendi) thought the next legitimate heir Duarte (descended from a daughter of Carlos IV who married João VI of Portugal); some wanted the descendants of Francisco de Paula (younger brother of Fernando VII), which would have meant Alfonso XIII; others favoured Juan. But the *Juanista* solution was bitterly opposed by veterans and military elements, who wanted the succession to pass to the female closest to the last male (they invoked the 'Semisalic Law of Felipe V'), ie to Blanca, eldest daughter of Carlos VII, now an Austrian Archduchess, and to her heirs (Oyarzun, *Carlismo*, 470–1; Melgar, *Escisión dinástica*, 136).

213 Oyarzun, *Carlismo*, 467–8; *Documentos de Alfonso Carlos*, 295; *HCE*, II–9, 421; Lizarza, *Memorias*, 192. The idea was suggested and the decree drafted by Larramendi. The Regent and the eventual successor were to swear publicly to uphold 'the foundations of Spanish Legitimacy, to wit: I. The Roman Apostolic Catholic Religion, with the unity and juridical consequences with which it was traditionally beloved and served in our Kingdoms. II. The natural and organic Constitution of the States and public bodies of traditional society. III. The historic progeny of the diverse regions and their *fueros* and liberties, components of the unity of the Spanish *Patria*. IV. The authentic traditional Monarchy, legitimate in origin and exercise. V. The principles and spirits and, insofar as is possible in practice, the same state of law and law-making anterior to the evil so-called new law.'

214 Oyarzun, *Carlismo*, 465–6; Galindo, *Los partidos*, 307. The Navarrese, Basque and Catalan delegates opposed adherence to the *Bloque*.

215 *Documentos de Alfonso Carlos*, 299–301: Alfonso had refused to abdicate, and neither he nor his sons had shown any inclination to accept Traditionalism. In a letter written to Fal Conde on 8 July 1936, but never sent, Alfonso Carlos stated that he favoured Javier as his successor (*Documentos*, 319–20).

216 Lizarza, *Memorias*, 193; Melgar, *Escisión dinástica*, 139. Archduchess Blanca was keen to uphold her sons' rights, and in Vienna on 30 May her youngest son signed the principles of Traditionalism in the hope of becoming Carlos VIII. The *Cruzadistas* (ie the dissidents of *El Cruzado Español*) officially styled themselves *Comunión Carlista—Núcleo de la Lealtad* (*ABC*, 4 Feb 1936).

217 Redondo & Zavala, *Requeté*, 345–8; Romano, *Sanjurjo*, 202. The Junta consisted of: Gen Muslera, Cols Rada and Baselga, Regional Inspectors of *Requetés* and Capt Sanjurjo (the General's son). Exactly when Varela became Sanjurjo's delegate is not clear.

218 Redondo & Zavala, *Requeté*, 416: its members were asked to resign, but they said they were in permanent session, and ate and slept in the building. *El Debate*, 12–13 Mar 1936, reported that the government wanted to put in its own nominees, thus in effect ending the *régimen foral* so far as the people of Navarre was concerned.

219 Quoted in Del Burgo, *Requetés*, 175.

220 Redondo & Zavala, *Requeté*, 348–9; Galindo, *Los partidos*, 322; Lizarza, *Memorias*, 61; Iribarren, *Mola*, 75.

221 Redondo & Zavala, *Requeté*, 349–50; Iribarren, *Mola*, 75; Galindo, *Los partidos*, 321, who says Sanjurjo was to lead the *Requetés* from Cáceres on Madrid.

222 Félix Maíz, *Alzamiento*, 39–41 & 64–9; Lizarza, *Memorias*, 109; Cacho Zabalza, *UME*, 19 & 27. It is generally agreed that Mola had no contact with the Carlists till early June; in view of the Carlist plan, of the UME officers and of Mola's desire for civilian support, it seems odd that there was no contact earlier.

223 Redondo & Zavala, *Requeté*, 352–3. A sentence is quoted from Sanjurjo's letter to Mola: 'I need your decision; if you decide, I want you to represent me.' As Sanjurjo approved of Mola making military plans in the north from late April, and Javier visited Estoril in May, the 'decision' surely cannot refer to whether or not Mola would rise; possibly it referred to the political aims of the rising. An unpublished source (quoted in Payne, *The Military*, 323) suggests that Sanjurjo decided in mid-May that a rising by Mola with Carlist support was the best bet.

224 Bravo, *Falange*, 165–6.

225 Iribarren, *Mola*, 44.

226 *O.c.*, 763–9.

227 *O.c.*, 1108. The local leader in Álava was at this time negotiating on his own account with the Army and the Right (Gil Robles, *No fue posible*, 717).

228 Payne, *Falange*, 102 & 110; *HCE*, II–9, 511; *HGL*, 447.

229 Redondo & Zavala, *Requeté*, 356.

230 Buckley, *Spanish Republic*, 200; Bravo, *Falange*, 199 & 201. At his trial he characteristically emptied an ink-pot over the clerk of the court.

231 Félix Maíz, *Alzamiento*, 195. Apparently the idea of a *coup* in Madrid was raised yet again. In April Mola had prevented a rising in Burgos, and at the end of May officers in Valencia had to be restrained (Iribarren, *Mola*, 51 & 68).

232 These decrees were attacked by Calvo Sotelo (*DSC*, 16 June 1936) as an insult to military dignity. On 23 June Franco wrote to Casares Quiroga complaining that they had undermined morale by ending

promotion by seniority and by permitting the reinstatement of
officers dismissed by the Army since Oct 1934; he claimed that
90 per cent of the officer corps had no confidence in the new
appointments (Arrarás, *Franco*, 171–4).

233   On this incident, see Calvo Sotelo, *DSC*, 16 June 1936; Atholl,
      Searchlight, 60; Gannes & Repard, *Spain*, 132; & J. L. Jalón, *El
      Ejército español* (2nd ed, Madrid, 1959), 11.

234   In mid-May the Republican Gen García Caminero visited Pamplona
      and advised the government to relieve Mola of his command and
      disperse the garrison (Iribarren, *Mola*, 49–50). In July Gen Batet
      (for the government) quizzed Mola at Irache; he had no choice but
      to deny that he was plotting an adventure (Iribarren, *Mola*, 87;
      Félix Maíz, *Alzamiento*, 249–52). In June Casares called Yagüe to
      Madrid and tried to persuade him to take a post abroad (Calleja,
      Yagüe, 75–6).

235   Cacho Zabalza, *UME*, 37–8. Capt Barba's *junta* in Madrid was de-
      tained for a time in June, but was replaced by a reserve *junta* (Cols
      Ortiz de Zárate, Ungría, Muñoz Grandes, Álvarez Rementería).
      The man most useful to Mola was 'The Technician' (Galarza of the
      UME) who used the Army's communications network in the service
      of the conspiracy.

236   Payne (*The Military*, 316–17) nevertheless believes there was a
      revival of the UME after the elections and accepts figures for March
      1936 giving it the allegiance of half the officers on active service.

237   Gil Robles, *No fue posible*, 727. Mola distributed commands as
      follows: North, Mola; Valencia, Goded; Madrid, Villegas (later
      Fanjul); Carabanchel, García de la Herrán; Saragossa, Cabanellas;
      Burgos, González de Lara; Valladolid, Queipo; Catalonia, González
      Carrasco; Cádiz, Varela and López Pinto; Málaga, Patxot; Córdoba,
      Col Cascajo; Africa, Franco, with Yagüe under him. Later in June
      a group of Generals in Madrid reassigned Queipo to Seville and put
      Saliquet in his place. (In July Goded and González Carrasco were
      switched round.) Only Mola and Cabanellas were in command on
      the spot.

238   Calleja, *Yagüe*, 82.

239   Félix Maíz, *Alzamiento*, 197.

240   Bernard, *Mola*, 103.

241   *HGL*, 450 (between St John's Day and St Peter's Day).

242   See *HGL*, 447; Iribarren, *Mola*, 55 & 76; & Vigón, *Mola*, 98–9, who
      says that the *consejo foral* was planning an armed demonstration,
      which prompted 'Garcilaso' to get three Carlists to see Mola and
      offer him 7,000 *Requetés*. Mola told them a rising should be for a
      national, not a *foral* cause.

243   Lizarza, *Memorias*, 85, 88, 91 & 99.

244   Lizarza, *Memorias*, 92–3; Redondo & Zavala, *Requeté*, 355. Zama-
      nillo was National Delegate for *Requetés* and carried the official
      proposals of Fal Conde, who was unable to be there himself. San-

jurjo had agreed with the Carlists to be President of a Military Directory, with two Carlist advisers and a cabinet of 'technocrats', including José Antonio as Minister for Corporations.

245 Lizarza, *Memorias*, 94–8; Redondo & Zavala, *Requeté*, 357–9; Vigón, *Mola*, 95; Félix Maíz, *Alzamiento*, 207 (the latter two give the date as the 16th). *HGL*, 430, seems to suggest that Fal Conde had agreed on a date for the rising (on 15 June?) but then threatened to withdraw the *Requetés* if his terms were not accepted. In June Oriol Urigüen put the *Requetés* of Álava and his own fortune at Mola's disposal (Arrarás, *HSRE* IV, 313; Gil Robles, *No fue posible*, 731—the date is variously given as the 4th or 27th).

246 *O.c.*, 1109–12 (negotiations with the military were only to be conducted at the highest level).

247 Ximénez, *JA*, 573; his ostensible objection to Calvo was that 'he does not know how to get on a horse'.

248 *O.c.*, 1113–14, for the orders of 29 June, saying the military were not to appoint the civilian authorities until three days after victory. This order was valid until 10 July; it was renewed on the 9th until the 20th (Payne, *Falange*, 113). Ximénez, *JA*, 771, refers to a plan to rise on the 10th, cancelled when the bearer of the watchword was arrested. See *El Debate*, 12 July 1936, for the Valencian episode and the Leftist rioting that followed.

249 Esteban-Infantes, *Sanjurjo*, 255.

250 Pemán, *Soldado*, 154.

251 Iribarren, *Mola*, 61, who says the 12th was the first choice, but S. Fermín did not finish until the 14th; & Calleja, *Yagüe*, 82, who gives 15–23 and says emissaries from the garrisons went to get final instructions under cover of S. Fermín. *HGL*, 450, also gives the date as the 15th.

252 Félix Maíz, *Alzamiento*, 224–5 & 229 (Mola thought Goded would be of more use in Valencia, but he insisted on going to Barcelona); & M. Aznar, *Historia militar de la guerra de España, tomo I* (3rd ed, Madrid, 1958), 85–7. Arrarás, *HSRE* IV, 316, says Mola first assigned Goded to Barcelona, but then changed him to Valencia; he changed him again when the plotters in Barcelona made it clear that they would not have the hesitant González Carrasco. According to his son, the plotters in both Valencia and Barcelona wanted Goded (Goded, *Un faccioso*, 29).

253 Thomas, *Civil War*, 167; cf Payne, *The Military*, 335–6.

254 Lizarza, *Memorias*, 100–4; Galindo, *Los partidos*, 334–6.

255 Lizarza, *Memorias*, 101–2, who says 'Garcilaso' arranged the meeting on the 9th; & Iribarren, *Mola*, 76 & 78, who gives the date as the 5th. It would seem that Rodezno assured Mola that the Regional Junta (under Baleztena) would be co-operative. Félix Maíz, *Alzamiento*, 279, says Rodezno assured Mola of the *Requetés*' support.

256 Lizarza, *Memorias*, 105–6; *HGL*, 430. Lizarza says Mola did not

believe Sanjurjo had written it. *HGL* explains this: Sanjurjo had not marked it with the agreed countermark; the letter was not therefore valid, and the emissary from Estoril was sent to be sure Mola knew the circumstances.

257 Lizarza, *Memorias*, 107–8, who says Fal Conde would have resigned if the rising had not been imminent; & Iribarren, *Mola*, 77–8. Javier actually said he would write to Alfonso Carlos in Vienna; if no reply came before the rising, they were to join it. Nothing was received from Vienna until after the rising. Alfonso Carlos said Carlists must join a rising for Religion and Country, and not insist on pressing his personal cause (*Documentos de Alfonso Carlos*, 305 & 310).

258 Iribarren, *Mola*, 79–80 (a compromise between Mola's wish to have the *Requetés* fully under military control, and the Carlists' wish to remain separate).

259 Lizarza, *Memorias*, 108–12.

260 Félix Maíz, *Alzamiento*, 278–84. Lizarza says that Félix Maíz's version is wrong. The text is therefore an attempt to piece the information together, not rendered easy by sometimes vague chronology. Lizarza says he gave his note to Mola on the 15th, though a close examination of his account rather suggests it could have been the 16th. In short, it would seem that the various Carlists and Mola were all to some extent carrying on rather different negotiations behind each others' backs. The above version would seem to fit with Iribarren, *Mola*, 81, who says negotiations were completed with the Carlists 14–16 July.

261 Bau Nolla (conversation), who was one of these emissaries; he was Traditionalist deputy for Tarragona and a close friend.

262 Vegas, *Calvo Sotelo*, 211–13.

263 Félix Maíz, *Alzamiento*, 168; Vigón, *Mola*, 102. The emissary was the ubiquitous 'Garcilaso'. An attempt was apparently made in July to persuade Calvo to leave Madrid for Navarre.

264 Bau Nolla (conversation). Bau had met Gens Villegas and Fanjul, Col Álvarez Rementería (UME) and the police chief Martín Báguenas near the Retiro.

265 Payne, *Falange*, 115. Cf Arrarás, *HSRE* IV, 399–400 (Mayalde's evidence). José Antonio expected to be sprung from gaol on the day of the rising and flown to Madrid.

266 Vegas, *Calvo Sotelo*, 220–1. 'The Technician' was by now setting things in motion from the War Ministry (Ansaldo, *¿ Para qué?*, 125).

267 Romano, *Sanjurjo*, 187, who was in Estoril at the time and says Sanjurjo intended giving power to Calvo; Sanjurjo commented: 'The enemy knows what he is doing. He has removed our best piece.' Jellinek, *Civil War*, 284–7, cites a document taken from a leading conspirator in Barcelona which named a Military Directory of Sanjurjo (President), Mola, Franco, Cabanellas, Goded, Queipo de Llano and Fanjul—with Salazar Alonso as High Commissioner

in Morocco. This was to be succeeded by a government led by Calvo Sotelo and including Franco (War), Mola (Interior), Goicoechea (Foreign Affairs), Albiñana (Agriculture), Gil Robles (Navy), Pemán (Education).

268 Salmador, *Ansaldo*, 90 (Gen Kindelán being the source).

269 *HGL*, 429 (on p 437 Franco is said to have approved of Sanjurjo as the nominal leader).

270 Galinsoga, *Centinela*, 189–91. In Cádiz he had found church-burning in progress. The Military Governor (a Colonel) said he had orders not to intervene; Franco told him he should disobey such orders in the name of a higher duty.

271 'El Tebib Arrumi', *El Caudillo* (Ávila, 1937), 32; by implication, he did not think this had yet happened. (Cf Mola's view in 1934: 'Indiscipline is justified when the abuses of power constitute oppression and infamy, or are leading the nation to ruin. Meekness is in the first case disgraceful; in the second, treason'—Vigón, *Mola*, 87–8.)

272 L. Ramírez, *Francisco Franco* (Paris, 1964), 194–5. Arrarás (conversation) also says emissaries returned from Tenerife without answers, much to the disquiet of Mola. Col Galarza could not get any clear idea of whether or not he was really with the conspirators (Gil Robles, *No fue posible*, 780). In Pamplona he was nicknamed 'Miss Canary Islands of 1936' because he would say neither yes nor no (Payne, *The Military*, 332).

273 Letter in Arrarás, *Franco*, 171–4.

274 Cortés Cavanillas (conversation) says Calvo Sotelo told him on 10 July: 'Franco has not decided.' Arrarás (conversation) says he knows of no evidence to show that his decision was made until the week before the rising. Vegas (conversation) says the task of telling Franco that the others would rise without him was entrusted to the diplomat Sangróniz—Ramírez, *Franco*, 203, says Sangróniz reached Tenerife on the 14th to tell him a plane had been arranged. Ansaldo puts the decision just before Calvo's death. The less cautious were infuriated by Franco's attitude, as they had been since at least 1934 —hence Sanjurjo's remarks: 'With or without Franquito, we shall save Spain!' (Ansaldo, *¿ Para qué?*, 121 & 125). According to Salmador, *Ansaldo*, 102, Mola sent Franco a message saying the movement had no room for parasites and 'the friend who is not a friend will be treated as an enemy'.

275 Kindelán asked Luca de Tena to hire a plane. On 5 July the latter rang up his London correspondent, Bolín, and asked him to see to it (£2,000 was waiting in a London bank). He and La Cierva got hold of a Dragon Rapide with a British pilot. The plane's orders were to wait in Casablanca until 31 July and return if no other instructions were given. Bolín and party left Croydon on the 11th, and the plane reached Grand Canary on the 15th. Gen Balmes accidentally shot himself on the 16th and Franco went to Las

Palmas. At 3 am on the 18th Yagüe telegraphed Franco in his
hotel. Franco proclaimed martial law and left Orgaz i.c. Canaries.
He left at 2 pm and stopped at Agadir and Casablanca *en route*
(L. Bolín, *Spain* [London, 1967], 10–52; Thomas, *Civil War*, 168;
Galinsoga, *Centinela*, 209–10; J. Díaz de Villegas, *Guerra de libera-
ción* [Barcelona, 1957], 54–5; J. Millán Astray, *Franco el caudillo*
[Salamanca, 1939], 21–3; *El Debate*, 18 July 1936; *News Chronicle*,
7 Nov 1936—the pilot's version; D. Jerrold, *Georgian Adventure*
[London, 1937], 370–3, for the details. There are the customary
discrepancies.)

276 Calleja, *Yagüe*, 80–4, says the Republicans in Morocco knew of a
plot on the 11th but Yagüe reassured them. His emissary to Pamplona returned unable to recall whether Mola had said the 14th or
the 15th. He was ready by the 14th, but instructions from the
Peninsula said the 17th at 17.00. He in fact began the rising at Dar
Riffien at 11 am, disregarding a new order to wait till the 18th
because the authorities in Melilla got to know the rising was imminent there. A rather different version, nevertheless giving a similar
impression of confusion, is R. Fernández de Castro, *El Alzamiento
Nacional en Melilla* (Melilla, 1940), esp 91, 97–8 & 145. Hills,
Franco, 236 & 258, produces evidence that Mola intended the
Moroccan rising to begin on the 18th—as does Gil Robles, *No fue
posible*, 733–4 & 774: the 18th was chosen after the Carlist troubles
had forced cancellation of Sanjurjo's original choice of the 14th.

277 Their failure to take preventive action against the Army infuriated
the Left (see Álvarez del Vayo, *Freedom's Battle*, 245; Largo Caballero, *Recuerdos*, 162; Thomas, *Civil War*, 168–9 & 176; Gil Robles,
No fue posible, 740–5).

278 Iribarren, *Mola*, 61; Bravo, *Falange*, 208; Aznar, *Historia militar*, I,
84. Since conspirators were nervous about the troops, the effect of
this reduction in military strength probably had little influence on
the plotters. The pretext was that the troops should go home to help
with the harvest.

279 *El Debate*, 19 July 1936; & *Claridad*, 18 July 1936. Lucía's note
read: 'As an ex-Minister of the Republic, as leader of the *Derecha
Regional Valenciana*, as a deputy and as a Spaniard, I lift up my
heart in this grave hour above all political differences to put myself
on the side of the authority which, in opposition to violence and
rebellion, is the incarnation of the Republic and the Country.'

280 *El Debate*, 19 July 1936.

281 Iribarren, *Mola*, 101–3; Bernard, *Mola*, 77; R. Fernández de
Castro, *Franco, Mola, Varela* (2nd ed, Melilla, 1938), 189–90;
E. Corma, *El general Mola* (2nd ed, Madrid, 1956), 23–4. Prieto
later said that Goded had been trying to negotiate with Azaña
(Payne, *The Military*, 509; cf Gil Robles, *No fue posible*, 624).

282 Thomas, *Civil War*, 194–6. Members of the extreme Left were
already armed and their presence in the streets of the capital was

very useful to Largo Caballero in sabotaging Martínez Barrio's 'government of capitulation' and in preventing the formation of a strong government on the lines advocated by M. Maura and others. Largo Caballero was apparently the only leading politician who wanted to arm the people. After Martínez Barrio's failure, Azaña asked Ruiz Funes to form a government, but the latter replied: 'If you force me, Mr. President, I shall throw myself out of the window.' See García Venero, *Fanjul*, 287–9 (using evidence of Feced); L. Romero, *Tres días de julio* (Barcelona, 1967), 193–6, 201–2, 229, 242–3 & 277; Jackson, *Spanish Republic*, 243.

283   Félix Maíz, *Alzamiento*, 314. Mola had said he would blow his brains out if the Carlists failed to turn up (*HGL*, 430). By this time Mola knew that Queipo had risen in Seville.

284   Plus odd buildings in Toledo, San Sebastián, Valencia, Gijón, Albacete and Jaén. For the risings of 17–20 July, see Thomas, *Civil War*, 181–217; Broué & Témime, *La révolution*, 82–102; Payne, *The Military*, 341–52; & Romero, *Tres días*.

285   Mola thought Goded's presence could have won the day in Valencia; Vegas (conversation) believes Lucía's attitude was a key factor there. In Málaga, Patxot took his men into the streets but was persuaded to bring them back in when Martínez Barrio convinced him that Mola was not going to rise (Iribarren, *Mola*, 103).

286   Vegas (conversation) stresses the confusion and lack of proper preparation; he describes the conspiracy as little more than an agreement between Generals. No instructions were sent to smaller garrisons, not even to one so close to the capital as Segovia. On the confused nature of the rising see also Gil Robles, *No fue posible*, 775–6. García Venero, *Fanjul*, chaps xv–xxii, catalogues the chaotic Madrid venture.

287   Hills, *Franco*, 240–3, provides interesting figures on military and police loyalties and shows that the insurgents ended up with less than half the officers in the Peninsula. The Army in Morocco was 24,000 strong.

288   On the 17th José Antonio called on his followers to rise for Spain with the Army (*O.c.*, 773–5). *Japista* 'militarisation' and/or participation is noted in Cádiz (Mariñas, *Varela*, 72), Burgos, Valladolid, Valencia, Málaga, Vitoria, Palma de Mallorca, Seville, Saragossa (Romero, *Tres días*, 42–3, 162–4, 199, 205, 259, 300, 302–3, 308, 317, 332, 397, 418 & 607), and Salamanca and Madrid (García Venero, *Fanjul*, 246).

289   Fal Conde and Javier sent a 'magnificent bimotor' to Alverça to fly him to Biarritz so that he could lead the *Requetés* from Pamplona. Mola sent Ansaldo and his Puss Moth with orders to fly him to Burgos. Sanjurjo significantly decided to take Ansaldo's plane to Burgos (where Alfonsine leaders awaited him; Ansaldo thought he would have restored the Alfonsine branch). Ansaldo had put down at a military aerodrome: the friendly Portuguese, under diplomatic

pressure, said he could not use an official 'drome. So he chose a ploughed-up racecourse near Cascais. Ansaldo himself believed his propeller broke on hitting a ridge on take-off. He cleared a row of trees but lost speed and hit some rocks when attempting a forced landing. His plane then burnt out (Salmador, *Ansaldo*, 122–32; Redondo & Zavala, *Requeté*, 379–81; Lizarza, *Memorias*, 116–17; Félix Maíz, *Alzamiento*, 275).

EPILOGUE

1   Mola's proclamation in Félix Maíz, *Alzamiento*, 306; Franco's in S. F. A. Coles, *Franco of Spain* (London, 1955), 175–7.

2   Melilla proclamation (in Franco's name) in Fernández de Castro, *Franco*, 80–2 (& his *Alzamiento*, 216–18).

3   Though some (Portela, Unamuno, Ortega) had second thoughts later.

4   The PNV issued a note explaining that, 'the contest being between citizenship and Fascism, Republic and Monarchy, its principles undoubtedly demand that it come down on the side of citizenship and Republic in consonance with the democratic and Republican régime that our people was deprived of in its centuries of freedom' (Sierra Bustamente, *Euzkadi*, 164). The Nationals were to maintain that the PNV was illicitly helping the enemies of religion against its defenders (eg I. G. Menéndez-Reigada, *La guerra nacional española ante la Moral y el Derecho* [Salamanca, 1937], 18–19). In Apr 1936 the PNV had contacts with military conspirators (Gil Robles, *No fue posible*, 728–9).

5   On the 'plot' evidence, see H. R. Southworth, *El mito de la cruzada de Franco* (Paris, 1963), 247–58.

6   *Cien años en la vida del Ejército español* (Madrid, 1956), 50. Article 2 of the 'Constitutive Law of the Army' defined its mission as 'to defend the Country from external and internal enemies' (quoted in F. Salvá Miquel & J. Vicente, *Francisco Franco* [Barcelona, 1959], 167).

7   Lerroux, *Pequeña historia*, 567–88. Lerroux had declined to join the conspiracy, but said he would support the Generals if they rose when government was in the gutter. He was warned of the rising by Martín Báguenas and crossed into Portugal on the 18th.

8   *Spain in Chains*, 11 & 15–16, where he argued that the Left had rebelled against the verdict of the polls in Nov 1933 (Oct 1934) and that the 1936 election was won by fraud: 'Whose fault was it that the Rightists should have withdrawn from a legal fiction which served only to annihilate them?' Catholics justified the rising with texts from St Thomas, Suárez, Vitoria, Pius XI's *Firmissimam*, etc (see, eg, *HCE*, II–9, 558; Menéndez-Reigada, op cit).

9   Gil Robles, *No fue posible*, 719 & 800–1. He was told in general

terms about the Generals' meeting on 8 March by the stockbroker Delgado, who had been a *Cedista* candidate in the elections. He knew *Cedistas* were among those acting as emissaries for the plotters, but says he only once discussed plans for the rising in a superficial way when the subject was raised by the *Cedista* deputy for Guadalajara, Capt Valenzuela. On the DRV see Gil Robles, *No fue posible*, 623, and Payne, *The Military*, 318. Lucía was imprisoned by the Republicans and later by the Nationals because he did not support the rising.

10 Gil Robles, *No fue posible*, 730.

11 Gil Robles, *No fue posible*, 787–9 & 798. He says he authorised the transfer of what remained of the election fund because he was sure most *Cedistas* by this time had despaired of legality; he thought Mola had asked for money. However, according to Arrarás, *HSRE* IV, 317, the money was offered to Mola's adjutant in late June by the Navarrese *Cedista* Aizpún. Both versions seem to agree that Mola neither wanted it nor used it.

12 Gil Robles, *No fue posible*, 733 & 790. He writes that Luca de Tena, an emissary of Mola, took him along when he saw Lamamié de Clairac on 12 July; however, according to an unpublished Carlist source (used by Payne, *The Military*, 335), Gil Robles and another *Cedista* visited Fal Conde on 5 July as 'emissaries' of the military.

13 Bernard, *Mola*, 71–2. Cf Franco: 'If the *coup* fails there will be a long and bloody civil war' (quoted by Coles, *Franco*, 192).

14 The President of the 'Junta of National Defence' set up in Burgos on 23 July 1936 was Cabanellas, the oldest General and a Republican. Its programme referred to a Military Directory, but did not mention the form of government. The old flag was not restored by the insurgents until 29 August. The 'accidentalist' Franco became Head of State on 29 September (Díaz-Plaja, *La guerra*, 173–6, 234–5 & 249–50). A statement by Franco published in *ABC* (Seville) as late as 23 July, ended: 'Long live Spain and the Republic!' (Tuñón de Lara, *España*, 443).

15 Standing for *Falange Española Tradicionalista y de las JONS*. The decree and the messages of adherence from the Carlists, Goicoechea and Gil Robles are given in Díaz-Plaja, *La guerra*, 398–408. Gil Robles's followers had hitherto been organised under a *Junta de mando de las Milicias*. Gil Robles officially brought his party to an end on 25 April 1937 in a letter from Portugal to La Calzada (text in J. Gutiérrez-Ravé, *Diccionario histórico de la guerra de liberación de España* [Madrid, n.d.], 84–5). In late Sept 1936 Gil Robles proposed that Rightist deputies draw up a constitution for National Spain, but the idea was turned down (*No fue posible*, 788).

16 Lizarza, *Memorias*, 49–50, refers to the purchase of large quantities of arms in Belgium, France and Germany, but these were held up in Belgium when the rising occurred. In late June the English publicist Jerrold was asked to obtain 50 machine-guns and half a

million rounds of ammunition (*Georgian Adventure*, 367). Rumours
of official German aid before the rising circulated by Republicans
were mistaken. Sanjurjo was contacted by German arms manu-
facturers and visited their factories early in 1936. In June he declined an offer by the businessman Bernhardt to buy Junkers on
credit (C. Foltz, *The Masquerade in Spain* [Boston, 1948], 39 & 46).
It seems likely that German nationals in Spain sold some small arms
to Rightists before the rising (*The Nazi Conspiracy in Spain* [Lon-
don, 1937], 227–8). Félix Maíz, *Alzamiento*, 264, refers to the idea
of La Cierva being sent to Berlin after the rising to approach
Admiral Canaris and one von Veltjens to get arms. *Documents on
German Foreign Policy 1918–1945*, srs D, vol III (London, 1951),
mention a private deal being negotiated in July with Feltjen, a
professional gun-runner. The first request to the German government for help is dated 22 July (pp 1–4).

The question of Italian aid is more complex. It seems that the
pact of 1934 had lapsed, apart from training some Carlists in 1935;
no arms were delivered (Foltz, *Masquerade*, 39). Cortés Cavanillas
(conversation) ascribes this to personal estrangement between
Mussolini and Alfonso in 1935, but Goicoechea invoked the pact
after the rising when he saw Ciano and Mussolini. Gutiérrez-Ravé
(conversation) says Alfonso immediately put money at Franco's
disposal to buy aircraft. Goicoechea and Sáinz Rodríguez secured
aid on 25 July, but Franco's emissaries, Bolín and Viana, asked
Ciano on the 22nd (Thomas, *Civil War*, 286 & 296; Bolín, *Spain*,
53 & 162–72). Yet a certain mystery remains. Pemán (*Soldado*, 141)
says the Italians gave permission for their embassy to be used for
the *coup* planned for April; it is not clear whether the matter was
referred to Rome. The Ambassador, Pedrazzi, was sympathetic towards the Monarchists, but in July he told Rome that a rising could
not succeed and advised Mussolini to cultivate Azaña (Payne, *The
Military*, 352). Goicoechea told Ciano that the usual Italian emissary
had been sent by him on the 13th to inform the Italians of the date
of the rising, but the emissary had been detained in Barcelona
(J. Gutiérrez-Ravé, *Antonio Goicoechea* [Madrid, 1965], 36).

The Portuguese government was sympathetic towards the insurgents but clearly was not sure whether the rising would succeed—
hence it gave way to Republican pressure and stopped Sanjurjo's
plane using an official airfield. However, the President, Marshal
Carmona, had previously invited Sanjurjo to be his guest at military
parades; when told on 14 July of the conspirators' plans he provided
Sanjurjo with a Portuguese security guard (Romano, *Sanjurjo*, 216).

17 Azaña on 17 July 1931, quoted by F. Sedwick, *The Tragedy of
Manuel Azaña* (Columbus, 1963), 100.

Appendix 1 ATTEMPTS AT DYNASTIC RECONCILIATION

August 1931 – January 1932

WITH ALFONSO XIII in exile and styling himself Duque de Toledo, another attempt was made to bring the dynastic schism to an end. From late May or early June 1931 representatives of the two branches met at the Vicomtesse de la Gironde's villa in St Jean-de-Luz to see what could be done for Monarchist unity. The representatives agreed on a Traditionalist ideological content for the restored Monarchy, but the vexed question of who should be King remained. The Alfonsine Danvila and the ex-Integrist Jaimist Gómez Pujadas were asked to approach the two Claimants. One result was a letter written by Jaime III (also styled Duque de Madrid) on 15 August in Frohsdorf. In it the Carlist Claimant urged a united Monarchist front against the Republic. To be effective such a front needed one leader: Jaime proposed to his cousin Alfonso that the latter should abdicate in favour of his son Juan, who should be educated in the principles of Traditionalism by Jaime. Jaime, if he became King, would then name Juan as his successor. Alfonso was impressed by this proposal but some of his advisers dissuaded him from acting precipitately.[1]

As a result of the meetings in St Jean-de-Luz Danvila and Gómez Pujadas drafted a six-clause pact for dynastic union. This document was signed by the two Claimants at Territet on Lake Geneva on 12 September. Both undertook not to support violent movements for a restoration and agreed to work for the election of new Constituent Cortes. Neither Claimant, nor Alfonso's sons, were to enter Spain until a new constitution had been introduced by these Cortes. Both promised to use their influence with their followers to get them to work together. Each promised to accept the decision of the Cortes as to who should be the King. If Alfonso XIII were chosen Jaime and his uncle Alfonso (Duque de San Jaime) would renounce their rights; if Jaime were chosen the Constituent Cortes would designate his successor.[2]

Jaime clearly wanted to end the schism, even going so far as to allow the Monarch to be chosen by election. The pact between the two cousins was kept secret: Villores, Jaime's Delegate, did not even inform the Supreme Junta of the Communion of its existence.[3] On 23 September Alfonso visited Jaime in his flat on the Avenue Hoche in Paris and two days later Jaime went to see Alfonso at the Hotel Savoy in Fontainebleau. At these meetings they made an agreement to form a 'united political front' against anarchy and Communism. Jaime told the French press about this but added that neither he nor his cousin had renounced their rights.[4] Nevertheless Jaime and Alfonso seemed to be progressing towards a solution of the dynastic question when Jaime died on 2 October.

The new Carlist Claimant was Jaime's uncle Alfonso, a younger brother of Carlos VII, who had fought in the Second Carlist War. He was 82 years old and childless. He became Alfonso Carlos I because to have taken the title 'Alfonso XIV' would have meant recognition of the legitimacy of Alfonso XIII's father, while to have assumed the title 'Alfonso XII' would have irrevocably alienated all Alfonsines.[5] Alfonso XIII immediately offered Alfonso Carlos the terms of the pact of 12 September. The latter, however, was deeply shocked at his nephew's flirtation with erroneous liberal ideas and could not sleep at night. He told Villores (his Delegate) that he would never have signed such a pact. As far as he was concerned no pact with Alfonso existed and the Carlists' copy was destroyed.[6]

Since he had no direct heir Alfonso Carlos put a counter-proposal to Alfonso: the latter should abjure liberalism, accept the principles of Tradition and undertake to abide by whatever decisions might be made by traditional Cortes convoked by Alfonso Carlos. Alfonso rejected this suggestion.[7]

At the end of November Alfonso and Alfonso Carlos met and agreed to work together for Spain and Religion though the schism remained.[8] A committee of Carlists and Alfonsines continued to meet in the Hotel Bordeaux in Bordeaux to work for the closest possible co-operation between supporters of the two Claimants. Another pact was drafted setting up a joint executive committee for the Monarchist movement. It also stipulated that, when circumstances required it, Alfonso Carlos as Head of the House of Bourbon and Regent would convoke Cortes to give Spain a régime inspired by Tradition. However, this document remained a dead letter.[9]

Although Alfonsines and Carlists worked together in Spain a solution to the dynastic question eluded Monarchists. In his manifesto of 6 January 1932 Alfonso Carlos attacked the Republic for its treatment of his 'beloved cousin Alfonso', but he advocated a full-blooded Traditional Monarchy. He stated that Alfonso would indeed succeed him after his death, but to be King it was incumbent upon him to accept Traditionalist principles. Alfonso XIII's manifesto of 23 January, which was the work of Vallellano (a member of the Bordeaux committee), proclaimed that he did accept the 'fundamental principles' upheld by his 'beloved uncle' Alfonso Carlos, whom he naturally recognised as the head of the Bourbon family. The manifesto went on to envisage a provisional government convoking Cortes to give Spain a new constitution. Alfonso was ready to reign again and would always submit to the national will.[10] Both documents were the product of the Carlist-Alfonsine discussions in Bordeaux.

Alfonso Carlos clearly acknowledged that Alfonso was his heir by the laws of heredity, but the Carlists refused to compromise on principles. Alfonso Carlos made it clear that his rights could only pass to someone 'who promises and swears to preserve intact traditional principles, which . . . are above persons'.[11] Alfonso XIII, who was in the Near East, said that he had no knowledge of the manifesto he allegedly signed at Mürren.[12] During 1932 hopes of ending the schism faded away as each Claimant fell under the influence of intransigent advisers.[13]

References

1 Melgar, *Escisión dinástica*, 105–10; *Documentos de Alfonso Carlos*, 216 (letter of 12 May 1933 to Sáenz referring to the document of 15 Aug —Galindo, *Los partidos*, 120, wrongly assumes that the document referred to was the pact of 12 Sept).

2 Text in Arrarás, *HSRE* I, 239 (and photo of signatures on p 244). See also Galindo, *Los partidos*, 117–18, & J. Danvila Rivera, 'Datos para la Historia', *ABC*, 20 July 1954.

3 J. M. Lamamié de Clairac, 'Negociaciones e intentos de pactos entre las dos ramas dinásticas', *Informaciones*, 7 July 1954.

4 Melgar, *Escisión dinástica*, 112–17. See also Galindo, *Los partidos*, 120–1, & *Documentos de Alfonso Carlos*, 171 (letter of 1 Dec 1931 saying he congratulated Jaime on a pact for joint Monarchist action—he confuses the dates of the two agreements).

5 Galindo, *Los partidos*, 123; Vegas Latapié (conversation).

6 Lamamié de Clairac, op cit; *Documentos de Alfonso Carlos*, 157 (letter to Villores, 2 Nov 1931) & 204–5 (letter to Sáenz, 8 Feb 1933). The Alfonsine Danvila (op cit) says Alfonso Carlos initially favoured the pact, but intransigent advisers soon turned him against it.

7 Melgar, *Escisión dinástica*, 125.

8 *Documentos de Alfonso Carlos*, 171 (letter to Oller, 1 Dec 1931).

9 *HCE*, I–4, 462 & Galindo, *Los partidos*, 135–8.

10 Texts in *HCE*, I–4, 460–3; see also Galindo, *Los partidos*, 138–48.

11 *Documentos de Alfonso Carlos*, 178 (letter to Supreme Junta of the Communion, 29 Feb 1932). *Ultras* like Cora Lira opposed Alfonso's succession whatever the circumstances.

12 Arrarás, *HSRE* I, 246.

13 Danvila, op cit, says Vallellano's manifesto represented the end of the episode.

Appendix 2 COMPONENT ORGANISATIONS OF ACCION POPULAR AND THE CEDA

THE GENERAL pattern to be observed is the formation of *ad hoc* Rightist coalitions in the provinces based on the ideological principles of *Acción Nacional* in Madrid. Until the foundation of the CEDA in March 1933 these 'umbrella organisations' sheltered convinced Monarchists; thereafter the Monarchists left them or new, specifically *Cedista*, organisations were set up.

The information which follows is drawn from *El Debate* (1931–6) and from Monge Bernal, *Acción Popular*, 936–1150. The abbreviations AN and AP are here used for *Acción Nacional* and *Acción Popular*: all bodies styled *Acción Nacional* were re-styled *Acción Popular* in April 1932. For convenience of reference organisations are listed by regions, divided where necessary into provinces.

ANDALUSIA

Almería. Organisation of AN began in Sept 1931 and AN *de Almería* was officially founded on 29 Nov 1931. Two of the founders were Traditionalists who left after the 1933 elections. The two leading figures were Gallardo Gallardo and Giménez Canga-Argüelles, the latter formerly a follower of the Conservative Sánchez Guerra.

Cádiz. AN electoral organisations were formed in May 1931 in Jerez de la Frontera and Cádiz: the latter began with 300 members and a further 2,000 asked to join in the first 48 hours. In Sept 1931 two separate permanent bodies were created: *Acción Ciuda-*

dana in Cádiz and the *Unión de Derechas Independientes* at Jerez. The former was run by Monarchists and declined to join the CEDA in March 1933; the Jerez organisation was therefore the AP provincial body.

Córdoba. The 'forces of order' formed an electoral organisation in May 1931 around the paper *El Defensor de Córdoba*. The permanent AN branch was founded on 9 June 1931. Development was hampered by closure for 4 months after 10 Aug 1932. It took the name AP *Agraria* in Oct 1933. Its *sección femenina* claimed 3,900 members in Jan 1932. A moving spirit in the branch was Medina Togores, a Sevillano aristocrat and leader-writer for *El Debate* (d 1934).

Granada. The *Unión de Derechas* was set up in Dec 1931/Jan 1932 with 200 members, some of whom were soon killed by Socialists. The organisation had a generally stormy passage throughout the Republic. Because of the inexperience of local men the driving force was Moreno Dávila, a lawyer-journalist sent down from Madrid as adviser. Though an 'umbrella organisation', the *Unión de Derechas* joined the CEDA in March 1933. After the 1933 elections a proper AP branch was created from it. It was supported by the paper *Ideal*.

Huelva. An AN committee came into being in May 1931. However, *caciquismo* remained quite strong in the province; the old politicians of the Monarchy went over to the Radicals or M. Maura in 1931. AP remained pretty insignificant until Jan 1935, when Pérez de Guzmán finally deserted Maura and took over AP, to which he added his *Agrupación Provincial de Derechas Democráticas* (founded in June 1932).

Jaén. A Rightist committee was formed in July 1931 which adhered to AN. In July 1933 AP claimed about 700 members, but serious organisation did not begin until Feb 1934. The AP paper *La Provincia* was started in Aug 1934.

Málaga. An 'umbrella organisation' adhering to AN, *Defensa Social*, was created before the June 1931 election. In 1932 it started a free meals' service but suffered a serious setback after 10 Aug; Monarchists were prominent in the leadership, some of whom were deported. AP, headed by Fernández Ruano, stayed in the CEDA, to which another entity, the *Agrupación Mercantil y Agraria*, also adhered in Oct 1933.

Seville. An AN electoral committee was formed in May 1931. In Nov 1931 the *Unión Ciudadana* was officially created as the AN branch. Although in Sept 1931 the organisation had only 664 members (47 of whom were not in the capital), the leadership considered the organisation complete in the city by Feb 1932; attention was then turned to the *pueblos.* The branch was hampered by unjust closure for 4 months after 10 Aug 1932. The chief figure was the Conde de Bustillo and prominent activists included the historian Pabón.

Aragón

Huesca. In Oct 1931 200 of the younger citizens were reported to be forming the *Agrupación de Defensa Social.* However, AP's strength in this Radical-dominated area was slight and no proper organisation existed even in 1935. Though there were by then two JAP branches, *Cedistas* decided to stay in the Rightist 'umbrella organisation' *Acción Agraria Altoaragonesa.*

Saragossa. AN here started before the June 1931 election as the successor to the pre-Republican Rightist electoral centre which included Liberals and Conservatives; it was now joined by Traditionalists and it became a real force on 8 Dec 1931 when the *Unión de las Derechas* was officially founded. The coalition with the Traditionalists ended with the formation of the CEDA, to which AP *Agraria Aragonesa* adhered. Its main personalities included Fr Guallar and Serrano Súñer.

Teruel. A Rightist committee appeared in Teruel in 1931 and AP *Agraria* was set up in La Estrella in Apr 1932. In June 1932 an 'umbrella organisation' for the whole province, the *Unión de Derechas*, came into being, out of which sprang AP *y Agraria* (officially founded on 21 Dec 1932).

Asturias

Oviedo. AN began as an electoral organisation in June 1931, but was officially founded on 14 Oct 1931. It was an 'umbrella organisation' including Monarchists and took the name *Agrupación Autónoma Asturiana de* AP. In March 1933 the Monarchists left and the body entered the CEDA as the *Agrupación Asturiana de* AP. It was keen to uphold the character of the region and drafted a statute in 1931. Its creator and leader was Fernández-Ladreda,

2D

Mayor of Oviedo under Primo de Rivera and later a Minister under Franco. The branch had a total membership of 52,800 in Dec 1935 (though it claimed 80,000 in Feb 1934).

BALEARICS

On 5 June 1931 the *Derecha Social* (including Integrists) was founded in Palma de Mallorca; it adhered to AN. In July it merged with the former Conservative Party and this *Unión de Derechas* claimed 1,400 members by Dec 1931. In Jan 1935 it became AP *Agraria* and then had 39,500 members. Its founder and leader was the Marqués de Verger. There was a separate organisation on Ibiza, the *Partido Social Agrario* (founded as an AN affiliate in Nov 1931).

BASQUE PROVINCES

Álava. The Rightist group here was the Traditionalist *Hermandad Alavesa.*

Biscay. A *Centro de* AN existed in Baracaldo from 1931, but there were no plans to start an organisation until 1934. An information centre was opened in Bilbao in June and AP *de Vizcaya* (subsequently called AP *Vascongada*) was founded in late Oct 1934 from Basque Nationalists who disapproved of Aguirre's drift to the Left.

Guipúzcoa. No branch was opened until 18 Oct 1934, when Lojendio (formerly a diplomat) founded the *Derecha Vasca Autónoma* in San Sebastián; 250 people were reported to have joined in the first eight days.

CANARIES

Las Palmas. AP *de Las Palmas* was founded with a largely working-class membership in Feb 1933; it had 1,000 members in Nov 1933 and 8,000 by Dec 1935. From Apr 1935 it had its own daily, *Acción.* AP worked closely with the local agrarian party founded in 1933 by Mesa López, who sat as a *Cedista* in the Cortes.

Santa Cruz de Tenerife. AP *Agraria* was founded in May 1932 and in 1935 had a total membership of 9,500.

CATALONIA

Relations between AP and the *Lliga* (supported by the Catalan clergy) were generally good and there seems to have been hope of some more formal understanding between them. The CEDA made no attempt to penetrate the region until 1934. (In July 1931 the *Derecha Social de Cataluña*, based on the remnants of Paláu's *Acción Social Popular*, sent its adherence to AN; in July 1932 the foundation of two AP-style groups was reported: the *Liga Ciudadana de Derecha* in Lérida and the *Derecha Arenyense* in Arenys de Mar.) *Acción Popular Catalana* was founded just after the rebellion of October 1934 as a result of collaboration between Gil Robles and Cirera Voltá (President of the *Instituto Agrícola Catalán de San Isidro*) against Companys's law on rural leases. The group attracted those who despaired of the *Lliga* as a force with which to oppose the *Esquerra*; in Nov 1934 it was joined by Fortuny's agrarian party which had committees in half the *pueblos* of the region. AP *Catalana* provided two Councillors for the *Generalidad* in 1935 (Interior and Labour).

EXTREMADURA

Badajoz. Three AN candidates were supported by the paper *El Correo Extremeño* in the 1931 election, but Leftist opposition apparently hampered organisation. A branch was started at Almendralejo in Apr 1932, but it was not until 24 March 1933 that the provincial branch was founded officially; it became AP *Agraria* in Sept 1933. The chief figure was Hermida, formerly a follower of the Conservative Sánchez Guerra.

Cáceres. The *Derecha Regional Agraria* was founded in Nov 1931 but there was no real organisation until 1934; it became AP *Agraria* in 1935. (In Trujillo in July 1933 about 1,000 workers reportedly left the Socialists and formed the Rightist *Unión Agraria Comarcal*.) The leader was Vega Bermejo who supported the *yunteros* in the Cortes.

GALICIA

Corunna. AP *de la Coruña* was created early in 1932 by Vázquez Gundín from the *Federación Católico-Agraria*. However, by then two 'umbrella organisations' were already in existence in other towns. The *Unión Regional de Derechas* in Santiago de Compostela was founded in Nov 1931 with 400 members. A group with the same name was founded in El Ferrol in Dec 1931 which claimed

20,000 members in July 1932. These three organisations were merged on entering the CEDA in March 1933.

Lugo. From the beginning of 1932 López Pérez (a popular ex-Mayor) built up the *Unión de Derechas Lucenses* with the help of the paper *La Voz de Verdad*. It was not until May 1933 that the *Unión de Derechas y Agrarios* (the basis of which was López Pérez's group) was considered properly organised.

Orense. In Nov 1931 the foundation of *Acción Ciudadana Gallega* was announced. In Jan 1933 an 'umbrella organisation', the *Unión Orensana de Derechas* was set up. A separate AP *de Orense* was founded in Aug 1933.

Pontevedra. In Jan 1932 Lis Quiben founded the *Unión Regional de Derechas,* an 'umbrella organisation' incorporating the AN branch started at Vigo the same month. The group, which claimed 30,000 members in June 1932, joined the CEDA in 1933. An awkward situation was created when its founder went over to *Renovación Española* in 1934. Leadership was assumed by Guisasola and the name was changed to AP in Dec 1935.

LEÓN

León. The AN electoral organisation was set up in May 1931 in the offices of the *Juventud Monárquica.* From AN and agrarian elements *Acción Agraria Leonesa* was formed on 30 Nov 1931. The revisionist campaign gave it a membership of 30,000 by Nov 1932. It became AP *Agraria Leonesa* in May 1936. Its principal activist was the social-Catholic reformer Álvarez Robles.

Salamanca. In this province there was a multiplicity of organisations and the situation was complicated. From June 1930 there was a Monarchist farmers' organisation, *Acción Castellana,* one of whose leaders was the Integrist landowner Lamamié de Clairac. This body turned 'accidentalist' and in May 1931 merged with other rural elements to form the *Bloque Agrario* (leaders Gil Robles, Casanueva, Lamamié de Clairac). By May 1933 it claimed 20,000 members. In Oct 1931 a separate AN women's organisation was set up which had 20,000 members in 1935. These two bodies formed the basis of the political 'umbrella organisation' set up in Feb 1932, the *Unión de Derechas Salmantinas.* On 26 Dec 1932 Gil Robles founded the *Derecha Autónoma Salmantina,* exclusively for 'accidentalists'. Its membership overlapped with that of the *Bloque Agrario* which continued to function as a farmers' organisation. The DAS was supported by *La Gaceta Regional*, whose editor (Cimas Leal) was one of its leaders; by 1935 it had won over most members of the *Unión de Agricultores*, a body committed to M. Maura.

Zamora. The creation of a branch in this province was slow. AP got under way in the spring of 1932. Its chief figure was Carrascal.

MOROCCO

Representatives from Ceuta and Melilla attended the AP Assembly in Oct 1932 and branches were opened prior to the 1933 elections.

MURCIA

Albacete. AP had only a few committees in the province by Nov 1933. The task of organisation was then carried out by Acacio Sandoval, elected as an independent Agrarian and coming of a wealthy Conservative landowning family.

Murcia. An AN branch was set up by two Propagandists sent from Madrid in May 1931. The organisation was built up with the help of the paper *La Voz de Murcia*. When the Monarchists left AP *Murciana* joined the CEDA. Its chief figures were the social-Catholic lawyer Salmón and Ibáñez Martín.

NAVARRE

Navarre. Unión Navarra was founded in March 1933 by the former *Maurista* Aizpún; it was keen to defend the regional personality and claimed not to be a political party but an organisation for those uncommitted to one. It had 7,000 members in Dec 1934 and changed its name to AP *Navarra* in Jan 1936. Its candidates topped the poll in the 1936 elections.

NEW CASTILE

Ciudad Real. Organisation was slow here, apparently owing to Leftist pressure. *Acción Agraria Manchega* was officially founded on 12 Jan 1933 and clashes with the Left were frequent. The chief figures were Mateo La Iglesia and Ruiz de Valdepeñas, an ardent defender of the wine interest.

Cuenca. An AN organisation was created for the 1931 election and developed into the 'umbrella organisation' *Acción Ciudadana y Agraria* in Dec 1931. This later became AP *Agraria*.

Guadalajara. An AN organisation based on the CNCA was created for the June 1931 election in opposition to the Left and the *caciques* of Romanones. It joined with Traditionalists to become the 'umbrella organisation' *Acción Regional Agraria y Ciudadana* in July 1931. The moving spirit of AP was Arizcún, removed from his post as chief provincial agronomist by Azaña's government.

Madrid. AN was founded by Herrera on 29 Apr 1931; 2,361 people joined in the capital in the first three days. It had 9,000 members by Jan 1932 and 42,000 when the Civil War started. The organisation in the province dated from the early summer of 1931 and was based on Catholic unions; its driving force was J. Martín Artajo, a lawyer and journalist specialising in agrarian questions.

Toledo. AN was set up in June 1931 in the offices of the *Centro de Defensa Social*. It developed into AP *Agraria* which had 100,000 members in March 1933. The leaders included the worker D. de Madariaga, Canon Molina Nieto and the Conde de Mayalde.

OLD CASTILE

Ávila. AN was founded on 6 Aug 1931 with 115 members. Its development was hindered by closure for much of 1932. Reorganisation was carried out in 1933 by an emissary from Madrid and it had over 1,000 members by late 1935. In Sept 1933 the *Bloque Agrario Abulense* also adhered to the CEDA.

Burgos. There was talk of starting an AN branch here in 1931 but there was apparently no wish to compete with Martínez de Velasco's organisation. *Acción Mirandesa* was formed at Miranda de Ebro in Jan 1932, but it was not until May 1932 that an 'umbrella organisation', *Acción Burgalesa de Derechas*, was founded in Burgos with 6,000 members. After the foundation of the Agrarian Party AP *Agraria* was set up in March 1934.

Logroño. AN started in May 1931 and became a strong branch under the name *Acción Riojana*. Its mainstay was the military engineer Ortiz de Solórzano.

Palencia. An AN committee was formed in May 1931; this led to the foundation of the *Unión Castellana Agraria* by the social-Catholic property-owner Cortés Villasana in June 1931. This organisation was dissolved in Jan 1932 when its members joined with Agrarian elements (led by Calderón, twice a Minister under the Monarchy) and UP-type Monarchists (led by Vallellano) to form the *Unión de Derechas Sociales y Agrarias*. The creation of a separate AP was reported in March 1934, but in 1935 the 'umbrella organisation' still existed and it was said that younger members were working for a proper AP branch.

Santander. The 'umbrella organisation' *Agrupación Regional Independiente* was founded in Apr 1931 and included Liberals, Conservatives, *Mauristas*, Integrists, Jaimists and Catholic trade-unionists. In Jan 1932 it had 1,600 members in the capital (its real strength lay among the rural workers). It was led by the Alfonsine Sáinz Rodríguez and in Feb 1933 it voted to stay out of the CEDA. In Sept 1934 Valiente and Pérez del Molino formed a separate AP branch.

Segovia. AN was founded in June 1931 with its headquarters in the *palacio* of its creator, the historian, poet, art critic and landowner the Marqués de Lozoya. Organisation was extended to all *pueblos* in the first month. In 1935 it had 600 members in the capital.

Soria. M. Maura's Conservatives were strong here. The formation of a *Bloque Agrario* was reported in June 1932. An emissary was sent out from Madrid in 1933 to ginger things up and an AP branch was opened in Dec 1933.

Valladolid. AN was started in May 1931 and relied mainly on support from the young. Among the latter was O. Redondo who left to form his own group; in 1932 his JONS attracted quite a number of youths from AP. AP was closed for two months after 10 Aug 1932 and became AP *Agraria* in June 1933. One of its leaders was La Calzada.

VALENCIA

The *Derecha Regional Valenciana* was founded by Lucía (editor of the *Diario de Valencia*) and a few friends in Dec 1929. The DRV officially adhered to AN on 14 June 1931 and subsequently became the model and inspiration for the CEDA. Its organisation extended over the three provinces of Alicante, Castellón and Valencia and it had 20,000 members in Nov 1931. Organisation in the region was considered complete by May 1932; the provincial semi-autonomous subsidiaries in Alicante and Castellón were styled *Derecha Regional Agraria*. The Alicante organisation had 41,000 members in July 1934. There was also a specifically working-class Christian party in Valencia from June 1931 called *Acción Democrática Social*.

THE AMERICAS

The first *Centro de la* CEDA in Spanish America was opened in Havana in Sept 1935.

Appendix 3 SOCIAL COMPOSITION OF THE MINORITIES OF THE RIGHT, LLIGA AND PNV

IN THE absence of biographical dictionaries for the period it is difficult to analyse in detail the interests represented by the Rightist deputies. The following tables are based on the occupations declared by deputies to *ABC* (20 Dec 1933 and 6 Mar 1936). Not all deputies complied with the paper's request for information. The occupations declared by those who did provide a good guide to their social standing but not to their material interests; for example, Lamamié de Clairac said he was a lawyer but did not say he was a stock-breeder in the west and therefore likely to be a vehement opponent of land redistribution. The sample for the Cortes of 1933–5 breaks down as shown on page 426.

The break-down of the sample for the Cortes of 1936 was as shown on page 427.

Only two conclusions can really be drawn from the two tables. Firstly, the parties of the Right contained a lot of lawyers, just as did those of the Left and Centre: the Second Republic was a Republic of lawyers. Secondly, the great majority of working-class deputies were Socialists. In so far as they are of any use the tables confirm the obvious.

Occupation	CEDA	RE*	Trads.	Ags.	Lliga†	PNV	Others‡	Total
Lawyers	44	9	10	17	11	7	83	181
Engineers	14	1	1	3	1	–	11	31
Academics	8	1	–	2	–	–	14	25
Journalists & writers	3	2	1	–	–	1	17	24
Physicians	5	1	–	1	–	–	16	23
Property-owners	6	1	2	3	–	1	2	15
Workers	2	–	1	–	–	1	11	15
Manufacturers	3	–	1	–	–	–	10	14
Farmers	6	–	–	2	–	–	2	10
Office-workers	1	–	–	–	–	1	7	9
Notaries	5	–	–	–	–	–	3	8
Priests	4	–	–	–	–	–	2	6
Architects	2	–	1	–	–	–	1	4
Army officers	1	–	–	1	–	–	2	4
Consuls & diplomats	–	–	–	–	1	–	1	2
Licenciados en ciencias	–	–	2	–	–	–	–	2
Inspectors of education	1	–	–	–	–	–	1	2
Property registrars	–	–	–	–	1	–	1	2
Publishers	–	–	–	–	1	–	–	1
Mariners	–	1	–	–	–	–	–	1
Ship-owners	–	–	1	–	–	–	–	1
Supreme Court clerks	1	–	–	–	–	–	–	1
Others	–	–	–	–	–	–	28	28
	106	16	20	29	15	11	212	409
(Total	117	16	21	29	25	12	255	475)

* Includes Pemán (originally independent Monarchist) and Albiñana (PNE).
† Includes Fons (Balearic Regionalist).
‡ Includes Rightist and other independents (as well as other minorities), eg Fr Gafo.

Occupation	CEDA	RE*	Trads.	Ags.	Lliga	PNV	Others†	To-tal
Lawyers	33	7	5	6	7	1	69	128
Workers	1	–	1	–	–	1	32	35
Academics	4	1	1	–	1	–	25	32
Physicians	4	2	–	1	–	–	24	31
Writers & journalists	3	–	–	–	–	–	20	23
Engineers	8	–	–	1	–	–	11	20
Manufacturers & traders	3	–	–	–	–	–	12	15
Civil servants	–	–	–	–	1	–	10	11
Farmers	3	1	–	–	–	–	5	9
Property-owners	3	1	–	1	–	–	3	8
Employees	2	–	–	–	–	–	6	8
Army officers	1	–	–	–	.	–	3	4
Diplomats	1	–	–	–	1	–	2	4
Architects	1	–	–	–	–	–	3	4
Notaries	3	–	–	–	–	–	1	4
Property registrars	1	–	1	–	1	–	1	4
Mariners	1	–	–	–	–	–	1	2
Priests	2	–	–	–	–	–	–	2
Supreme Court clerks	1	–	–	–	–	–	1	2
Magistrates	1	–	–	–	–	–	–	1
Others	–	–	–	–	–	–	25	25
	76	12	8	9	11	2	254	372
(Total‡	96	13	14	11	11	9	328	472)

* Including Albiñana (PNE).
† Including Rightist independents, as before.
‡ ABC collected and printed the information before the Cortes opened; some of those listed were subsequently unseated.

Bibliography

THE ORGANISATION of printed works into categories is particularly difficult where recent history is concerned. The following divisions are consciously arbitrary. Books which are primarily eye-witness accounts of events after 17–20 July 1936 but which contain information on the preceding period are listed in section E (ii) and not in D (i).

A. UNPUBLISHED SOURCES
Libro de actas de Renovación Española
Manifiesto del Bloque Nacional
  (both the above used by permission of D. Julián Cortés Cavanillas)
Malefakis, Edward Emanuel. *Land Tenure, Agrarian Reform and Peasant Revolution in Twentieth Century Spain.* D.Phil thesis, Columbia University, 1965.

B. DOCUMENTS
(i) *Cortes debates*
Diario de sesiones de Las Cortes Constituyentes de la República española, comenzaron el 14 de julio de 1931 (25 vols).
Diario de las sesiones de Cortes, Congreso de los Diputados, comenzaron el 8 de diciembre de 1933 (17 vols).
Diario de las sesiones de Cortes, Congreso de los Diputados, comenzaron el 16 de marzo de 1936 (3 vols).

(ii) *Newspapers and periodicals*
ABC (Madrid, daily), April 1931–July 1936.
Claridad (Madrid, daily), April–July 1936.
El Debate (Madrid, daily), April 1931–July 1936.

La Época (Madrid, daily), November 1931–October 1932.
El Socialista (Madrid, daily), April 1931–July 1936.
El Sol (Madrid, daily), April–July 1931 & February–March 1936.
Boletín de Orientación Tradicionalista (Madrid, weekly), July 1934–December 1935.
Blanco y Negro (Madrid, fortnightly), 1934–5.
JAP (Madrid, fortnightly—later weekly), October 1934–December 1935.
Bulletin of Spanish Studies (Liverpool), vols VIII–XIII (1931–6).
The Economist (London), 1931–6.

In addition, various single numbers of sundry Argentine, British and French dailies have been consulted; references are in notes where used in text.

(iii) *Printed documents*

Cortés Cavanillas, Julián. *Acta de acusación: epístolas, documentos, frases y diálogos para la historia de la segunda República.* Madrid (Librería San Martín) 1933.

Declaración colectiva del Episcopado español sobre el espíritu y actuación de los católicos en las presentes circunstancias. Madrid (Editorial Ibérica) 1932.

Díaz-Plaja, Fernando (ed). *La historia de España en sus documentos. El siglo XX. Dictadura . . . República (1923–1936).* Madrid (Instituto de Estudios Políticos) 1964.

— *La guerra (1936–1939).* Madrid (Gráficas Faro) 1963.

Documents on German Foreign Policy 1918–1945. Series C, vol. 5: March 5–October 31, 1936. London (HMSO) 1966.

— *Series D, vol. 3: Germany and the Spanish Civil War 1936–1939.* London (HMSO) 1951.

Ferrer, Melchor (ed). *Documentos de D. Alfonso Carlos de Borbón y de Austria-Este (Duque de San Jaime).* Madrid (Editorial Tradicionalista) 1950.

La Iglesia y la guerra civil española (documentos eclesiásticos). Buenos Aires (Editorial Ver) 1947.

Keogh, A. (ed). *The Pope and the People. Select Letters and Addresses on Social Questions by Pope Leo XIII, Pope Pius X, Pope Benedict XV and Pope Pius XI.* London (Catholic Truth Society) 1929.

Ministère des Affaires Étrangères. *Documents diplomatiques fran-çais 1932–1939. 2e série (1936–1939), tomes I–II (1er janvier-18 juillet 1936).* Paris (Imprimerie Nationale) 1963–4.
Ministerio de Justicia. *Causa General. La dominación roja en España. Avance de la información instruída por el ministerio público.* Madrid, 1944.
Pope Pius XI. *Encyclical Letter on Reconstructing the Social Order (Quadragesimo Anno).* London (Catholic Truth Society) 1957.
Unió Catalana d'Estudis Polítics i Econòmico-Socials. *Elements per a l'estudi de l'Estatut de Catalunya.* Barcelona (Editorial Políglota) 1931.

C. Anthologies, Collected Works and Speeches

Acción Española, tomo XVIII, no. 89. Antología. Burgos, March 1937.
Carlos VII. 'Mi testamento político a los carlistas', *El Correo Español* (Madrid), 24 July 1909 (supplement).
Cuartero, José. *Artículos de don José Cuartero: homenaje de 'ABC' a su insigne redactor.* Madrid (Imp Prensa Española) 1947.
Díaz Doin, Guillermo. *El pensamiento político de Azaña.* Buenos Aires (PHAC) 1943.
Donoso Cortés, Juan. *Textos políticos.* Madrid (Rialp) 1954.
Escobar, José Ignacio (Marqués de Valdeiglesias); Vigón, Jorge & Vegas Latapié, Eugenio. *Escritos sobre la instauración monárquica.* Madrid (Rialp) 1955.
Goicoechea, Antonio. *Monarquía y República (discurso pronunciado el 20 de abril de 1930, en la Plaza de Toros de Madrid.* Madrid (CIAP) 1930.
Gutiérrez-Ravé, José (ed). *Habla el Rey: discursos de don Alfonso XIII.* Madrid (Industrias Gráficas) 1955.
Herrera Oria, Ángel. *Obras selectas* (ed J. M. Sánchez de Muniáin & J. L. Gutiérrez García). Madrid (Editorial Católica) 1963.
Ledesma Ramos, Ramiro. *Antología* (ed A. Macipe López). Barcelona (Ediciones FE) 1940.
— *Discurso a las juventudes de España.* 4th ed, Madrid (Ediciones FE) 1942.
Maeztu, Ramiro de. *En vísperas de la tragedia* (ed J. M. de Areilza). Madrid (Cultura Española) 1941.

— *Frente a la República* (ed G. Fernández de la Mora). Madrid (Rialp) 1956.
— *El sentido reverencial del dinero* (ed V. Marrero). Madrid (Editora Nacional) 1957.
— *Liquidación de la Monarquía parlamentaria* (ed V. Marrero). Madrid (Editora Nacional) 1957.
— *El nuevo tradicionalismo y la revolución social* (ed V. Marrero). Madrid (Editora Nacional) 1959.
— *Antología* (ed F. González Navarro). Madrid (Doncel) 1960.
— *Un ideal sindicalista* (ed V. Marrero). Madrid (Editora Nacional) 1961.
Marrero, Vicente. *El tradicionalismo español del siglo XIX.* Madrid (Publicaciones Españolas) 1955.
Menéndez Pelayo, Marcelino. *Textos sobre España* (ed F. Pérez-Embid). Madrid (Rialp) 1962.
Mola Vidal, Emilio. *Obras completas.* Valladolid (Librería Santarén) 1940.
Pradera, Víctor. *Obra completa.* (2 vols.) Madrid (Instituto de Estudios Políticos) 1945.
Primo de Rivera, José Antonio. *Obras completas* (ed A. del Río Cisneros & E. Conde Gargollo). Madrid (Editora Nacional) 1942.
— *Textos inéditos y epistolario* (ed A. del Río Cisneros & E. Pavón Pereyra). Madrid (Ediciones del Movimiento) 1956.
— *Ultimos hallazgos de escritos y cartas de José Antonio* (ed A. del Río Cisneros & E. Pavón Pereyra). Madrid (Ediciones del Movimiento) 1962.
Redondo, Onésimo. *Obras completas* (*edición cronológica*). (2 vols.) Madrid (Publicaciones Españolas) 1954–5.
Río Cisneros, Agustín del (ed). *El pensamiento de José Antonio.* Madrid (Ediciones del Movimiento) 1962.
Romanones, Conde de. *Obras completas, tomo III* (*Memorias*). Madrid (Editorial Plus Ultra) 1949.
Torras Bages, José; Maragall, Juan & Cambó, Francisco. *La actitud tradicional en Cataluña* (ed J. B. Solervicens). Madrid (Rialp) 1961.
Vázquez de Mella, Juan. *Regionalismo y Monarquía* (ed S. Galindo Herrero). Madrid (Rialp) 1957.

Vegas Latapié, Eugenio. *Escritos políticos*. Madrid (Cultura Española) 1940.

D. Memoirs, Eye-witness Accounts and Biographies
(i) *Memoirs and eye-witness accounts*
Agire Lekube, José Antonio de. *Entre la libertad y la revolución 1930–1935: la verdad de un lustro en el País Vasco*. Bilbao (E. Verdes Achirica) 1935.
— [Aguirre]. *Freedom was Flesh and Blood*. London (Victor Gollancz) 1945.
Alcalá-Zamora, Niceto. *Los defectos de la Constitución de 1931*. Madrid (Imp. de R. Espinosa) 1936.
Álvarez del Vayo, Julio. *Freedom's Battle* (tr E. E. Brooke). London (Heinemann) 1940.
— *The Last Optimist* (tr C. Duff). London (Putnam) 1950.
Ansaldo, Juan Antonio. *¿ Para qué . . .? (De Alfonso XIII a Juan III)*. Buenos Aires (Vasca Ekin) 1951.
[Azaña]. *Memorias íntimas de Azaña* (ed J. Arrarás). 5th ed, Madrid (Ediciones Españolas) 1939.
Aznar, Severino. *Impresiones de un demócrata cristiano*. 2nd ed, Madrid (Editorial Bibliográfica Española) 1950.
Balbontín, José Antonio. *La España de mi experiencia (Reminiscencias y esperanzas de un español en el exilio)*. Mexico City (Colección Aquelarre) 1952.
Berenguer, Dámaso (Conde de Xauen). *De la Dictadura a la República. Crisis del reinado de Alfonso XIII*. Madrid (Editorial Plus Ultra) 1946.
Bolín, Luis A. *Spain: The Vital Years*. London (Cassell) 1967.
Bowers, Claude G. *My Mission to Spain: Watching the Rehearsal for World War II*. London (Victor Gollancz) 1954.
Buckley, Henry. *Life and Death of the Spanish Republic*. London (Hamish Hamilton) 1940.
Calvo Sotelo, José. *Mis servicios al Estado. Seis años de gestión. Apuntes para la Historia*. Madrid (Imp. Clásica Española) 1931.
Campoamor, Clara. *La révolution espagnole vue par une républicaine*. Paris (Plon) 1937.
Cano Sánchez-Pastor, Antonio. *Cautivos en las arenas. Crónicas de un confinado*. Madrid (Imp. de L. Rubio) 1933.

Cierva Peñafiel, Juan de la. *Notas de mi vida.* Madrid (Instituto Editorial Reus) 1955.

Conze, Edward. *Spain To-Day: Revolution and Counter-Revolution.* London (Secker & Warburg) 1936.

Cortés Cavanillas, Julián. *Confesiones y muerte de Alfonso XIII.* 2nd ed, Madrid (Editorial Prensa Española) 1951.

Cossío, Francisco de. *Hacia una nueva España. De la revolución de octubre a la revolución de julio: 1934–1936.* Valladolid (Editorial Castilla) 1937.

Dominique, Pierre. *Marche, Espagne.* . . . Paris (Librairie Valois) 1931.

Esteban-Infantes, Emilio. *La sublevación del general Sanjurjo. Apuntes para la Historia.* 2nd ed, Madrid (Sánchez de Ocaña) 1933.

Félix Maíz, B. *Alzamiento en España. De un diario de la conspiración.* Pamplona (Editorial Gómez) 1952.

Fernández de Castro Pedrera, Rafael. *El Alzamiento Nacional en Melilla. Hacia las rutas de una nueva España.* Melilla (Postal Exprés) 1940.

Gil Robles, José María. *No fue posible la paz.* Barcelona (Ediciones Ariel) 1968.

Guariglia, Raffaele. *Ricordi, 1922–1946.* Naples (Edizioni Scientifiche Italiane) 1950.

Gutiérrez-Ravé, José. *Yo fui un joven maurista (historia de un movimiento de ciudadanía).* Madrid (Gráficas Modernas) 1945.

Hidalgo, Diego. *¿ Por qué fui lanzado del Ministerio de la Guerra? Diez meses de actuación ministerial.* Madrid (Espasa-Calpe) 1934.

Hoyos Vinent, José María de (Marqués de Hoyos). *Mi testimonio.* Madrid (Afrodisio Aguado) 1962.

Ibárruri, Dolores. *El único camino.* 2nd ed, Paris (Éditions Sociales) 1965.

Jerrold, Douglas. *Georgian Adventure.* London (Collins) 1937.

Kindelán, Alfredo. *Mis cuadernos de guerra.* Madrid (Editorial Plus Ultra) nd.

Largo Caballero, Francisco. *Mis recuerdos. Cartas a un amigo.* Mexico City (Ediciones Alianza) 1954.

Lerroux, Alejandro. *La pequeña historia. Apuntes para la Historia*

2E

grande vividos y redactados por el autor. Buenos Aires (Editorial Cimera) 1945.

Lizarza Iribarren, Antonio. *Memorias de la conspiración. Como se preparó en Navarra la Cruzada, 1931–1936.* 3rd ed, Pamplona (Editorial Gómez) 1954.

López Ochoa, Eduardo. *Campaña militar de Asturias en octubre de 1934 (narración táctico-episódica).* Madrid (Ediciones Yunque) 1936.

Manning, Leah. *What I Saw in Spain.* London (Victor Gollancz) 1935.

Martín Blázquez, José. *I Helped to Build an Army: Civil War Memoirs of a Spanish Staff Officer* (tr F. Borkenau & E. Mosbacher). London (Secker & Warburg) 1939.

Maura, Miguel. *Así cayó Alfonso XIII....* Mexico City (Imp. Mañez) 1962.

Mendizábal, Alfredo. *The Martyrdom of Spain (Origins of a Civil War)* (tr C. H. Lumley). London (Geoffrey Bles) 1938.

Nadal, Joaquín María de. *Seis años con don Francisco Cambó (1930–36). Memorias de un secretario político.* Barcelona (Alpha) 1957.

Ossorio Gallardo, Ángel. *Mis memorias.* Buenos Aires (Editorial Losada) 1946.

Pérez Madrigal, Joaquín. *Pérez (vida y trabajos de uno).* Madrid (Instituto Editorial Reus) 1955.

— *El general Sanjurjo a presidio.* Madrid (Instituto Editorial Reus) 1955.

Picard-Moch, Germaine & Moch, Jules. *L'Espagne républicaine: l'œuvre d'une révolution.* 3rd ed, Paris (Éditions Rieder) 1933.

Reguengo, Vicente. *Guerra sin frentes.* 3rd ed, Barcelona (Editorial AHR) 1955.

Royo Villanova, Antonio. *Treinta años de política antiespañola.* Valladolid (Librería Santarén) 1940.

Ruiz Vilaplana, Antonio. *Burgos Justice. A Year's Experience of Nationalist Spain* (tr W. H. Carter). London (Constable) 1938.

Salazar Alonso, Rafael. *Tarea: cartas políticas.* Madrid (Sáez Hermanos) 1934.

— *Bajo el signo de la Revolución.* Madrid (Librería San Martín) 1935.

Serrano Súñer, Ramón. *Entre Hendaya y Gibraltar* (*noticia y reflexión, frente a una leyenda, sobre nuestra política en dos guerras*). Madrid (EPESA) 1947.
Young, Sir George. *The New Spain*. London (Methuen) 1933.

(ii) *Biographies*
Acedo Colunga, Felipe. *José Calvo Sotelo* (*la verdad de una muerte*). Barcelona (Editorial AHR) 1957.
Aguirre Prado, Luis. *Ruiz de Alda*. Madrid (Publicaciones Españolas) 1955.
— *Ramiro de Maeztu*. 2nd ed, Madrid (Publicaciones Españolas) 1959.
— *Vázquez de Mella*. 2nd ed, Madrid (Publicaciones Españolas) 1959.
Arrabal, Juan. *José María Gil Robles: su vida, su actuación, sus ideas*. Madrid (Librería Internacional de Romo) 1933.
Arrarás Iribarren, Joaquín. *Francisco Franco* (tr J. M. Espinosa). London (Geoffrey Bles) 1938.
Aunós Pérez, Eduardo. *Calvo Sotelo y la política de su tiempo*. Madrid (Ediciones Españolas) 1941.
Bernard, Ino. *Mola, mártir de España*. Granada (Editorial Prieto) 1938.
Boissel, Antony. *Un chef: Gil Robles*. Paris (Bloud et Gay) 1934.
Bravo Martínez, Francisco. *José Antonio: el hombre, el jefe, el camarada*. 2nd ed, Madrid (Ediciones Españolas) 1940.
Calleja López, Juan José. *Yagüe, un corazón al rojo*. Barcelona (Editorial Juventud) 1963.
Camba, Francisco. *Lerroux: el caballero de la libertad*. Madrid (Nuestra Raza) 1935.
Carner-Ribalta, J. & Fabregat, Ramón. *Macià. La seva actuació a l'estranger*. Mexico City (Edicions Catalans de Mèxic) 1952.
Coles, S. F. A. *Franco of Spain: A Full-Length Biography*. London (Neville Spearman) 1955.
Corma, Enrique. *El general Mola*. 2nd ed, Madrid (Publicaciones Españolas) 1956.
Corral, Enrique del. *Calvo Sotelo*. 2nd ed, Madrid (Publicaciones Españolas) 1956.
Crozier, Brian. *Franco. A Biographical History*. London (Eyre & Spottiswoode) 1967.

Esteban-Infantes, Emilio. *General Sanjurjo (un laureado en el Penal de Dueso)*. Barcelona (Editorial AHR) 1957.

Fernández de Castro Pedrera, Rafael. *Franco, Mola, Varela. Vidas de soldados ilustres de la nueva España*. 2nd ed, Melilla (Postal Exprés) 1938.

Galinsoga, Luis de & Franco Salgado, F. *Centinela de occidente (semblanza biográfica de Francisco Franco)*. Barcelona (Editorial AHR) 1956.

García de la Escalera, Inés. *General Varela*. 2nd ed, Madrid (Publicaciones Españolas) 1959.

— *El general Yagüe*. 2nd ed, Madrid (Publicaciones Españolas) 1959.

García Sánchez, Narciso. *Onésimo Redondo*. 2nd ed, Madrid (Publicaciones Españolas) 1956.

García Venero, Maximiano. *Vida de Cambó*. Barcelona (Editorial Aedos) 1952.

— *Melquiades Álvarez. Historia de un liberal*. Madrid (Editorial Alhambra) 1954.

— *Santiago Alba: monárquico de razón*. Madrid (Aguilar) 1963.

— *La Falange en la guerra de España: la Unificación y Hedilla*. Paris (Ruedo Ibérico) 1967.

— *El general Fanjul. Madrid en el Alzamiento Nacional*. Madrid (Ediciones Cid) 1967.

Goded, Manuel. *Un 'faccioso' cien por cien*. Saragossa (Talleres Editoriales Heraldo) 1938.

Gómez Oliveros, Benito & Moscardó, José. *General Moscardó (sin novedad en el Alcázar)*. Barcelona (Editorial AHR) 1956.

González Piedra, Juan. *Vida y obra de Menéndez y Pelayo*. Madrid (Publicaciones Españolas) 1952.

González Ruano, César. *General Sanjurjo*. 2nd cd, Madrid (Publicaciones Españolas) 1959.

Guinea Suárez, Carlos. *Víctor Pradera*. 2nd ed, Madrid (Publicaciones Españolas) 1956.

Gutiérrez-Ravé, José. *El conde de Barcelona*. Madrid (Prensa Española) 1962.

— *Antonio Goicoechea*. Madrid (Celebridades) 1965.

— *Gil Robles, caudillo frustrado*. Madrid (ERSA) 1967.

Hills, George. *Franco. The Man and His Nation*. London (Robert Hale) 1967.

Iribarren, José María. *El general Mola.* 2nd ed, Madrid (Editora Nacional) 1945.

Joaniquet, Aurelio. *Calvo Sotelo: una vida fecunda, un ideario político, una doctrina económica.* Santander (Espasa-Calpe) 1939.

Junta Local del Homenaje Nacional a José Calvo Sotelo (Tarrasa). *José Calvo Sotelo: fecundidad de su vida y ejemplaridad de su muerte.* Tarrasa (N. Flotats) 1957.

Manfredi Cano, Domingo. *Jaime Balmes.* Madrid (Publicaciones Españolas) 1954.

Mariñas, Francisco Javier. *General Varela (de soldado a general).* Barcelona (Editorial AHR) 1956.

Marrero, Vicente. *Maeztu.* Madrid (Rialp) 1955.

Martin, Claude. *Franco, soldat et chef d'état.* Paris (Quatre Fils Aymon) 1959.

Millán Astray, J. *Franco el caudillo.* Salamanca (M. Quero y Simón) 1939.

Olmedo Delgado, Antonio & Cuesta Monereo, José. *General Queipo de Llano (aventura y audacia).* Barcelona (Editorial AHR) 1957.

Ortega, Teófilo. *Presidente: Martínez de Velasco.* Barcelona (Araluce) 1935.

Ossorio Gallardo, Ángel. *Vida y sacrificio de Companys.* Buenos Aires (Editorial Losada) 1943.

Pemán, José María. *Un soldado en la Historia. Vida del capitán general Varela.* Cádiz (Escelicer) 1954.

Pensado, Berta. *El marqués de Comillas.* Madrid (Publicaciones Españolas) 1959.

Petrie, Sir Charles. *King Alfonso XIII and His Age.* London (Chapman & Hall) 1963.

Pi Navarro, Manuel. *Los primeros veinticinco años de la vida de José Calvo Sotelo (apuntes para una biografía).* Saragossa ('El Noticiero') 1961.

Pilar, Princess of Bavaria & Chapman-Huston, Desmond. *Don Alfonso XIII. A Study of Monarchy.* London (John Murray) 1931.

Prieto, Tomás. *Soldados de España: datos para la Historia.* Madrid (Ediciones Tormes) 1946.

Ramírez, Luis. *Francisco Franco. Historia de un mesianismo.* Paris (Ruedo Ibérico) 1964.

Requejo San Román, Jesús. *El cardenal Segura.* Toledo (Editorial Católica Toledana) 1932.

Romano, Julio. *Sanjurjo, el caballero del valor.* Madrid (Imp. de la viuda de Juan Pueyo) 1940.

Salmador, Víctor G. *Juan Antonio Ansaldo, caballero de la lealtad.* Montevideo (Prometeo) 1962.

Salvá Miquel, Francisco & Vicente, Juan. *Francisco Franco (historia de un español).* Barcelona (Ediciones Generales) 1959.

Santa Marina, Luys. *Hacia José Antonio.* Barcelona (Editorial AHR) 1958.

Sanz Díaz, José. *Escritores asesinados por los rojos.* Madrid (Publicaciones Españolas) 1953.

Sedwick, Frank. *The Tragedy of Manuel Azaña and the Fate of the Spanish Republic.* Columbus (Ohio State University Press) 1963.

Sencourt, Robert. *King Alfonso. A Biography.* London (Faber & Faber) 1942.

Sevilla Andrés, Diego. *Antonio Maura: la revolución desde arriba.* Barcelona (Editorial Aedos) 1954.

Silió, César. *Maura. Vida y empresas de un gran español.* Madrid (Espasa-Calpe) 1934.

Suárez, Federico. *Introducción a Donoso Cortés.* Madrid (Rialp) 1964.

'El Tebib Arrumi'. *El Caudillo, S.E. D. Francisco Franco Bahamonde, Generalísimo del Ejército y Jefe del Estado Español.* Ávila (Imp. Católica) 1937.

Valdesoto, Fernando de. *Francisco Franco.* Madrid (Afrodisio Aguado) 1943.

Valle, Florentino del. *El P. Antonio Vicent, S.J., y la acción social católica española.* Madrid (Editorial Bibliográfica Española) 1947.

Vallotton, Henry. *Alphonse XIII.* Lausanne (Payot) 1943.

Vegas Latapié, Eugenio. *El pensamiento político de Calvo Sotelo.* Madrid (Cultura Española) 1941.

Vigón, Jorge. *General Mola (el conspirador).* Barcelona (Editorial AHR) 1957.

Ximénez de Sandoval, Felipe. *José Antonio.* 2nd ed, Madrid (Gráficas Lazareno-Echaniz) 1949.

E. Other Books
(i) *Works published or written before July* 1936

Albiñana, José María. *España bajo la dictadura republicana (Crónica de un período putrefacto)*. 2nd ed, Madrid (El Financiero) 1933.

Alcalá Galiano, Álvaro (Marqués de Castel Bravo). *The Fall of a Throne* (tr S. Erskine). London (Thornton Butterworth) 1933.

'Anonymous'. *The Spanish Republic. A Survey of Two Years of Progress*. London (Eyre & Spottiswoode) 1933.

Arboleya Martínez, M. Annotated translation of Croizier, *Hacia un porvenir mejor*. Barcelona (Editorial Subirana) 1936.

Arrese, Domingo de. *Bajo la Ley de defensa de la República*. Madrid (CGAG) 1933.

Aunós Pérez, Eduardo. *La reforma corporativa del Estado*. Madrid (Aguilar) 1935.

Brandt, Joseph A. *Toward the New Spain*. Chicago (University of Chicago Press) 1933.

'El Caballero Audaz'. *Una española se casa en Roma (Diario de un hombre de la calle)*. Madrid (ECA) 1935.

— *La Revolución y sus cómplices*. Madrid (ECA) 1936.

Calvo Sotelo, José. *En defensa propia*. Madrid (Librería San Martín) 1932.

— *La voz de un perseguido*. (2 vols.) Madrid (Imp. de Galo Sáez) 1933.

— *El capitalismo contemporáneo y su evolución*. Madrid (Imp. de Galo Sáez) 1935.

Camba, Julio. *Haciendo de República*. Madrid (Espasa-Calpe) 1934.

Canals, Salvador. *De cómo van las cosas de España. Estudios políticos y económicos*. Madrid (CIAP) 1933.

Caravaca, Francisco & Orts-Ramos, Antonio. *La Iglesia contra el Poder civil*. Barcelona (Publicaciones Mundial) 1932.

Carrión, Pascual. *La reforma agraria: problemas fundamentales*. Madrid (Editorial Pueyo) 1931.

Casares, Francisco. *La CEDA va a gobernar (Notas y glosas de un año de vida pública nacional)*. Madrid (Gráfica Administrativa) 1934.

Castrillo Santos, Juan. *La orientación de la República*. Madrid (Javier Morata) 1933.

Castro Albarrán, Aniceto de. *El derecho a la rebeldía*. Madrid (Gráfica Universal) 1934.

Cortés Cavanillas, Julián. *Gil Robles, ¿ monárquico? Misterios de una política*. Madrid (Librería San Martín) 1935.

Fernández Almagro, Melchor. *Catalanismo y República española*. Madrid (Espasa-Calpe) 1932.

García Palacios, L. *El segundo bienio (España en escombros) 1933–35*. N.pl. (Ediciones Bancario) 1936.

Gomá Tomás, Isidro. *Antilaicismo*. (2 vols.) Barcelona (Rafael Casulleras) 1935.

Gómez Acebo Modet, Juan. *Origen, desarrollo y trascendencia del movimiento sindicalista obrero*. Madrid (Jaime Ratés) 1915.

Larraz, José. *La Hacienda pública y el Estatuto catalán*. Madrid (Editorial Ibérica) 1932.

— *El ordenamiento del mercado triguero en España*. Madrid (CEU) 1935.

Lucía Lucía, Luis. *En estas horas de transición hacia una política de principios cristianos, de afirmación de soberanías sociales y de preocupación por las realidades regionales*. Valencia (Diario de Valencia) 1930.

— *La Confederación Española de Derechas Autónomas*. Valencia (La Voz Valenciana) 1933.

Maeztu, Ramiro de. *Authority, Liberty and Function in the Light of the War*. London (Allen & Unwin) 1916.

— *Defensa de la Hispanidad*. Madrid (Ediciones Fax) 1934.

Maura Gamazo, Gabriel (Duque de Maura). *Dolor de España*. Madrid (?) 1932.

Maurín, Joaquín. *La revolución española. De la Monarquía absoluta a la revolución socialista*. Madrid (Editorial Cenit) 1932.

— *Hacia la segunda revolución. El fracaso de la República y la insurrección de octubre*. Barcelona (Gráficos Alfa) 1935.

Medina Togores, José de. *Un año de Cortes constituyentes (impresiones parlamentarias)*. Madrid (Editorial Ibérica) 1932.

Monedero Martín, Antonio. *La Confederación Nacional Católico-Agraria en 1920: su espíritu, su organización, su porvenir*. Madrid (V. Rico) 1921.

Monge Bernal, José. *Acción Popular (estudios de biología política)*. Madrid (Imp. Sáez Hermanos) 1936.

Moral, Joaquín del. *Lo del 'io de Agosto' y la Justicia*. Madrid (CIAP) 1933.

Ortega Gasset, José. *Invertebrate Spain* (tr M. Adams). London (Allen & Unwin) 1937.

— *The Revolt of the Masses*. London (Allen & Unwin) 1961.

Pascazio, Nicola. *La rivoluzione di Spagna. Dittatura, Monarchia, Repubblica, rivoluzione*. Rome (Nuova Europa) 1933.

Pemán, José María. *Cartas a un escéptico en materia de formas de gobierno*. 2nd ed, Madrid (Cultura Española) 1935.

Pradera, Víctor. *The New State* (tr B. Malley). London (Sands) 1939.

Quiroga Ríos, Domingo. *Contra los nuevos oligarcas. Quién es y adonde va Santiago Casares (Notas para la biografía de un político republicano)*. 2nd ed, Corunna (Imp. Moret) 1932.

Ramos Oliveira, Antonio. *La revolución de octubre: ensayo político*. Madrid (Editorial España) 1935.

Rodríguez, Teodoro. *El problema social y las derechas: nuevas orientaciones*. El Escorial (Imp. del Monasterio) 1935.

Royo Villanova, Antonio. *La Constitución española de 9 de diciembre de 1931, con glosas jurídicas y apostillas políticas*. Valladolid (Imp. Castellana) 1934.

Sáinz Rodríguez, Pedro. *La Tradición nacional y el Estado futuro*. Madrid (Cultura Española) 1935.

Semprún Gurrea, José María de. *República, libertad, estatismo (escritos, con sus fechas)*. Madrid (Imp. de Galo Sáez) 1931.

Silió, César. *En torno a una revolución: crisis de España, caída de la Monarquía, la República, la revolución socialista*. Madrid (Espasa-Calpe) 1933.

Tusquets, Juan. *Orígenes de la revolución española*. 3rd ed, Barcelona (Editorial Vilamala) 1932.

Vegas Latapié, Eugenio. *Catolicismo y República: un episodio de la historia de Francia*. Madrid (Gráfica Universal) 1932.

(ii) *Works published since July* 1936 (including general books)

Aguado Bleye, Pedro & Alcázar Molina, Cayetano. *Manual de historia de España, tomo III*. 6th ed, Madrid (Espasa-Calpe) 1956.

Aguirre Prado, Luis. *The Church and the Spanish War*. Madrid (SIE) 1965.

Alba, Víctor. *Historia de la segunda República española*. Mexico City (Libro Mex Editores) 1961.

Albert Despujol, Carlos de. *La gran tragedia de España, 1931–1939*. Madrid (Sánchez de Ocaña) 1940.

Almagro San Martín, Melchor de. *Ocaso y fin de un reinado (Alfonso XIII). Los Reyes en el destierro*. Madrid (Afrodisio Aguado) 1947.

Altamira, Rafael. *A History of Spain from the Beginnings to the Present Day* (tr M. Lee). New York (Van Nostrand) 1952.

Ansón Oliart, Luis María. *Acción Española*. Saragossa (Editorial Círculo) 1960.

Aronson, Theo. *Royal Vendetta. The Crown of Spain, 1829–1965*. London (Oldbourne) 1966.

Arrarás Iribarren, Joaquín (literary ed). *Historia de la Cruzada española, tomos I–II (volumenes 1–9)*. Madrid (Ediciones Españolas) 1939–40.

— *Historia de la segunda República española*. (4 vols.) Madrid (Editora Nacional) 1956–68.

Atholl, Katharine Duchess of. *Searchlight on Spain*. 3rd ed, Harmondsworth (Penguin Books) 1938.

Atkinson, William C. *A History of Spain and Portugal*. Harmondsworth (Penguin Books) 1960.

Aunós Pérez, Eduardo. *España en crisis (1874–1936)*. Buenos Aires (Librería del Colegio) 1942.

Aznar, Manuel. *Historia militar de la guerra de España, tomo I*. 3rd ed, Madrid (Editora Nacional) 1958.

Aznar, Severino. *Estudios religioso-sociales*. Madrid (Instituto de Estudios Políticos) 1949.

Bécarud, Jean. *La deuxième République espagnole, 1931–1936. Essai d'interprétation*. Paris (CERI) 1962.

Belforte, Francesco. *La guerra civile in Spagna. I: La disintegrazione dello Stato*. Milan (ISPI) 1938.

Beneyto, Juan. *Historia social de España y de Hispanoamérica*. Madrid (Aguilar) 1961.

Bernanos, Georges. *Les grands cimetières sous la lune*. Paris (Plon) 1938.

Bertrán Güell, Felipe. *Preparación y desarrollo del Alzamiento Nacional.* Valladolid (Librería Santarén) 1939.

Bolloten, Burnett. *The Grand Camouflage. The Communist Conspiracy in the Spanish Civil War.* London (Hollis & Carter) 1961.

Borkenau, Franz. *The Spanish Cockpit. An Eye-Witness Account of the Political and Social Conflicts of the Spanish Civil War.* London (Faber & Faber) 1937.

Brasillach, Robert & Bardèche, Maurice. *Histoire de la guerre d'Espagne.* Paris (Plon) 1939.

Bravo Martínez, Francisco. *Historia de Falange Española de las JONS.* 2nd ed, Madrid (Editora Nacional) 1943.

Brenan, Gerald. *The Spanish Labyrinth. An Account of the Social and Political Background of the Civil War.* 2nd ed, Cambridge (Cambridge University Press) 1962.

Broué, Pierre & Témime, Emile. *La révolution et la guerre d'Espagne.* Paris (Éditions de Minuit) 1961.

Bruguera, F. G. *Histoire contemporaine d'Espagne, 1789–1950.* N.pl. (Éditions Ophrys) 1954.

Burgo, Jaime del. *Requetés en Navarra antes del Alzamiento.* San Sebastián (Editorial Española) 1939.

Burgos Mazo, Manuel de. *Antología histórica.* Valencia (Editorial América) 1944.

Cacho Viú, Vicente. *Las tres Españas de la España contemporánea.* Madrid (Ateneo) 1962.

Cacho Zabalza, Antonio. *La Unión Militar Española.* Alicante (EGASA) 1940.

Calvez, Jean-Yves & Perrin, Jacques. *The Church and Social Justice. The Social Teaching of the Popes from Leo XIII to Pius XII (1878–1958)* (tr J. R. Kirwan). London (Burns & Oates) 1961.

Calvo Sotelo, José. *El Estado que queremos* (ed A. García-Arias). Madrid (Rialp) 1958.

Cardó, Carles. *Histoire spirituelle des Espagnes. Étude historico-psychologique du peuple espagnol* (tr R. Bonnafous). Paris (Éditions des Portes de France) 1946.

Cardozo, Harold G. *The March of a Nation. My Year of Spain's Civil War.* London (Right Book Club) 1937.

Carr, Raymond. *Spain 1808–1939.* Oxford (Clarendon Press) 1966.

Carrasco Verde, Manuel & others. *Cien años en la vida del Ejército español*. Madrid (Editora Nacional) 1956.

Castillejo, José. *Wars of Ideas in Spain: Philosophy, Politics and Education*. London (John Murray) 1937.

Castillo, José del & Álvarez, Santiago. *Barcelona, objetivo cubierto*. Barcelona (Editorial Timón) 1958.

Castro Albarrán, Aniceto de. *La gran víctima: la Iglesia española mártir de la revolución roja*. Salamanca (?) 1940.

Cattell, David T. *Communism and the Spanish Civil War*. Berkeley (University of California Press) 1955.

Checkland, S. G. *The Mines of Tharsis. Roman, French and British Enterprise in Spain*. London (Allen & Unwin) 1967.

Cleugh, James. *Spanish Fury. The Story of a Civil War*. London (Harrap) 1962.

Comín Colomer, Eduardo. *Historia secreta de la segunda República*. (2 vols.) Madrid (Editorial Nos) 1954–5.

— *De Castilblanco a Casas Viejas*. 2nd ed, Madrid (Publicaciones Españolas) 1959.

Crow, John A. *Spain, the Root and the Flower. A History of the Civilization of Spain and of the Spanish People*. New York (Harper & Row) 1963.

Dahms, Hellmuth Günther. *La guerra española de 1936* (tr A. Soriano Trenor). Madrid (Rialp) 1966.

Descola, Jean. *Histoire de l'Espagne chrétienne*. Paris (Laffont) 1951.

Díaz de Villegas, José. *Guerra de liberación (la fuerza de la razón)*. Barcelona (Editorial AHR) 1957.

Estado Mayor Central del Ejército (Servicio Histórico Militar). *Historia de la guerra de liberación (1936–1939). Tomo I: Antecedentes de la guerra*. Madrid (Imp. del Servicio Geográfico del Ejército) 1945.

Fernández Almagro, Melchor. *Historia de la República española (1931–1936)*. Madrid (Biblioteca Nueva) 1940.

Fernsworth, Lawrence. *Spain's Struggle for Freedom*. Boston (Beacon Press) 1957.

Ferrer, Melchor. *'Veinticinco años atrás . . .' el Requeté vela las armas. En el XXV aniversario del Quintillo*. Seville (Talleres Tipográficas Arzona) 1959.

Figueiredo, Fidelino de. *As duas Espanhas*. Lisbon (Guimarães Editores) 1959.

Finer, Samuel Edward. *The Man on Horseback. The Role of the Military in Politics*. London (Pall Mall) 1962.

Fogarty, Michael P. *Christian Democracy in Western Europe, 1820–1953*. London (Routledge & Kegan Paul) 1957.

Foltz, Charles (Jr). *The Masquerade in Spain*. Boston (Houghton Mifflin) 1948.

Foss, William & Gerahty, Cecil. *The Spanish Arena*. London (John Gifford) 1938.

Galindo Herrero, Santiago. *Breve historia del tradicionalismo español*. Madrid (Publicaciones Españolas) 1956.

— *Los partidos monárquicos bajo la segunda República*. 2nd ed, Madrid (Rialp) 1956.

Gannes, Harry & Repard, Theodore. *Spain in Revolt. A History of the Civil War in Spain in 1936 and a Study of its Social, Political and Economic Causes*. London (Victor Gollancz) 1936.

García, Regina. *El bulo de los caramelos envenenados*. Madrid (Publicaciones Españolas) 1953.

García-Arias, Amalio. *La armonía social en el pensamiento de Calvo Sotelo*. Madrid (Ateneo) 1957.

García Escudero, José María. *De Cánovas a la República*. 2nd ed, Madrid (Rialp) 1953.

García-Nieto Paris, Juan N. *El sindicalismo cristiano en España. Notas sobre su origen y evolución hasta 1936*. Bilbao (Editorial El Mensajero del Corazón de Jesús) 1960.

García Venero, Maximiano. *Historia del nacionalismo catalán (1793–1936)*. Madrid (Editora Nacional) 1944.

— *Historia del nacionalismo vasco, 1793–1936*. Madrid (Editora Nacional) 1945.

— *Historia de las Internacionales en España. Tomo II (Desde la primera guerra mundial al 18 de julio de 1936)*. Madrid (Ediciones del Movimiento) 1957.

— *Historia de los movimientos sindicalistas españoles (1840–1933)*. Madrid (Ediciones del Movimiento) 1961.

Garosci, Aldo. *Gli intellettuali e la guerra di Spagna*. Turin (Einaudi) 1959.

Georges-Roux. *La guerre civile d'Espagne*. Paris (Fayard) 1964.

Gil Munilla, Octavio. *Historia de la evolución social española durante los siglos XIX y XX*. Madrid (Publicaciones Españolas) 1961.

Gil Robles, J. M. *Spain in Chains* (tr C. de Arango). New York (The America Press) 1937.

Granados, Mariano. *La cuestión religiosa en España*. Mexico City (Las Españas) 1959.

Guardiola Cardellach, Enrique. *La anti-España*. Mexico City (México Nuevo) nd.

Guillén Salaya, F. *Historia del sindicalismo español*. Madrid (Editora Nacional) 1941.

Gutiérrez-Ravé, José. *Las Cortes errantes del Frente Popular*. Madrid (Editora Nacional) 1953.

Hennessy, C. A. M. *Modern Spain*. London (Historical Association) 1965.

'Hispanicus' (ed). *Foreign Intervention in Spain, Vol. I*. London (United Editorial) 1937.

Hobsbawm, E. J. *Primitive Rebels. Studies in Archaic Forms of Social Movements in the Nineteenth and Twentieth Centuries*. Manchester (Manchester University Press) 1959.

Hodgson, Sir Robert M. *Spain Resurgent*. London (Hutchinson) 1953.

Huerta, José Félix. *Defensa de España (discurso a la Nación española)*. Biarritz (Colección Complutense) 1964.

Hughes, Emmet John. *Report from Spain*. New York (Henry Holt) 1947.

Iturralde, Juan de. *El catolicismo y la cruzada de Franco, tomos I-II*. Vienne (Editorial Egui-Indarra) 1955–60.

Jackson, Gabriel. *The Spanish Republic and the Civil War, 1931–1939*. Princeton (Princeton University Press) 1965.

Jalón, José Luis. *El Ejército español*. 2nd ed, Madrid (Publicaciones Españolas) 1959.

Jato, David. *La rebelión de los estudiantes (Apuntes para la historia del alegre SEU)*. Madrid (CIES) 1953.

Jellinek, Frank. *The Civil War in Spain*. London (Victor Gollancz) 1938.

Kenny, Michael. *A Spanish Tapestry. Town and Country in Castile*. London (Cohen & West) 1961.

Kindelán, Alfredo. *Ejército y política*. Madrid (Aguilar) nd.

Laín Entralgo, Pedro. *La generación del noventa y ocho.* Madrid (Espasa-Calpe) 1959.

Legaz Lacambra, Luis & Buide Laverde, Ramón. *Universidad de Santiago, Cátedra Vázquez de Mella. Conferencias.* Santiago de Compostela (EUC) 1945.

Livermore, Harold V. *A History of Spain.* London (Allen & Unwin) 1958.

Loveday, Arthur F. *World War in Spain.* London (John Murray) 1939.

— *Spain 1923–1948: Civil War and World War.* Ashcott (Boswell Publishing Co) 1948.

Madariaga, Salvador de. *Spain. A Modern History.* 3rd ed, London (Jonathan Cape) 1961.

Manuel, Frank E. *The Politics of Modern Spain.* New York (McGraw-Hill) 1938.

Marañón, Gregorio. *Liberalism and Communism. The Background of the Spanish Civil War.* London (Spanish Press Services) nd.

Marcotte, V. A. *L'Espagne nationale-syndicaliste.* 2nd ed, Brussels (Imp. Aug. Puvrez) 1943.

Marrero, Vicente. *La guerra española y el trust de cerebros.* Madrid (Punta Europa) 1961.

Martínez Bande, José Manuel. *Communist Intervention in the Spanish War (1936–1939).* Madrid (SIE) 1966.

Martínez Barrio, Diego. *Orígenes del Frente Popular español.* Buenos Aires (PHAC) 1943.

Maura, Duque de & Fernández Almagro, Melchor. *Por qué cayó Alfonso XIII. Evolución y disolución de los partidos históricos durante su reinado.* Madrid (Ambos Mundos) 1948.

Melgar, Francisco (Conde de Melgar). *El noble final de la escisión dinástica.* Madrid (Publicaciones del Consejo Privado de SAR el conde de Barcelona) 1964.

Menéndez Pidal, Ramón. *The Spaniards in Their History* (tr W. Starkie). London (Hollis & Carter) 1950.

Menéndez-Reigada, Ignacio G. *La guerra nacional española ante la Moral y el Derecho.* Salamanca (Establecimiento Tipográfico de Calatrava) 1937.

Montalbán, Francisco J.; Llorca, Bernardino & García Villoslada, Ricardo. *Historia de la Iglesia Católica. Tomo IV: Edad moderna (1648–1963)*. 3rd ed, Madrid (Editorial Católica) 1963.

Montero Moreno, Antonio. *Historia de la persecución religiosa en España, 1936–1939*. Madrid (Editorial Católica) 1961.

Morrow, Felix. *Revolution and Counter-Revolution in Spain*. London (New Park Publications) 1963.

Mousset, Albert. *Histoire de l'Espagne*. Paris (SEFI) 1947.

Narbona, Francisco. *La quema de conventos*. 2nd ed, Madrid (Publicaciones Españolas) 1959.

The Nazi Conspiracy in Spain (tr E. Burns). London (Victor Gollancz) 1937.

O'Callaghan, Sheila M. *Cinderella of Europe: Spain Explained*. London (Skeffington) 1951.

Ortiz Estrada, Luis. *Alfonso XIII, artífice de la II República española*. Madrid (Gráficas Espejo) 1947.

Ossorio Gallardo, Ángel. *La guerra de España y los católicos*. Buenos Aires (PHAC) 1942.

Oyarzun, Román. *Historia del carlismo*. 2nd ed, Madrid (Editora Nacional) 1944.

Parker, A. A. *The Catholic Church in Spain from 1800 till To-Day*. London (Catholic Truth Society) 1938.

Paul, Elliott. *The Life and Death of a Spanish Town*. London (Peter Davis) 1937.

Payne, Stanley G. *Falange. A History of Spanish Fascism*. London (Oxford University Press/Stanford University Press) 1962.

— *Politics and the Military in Modern Spain*. London (Oxford University Press/Stanford University Press) 1967.

Peers, Edgar Allison. *The Spanish Tragedy, 1930–1936. Dictatorship, Republic, Chaos*. 3rd ed, London (Methuen) 1936.

— *Catalonia Infelix*. London (Methuen) 1937.

— *Spain, the Church and the Orders*. London (Eyre & Spottiswoode) 1939.

Peirats, José. *La CNT en la revolución española, tomo I*. Toulouse (Ediciones CNT) 1951.

Pérez Madrigal, Joaquín. *'España a dos voces'. Los infundios y la Historia*. Madrid (Edición EASA) 1961.

Petrie, Sir Charles. *Lords of the Inland Sea. A Study of the Mediterranean Powers*. London (Lovat Dickson) 1937.

— (with Bertrand, Louis). *The History of Spain*. 2nd ed, London (Eyre & Spottiswoode) 1956.
— *The Spanish Royal House*. London (Geoffrey Bles) 1958.
Pitt-Rivers, J. A. *The People of the Sierra*. London (Weidenfeld & Nicolson) 1954.
Plá, José. *Historia de la segunda República española*. (4 vols.) Barcelona (Destino) 1940–1.
Polo, Fernando. *¿ Quién es el Rey? La actual sucesión dinástica en la Monarquía española*. Madrid (Editorial Tradicionalista) 1949.
Puzzo, Dante A. *Spain and the Great Powers, 1936–1941*. New York (Columbia University Press) 1962.
Rama, Carlos M. *Ideología, regiones y clases sociales en la España contemporánea*. Montevideo (Nuestro Tiempo) 1958.
— *La crisis española del siglo XX*. Mexico City (Fondo de Cultura Económica) 1960.
Ramos Oliveira, Antonio. *Politics, Economics and Men of Modern Spain, 1808–1946* (tr T. Hall). London (Victor Gollancz) 1946.
Ratcliff, Dillwyn F. *Prelude to Franco. Political Aspects of the Dictatorship of General Miguel Primo de Rivera*. New York (Las Americas Publishing Co) 1957.
Redondo, Luis & Zavala, Juan de. *El Requeté (la Tradición no muere)*. 2nd ed, Barcelona (Editorial AHR) 1957.
Romero, Luis. *Tres días de julio (18, 19 y 20 de 1936)*. Barcelona (Ediciones Ariel) 1967.
Sáinz Rodríguez, Pedro. *Evolución de las ideas sobre la decadencia española, y otros estudios de crítica literaria*. Madrid (Rialp) 1962.
Sánchez, José M. *Reform and Reaction. The Politico-Religious Background of the Spanish Civil War*. Chapel Hill (University of North Carolina Press) 1964.
Seco Serrano, Carlos. *Historia de España, tomo VI: Época contemporánea*. Barcelona (Instituto Gallach) 1962.
Sencourt, Robert. *Spain's Ordeal. A Documented Survey of Recent Events*. London (Longmans, Green) 1938.
Sevilla Andrés, Diego. *Historia política de la zona roja*. Madrid (Editora Nacional) 1954.
Sierra Bustamente, Ramón. *Euzkadi de Sabino Arana a José*

2F

Antonio Aguirre. Notas para la historia del nacionalismo vasco. Madrid (Editora Nacional) 1941.

Silió, César. *Trayectoria y significación de España del tiempo al tiempo nuevo.* Madrid (Espasa-Calpe) 1939.

Smith, Rhea Marsh. *The Day of the Liberals in Spain.* London (Oxford University Press/University of Pennsylvania Press) 1938.

— *Spain. A Modern History.* Ann Arbor (University of Michigan Press) 1965.

Soldevila, Ferran & Bosch-Gimpera, Pere. *Història de Catalunya.* Mexico City (Col·lecció Catalònia) 1946.

Souchere, Éléna de la. *Explication de l'Espagne.* Paris (Bernard Grasset) 1962.

Southworth, Herbert Rutledge. *El mito de la cruzada de Franco.* Paris (Ruedo Ibérico) 1963.

— *Antifalange. Estudio crítico de 'Falange en la guerra de España: la Unificación y Hedilla' de Maximiano García Venero* (tr J. Martínez). Paris (Ruedo Ibérico) 1967.

Tamames, Ramón. *Estructura económica de España.* 2nd ed, Madrid (Sociedad de Estudios y Publicaciones) 1964.

Thomas, Hugh. *The Spanish Civil War.* 2nd ed, Harmondsworth (Penguin Books) 1965.

Toynbee, Arnold J. & Boulter, V. M. *Survey of International Affairs, 1937. Vol. II: The International Repercussions of the War in Spain (1936–7).* London (Oxford University Press/ RIIA) 1938.

Trend, J. B. *The Civilization of Spain.* London (Oxford University Press) 1944.

Tuñón de Lara, Manuel. *La España del siglo XX.* Paris (Librería Española) 1966.

Valynseele, Joseph. *Les prétendants aux trônes d'Europe.* Paris (author) 1967.

Venegas, José. *Las elecciones del Frente Popular.* Buenos Aires (PHAC) 1942.

Vicens Vives, Jaime. *Historia social y económica de España y América. Tomo IV, volumen 2: Burguesía, industrialización, obrerismo.* Barcelona (Editorial Teide) 1959.

— *Aproximación a la Historia de España.* 2nd ed, Barcelona (Editorial Teide) 1960.

Vigón, Jorge. *Historia de la Artillería española, tomo II.* Madrid (CSIC) 1947.
Vilar, Pierre. *Histoire de l'Espagne.* 4th ed, Paris (PUF) 1958.

F. ARTICLES AND ESSAYS

A.S. 'Comentarios a "La guerra civil española", de Hugh Thomas', *Revista de Estudios Políticos,* no 120 (Nov–Dec 1961).
Askew, William C. 'Italian intervention in Spain. The agreements of March 31, 1934 with the Spanish Monarchist parties', *The Journal of Modern History,* vol XXIV, no 2 (June 1952).
Aznar, Severino. 'Un pensador social español', *Revista Internacional de Sociología,* no 39 (July–Sept 1952).
Bentura, Benjamin. 'Hoy hace veinte años', *Ya* (Madrid), 13 July 1956.
Bolín, Luis A. 'Franco's flight into history', *The Reader's Digest* (London), Feb 1958.
Carr, Raymond. 'Spain: Rule by Generals', in *Soldiers and Governments. Nine Studies in Civil-Military Relations* (ed M. Howard). London (Eyre & Spottiswoode) 1957.
Corthis, André. 'Du couvent aux Cortès', *Revue des Deux Mondes,* 15 March–15 Apr 1936.
Danvila Rivera, Julio. 'Datos para la Historia', *ABC* (Madrid), 20 July 1954.
Dobby, E. H. G. 'Beneath the surface in Spain', *Time & Tide* (London), 29 Aug 1936.
Duff, David. 'The biography of Queen Ena—part II', *Homes & Gardens* (London), Nov 1960.
Entwistle, W. J. 'Background to the Spanish Civil War', *The Listener* (London), 12 Jan 1938.
Gil Robles, José María. 'Preámbulo su problema en España' to André Tardieu, *La reforma del Estado* (tr Conde de San Esteban de Cañongo). Madrid (ABF) 1935.
— 'The Spanish Republic and Basque independence', *The Tablet* (London), 19 June 1937.
Gutiérrez-Ravé, José. 'Algunas entrevistas históricas de don Alfonso XIII', *ABC* (Madrid), 28 Feb 1964.
Greaves, H. R. G. 'Politics in the Spanish Republic', *The Political Quarterly,* vol 3 (1932).
— 'A Soviet Spain?', *The Political Quarterly,* vol 7 (1936).

Jackson, Gabriel. 'The Azaña regime in perspective (Spain, 1931–1933)', *The American Historical Review*, vol LXIV, no 2 (Jan 1959).

Lamamié de Clairac, José María. 'Negociaciones e intentos de pactos entre las dos ramas dinásticas', *Informaciones* (Madrid), 7 July 1954.

Lerroux, Alejandro. 'Le destin tragique de la République espagnole', *L'Illustration* (Paris), 30 Jan 1937.

Lewandowski, Maurice. 'M. Gil Robles', *Revue des Deux Mondes*, 15 June 1935.

Moody, Joseph N. 'The socio-religious problematic of Spain', in *Church and Society. Catholic Social and Political Thought and Movements 1789–1950* (ed J. N. Moody). New York (Arts Inc) 1953.

Nadal, Jordi; Vicens Vives, Jaume & Martí, Casimir. 'El moviment obrer a Espanya de 1929 a 1936 en relació amb la crisi econòmica', *Serra d'Or*, Feb 1961.

Nicolas, André. 'Des élections a l'ouverture des Cortès', *Revue des Deux Mondes*, 1 Aug 1931.

— 'Élections espagnoles (16–28 novembre)', *Revue des Deux Mondes*, 15 Dec 1933.

Osorio García, Alfonso. 'El sindicalismo español anterior a 1936', *ACN de P* (Madrid), 15 May 1961.

Payne, Stanley G. 'Spain', in *The European Right. A Historical Profile* (ed H. Rogger & E. Weber). London (Weidenfeld & Nicolson) 1965.

Perpiñá Grau, Román. 'De economía hispana', appendix to Gottfried Haberler, *El comercio internacional* (tr R. Perpiñá). Barcelona (Editorial Labor) 1936.

Plaza Prieto, Juan. 'El desarrollo del comercio exterior español desde principios del siglo XIX a la actualidad', *Revista de Economía Política*, vol VI, no 2 (May–Aug 1955).

Primo de Rivera, Miguel. 'Génesis de la Dictadura', 'Constitución y labor del Directorio', 'La Dictadura civil' & 'Fin de la Dictadura española', in *El Debate* (Madrid), 21, 22, 23 & 25 March 1930 respectively.

Robinson, Richard A. H. 'Calvo Sotelo's *Bloque Nacional* and its manifesto', *The University of Birmingham Historical Journal*, vol X, no 2 (1966).

Romanones, Conde de. 'La République en Espagne', *Revue des Deux Mondes*, 15 July 1931.
— 'La révolution en Espagne', *Revue des Deux Mondes*, 1 Dec 1934.
Rossi, Vittorio G. 'Asturie turbolente', *Nuova Antologia*, 1 Dec 1934.
'Saguntinus'. 'Uomini e idee delle destre spagnuole', *Nuova Antologia*, 1 Sept 1933.
Sánchez, José M. 'The Spanish Church and the revolutionary Republican movement, 1930–1931', *Church History*, vol XXXI, no 4 (Dec 1962).
— 'The Second Spanish Republic and the Holy See, 1931–1936', *The Catholic Historical Review*, vol XLIX, no 1 (Apr 1963).
Schumacher, John N. 'Integrism. A study in nineteenth-century Spanish political thought', *The Catholic Historical Review*, vol XLVIII, no 3 (Oct 1962).
Starkie, Walter. 'Spanish kaleidoscope. A background', *The Fortnightly* (London), Dec 1936.
Thomas, Hugh. 'The hero in the empty room—José Antonio and Spanish Fascism', *The Journal of Contemporary History*, vol I, no 1 (Jan 1966).
Urbina, Antonio de (Marqués de Rozalejo). 'De los recuerdos que no se esfuman: Calvo Sotelo', *Punta Europa* (Madrid), no 31–2 (July–Aug 1958).
Valle, Florentino del. 'Trayectoria y significado social del P. Azpiazu', *Fomento Social* (Madrid), vol VIII, no 31 (July–Sept 1953).
Vegas Latapié, Eugenio. 'Maeztu y "Acción Española" ', *ABC* (Madrid), 2 Nov 1952.
Vicens Vives, Jaime. 'Espagne', in *L'Europe du XIXe et du XXe siècle (1914-aujourd'hui): problèmes et interprétations historiques* (ed M. Beloff, P. Renouvin, F. Schnabel & F. Valsecchi). Milan (Marzorati) 1964.

G. NOVELS AND SATIRE

Benavides, Manuel D. *Curas y mendigos. Prólogo de la guerra civil. (Reportaje)*. Barcelona (Imp. Industrial) 1936.
Estrada, Justo. *La gitana de Gil Robles. Reportaje humorístico. Diez conversaciones*. Madrid (?) 1935.

Foxá, Agustín de (Conde de Foxá). *Madrid de Corte a Cheka.* N.pl. (Ediciones Jerarquía) 1938.

H. DICTIONARIES

Diccionario de Historia de España desde sus orígenes hasta el fin del reinado Alfonso XIII. (2 vols.) Madrid (Revista de Occidente) 1952.

Gutiérrez-Ravé, José. *Diccionario histórico de la guerra de liberación de España* (*1936–1939*). (2 *folletos* published). Madrid (Ediciones Aspas) nd.

Acknowledgements

I AM indebted to the following for being so kind as to give up some of their time in order to provide me with information and talk to me about the period studied: D. Joaquín Arrarás Iribarren, D. José Antonio Balbontín Gutiérrez, D. Joaquín Bau Nolla, Mr Henry Buckley, D. Geminiano Carrascal Martín, D. Julián Cortés Cavanillas, D. Federico Fernández Castillejo, D. José María Gil Robles Quiñones de León, the late D. Manuel Giménez Fernández, D. José Gutiérrez-Ravé Montero, D. Enrique Jarero Alonso, Dr Salvador de Madariaga Rojo, D. Javier Martín Artajo, D. Juan Mercader, D. Román Perpiñá Grau, Sir Charles Petrie, Bt, D. Pedro Sáinz Rodríguez, Col Leonard Tomlins and D. Eugenio Vegas Latapié.

I should like to express my gratitude for his great help and guidance throughout the preparation of my work to the Warden of St Antony's College, Oxford; without his encouragement at times of weariness this book might never have been completed. I wish also to express my thanks to Mr Martin Blinkhorn, Mr Michael Hurst, Mr Brian Morris and D. Joaquín Romero Maura for reading the typescript, pointing out errors and making helpful suggestions; Mr Blinkhorn, with the benefit of his more intensive research, will doubtless at some future date correct certain of my statements on the Carlist movement and politics in the Basque Country. It goes without saying that I alone am responsible for whatever errors and shortcomings remain.

R. A. H. R.

List of Abbreviations

(i) POLITICAL PARTIES, TRADE UNIONS, ETC

AET	*Agrupación Escolar Tradicionalista*
CEDA	*Confederación Española de Derechas Autónomas*
CESO	*Confederación Española de Sindicatos Obreros*
CET	*Coalición Española de Trabajadores*
CMI	*Círculo Monárquico Independiente*
CNCA	*Confederación Nacional Católico-Agraria*
CNSCO	*Confederación Nacional de Sindicatos Católicos Obreros*
CNT	*Confederación Nacional del Trabajo*
CONS	*Central Obrera Nacional-Sindicalista*
DRV	*Derecha Regional Valenciana*
FAI	*Federación Anarquista Ibérica*
FE	*Falange Española de las JONS* (see below)
FET	*Federación Española de Trabajadores*
FNT	*Frente Nacional del Trabajo*
FUE	*Federación Universitaria Escolar*
ILE	*Institución Libre de Enseñanza*
JAP	*Juventud* (or *Juventudes*) *de Acción Popular*
JMI	*Juventud Monárquica Independiente*
JONS	*Juntas de Ofensiva Nacional-Sindicalista*
JSU	*Juventudes Socialistas Unificadas*
ORGA	*Organización Republicana Gallega Autónoma*
PCE	*Partido Comunista de España*
PNE	*Partido Nacionalista Español*
PNV	*Partido Nacionalista Vasco*
POUM	*Partido Obrero de Unificación Marxista*
PSOE	*Partido Socialista Obrero Español*
PSP	*Partido Social Popular*
SEU	*Sindicato Español Universitario*

SEV	*Sociedad de Estudios Vascos*
SOV	*Solidaridad de Obreros Vascos*
TYRE	*Tradicionalistas y Renovación Española*
UGT	*Unión General de Trabajadores*
UME	*Unión Militar Española*
UMN	*Unión Monárquica Nacional*
UP	*Unión Patriótica*

(ii) SOURCES

AP	*Acción Popular*
BOT	*Boletín de Orientación Tradicionalista*
BSS	*Bulletin of Spanish Studies*
DSC	*Diario de las sesiones de Cortes*
DSCC	*Diario de sesiones de las Cortes Constituyentes*
HCE	*Historia de la Cruzada española*
HGL	*Historia de la guerra de liberación* (*tomo I*)
HSRE	*Historia de la segunda República española*
JA	*José Antonio*
O.c.	*Obras completas* (of J. A. Primo de Rivera)

NOTE ON TITLES

Titles were officially abolished by the Second Republic; nevertheless many title-holders continued to use them. Persons are therefore referred to by the name most commonly accepted, eg Conde de Rodezno and Conde de Vallellano (and not Tomás Domínguez Arévalo and Fernando Suárez de Tangil), but José Antonio Primo de Rivera and General José Sanjurjo (and not the Marqués de Estella and General the Marqués del Rif).

NOTE ON PLACE-NAMES

Certain widely accepted Anglicised forms have been used, eg Catalonia for Cataluña, Corunna for La Coruña, Biscay for Vizcaya, Seville for Sevilla, Navarre for Navarra, Saragossa for Zarogoza, etc.

INDEX TO TEXT

Abadal Calderó, Raimundo de, 49, 50, 56, 91

ABC, 34, 38, 39, 40, 54, 68, 89–90, 111, 138, 147, 166, 167, 184, 194–5, 199, 269; suspensions, 42, 117

'accidentalism', 75, 107–9, 164–8

Acció Catalana Republicana, 50

Acción Castellana, 46

Acción Ciudadana (Cádiz), 117

Acción Española, 79, 98, 101, 130, 172

Acción Nacional: formation, 40; 1931 election manifesto and campaign, 45–6; links with other organisations, 46; candidates' defeat 1931, 54–5; becomes permanent body, 71; aims and programme, 71, 72, 73–5; diversity of members, 73; and 'accidentalism', 75; formation of organisations, 75–7; and Monarchists, 77–8, 79–80; campaign suspensions, 80–1; Socialist reactions, 81; local Rightist groups, 82; *see also Acción Popular*

Acción Obrerista, 77, 114, 163, 214–15

Acción Popular: 'legal tactic', 104; divisions of opinion, 1931–2, 105–6; government closure of offices 1931, 107; and Monarchists, 107–9, 110; development into political party, 107–10; and formation of CEDA, 113; suspension of meetings 1932–3, 118–19; Socialist attitude 1933, 135–6; and repeal of Law of Municipal Boundaries, 163

Acción Popular Catalana, 212

Acción Republicana, 139

Acción Social Popular, 25

agrarian problems: 1931–2, 85–7; 1933, 120–1

agrarian reform: views of *Acción Nacional*, 74; government inefficiency 1933, 121; debates in 1934, 162–3

Agrarian Reform, Law of, 1932, 87–9, 103; modification of 1935, 203–4; reintroduction of 1932 legislation 1936, 268

Agrarians: minority in Constituent Cortes, 57–8; and Constitution, 62, 67; and regional question, 62–3; and property rights, 63; and religious clauses, 64, 65; and agricultural aspects of economic crisis 1931–2, 85–6; and expropriation of *señorios*, 88; and Law of Agrarian Reform, 88–9, 203; concept of property, 88–9; and Court of Constitutional Guarantees, 118; attack on Carner's budget 1933, 119; and Law concerning Religious Confessions and Congregations, 123, 124; and rural leases, 127–8; and *Acción Popular*, 136; formation of *Partido Agrario Español*, 154–5; support Republican governments 1934, 155–6; and Catalan

Statute, 199; and wheat surplus 1934–5, 233–4

agricultural budget 1933, 120

Agrupación Socialista Madrileña, 261

Agrupación Regional Independiente, 117

Aguirre Lecube, José Antonio de, 48, 56, 69, 92, 93, 95, 145, 146, 185, 186, 191

Aizpún Santafé, Rafael, 188, 189, 212

Álava: and creation of a Basque State, 48, 93, 147, 185–6

Alba Bonifaz, Santiago, 32, 50, 57, 96, 240

Albiñana Sanz, José María, 35, 98, 156

Albornoz Liminiana, Álvaro, 262

Alcalá - Zamora Torres, Niceto: leader of Republican-Socialist coalition 1930, 33; and church burning 1931, 41; and civil status of the Church, 42; resignation October 1931, 59, 67; and religious clauses, 64, 65, 66, 67; first President of the Republic, 68; and Law concerning Religious Confessions and Congregations, 124; forces government crisis 1933, 126; withdraws support from Lerroux 1934, 159; and amnesty 1934, 160–2; and death sentences on revolutionaries, 195, 197; suspends Cortes 1935, 197; distrust of Gil Robles and hostility to CEDA, 197–8, 236; advocates moderate changes in Constitution, 207; entrusts formation of government to Chapaprieta 1935, 231; government crisis December 1935, 235–6; suspends Cortes, 240; asks Azaña to form government February 1936, 251; dismissed, 257–8

Alfonsines: and *Acción Nacional*, 78; and Traditionalists, 78, 79; and Sanjurjo plot, 97; resist

Acción Popular becoming political party, 109; and CEDA, 117; in favour of counter-revolutionary action, 129–30; military conspiracy 1932, 130–1; and Fascism, 132–3; and 1933 election, 143–4; hostility to Republican régime, 156; and 'accidentalism', 165; ideals in 1934, 172–3; and *Falange*, 179, 180; and Catalan Law of Farming Leases, 188; and Catalan Statute, 199; and hereditary Monarchy, 220–2; *see also Renovación Española*

Alfonso XII, 19

Alfonso XIII, 26, 28, 29, 30; attempt to return to 1876 Constitution, 31–2; supporters and opponents 1931, 32–5; leaves Spain, 37; and Monarchist supporters, 40; Bill of attainder against, 68; not involved in Sanjurjo plot, 97–8; and succession, 111, 117; refusals to abdicate, 113, 222; and CEDA, 117, 168–9, 222; supports conspiracy 1932, 130

Alfonso Carlos I: and Alfonsine-Carlist co-operation, 78; attacks 'atheist' Republic 1932, 78; and succession, 111, 113; opposed to Statute for Basque Provinces, 146; appoints Fal Conde Royal Secretary General, 175; orders suppression of TYRE, 176; manifesto June 1934, 176–8; designates Javier of Bourbon Parma Carlist Regent, 280

Alianzas Obreras, 183, 190, 271

Álvarez González, Melquíades, 32, 50, 51, 57, 96, 196, 197, 291

Álvarez Mendizábal, José María, 202, 257

Álvarez Robles, Antonio, 202, 203, 268

Álvarez Valdés, Ramón, 160

amnesty 1934, 159–61

Anarchism, growth of, 24

Anarchist risings 1931–3, 82, 122

Anarcho-Syndicalism, growth of 24
Anarcho-Syndicalists, 120, 183
Andalusia: unemployment and dis-
order 1933, 121; wheat crop
1935, 235; military rising 1936,
288
Anguera de Sojo, José Oriol, 189,
204
Ansaldo Vejarano, Major Juan
Antonio, 96, 97, 101, 130, 133,
180
Aparisi Guijarro, Antonio, 18–19
'Apostolic' Royalists, 15
Aragay Daví, Amadeo, 145
Arana Goiri, Sabino, 23
Aranzadi, 23
Araquistáin Queredo, Luis de, 150
arbitration, industrial, 29; see also
juries, mixed
Arboleya Martínez, Canon Maxi-
miliano, 25
Army: intervention in politics 1814-
1923, 27–8; military revolts 1930,
35; attitudes 1930–1, 25–6; 'accidentalist' attitude, 93; Azaña's
reforms 1931, 94–5; Orgaz con-
spiracy 1931, 95; Sanjurjo plot,
96–8, 100–4; Gil Robles' re-
organisation 1935, 227–8; con-
spiracy 1936, 277–90; conflict of
opinion on military intervention,
277–8; War Minister's powers
over appointments, 282–3; political aims of 'National Rising',
291–2; incomplete success, 293
Arranz Olalla, Gregorio, 72, 242
Asociación Femenina de Acción
Nacional, 75–6
Asociación Patronal Católica de
España, 215
Asturias: revolt of 1934, 190–1, 196
Ateneo, 41
Aunós, Pérez, Eduardo, 29, 221–2
Austria: Socialist rising 1934, 182
Ayats Surribas, José, 67, 72
Azaña Díaz, Manuel, 33; and
church burning 1931, 41; forms
second Provisional government,

67; proclaims Spain no longer
Catholic, 67; forms first government of Republic, 60, 68;
military reforms 1931, 94–5; and
Sanjurjo plot, 101, 102–3; reaction against his government 1933,
105; and Republicanism, 106;
confrontation with Gil Robles on
independence of judicial power,
118; government attacked over
Casas Viejas, 122; new government 1933, 126; resigns, 129;
opposition to Lerroux's government, 139; and 1933 election,
143; not against violence 1934,
153; and Socialist revolutionary
plans, 182–3; and Catalan Law of
Farming Leases, 188; and Catalan rising 1934, 190; acquitted of
providing Portuguese arms, 198;
reluctance to take power February 1936, 250–1; government
programme, 252–3; attempts to
appease parties, 257; President
of the Republic May 1936, 262;
and civil disorder, 260; government crisis, 263; removal of
Franco and Goded, 277
Aznar, Admiral Juan Bautista, 32
Aznar Embíd, Severino, 27, 36
Azpeitia Esteban, Mateo, 162, 235

Balbo, Marshal Italo, 97, 174
Balmes, Fr Jaime, 16–17
Barba Hernández, Captain Barto-
lomé, 226
Barcelona: revolt 1934, 190
Barnés Salinas, Francisco J., 267
Barrera Luyando, General Emilio,
96, 97, 100, 101, 174
Basque economic privileges, 186
Basque nationalism, 23–4
Basque Nationalist Party, see PNV
Basque Nationalists, 48–9, 185–6;
and Traditionalists, 49; meeting
with Orgaz 1931, 95; and Law
concerning Religious Confes-
sions and Congregations, 123–4

Basque-Navarrese, 62, 67, 72, 118, 128

Basque Provinces: General Statute of the Basque State 1931 (Statute of Estella), 48–9, 92; Constituent Cortes elections 1931, 56; 'Single Statute' 1932, 92–3; Draft Statute 1933, 146–7, 185–6; risings 1934, 191; statute of autonomy 1936, 267

Batet Mestres, General Domingo, 190

Bau Nolla, Joaquín, 287

Benavente, Jacinto, 217

Berenguer Fusté, General Dámaso, 31, 37, 38

Bergamín, Francisco, 103

Bergé, Ramón, 73

Bermúdez Cañete, Antonio, 100

Besteiro Fernández, Julián, 29, 60–1, 129, 137, 181, 198, 245, 261, 262, 263

Beúnza Redín, Joaquín, 56, 65, 66, 69, 73, 79–80

Biscay: and creation of a Basque State, 48, 93, 146

Blasquistas, 242

Bloque Hispano Nacional, 176

Bloque Nacional, 216–18, 227, 244, 280, 287

Budget: 1933, 119–20; 1936 proposals, 234–5

Burgos: wheat prices 1933, 120

Burgos Mazo, Manuel, 32, 96

Caballeristas, 245, 246, 262; accuse Right of provoking civil disorder, 269; and *Prististas*, 271–2

Caballero García, General Federico, 97

Cabanellas Ferrer, General Miguel, 279

caciquismo, 19, 52–4, 150, 163, 241, 249

Calderón Rojo, Abilio, 58

Calvo Sotelo, José, 29, 57, 79, 128, 191, 255; and *Maurismo*, 26–7; and economic crisis 1931, 84, 86;

attempt to end dynastic schism, 111; and Fascism, 131, 273; 1933 election campaign, 142; opposition to Rightist participation in government 1933–4, 156; and *Bloque Hispano Nacional*, 172–3; criticisms of Gil Robles, 172–3; and installation of Monarchy, 176; and death sentences on October 1934 revolutionaries, 196; and Catalan Statute, 200; and the *Bloque Nacional*, 216, 218; views on Parliament, 215–16; and regionalism, 219; and 'integrative State', 218–20; and 'accidentalism', 218; and the Army, 226; economic ideas 1935, 228, 229–30, 231; leader of Right 1936, 239; 1936 election, 242–4; threat of violence if defeated, 247; urges Portela not to give power to Left, 251; holds CEDA responsible for defeat, 252; and civil disorder 1936, 259, 260, 266, 273; need for unity of Right, 262; attacks on Casares Quiroga's government, 266; and Basque Statute, 267; and rural wages, 269; economic ideas 1936, 270; and Casares Quiroga's charges of subversion, 273, 274; murder of, 274–5; and military conspirators, 287

Cambó Batlle, Francisco de Asís, 23, 31, 49, 91, 144, 155, 187, 249, 256, 291

Cánovas del Castillo, Antonio, 19, 24, 28

Carlism, 15–16, 19, 21–2, 175

Carlists: disintegration of Catholic-Monarchist Communion 1880s, 20–2; and 1933 election campaign, 143–4; and succession, 176–7; ideas of 'New State' 1935, 222–4; and military rising 1936, 281–2, 283–4, 285–6

Carlist War 1833–40, 15–16; 2nd 1872–6, 19

Carlos V, 15–16
Carlos VII, 18, 21
Carner Romeu, Jaime, 83; budget
    1933, 119–20, 228
Carrascal Martín, Geminiano, 270
Carrasco Formiguera, Manuel, 67,
    72
Casanueva Gorjón, Cándido, 87,
    89, 103, 115, 155, 161, 162, 171,
    201
Casares Quiroga, Santiago, 198;
    Minister of the Interior 1933,
    122, 133; forms government May
    1936, 239, 263; and civil disorder,
    260, 273; and defence of Repub-
    lic, 264–5; attacks by Calvo
    Sotelo on his government, 266;
    and Calvo Sotelo's responsibility
    for subversion, 273; govern-
    ment's minimisation of disorder
    and military conspiracy, 288–9
Casas Viejas: shootings 1933, 122
Castillo, Lieutenant José, 274
Castro Albarrán, Canon Aniceto de,
    165–6, 168
Catalan nationalism, 23, 49
Catalan rising 1934, 190
Catalan Statute of Autonomy, 50,
    89–92, 198–200
Catalonia: Mancomunidad, 23;
    Constituent Cortes elections, 56;
    in 1932–3, 144–5; Law of Farm-
    ing Leases, 187–9; in 1936, 258,
    267
'catastrophism', 18
Catholic students' confederation, 27
Catholicism: sole religion of the
    State 1851, 17; late 19th century,
    24–5
Catholics: and political parties
    1929, 36; and Constitution 1931,
    60, 62, 70–1; and religious
    clauses, 61, 64–7; and property
    rights, 63; seek to institute second
    chamber of Parliament, 67; re-
    visionist campaign 1931, 71–82;
    and the Republic, 106, 166; and
    Law concerning Religious Con-

fessions and Congregations, 123,
    124, 125; endorsement of mili-
    tary rising 1936, 292
Cavalcanti   de   Albuquerque,
    General José, 101
Cebellos Botín, Pablo, 108
CEDA, 105; evolutionary tactic, 106;
    foundation 1933, 113–17; social
    policies, 114–15; and regionalism,
    115-16; and confessionalism 116-
    17; and Monarchists 1933, 117;
    Socialist charges against, 134;
    and Fascism, 134–5, 265; policy
    December 1933, 135; similarity
    of aims to Socialists', 138; Lar-
    roux's hopes of co-operation,
    139; and 1933 election campaign,
    143, 147; supports Lerroux 1933-
    4, 152; not seeking to govern
    1933, 154; support for yunteros,
    163; 'tactic' of 'possibilism', 167;
    papal support for 'accidentalist'
    views, 168; and Austrian experi-
    ment, 172; and Basque Statute,
    185–6; and Catalan Law of Farm-
    ing Leases, 188; and death sen-
    tences on October 1934 revolu-
    tionaries, 195–7; and social poli-
    cies 1934–5, 204–5, 215; col-
    laboration with Radicals, 205–7;
    following in 1934, 214–15; and
    the Bloque Nacional, 218; and
    wheat surplus 1934–5, 233–4;
    excluded from Portela's govern-
    ment 1935, 236; attack on Alcalá-
    Zamora, 236; and Portelista
    alliances 1936, 241–2; Republi-
    can Right alliances, 242; and
    Monarchists, 242–4; 1936 elec-
    tion, 244–5, 248; causes of defeat,
    251–2; and Azaña's government
    February 1936, 253–4; denies
    Socialist allegations of violence,
    255; and governmental reorgani-
    sation, 262; dislike of idea of
    national coalition government,
    263, 264; electoral malpractice
    enquiry, 256; withdrawal from

Cortes June 1936, 267; loss of influence, 276; disintegration 292
cemeteries, secularisation of, 69–70
censorship, 258
CET, 215
Chapaprieta Torregrosa, Joaquín, 228, 236, 240; Minister of Finance 1935, 230–1; forms government, 231–2; budget proposals for 1936, 234–5
Church: confiscation of property in 19th century, 15, 17; and Constitutions of 1869 and 1876, 20; and Republic, 42–4, 61–2, 74; property sales or transfer forbidden, 42, 43–4; state-ownership of property 1933, 123; and laicism in education, 125
Church burials, 69–70
Church burning 1931, 41–2
Cid Ruiz de Zorrilla, José María, 58, 155, 189, 256, 269
Cimas Leal, José, 108
Círculo Carlista, 113
Círculos Católicos, 24–5
Cirera Voltá, José, 212
Civil disorder 1931, 82; 1933, 119, 221; 1934 (Socialist general strike), 189–91; repressive measures, 194–7; 1936, 238, 249–50, 258, 266, 269, 270–1, 272; government debates, 259–60; distribution of arms to workers, 289
Civil War, 293
Claridad, 261
Clergy: state payment of stipends, 17, 161, 267
CMI, 40, 44, 54
CNCA, 25, 27, 54, 57, 87
CNSCO, 25, 77, 215
CNT, 25, 60, 77, 82, 119, 120, 138, 145, 190, 247, 249, 271–2; abstention from 1933 elections, 150; uprising 1933, 157; and Socialists 1934, 183; strike activities, 184
Comillas, Marqués de, 25
Common Lands, Law for the recovery of, 268

Communists: and Socialists, 183; and Caballeristas, 271
Companys Jover, Luis, 49, 145, 186–7, 188, 190, 198, 267
Comunión Tradicionalista Carlista, 93, 175–9, 224; and Sanjurjo plot, 98; and Alfonsines, 175, 176; reorganisation 1934, 178–9; and the Bloque Nacional, 218, 280; and succession question, 280; and aims of rising 1936, 284
Concordat of 1851, 17
Condés, Captain Fernando, 274
Confederación del Ebro, 86
Confederación Española de Sindicatos Obreros (CESO), 215
Confederación Regional de Trabajo, 190
Conquista del Estado, La, 35, 98, 99
Conservative party: collapse in 1913, 26
CONS, 181, 215
constituencies: reorgnisation 1931, 53–4
Constitution of 1812, 14–15; 1869, 20; 1876, 20; 1931, 59, 61–8, Ossorio's draft rejected, 61, regional issue, 62–3, property rights, 63, workers' rights and conditions, 63–4, religious clauses, 64–7, legislation implementing religious clauses, 68–71, reform advocated 1935, 207
Constitutionalists, 32, 39, 50, 96
corporativism, 209–11
Cortes: Constituent 1931, 55–6; Agrarian minority, 57–8; composition after 1933 election, 149; composition after 1936 election, 257; President's powers of dissolution, 257
Costa, Joaquín, 24
Court of Constitutional Guarantees, 118, 128, 198; and Catalan Law of Farming Leases, 187
Cruzado Español, El, 113
Cuatro Vientos: military revolts 1930, 35

Cuesta Cobo de la Torre, Ramón de la, 57

Dato, Eduardo, 26
Debate, El, 36, 38, 39, 40, 44, 54, 62, 72, 75, 87, 89, 90, 108, 122, 125, 127, 138, 148, 166, 172, 182, 184, 194, 197, 233, 235, 247, 252, 253, 262; suspensions, 42, 81, 117
Decree for the Intensification of Farming 1932, 121
Defence Law of the Republic, 60, 68, 118–19, 127
De la Taille, Fr, 165
Delgado Barreto, Manuel, 131
Del Río Rodríguez, Cirilo, 162–3, 202, 203, 204, 240, 242
democracy: Socialist attitude, 137–8
Dencás Puigdollers, José, 188, 190
Derecha Social (Mallorca), 46
Derecho a la rebeldía, El, 168
Diputación foral (Navarre), 212
divorce, 65, 70
Dollfuss, Engelbert, 172, 182, 220
Domingo Sanjuán, Marcelino, 87, 120, 121, 164
Donoso Cortés, Juan, 17–18
Doval, Major Lisardo, 196
DRV, 75, 109, 114, 116, 292; foundation and policy, 46; model for Acción Nacional, 81–2
Dualde Gómez, Joaquín, 200, 207
Durán Ventosa, Luis, 50, 91

ecclesiastical budget, 65, 66, 70; Law regulating incomes of parish priests 1934, 161
economic situation 1931, 83–4, 85–6; 1932–3, 119–22; 1935, 228–31, 233–5; 1936, 269–70
Editorial Católica, 27
education, 65, 67, 161, 123, 124, 125, 200, 267; views of Acción Nacional, 74
elections: Constituent Cortes 1931, 55–8; Cortes 1933, 148–51, campaign, 140–7, malpractice, 150; Cortes 1936, 247–9, alliances,

241–4, campaign, 244–7, malpractice, 255–6, new elections ordered in Cuenca and Granada, 256–7; Court of Constitutional Guarantees, 128; Municipal 1931, 36–7; malpractice, 53; Municipal 1933, 125–6, 146
electoral reforms: Decree of 1931, 53–4; Law of 1933, 148
Eliseda, Marqués de la, 130
employers: payment of wages to unemployed 1936, 269
Época, La, 176
Escamots, 187
Esperanza, La, 47
Esquerra, 50, 55, 89, 90, 91, 92, 139, 144–5, 153, 161, 164, 198, 199; withdrawal from Cortes 1934, 186, 187
Estat Català, 49, 190, 267
Estella, Statute of, see Basque Provinces: General Statute
Estelrich Artigues, Juan, 56, 91, 124
Euzkadi, 23, 48, 93
evictions, 86, 202–3, 268
Extremadura: unemployment and disorder 1933, 121; yunteros, 162–3, 200–1

FAI, 60, 145, 247
Falange de la Sangre, 180
Falange Española: foundation, 133; merger with JONS, 179–81; offers aid in Madrid revolt, 189–90; and the Bloque Nacional, 218; aims, 224–6; 1936 elections, 243; counter-terrorist violence and proscription, 238, 254; and military rising, 282, 284–5
Fal Conde, Manuel, 175; reorganisation of Carlist Communion, 178–9; and Right's 1936 election defeat, 252; support for Azaña February 1936, 254; Alfonso Carlos's Delegate-in-Chief in Spain 280; offers Sanjurjo leadership of Requetés, 281; and Carlist

participation in military rising, 284, 285–6
family rights, 65
Fanjul Goñi, General Joaquín, 57, 155, 195, 227, 236, 277, 279
Faraudo, Captain Carlos, 258
Fascio, El, 131–2
Fascism: Goicoechea's position, 130; Calvo Sotelo's admiration, 131, 273; government's attitude, 133; Gil Robles denunciation, 134–5, 140, 171
Federación de Derechas, 110
Félix Maíz, B., 282, 286
Fernández - Ladreda Méndez Valdés, José María, 107–8, 109
Fernández Pérez, General Emilio, 101
Fernández Ruano, Ángel, 107
Fernández Villaverde, Mercedes, 75
Fernando VII, 14–16
FET, 215
FET *y de las* JONS, 293
FNT, 215
Franco, Bahamonde, General Francisco: attitude to Republican regime, 93–4; refuses to support Sanjurjo plot, 100; deals with Asturian revolt, 190; opposes Monarchist plans 1934, 195; Chief of General Staff 1935, 227; vetoes rising 1935, 236; presses for 'state of war' February 1936, 250; opposes power for Left, 251; and 1936 elections, 256; posted to Canaries, 277; and military rising, 287–8, 291; 'Head of the Government of the Spanish State', 293
Franco Bahamonde, Major Ramón, 35
FUE, 132
fueros, 22, 23, 178

Gaceta del Norte, La, 48
Gaceta Regional, La, 108
Gafo Muñiz, Fr José, 25
2G

Galán, Rodríguez, Captain Fermín, 35
Galarza Morante, Colonel Valentín, 130–1, 226, 277
Galicia: statute of autonomy, 267
Gallegos Rocafull, Canon, 55
García Valdecasas, Alfonso, 132, 133
Generalidad, 49, 50, 90, 91, 199, 267; 1933 elections, 144–5; requests withdrawal of PNV from Cortes, 186; 1934 elections, 187
'Generation of 98', 24
Gil Robles Quiñones de León, José María, 27, 58; and Constitution, 62; and property rights, 63; and religious clauses, 65, 66, 67; seeks bi-cameral system of government and referendum procedure, 67; and withdrawal of Agrarians from Constituent Cortes, 72; and *Acción Nacional*, 72–3, 77, 82; 'accidentalism', 80, 116–17, 165, 166, 167; and economic crisis 1931, 84; and Catalan Statute, 90, 198, 199; and Sanjurjo plot, 103–4; 'legal' tactic, 104, 167, 169; and development of *Acción Popular* into political party, 105, 107–10; and the Republic, 106; 'possibilism', 106, 153, 194, 211; and formation of CEDA, 113–17; protests at detentions after Sanjurjo rising, 117–18; confrontation with Azaña on independence of judicial power, 118; and Law concerning Religious Confessions and Congregations 123; and 1933 municipal elections, 125; and Azaña's government 1933, 126; and Draft Law on Rural Leases, 128; Socialist attitude towards, 129–30, 134, 135; and Fascism, 134–5, 140, 171; and CEDA policy 1932, 135; and ban on *Acción Popular* rally, 136; 1933 election, 140–2, 144; and Electoral Law, 148; not seeking

Gil Robles—*cont.*
to govern immediately, 148, 154; and CEDA in government 1933–4, 152, 153–4, 157; and Martínez Barrio, 159; and amnesty 1934, 159, 160; offers CEDA help in amnesty crisis, 161–2; supports *yunteros*, 163; Monarchist accusations of insincerity, 167; and JAP, 171, 212–13; likened to Dollfuss by Socialists, 171–2; and evolutionary policy, 172–3; and *Falangistas*, 181; and Catalan Law of Farming Leases, 188, 189; and Socialist revolutionary outbreaks 1934, 191; and punishment of revolutionaries, 194, 195; asks for more portfolios in Radical-CEDA coalition 1935, 197; and *Cedistas'* attitude to Giménez Fernandez' measures on leases, 202; and Radical-CEDA coalition, 205–7; policies and aims after October 1934, 207–11; corporativism and parliamentarianism, 209–11; and regionalism, 211; Minister of War, 226; Army reorganisation, 227–8; economic ideas 1935, 228, 230, 231; and *'straperlo'* scandal, 232; wheat surplus, 1934–5, 233–4; and Chapaprieta's budget proposals, 234, 235; asks to be made Premier December 1935, 236; loss of CEDA followers, 238; 1936 election, 239, 245, 251–2, 255; disruption of Portela's governments 1935, 240, 241; and Monarchists 1936 election, 243; asks for 'state of war' February 1936, 250; support for Azaña's government, 253–4, 255; and President's powers of dissolution of Cortes, 257; and civil disorder, 259–60, 272–3, 276–7; and choice before government 1936, 262; and idea of national coalition government, 263; denies CEDA is Fascist, 265;

and Popular Front, 272–3; and Calvo Sotelo's murder, 276; endorses military rising, 291, 292
Giménez Caballero, Ernesto, 35, 132
Giménez Fernández, Manuel, 163, 197–8, 263; Minister of Agriculture 1934–5, 189, 200–2; and Law of Agrarian Reform, 203, 268; wheat surplus 1934–5, 233; and support of government 1936, 262; and 1936 electoral malpractice enquiry, 256
Giral Pereira, José, 289
Goded Llopis, General Manuel, 96, 97, 195, 227, 277
Goicoechea Cosculluela, Antonio, 55, 79, 156; and *Juventudes Maurista*, 26; and *Acción Nacional*, 45, 80; and Catalan Statute, 89; supports Sanjurjo, 97; resigns from *Acción Popular*, 110–11; and *Renovación Española*, 111–13, 117; and Fascism, 130; and 1933 election campaign, 143; and amnesty 1934, 160; and Italian aid to Monarchists, 174, 175; and Primo de Rivera, 180; and Catalan Law of Farming Leases, 187–8; and Socialist revolutionary outbreaks 1934, 191; and 1936 elections, 252, 255; support for Azaña February 1936, 254; and 1936 electoral malpractice enquiry, 256; speech at Calvo Sotelo's funeral, 275
Gomá Tomás, Isidro Cardinal, 168
González Carrasco, General Manuel, 100
González Mendoza, General, 291–2
González Peña, Ramón, 196
Grupo de la Democracia Cristiana, 27, 36
Guadalajara: wheat prices 1935, 234
Guadalhorce, Conde de, 29, 34, 159
Gua'lar Poza, Fr Santíago, 70, 77, 115; and religious clauses, 64, 65; and *Acción Popular* as political

party, 108, 109; attacks Largo Caballero on Ministry of Labour's 1933 budget, 120; and Law concerning Religious Confessions and Congregations, 124
Guipúzcoa: and creation of a Basque State, 48, 93, 146–7

Heraldo Alavés, 92
Herrera Oria, Ángel, 27, 36, 39, 45, 55, 115, 125, 167, 168; advocates ralliement, 44; and Acción Nacional, 71, 77, 82; and 'accidentalism', 75, 165
Hidalgo Durán, Diego, 190
Hoyos, Marqués de, 32, 36

Imparcial, El, 117
Incháusti, A. de, 214
Industrial arbitration, 68; see also juries, mixed
industrial unrest 1933, 119
Institute of Agrarian Reform, 87
Integrist Party, 21
Integrists, 46, 47
'Intellectuals in the Service of the Republic', 33–4
irrigation, 86–7
Isabel II, 16–18
Italy: support promised for overthrow of Republic, 174
Izquierda Republicana, 198, 245

Jaca: military revolt, 35
Jaime III, 22, 47, 78
Jaimists, 46–8; and Acción Nacional, JAP, 100, 114, 169–71; 1933 election campaign, 140, 150; not Fascist June 1934, 170; Movilización Civil, 170, 189; in 1935, 212–14; loyalty to Gil Robles, 213, 254–5, 265; shares some Falange views, 213–14; and Calvo Sotelo, 214; 1936 election, 244–5
Japistas: attracted to Falange 1936, 254
Javier of Bourbon Parma, 281; designated Carlist Regent, 280; 2G*

gives permission to mobilise Requetés under Mola, 286
Jesuits: expulsion 1820, 15; dissolution, 66, 68–9
Jiménez de Asúa, Luis, 62, 258
JONS, 97, 98–9, 100, 132, 179
JMI, 34, 39
JSU, 261, 271
Juan (son of Alfonso XIII), 111, 113, 176, 177, 222
Juntas Castellanas de Actuación Hispánica, 99–100
Juridical Statute 1931, 38–9
juries, mixed, 120, 121, 127, 204–5; CEDA policy, 114
Juventud de Acción Nacional, 76–7
Juventudes Mauristas, 26

Labour, Ministry of: 1933 budget, 119–20
labour arbitration; see juries, mixed
La Cierva Peñafiel, Juan de, 97, 111
Lamamié de Clairac de la Colina José María, 69, 72, 87, 90, 111, 118, 143, 179, 191, 201–2, 256
land redistribution: 87–9, 201, 203–4, 268–9
landlords: evictions of tenants 1935, 202–3
Lara Zárate, Antonio, 159
Largo Caballero, Francisco, and revolutionary methods, 83, 106, 142–3, 158, 182, 247, 271, 272; Law of Municipal Boundaries 86; and the Republic, 106; attacked on Ministry of Labour budget 1933, 119–20; President of PSOE executive committee, 129; ILO conference speech, 137; and democracy, 138; opposition to Lerroux's government, 139; seeks united front with extreme Left 1934, 183; leader of extreme Left 1936, 239; resigns from PSOE executive committee, 245; and Socialism, 246–7; and Prieto, 261, 264

Larraz López, José, 234
leases: Draft Law on Rural Leases
1933, 127–8; Catalan Law of
Farming Leases, 187–9, 267;
Law on Rural Leases 1935, 201–
3; new law 1936, 268
Ledesma Ramos, Ramiro, 35, 98,
99, 100, 132, 225
Left: attack on government over
Casas Viejas, 122; losses in 1933
election, 149–50; political distribution 1933, 150–1; attitude
to Cortes 1933–4, 164; and
'straperlo' affair, 232; protest at
repression of Asturian revolutionaries, 196; 1936 election,
245–7, 248–9; allegations of malpractice, 255–6
Leizaola Sánchez, Jesús María, 62,
63, 65, 67, 70
Lema, Marqués de, 45, 111
Leo XIII, pope, 17, 20, 223; policy
of ralliement, 165
Lerroux García, Alejandro, 31, 51,
55; leader of Radicals 1931, 33;
and civil status of the Church,
42; excluded from Republican-
Socialist coalition 1931, 60, 84–5;
refuses to rise against government
1932, 96; interpretation of 'Republic', 106; forms Republican
coalition governments 1933, 129,
139, 156–7; Socialist charges
against, 134; rejects Socialist-
Radical-Left Republican alliance
in favour of CEDA, 148 9, 152;
allies with CEDA and Agrarians,
157; re-forms government 1934,
159; declines to censure Alcalá-
Zamora, 162; and Basque Statute
1933, 185; forms government
October 1934, 189; declares
'state of war', 189; closes Cortes,
191; and re-establishment of
Republic after revolts, 193; and
death sentences on revolutionaries, 195–7; forms interim
government April 1935, 197;

and Catalan Statute, 198, 199;
and Radical-CEDA coalition, 205–
7; and 'straperlo' scandal, 232;
leaves government, 233; and
Chapaprieta's budget proposals
1936, 234; 1936 election, 242,
249; endorses military rising,
291, 292
Lerroux, Aurelio, 232
Liberal Conservative-Liberal bi-
partisan rotation in office, 19, 24
Libertad, 99, 100
Lizarza Iribarren, Antonio, 174,
175, 285, 286
Lliga Regionalista, 23, 39, 49–50,
56; and Catalan Statute, 49, 50,
91, 198–9; on regional issue, 62;
Generalidad elections 1933, 144–
5; withdrawal from Generalidad
1934, 187; and Catalan rising,
190; 1936 election alliances, 242
López de Ochoa Portuondo,
General Eduardo, 191
Los Reyes, Lieutenant Anastasio
de, 258
Los Ríos Urruti, Fernando de, 42,
61, 137, 262
Lozoya, Marqués de, 79
Luca de Tena, Marqués de, 41, 80
Lucía Lucía, Luis, 46, 188, 198,
235, 292; and Acción Popular as
political party, 109, 110; and
formation of CEDA, 113–17; and
confessionalism, 116; and regionalism, 116; supports government
position 1936, 289

Maciá Llusa, Francisco, 23, 49, 89,
92, 144–5, 186
Madariaga Almendros, Dimas de,
55, 58, 64, 71, 204; and Acción
Nacional, 72; and Acción Obrerista, 77, 214–15
Madariaga Rojo, Salvador de: and
amnesty 1934, 160
Madrid: general strike 1934, 189
Maeztu Whitney, Ramiro de, 34,
38, 79, 86, 220–1

Magescas, Armand, 131
Mangada, Colonel Julio, 97
Marañón Posadillo, Gregorio, 291
March Ordinas, Juan, 57
María Cristina, Queen, 15–16
Marín Lázaro, Rafael, 45
Martín Báguenas, Santiago, 130
Martín Martín, Pedro, 85, 145
Martínez Anido, General Severiano, 130
Martínez Barrio, Diego, 250, 263; informs Azaña of Sanjurjo plot, 101; attacks government over Casas Viejas, 122; forms Republican coalition government October 1933, 139–40; resigns from government and leaves Radical Party, 159; interim President of the Republic 1936, 258; forms government July 1936 and tries to compromise with Mola, 289
Martínez de Velasco, José: leader of Agrarian minority, Constituent Cortes, 57, 58; and laicist education, 66; and Agrarian withdrawal from Cortes, 72; and *Acción Nacional*, 72, 73; 1933 municipal election, 125; president of Right's electoral committee, 143; forms *Partido Agrario Español*, 154–6; allies with Lerroux 1933, 157; and amnesty 1934, 160; and Catalan Law of Farming Leases, 187, 188; and CEDA-Radical coalition 1935, 196, 197, 232, 234, 235, 236; and CEDA's inclusion in Portela's government, 240; 1936 election defeat, 249; endorses military rising, 291
Martínez García-Argüelles, Alfredo, 258
Martínez Rubio, Ginés, 178
Masquelet Lacací, General Carlos, 278
Maura Montaner, Antonio, 26
Maura Gamazo, Gabriel (Duque de Maura), 31, 32, 37, 38

Maura Gamazo, Miguel: leader of Republican-Socialist coalition 1930, 33; and church burning 1931, 41–2; and Segura, 43–4; and Bishop of Vitoria, 44; and separatism, 51; and 1931 municipal election malpractice, 53; resignation October 1931, 59, 67, 84; suspends newspapers, 92; and Azaña's government 1933, 126–7; breaks with regime 1934, 189; and CEDA-Radical government, 198; fails to form government 1936, 236; 1936 elections, 242; and idea of national coalition government, 263, 272
Maurín, Juliá, Joaquín, 245, 273–4
Maurismo, 24, 26–7
mayors: 'instruction' of, 53
Medina Togores, José de, 73, 108
Mendizábal, Juan, Alvarez, 15
Menéndez Fernández, Teodomiro, 196
Menéndez Pelayo, Marcelino, 20–1
Meseta: regionalism, 116; wheat prices 1933, 120
Miaja Menant, General José, 289
Minoriá Popular Agraria, 154, 166, 168
mixed juries, see juries, mixed
Mola Vidal, General Emílio, 35, 227; military conspiracy 1936, 277, 278–9, 281–3, efforts to control conspirators, 283, and Carlist participation, 283–4, 285–6, and inclusion of Franco, 287, refuses to compromise with Martínez Barrio, 289, proclaims martial law, 289, 291; and Civil War, 293
Molero Lobo, General Nicolás, 250
Moles Ormella, Juan, 274
Molina Nieto, Fr Ramón, 55
Monarchists: groups in 1930, 34–5; Alfonso XIII's attitude 1931, 40; and *Acción Nacional*, 77–8, 79–80; and Sanjurjo plot, 96–8; and *Acción Popular*, 105, 107–9, 110; and the Republic, 106; and

470   THE ORIGINS OF FRANCO'S SPAIN

Monarchists:—*cont.*

Renovación Española, 111–13; and 1933 election, 143, 148, 149; hostility to Republican regime, 1934, 156; and amnesty 1934, 159; and 'accidentalism', 166, 168–9; accuse Gil Robles of insincerity, 167; and CEDA's 'possibilism', 167, 237; seek Italian support for overthrow of Republic, 174; restoration and succession questions, 175, 176–7, 178, 222; and Catalan Law of Farming Leases, 187; and socialist revolutionary outbreaks 1934, 192; methods for dealing with Left, 194; wish for Army régime, 195; and death sentences on revolutionaries, 195–6; and Catalan Statute, 198, 199; and 1935 modifications to Law of Agrarian Reform, 203; and the *Bloque Nacional*, 217–18; and Primo de Rivera, 224; and '*straperlo*' scandal, 232; and CEDA's fall from power 1935, 237; and CEDA 1936 election, 242–4, 252; Republican alliances 1936, 244; and Azaña's government February 1936, 254; and 1936 electoral malpractice enquiry, 256; and civil disorder, 275–6; *see also* Alfonsines, Carlists, Integrists, Traditionalists

Monarchy: 1814, 14–15; succession question 1830, 15; 1817–1923, 19

Montiel, 51

Moral, Joaquín del, 97

Moreno Dávila, Julio, 109

Moreno Navarro, Captain Antonio, 274

Morroco: rising 1936, 283, 288

Moutas Merás, José Maria, 108

Múgica, Mateo, Bishop of Vitoria, 44, 61

Mundo Obrero, 42

Municipal Boundaries, Law of, 86; repeal 1934, 163

Mussolini, Benito, 174, 175

Mutualidad Obrera Maurista, 26

Nación, La, 117

National Assembly 1927, 29

National Cerealist Assembly, 120

national coalition government, plans for (1936), 239, 262, 263–4, 272

'National Counter-Revolutionary Front', 244

nationalism, 22–4

nationalist revival attempts 1930, 1931, 35

Navarre: and General Statute of the Basque State (Statute of Estella), 48, 49, 92, 93; and PNV, 146; *Diputación foral*, 212

Navarrese regionalism, 24

Nocedal, Cándido, 18–19

Nocedal Romea, Ramón, 21

'Nombela affair', 233

Olazábal, Juan de, 92, 111

Olazábal, Rafael de, 174

Oñate, Marqués de, 22

ORGA, 128, 139

Oreja Elósegui, Marcelino, 191

Orgaz Yoldi, General Luis, 95, 97, 277, 278

Oriol Urigüen, José Luis de, 93, 111, 146, 185

Ortega Gasset, José, 84, 291

Ossorio Gallardo, Ángel, 26, 27, 32, 51, 57, 61

Pablo-Blanco Torres, Joaquín de, 236, 240

'Pact of Salamanca', 193, 306

Paláu, Fr Gabriel, 25

Palencia: wheat prices 1933, 120

Palomo Aguado, Emilio, 148

Parliamentarianism, 209

Partido Social Popular, 27

PCE, 183, 245, 261

Pemán Pemartín, José María, 45, 79, 112, 172

Peña Nova (Governor), 162

Pérez de Laborda, José María, 170, 254, 256
Pérez Madrigal, Joaquín, 242
Pérez Platero, Bishop of Segovia, 70
'Persian' Royalists, 14–15
Pestaña Núñez, Ángel, 245
Pich Pon, Juan, 199
Pidal Mon, Alejandro, 20
Pita Romero, Leandro, 168, 242
Pius IX, pope, 17
Pius XI, pope: and Law concerning Religious Confessions and Congregations, 125; support for 'accidentalism', 168
Pizzardo, Mgr Giuseppe, 168
PNE, 35, 98, 101, 131, 218
PNV: foundation, 23–4; and statutes for Basque Provinces, 48, 146, 185–6, 267; and Traditionalists, 92, 93, 145–6; and Basque economic privileges, 186; and Socialist revolutionary plans, 186; and Basque risings 1934, 191; 1934–5, 211–12; 1936 elections, 242; support of Popular Front, 291
Ponte Manso de Zúñiga, General Miguel, 95, 96, 100
Popular Front, 245–6, 247–8, 249, 255, 256, 260, 262, 263, 272–3; 289
Portela Valladares, Manuel: Governor-General of *Generalidad* 1935, 199; governments 1935, 236, 238, 239–40; 'packing' of local government committees, 240, 241; dissolves Cortes, 240; 1936 elections, 241, 242; declares 'state of alarm' February 1936, 249; refuses to declare 'state of war', 250; refuses Gil Robles a place in government, 250; urges Azaña to take power, 250–1; resigns, 251; endorses military rising, 291
Portelista candidates 1936 election, 241–2
'possibilism', 16–17, 106, 153, 167, 194, 211, 237

POUM, 245
Pozas Perea, General Sebastián, 250
Pradera Larrumbe, Víctor, 27, 47, 175, 222–4
Prat de la Riba Serra, Enrique, 23
Prietistas, 271–2
Prieto Tuero, Indalecio, 66, 129, 137, 139, 188, 245; advocate of Socialist - Republican alliance, 1927, 29; and the Republic, 106; favours Basque Statute 1932, 146; and CEDA, 153; attitude to Gil Robles and CEDA 1933, 157–8; and amnesty 1934, 160; favours revolutionary methods, 181; advocate of evolutionary socialism, 239; and Largo Caballero, 261, 264, 272; refuses to form government May 1936, 263; and national coalition government, 263; and 1936 electoral malpractice enquiry, 256; and President's powers of dissolution of Cortes, 257; and civil disorder 1936, 260, 275
Primo de Rivera Orbaneja, General Miguel, 28–9
Primo de Rivera Sáenz de Heredia, Fernando, 282
Primo de Rivera Sáenz de Heredia, José Antonio, 131, 149, 156; leader in UMN, 34; and Fascism, 132–3; and *Falange Española*, 133, 179–80, 189, 235; views on socialism, 180; and CEDA, 181; Catalan Statute, 199; and Law of Agrarian Reform, 204; attitude to Monarchy, 224; and '*straperlo*' affair, 233; 1936 election, 243, 256–7; threat of violence if defeated, 247; offers services of *Falange* in event of Leftist coup, 249; and Azaña's government, 254; imprisoned, 254, 282; and *Falange's* part in 1936 rising, 282, 284–5, 287
Progressive Republican Party, 84
pronunciamiento procedure, 28

property rights, 63; views of *Acción Nacional*, 74; *see also* land redistribution
property tax, 268
PSOE, 33, 83, 129, 181, 245, 260–1, 263, 271
Public Order, Law Concerning, 127
Pujol Martínez, Juan, 72, 96

Queipo de Llano Serra, General Gonzalo, 35, 278–9

Radicals, 33, 51, 52, 84; Constituent Cortes elections, 55; and Casas Viejas, 105, 122; and Law concerning Religious Confessions and Congregations, 123; Draft Law on Rural Leases, 128; and 1933 election, 144, 148–9; resignation of members from Party 1934, 159; and clergy stipends, 161; disintegration and collapse of Party 1935, 193, 232–3; and death sentences on October 1934 revolutionaries, 197; and Law of Agrarian Reform, 204; collaboration with CEDA, 205–7
Rahola Molinas, Pedro, 56, 232, 236
ralliement, 165
Reacción Ciudadana, 35
Redondo Ortega, Onésimo, 98, 99, 100
regionalism, 22–3; provisions of Constitution 1931, 62–3; views of *Acción Nacional*, 74; CEDA policy, 115–16; Gil Robles'views, 211; Calvo Sotelo's views, 219; statutes of autonomy 1936, 267–8
religion, 14; Concordat of 1851, 17; freedom of worship, 20, 42, 64, 65; provisions of Constitution 1931, 64–7; legislation 1932, 68–71
Religious Confessions and Congregations, Law concerning, 105, 122–5, 161
religious instruction, 42, 65
Religious Orders: liberals' attack

1820, 15; dissolution of Jesuits, 65, 66; curtailment of activities 1933, 123
Renovación Española, 106, 117, 130, 131, 168–9, 176, 218
Republic of 1873–4, 19
Republicans: Socialist alliance 1927, 29; problems of government 1931, 30–1; Socialist alliance 1930, 33; and Constituent Cortes elections, 51–2; coalition in Constituent Cortes, 59, 60, 61; coalition government September 1933, 129; Monarchist alliances 1936 elections, 244
Republicans, Conservative: and property rights, 63; withdrawal from Cortes 1933, 126–7; anti-Marxist front with Right 1933 elections, 144
Republicans, Federal, 118
Republicans, Left: government of 1931, 30, 51; and Constitution, 59; and Republicanism, 106; in opposition 1933–4, 152, 153, 164; and clergy stipends, 161; and Socialist revolutionary plans 1934, 182–3; break with régime 1934, 189; and Law of Agrarian Reform, 204; governments 1936, 239, 289; 1936 elections, 241; and civil disorder and military conspiracies, 288–9
Republicans, Liberal Democrat, 50, 199, 200
Republicans, Liberal Right, 51–2; Constituent Cortes election, 55, 56; become Progressive Republican Party, 84
Republicans, Radical, *see* Radicals
Republicans, Radical-Socialist, 33; against religious teaching, 66, 124; demise in 1933 election, 149
'Republicans of 14 April', 50–1
Requetés, 47, 179, 224, 225, 281, 283, 286
'reserved annuities', 127
Rico Avello, Manuel, 159

Right: organisation and beliefs 1814, 14–15; neo-Catholic leadership 19th century, 18–19; 'regenerationism', 24; attempt at unification on Christian-Democratic principles, 27; state in 1931, 31, 39, 54; groups in 1930, 34–5; and agricultural aspects of economic crisis 1931, 85–7; and Catalan Statute, 90; and use of Defence Law of the Republic 1932–3, 118–19; divisions in 1933, 117; and municipal elections 1933, 125; and Socialism, 129–30; 1933 election, 140–4, 147, 148–9, 150; political distribution 1933, 150–1; divisions on agrarian reform, 162; acceptance of Republic, 193; differences on methods of defeating Left 1934–5, 194; and PNV, 211–12; divisions over economic policy, 228–31; and 1936 elections, 238, 244, 248–9, 251–2; support for Azaña, 253–4; allegations of malpractice 1936 elections, 255–6; 'national front', 256; and duty to government 1936, 292; united from without, 293

Rivas, Natalio, 250
Rocha García, Juan José, 233
Rodezno, Conde de, 56, 93, 111, 156, 161, 175, 286
Rodríguez del Barrio, General Angel, 278
Rodríguez de Viguri Seoane, Luis, 155
Rodríguez Jurado, Adolfo, 201
Rodríguez Tarduchy, Emilio, 132
Romanones, Conde de, 31, 32, 37, 57, 111, 155, 191, 242
Royo Villanova, Antonio, 58, 67, 72, 81, 85, 118, 120, 154; and regionalism, 62, 268; and religious clauses, 65; and Parliamentary supremacy, 68; and Catalan Statute, 90–1; and Law concerning Religious Confessions and

Congregations, 124; and Law on Rural Leases, 128; demands resignation of Alcalá-Zamora, 161; resigns 1935, 231
Ruiz Alonso, Ramón, 214, 256
Ruiz de Alda Miquélez, Julio, 132, 133, 224
Ruiz Funes, Mariano, 268–9
Rural Leases, Draft Law, 1933, 127–8

Saborit Colomer, Andrés, 129
Sagasta, Práxedes, 19, 24
Sáinz Rodríguez, Pedro, 58, 79; and Constitution, 62; and religious clauses, 64; withdrawal from Constituent Cortes, 72; and *Acción Nacional*, 73; supports Sanjurjo, 97; wishes Monarchists to remain in *Acción Popular*, 108; and future State, 221
Salamanca: mixed juries rulings 1933, 121
Salazar Alonso, Rafael, 162, 184–5, 232, 242
Salic Law, 15, 178
Salmón Amorín, Federico, 185, 205, 235
Samper Ibáñez, Ricardo: heads government April 1934, 162; and PNV, 186; and Catalan Law of Farming Leases, 187, 188, 189; resignation of government, 189
Sánchez - Albornoz Menduiña, Claudio, 204, 263
Sánchez Guerra, José, 32, 50, 51, 57
Sanchez Román, Felipe, 245, 262, 263, 289
Sanjurjo Sacanell, General José, 37; conspiracy and rising 1932, 96–8, 100–4; deportations and detentions, 103, 118; and UME, 226; and military conspiracy 1936, 279–80, 281–2, 285, 286; killed, 290
Sanz de Lerín, Colonel Eugenio, 93
schools, 65, 67, 123, 124, 125, 161, 200, 267

474 THE ORIGINS OF FRANCO'S SPAIN

Segovia, Bishop of, 70
Segura, Pedro, Cardinal Archbishop of Toledo, 43–4, 61, 168
Senate: proposal for creation, 207
señoríos, expropriation of, 88
Serrano Súñer, Ramón, 287
SEU, 181
Seville: economic state 1933, 121–2
Siglo Futuro, El, 34, 111, 166
Silió, César, 267
Sindicato Minero, 190
Sindicatos Libres, 25
'Sixfingers', 122
Social-Catholicism, 24–5
Socialism, 19th century growth of, 24
Socialista, El, 52, 129, 134, 136, 158, 182, 184, 247, 261, 275
Socialists: Republican alliance 1927, 29; Constituent Cortes, 30, 51–2, 55, 60; and Constitution, 62; and *Acción Nacional*, 81; evolutionary tactics, 82–3, 129; and agrarian problems 1931, 86; readiness to adopt revolutionary tactics, 106; and Law concerning Religious Confessions and Congregations, 123; and Draft Law on Rural Leases, 128; ousted from office 1933 'revolutionary phase', 129, 158–9, 164, 181–5; and fascists, 133, 136–8; and Goicoechea, 133–4; attitude towards Radicals and Lerroux, 134; attitude towards CEDA and Gil Robles, 134, 135; and *Acción Popular*, 135–6; and democracy, 136–8; similarity of aims to CEDA's 1933, 138; opposition to Lerroux's government 1933, 139; 1933 election campaign, 142–3, 146–7, 149–50; in opposition 1933–4, 152–3; and clergy stipends, 161; and repeal of Law of Municipal Boundaries, 163; division over methods of action, 181; seek united front with extreme Left, 183; and Salazar Alonso, 185; and PNV,

186; general strike 1934, 189–91, repressive measures, 194–7; and participation in Cortes 1934, 198; 1936 elections, 238, 241, 245–7; divisions of opinion 1936, 239, 245, 260–1, 271–2; demand power for Popular Front, 250; mobilisation of followers ordered, 289
Socialist Youth, 261
Sociedad de Estudios Vascos, 48
Somatén, 29
SOV, 25, 145, 191
'states of alarm and prevention', 1934, 184
'*straperlo*' scandal, 232
Strauss, Daniel, 232
strikes: 1934, 184; 1936, 270
suffrage, female, 67
'Support for the Republic', 51, 55
Supreme War Council, 227, 228
Syndicalist Party, 245

tenants: evictions, 86, 202–3, 268
Tedeschini, Mgr Federico, Papal Nuncio, 27, 42, 69, 165, 168
Toledo: wheat prices 1935, 234
Tornos Laffite, Cirilo, 109
Torras Bages, José, Bishop of Vich, 23
trade unions, 214–15; Catholic workers', 24–5, 270; CEDA policy, 114, 115
Tradition, 220, 222
Traditionalists: 19th century, 18–19; 1931, 46–8; and PNV, 47, 48 9, 92–3, 145–6; and creation of Basque State, 48–9, 92–3, 146, 185–6; support for Catalan State 1931, 49; and dissolution of Jesuits, 69; and *Acción Nacional*, 73, 80; and Alfonsines, 78, 79; adopt title of *Comunión Tradicionalista Carlista*, 93; and plans for *Federación de Derechas*, 110–11; and *Renovación Española*, 113; hostility to régime 1933–4, 156; and Catalan Statute, 199; 1936 elections, 244

TYRE, 113, 176, 218

UGT, 25, 29, 54, 77, 129, 181, 184, 205, 245, 261, 271, 289
UME, 226, 281
Unamuno Jugo, Miguel de, 291
unemployment: 1931, 84, 85–6; 1933, 121; remedial legislation 1934–5, 200–1, 205; enforced payment of wages to unemployed, 269
Unidades de Acción, 179
Unió Democràtica de Catalunya, 82
Unió de Rabassaires, 145
Unión Católica, 20
Unión Monárquica Nacional, 34
Unión Partiótica, 28–9, 52
Unión Regional de Derechas, 104
Unión Republicana, 198, 245
unions, see trade unions
Urquijo, José María, 146
Urquijo Ibarra, Julio de, 44
Usabiaga Lasquibar, Juan, 234

Valiente Soriano, José María, 76, 108–9, 168
Valladolid: wheat prices: 1933, 120; 1935, 234
Vallellano, Conde de, 27, 45, 72, 80, 97, 111, 240
Varela Iglesías, General José Enrique, 100, 224, 227, 236, 277, 278, 279
Vatican: attitude towards Republic, 42–4
Vázquez de Mella Fanjul, Juan, 21–2
Vegas Latapié, Eugenio, 34, 130, 165
Velarde, Ángel, 186, 242
Velayos Velayos, Nicasio, 202–4 231, 234

Ventosa Calvell, Juan, 32, 49, 91; attacks government economic policy 1931, 83–4; and Catalan Statute, 198; and 1936 budget proposals, 231; and 1936 electoral malpractice enquiry, 256; and Casares Quiroga's government, 265, 273; endorses military rising, 291
Vincent, Fr Antonio, 24–5
Vidal Barraquer, Francisco de Asís, Cardinal, 168
Vigón Suerodíaz, Captain Jorge, 130
Villalobos González, Filiberto, 57, 200
Villapesadilla, Marqués de, 278
Villegas Montesinos, General Rafael, 97, 277, 279
Villores, Marqués de, 47, 93

wages, 84, 121, 269
wheat prices: 1931, 85; 1933, 120–1; 1936, 268
wheat surplus 1934–5, 233–4
workers' rights and conditions: Constitution, 63–4; views of Acción Nacional, 74; migration of labourers prohibited, 86; CEDA policy, 114, 204–5

Yagüe Blanco, Colonel Juan, 190–1, 283, 288
Yanguas Messía, José de, 244
Young Propagandists, 39, 40, 45
yunteros: Extremadura, 162–3, 200

Zamanillo González Camino, José Luis, 284
Zamora: wheat crop 1935, 234